FIVE YEARS OUT!

BOOK 1: TO SEE THE WORLD

BY DELLA "DEE LEE" HOPLEY

The right of Della Hopley, AKA: Dee Lee, to be identified as the author of the work has been asserted by her following the Copyright Designs and Patents Act 1988.

Five Years Out! Book 1: To See the World

Copyright © D. Hopley 2014

Published by D. Hopley: hopley9@icloud.com

Dedicated to fellow travellers, and all the good people in the world - especially the street kids, truckers, bikers, and all true friends made on my journey so far… See you down the road!
D.

Table of Contents

INTRODUCTION:

I love to travel. It creates a state of perfect mindfulness - Every second bursting with endless possibilities, creating a complete awareness and appreciation of the eternal now. That's not to say it's all plain sailing! I've had many travel adventures, ranging from blissful to terrifying, and everything in between! The trilogy "Five Years Out" covers some of these early travel adventures...

CHAPTER 1:

PLANNING

I'd recently turned 17, and was bursting to see the world! What was this place that I had come into being on? So far, I was only aware of what my local surroundings had tried to shape me into, but I wanted an overview! I wanted to see, feel, taste, and experience what other wonders were out there on this tiny planet called Earth?! How else would I know where I truly fit into the greater scheme of things?

I figured that my late teens and early twenties would be the best time to go exploring, and maybe as I neared my mid' twenties I would be ready to settle down, have a family, and possibly a career in social work, as I always felt I wanted to help others in some way.

Since early childhood, I've always enjoyed writing, so I envisioned that once I was settled down, I would continue to write in my spare time, and maybe even share some of my adventure stories with the world one day, but first I needed to have some adventures to write about, and I considered that about five years out in the world should do it!

I'd finally left school and was planning to take off as soon as I'd got enough cash together to get going, and once I got going, I would simply volunteer work my way around the world. 'How else is it going to happen, if I don't make it happen?!' I'd often thought.

One afternoon I popped around to visit my dad – Geoff, to drop off my latest earnings to keep safe for me for my travel fund and have a chat about my upcoming travels. He had a giant map of the world on his kitchen wall which I loved to study, and would often imagine exploring every inch of the actual world it portrayed. My dad was always very encouraging and supportive of my travel plans. He had a very upbeat "Go for it!" type of attitude, which I loved!

BOOK 1: TO SEE THE WORLD

"Hiya Geoff here's another ten pounds to put in my travel-fund tin!" I exclaimed, beaming him a proud smile, as he greeted me at his front door. "Good job Del!" He answered, as he took it off me, and headed into his living room to put the ten-pound note in an old Chinese tea leaf tin that was hidden at the back of some books on a shelf in his living room.

After leaving School, I'd got a part-time job as a kitchen assistant at a local hotel, and I planned to work and save up as much money as possible to start my trip off. "So, where will you head first Del?" Asked my dad, as we sat down with our coffees. "Um, maybe to Aunt Freda's in the New Forest, she may have some work going for me, or if not, she may know of some work nearby. At least it'll be a start!" I answered enthusiastically.

"OK good, and where is your goal destination?" asked my dad, looking at me as if he was trying to gauge how serious I was about my travel plans. I playfully took a red coloured pin out of the side of his map, closed my eyes twirled my hand around and stuck it in the map. I opened my eyes and saw that it was pinned to a place in the USA called Oakland, which looked to be near San Francisco, California.

"Perfect! I love oak trees, so therefore Oakland is my goal destination!" I exclaimed facetiously! "Well, kind of, I mean, I really would love to explore the Americas first, to get the ball rolling so to speak, and then set off to other places afterwards "Basically, I want to go everywhere!!" I laughed.

"…But, yeah, the America's first for sure! I remember you and Mum always had good things to say about the Americans!" I said with a grin. While thinking how I'd always loved American TV shows and films, which made America feel very familiar, yet at the same time different enough to still be fun to explore! Plus, I'd grown up hearing stories about American soldiers who were based in my home town during WW2, and several of them had become a big part of my mum's family at the time, because her parents always had an open door and were very hospitable to all, especially to the American soldiers, as they were so far away from home. My mum had even been engaged to a GI named Jack Edward Anderson from Patchogue, Long Island, but sadly various circumstances had separated them.

"Yeah, I have great memories of the Yanks arriving in town when I was a boy! They were always so friendly, great guys!" answered my dad with a smile. He was eight years younger than my mum, but he had been old enough to remember them.

So, I was encouraged by the fact that both of my parents thought fondly of Americans, and I took this as a good sign to make the Americas my first overseas destination. Also, as well as my parents' positive stories about the American people, there was something about the geography of the Americas that drew me, I wasn't sure what exactly. It was just a feeling, a kind of magnetism.

As a child, I often had vivid dreams of my life as a young girl in an old American pioneer town. In these dreams, this place felt so much like home that I would often wake up feeling disorientated and confused by my surroundings.

Decades later, I received a copy of my family tree and I found out that I have American Pioneer ancestry. My great-grandparents - times nine or so, had emigrated to Massachusetts in the early 16th century and had raised a family out there. Their descendants had lived there for a few more generations until my great, great grandfather immigrated to the UK and settled. There was also some Native American DNA in the bloodline, so I had American ancestry on both counts, and I often wonder if my dreams were some kind of genetic memory. Maybe I was remembering my great, great... grandmother's life?

"So, what volunteering will you do to get by on your travels?" asked my dad, quizzing me. "I'll do anything as long as it's ethical! I could be a Nanny, an Au-pair, an English Tutor, a Hotel-Helper, a Fruit-Picker... whatever I can find!!" I answered enthusiastically, feeling totally up for the challenge.

I'd read backpackers did these kinds of volunteer jobs as holiday exchanges. The hosts usually provided room and board, and sometimes even an expense allowance, so these types of volunteer gigs would be perfect to help keep me afloat on my travels. I wasn't afraid of doing whatever it took to get out there, and see the world!

I never saw my lack of finances as a barrier. I wasn't from a well-off family, so from around eight years of age, whenever I needed some extra pocket money, I would simply go around the neighbourhood houses asking for odd jobs. I'd taken on hedge-cutting, lawn-mowing, car-washing, babysitting, dog walking, window cleaning, and running errands, so I felt that there would always be something I could do, and if there wasn't, I would create something!

My dad liked my enthusiastic spirit and sense of adventure and seemed to enjoy helping to mentally train me for my travels, often quizzing me on what I would do in various challenging situations. I always enjoyed lateral thinking, or "Thinking outside of the box" as they say. To me, these hypothetical scenarios seemed like fun puzzles to solve, and we often had a laugh at the same time!

He also taught me self-defence when I was younger, and would often show me how to fight off an attacker if need be. One time in particular stands out in my memory, from when I was around ten years old - The two of us were waiting for a bus, and there was no one else around, so he said "OK Del, imagine I'm a baddie about to attack you, how will you get away?"

"OK" I answered with a grin, as he took a few steps away from me in order to come back at me and start his "surprise attack" As he got ready, I stood there pretending not to see him, and then suddenly he was heading my way!

He was trying to look as dangerous and menacing as possible as he swaggered towards me and started to grab at me, this caused me to burst out into a fit of laughter, which then set him off laughing too, and the two of us wound up bent over laughing hysterically, as the bus pulled up we both climbed on board, out of breath and wiping the laughter tears from our eyes and trying to regain our composure, much to the bemusement of the bus driver - a slim, balding, middle-aged, serious looking man.

Over the years as I grew up, my dad also taught me how to fist-fight. He and his brother Derek had been championship boxers in their youth, so he knew a good trick or two, and when I was ten, he had also agreed to take me to Karate classes once a week, which I found a lot more exciting than boxing! – This, combined with his self-defence training would all come in very handy on numerous occasions during my travels.

Safety was obviously something to be concerned about, but I was determined not to succumb to fear. This world was my home planet, and I had as much right to see, and enjoy it as anybody else did, that was how I saw it, and I'd had the desire to travel and explore the world for as long as I could remember.

I had started school early; at four years old and it had all felt so unnatural. I just couldn't wrap my head around any of it! Why I was there? Why were the adults, who were essentially strangers, being so mean and bossy to me and the other kids? Why weren't they being nice and kind? Did they have a right to shout, and bully us like they did? What had we all done so wrong to deserve to be held for so many days of each week in such a strange place? What added to the confusion and stress of the situation, was being bullied by a few of the kids for being younger and smaller than them, but I fought back, and soon made friends with most of them - so I enjoyed the social aspect of school.

I was a tom-boy and loved playing with boys and girls, especially after school, where a gang of us would meet up to go exploring the town's alleyways, abandoned buildings, and climbing rooftops, or away into the local countryside, hiking, biking, making dens, and climbing trees. My love of exploring new places, seemed to grow from there.

I also enjoyed spending time alone in my bedroom being creative - writing stories, jokes, poems, drawing, daydreaming, or reading - especially Enid Blyton books.

I also had lots of pen-pals all around the world and I looked so forward to hearing about their lives in far-away places such as London, Wyoming, and Nigeria! These pen-pals felt like my extended family and added to the sense of the world being my home.

I went through a phase of writing stories, poems, jokes, and designing crosswords for a global pen-pal magazines, and it always gave me the sense that I was doing what I was meant to be doing - I was creating, and I loved it! I much preferred it to just sitting in a classroom learning about other people's findings, and what seemed like a bunch of meaningless facts and figures, all by rote! Such learning would send me into a zombie-like trance, and I would often be told off for being bored, i.e.: daydreaming, and not paying attention.

Most of my school reports read "Has the ability but doesn't use it" I never quite knew what they meant. I wondered if they liked being forced to do things that they had no desire to do. Wouldn't it be better to encourage and nurture a child's natural talents and interests? - Sure, we all need to learn the basics of reading, writing and arithmetic, but beyond that, I believed that there was so much more to life and to this world, and I couldn't wait to explore it for myself! No more learning about it from others!

I left my dad's place and headed home to the house I lived at with my mum – Lydia. She didn't seem too bothered either way about my plans to go travelling, as she was quite a passive type, and seemed to just accept things as they were. I was more of a pro-active type, and rather than be miserable about a situation, I would do my best to figure out a way to fix it!

We were very different in some ways, but we got along well in other ways, and we would often enjoy a laugh together at silly things; like me making a hand-mouth-puppet gesture if I found someone boring on TV, or having a little dance around the kitchen together to the Top of the Pops music chart show on the radio – Simple, but fun pleasures. She was also very generous, and would always share what little she had with anyone in need, and I always admired this about her.

BOOK 1: TO SEE THE WORLD

So, all in all, I had an average childhood, and by the age of seventeen, I was an average teenage girl. I was seeing a local boy named Matt, and I also had quite a few good friends who I enjoyed doing the usual teenage stuff with - mainly hanging out in parks, pubs, and clubs - drinking and dancing by night, and shopping for clothes, makeup and music by day, when not at college or work.

So, in many ways I was happy, but it just didn't feel like any of it was enough. I had a constant yearning to see and experience the bigger picture of the world around me, which I knew meant that I would have to sacrifice my life as I knew it, and step outside of my familiar little world, and step out into the great unknown!!

During this time, I was reading a book about a boy who was about to turn eighteen and who didn't want to spend another year doing exactly the same thing as the year before that and the year before that… I could totally relate to this, and I found this book quite inspirational and thought-provoking, to say the least!

When I was about fifteen years old, I'd also read the book "How to bring out the magic in your mind" by Al Koran. - It taught the power of visualisation, and it simply made sense to me. First, you visualise what you want to happen, then you feel it actually happening, and then you focus your energies on whatever actions are needed to manifest these visions into your reality. It seemed such a good method in which to harness, and focus one's attention and energy on life goals, rather than have it scattered all over the place. So, I would often spend my spare time lying on my bed and visualising my travels. Each time during a visualisation session, new ideas and thoughts would come to mind, bringing about lots of mini "Eureka" moments bursting out at various intervals.

One evening a few friends, whom I'd met on a media course that I was taking at the local technical college, alongside my part-time kitchen assistant job, and I took a taxi to a nearby town called Shrewsbury for a night out. The media course had initially been of interest to me because I was full of story ideas; for films, plays, comedies, and even advertising jingles! So, I'd thought that by taking the media course at the local tech' I would learn how and where to channel these creative ideas, but disappointingly most of the course was just spent watching the teacher fiddling around trying to set up a pathetic little film reel and TV set, completing tedious mind-numbing tasks, and talking about boring, dry, uninspiring subjects. So, as a result of this, myself and the other students had lost all interest in the course, and had taken to slipping off to the pub any chance we got!

We arrived in Shrewsbury after about a half hour's journey, and soon we were all shuffling into a pub that had New-Wave songs pumping out of the Jukebox. We all had a great night, laughing, joking, and dancing. At one point while feeling quite tipsy, I found myself chatting to one of my arty new-wave friends in a somewhat drunken philosophical manner... "Hey, I've had an epiphany! So, if we can travel the twenty miles or so to this town, why can't we travel another twenty miles to the next town, and the next town, and so on and so on, and just keep on going all around the world! I mean people are just people, right? So, what's so scary about that?" I rambled on excitedly.

My friend nodded in agreement, with an amused-looking smile on her face as if humouring me. "...I mean, we could just go, and go, and gooooo!" I exclaimed with a laugh. Even though I was tipsy, I knew the idea sounded somewhat ridiculous, but I also felt that it had a certain logic to it. I jumped up to go and have a dance, as if to celebrate my newfound key to the world!

As I danced, I felt that my friend thought that I was just joking around, but deep down I knew that I was serious! It was early March, and the weather would be warming up soon, so I decided that once it had warmed up enough, I would take off on my journey, and would simply think of it as going from "town to town" - one town at a time! - With maybe an ocean, or a mountain or two on route, but wherever I was, I would keep the same concept of "town to town" in my head to help keep me going and to make the idea of such an epic journey less overwhelming. I laughed at how ridiculously simple this psychological method was, and couldn't wait to put it to the test!

CHAPTER 2:

SETTING OFF!

Summer finally rolled around and I was still working as a kitchen assistant, and saving up for my travels. The media course at the tech' had become little more than a place to meet friends before heading to the local pubs and clubs. I was still seeing the same boy, and for the most part, I was having fun being a typical seventeen-year-old girl, but, all along, deep down I felt as if I was just biding my time, because more than anything, I was longing to set off on my travels.

One day in early June I met up with a cousin of mine, whom I'd nicknamed Gee, and she mentioned that she and her mum, my second cousin - who I thought of as my aunt, and whom I'd nicknamed Vee, were heading to Telford the next day. Telford was a town about 30 miles southeast of my hometown; Oswestry. My mind suddenly flashed to my travel the world from "Town-to-Town!" concept, and I spontaneously asked if I could join them.

She answered that she didn't see why not. and that we could go and ask her mum Vee. So off we headed to see her mum to ask her if I could go along with them. Much to my delight, she said, of course, I could join them, and that I could also stay with them at her son's house as well if I wanted to because I was also related to him, so I'd be most welcome! Feeling pleased with this response, I felt a surge of excitement that this could actually be it! - The start of my travels. Finally!

They would be catching a bus from Oswestry at 10 am the next day, so I would have to be at their place by 8 or 9 am at the latest. I had plans to go out with some friends that night, and we usually stayed out until the early hours of the morning, but I figured that I could still pull it off, even if I didn't get any sleep that night, I would just sleep on the bus on the way down! I told them that I would see them in the morning, and headed over to meet up with my friends at the Pub.

As the night went on, we went around the pubs and clubs and got tipsier as we went. I was having fun, but at the back of my mind, I was thinking about how I may actually be leaving my hometown, and all of my family and friends the very next day, and would possibly be gone for who knows how long? It felt quite daunting, yet at the same time exciting. I didn't say anything about it to my friends though, as I didn't want them to make a fuss!

At about 5 am I arrived home, and tiptoed up the stairs of our flat, so as not to disturb my sleeping mum. I suddenly felt a rush of sadness at the thought of leaving her, especially as she didn't actually know that I was leaving that morning, although I reasoned that I'd often talked about wanting to go travelling, so she did at least have an inkling that I may take off at some point.

Still feeling a little tipsy, I stumbled around in my bedroom gathering my things together and shoving them into my rucksack - It was an old army khaki-coloured rucksack that my dad had given me to use to go camping with a school friend five years earlier when I was twelve. He had let me keep it, because I loved it so much, as it felt like a proper adventurer's rucksack!

'Clothes, shoes, toiletries,' I thought to myself as I filled up my rucksack. "Passport! You'll definitely need that!" I told myself, half joking, half serious. 'Um, Walkman, music tapes, notebook and pen, what else? Oh, camera!' I thought, shoving the smaller items into my black coloured cloth shoulder bag along with my purse, and makeup which was already in there. Oh my god, I'm actually doing it! I'm going!" I thought, feeling a rush of excitement, as I put my passport safely into the back section of my shoulder bag. There was still lots of room in my rucksack, so I put my shoulder bag inside at the top figuring that it would be easier to carry the lot on my back. I pulled the drawstrings at the top of my rucksack together tightly, and fastened the cover-flap over it.

I was just about ready to leave when my thoughts once again turned to my mum, who was still sleeping soundly in her room, I felt really bad to be leaving in the early hours like this, especially as she would be left living all alone, but I felt I had to live my life and seize the day! I would be fleeing the nest someday, so why not today?! I needed to make a start on my travels, or else they wouldn't happen, and my cousins going to Telford seemed like the ideal opportunity to get the travel ball rolling...

I used my mum's notepad and pen in the kitchen, and went about writing a goodbye note to my mum. I told her that I was going with Gee and Vee to visit some relatives on my dad's side. My mum was also friends with Vee, so she would be ok about that, I added that I may continue onwards to look for work afterwards, but not to worry about me, I would be ok, and that I would keep in touch. I signed off "Lots of love from Della" with three kisses, and hoped that she wouldn't be too upset upon finding it.

I took the note to the kitchen and put it on a worktop next to the kettle, as I knew that she would head there to make a cup of tea when she got up. I checked the time on the clock, it was now after 6 am. I figured by the time I walked down the railway tracks into town it would be around 7 am, I could buy some snacks for breakfast and head over to my cousins for 8 am.

I tiptoed down the stairs of the flat, opened the front door, and stepped out into the cool early morning. I gently closed the door behind me, and started my walk down the long country lane, known as western avenue, until I reached the railway lines, where I started my twenty-minute walk into the town of Oswestry.

My mum had moved to a small village called Morda on the outskirts of Oswestry when I was fifteen, and it had been nice to move into a modern flat, but it was always a slight hassle getting to and from the town. The walk along the railway lines gave me time to wake up and collect my thoughts, and the excitement of what I was about to do grew with every step I took.

I arrived at my cousins and they were flapping around with last-minute bits and bobs, so I sat on the wall outside and ate some of the snacks I'd bought at a nearby shop. I was tired, but I was looking forward to the day ahead. I still couldn't quite believe that I was actually about to set off on my travels!

My cousin and aunt were finally ready, and we all started strolling into town to catch the bus to Telford. I suddenly realised that I had no money left on me, I'd spent my last couple of quid on snacks. My mind flashed to the money I'd saved up for my travels that was kept safe in the Chinese Tealeaf tin at my dad's house. By now, I had about a hundred and fifty pounds in the tin, and I decided that I should go and get it immediately!

'It would also be nice to see Geoff to say goodbye before I take off!' I thought as we neared his house, which happened to be on the same route as the bus stop. "I just need to quickly give my dad a knock to say goodbye, and to get some cash I've saved up!" I exclaimed as we got near his house. "OK!" answered Gee and Vee, as they both slowed down for me to run over to knock on my dad's house door.

I'd previously mentioned to my cousin and aunt that I would probably head off, and look for work down south after the Telford family visit, but I got the feeling that they hadn't taken me seriously, so they probably thought I just meant that I was picking up some spending money.

I knocked on my dad's door, but there was no answer. I knocked louder, but there was still no answer. I tried to open the door, but it was locked. I knocked again, but there was still no answer. Suddenly it dawned on me that it was Wednesday! He usually went out to a social club in another town on Tuesday nights, and he often stayed over at friend's houses.

"Damn!" I exclaimed out loud. 'What will I do? I have absolutely no money on me!' I thought to myself, feeling stressed and frustrated by the situation. I knew that once I got based somewhere my dad would be able to send my savings on to me via postal order, but what was I going to do for right now? My Cousins couldn't afford to lend me money, my only other option would be not to go, but the momentum felt so right! - I just had to go!

I took a deep breath and decided to not mention anything to my cousins, but instead to just walk with them to the bus as if all was well, and in the spirit of Al Koran's book; "Bring out the power of your mind" I would just stay calm, and visualise the bus fare materialising for me on my way there.

We crossed the street and started to walk into the town centre down Willow Street, and suddenly one of my brothers; Carl, appeared walking up the street towards us. We all stopped to greet each other, and I told him that I was going to visit relatives in Telford with our cousins and that I needed to borrow the bus fare if he had it. I explained that I had money saved up at our dad's house, but this trip had all happened so last minute, that I hadn't had time to get it, and that I really wanted to go as I was hoping to head south to look for work afterwards!

Carl knew about my travel longings and could see that I was genuine about my intentions, so he checked his wallet and had a five-pound note left in there. He took it out and handed it to me and wished me a good journey. I excitedly thanked him and told him to ask our dad to pay him back the fiver out of my savings. He told me not to worry about it!

I was very grateful for his kind gesture, as this was a lot of money for him to just give to me! My cousins started to look impatient to get going, so I thanked him again, we said our goodbyes, and I took off at a fast pace down the street with them.

BOOK 1: TO SEE THE WORLD

As we whizzed along in a hurry to get to the Telford bus, I suddenly spotted the boy I'd been seeing - Matt, standing leaning against a brick pillar across the street. 'Oh no!' I thought to myself. As I didn't want him to see me taking off.

I suddenly felt sad about leaving without a proper goodbye, but I figured it was all for the best, and once I got based somewhere for a while, I would write to him and explain, and who knows, maybe he would visit me? We were fond of each other, but it was very early days, and at seventeen I felt we were both much too young to be tied down.

He didn't spot me, which seemed odd, as we walked straight across his path of vision. Instead, he stared straight ahead as if his mind was far away, and besides he wouldn't have expected to see me in that part of town, at that time of day. I felt sad to think that this may be the last time I would see him for a long time, but I tried not to dwell on that thought, and I wished him well instead.

"There's the bus!" Shouted Vee, so we all ran to get on it. Minutes later we were riding out of town and onto the motorway. I felt another surge of excitement rise through me, as I realised that my dreams of travel were actually starting to become a reality! - and thinking of dreams. It was time for a nap!

I slept for most of the two-hour journey, only waking up slightly during stops and passenger pick-ups. Gee had nudged me awake when we arrived, and feeling groggy, I jumped up, grabbed my Rucksack, and followed Gee, and Vee off the bus.

The cold Telford air blowing across my face woke me up fast. "So where do we go now?" I asked, yawning, and looking around me and seeing nothing but a busy road, a small shopping precinct running alongside of it, and what looked like a never-ending housing estate surrounding us.

Vee answered that it was just a short walk to her son's house, as she picked up her suitcase and started to lead the way. Gee and I followed along, chatting about some of our favourite bands and music. We had both been into heavy rock in our early teens but were now more into punk and new wave. With Gee leaning more punk, and me leaning more new-wave, although ultimately, we both liked all kinds of music - As long as it sounded good to us!

After what seemed like a never-ending maze of alleyways through an infinity of council houses, we arrived at our relative's house. My aunt's son Jerry, and his wife Barb, came out to greet us. They both looked surprised, but happy, to see me.

Within minutes we were all sitting around the living room sipping on mugs of tea, while my aunt and cousins all had a chatty catch-up. I sat smiling and nodding at them all, but inside I was thinking about my travels and trying to work out the best time to leave. Should I stay for a few days here, or should I just stay the one night to catch up with sleep, and then take off? My gut instinct was to just stay the one night and to take off the next day. So, after a little more pondering, I decided that's what I would do!

I only had about £3 left on me from the fiver my brother Carl had given me, but I could head to the nearest motorway and hitch-hike! I'd done a lot of local hitch-hiking with my friends in my mid-teens - It was our main way of getting to various towns, pubs, clubs and parties in the area. I soon realised that as long as the driver was safe, it was a great way to get around! "You just stick out a thumb, and get transported from A to B – It's verging on magical! So why not use the same method to cover the rest of the alphabet!" I'd joked during one of our local hitchhikes to a nightclub up in the hills.

As I thought about my travel plans, my mind kept flashing to my mum at home. She would be up and about by now and would have read my goodbye note. I felt a wave of sadness at the thought of her being upset by reading it, but told myself to be strong, and that once I was based somewhere long-ish term, maybe she could visit me.

I imagined that if I liked certain places, then I would want to stay for a few weeks, or even months, which would hopefully give her time to visit me. I hoped that she would be ok on her own, as I had been the only one living with her after our family had split up when I was six. We were more like sisters than mother and daughter, which had its pros and cons.

"Della's going off to look for work after staying here, aren't you Della?" Exclaimed vee, and everyone suddenly looked my way. "Uh, yes, that's right" I answered, quickly coming out of my daydream. "Great, where're you heading?" asked my aunt's son Jerry.

"I'm going to head to my aunt Freda's in the New Forest first, and see if she has any work going, and er…take it from there!" I answered, feeling that at least it was a plan of sorts! "Great stuff!" he answered, with a big smile, and then continued chatting about other stuff with Vee, much to my relief!

A little while later we dug into a chip-shop feast of fish, chips and peas, washed down with cans of fizzy pop. Afterwards, we lounged around watching TV, drinking cups of tea, and munching on biscuits until evening. Around 6 pm we all set off for the local pub, which meant walking for what seemed like ages around the housing estate's maze of alleyways until we wound up at an open area with a shop, a laundrette, and a large pub.

We all tottered inside the Pub and spent the next few hours sipping on halves and pints of larger, eating pub snacks of crisps, nuts, and pickled eggs, and playing pool. I didn't have a clue how to play pool, but it was fun nonetheless, especially as Gee and I always managed to have a laugh at something.

Around midnight we arrived home, and our hosts showed us to our beds, mine would be the sofa, which I was happy enough to flake out on. - I slept like a log that night!

CHAPTER 3:

"TOWN TO TOWN!"

I woke up early the next morning. No one else was up yet, so I tiptoed to use the loo and have a wake-up wash. I found some instant coffee in the kitchen and made myself a big mug of it. I spotted an opened pack of digestive biscuits and grabbed a couple to have with my coffee. On the way back to the living room I noticed a wall clock. It showed just after 7 am on it. "Great, I've got some time to myself to wake up, and get ready to go!" I thought excitedly.

As I sat on the Sofa, sipping my coffee, and dunking my digestive biscuits into it, my mind kept hopping between images of myself hitch-hiking off down a motorway, and my mum back at home, was I really going to do this? My inner answer was an instant yes, almost as if I had no choice at this point. - I had started, so I would continue!

"Ooooh you're up!" said my aunt, as she appeared in the living room looking like she'd just woken up. "Yes, the kettle's not long boiled, and there are some digestive biscuits on the side, I hope it's ok that I've had some?" I answered, finishing off the rest of my coffee and biscuits. "Oh, of course it is! You're with family now!" Answered Vee with a warm smile.

Within the next hour or two the others were up and about, and everyone was merrily chatting away. My cousin Gee and I were having a laugh about something ridiculous as usual! – we both had a somewhat surreal, whacky Monty-Python-type, sense of humour, and together we would often wind up in hysterics over the most ludicrous of things, such as grabbing a potato each, and creating a "very serious" conversation between them…by the end of it one of the potatoes would be having to go to war to fight for its country, and the other would be staying home because of its bunions! Just silly, ridiculous stuff, but we would crack each other up!

I thought about how I was going to miss her, and our fun laughs together. 'Oh well, we'll be able to write to each other, and if I get based in some places for a while, maybe she can visit me too!' I told myself, before popping to the bathroom to have a shower and get ready for take-off.

"Right, I'm going to set off then!" I announced as I appeared back in the living room looking a little more put together than I'd looked before entering the bathroom. "Oh, you're not going yet, are you?" asked my aunt Vee. "Yep, I figure I should get going sooner rather than later! Where's the nearest motorway?" I answered first looking at my aunt, then automatically looking over at her son Jerry. He answered that there was a motorway just a couple of streets away, and gave me directions. I thanked him and went about picking up my Rucksack.

"We'll walk with you to the motorway" said Vee suddenly looking and sounding concerned about me. Maybe she'd thought I was just joking all along about taking off on my travels to look for work. Gee looked a little sad more than concerned but seemed mainly happy for me.

"Ok, let's go," said Vee, getting up, and heading towards the front door. Gee, and I followed her outside. I thanked Jerry and his wife Barb for putting me up, and we all started walking in the direction that he'd told me. Within 15 minutes or so, we were standing by a busy roundabout which led down to the motorway. I wasn't sure which way to start hitchhiking, so I went about reading the town and city names listed on the roadside signs nearby.

"Ah, Birmingham! That'll be south-east right?" I exclaimed to Vee and Gee. "Yes, that's south…" answered Vee, her voice fading out, and looking even more concerned than she'd looked earlier. "Does your mum know you're going?" She asked, as if in a last-ditch attempt to stop me from leaving.

"Yeah, kind of. She'll be ok" I answered, feeling that I'd pretty much always been free to come and go as I please, so what was the difference if I went a little further this time? "Ok, well, you take care, and keep in touch, won't you?" She responded warmly. "I will!" I answered, with a smile, as I stuck out my thumb, and started hitching.

Within seconds a car pulled to a halt about 50 feet ahead of us, so I ran to catch up with it, shouting goodbye to Vee & Gee as I ran. I opened the car door and asked the driver if he was heading to Birmingham. He said he was, so I turned and gave a thumbs up to Vee, and Gee, and jumped in the front passenger seat.

I glanced back to wave one more time as we drove off and caught a glimpse of Vee jotting down the car's licence plate number, which made me chuckle. Within seconds Vee and Gee became smaller and smaller and were soon obscured by other cars, so I turned around and got comfy in my seat.

"Thank you so much!" I said, turning to face the driver, who looked to be a nondescript, slim-build, middle-aged man, with mousy thinning hair, and glasses. "It's ok, I'm glad of the company" he answered, with a pleasant Welsh-sounding accent.

He had easy listening playing on his radio; Tom Jones, Shirley Bassey, Burt Bacharach and the like, and the atmosphere in his car felt safe and comfortable. We chatted away about this and that, as we zoomed along the motorway. "Town to Town…" I thought to myself.

CHAPTER 4:

NEW FOREST, NEW LIFE…

About six lifts and a handful of rest stops later, I arrived in a small town named Fording Bridge in the New Forest. My aunt Freda lived nearby, on a horse ranch she owned named "Hunters Moon" She had American Quarter Horses and had set up guest rooms for visitors to have "Working Holidays" where they would learn to ride a horse American-Western style and experience ranch life.

My aunt Freda had got the inspiration for her ranch from the time she'd spent in Montana USA with relatives as a girl. She loved Horses, and the New Forest seemed the perfect place for her to set up a ranch on the UK side of the pond.

I pulled my address book out of my rucksack and found her address, it read "Hunters Moon Ranch, Furze Hill, nr Fording Bridge" I remembered, from my childhood visit that it was just a couple of miles outside of the town, down a country road, and then up a long sandy lane that weaved its way into the forest, but I didn't have a clue which way to walk, as the last time I was there I was only twelve and five years seemed like a long time ago, and my memory was hazy.

"Excuse me, which way is Furze Hill please?" I asked a plump middle-aged lady who was strolling by. "Keep going straight, and you'll see it on your right!" She answered, pointing straight ahead. I thanked her and started walking in the direction she'd pointed.

It was a lovely sunny day, so I decided to hook up my earphones to my Walkman and pop a Donovan music tape inside of it to walk along to. I soon spotted the sign for Furze Hill and recognised the long lane up to my aunt's house.

As I walked along, the combination of the surrounding natural beauty of the New Forest, the sun shining down through the trees, and Donovan's song "Wear your love like heaven" created a strong sense of bliss, and I was on a natural high and feeling more alive than I had ever felt. "Yes, this is it! I'm finally doing it!" I thought to myself, as I glided along up the long sandy lane to my aunt's ranch house.

After several minutes of walking along on what felt like air, I neared a corral on my left that I remembered to be part of my aunt Freda's ranch. My mind flashed back to memories of our family visit here five years ago. The memories were Bitter-Sweet. She had seemed to be a very moody woman - Full of love one minute, full of hate the next! Our visit to her had felt like a white-knuckle rollercoaster ride!

My job back then had been to muck out the stables at 7 am, and in return, I got my meals and horse rides with my aunt Freda, her helper Liz, and the guests. Sometimes my mum would come along too, and all in all, we had some beautiful rides.

I also used to enjoy going out exploring on my own whenever possible, and one day I'd gone outside for a walk around 6 pm and discovered a herd of wild ponies grazing in a forest clearing. I loved horses so much that I couldn't resist gently approaching them to say hello and pet them.

They seemed ok with my presence and just continued calmly eating the grass. One of the wild ponies seemed to be friendlier than the others and started walking towards me snorting at the air as if to smell if I was ok. I smiled and warmly said "Hello!" as he approached me. He got close enough to touch, so I started stroking his mane and telling him how lovely he was.

He seemed to love the attention and moved even closer to nuzzle me. He got so close, that I felt tempted to jump on his back! I truly felt that he wouldn't mind and that he might even enjoy taking me for a little ride.

I started to slowly stroke his back, and softly press down on the area where I would sit if I were to mount him. He remained steady as if to say, "Go ahead, it's fine, jump on board!" "OK, here goes!" I thought as I used my arms to hoist my body up onto his back until I was draped over him like a blanket.

He stayed still and calm and didn't even flinch, so I slowly pushed myself around and turned to grab onto his mane as I swung my legs into place on either side of his belly, before sitting fully upright. He continued to stand firm and seemed unfazed that I had climbed up onto his back. The other Ponies didn't seem fazed either, they just glanced up for a second or two, then continued chowing down on their feast of grass.

BOOK 1: TO SEE THE WORLD

I took hold of his mane firmly, and gently nudged him to go forward while saying "Let's go!" He started to slowly walk on. I felt so excited to be riding off to explore the forest on a wild Pony! I was starting to feel like a true adventurer, and I loved it!

The sun was going down fast, and the daylight swiftly turned to dusk, and in no time at all, I found myself riding the wild pony through the forest by the moon and starlight. It was such an intensely magical feeling.

We continued strolling on in the moon and starlight, through the trees, and deeper into the forest until we reached an area with small dune-like hills, and clearings. The moon and star-lit sky opened up above us, and I was astounded by its beauty. I was purely in the moment and felt nothing but love for everyone and everything in the world! Nothing seemed to matter, but love.

This was the best feeling ever – until suddenly, I realised it was now quite late, and very dark, and that I didn't have a clue where I was?! I wondered how I would find my way back to my aunt's ranch. All I could see around me for miles and miles were hills and trees silhouetted against the moon and star-lit sky.

Panic started to set in, but I quickly realised that panicking wouldn't help and that it was probably best to just keep going until I spotted a house to ask for directions. The wild pony seemed very relaxed. As he trotted along, I would stroke his head and mane, and talk kindly to him. I asked him if he knew where we were and if he knew the way back to my aunt's ranch. He made a little snorting sound and calmly kept trotting along.

Suddenly, I saw a light through the trees and felt very happy to have arrived at someone's home. I would be able to ask them for directions to my aunt's ranch. I hoped I wouldn't be too late getting back, and that my mum and aunt Freda weren't wondering where I'd got to, as I was still only twelve after all!

As the wild pony trotted nearer to the house, I started to recognise my surroundings, "My goodness, this IS Aunt Freda's ranch!!" I'd exclaimed to myself. The wild pony started slowing down, as is to say "There you go, you're home now." I couldn't believe the wild pony had brought me back to my aunt's ranch, yet at the same time, it felt so natural.

I slid off his back, stroked his head, thanked him for the lovely magical journey that he'd taken me on, and thanked him for bringing me home. He seemed to be listening to me and gently nudged his head into my face and neck area. I gave him one last little hug, kissed his forehead, and said goodbye, adding that I hoped to see him again. He snorted, threw his head up, turned away and trotted off back into the forest. I felt truly blessed to have had such a beautiful experience.

Afterwards, I'd gingerly entered the kitchen of the ranch and found my aunt Freda and my mum chatting away about old times over a cup of tea. "Where've you been?" my mum asked casually, as they both looked over at me, although they didn't seem too bothered that I'd been gone for hours, much to my relief!

I told them all about my wild pony ride, and Aunt Freda said that I must have Native American in me, as they always rode bareback, and that it didn't come naturally for non-Native Americans unless they were a tribal people too. This seemed ridiculous, but at the same time, deep down it felt kind of true. "You never know!" I joked back. My mum looked non-pulsed and nodded her head casually and smiled as if to say "Well, that's Della for you!" – As she was used to my somewhat wild and woolly ways.

I was chuckling to myself at these memories from my last visit when I was twelve, and suddenly I looked up and saw Freda's ranch house right there in front of me - A pale blue painted bungalow, surrounded by a western-style fence with a big wooden wagon-wheel in the gate. A horse-shoe hung over the front porch and a dream-catcher hung inside the porch. The place had a strong wild-west movie feel to it. I hoped she wouldn't mind me just turning up, but she had said that my family and I were welcome to visit any time.

"Freda!" I started calling out as I got near the ranch. "Hello!" someone called back, and I turned to see her helper Liz coming up from one of the paddocks. "Oh, hi Liz, remember me?" I asked as she got nearer. "Are you Freda's niece Della?" she replied. "Yes, that's me!" I replied with a grin. "You've grown a lot, unlike me!" She said in a joking manner.

Liz was only about 5 feet tall if that. I laughed, and smiled back, then asked her where Freda was. "She's out riding, she'll be back any minute now!" Liz answered. "Would you like something to drink?" She asked as she passed me by, and started walking towards the ranch. "Yes please!" I answered as I followed along behind her feeling pleased that Liz was being friendly with me.

Suddenly I heard Galloping, and turned to see my aunt Freda arriving on a big black horse - Her blonde curls blowing in the wind, and her tanned weather-worn face contrasted by her big blue eyes. She was dressed like a cowboy and reminded me of the movie character - Calamity Jane.

BOOK 1: TO SEE THE WORLD

"DELLA!!!" She exclaimed with her very loud, somewhat posh-sounding voice. "Hi, Freda!" I shouted back with a smile. She galloped up closer jumped off her horse and came running over to give me a big hug. "I'm so happy to see you! I thought you were never coming back!!" She exclaimed sounding very emotional, and slightly winded. "Well, I'm looking for work if you have any" I answered, figuring I should get that point out of the way sooner, rather than later!

"Oh, we ALWAYS have heaps of work to do here!" Exclaimed Freda, "The thing is we can't pay you for it!" She added, laughing loudly. I laughed too, and thought even if she had no work for me, it was still nice to see her. I hoped that her moods would keep stable and that she and Liz didn't suddenly start fighting, as they had done quite a lot during my last visit five years earlier.

"Come in, come in! Liz put the kettle on and make us some tea!" ordered Freda sounding like the "Lady of the Manor" "Or Squash? - Would you like a cold drink or a hot drink?" asked Freda excitedly. "Could I have both please?" I answered, feeling that I could do with a cold drink after my walk, but that I would enjoy a cup of tea to sit down with and have a catch-up chat with my aunt Freda afterwards.

"Ok, Squash, and tea for Della! Just tea for me!" Ordered Freda, as Liz went about putting the kettle on, and clanking some cups and glasses around on the kitchen worktop.

The inside of the ranch house was stylish but on the rough-and-ready side. It looked very lived-in, with a combination of musty, and rustic smells of the animals, old furniture, and leather. The backdoor was open which let in a lovely floral and pine-scented breeze.

Even though it was all a tad ramshackle, it felt like a special place somehow. A place where my aunt Freda had turned her childhood dreams of being a "Cowgirl" into a reality! "Good for her!" I thought to myself, as I gazed around the kitchen at the Western-style décor and out through the window into the surrounding forest.

Liz hobbled over with our drinks on a tray like some kind of lowly servant and I was half expecting her to curtsy at any moment, especially as Aunt Freda had such a haughty personality, despite her wild cowgirl appearance. Aunt Freda was a character, that was for sure!

"Right, I'm off to stable Midnight, and water the horses!" Said Liz, after putting the tray of teas and my orange squash down on the table next to Freda and me.

She quickly finished drinking her own glass of orange squash, then hurried off out of the kitchen door.

"Don't forget to brush Comanche!" Shouted Freda, as Liz headed off out of the kitchen door. "Will do!" Liz shouted back as her voice faded away. "My goodness, is Comanche still around?!!" I exclaimed, remembering that Comanche had been my favourite horse to ride during my visit five years earlier. "Oh yes, where did you think he was?!" Exclaimed Freda, laughing at my comment. "Well, I guess, I mean I'd forgotten about Comanche until now?" I answered, trying to figure out what I'd meant for myself.

"Yes, Comanche, Midnight, and all of the others are still here, all going strong! Tommy-Tucker is about somewhere too! Do you remember him?" "Yes, I do!" I answered, with a vision of Tommy-Tucker the tortoise popping to mind.

"Your mother was given him on her sixteenth birthday, but she was never too interested in the animals her father gave her! She never rode her pony, and she hated the monkeys!" Said Freda, looking amused at her memories. My mum had told me stories about how her father always had a menagerie of animals, some of them exotic, around the house and backyard; monkeys, parrots, turtles, tortoises, tropical fish, cats and dogs…

"…So, when your mother showed no interest whatsoever in Tommy-Tucker, I told your grandpop, my uncle, that I would love to have him, and take him back to the Isle of Man with me…" Continued Aunt Freda.

"Gosh, so what age is he now?" I asked realising that he must be pretty ancient! "Oh, he's in his late thirties by now!" Answered Aunt Freda, as she pushed her chair back and stood up "Come one! I'll show you! We can go and say hello to Comanche too!" She added, leading the way out of the kitchen door. "Great!" I answered, as I stood up and followed her out of the kitchen door, and into the back garden.

Outside the air felt so fresh with a gentle breeze. The scents of various flowers pine, and shrubs hung in the air, as I hurriedly followed after Aunt Freda while simultaneously trying to savour the moment.

"My Manx-Cats! - The best in the whole of Great Britain!" Exclaimed Aunt Freda proudly as she strode off down the path into the back garden and waved towards what looked like a large caged area to our right. I glanced over, but didn't see any cats, and continued following along behind her feeling happy that she was in a good mood, and had been so welcoming towards me.

BOOK 1: TO SEE THE WORLD

"TOMMY! TOMMY! TOM! TOM!" Aunt Freda called out as she walked around a small garden area at the back of her ranch house. My eyes scanned the ground for signs of Tommy-Tucker the tortoise, but all I could see was grass, flowers, butterflies and bees buzzing around.

Suddenly there he was! RUNNING towards us on the grass along the side of the flower beds, he was making a beeline straight towards Aunt Freda. "Gosh, I didn't know that Tortoises could run like that!" I exclaimed. "Oh, yes, he's very fast!" answered Freda, as she swooped him up into her arms with his head facing me. "Della's here to see you!" She said loudly as she cuddled him, and stroked his head with one of her fingers. "Hello, Tommy-Tucker!" I said, as I smiled at him and reached out a hand to touch his head too. He seemed pretty laid-back and just stayed with his head out as we both made a fuss of him.

"OK, enough of Tommy-Tucker, let's go and see Comanche now!" said Freda, as she swiftly placed Tommy-Tucker back down on the grass, and went striding off past the flower beds. "Bye Tommy-Tucker!" I called out, as I ran to catch up with my aunt Freda.

"And here are my beautiful Manx Cats!" Freda exclaimed as she suddenly headed around the side of the garden, and back over towards the caged-off area. "I keep them in here at night, to keep them safe from predators, but they come out in the day, don't you, my beauties, come on, come back out and say hello to Della!" She exclaimed, as she opened the main gate to the cage and about nine or ten beautiful Manx Cats strutted out.

She called out their names to me as if I would remember them all, so I "Ooo'd, and Ahh'd", and reached down to pet them as they rubbed against my ankles, and purred loudly "Liz! Come and feed the Cats, while I take Della to see Comanche!" Shouted Freda loudly as she gave the cats one last pet, and rounded them all up, and back inside their pen.

I followed Aunt Freda back towards the garden area, looking forward to seeing Comanche. "Oh, and my pigeons are in the coop over there, you can see them later! Bertie is the oldest Pigeon in Britain!" Aunt Freda boasted loudly, as she strode off ahead of me, with her cowgirl swagger.

Aunt Freda led the way on through the garden, across the surrounding lawns, and down towards the paddock where a couple of horses were leisurely grazing. I recognised Comanche straight away, and my heart felt instantly happy to see him. "Comanche!" I exclaimed as I ran down the hill towards him.

Comanche looked up and stared at us. "Hi, Comanche!" I said gently, as I slowed back down to a walk as we got nearer to each other. He did a little heel kick, shook his head, and snorted before trotting over towards me. I felt sure he recognised me, as he came right up to me and made a whinnying noise while staring at me the whole time.

I smiled at him and stroked his head. "Hello Comanche, it's lovely to see you again," I said with a smile, and he made another whinnying noise. "It's like he remembers me!" I exclaimed to Aunt Freda as she joined us. "Oh, he remembers you all right! Horses are like Elephants, they never forget!" Answered Aunt Freda matter-of-factly.

"Liz, have you finished your chores yet? The cats need feeding" Freda shouted, as she spotted Liz walking between Stables. "Nearly finished!" Liz shouted back patiently.

"It's nearly supper time, you must be hungry!" Said aunt Freda, as she turned to head back towards the ranch house. "I am a bit!" I answered, suddenly realising that I was hungry, but not wanting to be a bother.

"Ok, come on, we'll have some supper soon!" answered Aunt Freda. I guessed it was around 6 pm, and it seemed a bit early for supper. To me, supper was a light snack just before bedtime. I guessed she meant what I would call tea.

"You'll have to sleep in the Caravan tonight!" Said Aunt Freda, as we walked back up towards the ranch house and past a small caravan parked up on our right. "Yeah, that's great, thank you!" I answered feeling excited to be there.

"So, how long are you planning on staying?" Asked Freda, as we walked on. "Well, I can stay for a few days, but I need to find some paid work as soon as possible really, as I only have a couple of quid left on me" I answered, hoping that Freda would understand why I couldn't stay too long if not being paid to work.

"Oh, I see, well, the hotels in Bournemouth will be hiring now, as it's the holiday season. Do you have any hotel experience?" She asked, sounding positive. "Yes, loads!" I answered, thinking about the time I'd washed glasses in a hotel for pocket money when I was 14, and how I'd recently worked part-time as a kitchen assistant in a hotel for the past year or so. "Wonderful! We can find you a job in no time then!" Answered Aunt Freda, sounding certain that I would have a job lined up very soon. "Great!" I answered, liking her positivity. Liz caught up with us as we entered the kitchen, and told Aunt Freda that she would feed the cats, and then join us for supper.

About an hour later we were all sat around the table eating a plate full of sausages, beans, and chips. 'Typical cowboy food' I chuckled to myself as I tucked in and listened to Aunt Freda and Liz chat about their day. They seemed like the best of friends one minute, and archenemies the next! "I guess it's just how they are" I thought to myself feeling mildly amused by their slight eccentricities.

That night, I bedded down into a slightly cold, damp, and musty-smelling Caravan. Aunt Freda had shown me how to use the gas heater if it got too cold and had given me a pile of extra blankets, so I figured that once I got into bed, I would be as snug as a bug in a rug!

I was soon cuddled up in bed feeling warm and cosy. I stared at the ceiling for a while thinking about my family and friends back in my home town. I hoped my mum was ok, and I wondered how my dad had taken the news that I was gone. I felt that he would be a little sad, but he would mainly be happy for me. I wasn't sure that my grandparents, or aunts and uncles, would be too bothered either way, as I didn't see them often, and I was sure that my brothers; Steve, Martin and Carl, would take the news easily, as we were all pretty independent.

My mind flashed to Matt, the guy I'd been seeing, I was sure he'd be ok. I thought about my old school friends: Sue LL, Sue L, Pauline E, and some of my new Tech' College friends, and I guessed they would probably be a little surprised, but I think they were all expecting me to take off at some point, going from my previous chats about it.

My thoughts then turned to the day's events: Waving goodbye to Vee and Gee, the vision of Vee scribbling down the licence plate number as I drove away with my hitched lift, the conversations with all of the different drivers who had picked me up while hitch-hiking, the reuniting with aunt Freda, and Liz, and seeing her animals again, especially Comanche and Tommy-Tucker.

As all of these thoughts and visions whirled around in my head, I felt a strong sense of being torn from the old and familiar, and of throwing myself into the new and unfamiliar, and although it felt somewhat daunting, and scary, it also felt somewhat wonderful, and liberating, and over all I was so excited to finally be starting my new life, in the new forest!

The following morning, I was up bright and early, and jumped out of the caravan in search of my aunt Freda, Liz, and coffee! I found all three in the kitchen of the ranch house and smiled and said good morning to Aunt Freda and Liz as I stepped inside. They greeted me, and Aunt Freda told me to help myself to cereal, coffee or tea. I grabbed a bowl of cereal, poured a cup of coffee, and went to sit with them at the kitchen table.

"Right, we're going to have to get you a haircut ASAP!" Announced Freda suddenly directing her gaze over towards me as if she meant business. I was shocked, as I didn't see anything wrong with my henna-coloured, spiral-curled long hair. "What's wrong with my hair?" I asked, feeling genuinely puzzled.

"Well, you can't find a good job with your hair looking like that!" Answered Aunt Freda abruptly. "What on earth could employers have against my innocent hair?" I answered on the verge of laughing at such a ridiculous concept, yet at the same time, feeling genuinely puzzled as to where she was coming from.

She seemed so certain that I wouldn't be hired looking so unconventional, and I started feeling that was fine because I wouldn't want to work with people if they had such a small-minded mentality! - I was always clean, and well-groomed, I just happened to have a slightly creative flare! "So, what's the big deal?" I asked feeling confused, and somewhat defensive.

"Well, to get where you want to be in this world, you have to play the game! Then, once you're where you want to be, you can dress and do as you please!" answered Aunt Freda matter-of-factly.

"Hmmm?" I answered, thinking that this seemed somewhat reasonable "Yes, but what if where I want to be is with like-minded, creative, free-spirited people!" I answered defiantly. Aunt Freda looked like she wasn't sure what to say to that, so I quickly thought that at this point it was best to just take on board what she was saying, especially as I did need a job as soon as possible!

"Ok, ok, I can play the game!" I answered facetiously, while rolling my eyes, "...Just as long as everyone else realises that we're playing a game and that what really matters is that we are good people!" I added as I shook my head, and rolled my eyes one more time, as a final act of defiance, before letting out a loud sigh and sinking my shoulders submissively.

Aunt Freda seemed to understand where I was coming from and nodded in agreement, and went on about the world being a crazy "Rat-Race" asking why I thought she was living in the forest with her animals and Liz! We all laughed, and then Freda went about getting her things together to take me into town for a haircut. I decided to think of it all as an interesting social experiment and to just go along with it, and see what happens. From now on my free will, would be set on a sliding scale with the greater world around me, so I may as well enjoy it!

After a short drive, we arrived in the village of Fording Bridge, and Aunt Freda parked her Station wagon car in a car park. Aunt Freda then led the way to a small hairdresser's salon just a couple of minutes walk away.

We stepped inside the salon, and a young woman came forward to greet us. "Hello, Sandra! This is my niece Della from Shropshire, she's down here job hunting, and needs to look the part!" Exclaimed Aunt Freda, for all the world to hear, much to my embarrassment.

'William Shakespeare was right about the World being a Stage!' I thought to myself, as I stood behind my aunt, smiling and nodding passively at the hairdresser like some kind of wayward youth who had seen the error of my ways and was finally on the verge of conforming. I tried not to laugh at this thought, and did my best to look serious, while in reality, I felt like some kind of dummy standing there!

'How far was I willing to take this social experiment?' I thought to myself, as Aunt Freda had a catch-up chat with Sandra. 'Maybe I am actually conforming? but if so, what am I conforming from?' I argued with myself, "I'm a good person! I help old people carry their shopping, I always hand in purses if I find them, and some of my friends and I even used to skive off school to go and cheer up people at the old folks home by leading jolly singalongs! So yes, I am a good person! So why should I be made to feel bad about having a bit of a wild hairdo? It's ridiculous!' I thought to myself, while still standing there nodding, and smiling, and trying not to let my grievances show.

"Ok, you can sit here!" Said Sandra, as she pulled out a seat for me. "Just a dry Cut" exclaimed Aunt Freda, obviously aware that she would be lumbered with the bill. I just continued nodding and smiling, like a dummy, and trying my best to just go along with it all. About a half hour later, I was leaving the hair salon with a much shorter haircut. All of my spiral curls and henna highlights were gone.

"I guess it wasn't too painful!" I joked to my aunt Freda, as we jumped into her car and headed back to her ranch house. She rolled her head back and let out a loud laugh. I chuckled and shook my head a little. This going along with things felt unnatural, but I was starting to see it all as part of my adventure…

"Oh, we'll have to pick up a paper on the way back, to look for a job for you!" Aunt Freda said as she started up her car. "What else do you need? do you need any toiletries or anything?" she asked, looking like she genuinely wanted to help me. I told her that I was ok, and had all I needed for now. She turned the radio on, and we both relaxed as she drove over to a nearby supermarket.

"I need to pick up a few things, and we can get a newspaper here too" she said, as she drove into the supermarket carpark. I was impressed by how helpful she was being, despite her tumultuous ways, I felt she did have a good heart underneath it all. I remember hearing stories of her helping the so-called "Peace Convoy travellers" after their caravans had been demolished by police during a Stonehenge riot. Apparently, even pregnant women had been beaten up, dragged off and arrested. Their mobile homes had been demolished in the process. Aunt Freda had taken them food and water, and pet food for the animals too.

She saw the Peace Convoy travellers as the underdog, and probably related to them in some way, being somewhat of a misfit from conventional society herself and living out in the forest as she did. She also had a soft spot for Native Americans and always spoke up for them if ever the topic came up. She was disgusted by what the Europeans had done to them, and I had to agree with her.

"We Europeans are not always the good guys, despite what our schools try to teach us!" Exclaimed Freda passionately. "Well, I guess crap can't smell itself!" I answered as I shook my head, feeling somewhat puzzled by this upside-down world. Aunt Freda laughed loudly at my analogy, then went about focusing on her driving.

As she drove, I slipped into a daydream and started to imagine life through the ages and all the wonderful and crazy things that had happened throughout all of time.

I pictured people living with nature in tropical jungles, eating fruit from the trees, and sitting around in a peaceful paradise, wanting for nothing. Then I imagined the humans moving on to caves and creating fire and clothes. Next, I saw nomadic tribes moving across vast landscapes and hoping to find a good base to camp, and bumping into fellow nomads, and having the wisdom to make peace, rather than war with each other.

I went on to imagine humans building towns and cities, creating technology, and commercial products, followed by wars starting over greed, resources, power, and corruption...

BOOK 1: TO SEE THE WORLD

'What was it all leading to? It all seems so bizarre and ridiculous! - Including my new haircut!' I chuckled to myself, suddenly coming out of my daydream as the car engine stopped, and Aunt Freda jumped out of the car to pop into a shop.

"I'll just wait here unless you need help carrying anything?" I shouted after her, feeling that I was enjoying just relaxing and pondering on life. "Ok, you wait here, I don't need help thank you, do you want the radio back on?" asked Freda, already out of the car. "No, it's fine thanks!" I answered. Feeling my thoughts were enough entertainment for the time being.

That afternoon, back at the ranch house, Aunt Freda scanned through the paper calling out local job listings to me. Most of them were in the nearby coastal towns and cities of Bournemouth, Southampton, and Swanage. For each job that I answered yes to she would circle with her pen. The idea was to get a few ready so that we could phone them all in a row.

"O.K, let's get phoning! Swanage Hilltop Hotel first!" Said Freda enthusiastically, as soon as I finished my coffee. My stomach started to tighten with nerves, as she started dialling the first number. I took a deep breath and slid to the edge of my seat as if ready for action. I wondered what questions I might be asked if some of them wanted to speak to me.

"Hello, I'm calling on behalf of my niece Della, she's from a very respectable family, her grandfather was the best dentist in the county, do you have a job for her?" Said Freda, in a commanding tone. I suddenly felt very awkward and put on the spot.

"Yes, she can do all of that! She's very bright, she can turn her hand to anything! Isn't that Right Della?" Said Aunt Freda looking over at me. "Yep!" I nodded and smiled back at her while cringing with embarrassment.

"Here, she wants to speak to you!" Said Freda, passing the phone to me. "OK, thanks!" I said taking the phone off her and clearing my throat to talk. The woman on the other end of the phone sounded almost as abrupt as Aunt Freda as she asked me about my previous work experience. I told her about my past hotel work and assured her that I was capable of the tasks she was rattling off. It all seemed a bit much, and although I was thoroughly capable, I wasn't sure that I actually wanted to do such a never-ending list of chores! 'But I do need a job - with pay!' I reminded myself and carried on agreeing to the lady's long list of demands.

31

"When can you start?" Asked the lady suddenly. "Um, well anytime!" I answered, nodding at Freda as if to say "Right?" "OK, well, if you arrive here on Sunday evening at 6 pm, you can start on Monday morning, how does that sound?" asked the lady. "Yes, that's great! Thank you!" I answered. Feeling excited to have got the job so swiftly! "I'll show you around when you arrive, and Yvonne will train you when you start the next morning, you'll soon pick it all up!" Added the lady briefly.

"OK, thank you, and what is your name please?" I asked as she was about to hang up. "Mrs Jones" She answered curtly as if she had been inconvenienced to have to spend an extra second to give me her name. "Ok, thanks again, see you Sunday!" I answered, before hanging up.

"Yay! Thanks, Freda!!" I said excitedly. Aunt Freda Smiled back and laughed. "Of course, they would give you a job, you come from a very good family!" She then went on to tell me about some of our family history regarding lords and ladies from Ireland who had descended from French royalty.

I joked that although it all sounded well and good, I hadn't inherited a single castle, or even a tiny trinket from any of them, adding that if I had, maybe I would be a guest at the hotel, not a servant!

Freda found this hilarious, and we were both laughing loudly like two fools when Liz appeared in the kitchen looking baffled and asking us what we were laughing at. "Della's got a job!" Answered Freda. "Well, there's a bit more to it than that!" I added, thinking that my getting a job wasn't THAT funny! And we all laughed.

That evening, I headed back to the caravan and jotted down the latest events in my journal, I had decided to keep a journal of my travel adventures and had enjoyed writing about the last couple of days' events.

I went to bed feeling on top of the world. As I fell asleep visions of my mum, dad, brothers, other family members and friends back in my home town whirled around in my head. I hoped that they were all ok with me leaving. It wasn't that I didn't love and miss them all, it was more that I also loved the world at large and wanted to see and experience it. I felt that they would understand, as they knew the type of person I was.

I woke up realising that I only had one more day to spend with Aunt Freda, Liz and the animals before I would be heading off to my new job at the Hilltop Hotel on Sunday.

The day was spent mainly helping with a few chores and chatting with Aunt Freda about our family. She loved to tell family stories from the past and was pleasantly surprised that I was familiar with some of them, like the one about the Irish wolfhound adopted by my grandpop, that had run out of the house in panic during a storm one night and was tragically hit by a train. The train driver had thought it was a horse because it was so large!

In the afternoon I went for a little walk alone into the forest with the hope of seeing my wild pony friend from five years earlier, but sadly, I didn't see him, so I sent a message of love to him out into the forest and hoped that it would reach him somehow.

Afterwards, I went to say goodbye to Comanche, Tommy-Tucker, the Manx-Cats, and all of the other Animals. I felt sad to be saying goodbye, but I was also excited by the thought that I would be moving on the next day.

That evening we made a phone call to my grandmother's house to give a message to my mum and dad to let them know that I was ok. Neither of my parents had phones, so this was better than nothing as a way to get in touch and pass on a message. My Grandmother was about ninety, so I didn't keep her on the phone for too long, but it was nice to hear her voice. She wished me well and told me that she would pass on my message.

Aunt Freda, Liz, and I all had another hearty meal of chips, beans, and sausages that evening, and we all had a good laugh and chat about life in general. Afterwards, I headed over to the caravan to pack my rucksack, while looking forward to setting off to Swanage the next day. I fell asleep fast, and it seemed seconds later that it was morning and time to get up. I jumped out of bed, used the tiny bathroom, quickly got dressed, grabbed my rucksack and hurried over to the ranch house.

Aunt Freda looked ready to go but told me to grab myself a coffee and help myself to some of the toast and jam that was on the table first. I gulped down my coffee and hurriedly ate the toast and jam while Freda went about tidying up the kitchen and getting her things together. Liz was nowhere to be seen, but I guessed we would see her outside on our way to the car.

CHAPTER 5:

THANK YOU; BENEDICT TAYLOR AND FELLOW KINDRED SPIRITS!

I followed Aunt Freda outside, and glanced around looking for Liz "We're leaving now Liz!" shouted Freda as she strode towards her car. "Bye Della! Good luck with your job!" Shouted Liz, suddenly appearing from way down on the other side of the paddock.

"Bye, Liz!" I shouted back as I waved to her and took one last look at my surroundings before running over to Aunt Freda's car and jumping inside ready for her to give me a lift to the local bus station.

As we drove along Aunt Freda was giving me advice on how to do a good job in order to make the money that I needed to do the things that I really wanted to do in life, and reminding me to "Play the game!" as she put it! Although I didn't like the idea of people being fake to each other, I had to admire her canny Spirit!

"Oh, and I want you to come to America with me at some point!" she exclaimed out of the blue. "Sounds good! When?" I answered "...late this year or early next year sometime, all being well. I'm looking to buy a ranch in Montana, Oregon, or Northern California, and I would like you to join me for company. Liz can stay home and run Hunters Moon" She continued, as if she had it all planned out in her mind.

"...Keep in touch by phone and mail over the next few months and one of the days, we can meet up in London to arrange our visas, you do have a passport, don't you?" She asked, sounding as if she knew that I did. "Yes, I've got it with me..." I started to answer "...Anyway, not to worry about that now, there's plenty of time!" exclaimed Aunt Freda, as if hearing my "Yes" was enough.

BOOK 1: TO SEE THE WORLD

Feeling pleasantly surprised with her invitation to join her in America I smiled to myself, and my mind flashed to my visualisations to visit America. "Must be the power of positive thinking!" I thought to myself with a grin.

We arrived at the bus station, and she told me what number bus to catch to Bournemouth, and explained that from Bournemouth I would need to take a ferry over to Swanage. This sounded fun, and I looked forward to my short journey.

Aunt Freda had insisted on paying my bus fare to Swanage. Saying that she didn't want me hitch-hiking in this day and age! I had tried to assure her that it was fine, but she wasn't having it, so I reluctantly took the bus fare off her.

Aunt Freda didn't want to stick around at the bus station, as she had her Animals to tend to, but she wished me all the best and handed me a couple of quid in change, as she gave me a big hug. "Thanks, Freda!" I exclaimed as she turned to jump in her car.

"Don't forget to phone and write!" She called out before driving off. "I won't!" I called out, as I waved goodbye, before turning to walk towards the bus she had told me to catch.

I was soon sitting on half-full the bus to Bournemouth leaning against my dad's old Rucksack and daydreaming of all the great adventures ahead of me. The sense of freedom once again created a natural high, which I felt sure that I was projecting out to all of my fellow bus passengers as they all seemed so happy too!

I felt so grateful for just being, as if all of my past, present, and future moments were in perfect balance and harmony, and I was blissfully riding the wave of the eternal now, and savouring every second as I went.

"Bournemouth Ferry Port!" Called out the Bus driver, suddenly bringing me out of my daydream state. I grabbed my rucksack, thanked the bus driver, and jumped off the bus. A ferry boat was sitting as if patiently waiting for its passengers to board, so I picked up my walking pace for fear of it suddenly taking off without me, and I quickly joined the queue of locals and tourists waiting to board it.

The ferry ride was short but sweet! It gave me a momentary sense of setting sail off to foreign shores, and I wondered what it would be like to sail across the oceans of the world. My fellow passengers and I all scurried off the ferry boat once it reached Swanage, and I stood looking around for a few seconds to get my bearings.

I spotted a newspaper stand, so I walked over and asked for directions to the Hilltop Hotel. The newspaperman directed me towards a steep road that seemed to be heading upwards alongside a clifftop. I thanked him and started walking.

It turned out to be about a fifteen-minute walk, which was good as it gave me time to take in my surroundings, and to gather my thoughts. Swanage had fresh salty air, and an uplifting feeling to it. I could see that it was a holiday spot for people from the South of the UK, as the majority of the holidaymakers around me had London-sounding accents.

I looked up to see a sign for the Hilltop Hotel on a post a few feet ahead of me. I took a deep breath and headed toward the entrance. It was an all-white painted, posh-looking medium-sized hotel. I gathered that the back of the hotel overlooked the Sea. There were detached, similarly, posh-looking hotels on either side of it, and the whole road seemed to be a hotel row!

As I walked up the hotel steps, a matronly-looking lady suddenly appeared "You must be Miss Hopley" she said abruptly. "Yes, that's me, are you Mrs Jones?!" I answered politely with a smile. "Yes, follow me!" She answered curtly, as she swiftly turned to lead the way.

Her manner wasn't very warm and friendly, it was cold and abrupt, as if she wanted me to get the message that she was the boss. I felt somewhat uncomfortable with her attitude, but I went about following her around the hotel as she told me what areas and rooms were what.

There was a large dining room which had a lovely view overlooking the Sea. A few tables had guests sitting at them, leisurely chatting, and sipping on their drinks. There were various lounge areas, and a bar area with plush red leather seats, where a couple of men sat on high stools chatting away.

She led me on to a large kitchen where people were busy preparing food. Some of them briefly glanced my way, but nobody smiled or even nodded any kind of greeting. They all looked stressed and unhappy. It all felt a bit overwhelming, but I figured that was natural for most new situations.

I followed her upstairs and she briefly showed me the guest rooms on the first floor. There seemed to be about twenty guest rooms. Then she led me up more stairs to what I presumed was the hotel workers' quarters.

"This is your room," she said opening the door to a small white-painted semi-attic room. "Ah great! Thank You!" I answered stepping inside, feeling happy to have a little room of my own.

"I'll leave you to get settled in, report to the kitchen at 6 am sharp. Yvonne will train you in, you'll soon pick it all up!" She said while looking ready to leave. "OK, thank you!" I answered as I got ready to close the door behind me. "Right then!" she said, and turned and swiftly walked away. I closed the door and turned to put my backpack down.

"Wow, my own little room!" I thought as I looked around, feeling so excited to have my very first home away from home! I suddenly felt very pleased with my new situation, despite the somewhat formal atmosphere. "This is great!" I thought, as I lay back on the bed, let out a sigh of contentment, and gazed up at the ceiling, once again feeling in perfect balance with the world.

After about twenty minutes of just lying on the bed and gazing at the ceiling, thinking about this exciting new phase of my life, albeit a somewhat daunting one. I jumped up and looked around the room to see where I could put my things away.

The first thing I noticed was the alarm clock on the bedside table, so I set it to 5.30 am the next day. I glanced around the room some more and wasn't sure if I liked the pale pastel-pink wallpaper or not. I noticed that the wall above the window seemed to be the start of the roof as it sloped up to the ceiling for a few feet and gave the impression that my room was part of a two-story attic or loft conversion. I assumed there must be one more level above me judging by the shape of the ceiling.

There was a slim white wardrobe in the corner to the right of the door where the ceiling was at its highest, and a white chest of drawers, across from the foot of the bed, near to the window where the ceiling curved down, and was at its lowest. There was also a small white table with a matching chair alongside of the wall opposite the bed. I envisioned mainly using it as a desk to write at and pictured myself writing in my journal and writing out cards and letters to family and friends.

My mum popped into my mind again, and I hoped that she was ok. I sat for a moment thinking about my friends and family back in my home town and hoped that everyone was doing just fine and that they were all happy for me, rather than worried about me.

After a few more minutes of thinking about my family and friends back in my home town, I took a deep breath, stood up, and set about unpacking my rucksack.

I hung my clothes in the wardrobe, placed my spare shoes on the wardrobe floor, arranged my toiletries neatly on the top of the chest of drawers and put the rest of my bits and bobs inside of the drawers.

Although I was tempted to put my journal on the desk-like table top, I decided to leave it in my shoulder bag, as I was getting in the habit of jotting down notes daily in it and wanted to keep it with me for most of the time.

Feeling pleased with myself I decided to go for a little walk around Swanage to explore my new homebase a little more. I touched up my makeup and brushed my hair, then headed out of my door. I spotted a couple of keys on a keyring hanging on one of the coat hooks on the back of the door and figured they must be for my door and the main front door. I grabbed the keys and then headed off down the hallway and the stairs to the ground floor.

I passed by a couple of staff members in the downstairs hallway and said hello, they said hello back, but they seemed very subdued. My overall feeling was that this hotel was not the happiest place to work, but hopefully, I would be able to hang in there and just "Play the game" long enough to save up some money to continue with my travels. My journey was still young, and I didn't want to ruin it! I would ask my dad to send my savings to me at some point, but I wanted to make sure that I was going to stay first.

I stepped outside into the fresh sea air and looked around me. A few fancy-looking cars were parked in the car park at the front. A white brick wall, topped with a lush green hedge surrounded the car park. The driveway led to a wide gateway for both cars and people to come and go to and from the Hotel, and the road outside sloped downwards towards the town.

I stood on my tiptoes and stretched my neck to look over the hedge and up the hill. More hotels on each side of the road for as far as the eye could see. I wondered if some of the other hotels were more fun than this one. 'Too late now!' I chuckled to myself!

I heard some bickering voices from inside the hotel behind me and thought I'd better get going quickly as I didn't like the sound of their tone. I moved fast and swiftly made it to the pavement outside of the hotel.

BOOK 1: TO SEE THE WORLD

I glanced back, to see Mrs Jones, pointing out an area on the porch to a sorrowful-looking female member of staff. 'I guess she missed a spot!' I thought, as my mind flashed to the old-fashioned brown and white uniform the staff at the hotel wore.

I laughed at the thought of myself in one of these uniforms, and had the sense of going from one extreme to another! 'One minute I'm a free-spirited, wild long-haired, creatively dressed punky new-waver, and the next I'm a full-on traditional maid! -Strange World!' I thought while laughing to myself at how ludicrous it all seemed as I trundled off down the road.

I strolled down the hill, past the numerous hotels, and down towards the beachfront. I didn't pass too many people on my way down the road from the hotel, I guessed that most of the hotel residents stayed within the hotel grounds, and maybe some of the hotels even had steps down to the Beach.

As I neared the beach front more people started appearing and milling about. There looked to be a fifty-fifty mix of what looked like holiday-makers and locals, This I could tell, not only from their attire, but from the expressions of their faces. - The holidaymakers looked like they had not a care in the world, as they strolled along the promenade that ran along the beachfront, while dressed in their bright and breezy clothes.

Meanwhile, the locals, dressed in dowdier, more practical clothes strolled along with their heads down as if in deep thought, or staring straight ahead as if in a hurry to get somewhere. I decided that for the time being at least, I was a holidaymaker, reasoning that my job hadn't actually started yet!

As I arrived in the centre beachfront area of Swanage, I felt my spirit start to lift, and my sense of well-being strengthen. Any woes I had instantly shrunk down to virtually insignificant specks, and a feeling of pure joy took over me. I was feeling great and on top of the world! I walked along until I found a nice spot to sit on the sand and just enjoy the day.

As I sat on the sand, I once again had the wonderful feeling of being at one with everything, from the tiniest grain of sand on the beach, to the whole of the universe! I gazed around me at my fellow beach loungers and wondered if they were feeling the same. The sky was a beautiful shade of blue, with a few white fluffy clouds just sitting still, as if placed there as a finishing touch by some grand designer.

I lay back on the sand and enjoyed my wonderful state of being. Tomorrow I would be jumping head first into the "Game" but for now, I was just me - and the whole of the Universe!

The next morning, I woke up to the sound of the alarm clock ringing at 5.30 am. It had a high-pitched frantic sound, as if in an attempt to immediately switch my gears, from sleep to action! I jumped out of bed wearing the long T-shirt that I'd slept in.

Once I got there, I used the loo and took a quick shower. I was never a morning person. I was always most awake in the evenings when I would feel energised for going out and about, or staying home and getting creative and maybe dabbling with some arts and crafts, or writing, and usually once I got into a project, I could easily get lost in it until 2 or 3 am, and only then would I start to get sleepy. So, to have to get up at 8 am for school, or a part-time job was always a struggle for me, let alone a 5.30 am wake-up!

The shower helped to wake me up a little, but back in my room, as I sat brushing my hair, and putting my makeup on I wondered what the world would be like if it was run by night people. All those poor morning people forced to stay up and work late! I chuckled at the thought, then realised, I'd better get a move on! I had to be fully dressed and ready to start by 6 am!

I quickly put on the brown and white uniform that Mrs Jones had left in my room for me. 'Oh, how I miss the carefree gal I was yesterday!' I joked to myself, as I had pulled the uniform into place, and brushed off any bits of lint.

I looked at myself in the mirror, and felt so ridiculous wearing the maid's uniform 'As If the hair thing wasn't enough? We have to wear costumes too!' I thought to myself, not knowing whether to laugh or cry! I left my room and hurried off down to the kitchen.

Most of the staff had already started working by the time I arrived in the kitchen, only Mrs Jones, and Yvonne stood chatting to one side. They greeted me with an impatient look, which I found unfair as it was only just 6 am on the dot. 'Maybe they expected me earlier?' I wondered to myself. '…If so, they should have said so!' I thought defensively as I walked over towards them.

"Good morning!" I said with a smile. "Morning" they both mumbled back at me. "This is Yvonne, she'll show you what to do!" announced Mrs Jones, before she sped off out of the kitchen towards the reception area.

BOOK 1: TO SEE THE WORLD

I smiled at Yvonne who was getting some paperwork together on a side counter. I glanced around me, taking it all in. A balding, chubby, middle-aged male chef was preparing some meats, while two young late teens/early twenties gals stood nearby chopping up vegetables. My mind flashed to my job at the hotel kitchen back near my hometown. It was quite an easy job, just preparing food and following orders, but I supposed the general atmosphere and pace of a place of a place is somewhat set by stress levels. This place seemed stressed out to start with, and the day had barely begun!

The two gals chopped away, both in silence as if afraid to speak. They also wore brown and white uniforms, but their hair was tied up under hair-nets, with a white hat on top. They looked like they could be sisters, they were both slim built, with pretty, but timid-looking faces.

I glanced around at the other kitchen staff to see if anyone would at least acknowledge my existence. - They didn't have to clap and cheer or anything, but a friendly nod with a smile would have been nice, instead, they all kept their heads down and continued working away.

"Right, put these on!" barked Yvonne at me at me suddenly. As she thrust something towards me. I took what turned out to be a hairnet and white hat from her hand, and chuckled out loud, quickly attempting to cover my chuckle with a question, and asking if there was a mirror anywhere.

"Here, I'll do it!" said Yvonne impatiently as she grabbed the hairnet and hat back out of my hands. "It's ok, I'll do it!" I responded, grabbing the items back again. "I was just asking if there was a mirror, I wasn't asking you to put them on for me!" I said in a bemused tone, as I pulled a puzzled face at her. I quickly put on the hairnet and hat, as I sensed Yvonne backing down a little.

Once my hairnet and hat were on, Yvonne started pointing out things in the kitchen. She explained to me that the hotel was "Silver-Service" and went about calling out the long list of my to-dos each day - "Set the breakfast tables. Take the morning teas to the rooms. Serve the breakfasts. Clear up the breakfast area after breakfast. Vacuum the breakfast and lounge area. Polish the bar and the glass tables. Help clear up the kitchen area. Then repeat the whole process for each meal. You finish at 8 pm, then you're free to do as you please!" said Yvonne after she'd finished with what seemed like a never-ending list of chores.

"Probably pass out!" I joked back. Yvonne stared back at me blankly. I awkwardly smiled, then went about following her around on a whirlwind tour, until we arrived back in the kitchen area. A tea trolly with two trays of tea in silver pots with white cups and saucers sat waiting patiently by the kitchen entrance. Steam was coming out of the teapot, so I gathered they were freshly made.

"Ok, take this tea trolly to the lift, go up to the guest floor, and take one tea tray to room two and the other to room seven" Ordered Yvonne, as if she was in the biggest hurry of her life. "OK," I answered, thinking 'This is easy enough' despite feeling like I'd landed in some 18th-century costume drama.

I wheeled the tea trolly towards the lift, feeling like all of the kitchen staff's eyes were on me as I went. I hoped that the tea trolly would run smoothly, but it felt heavy, and unbalanced as though the whole thing was about to crash and flip over. I told myself to just keep going and to try and act calm and composed despite feeling as though I was walking on a tightrope with an audience just watching - and waiting for me to fall!

Much to my relief I made it safely to the lift and made a great sigh of relief once I was inside, and the door had closed. At least I would have a few seconds to catch my breath before delivering the teas. I suddenly wondered if I was meant to knock on the doors, or just leave them outside. Yvonne hadn't specified. I decided that I would give a light knock, and hope for a response.

Each tray of tea was delivered successfully, as much to my surprise the guests in each of the rooms were already up and about. 'That's morning-people for you!' I chuckled to myself, as I headed back down in the lift with the empty tea trolly.

I felt quite pleased with myself that my first mission of the day had been smoothly accomplished. "That's done!" I announced as I arrived back into the Kitchen, ready for my next mission. Aside from a slight glance from one of the "Sisters" everyone just ignored me and carried on working. I stood there like a lemon for what felt like an eternity, before deciding that my best bet was to find Yvonne or Mrs Jones for my next instructions.

I found the two of them busy polishing the bar in the lounge. "Hello again! What shall I do next?" I asked with a smile. Yvonne and Mrs Jones rolled their eyes at each other, as Yvonne stepped forward and barked "Follow me!"

As each second passed in the company of Mrs Jones, or Yvonne I was feeling more and more that I didn't like this place one bit! but I kept remembering Aunt Freda's words to "Play the game" so I held my tongue, and docilely followed behind like a puppy dog in training.

'Why have they got such a rude manner?' I wondered to myself? '...I bet staff don't stay here too long!' I concluded, as Yvonne impatiently led me over to meet two other female maids aged around their late teens or early twenties who were hurriedly setting the tables for breakfast in the dining area.

The room was immaculate with around twenty round tables, each with a pristine white tablecloth draped over it. Half of the room was made up of large ceiling-to-floor windows that overlooked the sea. It was beautiful, and I felt that I would certainly much rather be a guest than a maid here!

My mind flashed to my joking with Aunt Freda about not inheriting any castles or even tiny trinkets from the ancestral royals, and I grinned to myself, as I wondered how Mrs Jones and Yvonne would be treating me if I was there as a guest instead of a worker. 'Very differently!' I thought to myself as I continued to look around the dining room.

"Della, this is Lisa and Mandy, they'll show you what to do. I've got to get back to the bar!" barked Yvonne, before hurrying off. The girls gave me a slight smile and nod but continued setting the table without saying hello, or giving me any instructions whatsoever. Once again, I hovered about feeling uncomfortable, with the feeling of not liking the place at all, growing by the second!

I looked over at the girls hoping that they would glance back, and give me some kind of signal or clue at least as to what I should be doing, but instead, they just carried on polishing the cutlery and setting the table and ignoring me. 'Maybe they resent me joining them?' I wondered as I continued to look their way, as I stood there doing my best to look ready for their instructions.

They were both slim and fair-skinned, with freckles and what looked like reddish-blonde hair. 'Maybe they're related too?' I pondered, reasoning that 'There is said to be safety in numbers' I laughed out loud, and had to pretend that I'd seen something funny outside. "Oh, look at that Pigeon!" I said, meaning Seagull, and they both gave me a deadpan stare. "Never mind, it's gone now! so what do you want me to do?" I asked, feeling as though if I didn't ask they would just continue to ignore me.

Mandy let out a sign, finished what she was doing, walked over towards me, and told me that we had to set all of the tables in a certain way, as the hotel was "silver-service" There was that phrase again, I still didn't have a clue what it meant, but was getting the impression that it just meant posh!

"OK," I answered, following her over to where all the trays of silver-coloured cutlery were. "You must make sure that each utensil is perfectly clean, so we polish them with a tea towel before placing them on the table" said Mandy coldly, as Lisa just carried on hurriedly setting the tables, in a manner that said, "We can't slow down, or we'll be in trouble!"

As Mandy went about showing me how to set the tables "Silver-Service style" my head started to spin with the rigmarole of it! it seemed that each person would have about seven pieces of cutlery each! - and each piece had to be in a specific order!

'Oh my god, get me out of here!' I thought to myself, as I followed Mandy around watching how she did it. "Here, you try!" Said Mandy shoving a set of cutlery at me. "OK," I answered, feeling like a deer trapped in the headlights.

As I placed the cutlery on the table, Mandy would say if it was correct or not. After a few goes, I suddenly got it, and it became easy. 'Ah, this isn't so bad after all' I thought to myself as Mandy eventually left me to carry on by myself.

I went into a daydream as I set the rest of my tables, but was rudely called out of it by Mandy announcing that the guests were here! Suddenly the doors flew open as what seemed like hundreds of people, mainly retired couples, piled into the dining room. I recognised one couple from my early morning tea delivery.

"Ok, quick, we have to go and take the breakfast orders!" Said Mandy shoving a note pad into my hand. "Get the table number as you take the order!" She called back as she hurried off to the nearest table.

I headed to a nearby table with my pen and notepad in hand. "Good morning, are you ready to order?" I asked with a smile. "Not yet, we've only just sat down!" answered a gruff-sounding, northern accent belonging to a 60-something balding man with a very large stomach, as his partner/wife, a meek-looking mousy-haired lady with glasses, smiled up at me apologetically. "OK, I'll come back!" I answered, looking around the room awkwardly, and feeling like a lemon once again.

Most of the people had only just sat down, but I guessed that Mandy and Lisa knew who the ready to order people were, unlike me, who didn't have a clue, so I just stood there awkwardly smiling at whoever glanced my way, aiming to give people a minute or two to decide what they wanted before asking for their orders.

BOOK 1: TO SEE THE WORLD

Suddenly Yvonne appeared and marched towards me angrily and I felt my defences instinctively go up. "Don't just stand there! Get to the kitchen and start collecting breakfast trays!" she barked while looking annoyed with me. "Well, I didn't know I was supposed to…" "Just Go!" she barked. "OK!" I barked back, feeling like I wanted to "Go" alright!

I headed towards the kitchen, shaking my head as I went. 'What a horrible place!' I thought to myself, feeling upset by her and Mrs Jones's rude, and abrupt manner. I took a deep breath and decided to just grin and bear it, and to do my best to just get on with it. I felt sure that from that moment on, my face would probably become just as miserable as the rest of them!

The rest of the day was a constant list of chores, and by 8 pm I couldn't wait to escape to my room and just flake out! I threw off the silly maid's uniform, put my long t-shirt on, and sat on my bed for a second to catch my breath, before almost collapsing into a sleeping position. "Oh my God, I have to do it all again tomorrow!" I thought to myself as I dozed off.

About an hour later I woke up feeling groggy. I looked at the clock, it was just after 9 pm. For a split second, I thought it was morning, and felt a sudden surge of panic, but then I noticed that it was getting dark outside, and realised that it must be nighttime.

I sat up on my bed and looked around my small room. Everything was still. All of the furniture, my clothes hanging over the chair, my toiletries on the chest of drawers, my little table/desk area by the wall There wasn't even a breeze coming in through the slightly open window.

I felt as though time was momentarily frozen while it waited for me to decide what to do next. Visions of my work day were whizzing through my head, followed by the dreadful thought that I would have to repeat it over again, and again until who knows when? The thought of endless days of repetition in such a hostile environment shocked me to the core.

'Forget this, I'm going out! - I'm not just here to work!' I told myself as I jumped up, and headed to the bathroom across the hall. I quickly washed my face with warm water, then splashed my face with cold water a few more times, in effort to wake up. I went back to my room, and quickly got dressed into my fun new-wave style clothes. I put on my gold-coloured low-heeled slip-on shoes with a bow at the front, which I thought was a fun touch, and sat down at my desk/table, and started to do my hair and make-up.

As I put my make-up on, I started to feel a buzz of excitement, as I imagined checking out the nightlife around the town. I glanced at the clock; it was nearing 9.30 pm. I figured that I could be in the town centre by 9.45-10pm-ish, and spend a couple of hours out, before heading back around midnight to get some sleep, before my 5.30 am wake-up time.

'The night is young!' I told myself as I headed out of my room. There were a few more rooms on my floor, but I'd yet to see anyone come and go from them. I concluded that the other staff must get the kitchen extra early to please Mrs Jones and Yvonne. 'Creeps!' I thought to myself as I shook my head at how unfriendly they were.

After I locked my room, for some reason I felt the need to virtually tiptoe, almost as if I would be in trouble if I was spotted leaving the premises so late. 'Gosh, this is like some kind of legalised slave labour!' I thought to myself, as I realised how silly it was that I felt bad just for wanting to go out in the evening at seventeen years of age!

As I tiptoed passed the stairs leading up to the loft above my room, I heard punk-rock music playing. 'That's weird, this place does not seem like it would have Punks staying here!' I thought to myself and chuckled at the vision of a bunch of punk rockers dining with the middle-class retirees in the lounge. I tiptoed down the stairs and onto the guestroom floor.

All was quiet, with no sign of life. I was relieved that no one was around and hurried down the last flight of stairs and into the ground-floor hallway. I couldn't see anyone around, but I could hear people laughing and chatting in the bar lounge area. 'That must be where they all go at the end of the day' I thought to myself and I hurried out of a side door that I'd spotted from the hallway.

Finally, outside, I took a deep breath of fresh air. 'It must be about 9.40 by now' I thought to myself, as I picked up pace and started heading down the hill into the town centre. 'I hope there are some fun clubs in town, I need to let what's left of my hair down fast!' I thought as I nearly broke into a run, with a strong sense of escaping from the strict hotel rising inside of me.

The town lights sparkled in the dusky light like a welcoming beacon signalling a place of much-needed respite. As I headed down the hill in search of some fun nightlife, I felt happy to be free again!

As I neared the town centre, I spotted a film camera crew down on the beach to the far side of the pier which seemed to be wrapping up for the day. "Excuse me, do you know what they've been filming?" I asked a smartly dressed middle-aged man as he walked towards me from the direction of the camera crew. "Beau Geste, with Benedict Taylor!" He answered politely as he kept on walking.

Beau Geste rang a bell, but I wasn't too familiar with it, but the name Benedict Taylor was more familiar to me. - He was a good-looking young actor who had been in a TV series called Barriers. "Thanks!" I answered as I kept on strolling into the town centre area.

There were quite a few lively bars, restaurants, and clubs around. I mainly wanted to dance, so I scanned the area for nightclubs, rather than pubs. I spotted a place that had some good pop tunes coming from it and a fun, friendly-looking crowd heading inside it. 'Ah, that looks like the place to be!' I thought to myself, as I headed towards the entrance.

Once inside the Nightclub I headed to the bar and bought myself a half of lager. I was still low on money, so I figured I would sip it slowly, and just have fun dancing. I was soon out on the dancefloor surrounded by punky-looking guys stomping their feet, and new wave-looking gals dancing around their handbags while sipping on their lager and limes. The music was mainly new-wave which I loved. 'This is more like it!' I thought to myself as I took a sip of my lager and started to dance around to a Human League song.

I managed to finish my half of lager faster than planned and was soon back at the bar ordering another one. 'Oh well, I've got to have SOME fun!' I told myself as I waited patiently for the bartender to serve me. Just then a tall slim girl, with thick brown curly hair appeared at the bar next to me and placed her empty half-pint glass down on the bar next to mine.

"Thirsty work!" I joked, glancing at her empty glass, then nodding over towards the dance floor. She laughed and nodded her head in agreement. "Where are you from?" She asked, in a mild Scottish accent. She had to shout as the music was so loud. "Oswestry, in the north-west midlands! I'm here to work at a hotel to save some money to go travelling! How about you?" I shouted back. She smiled, nodded, and looked impressed. "I'm from Scotland, I'm here to work too. I'm at a hotel up the hill!" She shouted back. "That's where I am - Hilltop Hotel!" I exclaimed, "I'm right next door at Sea View!" she shouted back, and we both laughed. "I'm Heidi, what's your name?" she asked with a big smile. "Della, nice to meet you, Heidi!" I answered feeling pleased to finally be meeting a nice person!

We were eventually served our drinks, so I turned to head back to the dance floor, and was just about to say "See you later!" to Heidi when she leaned over and said, "Do you know Benedict Taylor is here?" "No, but I saw the film crew near the pier earlier" I answered. "Come on, I'll introduce you!" she said giving me a fun-spirited look before leading the way through the crowd. "OK!" I answered as I followed her along while feeling excited to be out and about and socialising!

I wasn't a big fan of Benedict Taylor, but I didn't dislike him either, from what I'd seen of him on TV he seemed a pleasant guy, and meeting him seemed a whole lot more fun than mopping hotel floors for sure! Heidi led me over to a slightly relaxed area of the club where people were sitting, drinking, and chatting, on a bench seat that lined the wall.

"Benedict, I'd like you to meet Della! She's working at the hotel next to mine would you believe?!" I stood behind Heidi, smiling and feeling kind of awkward, and not sure of what I was supposed to say or do. "Great to meet you, Della!" Said Benedict as he shuffled over to his left and made room for me on the bench next to him. "Would you like to sit down?" He asked with a big smile "Um, hi, nice to meet you too! Yes, ok, thanks, um, but where will Heidi sit?" I answered, as I hovered, feeling happy to be making a new friend, famous or not, but awkward at sitting down before Heidi, especially as she had brought me over there.

"I'm fine, I'll squeeze in here!" answered Heidi with a smile as she sat down in between Benedict's male friend who was now on my right, and another guy, who was sitting at the end of the bench.

Soon we were all laughing and joking and the lagers kept flowing compliments of Benedict's friends and crew. Benedict turned out to be a really lovely guy, and I thoroughly enjoyed his company and the company of his friends - I had the feeling that I was finally amongst kindred spirits, which was amazing to me, as I'd never experienced that feeling in my life before, aside from maybe during chats with my dad. We were all on the same wavelength, and it was so refreshing to finally be around people who seemed to get my sense of humour and fun-spirited personality!

In school, I'd often been reproached for my humorous disposition, but now I was actually being liked for it! It was such a pleasant surprise, and it felt really good to feel not just accepted, but appreciated! This gave me the feeling that I was on the right track, and I felt reassured that setting off on my travels had been the right thing to do!

We all spent the next couple of hours drinking, chatting, laughing, joking and dancing until I suddenly realised that I had to be up at 5.30 am! "Hey, I've got to go! I've got to be up at half-five!" I announced, feeling bad to be leaving my lively group of new-found friends. I remembered I had my camera on me, and thought a group photo would be nice. As I took the camera out of my bag Heidi offered to take a photo of me with Benedict and his friend Jonathan, who was also an actor. I appreciated her offer but had hoped that Heidi would have been in the photo too, but everything happened so fast. Benedict gave me a sweet hug before I stood up, and everyone waved goodbye.

I felt sad leaving them all, and hoped for lots more fun nights, if not with them, but with other Kindred-Spirits - Now that I knew that such people existed! Heidi said that she would drop by and see me at the hotel one of the days, and at that, I waved goodbye and started my journey back up to the hotel. It was after midnight, so I tried to be as quiet as possible as I entered the building and made my way up to my room.

CHAPTER 6:

WISH I WASN'T HERE!

The next work day was almost identical to the one before, and I found myself operating on autopilot feeling like some kind of biological robot going about my daily duties. As I laid out the many pieces of silverware for each individual diner, I pondered on why one person would need so many pieces of silverware. "Maybe they were afraid of their own germs?" I chuckled to myself.

It was my half-day, so I was finished by 2 pm. I headed to my room to get changed. It was still early enough to go to town and have a look around, and maybe do some shopping. On my way out I noticed some hotel postcards for sale at reception. I bought one to send to my cousin Gee. I figured I would buy some more for my parents & other family and friends in town.

The weather was just right. Sunny, with a light refreshing breeze. The town looked busy, but not too busy. People were sunbathing on the beach, and some were swimming in the sea. "Ah, this is nice!" I thought as I meandered along. I noticed that the film crew had gone, and guessed they had either finished filming or had moved on to a new location. I wished them well!

Benedict in particular had seemed like a really nice guy, and in hindsight, it would have been nice to stay in touch. I found a café to have a coffee and to write out my hotel postcard to my cousin. It was a little after 4 pm, so I would still have time to post it.

I got comfy at the café and sipped on my coffee, and looked at the hotel postcard. On the front was a nice photograph of the hotel, with a view of the sea to the side of it. I thought it was perfect because it would show my cousin exactly where I was. I got out my pen from my shoulder bag, and started to write.

As I wrote out the postcard, I found myself telling my cousin how ridiculous the hotel was! I told her all about how snooty they all were, and how bossy the owner and her assistant manager were. I went on to explain how every diner had about 100 pieces of silverware each! I wrote down my joke about them being afraid of their own germs! I told her that I couldn't wait to save some money up and move on! - I added that it wasn't all bad though! The town and beach were lovely, and I'd made a nice friend from the hotel next door named Heidi, and we'd been hanging out with Benedict Taylor and crew at a club the night before which was fun!

I asked how she was doing, and asked her to say hi to her mum for me. I also asked if she'd seen my mum yet. I hoped everyone was ok. I told her that I would keep in touch, wished her well, and signed off with an x for a kiss.

Feeling pleased with what I'd written, I finished my coffee, and went in search of the post office. It felt good to have a grumble to someone, and I felt that Gee would understand as she knew me well. She knew that I was quite a free-spirited type, and that I was not keen on being bossed around. I preferred people to be nice and treat each other with respect. I would go out of my way to help anyone, but I didn't respond well to mean-spirited, rude people, which it seemed often went hand in hand with bossy types! As if their two grams of power had gone to their heads! Not my cup of tea at all!

I found a post office, bought a stamp, and posted the postcard. Then I went off to browse around the shops and buy some more postcards for my parents, and a few other family and friends.

The next few days I mainly just worked, ate, and slept! I was too tired to do much else, besides, payday was still a few days off, so I needed to hang tight until then. At least I had food and shelter, and by now I knew the daily routine by heart, so I was left to get on with it without too much bother.

One morning I entered the kitchen to see all of the staff huddled around in a circle reading something. I assumed they were reading a hotel menu, or their daily horoscopes or something. but as I got nearer, they all turned and stared at me. Some of them had a look of disdain, others a look of amusement as if trying not to laugh. Feeling puzzled I gingerly said "Good morning!" and pulled a slightly puzzled face as if to say "What are you all up to?"

One of them held something out towards me and asked if it was mine. Confused, I glanced down at their hand to see what it was and reached out my hand to take it off them, still feeling baffled as to what it could be. As I took it off them and held it up to look at, I suddenly felt a rush of light-headedness and embarrassment as I realised that it was the hotel postcard that I'd sent to my cousin! I had got so carried away with complaining about the hotel and its snooty staff and guests, that I'd forgotten to leave a space to write her address, so the card had come right back to the hotel!!!

"Oh yeah, thanks!" I answered in a surprised tone, as I took the card and shoved it in my apron pocket. "Right, I'll go and serve the teas!" I added, trying my best to act casual, when I felt as though my whole being was absolutely mortified!

After I clocked out that day, I went to my room and got changed to head out for a walk about in the town. I felt as though I wanted to avoid all the other hotel staff after such an embarrassing incident! It was still light outside, as we'd finished a little earlier than usual, and I definitely felt like I needed a walk to clear my head.

As I headed out of the hotel, I was pleasantly surprised to bump into Heidi in the hotel driveway. "I was just coming to see if you were about!" she said, looking pleased to see me. I was very happy to see her and desperate to share my returned postcard story with her as we headed down the hill into town. She burst into laughter as soon as I told her what had happened, and soon I was crying with laughter too. By the time we reached the centre of town the two of us were in hysterics. "Let's go for a drink!" exclaimed Heidi between bouts of laughter. Feeling tipsy from laughter alone, I thought "Why not!" I answered, knowing that I still had enough change left for a half or two. I followed her to a nearby pub with a beer garden at the back.

We were soon sitting out in the beer garden sipping on our drinks, and still laughing about the postcard incident. A few other people were sat about at the other tables chatting and laughing and sipping on drinks, as the sun was slowly setting.

"This is lovely!" I said once our laughter had finally subsided. "Isn't it grand!" answered Heidi looking happy to be out and about too. "So, what's your hotel like?" I asked her curiously. "It's not too different from yours, that's why I'm so glad to have a fun lass to hang out with!" she answered with a smile. "Where is she, can you introduce me to her?" I joked, and we both laughed. "Cheers!" exclaimed Heidi. "Cheers!" I exclaimed back, and we clinked our glasses together in solidarity.

We spent the next couple of hours talking about our hopes, dreams, and aspirations. The topic of boys popped up once or twice too, but like me, she wanted a bit more from life than the usual; job, marriage, and kids. She wasn't sure exactly what she did want yet, but she was sure of what she didn't want. I agreed as that was exactly how I felt. "I mean, how can we know what we want if we've yet to see all there is to choose from?!" I exclaimed, as we finished off our lagers and started to get up to leave. "Exactly!" Exclaimed Heidi, with a big nod.

We pencilled in plans for Heidi to call for me to go dancing at the same club we'd met at for the following weekend, and then we strolled back up to our hotels. I felt happy to have made a friend in a similar situation to me at the hotel next door. We could give each other some moral support, and have a bit of fun while we're at it!

Finally, it was payday and another half-day for me. I was due to meet up with Heidi later on for a night out on the town. I was just about to go to my room to have a shower and get ready when Heidi suddenly appeared at the side door of the hotel. I was happy to see her and opened to door to see why she had turned up a few hours earlier than expected.

"Do you fancy going to Alcatraz tonight?" Asked Heidi sounding enthusiastic. "Well, I thought this was prison enough?" I answered, as I rolled my eyes, and nodded my head at the hotel around me. "No, you daft thing!" answered Heidi laughing. "Alcatraz nightclub in Bournemouth! A few girls from the hotel across the way are going, and it should be a right laugh!" she added enthusiastically.

"Yeah! That sounds great!" I answered just as enthusiastically. "Brilliant! I'll call round for you at 7! We have to catch the 7.30 ferry, so be ready!" said Heidi with a big smile. "Great, I'll be ready and waiting outside for 7!" I answered, feeling excited about having a night out in Bournemouth. We gave each other an excited little wave before we both headed off to get ready.

Up in my room, I turned the radio on, and was soon dancing around to the Toya Wilcox song "I wanna be free!" it seemed very fitting, and it helped to energise me as I sorted out my clothes to wear for our night out.

I was soon showered and dressed up in my colourful, punky, new-wave/hippy clothes. I was starting to get hungry and remembered a packet of crisps I'd put in a dresser drawer. I didn't fancy heading to the bar for a snack, as I felt the staff would probably be looking me up and down and would be nosing as to where I was off to.

The atmosphere had been more awkward than ever since the postcard to my cousin Gee had come back to the hotel - on some level I felt as though I was counting the days until I could get out of there! 'Maybe, the boss was too?' I laughed to myself. We were not a good match! That was for sure! Although I had finally met the guy, from the loft above my room, who had been playing Punk rock music, and at first it seemed like we might click as friends until he mentioned that he was the boss's son, so I decided it best not to get too involved, although we did say hi whenever we met.

Around 6.45 I grabbed my shoulder bag, checked the mirror one more time, and headed downstairs. I felt a bit silly all dressed up, with my hair teased out, and full make-up on. I hoped I didn't bump into anyone from the hotel, as this was "me-time" and I was in "me-mode" not in "servant robot mode" which made me feel like a completely different person, because it was so far removed from my true self!

As I headed downstairs, I pondered on the many different roles that people play in the world, and wondered if I would ever find some roles that I actually enjoyed out there! I pictured myself doing things that I would enjoy for a living, things like writing, making films, designing, and inventing, as I had so many creative ideas! I pictured myself churning out all sorts of creations from my garden shed one day, and chuckled to myself at the vision, as I headed out the side door. Just as I was going through the door, I thought I caught a glimpse of someone at the far end of the hallway, but I didn't stick around to find out who!

Fresh air and freedom were what I wanted! 'I'm bored, I don't want to go to school! Don't wanna be nobody's fool! I wanna be me, I wanna be freeeee!!!' I sang in my head, thinking that this particular song by Toyah Wilcox must have been written especially for me! ...and all of the other creative free-spirits out there.

I headed swiftly to the end of the hotel driveway and found a little wall to sit on and wait for Heidi and the other hotel girls. I wondered what the other girls would be like, but I guessed they would naturally be nice if Heidi had befriended them.

I was sitting gazing up at the sky and daydreaming about future travels when I suddenly heard a high-pitched scream, followed by hoots and hollers of laughter and giggles. 'That must be them!' I thought as I turned to look up the hill to see a group of five girls heading down the hill towards me. I recognised tall Heidi at the centre of them all, and as soon as I looked their way, she started waving at me and excitedly calling out my name.

They were all dressed up and were nearly tripping over their high heels as they walked. I was wearing my "Gold Shoes" they weren't high heels, but they were my party shoes! and I always felt a sense of fun sweep over me whenever I put them on!

"Girls, this is Della, Della these are the girls!" Announced Heidi as they all slowed down to a hover around me. "Hi, Girls!" I answered, as they all said "Hi Della!" back in unison, before bursting into more laughter, hoots and hollers, I joined in the laughter, and merrily we all made our way down the hill.

"These Girls only started on Monday, I met them during a ciggy break on a bench across the street from my hotel," said Heidi as we all tottered along, by now we had broken up into pairs with Heidi and me lagging behind a little. "They seem nice! It's fun to have a night out again too!" I answered, feeling that THIS was what life was all about! - Making new friends, exploring new places, and having fun!

The Ferry ride over to Bournemouth was a laugh, especially as one of the girls was carrying a bottle of rum and coke in her handbag and was happy to share. We all took swigs of the rum and coke like mischievous pixies and would let out a giggle if ever we thought any of the other passengers had spotted us.

We arrived in Bournemouth and decided to go for a few lagers at a pub first, rather than go straight to the club. I spotted a chip shop, and because I was still hungry, I said that I would get some chips and meet them afterwards at the pub. It turned out that Heidi was hungry too, so we split from the other girls to go and grab some chips.

We both sat eating our chips on the picnic bench outside the chip shop, having a fun catch-up chat, then headed over the road to join the others at the pub. The pub was crowded but had a great atmosphere. Guys kept coming over to chat us up, and we joked that maybe we would see them for a dance later at Alcatraz.

We finally made it to Alcatraz, and had a fabulous night dancing, laughing, joking and having fun! A couple of the girls got off with some of the guys we'd seen at the pub earlier, but I wasn't interested in any of the guys who had tried to chat me up. They seemed nice enough to have a laugh with as pals, but it was rare that I ever really liked a guy, which was just as well because I wanted to focus on my travels!

At the end of the night, we somehow all made it back home to our hotels and said that we should do it again next weekend. I made it back to my room and flaked out on the bed, happy not to have to get up early the next day - I slept until noon!

I had a lazy Sunday, as I was feeling exhausted from the busy week, and the late night out, although I did manage to do a little hand laundry that afternoon, and had a short stroll downstairs to get some food from the kitchen. I spent some time just relaxing and journaling in my room, before vegging out flat on my bed, to read a magazine and listen to music.

After a while, I put the magazine down, and just lay on my bed staring up at the ceiling and started weighing up the pros and cons of staying on at the hotel. A few of the staff were nice, but the boss and her "Flying Monkeys" were always cold and abrupt, especially after they had found that postcard! So, all in all, I wasn't happy there.

After giving it some serious thought, I decided that I would leave that week and head over to Bournemouth to look for work and a place to stay there. I had enjoyed my night out in Bournemouth and it looked and felt like a fun, friendly city, and I felt sure that I would find something. I just couldn't stand much more of this formal, rigid atmosphere! I realised that I would miss Heidi and the girls, but I was happy that she had some nice new friends to hang out with now, and hopefully, we would keep in touch.

The next morning, I woke up with a strong feeling of apprehension about the work day ahead of me. It was as if all the negative things about the hotel, and the boss and co' had come to a head, and had suddenly hit me like a sledgehammer! 'Blow it, why wait? I'm getting out of here today!' I suddenly thought, just knowing that I could not stand another day there.

I hoped that I would still be paid any money that was owed to me, but either way, I was leaving pronto! I quickly got dressed with a sense of urgency rising up from my stomach, I hurriedly packed my rucksack and quickly wrote a note to the boss.

The note was polite enough. I simply explained that I had appreciated the job, but I didn't feel that it was quite right for me. I wrote down my dad's address at the bottom of the page and asked that they please send any money that was owed to me there. I wished them well and signed my name. I placed the note on top of the dressing table and put a cup on top of it to secure it from any breeze that might come in when the door was opened. Then, feeling like I was escaping from the actual Alcatraz, I tiptoed off down the hallway and down to the side door.

It was still early, just before 6.00 am so hopefully the boss and most of the staff would still be in the kitchen gearing up for the day and wouldn't notice me slipping away. I managed to make it outside without bumping into anyone, and sped off down the driveway, hoping that I wasn't being watched. Not that it really mattered anymore, but I had a strong feeling that I just needed to get down that hotel driveway and around the corner as fast as possible, in order to feel that I was finally free of there!

I turned the corner out of the driveway and onto the public footpath and a wave of happiness came over me. 'Thank goodness I'm out of there!!' I thought to myself joyfully, as I ran down the hill and towards the town. 'Bournemouth here I come!' I thought with a grin.

CHAPTER 7:

BOURNEMOUTH AND SOUTHAMPTOM; FRIENDS & FOES, AND A CRAFTY OLD BILL!

As the Ferry set sail, I breathed out a sigh of relief as I sat there curled up over my rucksack, feeling like some kind of fugitive on the run! I nervously looked around me hoping not to see anyone from the hotel. I did feel a bit bad for doing a runner, so I reminded myself of the reasons and felt a little better.

Once I was sure that nobody from the hotel was on board with me, I stretched out my arms and legs and yawned myself into a more comfortable sitting position. I leaned my head back and stared up at the ferry room ceiling to reflect on my time in Swanage. My mind flashed to the abrupt boss, her bossy assistant, some of the unfriendly staff, and the dreaded postcard scene! I did see the funny side though, thank goodness, and started to chuckle at the thought of the incident, which led to my memory of Heidi and I laughing our hats off about it all the way into town that day.

I suddenly felt a sense of sadness that I would miss Heidi. I hoped she wouldn't be upset that I'd gone. I felt sure she would figure out why. She knew I wasn't happy at the hotel. I wondered if I could drop her a line at her hotel, but she may be gone by the time I get based somewhere, or maybe I could look her family up in the phone book. I was just about to rack my brains to try and remember her surname, and the town in Scotland she came from when it was announced that we were about to dock in Bournemouth. I grabbed my rucksack and jumped up.

BOOK 1: TO SEE THE WORLD

As I queued with my fellow passengers to disembark it dawned on me that the other passengers probably all had specific places to go and people to see, whereas I had nowhere specific to go, and certainly no one to see! I found this thought both amusing and startling at the same time. 'Well, something has to happen!' I reasoned with myself, as I headed down the gangway and onto the street.

It was a beautiful sunny day, so I figured the best place to head for would be the town centre park. All UK towns had one, so I knew it would be the perfect place to relax and even do a little sunbathing, while thinking about what to do next.

I soon found the park and a lovely spot to sit down on the grass. Other people were sitting, and sunbathing around me. 'This is lovely!' I thought to myself as I lay back, propped my head up on my rucksack and stretched out.

The sense of freedom was so strong, that I wasn't worried that I had no home, or family and friends nearby. Instead, I felt full of gratitude for having regained the whole world to explore! I lay there for an hour or so in a state of bliss and contentment, just gazing up at the blue sky and white clouds floating by.

The sun warmed my skin and felt like nature's blanket. 'Maybe I don't even need a home?' I pondered. '…Maybe it's just about just getting in sync with nature, people, the planet and everything?' I thought, feeling as though I'd reached an epiphany of sorts.

Suddenly a football bounced on and off my leg. I sat up with a start to see two guys playing football nearby. One of them ran over towards me, as I lifted the ball to throw back to him. "Sorry about that!" He exclaimed as he came to a stop a few yards from me. "No worries!" I answered as I threw the ball up to him.

"What's your name?" He asked smiling. "Della, what's yours?" I answered smiling back. "Shane, and that's my brother Lee over there!" He answered, looking over towards the other guy. I smiled and gave a little wave to his brother Lee as he was standing across the grass watching us chat. As I waved, he waved back and started to walk over towards us.

"Is it ok if we sit with you for a bit?" asked Shane as Lee joined us. "Sure" I answered, feeling glad of some company. His brother Lee joined us and sat down too, and we were soon chatting away, and sharing our stories of how we had come to be there.

The brothers were from up north, near Manchester, but had come down looking for work for the summer. They'd found a job selling jewellery on the beach and said that their boss may be able to give me a job too.

"So, do you have a place to stay?" asked Shane, while glancing at my rucksack. "Yes, the Park" I answered jokingly. "You're welcome to stay on our couch, and chat with our boss about work in the morning if you want?" answered Shane, while glancing at Lee, as he nodded in agreement.

They seemed like decent guys, and I didn't get any weird vibes off them, so I was curious about their offers. "Sounds good, thanks. How much rent will you want?" I answered. "Oh, just chuck us a fiver here and there, no worries!" answered Shane casually. "Great thanks!" I answered as I was starting to feel even more positive about my decision to leave the hotel. I went on to tell them about the hotel job I'd just left in Swanage adding the story about the returned hotel postcard, and we all cracked up laughing.

After a while, I got hungry and said that I wanted to go and find something to eat. Shane said that they knew of a cheap café with good food not too far away and that they were getting hungry too. So, I grabbed my rucksack and we all strolled over there.

I was in a good mood and felt comfortable with the brothers. So, all in all, I was happy to have made some new friends, and the idea of a new job AND a place to stay, felt so much better than being cooped up as a live-in hotel slave!

The Café was a bit of a "Greasy Spoon" but the staff were friendly, the atmosphere was lively, and it had some good tunes playing on the radio. We found a table, and each ordered sausage, chips and beans, which reminded me of my meals at Aunt Freda's ranch house. I hoped that she and Liz, and all of the lovely animals were doing ok!

Our food arrived, and I suddenly realised how hungry I was! I had been thinking about going vegetarian over the last few years, but it never seemed a convenient time to do so, especially if I was low on funds, or broke, and having to eat what was available.

'Still, it just doesn't seem right for another creature to have lost its life so that I can have mine!' I thought as I gazed at the sausages on the plate. 'Don't think about it!' I told myself and tucked into the massive plate full of food. - The brothers were right; it was cheap and good!

"Aren't your mum and dad worried about you being down here on your own?" asked Shane as we sat chowing down. "Maybe a little bit, but I told them I was going travelling after I left school!" I answered with a shoulder shrug. "Yeah, they probably didn't think you'd actually do it though!" Joked Lee. "Especially at, what are you, seventeen, eighteen?" added Shane. "Yeah, seventeen, I'm ancient!" I answered with a grin and we all laughed.

"How old are you two?" I asked looking at them slightly challengingly, as if weighing them up. "I'm 23, Lee's 21" answered Shane proudly. "Oh well, we're all in the same moment of time, and that's the main thing!" I quipped back. The brothers looked puzzled for a moment then cracked up laughing. "She's not wrong!" exclaimed Shane as he finished off the last of his food.

"Where shall we go now then?" I asked cheekily, feeling as though we should go somewhere, but not having a clue where. "We'll show you around Bournemouth if you like?" Answered Shane, while Lee nodded approvingly.

We all downed the last of our drinks and then set off to have a walkabout. "Shall I carry your backpack for you?" Asked Shane with a smile. His gentlemanly gesture warmed my heart, but I figured that I should carry it, as I needed to get used to it being a part of me. "It's ok, it keeps me fit to carry it! Thanks though!" I answered with a smile.

We headed into the town centre of Bournemouth and I looked around at the bustling streets, and the grand buildings that lined them. There was plenty of greenery too. Lots of mini parks, and strips of vegetation and flowers. 'What a beautiful City!' I thought to myself '…With a Beach to boot!' I added.

"It's REALLY nice here!" I exclaimed to the guys. "Yeah, it's a good town! We like it!" answered Lee. "Is it a city or a town?" I asked, curiously. "Not sure really?" answered Lee looking over at Shane for answers. "I think it's a city?" answered Shane. We all laughed at the idea of not knowing if the place we were at was a town or a city.

"Well, it's either a large town or a small city!" I exclaimed, and the guys seemed to agree with that, as we laughed and continued with our stroll around. At some point, we passed the nightclub, Alcatraz. "Have you ever been there?" asked Shane, just as I was recognising it. "Yeah, just once with some gals from the hotels next door in Swanage. It was fun!" I answered. "Yeah, it's a great club!" answered Shane, as Lee nodded in agreement. 'It looks different in the daylight' I thought to myself. It looked as if it was all sobered up, and going about its daily business. 'Just like me!' I thought to myself, as we strolled along.

We found a pub with outside seating, not too far from the beach, and decided to get some lagers and hang out there for a while. It was quite a busy pub and had some lively music playing on the jukebox, so it seemed the place to be!

As we sat sipping on our lagers, with the sea breeze gently brushing over us, I went into a slight daydream and found myself enjoying the simplicity of the moment 'This is what it's about!' I told myself with a contented smile.

A little later on. some acquaintances of the brothers joined us, and we seemed to be having our own little party, especially as more people joined us as the afternoon went on. When it got too cold, we moved inside and continued on with our party until later that eve when at some point Shane suggested we head home, because their boss Liam was due to call round to pick them up the next morning around 9 am.

"He likes to get an early start on the Beaches" Explained Lee trying to look sober. I couldn't help but laugh at his face. "What are you laughing at!" Slurred Lee as he cracked up laughing too, this triggered Shane off laughing, and for the next few minutes, the three of us were crying with laughter like fools, at nothing in particular.

At some point we eventually made a move and staggered off out of the pub, waving goodbye at the other party people. It seemed quite a long walk over to the brother's flat, but it was probably because it was uphill a lot of the way, as in reality, it wasn't too far from the city centre. It was just on the outskirts, in a nice-looking leafy neighbourhood.

Shane opened the front door, and we all tottered inside. "Does anyone else live here?" I asked, worried about disturbing people. "Nah, just Lee and me. His bedroom's at the back, mine's upstairs, and we share the kitchen and living room.

"That's your room!" said Shane, as he opened a door on our left-hand side. We all stumbled into a nice-looking living room with a comfy-looking big sofa and a TV set on a stand in front of the window. "There's a loo at the end of the hall, with a bath in there too, Goodnight!" Added Shane as he left the room, and stumbled off up the stairs. "Oh Lee, give her a blanket and pillow will ya!" He shouted back. "Yeah, will do!" answered Lee, as he stumbled off to his room which was a little-ways down the hall from mine.

He soon appeared with a big red blanket and a worn-out-looking pillow. I thanked him, as he threw them down on the Sofa. "Goodnight!" he shouted as he stumbled off out of the living room, and towards his room. "Goodnight! Thanks!" I called back, as I gently closed the living room door and looked around the living room. 'This is nice!' I thought, feeling quite pleased with myself that I'd somehow managed to land on my feet again.

I sat on the Sofa just taking it all in, before deciding to tiptoe to use the loo and drink what seemed like a ton of water straight from the tap. I figured I would have a bath and get changed the next day, and tiptoed back to crash out on my new sofa bed. I wondered what the hotel boss and staff had made of my sudden disappearance. I drifted off to sleep with random visions of the hotel staff, and my time at the hotel floating around in my head.

I woke with a start to the sound of someone knocking loudly on the living room door. "Yeah?" I called out, feeling completely disorientated. "I'm making some coffee if you want some!" shouted Shane. "Er, yes please!" I answered sitting up feeling confused, groggy, and hung over. I glanced at the clock on the mantelpiece and saw that it was 8.20. I remembered the brothers telling me that their boss was calling for them at 9 am and that they would ask him if I could work for him too. I felt a sudden urgency to get up and dressed and wondered if there was even enough time for a bath.

I quickly folded up the blanket, and put it and the pillow together at the end of the Sofa. I was still dressed, as I'd slept in my clothes, so I decided to first pop to the loo, and then go and get a cup of coffee in the kitchen, and ask Shane if there was time for me to have a bath. I found the kitchen at the end of the hall on the left, just passed Lee's bedroom. Shane was in there eating a bowl of cereal, and swigging on a cup of coffee. He looked as rough as I felt. "There you go!" he said shoving a mug of coffee across the table towards me. I thanked him, and sat down to take a sip, "Want some cereal?" Shane asked as he got up to take his bowl to the sink. "No, thanks the coffee's enough" I answered, feeling too fragile and hung over to eat.

"Do you think there's time to take a bath?" I asked, gulping down my coffee. Shane glanced at the clock and answered "Maybe not a bath, but a shower. There's one upstairs on the left. My room is right next to it. The other rooms are the landlords, they store stuff in there, so they're locked up. You'll figure it out" Answered Shane, as he made himself another cup of instant coffee.

I thanked him, and quickly finished the rest of my coffee, before heading back to the living room to rummage in my rucksack for a change of clothes. I grabbed my hairbrush and make-up and hoped that there was soap and a towel in the bathroom as I hadn't packed either.

I darted upstairs and into the shower room. It also had a toilet in there which I thought was handy. "Get up! Liam will be here soon!" I heard Shane shouting at Lee, just as I was getting into the shower. I chuckled to myself and turned the shower on. It was freezing and took ages to warm up, and then it suddenly got too hot!

I finished as quickly as possible and spotted a few towels hanging on a rail. 'Hopefully, they won't mind if I use one, at least I'm clean now!' I thought to myself with a grin, as I quickly dried off. I was soon dressed, with my hair and makeup done, and just as I was about to head back downstairs there was a loud knock on the front door. 'That must be Liam!' I thought to myself as I quickly darted down the stairs.

Shane appeared just in front of me to go and open the front door and I caught a glimpse of a bedraggled-looking Lee swigging coffee at the kitchen table where I'd been sat earlier, just before I turned into the living room to put my worn clothes back in my rucksack, and my makeup bag back in my shoulder bag and take a breather before meeting Liam.

I had just finished shoving my rucksack out of the way into the gap between the Sofa and an armchair as Shane entered the living room followed by a slim-looking fair-haired man who looked to be about thirty-something. "Liam, this is Della, Della this is Liam!" Announced Shane. Liam, and I nodded and said hello to each other as I twirled myself around to sit up on the armchair.

Liam sat himself down on the Armchair on the opposite side of the room, and Shane sat on the sofa between us. "Della's looking for work, so I thought maybe she could help us sell the Jewellery?" Said Shane, earnestly. Liam shot me a glance. "Sure, have you told her the Spiel?" Liam answered. "Not yet, I thought I'd check with you first innit?" Shane answered.

Liam nodded and went on to rattle out a full sales pitch/spiel on what to say when selling the Jewellery. My head was spinning with the information overload, but I was mainly feeling excited about having found a job so quickly!

As Liam was telling me the spiel, I heard Lee charging back and forth between his bedroom and the bathroom and guessed that he was getting ready. "Right then," said Liam, as he unzipped a small sports bag and pulled out several small bags of Jewellery.

"Ten bags each? For now, alright?" he said, as he counted out ten bags and carried them over to me. "Thanks, they should fit in my shoulder bag," I said, as

I took them off him, and reached down for my shoulder bag which was on the floor next to my feet.

"Good!" answered Liam, as he counted out another ten bags and passed them over to Shane, who jumped up to go and get a plastic carrier bag from the kitchen. Just then Lee appeared looking a little more scrubbed up than my vision of him a short while earlier. "Grab me a bag too Shane!" Shouted Lee, as he greeted Liam and sat down on the sofa.

Shane arrived back in the living room and handed Lee a plastic bag, and Shane and Lee went about putting their ten bags of jewellery into the carrier bags. I sat on the edge of my seat smiling and awaiting instructions.

"Got a purse?" asked Liam. "Yes, I do" I answered. "Right, take your own money out of it and put this five quid worth of fifty Ps in it. You'll need a float for change" "OK" I answered, and I rummaged through my bag to find my purse. I took my money out and put it into a zip compartment in my shoulder bag, and put Liam's five pounds worth of coins into my purse.

"So, you sell each bag for two pounds fifty, and you keep a pound commission, the rest you give back to me along with the five quid float, alright?" Said Liam cooly, as I finished zipping up my Shoulder bag, and putting the flap back over it. "Yes, that sounds good to me" I answered. Hoping that the Jewellery would sell!

"Right, everyone ready? Let's go!" exclaimed Liam as he stood up and brushed his trousers down. "Yep, ready!" we all answered, as we followed him out of the living room, down the hallway, and out into the front garden that led to the street. "We'll take a shortcut to the beach," said Liam, as we crossed the road and he led the way down a side street.

It was another lovely sunny day, and the fresh air helped to wake me up some more. We all marched along like soldiers on a mission, and I felt quite pleased with myself for somehow gaining a job, a place to stay, and a little crew, all in a day!

We arrived at the beach, and Liam stopped to give us instructions on what parts of the beach we should each head to, and that we were all to meet up with him at 12 o'clock at the pier to pick up some more jewellery.

Liam instructed me to head up to the far west side of the beach and then to backtrack back. Shane was sent to the far east of the beach and, was also told to backtrack back, and Liam and Lee would start out from where we were, but would both head in different directions. We were all to meet up at 12 o'clock by the pier. We all said "See you later!" and headed off in our different directions. I was glad to be having a bit of a walk first before starting my sales, as it would give me time to rehearse the spiel in my head.

I walked along the sand and breathed in the fresh salty air and looked around me to see happy people sunbathing, playing beachball, or just arriving to find their spots on the beach. 'This is much better!' I thought to myself, comparing how I now felt, to how I had felt at the hotel. I smiled to myself as I walked along while practising the jewellery-selling spiel in my head: '…Hello there, I have a special jewellery offer for you today! First, I have the King Charles rope chain, which is top quality 925 silver…'

After I'd walked for about twenty minutes, and as the people on the beach lessened, I decided, now was a good time to turn around, start making my way back, and hopefully start selling my wares

I made a swift U-turn and started to stroll back towards the way I'd just walked. Nearby I spotted a happy-looking young couple sitting on a picnic blanket, laughing and joking with each other, and felt that they would be ok to approach.

As I neared them, they glanced over at me, both smiling. I smiled back and went into my spiel. I was pleasantly surprised when before I'd even finished, the guy reached into his wallet and said "Sure, I'll take a pack!" The girl looked pleased and joked that hopefully a couple of the necklaces were for her. The guy joked back of course they were, as he only wanted the King Charles rope chain. "Keep the change!" said the guy, as he placed three-pound notes in my hand. "Great, thank you!" I answered, as I gave him the pack of Jewellery, and took the money off him.

I waved goodbye, and strolled away feeling as if I was on cloud nine! "Wow, I wasn't expecting a tip!" I thought to myself as I, put fifty pence from the float into the zip section of my shoulder bag where the rest of my personal money was.

I spotted a group of about six friends sitting and sunbathing a few yards away and started to head towards them. I smiled hello as I approached, and most of them smiled back, but a couple of them weighed me up and down suspiciously. I burst into my sales pitch spiel, and they all listened intently.

"Let me see!" said one of the girls as I leaned over dangling the chains in front of her. She grabbed them with her hand and inspected them "Yeah, I'll take two packs, please! They'll be good presents! I've got my brothers birthdays coming up!" She said eagerly, as she searched in her handbag for the money.

The others gathered around me to inspect the chains. "I'll have one!" Said one of the guys, as the others ummed and ahhed. A few minutes later I was leaving the group having sold five packs of chains. "Wow, that's a fiver for me!" I thought proudly as I cooly strolled on down the beach with a beaming smile!

By the time I arrived at the meet-up point I'd sold all of the jewellery packs, and had made ten pounds to keep, plus a few quid in tips. Most of the people had been friendly, and had either politely declined to buy anything, or had been eager to buy something which made me feel as if I was doing them a favour by bringing their jewellery shopping to them!

Only one guy had made a cocky remark; asking if the chains would turn green in the bath? I'd answered that I didn't know, but if they did, be sure to shout "Eureka!" He'd looked at me puzzled, as I strode off feeling just as cocky as him!

The guys were back at the meeting point sitting on a bench, chatting, and counting out their money. We'd all sold up, which Liam was very pleased with. He shared out five more bags each and suggested we all just scatter and look for people who've recently arrived. We arranged to meet back up in an hour or so, and then we'd be free to do whatever we liked.

"What a great Job!" I thought to myself as I headed back out to the beach in search of punters, as Liam called them! The rest of the packs of jewellery sold swiftly, and I was soon back at the meeting place just sitting on the bench waiting for the others. It wasn't long before they each turned up. We were all full of smiles and congratulated each other, on selling out so fast.

"We'll do a few more days on the beaches, then we'll head to Southampton next week," said Liam intensely. I felt so proud to be in the fold, and sat nodding seriously, and trying not to break into a smile at my joy of earning fifteen pounds plus tips, all for a day of sun, sand, sea, and socialising!!

The next few days whizzed by, and as each day passed, I felt that I was growing more confident and relaxed with my sales pitches. I didn't feel nervous so much as excited about approaching strangers on the beach. I even enjoyed some of the cheeky ones, and would usually end up having a fun banter with them.

When our day off on Monday rolled around, the boys took off to meet up with some friends, and I used the free time to catch up with my laundry, some journaling, and writing letters to family and friends back home. I told them that I had a new address and a new job! I told them that the hotel job hadn't worked out, but how happy I was in Bournemouth selling jewellery on the beaches. I hoped that they would be happy for me and not worry about me. I told my dad that I didn't need my savings sent to me, as I didn't need them just yet, and I would rather they were kept safe with him. I also managed to make a phone call to my grandparents' house when my mum happened to be there, and we had a nice little chat. She seemed ok with me being away, but she sounded a little sad too.

Deep down I felt bad, as if I'd abandoned her, but I reminded myself that she had other family and friends around and that if I didn't make an effort to go and see the world, then it simply wouldn't happen! I hoped she would understand. I went to sleep that night feeling like I was all caught up with everything and I was feeling very happy with my lot. I looked forward to heading over to Southampton the next day to sell our wares!

Liam picked us up at 9 am sharp on Tuesday morning, and we sped over to Southampton in what seemed like seconds! On the way there Liam instructed the guys on what parts of the city to head for, and they eagerly agreed.

"Della, you come with me! I want you as my lookout!" "Look out?" I asked, feeling puzzled by his meaning. "Yeah, the old bill don't like us selling in Southampton without a hawkers licence, so we gotta move quick if we spot 'em!" answered Liam, sounding serious.

"Oh right," I answered, still feeling slightly puzzled. I couldn't see any harm in swapping Jewellery for cash with people, surely, it's the people's business and no one else. I just kept on nodding and agreeing with whatever Liam was saying, while mainly looking forward to a day out in a new city.

Liam parked up in a side street, and we all got out of the car. Shane and Lee were joking around, and still seemed a bit drunk from the night before! They drank booze and smoked weed pretty much every night, which was way too much partying for me, I enjoyed a couple of lagers, or a cocktail or two, and that was about it, but 'Too each their own!' as they say, I thought as I looked around the street, trying to get a feel for what was to me, a brand-new place! – One of my favourite things!

Liam gave the guys twenty bags of jewellery each and told them where we would be. "Come back there when you've sold out, otherwise, see you back at the car at four!" Said Liam sounding as organised as usual. He took out his sports bag, and a fold-up table, and slammed the boot of the car shut.

"Shall I carry something?" I offered, thinking it was unfair for Liam to have to carry everything. "No worries, let's go!" answered Liam, enthusiastically. The guys took off ahead of me and Liam, and we followed swiftly behind them.

I felt excited to be in a brand-new place! I glanced around me at the side streets that we were cutting down. There wasn't a whole lot of activity, mainly people parking up their cars, like we'd just done, and a few people heading either towards or away from us, as if in a hurry to get wherever they were going.

We soon arrived at the centre of a pedestrianised shopping street, and it was busy! There were people of all ages, shapes and sizes milling about everywhere. "Wow, busy place!" I said to Liam as he marched up the centre of the street with me hurrying to keep pace with him. "Yeah, it's a great city is Southampton!" answered Liam matter-of-factly.

Liam found a spot near a couple of benches, with little brick walls about 3 feet high, with flower beds inside of them. "You good at climbing?" asked Liam suddenly. "Yeah, I love climbing, why?" I answered puzzled by his question. "Right, jump up on that flower bed, and keep a lookout for the old bill all right?" He instructed. "Oh, yeah ok!" I answered, feeling a bit bemused, but also a bit excited, by my latest surprise job development.

As Liam set up his table a crowd of people started to form around him. I stood on top of the flower beds scanning the crowds for any sign of the Police. I wondered how much he would pay me if anything, and figured that either way, it was a new experience, and at least I now had some money coming in again and a place to stay - and what else would I be doing with my day?

A group of teenagers turned up and started horsing around to the side of the flower pot where I was standing. "What you doing up there?" asked one of the boys, looking at me with a curious grin. "I'm his lookout" I answered with a mischievous smile, as I looked side-eyed, and gestured towards Liam jokingly.

The boy laughed and told his friends that I was Liam's lookout. They all thought it was hilarious, and cracked up laughing, I was laughing along with them, and we were soon all chatting and making friends.

They asked me questions about where I was from, my travels so far, and the jobs I'd had. "I wish I could do that!" Exclaimed one of the girls. "You'd get as far as the train station, and be hungry for mums cooking!" laughed the boy I'd been chatting with. "Sod, you!" laughed the girl. "She's my sister!" said the boy, as if he wanted me to know that she wasn't his girlfriend. "You look around the same age" I answered, with a smile. "Yeah, she's a year younger than me," said the boy smiling back.

Just then I spotted a Policeman's helmet far off in the distance heading our way. I quickly started making a Psssst!!! noise to Liam to warn him, but he didn't hear me. So, I leaned over and called out "Liam!" loudly, but he still didn't hear me.

When I straightened up again the Policeman had disappeared. 'Thank goodness!' I thought to myself feeling relieved. I was just starting to relax, and carry on my chat with the teenagers, when the Policeman suddenly appeared again, right in front of Liam's crowd! I nearly jumped out of my skin!

He was carrying his helmet under his arm to hide it. 'The crafty thing!' I thought to myself as I slowly started to lower myself down from the wall to blend in with the group of teenagers in the hope that the Policeman wouldn't spot me and realise that I was with Liam.

"Quick, come with us!" said the boy, as he and his sister surrounded me to make it look like I was with them. "Thanks!" I answered as we started to move away from the scene. I felt a bit bad leaving Liam, but what else could I do?

As we shuffled off down the street, I caught a glimpse of the policeman arresting Liam, I assumed that he may have to pay a fine, or be locked up for the night or something like that. 'Oh dear' I thought, feeling terrible. Just then the teenagers all burst into fits of laughter, and suddenly I couldn't help but see the funny side too, as I started laughing along with them.

We spent the next ten minutes or so just laughing our hats off as we walked along. They took the mick out of me saying things like "Some lookout you are!" and "How come you didn't spot the copper sooner; do you need glasses?" and I was bent over crying with laughter because they were right!

"Yeah, I did spot him, and I tried to warn Liam, but he didn't hear me! And then the policeman took his helmet off!" I protested, through my laughter. "He did, didn't he the crafty sod!" said the boy I'd been chatting with earlier, in my defence.

"What's your name?" I asked feeling relieved to have some company at such a stressful time. "I'm Paul, that's my sister Cathy" he answered with a smile. "And, that's John, Eddie, and Sue" he continued. I smiled at them all, as we found ourselves some benches to sit down on and catch our breaths.

Suddenly a chubby, punkish-looking girl appeared and some of the teenagers made a beeline and crowded around her. "Who's that?" I asked Cathy, as she stayed sitting on the bench next to me. "Oh, that's Sal, she's the best shoplifter around! She swipes clothes and stuff, and sells 'em to us lot cheap!" answered Cathy casually. "Oh, I see" I answered. Feeling curious about these teenagers, as they seemed like really nice, fun, normal teenagers, not ruffians. I figured that they must just be broke and desperate!

"Where will you stay tonight?" asked Cathy, looking concerned. "I haven't really thought about it. I suppose I'll get the bus back to Bournemouth" I answered, suddenly feeling a little uneasy as I anticipated the atmosphere at the brothers house, after what had happened to Liam.

"Well, if you're stuck for a place to stay, you can stay at ours. Mum won't mind, we've got a big couch!" "Thanks, Cathy, that's good of you!" I answered, feeling a sense of reassurance to know that I had somewhere else to stay if I was going to be sacked for not alerting Liam to the Policeman in time!

I Told Cathy that I would head back to Bournemouth, but if there was any trouble I would come back if that was, ok? Just then Paul joined us, showing off a new pair of jeans that he'd bought off Sal. "Della can stay with us if she gets sacked can't she Paul!" Said Cathy as Paul got nearer.

"Of course, she can, mum won't mind, she likes the company!" answered Paul warmly. "We can walk over there now if you like, so you know where we live if you come back!" added Cathy, with a big smile. I thanked them both, and felt really happy to have made some lovely fun-spirited new friends.

After seeing where they lived; a nice council house on the outskirts of town, and briefly meeting their friendly mum: Jill. I thanked them again, and decided to head back to Bournemouth and face the music! I hoped things wouldn't be too bad! I said goodbye to my new friends, and added that I may see them soon, then went in search of the bus. I soon found it nearby and jumped on board, paid my fair, and found a seat.

I Arrived back at the brothers house, and sheepishly opened the front door. I could hear the brothers had loud music playing, and they were shouting and laughing and sounded quite drunk. "Hiya!" I said as I entered the living room. "Ooooooo, Liam's not happy with you!" Shouted Shane, looking very drunk.

71

"You're bloody done for mate!" added Lee, looking just as drunk. "It wasn't my fault! The Policeman took off his helmet so I couldn't see him!" I protested, feeling under attack.

"You should have seen him though!" Shouted Shane, in a teasing, reproachful manner. "He's bloody fuming!" Added Lee, as if enjoying the drama. "Where is he?" I asked, curious as to how they knew all about it. "He's home now, but he had a whopper of a fine! They were going to put him in the slammer otherwise!" added Shane. "It's your fault!" shouted Lee, in a goading tone.

"No, it isn't my fault! If what he's doing is illegal then it's his bloody fault!" I shouted back, feeling upset and angry that I was supposed to take the whole blame for Liam being caught. The brothers seemed stunned that I was defending myself and went quiet for a moment. "Anyway, I did try to warn him, but he didn't hear me, and then the policeman took his helmet off and hid in the crowd until he suddenly appeared in front of Liam's table" I added, hoping that they would at least see my side of the story.

"Nah, you're gonna be in F-ing trouble!" Shouted Shane bouncing back to his reproachful, mocking mode. "Yeah, you're gonna be in F-ing trouble!" echoed Lee, and they both started chanting it, as if they were at a football match. "You're gonna be in F-ing trouble! You're gonna be in F-ing trouble!" They continued chanting, as they swigged on their lagers, and danced around the living room.

I sat on the Sofa, let out a big sigh, and just stared into space feeling like absolute rubbish. "Here have some of this Skunk!" said Shane pulling some weed out of his pocket and passing it to Lee. Lee took the bag and sat at the coffee table to roll a joint.

'Oh no!' I thought, sensing they were only going to get rowdier and rowdier, the more off their heads they got, and thinking about how the living room was also my bedroom. I wondered what to do - I could either go out, go to the kitchen, or just hang tight while they partied and wait for them to burn themselves out.

I was too tired to go back out, and the kitchen was freezing, so, I decided to just hang tight, and hope that they calmed down a bit after a while. So, I got comfy on the sofa and made an effort to chat with them.

"How did your day go?" I asked, optimistically, hoping it had gone better than mine. "We sold out, then had to catch the bus home because Liam didn't show up at the car" answered Shane. "Because of you! You! You!" shouted Lee aggressively.

I felt really uncomfortable, and upset with their teasing, but decided to just shrug my shoulders and sigh, and hang in there. Shane turned up the volume of the music, and the brothers took big hits of the joint while jumping around the room and getting rowdier by the second.

"I need a piss!" Shouted Shane, and started peeing against the wall. "Me too!" shouted Lee, as he too started peeing against the wall. "Wayhayhaaay!!!" Shouted Shane as he started spraying his pee all around the room, with some of it catching me. "It's pissing down!!" Shouted Lee, and they both cracked up laughing. I jumped up and I darted out of the room, and into the bathroom to wash the splash of pee off my Leggins.

'What a nightmare!' I thought to myself, wondering what the heck I was supposed to do. I could hear the brothers laughing like two lunatics, and I decided I didn't want to go back in the living room until they had gone to bed. I decided that I would go to a nearby chip shop and get some chips and a can of pop and just hang out there for a couple of hours. I figured that the brothers were so drunk and high that they were bound to pass out at some point.

I crept out of the bathroom, and past the living room where the brothers were now chanting what sounded like more football-type chants, I slowly opened the front door, tiptoed out, and closed it quietly behind me. I let out a sigh of relief as I hurried off out of the gate, and down the street. Thankfully I still had my shoulder bag on me, with my purse and keys inside it.

Feeling really shaken-up by their behaviour, on top of an already stressful day, I strolled to the chip shop feeling upset, disheartened, and unsure of what I was going to do next. I ordered a plate of chips and mushy peas, and a can of orange pop, and found a seat in the corner of the café part. I sat at the back, and away from the windows, as I was worried of the brothers spotting me if they decided to go out.

I sat slowly eating my chips and peas, feeling utterly dejected. I was so disappointed to think that I had just got into the swing of things here, and had been really happy and enjoying myself, but it had suddenly all turned to crap!

My mind flashed to my new pals in Southampton, and I smiled at the thought of them. I remembered Cathy telling me that I would be welcome to stay at their place, and felt so grateful for that, especially as it was starting to feel like, aside from heading back to my aunts in the new forest, or my home town, it was my only option at this point. I wondered if I could maybe stay with them for a few days while I look for work, and once I had some money coming in, maybe rent a room somewhere in Southampton while I save up money for my world travels. It seemed feasible.

My mind flashed back to my enthusiastic travel chats with my dad. 'I can't turn back now; I've only just begun!' I thought to myself, feeling determined to keep on going, no matter what! I kept checking the clock on the wall, and wondering if the brothers would be crashed out yet. There was no way wanted to bump into them again tonight! Or ever again for that matter!

After a few hours had passed, I decided to slowly make my way back to the house and check if the coast was clear. I got to the front door and listened for sounds. All was quiet, which was a good sign. I put the key in the lock, and slowly turned it and tiptoed inside. I peeped into the living room and it looked like a bomb had hit it, but at least the brothers weren't in there anymore. It was nearly midnight, so I decided to try and get some sleep, but to take off early in the morning to avoid seeing the brothers, or Liam.

I tiptoed to the bathroom and back, then turned the cushions on the sofa over in case they had been peed on it, and quickly checked my rucksack to make sure it was ok. Thankfully it was still tucked away in the space between the chair and the sofa and had remained safe from the brothers' destruction. I lay down on the sofa, feeling exhausted, and quickly fell fast asleep.

CHAPTER 8:

SOUTHAMPTON SANCTUARY

I woke with a start at 6 am. I was glad to be awake early, as I wanted to get out of there as soon as possible! I got up and tiptoed to the bathroom, and within ten minutes, I was washed, dressed and ready to take off!

I decided that I would get some breakfast somewhere on my way. I just needed to go fast! Normally I would think to write a note explaining why I'd gone, but I felt there was no need at this point, as it should be obvious. Feeling down, I picked up my rucksack and put it on my back, left my key on the sideboard, and somewhat sadly made my way out of the house, and quietly closed the front door behind me.

I picked up pace once I was out in the street, and suddenly broke into a run! The running gave me a sense of liberation, and I was glad to be on the move again, especially after things had turned so sour. I arrived back in Southampton and found my way back to Cathy and Paul's mum's house, and knocked on their door.

"Della!" exclaimed Cathy as she opened the door looking like she'd just woke up. She welcomed me inside, and within the next couple of hours, her brother Paul, and their mum Jill joined us in the living room, as I told them how crazy the brothers had been, and how according to them, Liam was fuming with me for letting him get caught by the policeman.

"It wasn't your fault though, he didn't hear you when you did try to warn him, and the copper took off his helmet and hid in the crowd!" Exclaimed Paul, looking angry with the situation. "I know! ...and it's not my fault if Liam is doing illegal stuff in the first place either!" I answered, feeling indignant about the whole thing.

Cathy and her mum sat smiling and nodding, and it felt so comforting to be welcomed to their family home with open arms. It was just what I needed after things had ended so roughly with Liam and the brothers.

Feeling a little fragile after my ordeal, I spent the next couple of days at home with them, just going to the local shops, eating snacks, and watching TV. I didn't want to chance going into the city centre for fear of bumping into Liam and the brothers, not because I'd done anything wrong, but because I just felt sick of the three of them! Cathy's family had kindly taken me under their wing at my time of need, and I was so grateful for them, and that was all that mattered while I rested up, and licked my wounds.

After a few days of rest and relaxation, Cathy, Paul, and I headed to the town centre to hang out on the main street. I said that I would start looking for work, as I wanted to find a bedsit and save up for my travels. They insisted that I could stay as long as I wanted on their sofa, which was so kind of them but as much as I appreciated their offer, I did like my own space too.

Once we got to the town centre, we soon bumped into the local teenagers that hung out there and they warmly welcomed me back. I felt surrounded by new, but true friends, and I was grateful for their moral support. After the initial greetings had died down, one of them told me that Liam and the brothers had been looking for me, because according to them I'd stolen some of Liam's Jewellery!

"What the heck are they talking about?" I exclaimed, feeling absolutely confused, as I went about looking in my shoulder bag, just in case some jewellery was still in there from our last beach day. I unzipped the inner area at the back and was horrified to see about six small bags of jewellery there.

"Oh no! I do have some of their jewellery!" I exclaimed, feeling like crying with the stress of my discovery because I wanted nothing more to do with them or their stupid jewellery! They all laughed but also looked a little sorry for me.

Suddenly Sal the shoplifter turned up and seemed happy to see me. She seemed to find it hilarious that Liam and the brothers were searching the streets of Southampton looking for me, as word on the street was that I had stolen some jewellery!

"Yeah, but it's not true! I didn't realise it was in my bag!" I exclaimed desperately. "Yeah, that's what I always say!" Quipped Sal, and everyone roared with laughter. I wasn't sure whether to laugh or cry and right there I decided the best thing to do was to head back to Bournemouth to drop off the jewellery, as I just didn't want the hassle of still being linked to Liam and the brothers!

"I'm gonna take it back! I don't want it!" I exclaimed angrily. Sal and most of the teenagers were saying I should just keep it! But Cathy and Paul seemed to understand where I was coming from. I decided to put my job search on hold, as we headed back to Paul and Cathys to tell their mum Jill about what had happened.

We were soon all sat around the living room telling Jill of the latest goings on, and I felt as though they were all very understanding, which I appreciated. We even had a little laugh about things, which helped to ease the tension, of what felt like the seriousness of the situation.

Cathy said that she would come with me to drop off the jewellery if I wanted, and I took her up on her offer, feeling glad of the back-up. The next day would be the brothers day off, so early in the morning we took the train back to Bournemouth, as it was quicker than the bus, and headed over to the brother's house.

I knocked on the door and Shane opened it. He looked surprised and amused to see me. and called out for his brother Lee to come and see who was at the door. Lee also found it amusing to see me, and the two of them weren't as aggressive as they'd been the night they'd been off their heads, but they still had another laugh about my situation and told me how Liam was gunning for me for stealing his jewellery as if trying to scare me.

I explained that it was a mistake and that I had put the Jewellery in the back of my shoulder bag as usual, and forgotten it was there. I reached into my shoulder bag, took out the jewellery, passed it over to Shane, and asked him to give it to Liam when he saw him next.

He took it off me with a grin and said that he would give it to him. I thanked him and calmly said goodbye. Cathy was standing behind me the whole time, and I was glad that someone had witnessed me giving the jewellery back. We both gave a quick wave, turned around, headed out of the garden gate, and took off quickly towards the train station.

When we arrived back in Southampton, I felt relieved, as if a big weight had been lifted. Cathy, Paul, and their mum Jill, all agreed that it was all for the best and that I could relax now that Liam and the brothers would no longer be after me! We had to laugh at the concept of three thugs being after me as if I'd been involved in some serious underworld activities when all that had happened was, I'd simply forgotten to give Liam his cheap jewellery back, which was probably only worth a fiver at most!

In Southampton, I felt free to start my job search again without the worry of bumping into Liam and the brothers! I'd made some nice new friends, and I was happy enough for the time being, although I soon discovered that jobs were hard to come by though, so Cathy and Paul's mum: Jill helped me to put in a claim for a social allowance to tide me over while I was looking for work in the area, they also helped me to find a bedsit to rent at an BnB near to their house. So, within a week or two I was set up in a nice little bedsit and had a little pocket money to help keep afloat until I found work.

Meanwhile, my teenage friends on the street just wanted to hang out, and as a teenager myself, that was pretty hard to resist, especially when it was such fun! Southampton was fantastic! And even when I wasn't spending time with my friends, I enjoyed exploring the city streets. It was an uplifting, cosmopolitan city, with a great cross-section of people, and I felt very comfortable there.

One day while sitting on a park bench journaling, I got chatting with a handsome American guy, who had been sitting on the bench next to me. He looked to be in his mid-twenties and had a youthful energy about him. He was in Southampton on vacation and was loving exploring the UK. We introduced ourselves, but I didn't quite catch his name. He was fun to chat with. He told me that he was a race car driver in the US, which sounded exciting. I told him I hoped to include the US in my world travels, which he seemed pleased to hear.

We were getting along great, so when he said he invited me to join him for a burger at a wimpy burger. I said sure, and looked forward to it, as I'd yet to go to a burger bar. "What was your name again?" I asked as we strolled along. "It's Skid Martin!" He answered with a big grin. "Ah, a perfect name for a race car driver!" I grinned back. He nodded and laughed.

Skid had parked his flashy sports car that he'd hired near the park and suggested that we drive over to the burger place as it was on the other side of the town centre. I said ok, and jumped into the open-top sports car. "This is fun!" I exclaimed as we whizzed along the leafy residential streets around the outskirts of Southampton. "Sure is hun!" Exclaimed Skid, seeming happy to have some company. We were soon coming to a halt outside of Wimpy Burger, and people in the street stopped to look at Skids car, and at us.

Skid had an aura of celebrity about him and seemed used to attention, whereas I felt a little embarrassed that people were staring at us. "Come on hun!" Exclaimed Skid, as we headed inside the Burger bar. "I've never had a burger before!" I said, feeling excited to be trying one for the first time.

"What? Then you gotta have a whopper! -Two Whoppers, with the works!" Exclaimed Skid to the teenage boy behind the counter waiting to serve us. "What's the works?" I asked, feeling confused by his jargon. "You know, everything! Salad, Cheese, Pickles, Mayo! You do like pickles, don't you? Pickled gherkins, a kind of cucumber in vinegar" asked Skid, suddenly sounding unsure. "I'll soon find out!" I joked back.

We found a booth, and I was soon tucking into what turned out to be a very tasty, yet strange mixture of flavours to me. I wasn't overly keen on the pickles, so I took most of them out of the burger but left a couple of slices in because they did add a little kick to the burger. There was also a big carton of thinly cut chips, or French Fries as they were called, to share on the table between us, and we each took turns grabbing a few of them during our chats.

"So how come you've never had a burger before?" Asked Skid, as he chowed down on his burger, and took a swig of his coke. "There aren't any burger places in my home town, and I don't think they're too popular in the UK, because I haven't seen many of them – Well, not that I've noticed anyway. They seem to be mainly an American thing!" I answered, not really sure if there were many more burger places around, or if I just hadn't noticed them.

"Ah, the good old USA, bringing fine things to the world!" Said Skid with a laugh. I asked him whereabouts in the US he was from and he told me that he was originally from the South, but he lived in Los Angeles. I answered that I may just make it to Los Angeles at some point on my travels, and he told me that I would be welcome to visit him anytime, adding that he enjoyed my company!

He took out a pen and paper from his inner jacket pocket, and tore a piece of paper from a food bag, and scribbled down his name, and contact details on it, and gave it to me. I thanked him, and put the paper in my shoulder bag. "You're welcome! Let me know when you land at the airport, I'll come and pick you up, and show you the sights!" He said with a big warm smile. I felt comfortable in his company, he was a really nice guy, and I liked his friendly way, aside from American kids who had visited my home town when I was younger, he was the first American grown-up I'd ever met, and hoped that all Americans were nice like him!

"So, what were you writing earlier?" He asked with a smile. I told him that I was keeping a journal of my travels. "Oh, make sure you write me in as the handsome American!" He joked. "Of course!" I joked back, with a grin. His flirting seemed harmless, and my impression was that he was just happy to have someone to hang out with while alone in a foreign country.

"Shall we head back to the park? Where do you need to go?" Asked Skid, as we finished off the last of our burgers. "Um, I don't really have far to go from here, so I can walk thanks Skid" I answered, as I'd recognised a landmark building a few streets away as we'd entered the burger bar.

"Ok, well it was great to meet you, Della! I'm heading north tomorrow, to explore some more of Blighty, so I'm not sure I'll see you again, not on this side of the pond at least! Be sure to look me up if you make it to LA!" He said with a big smile, as he patted my arm. "Will do! Thanks for the burger!" I answered, smiling back as we headed out to the street.

We both waved and thanked the burger bar staff, as the door swung shut behind us. Skid gave me a little hug, then jumped into his car. "Bye Skid!" I shouted after him, as he waved and zoomed off down the road, and out of my day. I wished him well and wondered if I would ever see him again. As I walked along, I took out the piece of paper he'd written his contact details on. His writing was hard to read, as he'd written fast, but it looked like it read Mark "Kid" Martin, with a load of numbers, followed by; Sunset Boulevard, Los Angeles. I wondered if his nickname was actually Kid, and not Skid? but I was sure he'd said Skid, and Skid seemed more fitting for a race car driver! But then I remembered I'd asked him to repeat his name, and I thought he'd said "It's Skid Martin" but he probably said "It's Kid Martin" He must have found it amusing that I kept calling him Skid the whole time, but was probably too polite to correct me. I put the piece of paper back in my bag and strolled along.

I headed back to my BnB and decided to have a night in. I wanted to catch up with my journaling and write some letters and cards to my family and friends back in my home town. I gave my parents and friends my new address and told them some of the highlights of my latest adventures. I tidied up my room, and added "Skid's" address to my address book, in my mind he would forever be "Skid Martin" the friendly American race car driver who introduced me to hamburgers, French fries, and pickled gherkins! I got ready for bed. Feeling all caught up with my day's to-do list, I crawled into bed and quickly fell asleep.

A few days later a letter arrived for me from my mum. I was shocked and horrified to read that Liam was still gunning for me!?!? So much so, that he had written to my parents telling them that I had run off with his jewellery! I was in absolute disbelief, as this was a complete lie! I felt furious, and sick to my stomach as it dawned on me that the brothers had obviously kept the jewellery, and not told Liam that I had taken it back! I was so angry, I wanted to find them and punch their lights out.

I hurriedly wrote a letter back to my mum to explain to her that everything was okay, and not to worry about me, adding that I'd made some really nice friends in Southampton. I went on to explain what had actually happened with Liam's Jewellery.

As I was writing I had the feeling that I wanted to get going soon, so I added that, although I really liked Southampton and the friends I'd made there, it was best not to write back to me at that address, as I'd probably be leaving soon and would probably be heading over to London because I needed work to make some money for my travels. I explained that I had a little social allowance to help keep me afloat, but it wasn't much, and sadly there was just not a lot of work available for me in Southampton, so it was best that I move on. Which was all very true, but I also had a strong growing feeling to get away from the black cloud that I felt Liam and the brothers had created for me, but I didn't mention that as I didn't want to worry her. I asked her to please explain things to my dad Geoff, and anyone else who may ask about me. The main thing was, that I was ok, and for the most part, all was going well!

A couple of days later, I bumped into Sal in the street, and she told me that she was heading over to London, and asked if I wanted to go along with her as she didn't want to go alone, but she needed a change of scenery from Southampton. "Sure, that sounds good!" I told her, thinking of it as a reconnaissance trip, and if I liked it, I would wrap up my short-lived new life in Southampton, and head back over to London to seek work. It wasn't too far away, about 80 miles, so it seemed as though it would be easy enough to come and go to. I got the impression that this was a regular thing for Sal, and looked forward to our little excursion!

Sal was ready to go, and I didn't need to get anything from my bedsit, so the two of us strolled down to the motorway and started hitchhiking. A couple of hours later we arrived at Piccadilly Circus - bang in the centre of London. This was my first visit to London as an adult, and I loved the atmosphere! The place was buzzing with all sorts of people; tourists, locals, artists, musicians, students, backpackers… I felt as though I had arrived at exactly where I was meant to be!

We instinctively headed to sit down on the steps underneath the statue of Eros in the centre of Piccadilly circus, where loads of other interesting-looking people were also sitting - mainly punks, new-wavers, students, tourists and backpackers. I felt totally in my element, even though I had no notion of such a place even existing before we had arrived there!

I noticed a good-looking blond guy sitting nearby, I wasn't usually attracted to blond guys, I preferred dark-haired guys, but his hair was a nice shade of dark blond, and fell with effortless style, straight and layered lightly, down to his jawline on either side of his face. There was a certain something about him that I liked. More than his obvious good looks; with his fine chiselled bone structure, and stunning blue eyes. He also had a certain energy to him, which told me that he had a lot of depth and creativity and that there was far more to him than what meets the eye.

He seemed to notice me too, and casually came over to sit next to me with his guitar slung over his shoulder. He smiled, said hi, and told me his name was Bruno in a sweet Italian accent. He asked what my name was as he put out his hand to shake mine. I shook his hand and told him that my name was Della, and I glanced over at Sal to introduce her too, but she was happily chatting away with a curly brown-haired guy.

Bruno and I soon got chatting, He told me that he was from Milan and that he was in London to study music. He asked me where I was from, and I told him about my home town of Oswestry, and about my travels so far and the jobs I'd had along the way. He seemed impressed and got comfortable next to me.

After a while, Sal and the curly brown-haired guy joined in the conversation. His name was Tony, and it turned out that he was a friend of Bruno's. We had a joyful afternoon under the statue of Eros, just chatting, laughing, joking, and simply enjoying being. Bruno played his guitar and sang a few times, and I found his voice to be angelic. It reminded me a little of the singer Sting's voice from the band The Police, which was one of my favourite bands. Needless to say, my crush on Bruno was growing by the second!

That evening we were invited to a party at Tony's house, which was a massive fancy apartment in a posh part of London. Apparently, a former prime minister lived in the apartment below. Bruno and I were getting along well, almost too well! The chemistry between us felt very strong, and I felt butterflies every time he looked at me, or our hands touched. Part of me felt that I should just go with the flow, but deep down, I knew I wasn't into flings, and I didn't want to get drawn into a relationship when I was barely just getting going with my world travels.

After a couple of hours of drinking and merriment, I decided to crash out, and just ignore my feelings for Bruno. There was a guest mattress by one of the windows, so I lay down on it. Bruno came over and lay down too, it felt nice to have him next to me, but I resisted all temptations, and thankfully he was a gentleman and didn't try anything, aside from giving me a gentle kiss on my shoulder before we both fell asleep.

The next morning, I woke up with Bruno's arm resting protectively around me. I slowly wiggled free, and stood up and headed over to the bathroom. When I came out of the bathroom, I bumped into Sally in the kitchen and with a cheeky grin she asked me how things went with Bruno. She added with a wink that she and Tony got along great!

I told her that I really liked Bruno, but I didn't want to get involved, because I wanted to travel. Sal looked at me with a shocked expression "Bruno is a real looker! Some girls would kill to be with a guy like that! "What's wrong with you girl?!" She exclaimed. I laughed, and feeling awkward, changed the subject while telling myself that I must focus on my main goal which is to travel, and not fall for some extremely good-looking Italian guy that I just happened to meet under the angel of love statue – Eros. My heart hurt at the cruel irony of it all, but I took a deep breath and went about looking for some coffee.

Bruno suddenly appeared and staggered past us towards the bathroom. As he passed by, I felt butterflies in my stomach, and he looked over and gave me a sad look of regret, which I tried to ignore and act as if I hadn't noticed, even though deep down my heart felt as though it might explode at any second.

Sal's guy Tony emerged from the other room and gave her a big kiss, which she didn't ignore, and it swiftly turned into a full-blown snogging session, which made things even more awkward for Bruno and me, not that things could get any more awkward!

I automatically went into an aloof mode to cover up the feelings that were developing inside of me! I acted as though I was completely unaware of how awkward things were, and just started talking about how fun London was, Bruno seemed to pick up on this and did likewise, but there was tension beneath the surface between us, and the strong feeling that we liked each other, was impossible to escape from.

I kept reminding myself of my travel plans, which helped me to curb my feelings for Bruno long enough until we were ready to leave. Sal and her guy made loose plans to meet up again, while Bruno and I awkwardly told each other that we may see each other around. He looked a little hurt and confused as if he knew that we had a connection, but I tried to look as though I was ok with things.

We all waved our goodbyes to one another, and Sal and I headed outside, and into the street. The houses and apartments looked very grand, and affluent. 'How come Tony lives there?' I suddenly wondered. He'd mentioned something about his father owning the apartment the night before, but we were all too tipsy to pay much attention to what he was saying. He had a slight Italian accent too, so I figured that there was some kind of Italian connection between him and Bruno. 'Oh well, it doesn't really matter, as I'm free to continue with my travels now!' I told myself as we headed towards a tube station that would take us to the outskirts of London, where we would be able to catch a lift.

Sal and I came out of the tube station and headed over to a main road, I wasn't really paying much attention to where we were, as Sal seemed to know the route by heart. We both stuck out our thumbs and hitchhiked our way back to Southampton.

During our journey back Sal seemed to be on a high about meeting Tony, whereas I had mixed emotions about the whole experience. I decided not to tell Sal that I had actually really liked Bruno, but didn't want to get involved because I wanted to stay free to travel, because I knew she wouldn't understand, and would probably encourage me to get back there and go for it! But what would be the point? It would only cause problems; it wouldn't solve them.

That night I lay awake in bed wondering how I was going to deal with potential romances on my travels, especially as I wasn't into flings. I realised that I would have to be really strong to resist potential temptations, because if I gave into them, one thing could lead to another, and I could get drawn into a relationship, and my world travels would stop, and I just couldn't let that happen!

There would be plenty of time for romance after my travels, and if I did meet a guy who truly seemed like he may be the one, and I his one, then we would have to cross that bridge when we get to it! - Maybe he would travel with me, or we would stay in touch throughout my travels, and meet up at regular intervals until I finally got based somewhere? I fell asleep with visions of Bruno meeting up with me at various places around the world. My heart did feel a genuine connection between us, but it was probably too late now, and I wondered if I would ever see him again.

Over the next couple of weeks, I had a fun time with my friends in Southampton, but all along, I knew that I needed to get moving soon if I wanted to find work and make some money for my travels. Also, there was the ongoing threat of bumping into Liam and the brothers at any time. The other kids would usually warn me if they were about, but there was always the possibility of a chance meeting, which I dreaded to think about, as I knew Liam wouldn't believe that I'd dropped the jewellery off, and knowing the brothers, they would lie through their teeth, and I just didn't need the grief!

One day I met a friendly lorry driver named Frank in a local café and we got chatting about our lives in general. He had a pleasant demeanour and looked to be in his early forties, of average build, and looks, with greying brown hair, and a slight beard and moustache. He wasn't married and didn't have children, but he had a long-term relationship and seemed happy enough. I didn't get any pick-up vibes from him; I only got the sense that he was happy to have someone to chat to.

As we chatted, I mentioned that I should probably head to London to look for work soon, and he told me that he would be heading over to London the following Monday if I wanted a lift. I instantly realised that this would be great timing because I would have my social allowance on Friday, and rather than pay for another week of rent on Monday, I could keep the money to tide me over in London while I looked for work. This would mean having to do a runner of sorts, from my BnB, as they would be expecting the coming week's rent on Monday afternoon, but I would have been all paid up at least, so I wouldn't actually owe them anything. Still, I would feel a bit bad, just taking off, and leaving them at such short notice, without a tenant! I explained this to my Lorry driver pal, and he emphasised the fact that I would be all paid up, and not to worry, as they would soon find a new tenant. I guiltily agreed, and after a while of chatting about how I would go about it, we both had a laugh at the notion of me legging it over the garden wall at the crack of dawn!

We arranged for him to pick me up early on Monday morning to avoid the B&B owners seeing me leave. I still felt bad about just taking off, so I reminded myself that at least I'd been a good tenant - I'd looked after the place, and kept it clean and tidy. I was polite and friendly with the owners and fellow guests, and I wasn't noisy, and the main thing was I'd never missed a weekly rent payment, and I really did need the coming week's social allowance for my job searching trip to

London, as after it was spent I would have nothing. So I hoped that the Landlords would understand - I left them a nice note thanking them for their hospitality, and explaining my reasons for leaving. Then I quickly went about packing up my rucksack. I decided that rather than go out the front door where I would have to pass by the landlord's living area, I would go out the back way, through the kitchen, and into the back garden, and jump over the six-foot wall. Frank and I had joked about me doing this, and now I was really actually doing it!

With the help of a rubbish bin to stand on, I climbed up, and leaned over the wall with my rucksack on my back, swung my legs round, and jumped down the other side, then ran down the alleyway towards the street. I paused briefly to peep my head out of the alleyway, and look around the street before fully emerging and hoping that the landlords or any of their neighbours wouldn't spot me!

CHAPTER 9:

BACK TO LONDON: AND LOVE LOST FOREVER…

Thankfully Frank and his lorry were parked up a little way down the street waiting for me. I ran fast, jumped up inside the cab, and sat catching my breath on the passenger seat while Frank and I greeted each other with big grins. "I made it!" I joked, breathlessly. "Well done gal! You're like 007!" Frank Joked back, and we both laughed, as he started up the motor and pulled out into the street.

We had a good journey, full of fun and interesting chats, and lots of laughs and jokes. Frank was very easy-going and seemed grateful for some company, and I was grateful for the lift, so it was good all around.

We soon arrived in London and once again I felt excited to be there. I thanked Frank and said goodbye. I felt a little sad to be saying goodbye as we had had such a good journey together, and we got along so well, but I knew by now that these short but sweet friendships would be par for the course while travelling, so it was something I was going to have to get used to.

The first place I headed for was Piccadilly Circus. It still looked fun and full of life, but it didn't feel quite the same without Bruno there. A little of the magic was missing. I told myself not to dwell on that and instead to focus on finding work, as that's what I was there for!

I suddenly spotted Bruno's friend Tony, and for a split-second my heart skipped a beat as I assumed that Bruno must be around too. "Tony!" I called out, and he turned and looked my way. He looked very surprised to see me and hurried over to say hi and give me a hug. We sat down next to each other on the steps of Eros and had an excited chat about what we'd both been up to the past few weeks since we last saw each other.

He asked about Sal, and I told him that as far as I knew she was still in Southampton. He looked a little disappointed, so I added, that I was sure she would be back in London again soon, which made him smile. I cooly asked about Bruno, but he said he hadn't seen him around much lately, and that they were only acquaintances through mutual friends, as far as he knew he was serious about his music studies, and didn't socialise much, adding that he must have liked me enough to stay and hang out last time, as usually he didn't usually hang out for long. I laughed it off, as a wave of regret swept through me. I hid my disappointment, as I looked around me at the vibrant Piccadilly Circus scenery, secretly searching the crowds for Bruno.

I asked if Tony knew where there was any work going. He didn't have a clue and didn't seem to be bothered about mundane things such as jobs. I remembered that he was from a well-to-do family and that his family owned the large apartment we had partied at that night. I recalled that it was directly above a former UK prime minister's apartment; either Harold Wilson, or Edward Heath, but each time I was about to ask him about it the subject would change.

He told me I was welcome to crash there while I looked for work if I wanted to. I was grateful of his offer, but hoped that he wasn't expecting me to be interested in him in any way, other than as a human! He seemed okay, so I thanked him, thinking what have I got to lose? "If he tries anything on, I'll leg it!"

That night I crashed at his place. It was such a beautiful luxury apartment, which I was able to appreciate more now that I was sober. I noticed the fine wood-carved fittings, and antique looking furniture, and artwork on the walls. I felt so grateful that Tony was, for the most part, just a regular guy, he had no airs and graces, and he was decent in his behaviour with me, as much to my relief, he didn't try anything on, but for all the good things about him, I still didn't really feel comfortable staying there for some unknown reason? So, the next morning I picked up my rucksack, thanked him, and said I would head off to look for work further afield.

He was very laid back and didn't seem to be offended in any way, and just casually told me to come back if I got stuck. I thanked him, adding that I may see him around town, and took off.

I felt glad to be free again, and hopped on the nearest tube and decided to just pick a random stop, and look around for work there. I popped out somewhere in the East End and started to go for a walkabout. I spotted a church and decided to hide my rucksack there so that it would lighten the load for me to look around with just my shoulder bag. I soon found myself in a busy market place and I felt sure I would find some work there.

After meandering around for a while, I got chatting with a large Indian guy who was wearing dark sweatpants, and only a white vest on top, because the weather was quite hot. He had just been sitting there watching the world go by, so I'd approached him, and asked him if he knew of any work going. "Work?" He asked, in a strong foreign accent, as if he hadn't understood what I'd said. "Yes. Hotel work, maybe?" I added, hoping that he would recognise the word hotel, if not the word work. He nodded as if he knew exactly what I meant, and gave me the impression that he maybe worked in a kitchen himself and that they may have some work available for me.

"This way, follow me!" He instructed, in broken English, standing up, and starting to walk away. I didn't feel that I could fully trust him as he had a slightly off vibe, but I was curious to see what work might be going, so I followed him through the crowds of market stalls, vendors and shoppers as he gestured, and pointed ahead, while mumbling "Follow me" He led the way to a row of Indian restaurants, and my hopes perked up. Surely at least one of them was hiring, and if he would put in a good word for me, I may be in luck!

He stopped at a doorway in the middle of the row and unlocked a door with a key. I assumed that it was the private live-in area for the restaurant staff, and hoped that he was taking me to introduce me to his boss, although deep down I was feeling very wary as I followed him up a dimly lit stairway. At the top, he opened a door into what turned out to be a dingy little bedsit.

I was about to turn and leave, but the lay anthropologist in me was curious as to what his behaviour would be, while at the same time trying to give him the benefit of the doubt, and reasoning that maybe he was going to phone his boss for me, or something like that? I followed him inside, feeling strongly that I was flirting with danger, and that I should just go while the going was good! But it was too late now, I was inside.

He closed the door behind me and gestured for me to sit down on the bed. I sat down, feeling that I was giving him the chance to prove himself to be a decent human when suddenly he lunged at me. "NO!" I yelled as I pushed him away, but, instead of stopping, he got more aggressive and lunged at me again. I quickly showed him the cross I was wearing in the hope that he would have some respect. I considered myself to be spiritual, more than religious, but the cross had been a gift from my mum and had sentimental value to me, and I hoped that he would glean some kind of message from it, that told him I was saying "NO!"

He looked at the cross with a confused look, then lunged at me again, so again I pushed him away and this time I made a run for the door, but he managed to get there just before me and put all his weight against it. He was very large and strong, but I was so angry that he was trying to trap me that I used all of my strength to pull the door open against him. He pushed back against it with all of his might, but once I got a grip on the other side of the door, I was determined to get it open, so I pulled as hard as I could, and was able to get it open just wide enough for me to squeeze out through the gap and run down the stairs at the speed of light!

I tore open the downstairs door and instantly found myself back in the bustling market out of breath, upset and angry. I headed back to the church to pick up my rucksack and feeling shaken up and dejected. I was glad that I'd left my rucksack hidden at the church, otherwise, if I'd had it with me, I wouldn't have been able to make such a swift getaway. I instinctively caught the tube back over to Piccadilly Circus. - It felt like my base camp somehow.

I sat on the steps Eros thinking about what had happened on my travels over the last few weeks. On the one hand, it seemed like such a lot, yet on the other hand I felt as though I was only just getting going. I figured it must all be relative to how long a journey is. I was pretty sure that some kids would have headed home at the first sign of hard times, but I was determined not to turn back, and felt I had to keep on going - rain or shine!

My mind flashed to Bruno, and how I'd subtly rebuffed him. He was a stunning-looking guy, with a lovely sweet, creative personality on top, and he was the first guy I had really liked so far on this trip, but even so, I had not even given him a chance, plus I'd been offered a lovely place to stay by his friend Tony, but I'd turned that down too! And instead, I chose to go off on my own, and somehow wind up stuck in some little bedsit with a beast of a guy trying to assault me!

'Why did I always seem to take the hard road?' I thought to myself, feeling confused. I thought about how I had gone into that guy's bedsit, despite all of his dodgy vibes, and remembered that on some level I seemed to think of myself as some kind of independent anthropological research writer, throwing myself out into the world at the tender age of seventeen, almost as some kind of a social experiment, curious to learn about human nature. I thought about how I kept my journals and remembered that maybe I would write about my travels someday and share my stories with the world. This thought made me feel a little better, as it gave a sense of purpose to my life and my adventures...

As I sat there daydreaming and thinking about my journey so far, and all the people I'd met, I noticed it was starting to get dark, and I suddenly wondered where I would stay that night. I looked around me and felt sad not to see Bruno, or even Sal and Tony. It was as though a whole new wave of people had arrived, and washed the old wave of people away. I wondered where Bruno was at that moment. I remembered that he told me he had spent time in Boston, USA and had loved it there.

I wondered if I would ever make it there, and went about imagining how special it would be for us to both meet up again in Boston by chance. It was a strange sensation to feel as though I was on the verge of falling in love with someone who I would probably never, ever see again! "Good ole me!" I thought with a laugh, thankfully seeing the funny side!

My mind went back to wondering where I would stay that night, and I thought about heading over to Tony's. I wasn't exactly sure where his house was, but I figured that I would hopefully remember which tube trains to take if I tried. I'd seen a sign for Knightsbridge at the tube station a few streets down from his apartment, so I was sure I would find it if I tried, yet at the same time, I wasn't sure that I wanted to. It would feel like going backwards somehow, and I wanted to keep moving forward.

I decided that I would just tough it out, and go with the flow, and that it was all part of the adventure after all, and that all my travel experiences would be part of my bounty of material to learn from and write about! I continued to stay sitting under the statue of Eros, in the centre of Piccadilly, in the centre of London, surrounded by people, yet feeling completely lost, and alone. I knew that no matter what, something would have to happen sooner or later!

The next few days I spent on the streets of London hanging out with the street people - the misfits, the odd-bods, the homeless punk-rock kids, and the down and outs. Most of them were rough diamonds, and all of them seemed to look out for each other, and without question they took me under their wings, and would share their cheap digs, or squats with me, and give me a place to lay my head.

One night, I found myself in an all-night café full of cross-dressers. I'd never met such people in my life before, and I felt as though I was in a strange dream, but more than that, I felt safe. These exotic people fussed over me, and made sure that I was protected, and well looked after for the duration of the night. The next morning, one by one, we all went our separate ways, but I knew that I would never forget them and the care they showed me.

One day while sitting at Piccadilly Circus under the statue of Eros, which became my main haunt to rest and regroup between crashing out at random places, and looking for work, I got chatting with a girl a little older than I was, and in the course of the conversation, I told her that I was looking for work, and asked if she knew of anything going?

She told me there were jobs available a nightclub called Stringfellows. It was just a ten-minute walk away which seemed ideal. I was curious about it and asked what the job entailed. She said it was cocktail waitressing, and that it was easy, all I would have to do was take drink orders from the tables over to the bar and then take the drinks back over to the tables. She added that the tips were good too!

Feeling excited by the prospect of a fun job, with tips on top, I asked her for directions and decided to head over there straight away. She told me how to get there, and I thanked her and set off. I got a little lost on route, and instead of finding Stringfellows, I found another nightclub called Samanthas. It looked like a fun and friendly place, with a colourful décor, and I noticed that the people coming and going from there had good friendly vibes, and good music was playing inside.

I spotted a small "Help wanted" sign in the corner of the window, which as I took as a sign, on both levels, so chuckling to myself I walked inside, figuring that a club was a club, whatever the name, and hopefully the pay here would be similar to the Stringfellows club the girl had told me about.

A smartly dressed brown-haired man, of around thirty who I assumed was the manager walked towards me as I entered. "Hi, I'm interested in the job in the window!" I exclaimed, with a big smile. "Do you have experience in club work?" he asked smiling back. "Yes, I've worked at hotel pubs and clubs since I was fourteen, usually helping out in the kitchen, but it involved a little bar work and waitressing too!" I answered positively. He asked me a few more questions about my past work experience and seemed happy with my answers and much to my delight, I was hired on the spot!

"Great thanks!" I exclaimed. "My pleasure, can you start tonight?" He asked. "Yes, what time?" I answered eagerly. "About six" he answered, also looking pleased. "Great, see you at six!" I answered and took off out of the door. "Bye for now!" he called after me. I walked away feeling very happy to have a job again! - Now all I needed was somewhere to live!

I didn't have to start work for a couple of hours, so I headed back to Piccadilly Circus to sit on the steps of Eros and collect my thoughts. What would I do next? Where would I stay that night after work? I thought again about going to Tony's, but for some reason, I still wasn't keen on the idea. Deep down, even though he'd been hospitable, maybe I thought that he would expect something from me, especially as Sal had been so eager to be with him, but if I didn't let anything happen with Bruno - a guy who I actually felt strong chemistry with, then I sure as heck wasn't going to let anything happen with Tony, a guy I felt zero chemistry with! So going to Tony's felt like a big no-no!

As I was pondering on my next move, a guy came and sat next to me and said hello. I looked up to see a friendly-looking dark-haired guy a little older than me. He had an accent which I couldn't place. I said hello back, and asked where he was from. he said that he was from Portugal and that his name was Erick. He added that he was in London as a student.

He was very easy to chat with, and he asked why I was there, so I wound up telling him my travel story so far. He seemed impressed that I was so brave to just be going for it with no family or friends for support. He told me that he had also done a little travelling, and had spent time in the US, adding that he was hoping to go back there someday.

I told him I was hoping to travel the world possibly starting with the Americas. I added that maybe I would go to Canada first, and then volunteer work my way all the way down to the tip of Argentina! He found this hilarious, as did I, and we laughed at the idea of travelling the world with just our wits to get by on! Making random jokes about washing dishes, and picking potatoes and turnips on route to keep afloat. "Yeah, whatever it takes!" I'd exclaimed, through tears of laughter.

As we chatted, I mentioned that I was looking for a cheap bedsit or room to rent if he knew of anywhere, and he told me that he had a spare room and that I was welcome to it if I would chip in towards the rent. I was elated at this idea, so I eagerly agreed. I told him I was to start work that night at a nightclub called Samantha's and that this was perfect timing!

He gave me his address and told me that he would leave the door open that night, and tomorrow, he would sort out my keys. I was very happy with this arrangement. He didn't seem to have any ulterior motives, much to my relief, he just seemed to be a genuine fellow adventurer of sorts!

That night I started my new job at Samantha's night club. I was now a cocktail waitress and my job was to go around the tables looking for people who were ready to order their drinks. This was very easy, as most people would wave me over as soon as they spotted me.

The atmosphere was very upbeat and friendly, as everybody was out to have a good time. Popular chart music would be playing all night, and I was so happy to finally have a good job, with nice people who liked and appreciated me!

The pay was £20 a night, and the tips were piling up too! During a break at the side of the bar I got chatting with a guy who said his sister was Erika Roe; a girl who was made famous for streaking across a rugby pitch, during a game earlier in the year which sounded hilarious.

As we chatted a French guy joined us, and told us his name was Pierre. Erika Roe's brother picked up his drink from the bar and headed into the club, saying he may see us later, as Pierre and I continued to chat.

He told me that he worked at Harrods. He was quite good-looking and was very nice to chat to. I liked him a little bit, but certainly not enough to get involved with, plus I reminded myself that I wanted to travel, that was my main goal, not romance!

He gave me his number, and with a little wave and a smile I got back to work knowing that I would probably never call him, but he'd been nice to meet. Later I got chatting with a friendly table full of people. – I'd been dancing to some funky music as I served them, and suddenly they all jumped up to join me in a dance and I felt like I'd made an instant group of friends.

We were all getting along so well, that they invited me to sit with them for a drink. I was sure the club manager wouldn't mind, as no one was in need of a drink, and I was simply being hospitable, all part of my job! They asked about me, and I asked about them…

One of the girls said that she was Erick burdens girlfriend. I'd heard of him, and his band "The Animals" so I automatically started singing "There is a house in New Orleans…" "Yeah, that's the one!" she exclaimed, as she started to sing along with me. The others all joined in with the rest of the chorus, and we were all having so much that I nearly forgot to continue taking my table orders, but thankfully nobody seemed to care!

I felt no pressure from the club owner or the manager, or any of the bartenders. They all seemed happy enough, and would smile at me as they whizzed around. I got the impression that they were happy that I was contributing to the fun atmosphere, and that the drinks were flowing and the money was coming in! "This is my kind of job!" I thought to myself, as I jumped up, and bid my farewell, as soon as I noticed a table of people running low on drinks.

After I finished work for the night, I was paid a big wad of cash. "Thank you! Same time, same place tomorrow night!" I'd joked as I left. They all seemed very happy with me, as I was with them. I headed off towards the tube, feeling fantastic!

I jumped on the tube and made my way over to my new place. Erick had written his address, with very clear directions so it wasn't hard to find at all. I arrived and gently knocked on the door as I quietly opened it. I tiptoed inside. The flat was lit up with a lamp in the hallway, and another lamp in the kitchen, but the rest of the place was in darkness and I felt pretty sure that Erick had gone to bed. I tiptoed into the kitchen and spotted a note on the table.

The note read "Welcome Della, I've gone to bed. I'll see you tomorrow. Your room is the one with the door open. I've fixed it up for you. Sleep well, Erick" I went to bed feeling so happy to have a room to myself! I slept like a log and the next morning I woke up to the smell of strong coffee in the air. I found my way to the bathroom to wash my face and wake up a little before heading to the kitchen.

"Good morning, Della, how did you sleep? Coffee?" Said Erick with a big smile. "Yes, please! I slept great, thanks!" I answered, and the two of us were soon sitting down on the sofa with a big mug of coffee each.

We had a good chat about my new job, about his studies, and his daily routine. He gave me a main entrance, and a front door key, and told me to make myself at home. My rent would be £10 a week and this would include bills. I instantly calculated that one night's work at Samantha's would more than cover this, and my groceries and personal items. The rest of my earnings from tips would be for my travels.

I had the impression that Erick had a student grant so the rent money I gave him would just be extra spending money for him, so it was a win/win for both of us!

Also, the fact that he seemed totally fine with a platonic friendship was reassuring. It would be nice to have a housemate who is also a friend. I was so glad that I had taken a leap of faith, and just jumped into London feet first!

For the next few weeks I mainly just worked, ate, and slept. I was saving money for my travels so I didn't go out clubbing. Not that I needed to, as my cocktail waitress job at Samantha's scratched that itch for sure!

Whenever I passed by Piccadilly Circus and the statue of Eros it didn't look the same to me anymore. Instead of the free-spirits, musicians, artists, students, and backpackers, there were glue sniffers, sad-looking homeless people, and drunks. There were always a handful of tourists and free-spirited types, but they looked lost, and out of place.

I missed the time when I had first arrived there to such a magical sight of life in motion. Meeting Bruno and his sweet singing and guitar playing, the people around us laughing, joking, and having interesting conversations in accents and languages from all around the world.

It had been such a warm welcome to the city of London and had created a memorable first impression for me, but now it looked deflated and sad. but that was okay, I told myself because I was going to be moving on soon - and hopefully, London will too!

I had been sending postcards and letters to family and friends to keep them updated on my adventures, but I would only phone my grandparents on occasion to chat to them, or to my parents if they were there. They all seemed happy for me and always wished me well.

I phoned Aunt Freda regularly too, to check the latest on our proposed USA visit. One day I phoned her, and she told me that she would be in London the following week to arrange our visas. She told me that she would be buying my ticket in return for my accompanying her on the trip, which would be sometime between December and June. She mentioned how fun it would be to visit Macy's at Christmas time. I wasn't sure what she meant, but she carried on speaking before I had a chance to ask about it.

We arranged a meet-up time and place, and I figured that we would have a proper catch-up when we met up "Must dash now, I have to feed the horses! See you soon, God Bless!" She said, before hanging up. "Bye Freda, god…" I answered as she hung up.

The following Tuesday we met up near Hyde Park, and she hurriedly led the way to the American Embassy to sort our visas out. The appointment went smoothly, and once our passports were stamped. We had some free time left over for a stroll around London city centre.

As we walked, she asked me questions about my life in London, adding that she could never live in a city, because she loved nature too much, and besides, where would all her animals stay? She laughed as if picturing them all in a city high-rise building. I told her that I was enjoying living in London, but I loved the countryside too. "They both have their pros and cons!" I answered with a grin.

"Well, I must get back to Hunters Moon, my animals will be missing me!" Said Freda suddenly, as if she'd had enough of London. "OK, well I'll keep in touch to plan for our trip!" I said feeling excited at the prospect of travelling around the USA with Aunt Freda, even though she hadn't been in my travel visualisations! "I guess it's good to allow for a few surprises!" I joked to myself.

"Oh yes, there's plenty of time for that, now where do I catch the tube back to Borehamwood where my car's parked?" She asked as if our trip to America was no longer of great interest to her. We asked a couple of locals for directions and were directed to Kings Cross, and soon I was waving goodbye to her as she sailed off down an escalator to catch her tube train. I walked around King's Cross for a while just collecting my thoughts and feeling excited about how things were going. I was learning that ups and downs were certainly par for the course on my journey, but the main thing was, to keep going!

CHAPTER 10:

LEAVING LONDON

After a few more weeks of working at Samantha's and saving up money. I phoned Aunt Freda to say hello & check on the latest. We had a nice little catch-up chat, and then she suddenly told me that our America trip would have to be put on hold because of something or other to do with her Animals. I felt very disappointed but told her ok, and asked her to keep me posted, as I would continue to phone her regularly.

I hung up the phone feeling deflated and let down, but as I started to walk it dawned on me that I could still go ahead to the Americas, and maybe Aunt Freda & I could meet up over there! After all, I had been planning my travels solo way before Aunt Freda suggested I travel with her. These thoughts brought a smile to my face and a spring in my step as I glided along the pavement. I loved the feeling of "The world is your oyster" as the saying goes, although, I never quite understood how it meant what it did! I decided that now was the best time for my dad to send my savings to me, as I would need every penny I could get to embark on my overseas travels.

As soon as I got back home to Ericks, I wrote a letter to my dad and asked him to send my savings to Eric's address. I told my dad that I was hoping to head to the Americas soon - I wasn't sure exactly where yet, but I would keep him updated. I knew that my dad would be excited for me, as he knew that I'd been dreaming about world travel, starting with the Americas since childhood. I asked him to send the money as a postal order by recorded delivery, as it would be the safest way. Still, I was a little anxious about it being sent by post, as it was £150 and I didn't want it to get lost! but I needed it, as I knew it would come in very handy, along with the few hundred quid I'd saved up working at Samantha's.

I felt very pleased with myself for having saved so much money. When Erick came home, I told him that I had written to ask my dad to send me my savings by postal order, as I would probably set off for The Americas soon. Erick didn't take the news so well, which confused me, as he knew right from the start that I was planning more travels. I wasn't sure if it was because he secretly liked me, or if it was because he would miss my rent money!

Over the next few days, Erick started acting strange. Whenever we were both home at the same time, he would drink a lot of alcohol and get very drunk. He suddenly started making passes at me in an awkward and very irritating way, almost falling on me, and clumsily trying to hug and kiss me. I told him not to be so ridiculous and reminded him that we were just friends, but he was getting more and more obnoxious, to the point where I was dreading being around him.

One night in particular he was very rude and was acting way out of order. His behaviour reminded me of the Bournemouth brothers; Shane and Lee, and I instantly knew I had to get out of there! I went to bed that night not feeling safe. I felt as though I had to sleep with one eye open.

I was so upset that Erick had turned out to be such a creep! I didn't know if he'd always been that way, but had just been pretending to be a nice guy, or if he was a nice guy, but the booze had brought out the creep in him. This felt more likely, but either way, I knew I needed to get out of there! That night I decided not to sleep, I would lay on my bed, wait until the early hours, and then pack up and go around 3-4 am. Once I knew that Erick was fast asleep!

Thankfully Erick didn't bother me after I went to bed, and around 3 am I tiptoed out of my room to use the bathroom. I paused by Erick's room and could hear him lightly snoring. Feeling a sense of relief, I quickly used the bathroom, without flushing the loo, and freshened up, before heading to my room to pack the last bits and bobs into my rucksack and get out of there!

I wrote Erick a little goodbye note and left it on my bedside table, and put the spare flat keys on top of it. I felt a wave of excitement at the thought of moving on. Especially as I now had enough money saved up to head to the airport and get on a plane!

I had decided on Canada as the first place to explore within the Americas. From what I'd read, and seen on TV, it seemed a lovely country - a perfect blend of Europe and America, the people seemed polite and friendly, and as it was mainly English-speaking, I felt it would be a great place to start my overseas travels. Also, I would be right next door to the USA, and sort of on standby ready for when Aunt Freda wanted me to join her. It was perfect!

With my rucksack on my back, I tiptoed past Eric's bedroom door, he was still snoring. I glanced around the flat, and in my mind, I thanked it for giving me shelter over the last few weeks. I opened the front door, and gently closed it behind me, then raced off down the hallway, down the steps, and out of the building. It was still dark outside as I hurried along the maze of council flat tower blocks pathways, and out onto the main road.

As I made my way towards the tube Station my heart beating fast, and I felt as if I'd made a lucky escape! What was wrong with these guys?! Why were some of them such creeps??!! 'My God, they need to learn how to treat ladies properly, and maybe then they would have better luck!' I thought to myself, my fear turning to anger. Either way, it wasn't my problem, I was out of there!

I found the tube train to Heathrow and jumped on it. By now it was around 4 am. The tube was due to arrive at Heathrow around 5 am. For once it wasn't busy. Just a few bleary eyes passengers dotted about. I sat down next to the door and put my rucksack on the seat next to me. I sat back, and let out a gentle sigh of relief. Feeling so glad to finally be on my way again!

I thought about the goodbye note I'd left for Erick; thanking him for renting me his spare room, and mentioned that his behaviour when drunk had put me off staying there any longer, but I wished him well. I'd left my bedroom door wide open, so he would instantly see that I was gone. I wondered what he would make of me leaving so suddenly. Hopefully, he would get the message that he had been way out of order!

I slipped into a daydream wondering what Canada would be like, and seconds later Heathrow was announced. I grabbed my rucksack and jumped off the tube. I followed the other people with luggage, and headed inside the airport. I'd never flown before, heck I'd never been out of the UK before! I didn't really know how any of it worked, but it seemed logical to me, that if you want to fly to another country, then the airport must be the place where you buy a plane ticket!

I spotted a desk with a lady standing behind it serving people, so I made my way over to join the queue. "Do you have a ticket for Canada please?" I asked the lady politely when it came to my turn. The lady looked puzzled at my request.

"So, er, ...whereabouts in Canada?" she asked. Still looking puzzled. I hadn't really thought of a particular place I just wanted to go to Canada! - I wanted to explore, have a look around, and afterwards travel down to the USA, meet up with Aunt Freda, and explore some more! ...and afterwards, head down to

BOOK 1: TO SEE THE WORLD

Mexico and the rest of Central and South America! - Basically, I wanted to explore the Americas! So, to name just one city in Canada seemed silly!

Although, judging by her confused look, I doubted that she would understand any of that, so I just took a deep breath and tried to narrow down my travel visions to suit her request. "Um, where in Canada are the planes flying to?" I asked, feeling that my query was a reasonable one. At that she looked more confused than ever, as she nervously checked her books, and impatiently rattled off a bunch of city names in Canada.

I felt the name of the game was to shrink down all of my visions of world travels, and to simply pick a place, and try and make it sound as normal as possible! "Okay Montréal please!" I answered calmly while feeling frustrated, and somewhat suppressed by the situation.

"Doesn't she realise that I'm literally on the verge of finally realising my childhood dreams of setting off to explore the world?!!" I thought to myself, starting to see the funny side of the situation, which eased the tension a little.

"Okay" she answered, still seeming puzzled by my request. I couldn't help but find her attitude annoying and small-minded. Surely it wasn't such a bizarre thing to want to visit Canada? And that was without even mentioning my other world travel goals! "Maybe she was used to people just going on small conventional holidays? Not free-spirited explorers?" I thought to myself, trying to have some understanding as to where she was coming from. I took another deep breath and tried to just be polite and patient as she made up my ticket.

"Five hundred pounds please," she said as she shuffled a bunch of paperwork together on the countertop. "Five hundred!!" I thought, feeling shocked at the price! I only had a little over five hundred on me! I suddenly remembered the money I'd saved up that my dad was sending to me at Ericks. It hadn't arrived yet.

I briefly wondered if Eric had been acting badly on purpose to get rid of me so that he could keep my money. I felt sick to my stomach at the thought of Erick keeping it and leaving me with next to nothing after paying for the plane ticket, but I couldn't back out now!

"Ok, thank you" I replied, as I counted out my money on the counter. "Thank you!" She answered a little more nicely and looking reassured by the fact that I actually had the money. She handed me the ticket and some other paperwork and directed me over towards the waiting lounge. I thanked her and walked away feeling a strange mixture of stress and joy.

"All part of the adventure!" I told myself as I headed towards the lounge, and had my tickets looked at by a member of staff who seemed to be the lounge gatekeeper. I found a seat and sat down. I let out a sigh of relief, and sat there feeling a sense of numb excitement, as though I was on the verge of a big life change, but was quietly sitting waiting, in a state of limbo, for it to happen.

It suddenly hit me that I was about to do something massive! I was about to fly halfway across the world and into the complete unknown! The thought alone was scary and exciting at the same time and made me grin from ear to ear.

'Wow, I'm finally leaving the UK, and it's only three months after leaving my hometown! Not, bad going, and I'm still only seventeen! There's plenty of time to have a good look around this place called Earth!' I thought to myself, as the stress from the ticket sales interaction started to wear off, and the excitement of a whole new adventure started to take its place.

The next couple of hours were spent fluctuating between travel daydreams, and the sense of just waiting. I'd never flown before, so I didn't know what the procedure was. I figured I would just follow instructions as they arose.

I decided to have a little walkabout and spotted a booth selling postcards and stamps. I thought it would be a good idea to send a couple to my parents to let them know that I was heading to Canada. I bought two postcards with stamps and managed to write them out just before my flight was announced. I popped them in the post-box feeling pleased that I'd managed to do that before take-off!

I saw a line of people starting to form across the far side of the lounge, so I hurried over to join them. I was soon boarding the plane, and feeling as though I was in a dream of sorts, I walked down the aisle and found my seat by the window. I was excited to finally be on the plane, but I was a little bit nervous too. "Hi, I'm Harry!" Said a friendly-looking man as he sat down next to me. "Hi, I'm Della!" I answered back, as we shook hands, and got comfortable in our seats.

After a few minutes, the plane started to move and seemed to be picking up speed. "First time flying?" asked Harry. "Yes, it is" I answered as I looked out the window nervously to see the runway speeding by. "Oh, don't worry, I fly all the time! It's great! You'll love it!" said Harry, in a calm, and easy-going tone.

Feeling a little reassured. I took a deep breath, sat back, and tried to relax. Harry was from Canada he was very nice, and chatting with him made me feel at ease. He told me that he lived in Montréal, but travelled a lot for his job. He asked about my life, and I told him that I was off to see the world while I was still young! "That's the way to do it! don't let anything get in your way!" He answered heartily.

I like his spirit, and we got along great. "Wanna smoke?" He asked, offering me a Winston cigarette. "No thanks, I quit smoking a year ago" I answered, feeling that it was nice of him to offer. "You quit smoking a year ago? When did you start? When you were five?" He asked with a laugh.

"Well, I started at fourteen, and quit at sixteen" I answered with a grin. "Ah, so you're still only seventeen!" He answered nodding. "Yep! I never really wanted to smoke, but it seemed the thing to do when I was out and about with friends, everyone smoked like it was normal, but by the time I got to sixteen I decided it was best to quit sooner, rather than later!" I answered, glad to be chatting, and not thinking about the fact that we were getting higher and higher up in the plane. "Very wise! I should have quit a long time ago too!" answered Harry looking like he was giving it some serious thought. "Yeah, it wasn't easy! I had to plan a date to quit a few weeks in advance so that my mind and body were as ready as possible by that date!" I answered, hoping I may inspire him to quit too.

"So, then you just did it? You just quit, just like that?" asked Harry, looking amazed. "Well, yes, and no!" I answered laughing. "Go on!" said Harry laughing. "Well, on the morning of the day I'd decided to quit, I went a few hours without a cigarette, but then the craving got too much for me, so I lit up a cigarette, but because I'd gone a few hours without having one, it made me feel sick and dizzy, so I put it out, and told myself that I want that to be my last memory of having a cigarette, so hopefully I would never want one again!" I answered, still hoping to inspire Harry to quit smoking, while at the same time taking my mind off the flight.

"Well done! I may try that sometime answered Harry nodding earnestly, as he puffed on his cigarette. We chatted with ease, about all sorts, in between little bouts of rest, and after a while, I relaxed into the flight.

The flight turned out to be a good one and I enjoyed the meal and drinks that were served to us, especially as much to my surprise they were included in the price of the ticket, "…but then again it was a very expensive ticket!" I reminded myself with a sigh.

CHAPTER 11:

OH CANADA!

Suddenly lights appeared in the blackness below. "Are we there?" I asked Harry, with anticipation. "Yeah, that's Canada!" answered Harry with a big smile. I felt very excited that we were nearly there, I couldn't quite believe it. I found myself suddenly asking Harry loads of questions about Canada, thankfully he seemed happy to answer them! I asked about the weather, I asked if the people were friendly, I asked about the music, and I asked about the food, I was just so excited to be on the verge of arriving in a completely different country, on a completely different continent!

The plane landed smoothly, and we were instructed to disembark. Harry gave me his card and told me to call him if I ever needed anything. He added that we would probably lose each other going through customs and immigration, so it's best to say goodbye before that happens. I thanked him, said goodbye, and waved at him as we shuffled along, and sure enough got split up as I joined the queue for non-Canadians visiting Canada.

Because I'd never flown before I was just copying the people ahead of me. I noticed that everybody had their passports in hand, so I got my passport ready to show to the passport people waiting to meet us at the counters. When it was my turn, the guy looked a little puzzled at my passport and asked me to follow him. Feeling a tad anxious I followed him as he led me to a small office nearby.

"Sit down please," he said, as he went around the other side of a large desk. I sat down opposite him and felt my heart start to beat fast as I wasn't sure why I was in this room, but whatever it was, it seemed serious. We both sat in silence for what seemed like an eternity before he looked up at me and in a French accent said "You are only seventeen years old?" Then he went on to bombard me with questions "Why was I there? Who was I visiting? Why didn't I have a return ticket?"

I answered as fast as I could and I told him I didn't have a return ticket because I was visiting family in Vancouver, and would probably fly back from there. This came to mind because I suddenly remembered that I had an aunt on my mum's side who lived in Vancouver, so, in that second, I reasoned that maybe I would visit her! He asked if anybody was meeting me from the airport. This seemed to be a very important factor, and my American friend Skid Martin suddenly popped to mind, as I remembered him saying if I made it over the pond to LA, he'd meet me at the airport, I just happened to be at a different airport!

"Yes, my friend Skid Martin is meeting me" I answered quickly. "OK, I'll go and page him for you now" answered the man, as he stood up "Skid Martin?" He repeated, "Yes" I answered nodding. "OK, I'll be back soon" He, said, as he left the room. I stayed sitting there wondering what was going to happen next, as I hadn't expected any of this!

After several minutes the man came back into the room saying that nobody had responded to the page. "He's probably waiting for me outside" I answered, imagining Skid waiting for me in his sports car outside the airport. There was an awkward silence, so I mentioned that I noticed his accent was French. He answered and explained to me that in Montréal French is the main language. I answered that I had a hazy notion that French was spoken in some parts of Canada, but I didn't realise it was the main language in Montreal.

I was feeling genuinely surprised, and impressed by my new learnings, so I went on to tell him that my father and his brother had made a documentary in France, and when they came back to England, they told me that France was a beautiful country.

I went on to tell him that my dad had brought some Gitanes cigarettes back for my mum and that I was only eight at the time, but I was curious to try one when my mum was upstairs, it made me cough, so I put it out quickly, but when my mum came back downstairs it was still smouldering in the ashtray! He found this amusing and chuckled to himself, then his face broke into a smile. I chuckled too and smiled back at him, and for a moment it felt like we were friends.

He stared down at my passport as if in deep thought, then asked me about my seven names which he seemed to find interesting. He asked if I had any Romany heritage. I said that I did on my grandmother's side. He smiled a knowing smile and gently nodded his head as he continued to stare at my passport which he held in his hand like an open book.

We sat in silence for a few more seconds and then he suddenly said "Follow me!" I stood up and followed him out of the office, and down into the main airport area. My heart was beating fast again, as I wasn't sure what was going to happen next. Much to my surprise he led me all the way to the exit. Opened the door and wished me luck! My heart felt instantly elated, and with a big smile, I thanked him and wished him luck also, feeling that on some deeper level, I felt I had indeed made a true friend.

I walked out into the street and suddenly felt amazed by the fact that I was actually in the Americas! I couldn't quite believe it! I checked my purse and had £15 left "Better than nothing!" I joked to myself. I glanced at the street, half expecting to see my friend Skid Martin waiting for me, but of course, he wasn't there, so I went in search of a money exchange bureau and converted my £15 into Canadian money. Much to my delight, it suddenly doubled in value, so I took this as a good sign! So, with a skip in my step, I was off to explore Canada!

I decided the library was a good place to start, as I figured it would be perfect to regroup and get my bearings. After asking a couple of people for directions, I was soon strolling into a grand-looking library. I looked around to see all sorts of people inside, ranging from scholars, students, and artists, and homeless people. I'd found a shop selling postcards nearby and bought a few to send to family and friends, and figured that I could write them out inside the library.

I found a nice table and seat to sit at collect my thoughts, and write out my postcards. I was still feeling a little bit shaken up after being questioned upon my arrival. I had no idea that such a thing could, or would happen. I had just assumed that once I had my ticket, and passport, then all was in order. I felt bad for fibbing a little bit, but I had felt on the spot, and had just panicked!

I slowly realised that I could have just told him that I would be meeting my aunt Freda down in the US soon, but I wanted to visit Canada first, as that was the truth, but I'd felt so taken aback, that I was just saying whatever came out! I started to chuckle at how we'd sat in awkward silence for what seemed like an eternity, and my heart warmed as I thought about how he'd turned out to be a kind soul who seemed to sense and understand that, for whatever reason, I just needed to be there.

I took out my pen and wrote out my postcards. All in all, I felt good. I wasn't worried about where my food and shelter would come from as I trusted my instincts and knew that I would find a way to get by.

BOOK 1: TO SEE THE WORLD

After I'd finished writing my postcards, I asked for directions to the nearest post office. I headed to the post office and posted my cards. The streets of Montréal were beautiful and the people were well dressed and had good manners, which created a lovely atmosphere. I spotted a bar and decided to go for a drink. Maybe I would make some new friends?

There were only a handful of people in the bar. A couple of guys playing pool, and a couple of guys sitting at the bar. One reading the newspaper and the other chatting with the bartender I found a free stool at the bar and sat on it. The bartender came over to me and I ordered a cider. The cider swiftly arrived I paid for it and took a sip. I was shocked to discover it wasn't actually cider as I knew it to be, but apple juice! I asked the bartender if they had any alcoholic cider and he looked puzzled. I decided the apple juice would be okay. Middle of the road, easy-listening music played on the jukebox, and it helped to create a relaxed atmosphere.

I sat sipping my Apple juice, feeling thrilled to have arrived on the other side of "The Pond" as Skid called it. I wondered what I might do after I'd finished my drink, but in a way, it felt good not to know, as I loved the feeling of having a blank slate. Just then a guy who looked a couple of years older than me sat down on the barstool next to me and said hi. I said hi back. He noticed my accent and we got chatting. His name was Joe. He was friendly, but also a little annoying in the way that he would ask personal questions. I would just laugh them off, and try and change the subject because, in a way, I was happy to have someone to chat to - albeit a slightly annoying someone! Joe ordered a picture of beer and invited me to join him for a drink. I thanked him, thinking 'Why not!' The next hour so we spent drinking beer and chatting about random things. The bartender would join us occasionally and seemed to be weighing Joe up as if he was thinking that he may be up to mischief. I felt okay though, and I figured I would just go with the flow.

More people came in and a few people more joined us. They all seemed to know Joe, which was reassuring. At some point, one of them suggested we go and get some food and maybe go to a club not too far away. I was by now one of the gang, so I went along with them. We found a place to eat where they also served beers, and I was happy enough to still be going with the flow. Afterwards, we all went to a club and I wondered if maybe one of them would let me crash at their place afterwards. Figuring that in the morning I would decide where to go, and what to do next.

By the end of the night, most of the crowd had gone home and I was just left with Joe. He told me he knew a place I could crash at, and although I found him annoying, I didn't feel threatened by him, so I said thanks, and we headed off out of the club. I followed him down the main streets, and out of the city centre to a poor rundown looking neighbourhood. Things weren't looking too great, but I was curious to see where we were going.

Eventually, we came to an old abandoned derelict lot, and Joe pushed open the gate and started to walk inside. I asked why he was going in there and he said he had a van parked up in there that we could crash out in. Although feeling wary, my options at this point were very slim, so I followed him, knowing that if he tried anything on, he would regret it! We got to the end of the lot and there was an old van parked up in the corner. Joe opened the side door and told me to go on inside. I climbed inside. It was pretty dark, but I could see that there was a large mattress taking up most of the space, he told me it was where he crashed out. He was a casual labourer and just took whatever work he could get, and with the money he made he spent it on beer as he had no other commitments. He seemed happy enough with the situation. I felt a little uncomfortable, but at the same time I was glad of the shelter and somewhere to sleep, so I thanked him and lay down on the far side of the mattress and said good night. I was exhausted and happy to have somewhere to lay my head for the night.

Just as I started to drift off Joe made a move on me. I pushed him away and told him to leave me alone. He persisted, so I pushed him away some more. Eventually, we both fell asleep for a few hours, until I was woken up by Joe making yet another move! This time I was angry, I pushed him quite hard and told him to lay off! He knew I meant business as he looked a bit shaken up. I grabbed my rucksack and told him to F off! then jumped out of the van slamming the door hard behind me. I walked away feeling upset, hurt and angry that he'd turned out to be yet another creep. 'If he comes chasing after me, I'm gonna do him some serious damage!' I thought to myself, as I marched on, feeling enraged. I kept walking, and thankfully, for both of us, he didn't come after me. It was dawn, I guessed I'd had about four hours sleep, but I still felt tired, because I hadn't slept for a couple of nights before arriving in Canada. I spotted a sign that read Toronto and felt a sudden urge to head there. Although Montreal was a beautiful city, I suddenly felt a strong need to get away from there as fast as possible because of the bad experience I'd had with Joe. So, I followed the sign onto the opening of a motorway.

CHAPTER 12:

TORONTO - ALPHA OMEGA

As the Sun was rising so were my spirits. 'Don't let anything get in your way!' I thought to myself, remembering Harry's words. I put my rucksack down and stuck out my thumb. I soon got a lift with a guy named Dave. He told me people weren't supposed to hitchhike on the highway. I joked that I could get out of the car, and walk back to a surface street if he wanted to drive around and pick me up there. We both laughed, as I jumped inside the car.

I was happy to have got a lift so quickly. Dave put some music on the radio, and as we drove along, we chatted about this and that. Although he was friendly enough, I sensed something was slightly off about him, but I played it cool and focused on getting to Toronto, but I felt my guard was up the whole time.

We seemed to drive for hours and hours, and Dave was chatting less and less, which made me feel uncomfortable as if he was up to something, and although this was slightly nerve-wracking, a part of me was curious to see what would happen, as I slipped back into my "independent human behaviour researcher" mode! Plus, I also wanted to give him the benefit of the doubt, and a chance to prove my suspicious instincts wrong, but the sense that he had bad intentions in mind was very strong.

He kept driving until we seemed to be in the middle of nowhere. We were surrounded by deep snow, and the area was very desolate with no people, houses or towns for as far as the eye could see. He suddenly pulled over on the side of the road and parked the car. I felt sick to the pit of my stomach and braced myself for a fight.

"Wanna have a little fun?" He asked arrogantly. "No thank you, I just want to get to Toronto, are we nearly there yet?" I answered politely. I knew we weren't but, I felt it was best to play dumb while weighing up my escape route.

He suddenly leaned over and tried to make a pass at me despite my telling him I wasn't interested. "No!" I shouted, as I pushed him away, grabbed my rucksack and jumped out of the car. "You should be ashamed of yourself!" I shouted, once again feeling my blood rocket to boiling point as I felt ready to tear him apart if he came after me.

He looked shocked and confused as to what to do next. I stormed away fuming with anger, and not caring that I was in the middle of nowhere, but just needing to get away from him! I had the feeling that he hadn't expected me to jump out of the car because we were in such an isolated place, but he obviously didn't know me! "F You!" I shouted as I marched off into the infinite white snow.

His car stayed there for what seemed like ages as I walked further and further away into the nothingness. I wondered if he would come after me, or just drive away. If he were to come after me, I felt that I would knock him out, as I was so angry! I wasn't just angry. I was feeling very upset, and disgusted with the human race, especially the male side of it! My independent research into human behaviour was proving to be most disappointing, to say the least!

I kept walking and walking until eventually I got to a crossroad that looked like it may be a main road as the snow had melted to mush, and the tarmac was showing, although there was no traffic in sight, I just stood there waiting to see if anything would turn up. There was no sign of Dave, so I assumed he'd continued on the desolate road that we'd been on. Maybe he lived up that way or took a different route to avoid me.

A few minutes passed and a small pick-up truck came trundling along. I stuck out my thumb and the pick-up truck stopped. I ran to catch up with it. I opened the passenger door and took a split second to see if the driver seemed okay. Thankfully he did! He was an older jolly spirited country guy, and I felt safe with him, as there were no weird vibes at all. I jumped into the passenger seat and slammed the door shut feeling so happy to be away from Dave, and the desolate snow.

"Hi, are you going to Toronto?" I asked with a smile, determined not to let the incident with Dave change my demeanour. "Sure am!" He answered with a smile, and I let out a sigh of relief. "Great thanks!" I answered, as I jumped into the truck, and got comfortable in the passenger seat.

"I'm Al, what's your name?" He said as he reached out his hand. "Hi Al, I'm Della!" I answered as we shook hands. "Nice to meet you too Della, where are you from?" He asked as we got comfortable in our seats, and he stepped on the gas. "I'm from England, but I'm off to see the world starting with the Americas!" I answered dramatically, with a laugh. "Wow, that is amazing! All on your own!" He answered, looking shocked. "Yep, just me, myself, and I!" I answered casually with a smile, while on some level, not believing that I was doing it either!

As we drove along, I told him what had just happened to me with Dave, and he looked very upset about it. "Snakes in the grass!" he answered with a sigh, as he shook his head. "Well thank goodness for good people like you!" I replied, trying to make him feel better. He smiled, and we sat back in our seats and spent some time in comfortable silence just admiring the views.

As we drove along, every now and then we would start chatting away like old friends. He was the type of person who felt safe, and comfortable to be around. A genuine good guy. He was kind enough to treat me to a nice meal and a hot drink at the first roadside café we came to, and told me that he would drive me all the way to Toronto to make sure that I was safe! I told him that I was so grateful for his help and that people like him made up a thousand-fold for the bad people in the world. He smiled and wistfully nodded his head. I made a mental note of this to my "Independent human behaviour researcher" findings, and my heart warmed at the thought.

We arrived in Toronto, and Al dropped me off on a street called Young Street. It was right in the centre of Toronto, and I felt a rush of excitement to be there. Al took five dollars out of his wallet and wrote his number on a piece of paper. "Take Care Della, call me if you ever need any help" He exclaimed, as he squashed the money and the piece of paper into my hand. "Thanks, Al, I'll be ok!" I answered confidently, as my London street-life days flashed to mind.

"OK, Watch out for the snakes!" Al shouted as I jumped out of the pick-up truck, and slammed the door behind me. "I will! Thanks, bye Al!" I exclaimed, as he drove off and we waved goodbye to each other.

The Toronto streets were full of life, and I loved the atmosphere. The architecture was a mixture of traditional, modern, and eclectic, with people of all ages, and races milling about. It seemed a very upbeat cosmopolitan city and I instantly knew I was going to like it there.

I decided to walk around and explore, and at some point, I arrived at an area called Kensington Market. This was a lively place with colourful market stalls, cafes and bars, cool alternative creative types of people strolled around or sat outside café-bars and restaurants. I spotted a café-bar called Tropical Paradise and headed inside.

The Café-bar had a very friendly atmosphere. I ordered a half of lager and was surprised to be asked for my ID! "What do you need to see my ID for" I asked, feeling puzzled. "Oh don't worry about that, come and join us!" Called out a flamboyant-looking guy who was picking up a pitcher of beer off the bar nearby. "Ok, thanks!" I replied with a smile, and gave a cheeky little wave to the bartender, as I followed the flamboyant guy. The bartender didn't seem bothered and carried on serving others.

The flamboyant guy led me towards a table with a few other interesting people sitting around it. "My name's Brian what's yours?" said the flamboyant guy as we neared the table. "Hi Brian, my name's Della!" I answered with a smile. "I love your accent!" answered Brian, excitedly. "Everybody this is Della, Della - Everybody!" announced Brian as we both sat down next to each other at the large table. They all looked up smiled, and said hi. I said hi back, as Brian handed me a plastic glass of beer. "Thanks!" I said feeling grateful for his hospitality.

"You're welcome! So, where are you from?" asked Brian eagerly. "Oswestry, Shropshire, in the North West Midlands of England, on the border of Wales, between Liverpool and Birmingham" I answered swiftly, before taking a sip of beer. "Ooooh, lovely! I'm from the deep south in the US of A, but I spend most of my time in Canada because I love the lifestyle here!" Answered Brian with a big grin. "Oh, and this is Lyn and Paul, Lyn is from England too!" said Brian, nodding his head towards a couple who were sitting at the table. They looked over and smiled, so I smiled back.

"Lyn's pregnant, and they want to get married, but they can't until Lyn's divorce goes through in England!" added Brian looking over towards the couple in a sympathetic way. "Gosh, that sounds complicated!" I said, feeling how frustrating that must be for them. The couple nodded and sighed as if they were finding it very difficult.

Soon we were all chatting away like old friends, and I felt so happy to have stumbled upon such a warm, friendly, fun place, where I felt completely in my element! A few other people joined us, and seemed relaxed and unfazed by me; "The newcomer in their midst" which I liked, as it made me feel at ease, and not at all self-conscious about being there with them.

At some point, a young, good-looking, dark-haired guy entered the bar, and I felt an instant attraction to him. He was holding a hockey stick, which I found

BOOK 1: TO SEE THE WORLD

amazing! I'd heard that Ice Hockey was a popular game in Canada, but it had felt like some kind of myth to me for some reason, so to see an actual real live Ice Hockey player so soon upon my arrival in the country, gave me a slight thrill!

The guy handed the Hockey-Stick over the bar for safekeeping and bought a pitcher of beer. As he turned to look for somewhere to sit, Brian waved him over to join us, which I was really pleased about. He sat down next to me, which I was even more pleased about, we smiled at each other, and when our eyes met, I felt butterflies, and I wondered if he did too.

"This is Jeff, he's one of Toronto's finest young hockey players, and this is Della, she's here to change the world, starting with Canada!" Announced Brian, with a big smile. "Gotta start somewhere right?" I joked back, grinning. Jeff laughed nodded his head in agreement and said "Hi!" with a lovely smile. "Hi!" I answered, smiling back, while feeling some chemistry between us. 'Today is getting better by the second!' I thought to myself, as I sat next to Jeff sipping on my beer, and enjoying the company.

The next couple of hours we all got very tipsy, and merry and had a great time. The feeling of being with old friends stayed with me throughout, and in some way, I felt as though I had reached my final destination, which was very odd, because I knew that in reality, my world travels had barely begun!

"My dad's name is Geoff, spelt G.E.O.F.F, how do you spell your name?" I asked Jeff as we sat drinking our beers. "J.E.F.F" he answered, with a cute smile. "That's nice, you spell it exactly as it sounds! I don't know why they pop and O in there in England?" I answered, and we both laughed. "So how old are you?" he asked, sounding as if he was genuinely interested in me. "I'm seventeen, how old are you?" I asked, loving how good it felt to be sitting next to each other. "I'm nineteen. Wow, you're young!" He exclaimed, looking surprised. "Yeah, just like the night!" I joked back, and he laughed.

The more we chatted, the more attracted to him I felt, and the attraction seemed mutual. He was very friendly and fun and we enjoyed chatting with each other about all sorts of random things. We just got along with such ease, which I loved. At some point he said he had to leave, adding that he lived nearby, so he was a regular at The Tropical Paradise, and that he was sure that we would see each other again. I felt a little sad that he was leaving, but I was happy that we'd met. We said our goodbyes, and as he left, I hoped to see him again soon. As the night went on, more and more people joined the café-bar and everybody seemed to be very friendly with each other, which created a comfortable, easy-going, relaxed atmosphere.

Towards the end of the night, a woman entered the bar looking very drunk. Lyn and Paul both pulled a face, and Lyn mumbled to me "Don't bother with her, she's an alkie, and she's bad news!" The woman ordered at the bar, then went to sit alone at a table with a picture of beer while looking like a sad, lost soul. I felt sorry for her, and felt that ignoring her surely wouldn't make things any better, only worse!

Just then Brian came out of the toilets and spotted the woman, and Brian Being Brian, immediately shouted out "Karina! Why don't you come and join us!" I grinned to myself and found this very heartwarming, and I liked Brian for it. Karina looked up, waved, stood up, and headed over to join us. We all shuffled our chairs over and made room for her to sit with us. Lyn and Paul barely said hello to her, but Brian gave her a big smile and was happy that she had joined us. A guy who had been sitting with us chatting to Paul quickly turned his attention towards Karina, and they were soon chatting away as they drank their beers.

"I love your style of dress!" Exclaimed Brian, suddenly looking me up and down. "You wear bright colours so well!" He especially seemed to like the red bandanna I had tied around my thigh at the top of my light purple jeans, which I had originally worn to match my red jumper, but I'd got used to tying it around my jeans whatever I was wearing, just for the fun of it!

I happened to be wearing my red jumper again, so I figured I must be looking somewhat colour-coordinated! "Thanks' Brian! I like your style of dress also!" I answered, admiring his interesting mix of indigo jeans and what looked like a tweed blazer, and a blue tee-shirt underneath, but what really gave him his flamboyant air, was his thin handlebar moustache! I loved people who dared to be different, and he was just the right amount of eccentric to be very likeable, and great fun!

"I do love your English accent too! Will you teach me how to speak proper English?" He asked eagerly. I found his request hilarious, as I didn't consider myself to speak "Proper English" So I reiterated that I was from the Northwest Midlands, and didn't speak the "Queens English" but more of a kind of North Midlands mix! He didn't seem to care and insisted I teach him some words. "TOM MAR TOES! TOM MAR TOES!" he kept repeating. "OK TOM MAR TOES!" I answered in an exaggerated posh English accent, and we both laughed.

"Let me try it your way too! TA MAY DOES!" I exclaimed, and we both cracked up laughing.

"OK, OK, HERE'S ONE! HOW DO YOU SAY CAN'T!" He exclaimed excitedly. "CARNT!" I answered, in my exaggerated posh English accent. "OH I LOVE IT! CARNT!" answered Brian proudly. "NOW ME, CAN'T!" I exclaimed, trying to say it his way, causing us both to crack up laughing again. "BUDDA!" "BUTTAH!" "WARDER!" "WARTAH!" and so on we went, until we were both crying with laughter. as we each tried to learn the other's way of saying things.

Karina seemed to find our antics funny, and as the guy she'd been chatting with left, she started to join in our silly conversation, adding some of what she called "Valley Girl Speak" Which sounded like a drunk American speaking, or maybe it was just because Karina was drunk? Either way, we all found it hilarious, and laughed until we cried trying to copy her saying ridiculous things such as "Gag me with a spoon!" "What-Ever!" and "Totally Bitchin!"

After our Valley Girl Speak lessons, we got chatting some more, and Karina told us that her boyfriend was down in "La-La Land" and that's probably what he was hearing a lot of! "Where's that?" I asked curiously. "Oh, it's a nickname for LA, you know - Los Angeles!" she answered, looking fed up. "Oh, I see!" I answered, suddenly seeing the connection. "I prefer to call it La-La Land because everyone's away with the fairies down there!! She exclaimed. I laughed at the idea of a whole city of people living in some kind of fairyland commune and asked her why she wasn't with her boyfriend down there. "Too much red tape!" She answered as she took a big swig of beer, which gave me the feeling that was probably the reason why she was depressed and drinking a lot. "I'm gonna go use the little girl's room!" announced Karina, suddenly standing up and heading towards the bathroom, while Brian jumped up and went to order more beer at the bar.

While they were both away, I got chatting with Lyn and Paul again. It seemed that they were having problems with red tape too. Lyn explained that she would have to go back to England to finalise the divorce before she could marry Paul, but the problem was, that once she left Canada, she might not be allowed back in! This seemed like such a sad and difficult predicament to be in. Brian arrived back at the table with a pitcher of beer, and must have overheard our chat, as he chimed in "It's the same for me, you know! I have to pop back and forth over the border at least once every six months! - Your best bet would be to get married if you want to stay here!" He exclaimed to me, before taking a swig of his beer.

"…There's just too much red tape everywhere! Red tape! Red tape! Red tape!" he exclaimed, almost in an operatic-like song, and I wasn't sure if I wanted to laugh or cry!

We soon all got chatting about world politics and we all agreed that people should have the freedom to be wherever they wanted to be on their home planet, as long as they're not breaking any laws! "We are all part of the human family, and this world is our home! - It's like a big house, with a beautiful garden! Cheers everyone!!" I exclaimed, feeling tipsy, as everybody raised a glass and said "Cheers!" "…I believe there's just one race, and it's the human race! Here's to us!!!" I added before taking a big swig of beer, and they all laughed and nodded in agreement.

We partied on till late, all of us behaving as if we didn't have a care in the world, while at the same time trying to solve all of the problems of the world! "You can come and crash at mine if you want somewhere to crash!" Said Karina, as she stood up to leave. "Oh, thanks!" I answered, sipping the rest of my beer, and glancing over at Brian to see if he approved. "Brian, you can crash too if you want?" she added. "I'd love to!" exclaimed Brian with a big smile.

The three of us said our goodbyes to everyone that was left at the table, and in the surrounding area and headed off out of the front door, turned right, and set off up the street. Each of us very tipsy, with our arms linked like three old friends, laughing, joking, and singing songs as we went. I truly did feel I was home. Karina only lived a couple of minutes' walk away, and she was soon leading us across the street, and up some steps to what looked like an oldish building made up of flats.

She opened the door to her flat, and as we all piled in, she pointed to a door and explained that the basement was empty and that I could crash down there as there was a bed, and Brian could sleep on the sofa in the living room. Brian and I both thanked her, and I headed straight towards the door she'd pointed at, wished them both goodnight, and said that I would see them in the morning. "Goodnight/Sweet dreams!" they shouted back as their voices disappeared into the distance. I headed down to the basement in my tipsy state. I quickly found the light switch, flicked on the light, and immediately spotted the comfy-looking bed. I was so happy to have a bed for the night again! I put my rucksack down, and without using the bathroom to wash up, I lay down on the bed, and I fell asleep instantly.

I woke up at some point the next morning and propped myself up on my elbows to look around me. There was a small window at street level that let the light in, and I spotted a sink to the side of it, and a wardrobe in the corner. This must be a communal spare room that the residents have for their guests I reasoned, as I lay back and yawned and stretched out, with visions of our tipsy shenanigans from the night before popping into my mind.

I laughed at the memory of Karina, Brian and me all arm in arm having a tipsy singalong on the way up the street to Karina's. I was pretty sure I asked Brian to lead the country song "Oh Susanah" because he said he was from the US South, and I had a hazy memory of trying to teach Karina, and Brian the old English singalong song "My ole Man's a dustman!" but we were laughing most of the way through it, because of our ridiculous cockney accents.

I suddenly remembered Jeff and felt the butterflies again, which made me smile even more. The basement felt peaceful, and I was feeling so happy to have my own little space and to have made some lovely new friends. I wasn't sure how long it would be for, but I would enjoy it while it lasts!

I sat up and saw my rucksack at the end of the bed on the floor. Thank goodness I had remembered to bring it with me from the café-bar, I thought to myself. I got out of bed and stood up and headed over to the sink to wash my face and wake up.

I could smell coffee, so I headed upstairs to see what was going on. Karina was in her kitchen drinking coffee and smoking a cigarette "Good morning!" I said with a smile, as I entered the room. "Good morning!" she answered, with a smile, and we both laughed as if finding the situation of us suddenly being housemates "of sorts" a little funny - especially now that we were all sobered up.

"Where's Brian?" I asked looking around me, and realising there was no sign of him. "He left about 20 minutes ago! Wanna coffee?" said Karina, getting up to pour herself another cup of coffee. "Yes please" I answered, as I sat down at the table across from where she'd been sitting. "Sure, and help yourself to cereal or toast!" she said as she lit up a cigarette, and placed a cup of black coffee down on the table in front of me. I thanked her and said the coffee was enough for now. She sat back down at the table with her coffee and cigarette, and we got chatting about the night before, and what fun it had been.

We chatted away, and we seemed to really connect on lots of levels, and after an hour or two I felt that a bond was being made between us. She was very intelligent, funny, and interesting to talk to. "Wanna see my artwork?" She said suddenly. "Sure!" I answered, pleasantly surprised to find out that she was an artist. She stood up and led me to the adjoining room. Against the wall sat a bunch of artworks. I stood near as she flipped through them telling me what each piece was about.

"These are amazing!" I exclaimed as she flicked through paintings of flowers, nature, vases, and people all in vibrant colours, scaled to perfection. She told me she saw them worldwide, but sales would fluctuate, and sometimes she would have no sales, and no money and other times she would have lots of sales and lots of money!

We both found this funny and laughed at what seemed for ages at how fickle the world could be! "So, what are you going to do Della!" She asked me after we stopped laughing and headed back to the kitchen table. "…Are you going to stay in Toronto?" She added as she topped up our coffees.

"I'm not really sure what I'm going to do?" I answered as I sat down, and took a sip from my second cup of coffee. I explained to her that I wanted to travel the world, starting with the Americas, but I really liked Toronto, and her, and the other friends I'd made, and about how I'd felt instantly at home there. I explained my earlier thoughts of feeling as if I had arrived at my final destination, which was really strange because, at the same time, I had the awareness that my world travels were barely just beginning!

"Wow! How are you going to travel the world?" Karina asked sounding amazed. "I don't know. I guess; town to town!" I said while grinning at my little inside joke. "Well, you got guts girl, that's for sure!" she said as she put her cigarette out. "I guess!" I said, as I smiled and shrugged my shoulders. Karina laughed and headed to the sink to wash out her cup.

"I'm going to take a shower and get dressed. Help yourself to more coffee, and food if you want it, and I'll see you in a bit!" She announced, before disappearing off towards the living room. "OK, thanks, Karina!" I called after her.

Feeling a little bit hungry I put some bread in the toaster and made some toast with peanut butter, and poured myself another cup of coffee. I sat there collecting my thoughts and wondering what to do. I really did like Toronto and the friends I'd made, but I really wanted to keep travelling too.

Just as I was pondering on my predicament, Karina arrived back in the kitchen looking all spruced up. "Wanna go look for some work?" she asked looking optimistically at me. "Work?" I answered as if this was a strange concept. "Yeah, to get us some beer money!" She joked.

"Well, yeah, but because I'm backpacking from overseas, I think I can only do volunteer stuff" I answered while trying to remember the information I'd read up on in my local library about volunteering abroad. "That's fine! We can volunteer to help out, and they can volunteer to thank us with diamonds and pearls!" Karina answered with a big laugh. "Yeah, and some chocolate!" I joked back. "There are tons of Italian restaurants around here, and they often need help, they'd be happy for us to lend a hand. They don't pay a lot, but you usually get fed, a bit of cash in hand, and sometimes even a bottle of wine too!" she said casually, with a grin. "I guess that would be good!" I said realising that I probably only had about $10 left on me. "...Yeah okay, I'm game" I answered, with a smile. "Right if you wanna use my shower, I've got some clothes you can borrow?" "That would be great!" I answered, feeling excited about the new day.

I thought about how I had some clothes, in my rucksack, but they were mainly practical travel clothes, not smart clothes to go job hunting, so I was pleased with her offer. "Sure," said Karina, then headed off to the bedroom to grab some clothes for me to look through. A few minutes later she was back with a big pile of clothes "Help yourself!" she said as she placed them on the kitchen table. I dug through the pile and found a dress that I thought would go nicely with my gold shoes

"Would it be okay to borrow this one?" I asked as I held it up against me "Of course! it looks good on you!" she said, with a smile. "Thanks, Karina!" I said as I stood up to go and take a shower. "Do you need a towel?" "Oh, yes please" I replied, remembering how I still didn't have a towel on me. "Sure!" she answered, as she took off to the other room.

"There you go!" She said as she handed me a large purple towel. "Thanks!" I answered, as I took the towel off her, then headed towards the bathroom with my clothes, and make-up, and quickly took a shower. It felt so good to get cleaned up again, especially after my last couple of days of being on the move. After the shower, I quickly got dressed, did my hair and make-up, and started to look and feel a little more like myself again.

When I came out of the bathroom, I spotted Karina coming out of her bedroom looking like she was dressed to the nines. She'd got changed again, and put on some more makeup. "Hey Karina, you look fab!" I exclaimed, with a big smile. "Wow, so do you!" She answered, smiling back.

"Look at us! Don't we look good!" she exclaimed, as we both checked the long mirror in the hallway. "We sure do!" I answered with a laugh. I was really pleased that the dress I had chosen fit me just right, and it matched my gold-coloured shoes! Karina was a similar size to me, and I guessed she was maybe only two or three years older than me, and the fact that we had similar taste in clothes, was really handy! "Let's go!" said Karina, as she grabbed her handbag "Okay, hold on!" I answered as I put my bits and bobs back into my shoulder-bag, and quickly followed Karina towards the front door.

With a spring in our heels, we trotted off down her front steps, and into the street. "Okay, let's go this way!" said Karina leading us in the opposite direction to the tropical paradise café-bar. We headed to the corner of the street and turned left. As we walked along, I noticed lots of Italian restaurants lined the pavements on both sides of the street, and I remembered Karina telling me there were loads of them around the neighbourhood. 'She wasn't wrong!' I joked to myself.

"This one! Let's go in!" Exclaimed Karina, pointing towards one of the restaurants, as she led the way inside. I followed her, curious to see what would happen next. "Need any help here?" asked Karina confidently, as I stood back smiling meekly, as I didn't want him to think we were troublemakers. "What do you do?" asked the guy who I presumed to be the owner or manager, as he paused from laying the tables. "Well, we can wait tables, meet and greet..." Said Karina, looking over at me "Yeah, and we can wash dishes, and clean" I added enthusiastically. "...Help out in the kitchen, whenever you need us to do!" Added Karina, as we both stood there looking raring to go.

"Do you have any Restaurant Experience?" he asked, sounding interested. I told him that I had been a kitchen assistant in England, and I'd helped out at a couple of hotels there also. Karina told him that she too had experience at restaurants and bars. he seemed pleased with this and told us to come and take a seat with him at a table.

As we all sat down, he told us his name was Tony, and that he was the co-owner, as he reached out to shake our hands. We introduced ourselves, and within ten minutes we were hired. We would start the next day and help out for the evening shift. We thanked Tony and left with even more of a spring in our step than we'd started with.

"Let's go celebrate!" Exclaimed Karina, as we found ourselves automatically heading towards the tropical paradise café-bar. We arrived quite early, although Lyn and Paul already had a table at the back. They glanced over at us as we entered. I waved at them as Karina headed to the bar to buy a picture of beer, and they waved back, as I quickly followed behind her, to chip in, and carry the glasses, which were not actually glasses, they were clear plastic beakers, and I assumed it was a safer option for a bunch of tipsy. and drunk people!

We sat down near the window, both pleased with ourselves for getting our new jobs! As we sat grinning from ear to ear, and sipping on our beers, I asked her what she was going to do about her boyfriend in LA. "Will you join him eventually?" I asked, thinking that it seemed the logical thing to do. "It's too difficult, in order for me to join him he would probably have to marry a Yank, get things sorted for himself first, and eventually I'd be able to marry him, but it could take years! - makes you sick!" she exclaimed, before swigging down her beer and looking fed up with the situation. I felt fed up, and exasperated for her, and let out a sigh, as I took a swig of my beer too.

"It's such a shame! Why do people create these problems of being restrained to certain parts of the planet, and limited to other parts? I can understand if people are criminals. They need to be restrained! but for decent human beings to have such red tape hassles seems ridiculous!" I exclaimed, thinking about Lyn and Paul, and Brian too, and possibly myself in some potential future scenarios.

I imagined red tape all around the world, entangling everyone, and just couldn't make sense of any of it. "Yeah, make's ya sick!" repeated Karina, as she gently thumped the table. "Oh well, at least we'll have some more beer money coming in soon!" I said with a grin, and we both cracked up laughing.

"I have to pop to the loo!" I said as I jumped up and headed over towards the washroom. "You look great! Who is that girl you're with?" asked Lyn while nodding towards Karina, as I passed by her and Paul's table. "Thanks! Oh, that's Karina, we both went to find a restaurant that needed help today, and we found one!" I said still feeling pleased with ourselves. "Karina? That's not Karina!" She exclaimed in disbelief. "Yeah, it is!" I answered with a grin. Lyn and Paul looked puzzled as if they couldn't believe that this well-dressed, beautiful woman was the same woman as the usually drunk and messed-up Karina. I continued on to the washroom, not knowing what to make of their reaction.

I used the loo and washed my hands. I noticed that there was a long mirror in the bathroom, so I paused to check myself. I was so pleased at how much the dress suited me. It was coloured dark brown and gold and hung just below the knee. I loved how it matched my gold shoes perfectly! My hair was looking okay, now that it was growing out again, and I was happy to see my waves returning. I finger

121

combed my hair, and touched up my make-up and all in all, I felt pleased with how I looked. I wondered if Jeff would drop by. 'Maybe he would be pleased too!' I thought to myself with a smile.

I came out of the bathroom and started to head back towards Karina. "Sit with us!" Exclaimed Lyn, as soon as I got near their table. "OK, thanks!" I answered as I waved over at Karina to join us. I got the impression that Lyn and Paul seemed curious to see if Karina really was Karina. Karina poured what was left of the beer into our glasses, picked them up, and headed over towards us. "Hi!" she exclaimed, as she sat down, and passed me my beer. "Thanks, Karina!" I said as I took a sip of beer. "You're both looking great!" exclaimed Paul, as Lyn nodded approvingly. "Cheers/Thanks!" Karina and I answered as we clinked our plastic glasses together.

"So, which restaurant will you be helping out at?" asked Lyn curiously. "Karina told her the name of the place, while I glanced around the room to see if Jeff and Brian were around yet, as I looked forward to hopefully seeing them both. We told Paul and Lyn all about our day until the conversation progressed to other things, and once again I felt as if I was where I was meant to be. During a beer-sipping pause in the conversation, I mentioned that Karina was a great artist, and Lyn and Paul looked surprised and asked her about her art. Karina went on to tell them about it, which led to an interesting chat about world art and literature, of which Karina was very knowledgeable. Lyn and Paul looked absolutely dumbfounded, as if they couldn't believe that this high-brow intellectual artist, was really Karina, the person who they seemed to think of as "The Drunk!"

After finishing her glass of beer, Karina excused herself to go and use the washroom, and Lyn and Paul looked at me in utter amazement. "You must be a good influence on her!" Exclaimed Paul, as Lyn looked wide-eyed, and nodded in agreement. "No, it's just the way she is! You've only seen one side of her before is all!" I exclaimed, and laughed it off, as Karina came back from the washroom, and sat back down next to me looking happy.

Soon we were all chatting, laughing and joking about all sorts once again. "Brian!" shouted Karina suddenly, and I looked up to see Brian coming in all dressed up to the nines, with a bright yellow bandanna tied around his thigh! This made me chuckle. "Oh, you've got one too!" I joked. He laughed and said "Of course, it's the latest trend you know!" as he came and joined us at the table, and the pitchers of beer continued to flow along with our merriment!

BOOK 1: TO SEE THE WORLD

At some point, Jeff arrived, along with the butterflies in my stomach, and as soon as he bought a pitcher of beer, he came and joined us at our table, sitting right next to me, which I was very happy with. "You look nice!" He said with a lovely smile. "Thanks, cheers!" I answered, holding up my glass to click his. He held up his glass and clinked my glass back, but being plastic, it was more of a tap than a clink! I felt so happy that not only had he turned up, but he was sitting right next to me again, and we were once again getting along so well.

The next couple of hours were filled with more laughter and merriment. As we finished the last of our beer Jeff suggested that we go to a bootleg club. I asked what that was, and he explained it was like a speakeasy. I asked what a speakeasy was and we both laughed. "Come on, let's just go, you'll like it!" He exclaimed, as I found myself automatically standing up and getting ready to leave with him.

We asked if the others would like to come along, but they all seemed happy enough to stay at the tropical paradise, so we said our goodbyes and started heading towards the exit. "Buzz me up, if you need a place to crash!" Shouted Karina, as we left. "OK, thanks, Karina!" I shouted back, as I followed Jeff out of the door, and to the left, and on down the street. As we walked, he explained to me what bootleg, and speakeasy clubs were, and I said they sounded like great fun!

As we walked along my butterflies intensified, but I didn't let on, I decided it was best to play it cool for now, especially with my travel plans, but I was just happy to have made a new friend "Why complicate things with romance!" I thought to myself, as we hopped on a bus on Young Street. We sat close to each other on the bus, and I liked how natural we felt together. I took this as a good sign. We were both quiet for most of the journey as if simply just enjoying sitting next to each other, which was another thing I liked about him. He felt good to be around, whether we were talking or not, and he seemed to feel the same about me.

"This is it!" Said Jeff, as he suddenly stood up and pressed the bell to stop the bus. I followed him, and we both thanked the driver and jumped off the bus. We seemed to be on a quieter part of a long city street, and I wondered where this club was.

"This way!" said Jeff, as he led the way down the street. I followed along feeling just as excited to be on a date "of sorts" with Jeff, as I was excited to be going to a speakeasy club! Jeff suddenly headed over towards what looked like a closed clothing store and knocked on the front door. "Why are you knocking?" I asked puzzled. "The club's at the back!" he whispered. "Oh, I see!" I answered, feeling intrigued as I hadn't really expected it to be so quiet.

After a few seconds, the door slowly opened, and a bouncer-guy opened it and looked us both up and down. Jeff said a few words, and they seemed to work and next, we were swiftly led inside. We had to walk in the dark through the clothing store. I could hear muffled music but it wasn't very loud, so I assumed it must be like a small private party.

The bouncer led the way until we got to a door at the very back of the store. "Enjoy your night!" He exclaimed as he opened it. "Thanks!" we both answered, as we headed into the club.

The music suddenly became very loud as we entered, and I looked around me to see a huge warehouse full of people having fun, dancing, and drinking. There was a bar on the left and great music playing. "Wow!" I exclaimed, not quite believing my eyes. "I'll get us a drink, you hang tight!" said Jeff, as he gave me a little side shoulder hug, and headed towards the bar. I sat down, leaned against the wall, and looked around me.

I felt so excited to be at this secret club! I was also looking forward to spending some time with Jeff, and having a dance! Jeff soon came back with our drinks and sat down next to me. Once again, I was aware of how comfortable I felt with him sitting close to me, and I liked it. "Do you know the band "Men at Work"?" asked Jeff as he handed me a drink. "Thanks! ...Oh, I think so, they're from Australia right? What's that song they do?". I answered as I took a sip of what seemed to be some kind of delicious fancy cocktail, and Jeff looked like he was trying to remember the name of the song too.

"A land down under!" I exclaimed, suddenly remembering the song. "Yeah, that's it! They're over there at the bar!" Said Jeff, nodding over towards the bar. "Oh great, maybe they'll sing us a song!" I joked as I looked over towards the bar, to try and see who Jeff was gesturing at. Jeff laughed, and as we sipped on our drinks, he asked me about my life in England. "So, do you have a boyfriend?" He asked curiously. "Well, I did have, kind of, but I left to go travelling," I answered, remembering how Matt and I had been seeing each other for a few months before I left my hometown. "Not in love then?" Jeff asked, looking puzzled, as if he was trying to make sense of why I would leave a guy I was in love with. "Well maybe a bit, but it was very early days, and I still wanted to travel" I answered, with a shoulder shrug.

"How about you? do you have a girlfriend?" I asked, curious to find out. "Not anymore! We broke up a few months ago. Her family moved to Vancouver" He answered, looking sad for a moment. "So, do you think you may move to Vancouver as well?" I asked trying to help him with what seemed an easy solution. "No, it's over! I think she's found somebody new" he said sounding sad again, "but I'm glad I got to meet you!" he quickly added, looking happy again. "Yeah, it's nice to meet you too!" I answered, feeling a little uncomfortable, but at the same time curious as to where this conversation was leading.

Jeff snuggled up a little closer and put his arm around me. I nervously took a sip of my beer, not sure how I felt about him getting so close. As I turned to look his way, he leaned over and gave me a little kiss. The butterflies were happy, but I felt a little surprised. "Just thought I'd break the ice!" said Jeff, as he gave my shoulder a little squeeze. I sipped on my beer and smiled, not really sure of what to say, or do next.

"Shall we go and dance?" I said suddenly finding a way out of what felt like a slightly awkward situation. "Sure!" Jeff answered as we both jumped up and, with our arms around each other, went over to the dance floor. The music was loud, and we started a fun dance. By now I was feeling tipsy and happy to be there having fun with Jeff. I got glimpses of the guys from the band Men At Work standing by the bar and noticed that a lot of people were crowding around, and making a fuss of them, but Jeff and I just wanted to dance with each other.

We didn't leave until around 6 am and arrived on Karina's doorstep around 7 am. I buzzed the buzzer hoping she wouldn't be too annoyed at being disturbed. Within a few minutes, a sleepy-looking Karina opened the door. "Hi Karina, is it okay to crash in the basement," I said sheepishly. "Sure, go on in," she said with a yawn. "Thanks, Karina" I answered quietly, as Jeff and I tiptoed down to the basement together.

We lay down on the bed, and in seconds we were both out like lights. I woke up around noon, to see Jeff getting ready to go out. "Hi Jeff' I mumbled sleepily. "Hi Della, I've gotta get to work. I'll see you tonight at tropical paradise" he said quietly, as he gave me a little kiss on my forehead, before he quickly took off. 'I love Toronto!' I thought to myself as I lay there, half awake. 'I feel so at home here! I love my new friends, and I really like Jeff' I thought to myself, feeling so content and happy, but then I suddenly remembered that I wanted to travel and see the world, and once again I felt torn. I sighed, yawned, and stretched, before getting up, washing my face, and heading upstairs.

In the kitchen, I found a note that Karina had left telling me to help myself to food and coffee and that she'd see me at the TP later. We didn't have to help out at the Italian Restaurant for a couple of days so I decided to have a free day to explore the city. I helped myself to a coffee with some toast and peanut butter, took a shower, changed my clothes, and headed out into the new day.

I decided that I would just stroll around, with no particular place in mind to head for. I would just explore, and see what I find. As I walked along I was once again aware of how much I loved the atmosphere in Toronto. It was very vibrant, and uplifting, with a positive energy to it. I looked around at the cafés, shops, and bars, and everyone seemed so upbeat and in good spirits. The people seemed to have the perfect balance of work and play.

I suddenly spotted an interesting-looking tower nearby. I had seen it in the distance before, but never so close up. I decided to go and see if it was possible to take a lift to the top, as I imagined the view would be fantastic. As I got nearer, I noticed a sign that read; CN TOWER, and I was excited to find out if a lift to the top was allowed. As I entered the building, I noticed a queue of tourists waiting to buy tickets to the top, so I joined the queue and soon had my ticket. I got inside the lift with some of the tourists, and we rode up to the top. We were all smiling and chatting about how high it looked, and how great the views must be. Soon the lift stopped and we all walked outside to look around.

The first thing I noticed was the strong wind blowing, but the breathtaking views soon took my mind off the wind. 'Wow! This is fantastic!' I thought to myself, as I walked around the tower looking out to see as far as the eye could see. I noticed a lake with boats sailing gracefully around it, which surprised me as I hadn't realised that I was near a lake. 'Toronto is full of surprises!' I thought as I stared out watching the boats sail around on the lake, with a contented smile on my face.

The tourists were mainly from Asia, and they strolled around the tower, chatting, and sometimes stopping to admire the view, but I was lost in a world of my own, and savouring the moments. I found a little gift shop and bought some CN Tower postcards to send to my parents. One of the postcards was a double postcard, which folded over to create an envelope, with a little card inside to certify that someone had been to the top of the CN Tower. I bought one to send to my dad, feeling that he would love to know that I'd visited the top of the CN tower, and even had a little certificate to prove it!

BOOK 1: TO SEE THE WORLD

I suddenly felt hungry and looked around to see where I could get something to eat. There was a restaurant inside, so I decided to go and get a snack. I sat by the window and continued to admire the view. Much to my surprise I discovered that the restaurant was rotating, as I noticed the view was ever so slowly changing around me. 'Wow! This is fab!' I thought to myself as I gazed out of the window, feeling so happy to be there.

"What can I get you!" Said a twenty-something, brown-haired waitress, who seemed to arrive at my table from the ether! "Um, I'd like a coffee and toast with butter and jam please" I answered with a smile. "Sorry, this area is for diners only" answered the waitress somewhat coldly, which puzzled me, because as far as I was concerned, toast was food! Especially with butter and jam! "Oh, so where do I go if I want toast with jam, and a coffee then please?" I asked, feeling like I had done something terribly wrong, and was now in trouble for it. "Well, if you take a seat on the inside, we can serve you there" she answered, as I stood up and she ushered me towards some inside seats away from the window. "Okay, thank you!" I answered, as I stood up, walked across to an inner table, and sat down. All the while, feeling self-conscious and confused, as to why I'd been asked to move. It wasn't as if the place was full, or they had needed my table for some Arabian Prince or something!

I got comfortable at my new table, and read the menu just to see if toast was actually listed, as her reaction to my order had been one of confusion and mild disdain. I suddenly noticed that "Continental Breakfast" was indeed listed, and felt instantly justified, as it literally was; tea or coffee with toast, butter and preserves, aka: Jam!

She came back to take my order, and although by that point I was starting to feel as though I was some kind of nuisance to her, I reminded myself that I was a customer, and had actually done nothing wrong, aside from apparently sitting in the wrong place unintentionally! "I'd like the continental breakfast, with coffee please!" I exclaimed confidently, ready to stand my ground and fight my corner over pedantises if need be! The penny seemed to drop for her, as she suddenly seemed to realise that my original order wasn't so strange after all! Looking a little embarrassed she scribbled down my order and headed off towards the kitchen area. I let out a sigh, got comfortable in my seat, and wrote out my postcards, feeling all was once again well with my world.

I enjoyed my continental breakfast albeit, away from the view. Afterwards, I paid up and went for a little walk about the tower again. I noticed lots of names were written on the walls of the stairwell. So, I decided to write my name, my brothers names, and my mum and dad's names. 'Why not!' I thought to myself, thinking how the family had split when I was a small child, '…but up here we could be together forever!' I smiled to myself contentedly, as I strolled away and back towards the lift. I had one last look at the view, before stepping inside the lift, riding it back down, and strolling out of the building, and back into the street.

I found a Post Office nearby, and posted my postcards off to my parents, then carried on with my leisurely stroll. 'I may as well head over to the tropical paradise' I thought to myself with a smile. Looking forward to seeing Jeff, and my other new friends. I opened the door of the tropical paradise and looked around. I didn't recognise anyone, so I strolled over to the bar and ordered a pitcher of beer, by now I was treated as a local, and they never asked to see my ID.

I took my pitcher, and a glass, and found a table to sit and collect my thoughts. I poured myself a drink, let out a relaxed sigh, and looked around the room. There were some people who had been shopping at the market nearby looking at their clothing items with the pride of the bargain hunt. They seemed to be from the same family and were all looking very happy with their purchases. Their joy made me smile. I continued to look around the room, as it was interesting to see a whole different crowd in The Tropical Paradise at this time of day. There was an older guy in the corner sipping his drink slowly and looking lost in thought. I glanced across from him to see a couple of young office worker gals, excitedly chatting about guys they'd met recently.

None of my eclectic mix of pals were in yet and I was missing the atmosphere that their free spirited fun and playful ways created. Just then two young guys walked in - They looked more my type, and I instantly sensed them to be on my kind of wavelength. They looked a couple of years older than me and were both dressed in an alternative style. One had dark brown hair, in a curtain hairstyle, with glasses and the other had short brown hair. They both look very arty which I liked, as arty types were usually interesting to chat with, and fun to hang out with. They ordered a pitcher of beer, and came and sat at the table near me.

"Hello!" I said as they glanced my way. "Hi! Where are you from?" asked the guy with the curtain haircut. "England, how about you?" I asked with a smile. "Local, do you mind if we join you?" asked the guy with the curtain haircut, smiling back, while the other one smiled as well and looked on curiously. "Oh course not! I'd be glad of the company!" I answered with a smile. "Hi, I'm Kyle, that's Dave!" Said the curtain-haired guy. "Hi Kyle and Dave, I'm Della!" I answered as I shook hands with them. We were soon chatting away and sipping on our beers, and having a laugh at random things.

"So, what's the music scene like in England?" Asked Kyle with an earnest look on his face, that told me he was a music connoisseur of sorts. "Well, there are all sorts of music scenes going on, it depends on what people are into. There's Punk, New-Wave, New-Romantic, Motown, Heavy-Rock, and even Disco!" I answered, feeling as though I was of no help at all!

"Kind of like here then!" exclaimed Dave with a grin, while Kyle sipped on his beer as if thinking about what I'd said. "Yeah, I suppose so. I've always been into all sorts of music though, so I've never just stuck with one scene - As a little kid I loved Elvis and the Beatles, then I was about fourteen I got into the tail end of the hippy folk-rock stuff like Donovan and Joni Michel, and then I got into heavy rock like Led Zepplin, and Black Sabbath, after that, I got into a bit of punk, Ska and new-wave… I even like a bit of disco to dance to, as long as it's the funky stuff, like James Brown, I'm not so much the cheesy disco stuff though. How about you both?" I said, feeling enthusiastic about talking about one of my passions.

"Well, I'm mainly into obscure, underground music, but I do like some of the UK punk and new-wave bands, and even some of the New York punk scene, can't say I'm into disco though" answered Kyle, with a grin. "Yeah, my tastes are a bit broader like Della's, and I like a bit of a boogie too!" Joked Dave, and we all had a laugh.

We continue to chat about all sorts of topics, from music to art, from art to travel. It turned out that they wanted to go to Europe at some point. They just needed to save up some money first. I suggested that they volunteer work as they go along, and they found this concept hilarious. I laughed along with them; even though I was doing just that!

After a while, they seemed to get restless, and they asked if I wanted to go to the next bar with them. "Sure, I've got nothing else to do!" I answered swigging down the last of my beer. "Fair enough!" they answered, with a laugh, as they led the way, and I followed them out of the front door, I waved goodbye to the bartender as we went, and he smiled, and waved back.

The next bar was just a few doors down to the left, it was called The Spot, which I found to be an interesting name. I followed them inside feeling happy to have made some new pals. It was kind of dark and dingy, but it had good tunes playing, and the bartender was nice and friendly, and I liked the atmosphere.

There were only a couple of other people in there, drinking in the shadows. We each climbed up on a barstool and ordered our drinks. "What's that?" I asked, pointing at some weird-looking stuff in a jar on a shelf behind the bar. "Oh, that's Octopus," said Dave casually. "Oh yuck!" I answered, confused as to why it was chopped up in a jar.

"It's pretty tasty, wanna try it?" said the bartender, as he picked up the jar, unscrewed the lid and passed it my way. "Oh no thanks!" I said, feeling sick at the thought. "Go on try it!" Said Dave with a big grin, "Yeah it's nice!" Said Kyle laughing.

"Really it's tasty!" Said the bartender, as he picked up a fork and took a piece out and ate it. "Okay, I'll try it!" I answered feeling partly repulsed, but partly curious, and thinking 'Why not!' The bartender picked up another fork and another piece of octopus and passed it to me.

I took the fork off him and looked at the piece of octopus. It was so strange looking, like a chunk of fat! "Okay, here goes!" I said, cringing, as I put the piece of octopus in my mouth in one quick go. The taste was awful! Like a cross between pork and salty fish.

I quickly ate it, just to have done it, and the guys clapped their hands and cheered. "That was awful! I'm not eating that again! In fact, I might stop eating animals altogether it all seems so barbaric and crazy!" I exclaimed, as the beer kicked in, and the idea of eating other creatures suddenly seemed so bizarre and unnecessary to me.

"Well done, Della! You deserve another drink!" Exclaimed Dave as he filled up my glass with beer from a pitcher he'd just ordered. The beers flowed, and we had a great time laughing and chatting and enjoying the fab music that was playing – Cool eclectic stuff, even Kyle seemed to be enjoying it, so it must have been good!

After a while, we decided to head back to the tropical paradise to see who was about. As we entered, I was happy to see my gang there, and we all greeted each other with big hoots, hollers, and hugs. My friends seemed to know Dave and Kyle a little bit, so we all sat together and continued our party.

Suddenly Jeff appeared and came and sat next to me with his drink. He gave me a little side hug, and a kiss on the cheek, and looked a little bit unsure about Dave and Kyle sitting next to me on the other side as if he was wondering if I was interested in one of them, but he was still his lovely friendly self, and we all had a good time laughing, joking and being just as silly as ever!

A little later on Karina appeared and joined the party and during a little catch-up chat, she reminded me that we had to help out at the Italian restaurant in a couple of days. I felt happy at the thought, as it meant my pocket money would be topped up, plus Karina and I would have a laugh, as we always did!

Somebody announced that there was a house party nearby and that we were all invited. We all cheered, finished our drinks and jumped up and followed the leader off out of the tropical paradise, I again waved goodbye at the bartender as I left and he waved back at me, with a big grin on his face as if he was happy to see me having fun.

'I really do love it here!' I thought to myself as we all walked along. By now it was dark outside, and as the group of about ten of us walked off down side streets and alleyways somebody lit up a joint and passed it around. I was wary of smoking because I didn't want to get hooked on cigarettes again, but as we were all so tipsy, and having fun, I took a couple of puffs just to join in with the merriment and within seconds I felt completely zonked out, and felt sure that I was walking along lopsided! I didn't like it at all, and I couldn't wait to get to the party and drink some water, and just chill out somewhere until if wore off.

Jeff put his arm around me and we walked as if to keep me safe, which was so sweet of him, and it reminded me of one of the reasons that I liked him. He was so thoughtful and kind, and easy to be around. We walked for what seemed like years until we finally got to the party.

As we entered the house, the party was in full swing with good tunes playing, and people dancing and having fun, but I was feeling way too tipsy and zonked from the joint to enjoy it, all I wanted to do was lie down, and to go to sleep! but we had only just arrived, so I felt I had to just hang in there. Jeff seemed to notice that I wasn't really in the mood for the party and as we were sitting next to each other on an old sofa, he put his arm around me as if to comfort me some more. I appreciated his kindness and rested my head on his shoulder. All I wanted to do was go to sleep! "We can go and stay at my friend's place if you're too tired to party," said Jeff considerately. "OK," I answered, pleased at the thought of being able to catch some sleep. We both got up and headed back outside. I didn't see any of our friends to say goodbye to, but I figured I would see them again sooner or later.

Feeling like a zombie, I leaned on Jeff as we walked with our arms around each other. We cut down some side streets until we reached what Jeff told me were the projects. I wasn't sure what he meant, but it looked like what in England is called a block of council flats. "My friend lives in this one, he won't mind if we crash!" Said Jeff, as he pressed a buzzer on one for one of the flats. His friend soon let us in, and Jeff introduced us, his name was Danny, and he seemed nice at first, but turned out to be a bit of a creep, and was making passes at me every chance he got, which I found to be weird and disrespectful, not only to me, but to Jeff also!

Danny said that we could all crash in his bedroom, as he had a huge bed and a thick carpeted floor. He suggested that I crash on the bed, and he and Jeff would crash on the floor, with pillows and blankets. We all agreed to this, but just as I was starting to doze off, Danny snuck onto the bed and made another pass at me. I gently pushed him away, and climbed down onto the floor, to sleep next to Jeff instead.

The next morning, I woke up, and much to my delight Danny had left and Jeff was in the kitchen making a drink. "Sorry about my friend, sometimes he's like that with girls. I'm glad you chose to sleep next to me rather than next to him" Said Jeff, as he gave me a little hug and a gentle kiss on my forehead. "Well, I didn't really like Danny, because he was bugging me most of the night, but I do like you!" I said to Jeff with a cheeky grin. He smiled and gave me another little kiss.

We both sat side by side on a bench at the dining table in Danny's kitchen with our coffees, slowly sobering up from the night before. "What are you up to today?" asked Jeff, as he held his arm affectionately around my shoulders. "I have a free day, until tomorrow, then Karina and I are helping out at the Italian restaurant, what about you" I answered, as I put my arm around him too. I liked the way we always felt so natural and comfortable together.

"I have to go to work, but I'll see you around four at the TP!" Said Jeff, as he gave me a little squeeze. "Sounds good!" I answered, and sipped on my coffee, as the butterflies fluttered around in my stomach. We finished off our coffees, and we left his friend's apartment. Jeff walked me so far back to downtown and gave me directions on how to get back to the tropical paradise from there.

He gave me a big hug and a kiss before he headed off in one direction, and I headed off in another. As I walked along, I had the feeling that Jeff and I were becoming a couple, and I wasn't sure what to make of it. I decided to try and not think about it, by just walking, and exploring Toronto. After a couple of hours of wandering around, just enjoying the sights and sounds of the city, I decided to head back to the Tropical Paradise for a beer. I got a little lost, but eventually found my way there, and strolled inside and got myself a drink.

There was a different bartender on duty, an older man, who was nice enough, but very quiet and seemed in a world of his own most of the time. I took my pitcher of beer and sat down by the window. None of my friends were there yet, but there was an interesting-looking man sitting at the table next to mine and at some point, we smiled at each other and said hello. He noticed my accent and asked where I was from. I told him I was from England and we got chatting…

His name was Don, and he was very easy to chat with, so the conversation flowed into all sorts of areas, from travel and music, and on to art and philosophy. We both seemed especially interested in Philosophy, and I found myself telling him that one of my earliest memories was of being about three years old, looking out of the window of the living room house where I lived with my parents, and watching the cars, and people go by, and having the sudden realisation that the only moment that existed was "now!"

I told him how I clearly remembered repeating "now" every few seconds as I watched the world go by, as a way to capture each moment in time, and how over the years since then, that thought has often popped into my mind, and how it made me realise that even if we were immortal, all we would have is "Now!" - adding that even when people pass away, the only moment that exists for them as a living being, is the moment they pass because all other moments have ceased to exist anyway! So, what the point of it all if all we have in reality is a split second of existence?!" I quipped.

We both had a good laugh and at some point, he told me that a lot of my thoughts and questions were what some of the great philosophers had thought about and questioned. "Well, I wish I had the answers!" I joked, "So do I!" he answered, and we both laughed some more. He went on to tell me that he was a philosophy professor at a local university and that he was often invited on various radio shows to be interviewed about his work. I really liked him, as we seemed to be on a similar wavelength, and I found our conversation to be very stimulating, and totally my cup of tea! As we chatted away, one by one the gang slowly appeared and joined us at our table, We were soon all having our usual chats, jokes and laughs, which Don seemed to enjoy being a part of.

Eventually, Don said he had to get going and hoped to see us all again soon. We all waved our goodbyes, and after he left, Brian told me that he was a renowned philosophy professor; Donald Dwight Evans, and that he was often on local TV and radio, confirming what Don himself had told me. I felt privileged to have spent some quality time with him!

Much to my surprise Dave and Kyle suddenly appeared and joined us at our table. I was happy to see them again, and they seemed happy to see me again too. We all made room for them at the table, and we picked up where we left off on our chats about music art and travel. Dave suddenly mentioned that he had some records to sell and that if a couple of us could help him in the morning to carry them to the market where he was pretty sure he would be able to sell them. He added that he would share the money with us, and we could use it for a beer! I said that I was game, as I didn't have to help out at the restaurant until the afternoon the next day, so we had a few more drinks.

Jeff suddenly appeared, and sat next to me, giving me a little hug and kiss once his beer was secure on the table. Dave asked Jeff if he was up for helping lug the records to market in the morning. I said that I was going to help, and added that we'd get some beer money out of it. "Sure" answered Jeff with a grin, and we all laughed at the idea of swapping records for beer money.

"Shall we head over to my place now then? We can have a few more drinks there, and you can crash at my place, and in the morning, we can take the records to sell" said Dave, looking like he wanted to get the wheels of his record-selling plan in motion.

"Sounds like a plan!" I exclaimed, "Sure!" Said Jeff, as we smiled at each other, and I felt the butterflies in my stomach take flight once again. We gave each other another little hug and kiss, as we stood up to follow Dave, and Kyle off out of the door. Karina, Brian and the others stayed behind, and we waved and called out goodbye, before setting off down the street to head for Dave's place.

Daves's apartment wasn't too far away, and we were soon all piling inside. His apartment was modest, but stylish and had a relaxing atmosphere. Dave was an excellent host and swiftly gave us each a drink, and put on some good music on.

We all sat around and relaxed, casually chatting, and listening to the tunes. Jeff and I sat next to each other on the floor leaning against a wall. Jeff had his arm around my shoulders, and I rested my arm on his thigh. He seemed more relaxed to see that Kyle, Dave, and I were only friends.

Eventually, we all crashed out. Dave in his bedroom. Kyle on the sofa, and Jeff and I next to each other on the carpet with cushions and a couple of blankets that Dave had given us. I slept like a log, until the next morning when I heard Dave clanking around in the kitchen. I got up to go and use the bathroom. By the time I came out of the bathroom, the smell of fresh coffee brewing was in the air. Jeff was now sitting up, and gave me a sweet smile as he spotted me. I smiled back and went to sit next to him. We gave each other a little hug and kiss, then he jumped up to go and use the bathroom too.

Kyle was still asleep on the sofa. Dave came over from the kitchen area with a couple of cups of coffee for Jeff and me, and as he passed Kyle, he gave him a gentle kick on his foot and asked if he wanted a coffee. "Yes please" groaned Kyle, as he slowly rolled over.

Soon we were all sitting around sipping on our coffees, and looking like we'd all been dragged through a hedge backwards. "Does anyone want some peanut butter and toast?" Asked Dave as he headed back towards the kitchen area. "Yes please!" We all answered in unison. "Shall I help?" I asked, jumping up and heading towards the kitchen. "Ok, thanks, maybe make some more coffee" Answered Dave as he rummaged in the cupboards to get some plates out. "More coffee any...?" I asked, "Yes please!" answered Kyle and Jeff before I'd even finished my sentence.

After breakfast, Dave said he would go and get the records, and went about bringing four large piles of albums into the living room. "One pile each!" I joked while hoping they weren't too heavy! "Yep, we should make at least $40 for the lot, so that's $10 each!" Exclaimed Dave proudly. I was pleased with this and so was Jeff. I jumped up and went to use the bathroom to freshen up and do my hair and make-up, and by the time I arrived back in the living room, the guys were nearly ready to go. Kyle quickly popped to use the bathroom, while I helped Dave wash up the dishes, and tidy up.

"OK, let's go!" exclaimed Dave, as we all grabbed a pile of records each, and headed out the front door in single file, with Dave leading the way I found this kind of comical, and so did Jeff, but we tried not to laugh too much for fear of dropping the records!

Eventually, we made it to Kensington Market, and Dave led the way to the record stall. Dave had a friendly chat with the owner about selling the records, and quickly a deal was made and we were all shoving $10 each into our wallets and purses. Dave had a little extra, which I was pleased about, especially as they were his records. Feeling pleased with our work we all headed over to the tropical paradise in fun spirits to celebrate!

Around 1.30 Karina arrived in the doorway of the Tropical Paradise and scanned the room as if looking for me. As soon as she spotted me she waved and came hurrying over towards me. "We've got to be at the restaurant at two!" she exclaimed, sounding a little anxious to see me casually hanging out with the gang. "Yes, I know!" I answered downing my last drop of beer. "Here have some more!" said Dave as he filled up my glass. "I don't know, I don't want to be tipsy going into the restaurant!" I protested with a laugh. "Well, I'll have it!" exclaimed Karina with a mischievous grin. "Good idea! I've already had a couple, and Kariana's only just arrived, so why not it's only fair!" I exclaimed.

At about 1:45 Karina and I said our goodbyes to the gang, took off out of the door, and ran all the way over to the Italian Restaurant. We just about made it on time, and Tony looked happy to see us. Tony quickly gave us aprons to wear. "Just clear the tables please ladies" he instructed, with a warm smile. "OK, Tony!" We answered, as we smiled back, and went about clearing the tables and taking the plates into the kitchen, where we piled them up for the dishwasher to deal with.

The restaurant was very busy, and each time we thought we'd finish clearing the tables, more tables needed clearing! Karina spotted that someone had left a half bottle of wine and cheekily poured us both a glass. We grinned mischievously at each other, said "Cheers!" and clinked our glasses and both took a sip of wine.

We carried on taking sips of our wine in between clearing tables, and at some point Tony noticed, but much to our delight, he just grinned over at us as he went about taking orders. He was very pleased with our help, and didn't seem to begrudge us having a little fun! 'This is so different to the stuffy English Hilltop Hotel in Swanage!' I thought to myself, feeling so happy to be helping out someone who was so nice, with such a fun friend to boot. My mind flashed to Heidi, and I hoped she was doing ok wherever she was.

The time seemed to fly by and in no time at all. Tony was given us $12 each as thanks for our help. We were both very happy with this. We thanked him and made arrangements to be back at the same time the next day. We took off down the street, and headed back to the tropical paradise to celebrate!

Karina and I arrived at the Tropical Paradise before any of our other friends, which was nice, because it gave us time to catch our breaths, and have a one-on-one chat with each other. Karina told me that I was welcome to stay as long as I wanted or needed in the basement at her place, which gave me a great sense of security. I asked her if it would be ok to give her address to my family and friends in the UK, so that they had a contact address for me, and she assured me that it was ok, which was so good of her. She was a new, but true friend, and I genuinely appreciated her friendship.

Over the next few days, I caught up with my journal writing and sent letters to my parents with the latest updates. I told them that I would probably stay in Toronto for a few more weeks at least because I really liked it there, and I told them about the friends I'd made, hoping that they would be reassured that I was safe, and in good company. I added that it would be ok to send mail to me at Karinas, and I asked my dad if he had sent my savings via postal order to Erick's address in England, and if so, had Erick sent it back to him? I had a sickening feeling, that I would never see that money again, but still held on to little hope.

The next few days were spent clearing the tables at the restaurant in the afternoons and celebrating at tropical paradise in the evenings, with the odd house party here and there. I was loving my Toronto life very much – The city, the people, my friends, and Jeff. I felt sad whenever I thought about moving on with my travels, so I would shove those thoughts to the back of my mind.

One day a letter arrived from my dad, telling me that he was happy to hear that I was having such a good time in Toronto and that my friends sounded like a great crowd. At the end of the letter, he added that he had sent the postal order of my £150 savings to Erick's address, and sadly it had yet to return. He told me that he would do his best to retrieve it, and I knew that he would. I assumed he would write to Erick asking that the mail be returned, he probably wouldn't even mention the postal order inside, in the hope that Erick was unaware of the contents, but I had already mentioned it to Erick, so he would have known about the postal order inside, and if he'd been a genuinely decent guy he would have returned it straight away, but by now a few weeks had passed, so my guess was that he'd kept it, and probably forged my signature.

I felt so angry at Erick and hoped that my dad didn't resort to paying Erick a visit, as the outcome would not be a good one for Erick, and could lead to my dad getting in trouble with the law. Rather than dwell on such negative things, I decided to focus on the good things in my life, and told myself that it was a case of "Win some, lose some!" and that my life in Toronto was priceless, and that I wouldn't change a thing!

I had a free day, so I wrote my dad a letter back, telling him not to worry about it, and that if Erick didn't send the letter back, it was probably because he'd gone back to Portugal already. I fibbed and told him that he had been due to go back to Portugal a couple of weeks prior, in the hope of putting my dad off any ideas he might have of heading down to London, to get my money back. I added that I was so happy in Toronto and that if I hadn't left London when I did, and if I'd stayed waiting for the postal order to arrive, I might not have found Toronto, and my friends there. I knew he would understand that I was essentially saying "Win some, lose some!" and would see the bigger picture, and be happy for me.

I headed to the post office to post the letter and then decided to go for a walk and explore some more of the city. I went to a park area and sat down to watch the world go by. Not long afterwards, a young girl of about sixteen came and sat near me. She had lovely light brown curly hair, and was kind of unusual looking, and reminded me of the cherubs that I'd seen in church paintings.

We smiled and said hello to each other, and she noticed my accent and asked where I was from. I told her I was from England, and asked her where she was from. She told me that she was from another part of Canada, and had run away to Toronto, where she had managed to get a cheap room and odd jobs to get by.

"It's tough at times, but at least I'm free!" She said with a look that said, she'd been through a lot back home. "I know what that's like!" I said with a laugh, feeling like an older sister, while in reality, I was only a year older if that! "My name's Janie, what's yours?" She asked, still smiling. "Della" I answered smiling back. "Nice name, have you been to any clubs and bars yet?" She asked with an enthusiastic smile. "Um yeah, The tropical paradise, The spot bar, and a speakeasy on Young Street" I answered smiling back. "…Oh, and a few parties!" I added, remembering some of the house parties I'd been to. She seemed impressed and asked if I'd been to some other bars and clubs around the city. The names didn't ring any bells. "No, I haven't been to those places" I answered, feeling curious about them. "Wanna go to some?" she asked, with a grin. "Sure! I'm free today, and have no plans" I answered grinning back. "Let's go!" She answered as we both jumped up, and she led the way.

After walking for a little while, we arrived at the downtown area and Janie led the way into a bar. It was a little on the rough side and didn't have the same creative atmosphere as The Tropical Paradise, The Spot, or the Speakeasy, but I was intrigued to find a new place, just the same. Janie seemed to know a few of the locals, and soon we were chatting, laughing, joking, drinking beer, and playing pool with a few of them. After a while Janie seemed to get bored and

138

suggested that we go to some other bars, which led to a tipsy blur of more clubs and bars, and fun shenanigans as we drank beer, chatted, laughed, joked, and danced our way around downtown.

At some point, she met up with a guy she seemed to know, and we all tipsily made our way back to hers. She said I could crash out on the bed as it was very large, and there was plenty of room for all three of us to crash out on it. I was feeling very drunk and exhausted at this point and just wanted to flake out. I soon drifted off to sleep.

When I woke up the next morning the guy was gone, and Janie was down the hallway in the kitchen clanking around. I went in search of the bathroom to wash my face. "Morning Janie!" I called out as I spotted the bathroom nearby. "Morning Della, Coffee?" she shouted back. "Yeah, thanks!" I answered as I headed into the bathroom.

After using the bathroom, I headed back to her bedsit, to sit on her little sofa with her. She'd put two cups of coffee on the little coffee table, and I thanked her, before taking a sip. "Wanna smoke? she asked picking up a pack of cigarettes. "Yeah ok, thanks!" I answered, as I took a cigarette and she lit mine, then hers up. I took a drag and the smoke tasted awful, and I wondered why I'd accepted a cigarette, while suddenly remembering that I'd quit a year ago. I figured it was because I was half asleep and hungover, and maybe because I'd had a couple of puffs on a joint on the way to the party that night. I wasn't really enjoying the taste, so I only took very light puffs, before putting it out, and hoping that I wouldn't get addicted to cigarettes again.

We sat sipping on our coffees, puffing on our cigs, and talking about the night before. "That guy was nice, is he your boyfriend?" I asked, curious to know more. "No, he's just someone I see" she answered casually. "How about you? You seeing anyone?" She asked grinning. "Kind of, but kind of not" I answered, thinking about Jeff. "What's that supposed to mean?" She asked laughing and looking confused. "I don't know?" I answered, and we both burst out laughing. "Do you wanna come over to the tropical paradise with me, and meet some of my friends?" I asked, thinking it would be fun to introduce her to the gang. "Sure!" she answered, and we got ready, and set off down some side streets of what looked like quite a poor part of town.

As we walked, Janie bumped into the guy she'd brought home and got chatting with him about scoring some smoke. "Hey Della, I'm going to go with Jake. I may see you later though!" she said, sounding as if she was suddenly on a mission. "Ok, it's called; The Tropical Paradise is in Kensington Market if you do drop by later!" I shouted, as we waved goodbye to each other, and took off in different directions. I wondered if we would ever meet up again. She was a nice girl, but from a whole different scene to me. Her crowd was a little rough around the edges, whereas my crowd was more on the light-hearted, fun, and creative side, but as long as people were nice, I didn't care what scene they were from!

I carried on walking and spotted a sign that read "Models wanted, good pay!" Feeling curious, but not expecting it to be for me as I wasn't tall enough, I walked inside the building just to see what would happen. "Are you here to try out for the modelling position?" asked a glamourous-looking blonde lady behind a desk. "Um, yes!" I answered, wondering what would happen next. "OK, just fill in this form!" she said handing me a paper and pen. "Thanks!" I answered as I sat down on a nearby chair to fill out the form.

I quickly filled out the form and sat waiting for - I had no idea what? After about five minutes another door opened and some young girls around my age walked out smiling and chatting to each other. A guy came over towards me, and picked took the form I'd just filled out, and looked at me with a welcoming smile. "Okay, follow me!" he instructed.

I stood up and followed him into the other room, half of me feeling curious to see what would happen, the other half of me wanting to run! Inside the room was a panel of about three women and two guys sitting facing a runway. As I stood there smiling and nodding hello at them, they took turns to ask me some questions, my name, my height, my weight, my age... "Have you ever modelled before?" asked the guy who'd led me to the room. "No, not yet!" I answered, and they all laughed.

"Okay, all you have to do is walk up and down the runway!" instructed one of the women. I said ok, as I took the steps up to the runway, then feeling very silly and self-conscious, walked along it. "Okay, now turn!" Instructed one of them. I felt absolutely ridiculous, and couldn't wait to get out of there!

"Okay, that's good, thank you, take a seat!" said the guy who'd greeted me. I sat down feeling like a dummy, and wondering what would happen next, as they chatted among themselves. Eventually one of the women came over towards me.

"You have very good potential! You're very pretty, you have great cheekbones, and we LOVE your style and personality! You're also in great shape and have a beautiful figure, but for modelling you would need to lose about ten pounds, please don't be offended, it's just the way it is in the industry!" She said looking at me as if she wanted to hire me, but I needed a few tweaks first.

"Thanks, but I didn't think I was tall enough for modelling?" I answered, feeling confused by how enthusiastic they seemed to be about me, aside from the ten pounds. "Oh, that's only in some cases. We work with girl's magazines, catalogues, and some TV shows, and height isn't really an issue. What counts is looks and charisma, and you have both!" She answered enthusiastically. "Really?" I answered, with a laugh, feeling confused that they saw such potential in me. I just thought of myself as okay-looking, but nowhere near the level they seemed to be seeing me at. "So here are our contact details, get back to us if and when you're ready, and we'd be happy to hire you!" She said as she gave me a card with the model agency's details on it. I thanked her, and headed towards the exit, waving goodbye at the others as I left.

"Thanks!/Goodbye/ See you soon!" we called out to one another as the door closed behind me, I knew I had no intention of going back there ever! It all felt too bizarre to me, I had only gone in there out of curiosity! I got back to the tropical paradise and felt as though I was finally back in my element. I couldn't wait to tell the gang what had happened at the modelling place.

Brian found it hilarious, as did the others, and for the next couple of hours, my very short-lived modelling career was a running joke, as they all took turns to do "model walks" to the bar and back, and later that eve as I was tucking into a burger and fries, Brian teased that I was never going to lose the ten pounds that way! "Well, at 5 foot 3, and weighing about 9 stone, I think I'm slim enough! And anyway, most of my weight is muscle which I needed to be strong, especially for backpacking around the world!" I exclaimed, mock indignantly. "You have a point!" answered Brian with a laugh. I caught a glimpse of Jeff looking sad for a moment, which made me feel bad at the thought of leaving him, my other friends, and Toronto to continue with my travels.

One day at the bar somebody mentioned they were heading up to Niagara Falls and my ears picked up. I quite fancied having a look at Niagara Falls! "Give you a lift if you want?" said the guy, noticing my look of interest. His name was Don, and he was an acquaintance of Paul's, so I felt I could trust him, especially if Paul and the others knew that I had taken a lift with him. "Thank You! That would be great!" I answered with a big smile, feeling my passion for travel starting to stir. We chatted about the day trip for a little while, and he arranged to pick me up the next day at 11 am, on the corner of the street near Karina's apartment, and we would be back in the evening.

I excitedly told the others that I was off on a day trip to Niagara Falls. They all seemed happy for me, aside from Jeff, who looked a little hurt and confused, but I felt he had no say, as we weren't a proper couple, we were just friends - with butterflies.

"I'll see you all when I get back!" I said as I got up to leave and go and get my things ready for the morning. "You'd better come back!" said Karina laughing. "I will! I just want to have a look at the falls, they look amazing. I've only ever seen photos, and films of them!" I answered excitedly.

"See you back at yours later, or in the morning or tomorrow eve!" I shouted to Karina, who was by now having a fun time chatting and drinking with friends. "OK, see you later!" she called back with a big smile on her face. It warmed my heart to see her happy. "I'll walk you home!" said Jeff suddenly, as he jumped up and started heading towards the exit with me. "Ok, thanks" I answered, liking his chivalry.

"Are you sure you're coming back?" He asked as he put his arm around me and we walked up the street together, towards Karinas. "Yeah, I'll be back tomorrow evening!" I answered as I put my arm around his waist. "Ah good, coz I'm gonna miss you!" He said as he gave me a little squeeze. "I'll miss you too, but I'll be back soon!" I answered, feeling a little awkward about the situation. We had never chatted about becoming a couple, but somehow it was starting to feel like we were a couple, and what made it harder to resist, was that we felt so right together.

CHAPTER 13:

NIAGARA FALLS NANNY, TOMATOES AND SUGAR

The next morning, I quickly got ready, grabbed my bag, left the apartment, and ran down the street to meet Don. There'd been no sigh of Karina or Jeff when I left, which I was kind of glad about, as I was able to make a swift getaway!

I spotted Don, standing outside of his pick-up truck, and we instantly waved at each other. "Hi, Don!" I said as I got nearer "Hi Della, ready to go?" He asked with a smile. "Yep!" I answered as we both climbed inside his pickup truck.

He started the pick-up truck up, and we took off. He seemed to be carrying a small load in the back of the truck, which was covered up in a tarp, as I looked back at it as if reading my mind, he said that he had some work to do on the outskirts of Niagara and that he would drop me off so that I could go and see the sites, and meet him back at 6 pm. That sounded like a good plan to me! We had a pleasant chat along the way about all sorts of random things. He was a really nice, friendly easy-going guy, and I enjoyed his company. The time flew by, and we arrived in Niagara Falls in no time!

"Ok, Della, I'll meet you back here at six, downtown is that way!" Said Don, as he dropped me off. I thanked him, and waved goodbye, and strolled off down the side street and into what seem to be the centre of Niagara Falls Town.

The town had a really nice laid-back atmosphere, and the air felt very fresh. I walked along feeling happy to be visiting somewhere new. As I came around the corner I could see crowds of people over to the right of the street. As I got nearer, I caught a glimpse of the falls through the crowd and felt a rush of excitement. A lot of the people were taking photos of each other, and there was a strong buzz of excitement in the air.

I weaved my way through the crowd until I reached the wall with a safety railing, which bordered the river and the falls. The view was amazing! The falls seemed to have an almighty energy as they burst over the top and cascaded downwards into the river below, which was shrouded in mist. It struck me as fascinating to think the falls were in constant motion. I gazed around at the view, feeling so excited to be there.

"Howdy" Said an older slim guy, with thinning fair hair standing next to me "Howdy!" I said back with a smile. "Did you hear about the tragedy?" He asked, looking concerned. "No, what tragedy?" I answered, feeling a little anxious over what he was about to tell me. "Yesterday a lady threw her baby over the falls!" He said, sadly shaking his head. I felt instantly sad and sickened at the thought, and wasn't sure if he meant the lady had jumped over the falls holding her baby, or if the lady had thrown her baby over alone. Either way, this was very sad, so I felt it wouldn't be right to question the details.

He went on to tell me that people did it all the time, that they just had enough and jumped over the falls. "It's been going on for years!" He said shaking his head, "...And they even go over in barrels for fun!" he added, as if trying to make a joke to lighten the mood. "Gosh, what a place!" I answered, not really sure what to say. "Well, I'd better get going! Might see you around, bye for now!" I said, as I strolled away, and continued on with my little walk.

As I walked, I thought about the poor little baby in the falls and assumed the baby's mother must have been in a very bad way to do such a thing. I felt sad thinking about it, but as I looked around at the happy locals and tourists, and beautiful waterfalls and rivers, my mood lifted a little, and I tried to focus on this feeling, and put my sad feelings to the back of my mind.

As I walked along, I spotted a grassy park area with a little tower on it. 'That looks interesting!' I thought to myself, as I automatically headed towards it. I was soon heading up to the top and had to smile when I noticed a sign for a revolving restaurant, as my mind flashed to my visit to the top of the CN Tower. I realised that I was hungry, so I decided to stay for lunch. This time I sat by the window, and wasn't moved to another table!

After my lunch with a fantastic view, I walked back down the steps and decided to go for a walkabout in the town centre of Niagara Falls. I liked it, it was very down-to-earth and rustic with character. It had a bit of a wild-west feel to it somehow, which I loved! The people were friendly, the weather was fresh and there were lots of nooks and crannies to stroll about and explore.

BOOK 1: TO SEE THE WORLD

I came across a poster store which looked very interesting so I stepped inside. All sorts of posters of movie stars, sportsmen and women adorned the walls. "Howdy!" said a friendly-looking older man who came out from the back. "Howdy!" I answered back liking the way everyone said Howdy, instead of hello, or hi in greeting. We soon got chatting, as he was very nice and easy to chat with. He mentioned some connection to the boxer Jack Dempsey, but I didn't really catch what he said or quite know who that was, but he seemed to think that I would have heard of him, so I just smiled and nodded. He invited me to have a coffee with him, so I accepted, and we sat chatting some more. He asked if I was staying in town for long, and I said I hadn't really planned on it, but it would be nice to spend a little more time, as it was such a lovely place!

He told me that he had a spare room upstairs and that I would be welcome to crash there for a few nights if I wanted to spend more time in Niagara Falls. He seemed genuine, I didn't sense any dodgy vibes from him, and I felt pleased with his offer, so I asked if he was sure. "Sure, it's no problem to me at all!" it's just an empty room, with a bed in there, and a cupboard, but you're welcome to it!" He said warmly. I asked if he wanted some money for my stay. "Of course not! You're a guest from the old country, you're welcome!" He answered smiling. "OK, thanks er?..." I answered, not remembering his name. "Jack!" He answered as we both shook hands. "Della!" I answered, wondering if he was the Jack Dempsy that he'd mentioned earlier, or maybe a relative or a friend with the same name, but it felt too late to ask now!

"I have a key for you" He said reaching into a drawer at his desk and passing a key over to me. "You can come and go as you please. I'll show you the room. follow me!" He said, sounding happy to be my host. "OK, thanks, Jack!" I answered, feeling pleased to be on the verge of a mini holiday in Niagara Falls! I followed him to the back of the store, and up some wooden stairs. "That's my room back there!" He said as he pointed down a dark hallway. "...And that's your room in the front!" he said sounding upbeat. "Great, thanks!" I answered as I went to look at the room. It was a simple room, with wood floors, bare walls, a little single bed a bedside table, and a cupboard, but no wardrobe. It was at the front of the store so it looked over the main street. "This is great!" I exclaimed, feeling excited to suddenly have a little room all to myself in Niagara Falls! "Glad you like it!" he answered, with a big smile.

I still didn't get any weird vibes from him, and felt very comfortable around him which was a good sign. He reminded me of my grandad on my dad's side and had a lovely country way about him, no airs and graces, just a very down-to-earth manner. We went back downstairs, had another cup of coffee, and chatted some more. He asked me about England, and he told me about Canada, and a little bit about the United States. "So what are your long-term plans Della?" he asked curiously. "Well, I just want to take a few years out to travel and see the world, I have a rough sketch of the places I'd like to see, but no set plans, so I can enjoy the freedom to do things like stay in Niagara Falls for a few days!" I answered with a grin. "A true adventurer!" He answered with a look of admiration. "Cheers, Jack!" I answered, and we both laughed, and we clinked our coffee cups! I loved the sense of freedom my travels so far were giving me, and he seemed to totally understand, and get that.

"Thanks for the coffee, I'm going to go for a little walk about, and I'll see you later. Thanks again for letting me stay for a few days!" I said as I stood up to look where to put the coffee cup. "I'll take the cup! Enjoy yourself! Come and go as you please!" He exclaimed as he took my coffee cup off me. "OK, thanks, Jack!" I answered as I headed towards the front door. "See ya later!" I called out, as I headed out of the front door and went strolling off down the street feeling on top of the world!

I suddenly wondered if my friends in Toronto would be worried about me, and decided it was best that I meet up with Don and explain what had happened and hopefully, he would tell the others. I was sure they would understand, especially as by now they knew me pretty well, and knew that my main objective was to travel! I hoped they wouldn't think that Don had done something bad to me! 'Poor Don!' I thought with a chuckle, as he was such a nice guy. My mind flashed to Jeff, and his sad-looking face when I'd mentioned my travels, and I felt a pang of sadness in my heart, but told myself not to think about him, and carried on with my walk.

I strolled around Niagara Falls feeling I hadn't a care in the world, but my thoughts kept turning back to Jeff and I realised that I was starting to feel more and more torn between my developing feelings for him and going with the flow of my travels. 'Don't' think about it! Just keep going with the flow!' I told myself as I carried on walking. I turned a corner and found a little bar, and decided to go inside for a beer. Hopefully, they wouldn't ask for ID! There were a few people in the bar, and it had a jukebox playing some heavy blues rock music, which I liked the sound of.

The people in the bar looked like blues rock 'n' roll fans, as nearly everybody wore denim and check shirts, with a few denim jackets, and a few cowboy hats here and there. I felt as though I had walked into a bar from the wild-west that had been nudged slightly on to the modern age, and its blues rock music, but was still clinging on to its original style, which I liked! I walked up to the bar, sat on a barstool, and waited my turn to be served. Just then a pretty blonde girl a few years older than me and a good-looking, dark-haired guy also a few old years older than me came into the bar full of laughter and sat next to me.

"How are you doing?" said the girl, as she swayed onto her seat next to mine. "Okay thanks, how are you?" I answered, grinning at how tipsy they both seemed. "Are you from England?" She asked, her eyes lighting up with curiosity. "Yep!" I answered, with a smile and a nod. "What are you doing all the way over here in Niagara Falls?!" she asked as if finding it amusing that I was somehow right there on the bar stool next to her.

The guy she was with ordered a picture of beer, and asked for three glasses, as the bartender looked my way, I started to order a drink, and the girl said "No you're welcome to join us!" I thanked her, and they introduced themselves as Suzie and Billy. I was soon drinking beer with them and chatting about their lives in Niagara Falls, my earlier life in England, and my current travels. "Wanna play pool?" asked Suzie, suddenly turning towards the pool table. "Sure, I'm not a good player, but I guess it's good practice, right?" I answered with a grin. "Right!" She answered with a laugh.

As she set up the pool table, Billy went to put some more tunes on the jukebox. "John Cougar Mellencamp, sweetheart!" Suzie called out to him as he went, and I got the impression that he was one of her favourite singers, especially as Billy looked a little like a picture, I'd seen of John Cougar Mellencamp!

We started to play pool, and as we played, we chatted, laughed and joked about all sorts of things. I was enjoying getting tipsy in such a fun easy-going down-to-earth bar. I started to realise that I felt more at home in Canada than I had felt in the UK! I seemed to fit in more with the easy-going, and friendly way that they had. The people seemed much more laid back, and not as formal as the Brits, although my friends in the UK weren't typical Brits either, they were more on the fun and creative side, but generally speaking, Canada felt more like me, and I liked it!

"We're heading over to Joe's next if you wanna come along?" said Suzie as she finished her beer. "Where is that?" I asked curiously. "It's just a bar on the other side of town. They serve good food!" she answered with a big smile. "That sounds good to me! I answered enthusiastically. We finished off our beers and headed off out of the door, waving at the bartender as we went.

It seemed that we would go past Jack's Poster Shop on our way, so I waved to Jack, and quickly popped inside and told him that I made some friends and that we were on our way to Joe's bar. He seemed to find this amusing. "Have a good time! Do as you please, see you later!" He called out, looking happy for me. "Thanks, Jack!" I called back, then let the door close, as I ran to catch up with my new friends.

Suzie and Billy led the way to a large bar and restaurant with a vibrant atmosphere. A lot of people were eating from baskets, and I tried to make out what they were eating, on closer inspection it looked like they were eating fried chicken drumsticks, fries, and coleslaw, with crips or potato chips as they called them on the sides. 'Tasty!' I thought to myself, as we found a table and sat down.

"Order whatever you like, our treat!" said Suzie, gleefully as she passed me a menu. "Are you sure?" I asked, feeling kind of awkward at being treated by them. "Sure, you're a visitor here, and we like to treat our guests right don't we Billy!" exclaimed Suzie, looking at Billy with a big smile. "We sure do!" answered Billy smiling back. "Okay, then I'll buy the next picture of beer!" I answered, trying to do my bit to chip in. "Oh no you won't!" said Billy, as he ordered a large picture of beer, and once again asked for three glasses.

I felt pleased to have found such warm, friendly, easy-going people to hang out with, just as I had in Toronto. I was starting to feel as though I had found my place in the world in Canada, but it was way too soon! I had barely started my travels! My mind flashed to my world travel plans, and the places I wanted to visit, and I reminded myself that I still wanted to see the United States, Mexico, Central America, and South America, and maybe later I could take a boat over to explore South Pacific, then East Assia, and Africa, and some more of Europe before circling back to England to visit family and friends, and regroup!

Hopefully, by then I would have found the right place for me to make my long-term home base and would be making plans to move back there, wherever it was. These travel thoughts really appealed to me, but then my mind returned to where I was in Canada, and how happy I was to be there, and I felt as though a big part of me never wanted to leave. I brushed these thoughts and feelings to the back of my mind and went about having a fun afternoon with Suzie, and Billy.

Just after 5.30 pm, I told them that I had to pop over and tell Don that I wouldn't be heading back to Toronto with him. By now they knew all about my friends in Toronto and agreed that it was a good idea to go and tell Don of my plans to stay for a while. I said I would meet up with them a bit later and took off to find the street where Don and I had arranged to meet. Thankfully the town wasn't too big, and I found it pretty easy to navigate my way back to the meeting place.

By 6 o'clock I was there ready to meet Don, and he showed up within seconds of my getting there. "Hi Don, I hope you've had a good day! I've made some friends, so I'm going to stay in Niagara Falls for a few days. Will you tell the gang back at Tropical Paradise please?" I said, as soon as Don jumped out of his pickup truck. "Will do, I don't blame you a bit!" He answered, looking happy for me. "Thanks, Don!" I answered, grateful that he would relay my message to the others. "No problem! Have fun!" he exclaimed, as he jumped back in his pickup truck. "Thanks again, Don!" I called after him, as he took off. We waved goodbye to each other. Afterwards, I headed back to meet Suzie, and Billy at the bar.

We had a great evening of eating and drinking, and later we went over to another bar for a nightcap. There was a blues rock band playing, and we all automatically started dancing on the floor. "What a fun town!" I said to Suzie. "It sure is! That's why I don't go anywhere else! she said, with a laugh, as she gave Billy a hug and a big kiss. "Billy has to go away though, don't you Billy!" she said, sounding pretend sad. "Yeah, but I always come back, don't I!" he joked back. He was a truck driver like Don and spent a lot of time on the road. I got the impression that truck driving seemed to be a popular profession for guys in these parts. Which seemed very fitting, as they had a kind of cowboy spirit about them, and I thought the trucks must be like modern-day horses in a way.

"Do you ever go along with him?" I asked Suzie, thinking that's what I would probably do if my guy was a truck driver. "No, I got a kid! Gotta stay home with him, he's a good boy though! ...Did you ever think of being a nanny?" she asked me looking interested in the possibility. "Not really as a proper profession, but maybe as a volunteer gig on my travels?" I answered, remembering that it was one of my previous volunteer gig ideas to keep afloat on my travels. "Well, my mom usually helps me with running my house, but she's away for a couple of weeks. Would you be able to help out by any chance? I can't pay you, but you can have room and board, and a bit of pocket money here and there for times when we go out like this!" She said persuasively.

I felt excited by the offer, but my mind suddenly flashed to Jeff, and my friends in Toronto, and I suddenly felt torn, and unsure of what to do. Once again, I had to remind myself that I was travelling to see the world to meet different people from different cultures, to experience new things, and to have adventures and that the only way to do that was to go with the flow and to be open to new

149

opportunities. After all, that was the whole point of my travelling, it was not to get stuck in one place, in the same old routine!

"That sounds great!" I answered, deciding that I would just go for it! "Yeah, Della's gonna be our nanny while mom's away!" announced Suzie, as she raised her glass to me and Billy as he re-joined us. "Cheers!" We all exclaimed as we clinked our glasses together. We spent the next couple of hours dancing, and drinking, and having a great time! I told them I would spend the night at Jack's, and meet them the next day. I got back to Jack's after midnight, and tiptoed to my room and fell asleep fast.

The next morning I met Jack in the kitchen, as he was putting a pot of coffee on. "How was your night out? Want some coffee and toast?" He asked in his usual easy-going manner. "Yes, please Jack! I had a great time thanks, and they've asked if I'll be a nanny for their son for a couple of weeks while her mom's on holiday!" I answered excitedly. "Wow you move fast!" answered Jack, looking please for me. "Yeah, I really like it here!" I answered, feeling so happy to be in such a friendly, fun place. It had the same friendly vibes as Toronto but was much smaller, so it had a small-town feel to it, which I found quite cosy and familiar, as my home town Oswestry was a small town too.

We sat and chatted over breakfast, and then I went back upstairs to tidy up my bed, have a shower, and get ready for the new day ahead. It suddenly dawned on me that my rucksack and all of my clothes were still at Karina's. I only had my shoulder bag with me, with my usual; cardi, money, keys, comb and make-up inside. I was sure that my things were safe at Karina's, and hopefully Suzi, would have some old clothes that I could borrow. I went back downstairs and sat chatting some more with Jack. I told him I would drop by to say hi from time to time over the next couple of weeks, and once again, thanked him for his kind hospitality. He told me that I was most welcome, and we bid each other goodbye.

The next couple of weeks spent helping out at Suzie's house was great fun, and very easy! All I had to do was watch her son Mikey for a few hours in the afternoon while she was at work, and sometimes when she and Billy wanted to go out in the evenings. In exchange, I had my own bedroom, food, and a little bit of pocket money here and there. Sometimes Billy would babysit so that Suzie and I could pop out for a beer. They were a fun, friendly, easy-going couple and their little boy was very sweet, and a pleasure to look after. Mikey and I mainly spent our afternoons drawing pictures, playing games, or watching cartoons.

While I was there Suzie introduced me to toasted sandwiches, with mayonnaise and large "Beef" tomatoes sliced up. They were so simple, yet delicious, and they quickly become a favourite of mine! All in all, we became one big happy family, although the only thing that I wasn't too keen on, was that sometimes Suzie and Billy would do hard drugs in the kitchen!

The first time I saw Suzie, heating up a spoon I asked her what she was doing, and she explained she was heating up some sugar to shoot up. I was shocked because it was obvious, she didn't mean table sugar, and they hadn't seemed like hard drug users to me, especially as they had a young child, but they did love him, and take great care of him, and their home. So, I assumed that it must be some kind of recreational thing that they did on occasion, on a par with alcohol.

They never invited me to join them in their drug taking, which I was glad of, because it wasn't my scene, and I wouldn't want them to think I was being judgemental of them. I think they just sensed that it wasn't for me, also I was the one looking after their child during their party time, so it wouldn't have been wise to invite me to join them!

In my free time, I would go on walkabouts, and sit by the Falls and look over at the United States. It was so strange to see the US across the river. There was a bridge called The Rainbow Bridge, where people from both sides would walk back and forth, and there was always a good atmosphere there.

I would sometimes visit Jack at his poster to shop for a coffee and a chat, which was nice, although one afternoon I was surprised that he seemed to be hinting about looking for a girlfriend. I didn't know what to make of this and wondered if he was just making conversation, or if he was trying to show an interest in me. Either way, it felt kind of weird, so I just laughed it off, and told him I would look out for a gal for him then! He laughed too, and I left that day feeling a little uncomfortable, so I never went back.

After a couple of weeks of helping out as a Nanny for Suzie and Billy, Suzie's mum came back from her vacation and was once again available to babysit for Mikey in the afternoons. Suzie and Billy said that I was still welcome to stay there, and I thanked them, but I said that I was missing my friends in Toronto so I would head back there.

That night we all said our goodbyes to each other, and I told them that I would get an early start the next morning, so I probably wouldn't see them. I told them that I would keep in touch, and thanked them for everything. They all gave me a big hug, and Suzie gave me a little extra cash as thanks. I felt a little sad to be leaving them all, but I looked forward to seeing the gang back at The Tropical Paradise.

Early the next morning I packed up what little I had into my shoulder bag, tiptoed out of the house, and headed out to the highway to hitchhike back over to Toronto. I got a lift with a quiet older man named Davey in what looked like an old car. He drove slowly, and we chatted about this and that. He lived on the outskirts of Toronto and was married, and he and his wife were retired and mainly spent their days taking care of the house and garden and looking after the grandchildren. He was on his way home, after helping his son with DIY jobs at his house in Niagara Falls.

We stopped for a leisurely breakfast on the way. We weren't in a rush to get anywhere, and it was nice to feel that sense of freedom again. As much as I had enjoyed my time in Niagara Falls, and had really liked the friends I'd made there and the little boy I'd been looking after, I had started to get into a routine of sorts, which was starting to feel a little boring to me, plus I was missing my fun Tropical Paradise friends for sure! After breakfast, Davey and I used the washrooms, before strolling back to his car and continuing on with our journey. Finally, we arrived back in downtown Toronto, and I thanked Davey, and we wished each other well before I jumped out of the car, and we waved goodbye to each other.

I felt so excited to have arrived back in Toronto! I felt so at home there, and I couldn't wait to get to the tropical paradise and see the gang, and tell them all of my latest adventure! It was quite a walk, as I'd been dropped off on the other side of the city to the Tropical Paradise, but this was ok, as I loved the refreshing feeling of walking in Toronto, I couldn't pinpoint why, there was just something uplifting about the atmosphere I liked.

Around noon I found myself finally entering the doors of the Tropical Paradise and scanning the room for my friends. "Della!" Called a familiar voice and I looked over to see Brian's big smiling face looking over at me, as he was waving his arms, and running towards me to give me a big hug. "Where have you been? What did you do? Who did you see? You must tell! Come and sit down and have a beer, and tell me all about it! It feels like you've been gone so long!" he said excitedly, as he ushered me over to his table.

"Hi Brian, where are the others?" I asked, noticing that he was with some people I didn't know. "Karina's working most days now, and Paul and Lyn haven't been in lately" he answered, still looking pleased to see me. "...Oh and Jeff's probably at work!" he added and as if reading my mind. "Ah good, I'll probably see them all sooner or later then!" I answered with a big smile while feeling elated to be back.

He introduced me to his new table of friends and we all smiled and shook hands with each other as I sat down to join them. I loved how Brian was friends with all sorts of people. He was the star catalyst of the Tropical Paradise. "So, tell me all about your latest adventure!" said Brian excitedly, as the others stopped chatting to listen to my reply. I told him all about my visit to Niagara Falls, and how I'd wound up being a nanny for two weeks. He seemed to find this hilarious, and roared with laughter, "So, no more modelling, now you're Mary Poppins from England!" he exclaimed. "'Oh yes that's me!" I joked back before taking a swig of my beer, and we all cracked up laughing. It felt good to be back!

"So, what will you do now? will you stay, or will you go??" asked Brian sounding excited for me. "I don't know what to do?" I really love Toronto, and all the friends I've made here, but at the same time, the whole point of my travels was to explore and see the world! ...Argh, I really don't know what to do. I feel so torn! I know if I go, I'm going to really miss you, and the others!" I said, pulling a confused and sad face, as I shrugged my shoulders in exasperation.

"Oh, travel, travel, travel! A world of adventure awaits you! - Don't worry about us!" He exclaimed dramatically, as the others nodded in agreement. "Cheers Brian!" I answered. appreciating his understanding, and his not feeling offended if I chose more travels over staying. I got the feeling that he knew it wasn't anything personal, and maybe because he too was a traveller of sorts he completely understood where I was coming from.

"I'll be heading back to the southern states soon to visit my folks! And afterwards, I'll return with my new visa for Canada, and be good to stay for another six months!" He exclaimed proudly. "Sounds good! Hey, maybe I'll see you down south!" I joked, and he squealed with laughter. "Now, that WOULD be fun!" he answered with a grin. Just then Karina entered the bar, and her face lit up with a big smile to see me. My face lit up with a big smile to see her too, as I jumped up and ran over to greet her, we gave each other a big hug, and she asked me all about my trip as she walked with me to join us at our table. One of Brian's friends poured her some beer, as if to welcome her, while Brian went to buy another picture, we all chipped in a few dollars and put it on the table next to where Brian was sitting, for him to pick up when he got back. I loved how we all automatically chipped in for our shared pitchers of beer, there was no fuss about "Who's round is it?" like in the UK. Things, including the beer, just flowed more naturally somehow!

I asked Karina how things had been going for her, and she seemed to be doing great, which I was pleased to hear. I told her that I hoped Tony the Restaurant owner wasn't mad at me for taking off, and she laughed and said he was fine with things, as he knew I was on my travels. She added that she had missed a couple of days here and there too, and he had been cool about it. He just seemed to appreciate the help when she did turn up. Soon we were all laughing, joking and chatting away like "old times"

As the day went on more familiar faces appeared, including the philosophy professor; Don - he waved and sat down at his usual table, so, I went to say hi, and have a little chat with him on my way to the washroom. I quickly filled him in on my latest little adventure and mentioned that I may be heading off on some more travels again soon. He seemed to understand my need to travel, and wished me well on whichever road I took! I thanked him and wished him well too. Later on, Lyn and Paul arrived and they seemed happy to see me too. Deep down, each time the front door opened, I was hoping to see Jeff, but I felt bad for being away for, what felt like, so long, and wasn't sure how he would behave towards me if he did turn up.

There was no sign of Jeff at all that night, and as I walked back to Karina's with her I felt that it was probably for the best, and once again, reminded myself that I was there to travel not to stay! Karina said I could go to the restaurant with her the next day to see if they needed any extra help if I wanted? I agreed to go with her, so the next afternoon the two of us got dressed up as usual and headed down to the restaurant. Tony the owner looked pleased to see me, and gave me a big hug, and welcomed me back. He was totally okay with me not being there the last couple of weeks and seemed to understand that Karina and I were both free-spirited types and not always able to stick to a routine. Thankfully he let me help out for the next few hours, and I soon had a little more pocket money on me.

We headed back to the tropical paradise after helping out at the restaurant, and as we walked down the street, Karina asked me what my plans were. I explained to her how I felt totally torn, on the one hand, I was very happy in Toronto I loved the city, and my new friends there, including her, adding that I had some special kind of feelings developing for Jeff, but I was also still longing to travel. "Oh girl, what are you going to do?" she said in a sympathetic way, as if totally understanding my dilemma. "I don't know. Let's drink some beers and see!" I answered, and we both laughed as we entered the tropical paradise The first face

154

I saw as we entered was Jeff's. I felt instant butterflies in my stomach and my face flushed red. I suddenly felt awkward and embarrassed and felt as though I needed to hide my feelings, but I wasn't sure that I was succeeding.

"Della!" Exclaimed Jeff, as he came rushing over towards me and gave me a big warm hug. "Hi" I answered, as I hugged him back in a slightly aloof way while feeling terrible about it on the inside. He instantly seemed to notice that I was behaving a little standoffish. "I'm gonna go back and join my friends, and give you some space!" He said, sounding a little hurt, as he turned and headed back towards the area he'd come from. "OK, see ya!" I answered cooly.

Karina and I found a table to sit at, and we continued on with our girl talk. I asked her about her boyfriend in LA, and if there was any news. "Same ole, same ole!" she said looking downhearted. "Surely you can work something out?" I answered, feeling fed up for her. "Not for a while" she answered sounding sad as she drank her beer down almost in one go, and gave out a hearty sigh.

"Della! Karina!" shouted Brian as he entered the building. Karina and I looked up and smiled, both of us happy to see him, as we waved and beckoned for him to come and join us. He gestured that he would join us after grabbing a glass from the bar, and once again, I was reminded of how much I loved the way we all just shared our pitchers of beers, and had a good time together!

The place got more and more crowded, and more familiar faces started to turn up, including Dave and Kyle. The atmosphere got more fun as the music was turned up, and some people started dancing, while others were chatting, laughing, and joking. Everyone was happy including me, although deep down I felt a little sad about Jeff, and would catch myself glancing around the room looking for him, but he seemed to have disappeared. I felt so bad for not being more friendly with him when he'd greeted me.

After a while, Paul and Lyn joined us at our table and seemed amused that I'd stayed in Niagara Falls for two weeks helping out as a nanny. They told me that Don had told them as soon as he got back, and that they were meeting him there that night, and that he would be pleased to see me. I asked Lyn what the latest was with her and Paul, and she said it looked like she would have to go back to London soon, and hopefully, they would be able to work things out. I wished her well, and she asked me what my plans were. I told her I had quite enjoyed my stint as a nanny in Niagara Falls, and that maybe I would look for more volunteer nanny gigs. We both agreed that it was a handy little gig for travelling!

155

Just then Don arrived. He was happy to see me and asked how I'd enjoyed Niagara Falls. He sat next to me and I told him all about my two weeks stay there. I told him that I may look for more nanny gigs, as I had quite enjoyed it. He mentioned that his sister often needed some extra help with the house and that he could give her a call if I wanted. I asked where she lived, and he told me she lived near a town called Fort Erie, about ninety miles away, south of Niagara Falls, and that he was going there in a couple of days, and would give me a lift if she needed the help, and if I wanted to help of course? I thanked him and said it sounded good. he told me he would phone her and get back to me.

Suddenly, I felt somebody massaging my shoulders and I turned around to see Jeff. My heart melted a little, and we had a special moment as we smiled at each other, but I instantly felt sad because I knew that I would be travelling on soon. Somebody passed him a chair, and he squeezed in next to me and put his arm around me, and for a short moment in time I felt as if we were a proper couple. In my heart I felt happy, but in my mind, I was still feeling torn and confused.

Karina suddenly stood up to go, and asked if I wanted to go with her and crash out at her place, and maybe help out at the restaurant with her the next day. I said yes and quickly stood up as well, and said goodbye to everybody. Jeff looked confused, so I told him I'd see him soon, and once again things felt a little awkward between us. I tried to act cool and not show any emotions, as Karina and I waved at everyone and quickly left out of the front door, and headed up the street, back to her place.

The next day we helped out a few hours at the restaurant, and once again we had some pocket money to spend, and headed back to the Tropical Paradise to spend it! Don was at the bar when we arrived and looked eager to see me. We headed over and stood next to him to order our beer and pick up our glasses. "I spoke to my sister Jane," Don said, excitedly, momentarily reminding me of the girl named Janie that I'd met a few weeks earlier. I hadn't seen her since but I hoped she was doing ok. "...and she said she would be glad of the help, they have a spare room and a cupboard full of food, and would be able to give you little pocket money on top, are you still interested?" continued Don, his face looking full of enthusiasm.

For a split second, my heart felt torn, and I felt confused and not sure if I wanted to leave Jeff, and my Toronto friends again, especially so soon! "Thanks, that sounds great! When does she need the help?" I heard myself say. "Well, I'm heading down there tomorrow afternoon, I can give you a lift if you want?" answered Don swiftly. "Wow, that's great!" I answered, trying to look pleased while feeling sad. "OK, where shall I meet you?" I asked with a smile, while nervously glancing around to see if Jeff was about yet. "4 pm, at the same place as last time if you like?" Answered Don, smiling back. "That would be great!" I answered, thinking how handy it was that it was just on the corner from Karina's apartment. "OK, see you tomorrow!" exclaimed Don, as he finished his drink, and bid his farewells to his friends.

I quickly found Karina and told her my news. she seemed happy for me, but a little sad as well. I said I felt the same, and I told her I could still visit, and maybe she could visit me too! I dreaded telling the others, especially Jeff, but by the end of the night, everybody knew I was heading off to my next nanny gig the very next day! They all wished me well and told me to come back often, and I said I would. Jeff was the only one who didn't seem happy for me, he seemed a little standoffish and hurt, which I felt bad about, but I put on a brave face and acted like I didn't really care.

That night Karina and I left the bar and waved goodbye to everybody. Jeff suddenly came rushing over towards us, as if in a last-ditch attempt to stop me from going and we gave each other a big hug. I reassured him that we could visit each other, but he didn't seem convinced and as we kissed goodbye, I saw a sadness in his eyes, which I felt terrible about. Little did he know, that I felt just as sad too.

As Karina and I walked up the street to her apartment, I felt a strong mixture of sadness over Jeff and excitement about new travels. As we walked along, the fresh breeze on my face seemed to ease my confused heart and mind, and I looked forward to a good night's sleep, and heading off on a new adventure the next day. As I drifted off to sleep, I was still feeling very sad to be leaving Toronto, Jeff, and my friends there, but I reminded myself that I had also left my family and friends back in England as well. 'You've done it before, you can do it again!' I told myself, as I restlessly tossed, and turned.

I knew that in order to gain anything in this world, I would have to make space for it by letting go of something else. It was a natural science of sorts, and in my case, I really wanted to travel, which meant letting go of family and friends. I hoped that the bonds between us would stay strong and that one day when I was based in my long-term home, wherever that may be? We would all meet up again, many more times. I eventually fell asleep, with a vision of Jeff's sad face as he kissed me goodbye, in my mind.

The next morning Karina and I had breakfast in her kitchen and chatted about life in general. She asked if I wanted to go to the Tropical Paradise for a drink before I left, but I decided that it was probably for the best that I didn't. She understood, so we hung out at her place for a couple of hours just chatting in general, until she had to pop out to run some errands. I told her I would go and pack my rucksack and hopefully see her before I left.

After I finished my cup of coffee, I washed up the dishes and headed down to the basement to get ready to go. I looked around the room that had given me shelter for the past few weeks, and felt sad, that I was to be leaving soon, but I felt excited at the same time. I was fast learning that my travels were a bitter-sweet mixture of the joy of arriving, followed by the sadness of leaving. I took a shower, packed up my rucksack, tidied up the room, did my hair and makeup, and headed back upstairs. It was now nearing 3.30, just a half hour before I was to meet Don. I hoped Karina would come back soon, and just around 3.40 I heard the front door opening, and a few seconds later Karina arrived in the kitchen.

"Hey Karina, I'm glad you made it back before I leave!" I exclaimed, feeling happy to see her. "Me too, wanna beer?" She asked as she put her shopping down on the side, and opened the fridge door. "Sure, thanks!" I answered, thinking it would be nice to have one for the road. She got us both a small bottle of beer and we both sat at the kitchen table together, in a kind of happy-sad limbo mood. "Cheers!" I exclaimed. "Cheers!" answered Karina, as we both clinked bottles.

"Well girl if you don't come back, and if you do keep travelling and end up in La-La Land, say hi to Gerry for me!" she laughed. "Will do!" I answered, as we both clinked our beers together again and laughed. "Well, I guess, I'd better get going!" I said, as I finished my beer, and stood up "OK!" answered Karina as she stood up with me. We hugged each other goodbye, and I headed towards my rucksack.

My heart started to beat faster, at the prospect of leaving, especially as I still felt so torn. I thought about how my friends in Toronto were all such lovely people, and Jeff and I had something that seemed special developing between us, and I was so happy there, why on earth was I leaving just because I'd previously decided I wanted to travel? Why were things so complicated? "OK, so if I wind up in LA I'll keep a lookout for Jerry for you, but hopefully he'll be back to spend some time with you soon!" I said, with a laugh, trying to lighten the mood. "Maybe!" she answered, as she smiled a sad smile, and shrugged her shoulders.

BOOK 1: TO SEE THE WORLD

"Thanks again for everything!" I exclaimed as I headed towards the front door. "You're welcome!" she answered, as we gave each other another big hug, I grabbed my rucksack, and opened the front door. Karina, sat back down at the kitchen table opening another beer and looking lost. I felt so bad to be leaving her. "See you next time!" I said giving her a little wave. "Later girl!" she called out, as she waved back. I smiled and closed the door behind me.

It was nearly 4 pm, so I was just about to make a run for it when Karina opened the front door. "Wait!" she shouted, as she hurried over towards me and gave me another big hug. "Thank you for being my friend!" she said, as we stood there hugging. "Thank you too, Karina!" I answered, feeling terrible to be leaving her, Jeff, and the others. "We can keep in touch, and meet up down the line!" I said, trying to sound optimistic, while at the same time wondering if and when we ever would meet up again. "Bye for now then!" I said as we gave each other one more quick hug. "Bye for now!" answered Karina sadly. "See ya!" I called out, as I took off down the drive, and onto the street. "See ya!" she called back, as we waved at each other one last time before I took off running to meet Don.

As I ran, I felt very sad and was on the verge of tears, but I held my emotions in and started running faster towards the arranged meet-up point for Don. As I ran, I wasn't sure if I was running to be on time for Don, or running to get away from my emotions. I felt it was a mixture of the two.

As I turned the corner at the end of the street, I slowed down and started to walk towards the meet-up point, although I was still feeling sad, I started to feel that old familiar feeling of freedom rising in my gut. It was some kind of chemistry in me that I seemed to be becoming addicted to. I pondered on the idea of this feeling being similar to a drug of sorts, or at least the chemicals being released in my body were maybe similar to, or the very same chemicals that various drugs release. 'At least it's not "Sugar!' I joked to myself, with a grin, as my mind flashed to my memories of Suzie and Billy in their kitchen, getting ready to go out partying.

I went and stood at the meet-up spot, and looked up and down the street for Don's pick-up truck. Within seconds he arrived and parked his truck in front of me. We smiled and waved at each other, and I opened the passenger door. He had lively pop music playing and was in a good mood. "Hi, Don!" I said as I jumped in the passenger seat. "Hi Della, how are you doing?" he answered with a big smile. "OK, thanks! Thanks for picking me up, again!" I answered, and we both laughed, as he started up the truck, and we took off up the street.

As we drove along, he said he was hungry and wanted to stop at a truck stop for some food and asked if I would like some food too. I said that would be nice, and thanked him. Soon we pulled up at the truck stop and strolled into the Diner. We found a booth to sit at and read the menus. "Order whatever you want!" exclaimed Don generously. "Thanks, Don!" I answered, as I eagerly scanned the menu, as I was by now pretty hungry too.

"So, what's your sister Jane and her family like? I assume they're nice if they're anything like you!" I asked curiously, once we had both decided what to order. "Oh my sister and her family are lovely, you'll all get along great! You'll love 'em, and they'll love you!" he answered with a big smile. "Aww, I can't wait to meet them!" I answered, smiling back. "John's a truck driver, and is away a lot, so Jane will be so glad of your help, especially with Christmas coming up, and she'll be glad of your company too!" He added with a smile. "It'll be my pleasure!" I answered looking forward to meeting what sounded like a wholesome Canadian family. I felt it would be a great chance to experience family life in a different culture from the one I'd grown up in. "So, do they live in a town, a suburb, or the countryside?" I asked, curiously. "Well, it's a little of all three!" he answered back, and we both laughed. "It's a nice area, it won't take us too long to get there, about an hour and a half or so!" He added reassuringly, and I looked forward to our journey, and to my new adventure.

The young fair-haired waitress suddenly appeared, and we both ordered grilled cheese sandwiches, fries with tomato ketchup, and a large coffee each. We were soon sitting, happily eating and chatting away. I liked Don, he was very easygoing and nice to chat with. I felt comfortable in his company and hoped that his sister Jane was similar to him. I felt sure that she would be, somehow.

After our meals, we had a few coffee top-ups and chatted some more as we let the food go down. Don seemed to like my free-spirited way, and I didn't get any weird vibes from him which helped me to feel relaxed and at ease with him. I felt that on some level he may be looking for inspiration from me to maybe set off on his own travels someday.

"OK, we should get going!" announced Don suddenly around 6 o'clock, so we both stood up and headed off to his truck and jumped inside. Soon we were once again on the highway cruising along. "Gosh, it's getting dark quickly!" I exclaimed, suddenly realising that the sun had gone down. "Yeah, I'll take a shortcut to save us some time!" answered Don, as he took stepped on the gas, and cut down a side road. He turned the radio up, and we both sat back and relaxed in our seats. I was enjoying the music and slipped into a daydream about hopefully meeting up with Jeff, Karina, Brian and the others again, sooner or later. I smiled to myself and chuckled at the thought.

I suddenly noticed that Don seemed to be taking more and more back roads to get to his sister's place, and as it was dark it was hard to see where we were going. He continued driving down the back roads with confidence, until at some point he started to seem a little lost and frustrated. "Are you lost?" I asked gingerly not wanting to offend him. "Yep!" he answered with a sigh. "Oh no, how come?" I asked, feeling puzzled, as surely, he knew the way well. "I usually go the main way, but I thought this was a shortcut!" he answered, sounding baffled, and we both instantly saw the funny side and started to laugh. "I'm gonna have to try and find the highway, these roads are getting us nowhere!" he exclaimed, sounding defeated. "Yeah, probably for the best!" I answered encouragingly. Don made a right turn at the next street and stepped on the gas.

As we were speeding along, I noticed a sign that read Buffalo. "Buffalo, isn't that in New York?" I asked, remembering that during my time in Niagara Falls, I was told that Buffalow - New York, was across The Rainbow Bridge from Niagara Falls. "Yeah, we can cut through Buffalo to get down to my sister's place!" answered Don, sounding like a man with a plan! "How fun, I'd better get my passport handy!" I said with a chuckle, thinking it funny that we would casually be taking a shortcut through the US to reach his sister's house. "Oh yeah" Answered Don, as if it hadn't even crossed his mind. "The border check is around here somewhere, it's been a while since I came this way" said Don, once again looking a little lost.

I went about rummaging in my backpack to get my passport ready. I was pleased that my aunt Freda had organised our six-month visas a few weeks back when we met up in London, so mine was valid from early December, until early June, and as it was now the first week of December it was perfect timing, plus there was still plenty of time for aunt Freda to pop over and meet up with me at some point. I started to feel excited about our fleeting visit to the US, as I continued rummaging in my backpack.

My passport wasn't in the front pocket where I usually kept it, when it wasn't in my shoulder bag, and just as I was starting to panic that I'd left it in Toronto, I found it squashed between my journal and a magazine at the bottom of my backpack. I remembered that I'd hidden it there for safekeeping, as the front pocket wasn't always the safest place for it. I quickly grabbed it and sat up straight, ready to show it at the border check.

We reached what looked like a large gateway. "I think this is it?" Don mumbled as he looked around with a confused look on his face while leaning forward off his seat to get his wallet and ID out of his back jeans pocket. I looked around, but there was nothing much to see. Just trees, and grass, and a few cars on a highway in the distance.

No one was around, aside from two men standing about forty feet away chatting and smoking cigarettes in the dark near some trees. Don slowed down to see if they were the border people, and one of the men turned and walked towards us. As he got nearer, I could see that he had some kind of uniform on, so I assumed he must be the border checker, so I opened my passport and held it up ready for him to check. Don rolled his window down, and they said hello to each other, the man smiled and said hello back and looked at Don's ID that he was holding up and glanced over at my passport that I was holding up. He smiled nodded his head, and waved for us to carry on. Don and I nodded, smiled, and waved, and continued on our way.

I felt excited to suddenly be in the US, and back out on the road on another adventure. "Gosh, so we're on the other side of the rainbow bridge!" I asked, as I spotted a sign that read "Rainbow Bridge" I was feeling completely confused, and turned around, yet at the same time excited, and amused! "We sure are!" answered Don, sounding a little more relaxed now that we were back on the main roads again. "...So, my sister's house should be about twenty five miles south... I think?" added Don, suddenly looking and sounding just as confused as he'd been before we took the shortcut. "Hey, getting lost is all part of the adventure!" I joked, and we both laughed.

"So, when was the last time you visited your sister?" I asked curiously. "Oh it was a few months back, but I usually head south then east, and this time I tried to cut across di-ag-a-nolly" he explained, as he struggled to say the word diagonally. I tried to help, but I wound up getting the word just as muddled as him, and we both laughed with the frustration of not remembering how to pronounce the word. "...Or, maybe I just missed a turn!" he said with a laugh as if giving up on that word. "Yeah, probably!" I answered, and we both laughed, as he turned the radio up, and we both sat back to enjoy the journey once again.

"Are we anywhere near Boston?" I asked, my mind suddenly remembering Bruno, and how he'd told me that he loved Boston, so much so, that I had felt curious to visit when he'd told me about it. "Boston's about a six or seven, hour drive away" Answered Don casually. My heart started to race at the idea of a visit there, who knows maybe I would bump into Bruno? I thought smiling to myself at such a romantic notion.

"Is there any chance we can pop over there just for a look around before we go to your sisters?" I asked excitedly. "Well, we could, but it'd take us a good twelve hours or so, there and back, so I'm not sure if that qualifies as a pop, as you put it?!" answered Don, seeming amused by the idea. I suddenly didn't care if it was a long drive there and back, I was excited by the chance to see Boston, and maybe even Bruno too! "I don't mind, if you don't, it'll be a fun side trip!" I answered enthusiastically. "OK, Boston it is!" Exclaimed Don as if happy to please me, and secretly up for a bit of adventure himself. "We will have to find a restaurant so I can call my sister first!" He added as if suddenly remembering our original destination. "Oh yeah, that's a good idea! 'I answered nodding, with a big grin on my face, the adventurer in me feeling very excited at this new development, but a little bad at postponing our arrival at his sister's. 'All part of the adventure!' I told myself with a grin.

CHAPTER 14:

CAN'T FIND BOSTON! - NEW YORK IT IS THEN!

We followed the highway signs east until we spotted a roadside restaurant. "Hungry?" Asked Don, as he started slowing down. "I am a bit!" I answered as he pulled into the restaurant's driveway. The restaurant was very old-world looking, and reminded me of Country Inns in the UK, only with an American flavour. I was curious to see what it was like inside.

"Are we still in the US?" I asked Don jokingly, feeling confused, and wondering if we'd arrived at some English-influenced part of Canada. Don turned and asked the bartender where we were. "Well, you're not on the moon, I can tell you that!" Joked the bartender. "Well, I know that, but where are we?" I laughed back. "Sunny Buffalo, New York, what can I get you both?" Said the bartender with a smile. "Two beers" answered Don, as we walked towards a table nearby and sat down. As we were looking at the menu, the beers arrived.

As I sat looking around at the cosy bar, I was starting to sense a slightly different atmosphere to the one in Canada. The bartender was just as friendly as the Canadian bartenders, but he also seemed a little more playful, although I realised that it could just be a one-off and just his personality. "So how far is Boston?" I asked again, as we swigged on our beers straight from the bottles. "It's about three hundred and fifty miles from here, I reckon?" Answered Don, looking as he was calculating how far we'd travelled already. "Wow, a bit of a ways then!" I answered, nodding my head, sipping on my beer, and grinning with excitement at the thought of going to the very place Bruno had told me about just a few months earlier.

We ordered our food, and then Don went to use the pay phone to call his sister to explain what had happened. I sat sipping on my beer, and daydreaming about my visit to Boston. I imagined bumping into Bruno somewhere there, maybe in a bar, in a park, or on the street. How strange, yet wonderful that would be!

I pondered on whether I would be open to a romance with him this time, and if he would still be open to a romance with me, but my mind suddenly flashed to Jeff in Toronto, and I felt a wave of guilt and sadness rush through my heart, followed by a strong feeling of being torn between people and places, here, there and everywhere! I took a deep breath, and I once again questioned if my love of travel meant that I would constantly be having to sacrifice romances, friendships, and places.

I wasn't interested in flings, only real love, or at the very least infatuation! I hoped that things would work themselves out along the way. 'Maybe one day I will fall for a person and a place together. That would be perfect! …Yeah, like what just happened in Canada!' I thought to myself, feeling stumped. '…I love Toronto, my friends there, and I had feelings developing for Jeff, so what the heck am I doing in some bar on a highway in the US on the road to Boston?!' I thought feeling as if I didn't know whether to laugh or cry, so I took another swig of my beer instead, and as the tipsy sensation took over, it made me feel like I didn't really care. 'Just go with the flow!' I told myself, trying to suppress my feelings of confusion and sadness, while quickly developing a strong understanding of why Karina liked a drink!

Don suddenly came back and sat down at the table looking like everything was hunky dory. I asked if his sister was okay with our little excursion. He explained that she was fine and that he had told her that we would probably see her tomorrow sometime, who knows? He laughed casually. I was happy with this news and got the feeling that his sister was as easygoing as him. We dug into our meals of steak and fries.

"Ready to hit the highway?" asked Don, as we finished the last of our beers. "Yep, I'm ready!" I answered. My head was looking forward to checking out Boston, but my heart was yearning to get back to Toronto. I stood up with Don, and as I was getting my things together Don went over to ask the bartender directions for the Boston Highway. The bartender had told him how to get there, and Don seemed to understand the directions pretty well - much to my relief! We both waved our goodbyes to the bartender and headed out of the door, and back to Don's truck.

Don put the music back on the radio, and we sat back and enjoyed the ride. We seemed to be driving down country lanes which reminded me a lot of my home town's surrounding countryside on the border of England and Wales, which seemed strange to me, as it had been the last thing that I was expecting the US to be like!

Eventually, we arrived at the main highway and saw the sign for Boston. My heart skipped a beat with the thought that we were actually on the road to Boston! I couldn't quite believe it, and felt like pinching myself to check it wasn't a dream! But again my mind instantly flashed to my Toronto friends, and I felt very sad to feel as though I was moving on from them. Then my mind flashed to my family and friends in the UK, and I realised I was missing them all too, especially my mum, it always pained my heart to think of her on her own, so I had to remind myself that she had other family and friends around her. I hoped that she and they were all ok. It was strange to feel so happy, and sad at the same time. I'd never felt such a contrasting mix of feelings before setting off on my travels.

Don followed the signs for Boston, and we had a nice chat about all sorts as we drove along. The roads started to get busier, and I felt that it probably meant that we were getting nearer to Boston City. I felt thrilled at the thought and wondered what it would look like. I wondered if it would be similar to UK cities, more similar to Canadian cities, or not like either. 'I'll soon find out!' I thought to myself with a grin.

At some point, the highway we were on merged with other highways, and I realised that we hadn't seen the sign for Boston in a while. I mentioned it to Don, and he seemed very puzzled about it too. After a while the highway got less and less busy until it seemed as though we were back on the country lanes again, so eventually we turned around and headed back in the direction we had come from. I started to feel my excitement changing into disappointment, and we seemed to be driving and driving, but getting nowhere.

Eventually, we got back to the main junction and saw a sign for Boston again. My mood lifted, as we headed off towards the direction of the sign. Don seemed happy that I was happy, and he wasn't showing signs of stress at the situation. He seemed like a genuinely good guy, and I felt as though he was simply being a good Canadian host to me, I felt as if he was acting as an ambassador of sorts, his words and deeds seemed very genuine, and I still didn't feel any bad vibes, or ulterior motives from him. It was nice to have a genuine friend. I also got the feeling that he was fulfilling a little of his wanderlust desires too.

BOOK 1: TO SEE THE WORLD

We saw more and more signs for Boston as we went along, so once again we relaxed into the journey. and sat back listening to music on the radio, but after a while, suddenly around the same time, we both seemed to notice that we'd stopped seeing the signs for Boston again. "What is going on?" exclaimed Don, sounding confused with the situation. We both looked at each other with confused faces and shook our heads, once again I didn't know whether to laugh or cry! "It's so weird?" Was all I could answer, as we wound up in a desolate area, away from all the main traffic and signposts and back on what seemed to be a quiet country road again.

So, once again Don turned around and headed back towards the main junction to try again. "This is just crazy!" He said, shaking his head, and sounding frustrated for the first time, I felt so bad for him, as he was mainly doing this for me, but within a split second, we both seemed to see the funny side, and we both started laughing. "If at first, you don't succeed…" Said, Don. "Try, try a hundred times!" I added, and we both cracked up laughing some more. "Or a thousand times!" added Don, and we both roared with laughter, as we started looking for Boston signs again!….

After several more tries, and for some reason simply not finding Boston, I noticed a sign for New York, and at this point feeling delirious with the combination of beer, fatigue, and laughter, I suddenly felt tempted to head there instead! That was if Don was game of course. "What about New York?" I suddenly said to Don, with a mischievous look of optimism on my face. "New York?" he asked curiously. "Well, seeing as we're in the US now, and we can't find Boston, then, why not make the most of it, and go and see New York instead!?" I said with a giggle. "Right!" he answered slowly while nodding his head as if seeming to agree with my fun sense of logic.

"New York it is!" he exclaimed, as he suddenly changed highway lanes, sped up, and started following the signs for New York. I felt a little sorry for him, that he'd tried so hard to take me to Boston, and I hoped he didn't feel bad about us not being able to find it, but it was not for lack of trying, that was for sure!

This time we saw New York signs all along the way, and the roads got busier instead of quieter. Don suddenly switched on his CB radio, and we suddenly heard lots of people chatting on CB radios all around us. Don picked up a mic and started chatting to some of the other truckers. I loved hearing all the different accents from the New York area, as I'd only ever heard such accents on television before, so it was exciting to hear them in real life. I felt as though I was in some kind of bizarre movie!

"So, what will we do when we get there?" asked Don suddenly. "Isn't it the city that never sleeps? There must be loads to do?!" I answered dramatically, and we both laughed. "…I guess we will see when we get there!" I added shrugging my shoulders. Don laughed and nodded. He seemed to enjoy my free-spirited nature.

We drove towards New York and found a truck stop on the outskirts of town across the river in New Jersey. Don parked his truck and we went inside the Truck-stop café. By now it was early in the morning, about two am. We ordered some food and coffee and I sat feeling in a kind of dreamy limbo.

We chatted about our journey, and how weird it had been that we couldn't find Boston. We joked and laughed about this for quite a while. At some point, Don stretched out his arms towards the ceiling and yawned. He slowly announced that he had decided that he would head back to Canada from the truck stop and asked what I wanted to do. Did I want to stay, or head back with him?

I suddenly felt totally confused, and not sure what I wanted to do, especially as I was so near to the world-famous New York City! How could I not stay and have a look around? I had the overall feeling that I had to stay, so told him that I wanted to stay for a couple of days, and check out New York, but afterwards, I would head back to Canada, and if his sister wasn't mad at me, and still wanted my help, I'd be happy to help!

He seemed to understand, which made me feel a lot better. He explained that he had some appointments lined up over the next couple of days and he didn't want to miss them, so it was best that he get back sooner rather than later. He added that if he'd had more time, he would have loved to visit New York with me as he hadn't been there in a long time.

He wrote down his sister's address and phone number on a small piece of paper, and added some more details on the other side about the best time is to phone. He also told me to call him any time if I needed anything. I thanked him and felt grateful that he was so easy-going.

We stayed chatting until dawn, and as the sun rose Don said that he would start getting back. He added, that if I wanted, he would give me a lift through the tunnel to the New York side and that he would take off from there. I thanked him, as this seemed like a good idea, so we left the restaurant and headed to his truck for our drive through the tunnel.

"We're now driving under the Hudson River!" said Don about halfway through the tunnel "Wow, I've heard of the Hudson! How exciting to think we're beneath it!" I exclaimed, feeling as though the movie I was in was turning into a dream! I still couldn't quite believe that I was about to visit New York City! I wondered if I would wake up at any minute and find myself curled up in Jeff's arms in my little bed in Karina's basement. My heart would have loved that!

Within the hour Don was pulling up his car to drop me off on the outskirts of downtown New York City. I suddenly started to get an anxious feeling that this was my last chance to change my mind and go back to Canada with him, but I kept calm and took a deep breath as he parked up his car.

I grabbed my rucksack and thanked him for the lift. He said I was welcome, as I opened the car door and we said our goodbyes. We said that we would see each other soon. I thanked him again and jumped out of his car, and was suddenly standing there all alone and cold as I waved goodbye to Don while watching his car disappearing off into the traffic.

'What the heck am I doing here?' I suddenly thought to myself as I realised that all I had to my name was the Rucksack on my back and a little bit of pocket money in my purse. I had no family, no friends, or even acquaintances to visit in New York City, and nowhere to stay! I suddenly felt full of fear and regret, yet at the same time a tiny part of me still felt excited to be there, these were more new conflicted feelings to me, which I found most intriguing!

I slowly strolled into the centre of Manhattan, and was amazed at how tall the skyscrapers were! I could barely see the sky in between them, just a thin blue sliver. The streets were very busy even though it was still early in the morning, and I was soon swept away by the crowds rushing about on the streets.

Once or twice, I tried to ask directions to an area I'd heard mentioned in the tropical paradise, it was called "Lafayette Square" and was in a part of New York known as "The Village" According to Paul and Lyn it was a really nice area, and they even had a friend there that they'd mentioned once or twice, and had told me to look them up if I was ever in that area during my travels. I couldn't remember the name of their friend, but I was hoping to find a similar bar or café to the Tropical Paradise, and that maybe the name would come back to me, or that I'd at least meet some kindred spirits to spend a little time with to help me get my bearings in the city.

I tried to ask people on the street for directions to get there, but each time I approached somebody to ask for directions, they just completely ignored me and kept on walking. It was the strangest thing! 'This behaviour is the opposite of the friendly people of Toronto! Surely, I don't look that threatening? - I'm a girl of seventeen with a rucksack on my back, and that's it! No weapons, drugs, booze, or even a menacing look! Just a friendly smile!' I thought to myself, as I walked along. Feeling a little hurt by their coldness, and not understanding why the people seemed so afraid to talk to me.

I suddenly saw a homeless man begging for money, and my heart went out to him, so I gave him a little change. I felt sorry for him. 'Gosh, if I hadn't been able to get any help all from the people on the streets of New York, what hope did he have?!' I thought to myself. He thanked me and gave me a sweet little smile. I felt a strong feeling of compassion rise up inside of me, and I suddenly wished that I could help all of the people in the world. 'That would be so wonderful, but sadly, I wasn't able to, I'm barely getting by myself! but at least I helped this man out a tiny bit' I thought to myself.

I walked along in a sleepy daydream, thinking about how the world would be paradise if humans made it into paradise! I wondered why the human race chose to create war and poverty, instead of peace and abundance. Obviously, all that the planet would ever have, was already in existence! I imagined it being like a giant ball of clay, and it was up to us what we chose to make of it.

I walked along pondering on these things, every now and then glancing up at the tiny slice of sky above me. I was in New York City, but I wasn't loving, or even liking it. It felt so rushed and hostile, and I wondered what was the point of living in such a place. I assumed that most people were there to make money, and then maybe move on to where they really wanted to be.

Eventually, somebody gave me directions to Lafayette Square in the village, and I strolled over there. I found a park to sit on a bench and rest. I hadn't slept all night and was suddenly feeling very tired. 'Oh well, it's nice to just sit and catch my breath!' I thought, feeling like I needed to rest up a bit. I took out my notepad to jot down some thoughts to later add to my journal and noticed that I had made a note of the building where Paul and Lyn had mentioned their friend lived in New York, but I'd scribbled it down, probably fast, while tipsy, and couldn't make much sense of it, other than Lafayette Square, The Village, NY. 'Oh well, at least I'm here!' I thought to myself with a sigh.

Once again. I felt lost and confused as I sat watching the people race by as if they had no time to stop for any person or thing. I didn't see any friendly-looking areas with people just hanging out and enjoying the day.

Everybody seemed in a rush to get somewhere! I missed my friendly, fun, easygoing friends from Toronto, and felt that maybe I had made a big mistake leaving them, but once again I reminded myself that this was all a part of my adventure! I took a deep breath and wondered what to do next. I suddenly felt hungry, so I found a nearby Deli.

I sat and ate my deli sandwich, and sipped on a coffee while taking stock of everything I'd experienced so far. My mind went back to my journey from my home town, which now seemed so far away in distance and time. Just then a guy in his twenties came and sat near me, and gave me a smile. This was such a welcome smile, after the hostility I'd experienced so far on the streets of New York. He overheard my accent as I thanked the waitress for the coffee top-up, and he asked where I was from. I told him I was from England, and we got chatting. His name was Joe, and he lived in The Bronx, New York.

I told him a little about my previous travels and explained what had happened with our failed trip to Boston which he found hilarious. He asked what I would do next. I told him I wasn't sure, and that I was supposed to head back to Canada and on to my next nanny gig, but as I was saying this, I realised that I was starting to feel very tempted to explore the States now that I was here! I had been planning to come down here at some point to meet up with my aunt Freda anyway, so why not get a head start? I felt as though I needed a day or two to think about things before making my decision.

I mentioned this to him and he nodded in an understanding way. "Have you got a place to stay tonight?" He asked, looking concerned. "No, I haven't planned that far ahead yet" I answered with a laugh. He laughed back and told me that I could crash on his sofa in the Bronx if I was stuck for a place. My mind flashed to all of the not-so-nice guys who had offered to help me out before, and I felt wary, but he truly did seem very genuine and he had kind, caring vibes, very similar to Don, and I didn't feel threatened by him at all.

I thanked him and said I might just do that as I hadn't slept all night! He seemed sorry for me and told me if I wanted, I could go and crash there now. I thanked him and said actually that would be nice! He said no problem, and to follow him. We finished our food and drinks, paid and left the café. Joe led the way to the subway, and we took a couple of trains to the Bronx.

Joe continued to lead the way to a rundown area of flats and empty lots of land, full of rubble and derelict buildings. kids were playing basketball at the side of some of the buildings, and it looked like a scene from a hard-knock movie. We went inside his building and up a few floors in the lift. Joe's apartment was humble but cosy. The sofa looked very comfy. Joe went to another room to get some blankets and a pillow. He threw them on the sofa and told me to have a good sleep "I Gotta go back out, come and go as you please!" he said as he threw some keys on the table. I got comfy on the sofa and fell fast asleep in seconds.

I woke up a few hours later, around four in the afternoon, and helped myself to some instant coffee, and a cheese sandwich, and sat on the sofa to wake up a bit more, and think about my current situation. I liked how Joe reminded me of my Canadian friend Don, and I was so happy to have met him, and grateful for his kind hospitality.

About a half hour later Joe arrived back home. He seemed happy to see me up and about. "You look like you've had a good sleep!" he said in a jolly way. I said I had, and I thanked him once again. He made himself a coffee, then came and sat down in the living room with me. "I hope you don't mind that I helped myself to a cheese sandwich and a coffee," I said a little sheepishly. "Of course not! I'm happy to oblige!" He said with a big smile as he sipped his coffee.

He told me he worked a night shift, so he wouldn't be home that night, but he was off work the next day if I wanted him to show me around. I thanked him and said that would be great! He made us both another coffee and came and sat on the sofa next to me, and put the television on. I felt relaxed with him as we settled back to watched old films and comedies, and have random little chats about various things from the movie, and from life in general. I still didn't sense any ulterior motives, he just seemed a genuinely nice guy, who was as happy to have a visitor for company, as I was happy to be there. When the movie finished Joe said he was going to take a nap, so I vegged out some more on the sofa watching TV, and thinking about what I might do next. Where would I go?

A few hours later Joe got up and rushed around getting ready for work. He checked if I was ok, and told me to make myself at home before he took off. I decided to relax on the sofa and watch television. It felt good to just do nothing, I hadn't done that in some time!

After a while, I got restless, so I decided to go for a walk and check out the neighbourhood. I put on my jacket, picked up the key that Joe had left for me, and headed outside. It was dark out, but people were still walking about. Some of them would nod hello as they passed, and I nodded back as if to let each other know that we weren't a threat to each other.

I walked down the street towards the main road. To be in an unknown city at night was a little daunting, but I figured I would be safe enough, as long as I stayed in the shadows, where I wouldn't be noticed by anyone with bad intentions. I got to the main street and decided to turn right just to see what there was to see. The Bronx had a whole different feel to it to Manhattan. It felt gritty, with a rough edge, but it was very real, and at least the people here were kind of friendly.

I was enjoying just walking around the streets in the dark looking in bars and cafes, and walking past apartment blocks. I felt as though I was in a dream, or some kind of ghost wandering around. Who would ever expect a seventeen-year-old girl from a small town in England to be strolling around the streets of the Bronx around midnight?

I passed what looked to be a small cafe, but inside a group of men were sitting around a small table playing cards. I thought this was kind of cool, and I liked the Bronx's spirit. It seemed to be a world unto itself! Eventually, I arrived at a giant stadium and got chatting to a friendly guy at a bus stop nearby. He was middle-aged and he seemed as if he was on his way home from work. I asked him what the stadium was called and he told me it was called The Yankee Stadium. I sat on the bus bench next to him and admired the stadium from afar, I had heard of it before, but I hadn't expected to see it on my little midnight walkabout!

Eventually, I got tired and found my way back to Joe's apartment. I used his key to go inside I made myself another cheese sandwich and poured a glass of milk. Watched TV until I got really sleepy, then crashed out on the sofa.

Around 7 am, I heard Joe's key opening the front door. I was still very tired from my walk-about and hadn't gone to sleep until about three, so I stayed resting with my eyes closed. Joe didn't disturb me. He quietly headed to the bathroom and a few minutes later I heard him open and then close his bedroom door. I turned over and went back to sleep for a few more hours.

At just after 10 am I woke up again. This time I felt energised, I wanted to go out and explore more of New York, and maybe even see some sites. I decided not to disturb Joe as he'd only gone to sleep around 7 am. I washed up in the bathroom, got a cup of coffee and some toast, and as I ate and drank I wrote a note to Joe thanking him for letting me crash, and telling him I was going to see some sites and that I would see him later. I left my rucksack next to the sofa, so that he would see I was coming back, picked up my shoulder bag, then headed out of his front door, and down the stairs and out into the street.

The Bronx looked different by daylight, but it still had the same gritty edge to it which I really liked. I loved that the US had such a real place and that it wasn't all shiny and perfect as it was portrayed in a lot of American movies. I found my way to the subway and caught a train back over to Manhattan passing through Harlem on the way, which I found cool, as memories of The Harlem Globe Trotters Cartoons, I used to watch as a kid popped to mind. It seemed to be a busy, vibrant area, and lots of young black guys were jumping on and off the train in a spirited and boisterous way, loudly laughing and joking, and calling out to people they knew.

Once again, I arrived back on the streets of Manhattan, where I suddenly realised that I felt like a tiny ant, surrounded by hornets, all of us trapped at the bottom of an oblong box, with only a thin slice of sky above to give me hope of better things to come. I wasn't keen on the claustrophobic feeling it gave me and wondered how the people around me weren't freaked out by such high buildings surrounding them. I guessed they must be used to it, but I wasn't sure that I could ever get used to such an enclosed environment.

As I walked along, I looked around for signs of community, but I still didn't see anywhere to just hang out with people. Everybody was just rushing around wearing grim faces, and they seemed to have no time for each other let alone for me!

I suddenly remembered The Statue of Liberty being a famous New York landmark and wondered how to get to it. I saw a newsstand walked over and asked the seller for directions. He told me that I would need to catch a bus, and then a ferry over to Staten Island. I followed his directions and eventually arrived at The Statue of Liberty! I was very excited to be there as this was very symbolic of the America that I knew and loved.

I walked around at the foot of The Statue of Liberty in a state of excitement, awe and wonder. I couldn't believe I was actually there - at the Statue of Liberty! My mind flashed to all of my travels so far - My family and friends in England, my new friends in Canada. All of the good, and bad people I'd met along the way. As these visions of my travels swirled around in my mind, I had a strong feeling that rather than belonging nowhere, I belonged everywhere! I was at the foot of The Statue of Liberty, but I felt on top of the world!

I noticed that men were working on the torch of the statue, and found out it wasn't possible to go up to the viewpoint in the torch, but people could take the steps up to the crown instead, which I decided to do. The spiral steps up to the crown seemed never-ending, and all I could see in front of me were the shoes of the person ahead of me as they walked up and up, and around and around. I noticed some little inlets on the side of the outer wall with seats to sit on to rest on. I decided that this was a good idea, so I took a rest about halfway.

I finally made it to the top of The Statue of Liberty and thoroughly enjoyed the view from the crown. I spent some time reflecting on where I was in the world. This was a dream come true, and I wanted to enjoy every second of it!

After a while, I headed back down the steps and bought some postcards to send to my parents and Aunt Freda. I sat down to write them nearby. I told them all where I was and suggested to Aunt Freda that she leave a message with my grandparents to pass on to me any news of her arrival date in the US as I would phone them from time to time, adding that for the time being I didn't have an address for her to write to. I posted the cards, then went on a walkabout some more.

I hoped that maybe if I walked around down side streets, and through parks, and random areas I would eventually come across some interesting nooks and crannies similar to London, which had been full of interesting places like Piccadilly Circus, Camden Town, Portobello Road, Covent Garden, Carnaby street etc... but sadly, I found nowhere of interest to me, just more streets full of busy hornets! I decided I would rather go back to the Bronx, where things felt more real somehow, so I found the subway and headed back over there.

When I got back to Joe's apartment, Joe was up watching television and was happy to see me. He asked me where I'd been, and I told him about my day. He said he would've taken me out, and that I should've waited for him! I thanked him but told him that I had felt restless, and just wanted to get going and that I didn't want to disturb him, which he seemed to understand.

He asked me what I thought of Manhattan, and I told him that I preferred the Bronx! which he found hilarious, I explained my reasons, and he smiled and nodded his head in agreement. I added that I was sure that if someone had friends in Manhattan who knew where to go and what to do it was probably a great place, but at face value, as an outsider, it was not so great!

"So, what made you go travelling from England?" Asked Joe, looking genuinely interested. "I just wanted to see that world!" I answered with a grin. "Yeah, but you're only seventeen, isn't it scary?" He asked, looking somewhat concerned for me. "Well, yes, and no! I'm just very curious-minded, and I like to write, so in some ways, I feel as though I'm some kind of independent anthropologist, conducting the social experiment of throwing a seventeen-year-old female out into the world with nothing but the bare essentials to see what happens! I'm both the subject and the researcher, it's great fun!" I said with a laugh.

"Too many big words for me there, you must be a brainy type too!" answered Joe, and we both laughed. "I don't know about that. I've never been interested in academics, I'm more of a creative type, I think?" I answered, and we both laughed some more. "So, what will you do with all this research?" asked Joe in a mock serious way, as if playing along. "I have no idea!" I answered, and we both cracked up laughing again.

"You're a trip! That's for sure! And you got guts! I don't know many full-grown men who would do what you're doing, let alone women, but a seventeen-year-old girl, that's something else!" said Joe, grinning and shaking his head in disbelief. "I just want to check out where I am!" I answered, with a shoulder shrug. "Yeah, most people check out their neighbourhoods and cities, and maybe a few other cities in the area, but the whole planet, that's dedication!" laughed Joe. "Hey, why stop at the planet!" I joked, and we both laughed. "I'll probably continue on with my travels tomorrow, I appreciate you putting me up though, it's been great to rest up and regroup with good company!" I said, with a smile. "No problem, you can stay as long as you want, I enjoy your company too!" answered Joe, smiling back. "Thanks, Joe, I'll probably head back to the nanny gig in Canada, hopefully, we can keep in touch though!" I answered, feeling bad to be moving on so soon. "So, don't you want to explore more of the US?" asked Joe, curiously. "Yeah, but I was happy in Canada, so it makes sense to be based there for a while" I answered, although, as I was saying it, I wasn't too sure if it was truly what I wanted to do. Once again, I felt torn and continued to wonder if I should just stay in the States and explore, now that I was here. I decided that I would make my decision the next day.

Joe had plans to go out and meet friends that evening and invited me along. I thanked him but told him I would rather stay in, catch up with my journaling, and get an early night for an early start the next day. He understood and told me to make myself at home and that he would see me later, or in the morning.

Joe was such a genuinely good guy, and for a second, I wondered if there was a chance that we could like each other, but my overall feeling was no. I really liked him as a person, and he was an attractive, fit, young guy, but I just didn't feel a spark, and maybe it was the same for him. It was nice to think that some people are just nice people, it doesn't always have to be about romance. I thanked him, and he took off with a smile and a wave. I had a nice evening catching up with my journal, relaxing and watching television, and around 11 pm I got my sofa bed ready, got comfy, curled up, and went to sleep.

I heard Joe coming in about an hour later, but once again he was very quiet and didn't disturb me. I woke up around six am the next morning. I was glad for an early start. I used the bathroom to shower and get dressed into some fresh clothes and then headed to the kitchen for some coffee and toast. I sat watching television for about an hour while I woke up some more. Afterwards, I went to brush my teeth and do my hair and makeup.

As I was getting my rucksack ready Joe woke up and came out of the bedroom. "Good morning," Joe said with a smile. "Good morning, Joe, I'm just getting my rucksack ready to leave!" I answered, smiling back. "I'll be with you in a minute!" answered Joe as he headed to the bathroom.

By the time Joe came out of the bathroom, I was ready to go. He asked me where I was heading, and I said I would head back to Manhattan and then I would decide. I told him that I still wasn't sure what I wanted to do, explaining how I was still feeling torn between exploring the States and being there ready to meet my Aunt Freda and heading back to Canada.

"Well, whatever you do, be safe!" Joe replied as he put his hand into his jacket pocket to get his wallet, he then opened it pulled out a $10 bill and gave it to me. "It's not much, but it may get you a little something to eat if you run low on funds" His gesture was so touching and heart-warming to me. I felt my eyes tear up a little. "Thank you, Joe, hopefully, I'll be able to repay you one day," I said, sincerely. "Don't worry about it!" He answered, as he wrote down, and gave me his contact details and a big hug. For a couple of seconds, I felt loved and safe, but instantly shook off the feeling, as I grabbed my rucksack, soldier-style threw it on my back, and started to march out of his apartment. Joe opened the front door for me, and as I left, he wished me all the best, "All the best to you too Joe!" I called out as I headed down the steps. I wondered if I would ever see him again.

Once again, I was back out on the streets of the Bronx. I headed for the subway and decided I would head into Manhattan, walk around one more time and see how I felt about everything. Hopefully, I would make my mind up about what to do once I got there.

I arrived in Manhattan around 9:30 in the morning and as usual, it was very busy. I walked around in a daze, not sure what to do. I felt as though I was waiting for inspiration to guide me. As I walked on in a semi-trance-like state, I somehow found myself in an underground shopping centre which I found interesting. I'd never been to a shopping centre underground before. I kept walking and went through the motions of window shopping, while still feeling completely lost and confused.

Suddenly the inspiration hit me - I would continue my travels in the USA. I knew this was the right decision, especially as in the bigger picture of things, my whole reason for doing what I was doing in the first place was to travel and see the world. Besides, Aunt Freda would be over at some point, and I would be ready to meet her, so why would I backtrack to Canada? 'Maybe because Jeff and the other good friends I've made are there, and maybe because I was so happy there, and maybe because I have the added security of a nanny gig lined up for me!' I thought to myself rebelliously, as my heart started to hurt a little at the thought of not going back.

My mind flashed to Don, and I suddenly felt bad for letting him, and his sister Jane down, I felt so torn between the two paths, but the feeling to keep going was just a little stronger than the feeling to turn back, so I hoped that they would understand. I decided that I would send a postcard to apologise and explain.

I had picked up a few extra postcards from the Statue of Liberty, so I found a coffee shop to sit down, write to Don, and explain what had happened. I asked him to please give my apologies to his sister, and to pass on my regards to Jeff and my other friends at The Tropical Paradise.

I hoped that by mentioning Jeff separately from my other friends, that Jeff would know that I did think something of him at least. I addressed it to Don C/O The Tropical Paradise and hoped that it would get there ok and eventually find its way to Don. I finished writing the card and drinking my coffee, then walked around the shopping centre some more. As I walked around the shopping centre, I suddenly wondered how I would actually get out of Manhattan. I didn't know which way to go to get back to the highway.

This seemed a bizarre predicament to me and laughed to myself about it. I decided I would simply ask somebody if they knew the way out of New York, 'How else could I phrase it?' I thought, trying to convince myself it was a perfectly reasonable question while feeling sure that I would start laughing in the middle of asking it, as in reality, it seemed such a ludicrous question!

"Excuse me," I said to a casually dressed man who was walking my way. I was relieved that he at least paused to see what I had to say. "Um, do you happen to know the way out of New York please?" "What do you mean by that?" he asked, seeming to find my question amusing. "Well, I want to get out of New York and back onto the highway so that I can hitchhike elsewhere!" I answered, trying to sound serious, yet at the same time, fully aware of how ludicrous it sounded.

"I've got the exact same problem! I'm trying to find me way out too!" Said an English-sounding male voice. I turned to see a young white guy, maybe a couple of years older than me, standing smiling at us both. He was also carrying a rucksack. I smiled back, and we both started laughing at our predicament, and the guy I'd been asking for directions started laughing too. "OK, guys, your best bet would be to get a subway over to New Jersey, because there's a truck stop in Hoboken where you can probably hitch a ride." Said that guy after giving our predicament some thought. I guessed it was the same truck stop where Don and I had stopped off. "Ah, yes, I think I know where you mean!" I answered with a knowing look. The English guy kept nodding and smiling, and looking hopefully at the two of us as we chatted. "Great thanks!" I answered. "Yeah, thanks!" echoed the English guy as we both turned and set off together towards the subway.

"What's your name?" asked the English guy as we walked along. "Della, what's yours?" I asked, curious to have met another English backpacker, in the same place as me, with the exact same predicament! "Dave, good to meet you!" he answered, as we shook hands. "So what do you think of New York?" I asked, curious to hear his opinion. "It's not all it's cracked up to be! I've been here a week, and almost no one has spoken to me!" He answered looking baffled. "Same! Well, no, I haven't been here a week, just three days, but no one would speak to me either!" I answered, and we both cracked up laughing.

"I get the feeling it's the kind of place where if you have friends to show you around and go to the right places, it's probably a great city because it has a lot going on, but as an absolute stranger, it's quite hostile, and I haven't really enjoyed it, although to be fair, I mainly mean Manhattan, because the Bronx was great! The people were really down to earth there. I met a guy named Joe who even let me crash out on his couch for a couple of nights!" I exclaimed.

"I wish I'd met Joe, I was staying at some dingy hotel!" joked Dave, and we both laughed. "So, how long are you over here for?" he asked curiously. "Well, I was in Canada for a couple of months, and now I've got a few months to look around the States, while I wait for my aunt Freda to come over. Then I'll meet up with her to look at some properties, after that, I'm hoping to carry on with my travels. Maybe Mexico next, then Central and South America... How about you?" I asked, enjoying chatting with a fellow backpacker. "I've got six months, and like you, I want to have a look around the States too. I haven't really thought about

Canada, or Mexico though, you must be a hardcore traveller!" He joked. "Well, I'm getting there!" I joked back, and we both laughed.

"So have you been hitchhiking everywhere?" He asked curiously. "Yeah, why pay money when you can hitchhike right?" I said with a laugh. "Yep! I hitchhike everywhere in England! Still takes guts for a girl though!" He answered, with a look of admiration. "I guess, but I don't see much difference really, we've still got to be careful whatever we are!" I answered, with a shoulder shrug. "True!" he answered with a nod.

"I trust my instincts. You can usually tell the dodgy drivers straight away, and most of the people who pick me up, do it for my safety! Or that's how it seems, do you get that feeling?" I asked, curious to hear about his hitchhiking experiences. "Yeah, you're right, you can usually tell if they're sound, and most people do seem worried about young people hitching, so it works in our favour!" He answered wisely, and we both laughed.

"So, how old are you?" I asked. "Nineteen, coming up for twenty, and you?" he answered curiously. "Seventeen, coming up for eighteen!" I answered. "Wow, only seventeen!" He answered, looking surprised. "Yeah, everyone seems to say that, but I don't know why. It's not like I'm seven! I'm seventeen, three years off twenty!" I answered shaking my head and pulling a puzzled face. "Fair play!" answered Dave with a grin.

"Hey wait, I've just got to post these cards!" I said suddenly, as I spotted a post office near the subway station. "Sure!" answered Dave, as he walked towards the post office with me. Thankfully the queue moved quickly, and my postcards were soon on their way to my family and friends in England and Canada. I headed back outside, and it was nice to see that Dave was still there waiting for me. "I'm ready!" I exclaimed as we headed for the train to New Jersey.

We jumped on the train to New Jersey and chatted about our travels as the train chugged along, I presumed, under the Hudson River. Dave had mainly travelled around the south of England, and this was his first overseas trip. He said that he had saved up some money, and just fancied a change of scenery. A feeling that I could totally relate to. The train stopped at New Jersey, so we both jumped off. Dave asked a station worker the way to the Hoboken Truck stop, and we eventually found our way over to there.

By now, it was late in the afternoon, and we were both hungry so we headed over to the Truck-stop diner and ordered some food and coffee. We figured it would be best to spend our time in the diner, while asking around for a lift. As we chatted, we both decided that we should head south, maybe to Florida as we both had the impression that it would be warmer, and more exotic than the northern States. This seemed like a fun plan, and we talked about what we each thought it would be like. We both envisioned palm trees, blue skies and sunshine, which would be a very welcome change from the freezing cold weather that we were currently experiencing.

Most of the truck drivers we asked for a lift were not going south so we just kept ordering more coffee and occasionally another order of fries to go with it. Around 10 pm a friendly-looking truck driver came in and sat at the table next to us. "Hi, are you heading south by any chance?" I asked with a smile, as Dave looked on eagerly. "Sure am, but not until six am, need a ride?" He answered, obligingly. "Yeah, that would be great, thanks!" I answered, feeling pleased that we'd finally met someone who was heading in the direction we wanted to go, even if it wasn't until dawn. "Frank!" He said as he stood up, and came over to shake hands. "Della/Dave!" we both answered with big smiles. "Mind if I join you with my coffee?" He asked as he turned back towards his booth to pick up his coffee cup. "Of course not!" I answered as I slid along to make room for him on my side of the booth. "Thank you kindly!" he answered, as he grabbed his coffee cup, and joined us in our booth. "So, I'm going as far as Maryland, where are you both heading?" He asked, before taking a sip of coffee. "Maryland is good enough for us, at least we'll be out of New York!" I exclaimed. Dave and I went on to tell him about our predicament, which he found highly amusing, and we all laughed and joked, about being stuck in New York City for days, weeks, months, or even years!

Around midnight Dave and I got very tired, and Frank told us we were welcome to sleep in the back of the truck if we wanted, but he warned us that it would probably be very cold! He explained that he only had room for him to sleep in the front sleeper of the truck. We thanked him, as the back of the truck would be better than nothing! He led us to his truck and opened the back door on the container, it was a very large truck, but it was empty, and seemed to be made of corrugated steel. It was now December, so the weather in New Jersey was freezing. We decided we would just try and take a short nap at least. We each found a spot in the truck to sleep. I curled up in a ball and fell fast asleep from pure exhaustion.

A couple of hours later I woke up absolutely freezing! I looked around the truck and saw that Dave wasn't there. I got up, grabbed my rucksack, opened the back of the truck door, jumped down to the ground, and quickly ran shivering from head to toe back to the truck stop café. I soon spotted Dave in the café and went to sit with him. "There you are!" I exclaimed as I sat down opposite him, still shivering. "I couldn't sleep in there, it was too bleeding cold!" He exclaimed, looking fed up. "Yeah, it was freezing! I don't know how I managed to doze off, I must have been exhausted!" I answered as the waitress appeared to pour me a welcome cup of hot coffee. I thanked her, took a sip, and hoped that it would warm me up fast! We spent the next few hours at our booth in the diner with our heads resting in our arms to give us a little place to drift off at least for a few moments of microsleep here and there, in between sipping on our coffees to keep warm.

Around 5 am we spotted Frank coming back inside the diner "Frank!" shouted Dave, and he smiled to see us both back in the cafe. "Too cold for you aye?" he asked as he joined us and sat down at our table. "Yeah, it was freezing!" We answered with a laugh. "Don't worry we will be hitting the road soon! Maybe you can get some sleep in the cab" he said with a smile. "That would be nice, thanks!" I answered while Dave nodded in agreement. "Have you guys had breakfast yet?" asked Frank, as he picked up a menu. "Not really, just coffee, we've been drinking coffee and dozing off on the table" I answered pulling a silly delirious face. "So would you both like something to eat?" asked Frank, grinning at my silly face-pulling. "Yes please/That would be nice thanks!" we both answered at the same time. "Order whatever you want!" answered Frank Generously. "Thank you! / Thanks!" we both answered gratefully. "No problem, I'll be glad of the company for the journey!" answered Frank, as if to make us feel ok about accepting his generosity. We all enjoyed a big breakfast and lots more coffee, before following Frank back to his truck. This time we were in the front with him he powered up the truck and drove out onto the road.

It felt so good to be moving again, after what felt like a very long detour to New York. "One of you can take a nap in the sleeper, and the other can take a nap on the front two seats!" exclaimed Frank, as his truck picked up speed. "Della, you have the sleeper, I'll be fine here!" said Dave generously. "Thanks, Dave!" I answered, as I climbed into the sleeper at the back of the seats and got comfy. I was so impressed that the truck's cabin had a mini bed to sleep in. 'What a great idea!' I thought, as I stretched out, and pulled a blanket over me. I was as snug as a bug in a rug and fell asleep fast. A couple of hours later I woke up, stretched out, and sat up to see Dave sleeping curled up on the front two passenger seats, and Frank quietly singing along to tunes on the radio. It was such a heartwarming sight and a pure demonstration of trust and goodwill between strangers. It reminded me that most people are decent and good. I decided, not to disturb them, but instead to lay back in the sleeper and relax, and daydreamed about my travels so far.

CHAPTER 15:

EAST COAST CRUISING

Dave and I had a good journey down to Maryland with Frank. It was great to see the open road again. Once again, I had the sensation of leaving the familiar and taking yet another leap of faith into the complete unknown, and I loved it! I loved the way all of my senses felt as though they were waking up from being on autopilot, alert and ready for the challenge!

We stopped at a cafe in Maryland for lunch, and Frank told us that he would be heading home from there so we would have to find another ride. As we ate, Dave and I chatted about our plans and Dave mentioned an historical fort in the area that was a place of interest to him. He told us that he'd decided to hitch over to visit it, and that he would maybe stay in the area for a few days, as he had always wanted to visit those parts of the USA.

He asked if I'd be interested in sticking around for a while too, but I wasn't feeling the same draw to the area as he was, so I told him that I would carry on hitching south towards Florida. We finished our lunches, then thanked and said our goodbyes to Frank, and headed over to the highway, as the café was low on diners so we doubted we would find a ride there.

We reached a crossroads and wrote down our UK addresses to swap with each other, and after a quick hug and wave, we each took off in different directions – Dave heading East, and myself Southbound. A feeling of sadness swept through me, as Dave and I gave each other one last wave. I realised that this was yet another friendship quickly made, and then gone just as quickly. Although I felt sad about this, at the same time, I was fully aware by now that this was just the way of the road, although I wasn't sure if I would ever really get used to it. I would just have to learn to live with it. I stuck out my thumb and soon found a lift with another truck driver.

BOOK 1: TO SEE THE WORLD

The Truck driver's CB handle was "Southern Gentleman" and he swiftly gave me the CB handle "Little Dimples" because he said that when I smiled, I had dimples in my cheeks. Something which I wasn't aware of, so I had to check the mirror and smile to see, and sure enough, I was surprised to see that in the centre of each cheek was a dimple! He laughed to see me checking for face dimples in the mirror, and I laughed too because it seemed so bizarre to have a facial feature that I didn't even know about!

He was a very nice man. and I got the feeling that he wanted to make sure that I was safe. I felt very happy, and comfortable in his company as he was very easygoing and mild-mannered. I travelled with him in his truck for a couple of days, and we had some great chats and laughs, and lots of singalongs to the radio - mainly western music.

Whenever I got tired, he would let me sleep in his sleeper bunk at the back of the driver and passenger seats while he continued to drive. Every time I woke up, we were somewhere completely different. I was amazed at how America seemed to go on forever.

The Southern Gentleman would often include me in his CB radio chats introducing me as Little Dimples. At first, I felt a bit shy, but I soon got into the swing of the chats and had a great time learning and practising some of the jargon "Breaker, breaker 1 9, anyone got a copy?"- Hello, can anyone hear me?"10 4 good buddy!" – Message received, and understood, "Smokey on the road" – Police on the road. "What's your handle?" – What's your CB nickname? etc...) It felt as though I had entered a whole other world, which I found it to be great fun, and I thoroughly enjoyed my time on the road with The Southern Gentleman.

When it came time for The Southern Gentleman to head west, he took me to a truck stop for a goodbye breakfast. While we ate The Southern Gentleman arranged my next lift with a trucker that he knew well, and trusted, he also warned me not to get lifts with car drivers, and advised that it was best to stay with the truck drivers only, because they were safe and that most of them, were what he called "Good ole boys". He added that the car drivers could be dangerous, and you just never knew who you were getting into a car with. I thanked him for his advice, and we exchanged contact details before saying our goodbyes. - Another short-lived friendship over.

The next trucker was a chubby middle-aged fair-haired man named Fred. He had a very easy-going manner, but he seemed a little shy and didn't say a lot. This was fine with me, as I could just relax back into my seat, and enjoy the scenery.

It was wonderful to see the small towns of the East Coast of America. They were so picturesque and had a quaint old-fashioned atmosphere to them. I bought postcards along the way whenever we stopped at a rest stop.

At one of the rest stops, when Fred popped to use the bathroom, I got chatting to a woman in her early twenties who was sitting alone at the table booth across from ours. Her name was Cathy, and she told me that she was driving to Florida in her car. I told her a little bit about my travels, and she said that I could ride with her if I wanted to.

This was great timing because Fred was about to head west soon, also I felt sure that the southern gentleman would approve of me getting a lift in a car with a nice young woman. I thanked her, and when Fred came back from the bathroom, I told him that Cathy had offered me a lift to Florida with her. He seemed happy for me, so I thanked him for his lift, and we said our goodbyes. "Give my regards to The Southern Gentleman next time you see him!" I called out with a big smile, as he was leaving. "Will do!" He called back, as he disappeared out of the exit.

My new friend Cathy and I got our bags together, popped to use the bathroom, and then headed out to her car. She told me that she was going to Tampa, Florida and that she would be glad of my company. She was very easy-going and comfortable to chat with although I noticed that she did seem a little anxious at times, as if she was tired, and the stress of her journey was starting to take its toll on her.

As we drove along chatting about this and that, at some point during the course of the conversation she told me she had family problems which had affected her badly, as she spoke, she took out a small jar of pills from the glove box and showed it to me, telling me that she had to take them to calm her nerves after having a lot to deal with the past couple of years. "They seem to help ease things a little!" She said with a sigh. "Well, as long as they're working, that's the main thing!" I answered, feeling sorry for how bad things must have been for her to have to start taking pills. After a while, we gradually stopped talking, and both sat back in our seats and got comfortable listening to music on the radio and enjoying the scenery passing by.

On one level I was feeling relaxed and carefree, but deep down, I was still feeling sad about leaving Jeff and my other friends behind in Toronto. Once again, I had to remind myself of the bigger picture, and the reason for my travels which helped to get things in perspective, but the sadness at leaving remained in my heart.

Eventually, we pulled into a rest stop to have a snack and a drink. "Della, would you mind driving for a while?" asked Cathy as we ate. "Um I don't know how to drive, but I could try!" I answered, optimistically, wanting to be of some help.

"Thanks, Della! It's an automatic car, so all you have to do is steer. It's easy, especially on the open highway!" she answered, sounding just as optimistic as me. "Yeah OK!" I answered, looking forward to the challenge.

CHAPTER 16:

FIRST DRIVE EVER… ON THE SUNSHINE SKYWAY BRIDGE!

After our meals, Cathy drove us out of the rest stop parking lot, and over to the main open highway. After driving for a few minutes, she slowed down and parked on the verge. "Wanna swap seats?" She said as she turned towards me. "Sure!" I answered feeling excited about the prospect of driving on an American highway.

We quickly got out of the car and swapped seats. Cathy explained to me that because it was automatic, I wouldn't have to do anything, but steer, which seemed like it would be very easy on the open highway. "OK, so remember, you don't have to do anything much, just steer, push on the gas to go faster, let off the gas to slow down, and hit the brake pedal to stop!" She repeated, as she took a couple of her nerve tablets, and washed them down with some soda pop. I nodded, taking it all in, and feeling raring to go!

I set off driving down the highway with the feeling that THIS was what adventure was all about! The highway looked long and never-ending, and wasn't too busy, within seconds I was driving along feeling like I'd been driving on American highways for years! "You're doing great! Just keep heading south towards Saint Petersburg, the place I'm going in on the south side of Tampa, I've been there before, a couple of years back, from the north side, but someone told me it's quicker to head to Saint Petersburg first, past Clear Water!" Said Cathy, as if I knew these places she was mentioning. "OK, I'll look out for Clear Water, and Saint Petersburg!" I answered, wanting to reassure her that I had some kind of clue at least.

Much to my surprise, after a few minutes of seeing that I was ok driving, Cathy got comfortable in her seat and fell asleep! I realised that her tablets must have kicked in! I felt so proud that she was trusting me to drive without her guidance. I drove along with ease, slowing down when necessary, and building up to cruising speed when safe to do so, it all felt pretty natural to me, and like Cathy had said, very easy!

After a half hour or so I saw signs for Clearwater and felt pleased that I was on the right track. I noticed the traffic was getting a little busier around us and assumed that meant we were getting nearer to the city of Saint Petersburg.

I carried on driving with ease. Loving the feeling of freedom it gave me, and feeling pleased with myself that I was managing ok, even with a sleeping passenger! After, about another half an hour or so, up in the distance, I spotted a very high narrow bridge that seemed to be going straight up into the sky like a rollercoaster, and I hoped that the road we were on was not leading to it!

I kept driving and tried to keep my calm as the road got busier with traffic. Soon I was surrounded by cars, and straight up ahead of us the bridge was getting nearer and nearer, and I soon discovered that we were right on course for it! "Cathy, wake up!" I exclaimed, starting to panic a little, but she was in a deep sleep. "Cathy, wake up!" I shouted again, as I started struggling to keep in the flow of the fast-moving traffic that was headed directly towards the sky bridge, but she would not wake up, so I had no choice but to keep driving, by now there was traffic on either side of me, and I didn't feel safe attempting to change lanes to avoid the bridge.

I soon found myself driving up and onto the bridge and doing my best to keep driving in a straight line, and stay in line with the flow of traffic. It was very narrow with only two single lanes for cars going in each direction. I felt that it was too narrow, and worried that I might scrape the side of the oncoming cars if I didn't steer the car perfectly straight, which was hard to do when feeling so nervous!

As the bridge was very steep, I felt as though I had to nearly hold my breath to steady my nerves as the car climbed upwards towards the sky. My heart was beating faster and faster, meanwhile, Cathy was still in a deep sleep oblivious to my distress. "Wow, my first time driving and I get this! Trust me!" I thought to myself, feeling in a state of shock and disbelief as the bridge seemed to go on forever. My instincts seemed to take over, as I took slow deep breaths, and did my best to keep on course, while I felt as though I was steering for our dear lives!

About midway across the bridge, I glanced into the rear mirror, and much to my dismay there was a police car right behind us! I suddenly felt lightheaded, and my heart started beating even faster. I clung onto the steering wheel tighter than ever, kept taking long deep breaths, and tried to just focus on the road and keep steering straight. It was petrifying, as by now we were very high up in the air, on a very long thin bridge trying to keep up with traffic, while oncoming traffic was speeding towards us in the other lane, and if all that wasn't enough, there was a police car, right at the back of us!

I could do nothing but keep going, and just hope we would be over the bridge one day! It finally started to dip down like a rollercoaster drop, and although it was still scary, it felt good to know that we were at least over the halfway mark. Every time I glanced in the mirror, I would see the police car right behind us, and the silhouettes of the two Policemen inside. Cathy was still in a deep sleep, and by this point, I felt it was best to just leave her sleep.

Finally, we were over the sky bridge, and back on a normal surface road again, but the police car was still behind us. I tried my best not to panic, to act normal, and to keep as calm looking as possible, but inside I was feeling stressed to the max! "I could do with some of Cathy's nerve pills right about now!" I joked to myself, starting to see the funny side a little.

Suddenly the police car turned off to the right behind us, and I let out a deep sigh of relief, and relaxed as much as I possibly could considering that I was now driving on outer city streets with many lanes of traffic, junctions, stop lights and even a few pedestrians here and there. We were no longer on the open highway. I drove for a little while more, before I spotted a good place to pull over and stop the car. I parked up and sat in silence collecting my thoughts. I couldn't believe what had just happened, especially as it was my first time ever driving a car, and in a different country to boot! I decided not to wake Cathy because she was sleeping so peacefully, instead, I quietly got out of the car and went to stretch my legs a bit, and sit nearby on a bench, to calm down and breathe in the fresh air.

After a while Cathy emerged from the car wiping the sleep from her eyes and sweeping her hair away from her face, I told her what had just happened, and she seemed to be taking in what I was telling her as she was slowly waking up. I told her all about how things had unfolded, and reminded her of how it was my first time ever driving - and suddenly I was driving over this extremely high bridge, in single-lane – two-way traffic, with the police right behind me! I added that it would have been scary enough for anyone, but for a first-time driver, in a foreign country it was absolutely terrifying! She, looked at me as if she was impressed that I had handled the situation very well, and suddenly we both burst out laughing!

BOOK 1: TO SEE THE WORLD

Once we had both calmed down and caught our breaths, she told me that we were now near Tampa and that hopefully, she would remember the way to the place she was going to. "OK," I answered, as I nodded, and smiled, feeling good to be somewhere sunny. My mind flashed to the cold winter streets of London, Toronto and New York as I looked around at the elegant palm trees, and open blue skies, and felt the warmth of the sun on my skin. Right then, I knew I had made the right decision to head south.

"Do you have a place to stay?" asked Cathy suddenly. "Not yet!" I answered with a laugh. "I'll be staying at a sheltered housing place, it's very nice, and lovely people run it, I'm sure they'll put you up if they have room" she answered. "Sound's good to me!" I answered with a smile, as we walked back over to her car and jumped inside.

CHAPTER 17:

TAMPA BAY - YOUNG BRIDE TO BE?

Cathy was finally back in the driver's seat, and I relaxed back into the passenger seat. She seemed to get her bearings quickly, and after twenty minutes or so, she drove into a lovely-looking residential area and parked up on a quiet street, lined with nice-looking, but modest, houses, and palm trees. We both got out of the car and she led us to a small bungalow and knocked on the door. A lady with a friendly face opened the door and invited us both inside.

Cathy introduced us to each other, her name was Janice and explained that I was her friend and that I needed a place to stay for a few days while I decided what to do next. Janice told me that I was welcome to stay, as the back bedroom was free and had two beds in it, so Cathy and I could share if we didn't mind sharing with each other. Cathy and I were very happy with this arrangement and thanked her.

Janice smiled and said for us to follow her as she led the way to a bedroom down a long hallway, and told us to make ourselves at home. We thanked her, and she left us alone. Cathy picked her bed, and I put my rucksack down on the other one "This is great!" I said to Cathy, beaming her a big smile, as I sat on my bed feeling happy with how the day was turning out.

"Yes, these are good people!" answered Cathy, looking just as happy. After we put our things away, we headed back out into the main lounge and sat down. Janice appeared from the kitchen and asked us if we wanted some coffee. "Yes please!" we both answered, in unison.

After a few minutes, Janice appeared again, this time with coffee and cookies on a tray, and joined us in the lounge. We all had a little get-to-know-each-other chat, and I found out this was a group home for people who were in between living situations. It was run by donations. There were six other people staying there who we would meet over the next few days. This was the perfect place to get my bearings and decide what to do next!

That evening I lay on my bed feeling so grateful for all the good people in the world and thanked the creator for my new temporary home. My mind flashed to my family and friends back in England, and up in Canada, and I realised that more and more I was feeling as though I truly was the "independent anthropologist researcher" in some kind of ongoing social experiment that I'd joked to Joe about. It was as if I was trying out different living environments like costumes, just to see how well I adapted. "So far, so good!" I joked to myself with a smile, before turning over, and going to sleep.

Over the next few days, Cathy and I mainly rested up and took things easy, as we both needed to rejuvenate after our previous road trip. One day I decided to go for a walk. Cathy was too tired to join me, so I said I would see her later. I strolled out of the residential neighbourhood and headed into what seemed to be a popular area with shops, bars and cafes, and found myself automatically walking into a rustic-looking bar.

There was a group of young people around my age in there playing pool and drinking beer. They all turned and looked over at me curiously, so I nodded, and smiled back at them, then headed over to the bar and asked for a bottle of beer. The bartender asked for my I.D., and just as I was about to make some excuse, a slim fair-haired guy from the group of young people appeared at the bar next to me. "Don't worry I'll get it" he exclaimed, as if anticipating that I may have a problem getting served. The bartender seemed okay with this and handed us both a bottle of Budweiser Beer.

"Thanks!" I said, with a smile, before taking a sip from the bottle of bud. "No problem, what's your name?" asked the guy, as he threw a couple of dollars down on the bar, and told the bartender to keep the change. "Della, what's yours?" I answered. "I'm Danny, come and join us!" he answered with a big smile, as he led the way towards his friends over at the pool table. "Howdy!" called out a friendly-looking blonde girl who was shooting pool. "Howdy!" I called back with a smile. "Jenny!" She exclaimed, as she reached out her hand to shake mine, after making her shot. "Della!" I answered as we shook hands.

"Sue! Called out the other blonde girl, "Jim" added the other dark-haired guy, as we all waved and smiled at each other. We were all soon chatting, joking and laughing, especially about our different accents! "You should come back to our place with us!" said Jenny as she came and sat down next to me. "…We're gonna shoot some shots, then go to a really cool dive bar, it's fun - they have good bands!" She added, enthusiastically. "Ok sure, thanks for the invite!" I answered with a smile. Feeling happy to have made some fun friends. We arrived at their house which was an attached bungalow, in a row of other bungalows, with another row of bungalows across the grass, at the far end, creating an overall L shape, that reminded me of army barracks.

Jenny explained that Danny and Jim shared the apartment and that she and Sue were just friends of theirs and enjoyed hanging out with them. She told me that there was another guy named Rick who also lived there, and he appeared just as she was telling me about him. He looked similar to Jim and had the same dark brown wavy hair and smiley face. He looked happy to see us all and seemed a little surprised and amused to see me, especially when he heard my accent.

We sat around and did shots of Tequilla, and had a great time before heading over to see the band at the dive bar. I felt very comfortable with these people as they reminded me of my Toronto friends, they were very open, friendly, and easy-going. It reminded me of making friends as a child - it just happened so naturally.

After the bar closed, Danny said that I could crash on their sofa for the night if I wanted, so I took him up on his offer. I hoped that Cathy, Janice, and the others back at the shelter wouldn't be worried about me and wonder where I'd got to!

The next morning, I asked Danny if it was ok to call the shelter to let them know I was ok. He said sure, so I quickly found the piece of paper that I'd scribbled the address, and phone number down on, and called them up. Janice picked up the phone.

"Hi Janice, it's Della, just calling to let you know I'm ok! I made some friends, and stayed over at their place last night!" I said, hoping that she and the others hadn't been worried about me. "Oh, that's good to know! As long as you're ok!" answered Janice, in her usual easygoing manner. "Thanks, Janice, oh and this is the phone number in case you need to get a hold of me" I said, as I read out the phone number. "Thanks, I've written it down. See you later!" answered Janice obligingly. "Thanks, see you later! Say hi to Cathy for me!" I said just before we both hung up.

After the phone call to Janice, I now felt I was free to relax and hang out some more with my new pals! Jim opened up the apartment door wide and suggested we all go and sit outside. We all stood up and followed him out to some garden chairs that were placed on the grass, to the right, next to a low-level garden table.

I sat down on one of the chairs and noticed that diagonally, in the bungalows over to the right, was a tanned, dark-haired guy sitting outside his apartment sunbathing. He looked about ten years older than us, but he was friendly, as he waved, and he came over to say hi and to see who I was, or so it seemed.

He sat down in a seat to my right and introduced himself as John, I told him my name, and we were soon chatting away. He told me that he was a paralegal, and I found him quite interesting to talk to, while the other joked around about some of their latest antics. At some point, somebody bought a pizza, and we were soon all sitting around eating pizza and drinking beers, with blues-rock music playing in the background I was enjoying the laid-back atmosphere, for sure.

John and I chatted away merrily, and we both got tipsier and tipsier, at some point, he told me that he used to be a cat burglar! "One of the best!" He boasted. "How the heck did you go from cat burglar to paralegal?" I asked with a laugh, finding the leap hilarious. "Oh, you know lawmakers and lawbreakers are two sides of the same coin, I just flipped sides!" He exclaimed nonchalantly. "Good for you! Cheers!" I exclaimed, holding up my beer bottle to clink his.

"Cheers, so what are your plans?" He asked curiously. "I don't have any! I'm just enjoying the eternal now!" I exclaimed tipsily, before taking a swig of my beer. "Well, if you want to stick around, I'm looking for a wife!" he said casually, and I wasn't sure if he was joking or serious. "For real, it would help cut my taxes, and you'd be able to stay and get residency if that's what you want, and of course, I find you very attractive too! How about you, would I be someone you'd consider as a husband?" He added looking like he was serious. "Gosh, I don't know. I mean you do seem nice, but we've only just met!" I answered, with a laugh, while feeling put on the spot, and not sure what to think or say. "Think about it!" said John, as he stood up, and waved goodbye to the others.

I pondered on his idea for a few moments, before telling the others about it. Their reaction was to drunkenly egg me on. "You should do it! You'd be able to live right here next to us!" Exclaimed Danny, "...and we'd all be able to hang out together and have a blast!" added Jenny. I laughed at their fun-spirited attitude, and how ridiculous it all sounded, but a tiny part of me started to seriously consider his proposal. "I'll think about it!" I answered with a grin.

As the day went on more and more friends of Danny and co joined us sitting around outside until it turned into a big party. By the evening, I was feeling totally drunk, and started to get swept away with the idea of getting married to John the former cat burglar / current paralegal! The more I thought about it, the more the idea appealed to me. 'Why not? We find each other attractive, and we seem to get along very well, so it wouldn't just be for practical reasons - we would be a real couple. It's actually a good idea, and everybody else seems to think so too!' I thought to myself excitedly.

"Hey, guys!' I exclaimed, standing up as if to make a speech. "...I'm seriously thinking that I should take John up on his marriage offer! I mean, we like each other, so it would be real, and it would mean that I could stay and hang out with you guys, and he would get his taxes reduced, so why not?!" I exclaimed drunkenly. "Go for it! You only live once!" exclaimed Danny. "Yeah, do it / Go for it!" exclaimed the others. "Cheers to that!" I exclaimed as we all clinked our beer bottles together. I laughed to myself, thinking how funny it would be to tell Cathy and Janice back at the shelter, all about my latest turn of events!

"I'm gonna go tell John!" I exclaimed as I strode over towards John's bungalow. The others cheered me on for every step of the way and fell silent as I knocked on John's door. After a few moments, John appeared at his front door with a white towel around his waist, as if he'd just got out of the shower.

"OK John, yes, I will marry you! So, what do we have to do?" I exclaimed in a tipsy slur, "That's great news! Don't worry about it, I'll sort it out, by the way, how old are you?" answered John looking serious. "Seventeen" I answered taking a swig of beer. "Seventeen?!" answered John, looking shocked. "Oh, this means we will need permission from your parents!" He added, looking a little concerned. "Oh right," I answered "Hopefully they will be okay with it?" I answered. Not really believing what was developing.

"Well, just tell them you've met a guy you like, and you need to get married to stay with him" answered John eagerly. "OK, I'll do that!" I answered excitedly. "Great, let me know how it goes, and we can take it from there!" answered John giving me a big hug. "Will do, see ya!" I answered, as I turned around, and staggered back to my friends who were sitting around staring over at us, as if trying to make out what we were saying.

"I told him yes!" I exclaimed as I arrived back to where my friends were. They all cheered for me, and Jenny cracked open a beer and passed it to me. "Cheers everybody!" I exclaimed as I went around clinking everyone's beer bottles. They all seemed genuinely happy for me, as they asked me how and when John and I would be getting married. "I've gotta get permission from my parents because

I'm seventeen, but after that, it should be fine!" I explained. "That's great news!" exclaimed Danny, as he clinked my beer bottle. "Yeah, we don't want to lose you, you belong here with us!" exclaimed Jenny tipsily. "Yeah, I do! I don't want to lose all of you either!" I exclaimed back tipsily, as I felt a genuine love for my new friends. The party eventually wound down, and I crashed out on the sofa once again.

The next morning, I woke up at about eight, and wrote a note to Danny and co to say thanks so much for their hospitality, and that I was heading back to the shelter, but I would see them soon. I wrote the phone number for the shelter at the end of the note, just in case Dan or one of the others wanted to call me. Then I took off.

Back at the shelter they were all happy to see me, and asked me about my mini adventure. "Well, I made friends with a lovely group of people, and then they invited me back to their house, and I was having so much fun, I just stayed for a couple of days, oh, and I'm getting married!" I announced with a big smile. "Wow, you move fast!" Said Cathy, cracking up with laughter, as we all roared with laughter at her response. Soon they were all congratulating me and wishing me well, as they seemed to understand that this was an overall good idea.

I explained I would need my parent's permission first, and I asked if they had any writing paper so that I could write to my mum and dad to explain things. Janice headed over to a nearby cupboard and passed me some writing paper, an envelope and a pen. "Thanks, Janice!" I exclaimed as I headed to the dining table to write the letters to my parents.

I sat at the table and wrote my letters explaining things. I didn't go into details, I decided it was best to take John's advice, and just tell them that I'd met a guy I liked, and we wanted to get married so that I could stay with him. I figured that my parents knew me well enough to trust me to make such decisions, and hoped that they would give their consent. I finished off the letter by asking how everyone was doing.

Just as I was finishing writing out their addresses on the envelopes Janice appeared, and told me that she would be running some errands in town the next morning, and would post the letters for me if I wanted. "Thanks, Janice! How much do you need for the stamps?" I asked. "Don't worry about it!" She answered as she took the letters off me, and put them on the cupboard shelf ready for morning.

They all seemed truly happy for me, and once again my heart was warmed by this welcoming American spirit, it was similar to the hospitality that I'd experienced in Toronto, so to be experiencing it again in Florida, I wondered if it was because they had descended from immigrants themselves, so maybe they wanted to extend the hospitality to people who were in a similar boat as they had once been in – Exploring pioneers from faraway lands, or maybe they were just good people? Either way, I felt very welcome and was impressed by their kind and generous ways.

Later that day I went over to visit John. As I walked over to his house, I wondered if we would both still feel the same about getting married, now that we had sobered up, I imagined that John too was sober at this time of day, and I was curious to see what would happen. I arrived at the bungalow complex and spotted John sitting sunbathing outside his apartment again. He glanced up and looked very happy to see me. "Hey Della, I have some forms for you to send to your parents to sign!" He exclaimed as he jumped up to give me a welcome hug.

"OK, thanks!" I answered, feeling as if on some level, I was just going along with things for the fun of it, as if curious to see how far we would take things. I told him I would add them to the letter I'd already written to my mum, as it wouldn't be posted until the next day when Janice ran her errands. "Hopefully they'll be ok with things, and sign the papers, I guess we'll soon find out!" I said with a grin. "Take a seat! Want some lemonade?" said John, as he started to head inside his house. "Yeah, thanks!" I answered, thinking a lemonade would be nice. He soon returned with a tray, carrying a jug of fresh lemonade, and two glasses, and sat down on the chair next to mine, and poured us both a drink. "Thanks!" I said as I took a sip of the delicious cold lemonade.

We chatted about our life plans in general, and about how we felt about each other. We determined that we did find each other attractive, so we figured that we could spend the time between the present, and the wedding as a kind of courtship phase to get to know each other better. "Well, I guess I'll head back to the shelter, say hi to the others for me if you see them!" I said, as I finished off my drink, and stood up to leave. There was no sign of Danny and co outside his apartment, and I assumed they were out at work, school, or playing pool. "Will do!" answered John, standing up to give me a hug. "See ya! Thanks for the lemonade!" I called out, as I took off.

I arrived back at the shelter and said hi to Cathy, Janice and the others who were all enjoying sitting out on the front porch. I headed over to the cupboard and picked up the letter for my mum, took it to the kitchen, where I was able to steam it open and put the forms that John had given me inside them.

I spotted some Sellotape in a tray of bits and bobs, so reinforced the envelopes with it, before putting the letters back on the cupboard shelf, ready for Janice to take with her the next morning. I wondered what my parents would make of it all, and had to laugh at the thought.

That evening, I spent some time with Cathy and Janice on the porch, just enjoying their company, and chatting about our lives in general. After a while, I headed to the bedroom alone and spent some time catching up with my journal. By now, I had fully sobered up from the night before, and although I was still feeling excited at the prospect of a brand new life in Florida, I started to wonder what had made me go along with the idea of getting married to John so easily? After all, I had turned down potential relationships with Bruno, and Jeff, who were two guys I had really liked, in order to keep on travelling, so what was so different now? Then it hit me - it was the SUN!

I suddenly realised that I had seemed to come fully alive in Florida, which I was sure was due to the gorgeous sunshine, blue skies, and laid-back people! It was a moment of self-discovery, as I realised that I'd never experienced life in a tropical climate before arriving in Florida. 'Yeah, but surely I can't base my relationships on the level of sunshine in the area?' I thought to myself with a chuckle, as I lay back on my bed to have a good think about everything. As I lay there, I started to remember the whole point of my travels was to see the world, and not to get stuck in a relationship, never mind a marriage! I suddenly remembered that I was supposed to be meeting up with my aunt Freda at some point too, and I was pretty sure that Florida wasn't on her itinerary! I felt as though I was being ruthlessly vacuumed away from my dream life in Florida, and back to the reality of my world travels.

'Damn, what do I do now? Do I stay here with John, and see how things work out, and maybe I'll continue on with my travels at some point down the line, or maybe John will want to travel with me? Or is THIS the end of the line?! But what about Aunt Freda?!" I thought, suddenly feeling a sense of panic and absolute confusion rising inside of me. 'I barely know John! What the heck was I thinking, agreeing to get married to him on a drunken whim, just so that I could hang out and get drunk with a bunch of fellow teenagers!' I started to laugh at the craziness of the idea.

My mind flashed to Jeff back in Toronto and I felt the usual butterflies he always gave me. 'Damn, if I'm going to marry anyone it should be Jeff! Not some random former cat burglar in Tampa!' I thought, shaking my head, and laughing to myself, at how ridiculous it all seemed now that I was sober. I lay there some more, just mulling things over, weighing up the pros and cons of leaving, vs the pros and cons of staying, and thinking about how John was quite nice and attractive, and how good it was that the attraction was mutual. I thought about my lovely new friends, and how fun they made the idea of me and John marrying sound. I thought about how gorgeous the weather was, and how good I felt living there, and suddenly I realised, that I wasn't sure of what I wanted to do, so I decided to go for a walk around the block, to clear my head instead!

By the time I got back from my walk, I'd decided that the next morning I would go and have another chat with John about the marriage. I wanted to be sure that we had genuine potential as a couple, as the more sober I was, the more I had the feeling of being swept away with something, that I wasn't one hundred per cent sure of, but at the same time, I didn't want to regret turning down, what could be a wonderful, life-changing opportunity! - I just wasn't sure what to make of it all!

The next day I headed back to Johns, and we had a serious chat about everything. The more we chatted, the more it did seem as if we did have a good chance of things working out between us. We hadn't known each other long, but we did like each other, we got along well, and hopefully, our feelings would continue to grow, so we both decided, why not give it a go! - The sunshine seemed to make anything feel possible! Within the next couple of weeks, I received a letter from my mum, along with the signed forms. She told me that she and my dad were okay with it, as they trusted me to do what was right! I'd had a feeling that would be their response, and I felt proud of their trust in me.

I headed over to tell John the news, and we pencilled in a date for our marriage on the Calander for a few weeks time. I wrote back to thank my mum and dad, and to tell them a little more about my recent travels, and my new friends in Tampa. As I was writing my letter, I realised that my journal was almost full, so I decided to post it to her with my letter and asked her to put it with my stuff at home for safekeeping.

I decided to wrap up my journal first, as I wanted to keep it private, for the time being. It was an A4 notebook, so it was quite large, and meant that I had to go and buy some wrapping paper, and a large envelope for it, before posting it to my mum. After it was posted, I went back to the stationary store and bought a new A4 notebook, a smaller notebook, and a couple of pens to continue on with my journaling. It had become one of my favourite hobbies and seemed to help me to keep things in perspective. I looked forward to filling up my new journal, with new adventures - of my married life in Florida!

Over the next few days, John suggested that I move from the shelter into his apartment, which seemed like a good idea, although I reminded John that I would like to still keep things platonic for now, during our getting-to-know-each-other phase, as I didn't want to rush anything. I figured that if our friendship hadn't blossomed into romance by the time the wedding date rolled around, we could simply cancel the wedding, what did we have to lose? He seemed ok with the suggestion and agreed that it was good not to rush into things. He told me I was welcome to sleep on the sofa, or on his extra-large water bed, so I chose the sofa.

The first few days of my stay at John's were fine, and we had a fun time hanging out with Dan and our friends next door. All was going well, until one night when John got drunk and made an aggressive pass at me. I had to use all my strength to fight him off. Thankfully, he was so drunk that he soon staggered off to bed, and passed out. I instinctively wanted to get away from him as quickly as possible, as I didn't trust him anymore. All of my dreams of living a happily married life in Florida disintegrated in an instant! So, feeling shaken and upset, I planned my getaway!

I quietly packed my rucksack, then sat on the sofa waiting for first light. As soon as I saw a hint of sunshine outside, I grabbed my rucksack, threw it on my back, and hurriedly tiptoed out of the front door, I quietly closed the door behind me, and just ran for it! I felt really sad to once again be leaving my new friends behind, but after John's physical attack, I just didn't feel safe with him, and the idea of even a romance developing with him had completely disappeared, let alone a marriage!

CHAPTER 18:

ON THE ROAD AGAIN!

I ran for quite a long time, with a strong feeling of escaping from a potentially harmful situation. Eventually, I slowed my pace down to a walk and walked until I found a highway sign. I headed over towards the entrance to it and stuck out my thumb. Just then one of the guys that had been at a few of Danny's parties, came walking down the street towards me. "Howdy!" He said with a smile. "Howdy! Mike right?" I said, smiling back. "Yep, Della right?" He answered, with a grin. "Yep, that's me, so where are you off to?" I asked curious to see one of the party crowd out and about so early.

I'm gonna hitchhike south and look for some work, I heard they need help cutting and selling Christmas trees down in Fort Lauderdale!" he answered optimistically. "I'm hitchhiking too! Not sure where yet, I just felt it was time to move on!" I answered, not wanting to talk about John's attack on me. "Come along with me if you like. My girlfriend was gonna come, but she's got stuff to do, and I know she wouldn't mind, she met you at Dan's a couple of times and she likes you!" He said warmly. "Oh right, Lisa, isn't it?" I asked, suddenly remembering seeing Mike with a slim ginger-haired girl a couple of times at Dan's. "Yeah, that's right!" answered Mike with a smile. "Oh, yeah, she's really nice too!" I answered, remembering that although we didn't chat with each other much, we always gave each other a little wave or smile whenever we spotted each other.

"Sounds good to me!" I answered with a smile. "Great, let's go!" answered Mike, as we both shifted our positions and stuck out our thumbs. "So how long have you known Danny?" I asked, curious to know his background with Mike and co. "Oh me and Dan go way back! I've known him since we both started high school!" answered Mike, as a pick-up truck slowed down to pick us up. "Oh, that's nice!" I answered as we ran towards the pickup truck.

"Hi, ya heading anywhere near Fort Lauderdale?" asked Mike, as he opened the pickup truck's passenger door. "I can get you down to Fort Myers!" answered the older-looking country gentleman. "That's great thanks!" answered Mike, as he beamed a smile at me, and we both climbed inside the pickup truck. "Thanks, what's your name?" I said once we got comfy in our seats. "Jack, but most people call me Jackie!" He answered, reaching out a hand to shake. "Hi Jackie, I'm Della, and that's Mike!" I answered as we all shook hands. "Is that an English accent I hear?" Jackie asked, as he got the car in gear, and then took off down the highway. "From me of Mike?" I joked, and we all laughed.

"I'd love to visit the old country one day! It sounds beautiful, except for the rain, is it true it rains all the time there?" asked Jackie as we glided along. "Well, it doesn't rain every day, but it does rain a lot!" I answered with a nod. "I'll have to go in the summertime then!" answered Jackie wistfully. "Well, it rains in the summertime too, but the rain is a little warmer then at least!" I joked.

"I'll bear that in mind!" answered Jackie with a laugh. "…So what kind of music do you kids like?" he added, as he switched on the radio. "Rock/All sorts!" answered Mike and I at the same time. "Rock it is then!" answered Jackie, as he turned the dial until some rock music blasted out. "Better turn that down!" chuckled Jackie, as he adjusted the volume, and we all stopped chatting and sat back in our seats to listen to the music and watch Florida whizz by.

After a couple of hours, I spotted signs for Fort Myers, and Jackie was soon pulling into a truck stop parking lot. We all jumped out and headed to the diner. "Order whatever you want!" said Jackie generously. "Thanks/Thank you!" we answered, as we went about studying the menus. We were soon all enjoying eggs over easy with hashbrowns, toast, and coffee.

"What's Grits?" I asked, after I'd finished eating, and picked up the menu for something to read while the others finished eating. The guys both laughed and looked at each other as if they weren't sure how to answer. "Well, it's kinda like oatmeal, but it's made from corn maize" answered Jackie, as he finished the last of his food. "I've never liked Grits!" exclaimed Mike, as he finished his food, and slid his plate away. "Oh, that sounds tasty to me!" I answered. "Yeah, I like Grits! You'll have to try them sometime!" answered Jackie, as he looked like he was getting ready to get up and go. "Well, I'm gonna get going, you kids be safe now, ya hear me? Here's a couple of bucks towards your trip, and hold on I'll write my number down in case you need to call me" Said Jackie and he put a couple of dollars down on the table and looked around for a pen. "Can I borrow your pen please?" he asked a waitress as she passed by. "Sure thing hun!" she answered obligingly as she handed her pen over.

Jackie scribbled his name and number on a napkin and slid it next to the dollars on the table. "Call me if you get stuck or need anything!" He exclaimed as he passed the pen back over to the waitress who was by now clearing the table next to ours. "We will, thanks so much! / Thank you kindly!" answered Mike and I, as we each took a dollar, and Mike slid the phone number my way. "No problem! Good luck kids!" answered Jackie as he took off towards the cash register to pay. "See ya!/Bye now!" Mike and I called out, as Jackie gave us one last wave after paying. "More Coffee?" asked the waitress, appearing back with a pot full of steaming fresh coffee. "Oh yes please /Sure!" answered Mike and me eagerly. The waitress filled our cups, and we sat back to relax for a while and enjoyed a little getting to know each other some more chat.

After a while of chatting, I told him what had happened with John, as it felt good to have someone to talk to about the incident. "I've never trusted that guy, I'm sure he's some kind of con man!" exclaimed Mike angrily. "Yeah, I thought he was ok and quite likeable at first, but now I feel like he manipulated me into nearly marrying him!" I answered, feeling as though I was finally coming out of some kind of spell that John had put on me. "Oh yeah, he's smooth, and all the kids like him and look up to him, but I've never really liked him!" answered Mike passionately, and it felt good to have someone on my side. "At least I found out sooner, rather than later!" I exclaimed. "Yep, count your lucky stars!" answered Mike, with a knowing smile.

After we finished our coffees, we asked around in the café for a lift southeast to Fort Lauderdale, but nobody was heading that way, so we strolled over to the highway and started to hitchhike again. "We may as well walk a little as we hitch!" exclaimed Mike, as we both started to slowly walk alongside of the quite county road. "Yeah, it's nice to walk a bit!" I answered. "Sure! Watch out for the Alligators though!" answered Mike, with a laugh. "The what?!" I asked, not sure if he was joking or not. "The Alligators! We're coming up on "Alligator Alley" right about now!" answered Mike, with a mischievous grin. "Oh my god, really?! What, so there are actual Alligators just strolling around here?" I asked, sort of believing him, but not wanting it to be true. "Pretty much!" he answered, still grinning. "Well, I hope we get a lift soon then!" I exclaimed, pulling an exaggerated scared face, as I glanced around me. "I'm sure we will!" answered Mike with a laugh.

We spent the next half hour or so, slowly strolling down the country road, with almost no traffic passing by at all, and of what little traffic that did pass by most of it was going in the opposite direction. One or two cars were heading our way, but the drivers just waved, as if to say sorry, but they couldn't pick us up. "They may be afraid because there's two of us, what if you walk on ahead, and I hitch alone, and when I get picked up I can ask the driver to pick you up too?" I suggested, as I was starting to feel fed up with no cars stopping for us, and tired from getting no sleep the night before. "Sure ok, but don't forget to pick me up!" answered Mike with a laugh, as he picked up his pace to head on down the road ahead. "I won't!" I answered, laughing also.

Mike headed off further into the distance, and I stood there alone waiting for a vehicle to come along. After a couple of minutes, I spotted a pickup truck heading my way, so I eagerly stuck out my thumb. Thankfully the driver stopped, so I ran and opened the passenger door. "Hi, are you going near Fort Lauderdale?" I asked the chubby, middle-aged, friendly, looking driver. "Sure am!" he answered obligingly. "Ah great, thanks! Um, my friend Mike is a little ways down the road, would it be ok to pick him up too?" I asked as I stood holding the door open in case he said no. "Sure, no problem!" answered the driver in a laid-back way. "Great, thanks!" I answered, jumping in the truck, and getting comfy in the passenger seat. "What's your name?" asked the driver, as he stepped on the gas, and picked up speed. "Della, what's yours?" I answered as we trundled along. "Nice to meet you Della, I'm Lenny" he answered, as he reached over to shake hands.

County music was playing on his radio as we glided slowly along, both of us on the lookout for Mike. "Gosh, where is he?" I exclaimed, not seeing any sign of Mike on the long road ahead. "Maybe he got a ride?" answered Lenny, as if trying to make me feel better. "I think you were the first truck that came along after he walked off ahead of me, and I don't recall seeing any traffic going the other way either?" I answered, feeling puzzled. "That is strange!" answered Lenny in agreement. "Yeah, I don't get I mean, where is he?" I answered looking at the vast empty-looking land to either side of us, and the long open road ahead. "So why did he walk on without you?" asked Lenny, sounding a little confused. "Oh, we couldn't get a lift for ages, so I suggested that he walk ahead and hopefully I would get a lift alone, and be able to pick him up when we got to him!" I answered with a mischievous giggle, feeling a little like some kind of trickster. "Oh, I hear ya, makes sense!" answered Lenny laughing along with me. "Maybe he went to use the bathroom in the shrubbery, do you think we could drive back just in case?" I asked, feeling that we should have seen him by now if he was on the road. "Sure, no problem!" answered Lenny, as he slowly made a U-turn, and turned around. "Gosh, I hope an Alligator didn't get him!" I exclaimed, suddenly remembering what Mike had told me about being near Alligator Alley. "Let's hope not!" answered Lenny, with a nervous laugh.

Lenny was very kind and drove all the way back to where he'd picked me up, but we still saw no sign of Mike. I felt terrible as if I had somehow managed to lose him! I hoped he was okay, and figured that maybe he had picked up a lift, or just hiked off somewhere else, but at the same time, I couldn't see how, because I was pretty sure that Lenny had been the only car that came along after Mike had left, so Mike's disappearance was a mystery! Lenny made another U-turn and started driving back in the direction that we were heading, but there was still no sign of Mike anywhere. We drove for several miles until we arrived at a rest stop and Lenny suggested we take a break for a coffee and a bite to eat. I felt I could do with a large coffee to keep me awake, as by now I was feeling very tired, and just wanted to curl up and go to sleep. I also thought there was a chance that we would see Mike there.

We headed inside the rest-stop diner, and I glanced around, hoping to spot Mike, but there was no sign of him. We found a window booth and sat down facing each other. "So, what will you do now Della?" asked Lenny, sounding concerned for me. "I don't know, Mike said they needed Christmas tree helpers in Fort Lauderdale, so I was just going along with him for something to do, but now I'm not sure I even want to go there?" I answered, with a laugh. "I hear ya, it's good to be free to go where the wind takes ya!" Answered Lenny, seeming to like my freewheeling sense of adventure. "I guess!" I answered, feeling exhausted from being up all night after John's attack.

We soon got chatting with another truck driver sitting nearby. He told us that his name was Franky and that he was heading northwest and that I was welcome to ride along if I wanted. This suddenly felt right to me, so I eagerly took him up on his offer. I felt that deep down I just wasn't so keen on hanging out in Alligator territory! I thanked Lenny for the lift and followed Franky to his trunk, and was soon headed back up north again. It felt strange passing by Tampa, and I felt the urge to get out, and go and tell my friends what had happened with John, and explain to them why I was taking off, but there was no way I wanted to risk seeing John again. I hoped that when Mike, hopefully, made it back home, he would tell them all what had happened. I suddenly remembered my parents had sent the signed marriage forms, and felt sad that I would have to tell them the wedding was off, but for now, that would have to wait.

BOOK 1: TO SEE THE WORLD

The next couple of days travelling north-west with Franky were a welcome escape from John! Franky was very nice-natured and kind. He let me sleep in the truck bunk behind the passenger seats while he was driving, and then when we parked up at a rest stop, he would sleep, and I would sit up in the Café drinking coffee. The servers and fellow diners at the truck stop cafes had a warm and welcoming American spirit which I admired, and I found that I was coming to love the USA more and more, as each day passed. When it came time for Franky to head home, he made sure to arrange a lift for me with another trucker friend of his before he set off. I felt safe with the Truckers, as they felt like true Knights of the Road.

My Trucker handle remained "Little Dimples" and on the CB radios, they would refer to me as such. I joined in on many fun, chats as I was charioted along the US highways, not exactly sure where I was going, but simply enjoying the journey! The truckers always made sure that I got a good safe ride with the next trucker, and I felt as though they looked out for me as if I was their little sister or daughter, and they all seemed to admire my adventurous spirit. One thing I noticed was, like "The Southern Gentleman" had, they all warned me against getting lifts with cars. They said that the truckers were the good guys, and they all looked out for each other and their passengers. They said that there may be the occasional lowlife, but most of them were good, whereas car drivers were too much of a gamble, and not worth the risk!

I spent the next week or so, zigzagging up the east coast with no particular plans, just enjoying the adventures of each new day as it unfolded. On route I picked up postcards to send to family and friends whenever possible to try and keep them updated on my adventures; Postcards from the US East Coast must have been landing on my family and friends' door mats regularly, with pictures on the front of places like; Baltimore, Maryland, Washington DC. Michigan to name but a few. In my first postcard to my parents, I broke the news that the wedding to John was off. I told them that I'd decided to carry on with my travels instead. I didn't mention that John had turned out to be a creep, as I hadn't wanted to worry them, but I knew they would understand.

One truck driver I rode with, named Ben, from Michigan told me that Michigan was where the Kellogg's cereal factory was which I found intriguing. He told me I was welcome to ride home with him to meet his family and spend Christmas with them if I wanted to. So I thanked him and took him up on his offer. A couple of days we arrived at his home, and I had the pleasure of meeting his wife Anna, and their two children; Dave and Jenny, who were just a few years younger than me. They were such a lovely wholesome family, and we got along instantly. I stayed with them for a few days over the Christmas holidays and enjoyed a home-cooked Christmas dinner, and felt privileged to be experiencing life with an American family, for such a special time. I wondered if my parents had sent any Christmas cards, and presents to me at Johns in Tampa, and I felt disappointed that I would not be receiving them.

After the Christmas holidays, Ben's family told me that I was welcome to stay with them for as long as I liked, which was so heartwarming and kind of them, but I just wanted to keep travelling and exploring. Besides it was way too cold up north! I wanted to head south again. The snow reminded me of Canada and the UK, and I recently discovered that I preferred the sun! I thanked them but told them that I felt restless and my feet were itching to move on with my travels. I wasn't sure they quite understood why I was travelling, but they wished me well, as we bid our farewells to each other. I wondered if I would ever see them again, while at the same time knowing that I probably wouldn't.

Ben gave me a lift to the nearest truck stop. I had no main destination, and spent the next few weeks riding along with the salt-of-the-earth truckers, going "Wherever the wind took me!" as Lenny had put it. I just longed for pure adventure and to live in the moment, I felt so alive and free and I loved the sense of my reality unfolding second by second. At times I would feel a sense of fear and vulnerability, at not knowing when I would have my next meal, or where I would sleep that night, but at the same time, I also loved the not knowing, because it meant that anything was possible!

CHAPTER 19:

RUCKSACK GONE - STRANDED IN NORTH CAROLINA!

One day while hitchhiking in West Virginia I became stuck for a ride. By now I'd decided to head west, as I felt I'd explored most of the east coast. I had a few offers of lifts north and south, but I didn't want to head back to the ground that I'd already covered, and I was feeling drawn to explore the west.

Hours passed by with no sign of any trucks heading west, so when a guy I got chatting with at the booth next to mine said that he could give me a lift west, I was pleased with his offer. He joined me at my table and we sat drinking our coffees, and chatting. He wasn't a truck driver, he was a car driver and was on a road trip for one reason or another.

In the back of my mind, I was remembering the warnings from my truck driver friends about not getting lifts with car drivers, and I started to feel unsure about what to do for the best. I was about to decline his offer, but then I remembered that I'd hitchhiked a lot in the UK, mainly with cars, so I changed my mind and decided to take him up on his offer. We finished our coffees and headed out to the parking lot.

I threw my rucksack in the backseat of his car and sat in the front passenger seat next to him as he drove off out onto the highway. His name was Ray, he was okay, but seemed a little odd, so I didn't feel totally comfortable with him, but I figured as long as I kept my wits about me, I could get out of a bad situation if one should arise.

Our conversations would come to awkward dead-ends, and I had the feeling that he wasn't used to socialising. Also, his awkward silence made me start to wonder if he was thinking of bad intentions for me, so naturally I became more wary of him, but at the same time, I wasn't afraid of him, as he just seemed to be a harmless odd-bod for the most part, and I felt sure I could defend myself from him if need be.

After a short drive, we came to a small town, and he pulled into a shopping precinct car park and asked if I needed anything. I told him that I was low on a few toiletries, and he kindly offered to buy them for me with his shopping, which was good of him. He mentioned that he could put it on his expenses, and led the way into one of the main general stores. He told me to pick out a few things, but nothing too expensive!

This seemed fair enough, so I conscientiously picked out a few toiletries, and showed them to him for the ok, before putting them in his shopping basket. He grabbed a few snacks and drinks and told me to do the same, which was very generous of him, and made me realise that he wasn't that bad, although I still kept my wits about me, as I was aware that his generosity could be an action to get me to trust him more.

We got back to his car laden with goods from the store. Both of our moods seemed lifted, and we once again took off down the highway, slurping on sodas, and munching our potato chips. The radio played middle-of-the-road tunes, and I felt a little more at ease with him, but I still had an uncomfortable feeling. After an hour or so on the road, he pulled into a motel car park and said that we could catch some Z's there. I had the underlying feeling that he may try something on, but still, I wasn't too bothered as I felt I could handle him if I had to.

The motel room had only one double bed in it, but at least it was large. I figured I would crash out with all my clothes on, and if he tried anything I would fight him off and get out of there fast. I made sure that my rucksack was near the door, and ready to grab if I had to make a run for it. We both lay down on top of the bed covers and as soon as I could hear him snoring, I allowed myself to doze off.

I was in a deep sleep when I suddenly felt someone trying to kiss me. I woke up and yelled "What the heck are you doing!" as I shoved him away. He mumbled that he was sorry, as I jumped up and headed to the bathroom locking the door behind me. I needed a few minutes to wash my face, wake up, and decide what to do next. I was ready to fight if I had to.

When I came out Ray was sitting up on the bed, all hunched over with his head between his hands, as if he was feeling bad about making a move on me. I still didn't feel afraid of him, so I sat in a chair nearby and told him I was fine, and not to worry about it. He apologised once again and suggested that we set off early, as we still had a couple of days before we would reach the west coast. I checked the clock and saw that it was 5.55 am and agreed that an early start would be a good idea. Besides, there was no way that either of us would get back into that bed again!

We picked up our bags in awkward silence and headed for the car parked outside. We drove for a short while before Ray stopped at a diner and got us both some breakfast. We ate and drank in more awkward silence, before hitting the road again.

Soon we were speeding along, having our usually dead-end chats, while middle-of-the-road music was back on the radio. I was aware of this being my only current reality, and hoped for a better reality down the line! Hopefully, I was on the right road! As the day went on, I got very tired and asked if I could have a nap in the back seat. Ray said that it was okay, so I climbed over the back of my seat, stretched out, and got comfy on the back seat. I still didn't feel afraid of Ray, he seemed more pathetic, than scary to me, and I soon fell asleep.

When I woke up we were parked up at a rest stop. I sat up bleary-eyed and looked over at the reception in the visitors centre, and saw Ray inside looking at a map. I decided to go and use the bathroom to wash my face to wake up a bit. When I came out of the bathroom I headed back towards the car, but there was no car! I couldn't believe my eyes! The car was gone, and so was my rucksack with ALL of my belongings inside it, including my passport! I only had the clothes that I was wearing - which were sweats, as they were comfortable to travel in. I stood there in absolute shock, looking around the car park hoping to see that he'd maybe moved his car or to see his car suddenly coming back into the car park.

"Are you okay hun?" asked a friendly voice, as I stood there in disbelief. I turned around to see the custodian of the rest station - A chubby round-faced, fair-haired, guy with a warm friendly smile. "I don't know, it looks like the guy I hitched a lift with has taken off with my rucksack, and all my stuff" I answered, feeling numb and in a state of shock. "Would you like to come inside, and have a cup of coffee?" he asked humbly, as if he was not sure what else to say. "Yes please" I answered, feeling on the verge of tears, as I turned and followed him across the car park towards the visitors' centre.

"Where are we?" I asked as we walked. "Virginia at the border of North Carolina" he answered, in a lovely southern accent. "Oh, I fell asleep for a while and lost track of where I was" I answered, hoping he would understand. "Oh, that happens! What's your name, mine's Billy" he answered warmly. "Della" I answered, still feeling as if I was in a state of shock.

Billy led the way to his office, poured us both a cup of coffee, and gestured for us to both sit down. "So what will you do next Della?" asked Billy, looking concerned for me. "I don't know. Maybe he'll come back once he realises I'm not in the back of the car. I'd been taking a nap on the back seat, so he might not have noticed that I was gone!" I answered, optimistically, while still feeling dreadful. "Well, if he doesn't come back you're welcome to come along with me to my mother's farmhouse a couple of miles away in North Carolina. She has a spare room, and you can rest up while you decide what to do" he answered, with a caring smile.

I was so grateful for his kind offer, and it warmed my heart that he was being so kind, especially in comparison to what had just happened to me, on top of some of my other not-so-kind experiences on my journey so far. "Thank you, Billy, that would be lovely!" I answered, feeling on the verge of tears once again. "You're welcome hun, would you like a magazine to read while you wait for me to finish work in an hour or so?" he asked, as he stood up, and reached for some magazines nearby. "Yes please, thank you" I answered, as I took them off him.

I spent the next hour or so half reading the magazines he'd given me, and half just staring at the pages and wondering if Ray would come back. I thought about all of my favourite things that were in my rucksack, my clothes and my gold shoes were now gone, possibly forever! Including the Rucksack itself, which had been one of my pride and joys ever since my dad Geoff had given it to me. I suddenly remembered my journal and felt so relieved that I had posted it to my mum from Tampa, at least it was saved, hopefully. I would ask her if it arrived ok the next time I spoke, or wrote to her.

Every few minutes or so, I would jump up and look out of the window, but each time there was no sign of Ray. I kept pondering on if Ray had taken off without me intentionally, or if he hadn't even noticed that I was no longer asleep on the back seat. I had no way of knowing the truth.

After Billy finished his shift, he drove me to his mother's farmhouse. We parked up in the driveway, and I hung back, as he entered the house to give him time to tell his mother about me. "Come in, come in!" Billy exclaimed, not wanting me to stay outside. "OK, if you're sure it's ok" I answered, as I followed him inside.

"Mom, this is Della, from England, she got left at the visitors center by a guy she'd hitched a lift with. He took off with all her stuff too!" said Billy, as he gently ushered me forward into the kitchen where his mom was cooking. "Oh honey, that's awful, have a seat while I fix you something to eat, are ya hungry?"

She asked, looking even more concerned for me, than Billy was. "Thanks, I am a little hungry" I answered as I took a seat at the kitchen table, feeling touched by her warm welcome. "There you go, have some bread and butter for now, and I'll be making some dinner soon" Said Billy's mum, as she placed a large plate of fresh bread and butter on the table in front of me. "Oh thanks, um what should I call you Mrs…?" "Oh, just Sally-Anne, that's my name!" she exclaimed with a little giggle. "Would you like some coke or another coffee?" asked Billy, as he went about looking in the cupboards for cups and glasses. "Coke please" I answered, feeling so grateful to be so welcomed by Billy and his mum.

"I'll show you the guestroom" said Sally-Anne, after I finished eating my bread, and drinking my Coke. "Ok, thanks" I answered, as I stood up to follow her. She led the way upstairs and opened a bedroom door. "You're welcome to stay here as long as you need to!" she exclaimed. Her kindness brought tears to my eyes, as I looked to see a big comfy bed with quaint old-fashioned bedding, and big comfy pillows. "Thank you" was all I managed to say.

That night, the rest of the family arrived and were just as warm and welcoming as Sally-Anne and Billy. Sally-Anne made us all a big dinner of mashed potatoes, meat, vegetables, gravy, and what Billy told me were biscuits, which were kind of like what I would call plain scones in England. I attempted to explain this to them, adding that what they call cookies, are called biscuits in England, but by the end of my explanation, everyone was confused, even me, so we just laughed and tucked into our food. Billy's dad was named Davy, and he looked like an older version of Billy, and Billy's younger Sister was named Annie, and she looked like a younger version of Billy's mum.

They were all very easygoing and made me feel completely at home. We all sat around the table chatting about various things, with the chat often turning back to Ray driving off with my stuff, as none of us could believe what had happened, and like me, they couldn't decide if he had intentionally left without me, or if he'd thought I was still asleep on the back seat? "I guess if he only glanced and saw my rucksack on the back seat in the corner of his eye, he may well have thought it was me?" I said, pulling a confused face. "True, but you think at some point he would have noticed that you were gone, and come back?" answered Billy, shaking his head. "Yeah, but maybe he couldn't find his way back? Last time I saw him he was studying a map!" I answered, and we all cracked up laughing.

Billy's family seemed to make everything feel all right somehow, and being with them gave me a strong feeling of security, as they behaved as if they wanted to genuinely take care of me, which was just the right tonic, after what I'd just been through recently. They were very wholesome and genuine, and they felt like an instant family to me. For the first time in a long time, I felt truly safe. "At least you're safe here," said Sally-Anne, as if reading my mind. "Thank you" I answered with a smile.

After dinner, I offered to help tidy up, but Sally-Anne wouldn't hear of it. I asked Billy if he had a spare notebook, or some paper and pen that I could have, and told him that I'd been keeping a journal of my travels. He found this interesting, and he kindly obliged and gave me a barely used notepad, throwing away the used pages, so after bidding everyone goodnight, I headed up to my cosy bedroom and spent the evening sitting up on my bed, leaning on pillows that were propped up against the wall, and jotting down notes on what had happened on my travels, since I'd posted my first Journal to my mum from Tampa.

 I was so happy that I'd posted my journal to my mum, as my other things would be a lot easier to replace than my stories from my travels, which I probably wouldn't be able to remember the details of if left to my memory alone. I wondered if, on some intuitive level, I had sensed that my luggage was about to get lost. I'd had precognitive dreams since childhood, so it felt as if it was a possibility at least, but then again, it had been nearly full, and I wanted to lighten my load. It would remain a mystery, just like the mystery of whether or not Ray had known I wasn't in the car when he drove away.

As I wrote, I had a strong sense that my childhood dreams of travelling the world were now an actual reality, which was mind-blowing, and made me grateful for ALL of the experiences I was having on my adventure, even the not-so-good ones! "It's all part of the adventure!" I thought to myself, as I put my pen and notepad down, turned off the bedside lamp, and fell asleep. As much as I loved Billy's family, and the comfort and security of staying there. I only stayed for a couple more nights, before deciding that I would continue to hitchhike west. It was as if I'd started the momentum to head west, so I had the natural impulse to continue on with it.

Billy's family seemed alarmed that I was planning to get going so soon, and told me I could live with them instead of going off alone travelling. They genuinely wanted to look after me and take me under their wings, as they saw me as a seventeen-year-old child, and wanted to keep me safe, but I saw myself as an intrepid world explorer and was itching to get going again. I was so grateful for their help, but I had such a strong desire to explore the rest of the United States, or as much as possible at least, as now that I was here, I wanted to make the most of it! I momentarily wondered when my Aunt Freda would be arriving, and realised that I no longer had her phone number on me, so I would have to write to my mum and ask her to send it to me once I was based somewhere long enough.

Billy and his family seemed sad about my decision to leave but slowly came around to accepting it. Billy's mother had previously laundered my travel clothes, while I had borrowed some of Billy's sister Annie's clothes, but on the morning that I was due to leave, I took a bath and put my travel clothes back on. I thanked Annie for letting me borrow her clothes, and she had said that I was welcome, and that I could keep whatever I liked. I thanked her and just kept a pair of socks, as I didn't think it would be fair of me to keep Annie's clothes.

Sally-Anne had made a lovely big fry-up breakfast as usual, this time with a bowl of grits on the side, which I was pleased to try. The grits tasted a little like corn-flavoured porridge, which I liked! In the living room, Sally-Anne had put some clothes, underwear, and toiletries together in a little pile, with a cream and pastel flowers zip tote bag next to it, and told me I could have them if I liked them. I thanked her, and as she had specifically put them aside for me, I didn't feel so bad about taking them. I was grateful to have some spare clothes again. The family also gathered some money together, and put it in a little purse for me, wrote their phone number down and told me to phone them if I ever needed help. I felt so touched by their kindness, and once again I felt tears come to my eyes. I thanked them as they each took a turn to give me a hug goodbye.

I headed out of the door with Billy, and he gave me a lift back to the main highway. I could tell he didn't like doing this, but I reassured him that I would be okay. He smiled and parked up for me to get out of his truck. "OK, Della, give me a call if you need anything," said Billy, as he leaned over to give me a little hug. "Thanks, Billy, I really appreciate how kind you and your family have been to me" I answered, as I hugged him back. "Oh, and I'd like you to have this to remember me and my family by" said Billy as he passed me a patch with "Virginia Custodian" embroidered onto it. "Oh, that's a lovely memento, thanks Billy! I'll never forget you and your family, that's for sure!" I answered as I took it from him while thinking that he and his family were genuine custodians and that I would always treasure the "Virginia Custodian" patch he had given me. I jumped out of his pickup truck and waved goodbye, as I walked down the highway that was heading west, and stuck out my thumb.

CHAPTER 20:

WHITEY CARSON - HAPPY TRAILS!

The first lift I got was with a friendly old truck driver named Whitey. He told me that he would be driving west for the next couple of days until Arizona, and then he would be heading north. This sounded good to me, so I accepted his offer and jumped up into the passenger seat.

Whitey was a lovely guy, and we chatted about all sorts of topics in a fun, friendly easy-going way, and we spent the next couple of days watching places like Memphis, Mississippi, El Paso, and New Mexico whizz by. The scenery was stunning! - from beautiful greenery and lush rivers to majestic mountain and desert landscapes. It felt great to be back on the road, especially with good company. I refused to let the bad apples ruin my beautiful world!

At night when I got tired, Whitey told me to feel free to climb into the bunk behind our seats and take a nap as he was used to driving way into the early hours before he would park up to sleep, so I would usually sleep for a few hours, and as he was pulling into a layby or a truck-stop, I would wake up, and jump back into the front seat, and we would have a little chat before Whitey would climb back into the bunk so that he could catch a few Z's too, and as it was usually still very early hours, around 3 or 4 am, I would get comfy in my seat, and continue to nap some more.

"Let's go get us some coffee!" Said Whitey as we arrived on the outskirts of Phoenix, Arizona early in the morning. He drove into a truck-stop parking lot, next to the diner. "Good idea!" I answered, as I yawned and stretched out, before opening the passenger door and jumping down to the ground.

"You must be a sporty type!" Whitey said, looking impressed by my jumping feat. "Yes, and no" I answered with a laugh. Whitey looked a bit confused. "I mean, I love climbing, swimming, hiking, biking etc... but I don't like competitive sports at all!" I said trying to explain "Gotcha!" He answered with a head nod as if totally understanding what I meant.

"How about you Whitey, are you sporty?" I asked as we entered the rest stop diner. "Well, I've been into lots of things in my time, I guess music is a big love of mine" He answered philosophically. "Ah nice, what kind of music..." "Good Morning, come this way!" Interrupted a friendly middle-aged woman with a big blonde hairdo, and heavy make-up.

We followed her along to a booth. She seemed to be swinging her hips every step of the way, which I found quite comical, I wasn't sure what Whitey made of it. "There you go sweeties, now what can I get for you" She said, as we followed her gesture to sit down in a cosy-looking window booth. "Well, Rose, to start we'd like a couple of coffees, right Della?" Said Whitey with a big grin. "Yes, please Rose!" I said, noticing her name tag on her apron. "Two coffees coming up!" answered Rose, as she turned and headed towards the kitchen area. I loved these American road diners, as the staff were always so friendly, and welcoming.

Whitey passed me a menu, and as usual, he told me to order whatever I liked. I felt so lucky to have met another lovely person. He and Billy made up for the John's and Ray's of the world for sure! I thanked him and went about studying the menu. "I'm gonna get me the full breakfast, and I reckon you should do the same, especially as you'll be hitchhiking on later," said Whitey, wisely.

"OK, thanks Whitey!" I answered, and we were soon both tucking into a massive plate of eggs, bacon, hashbrowns, pork and beans, grits, and toast! And the coffees kept on coming. I loved how at these diners the waitresses came around with a big jug of coffee and asked if we wanted a top-up every ten minutes or so. "What a wonderful country the USA is!" I thought to myself, absolutely loving the atmosphere, the scenery, and most of all, the people!

Whitey was very easy to chat to. He reminded me of a kindly grandpa type. He told me that he would soon be heading north, but he would drop me off at another truck stop on the other side of Phoenix, as I would be sure to catch another truck ride heading west from there.

We finished our breakfasts and thanked Rose. Then Whitey left her a generous tip, and we headed back out to his truck and climbed on board once again. As we drove along, Whitey, like my other truck driver friends, advised me to stick with truck drivers while hitching, and not to go with cars. I had previously told him about my experience with Ray, and he had pulled a face and shook his head as if to say, car drivers are bad news!

We arrived at the next truck stop, and he pointed out the trucks that were most likely heading west and suggested that I stand at a certain roadside spot to catch them, rather than waste time trekking around the truck stop asking for a ride. He explained that if a truck picked me up from that spot, then it was pretty certain that they were heading west.

I thanked Whitey for giving me a lift, and for his good company and generosity, and as I was about to open the passenger door, he reached into one of his boxes of personal items and pulled out a single record with a picture of a cowboy on the front. He grabbed a pen and wrote "Happy trails!" on the cover before giving it to me.

He said that it was his record, and he wanted me to have it, I wasn't sure if he meant he had sung the songs on it, or if he'd meant it was his possession. but either way, it was a lovely gesture. I took the record with a big smile and thanked him.

We said our goodbyes, and I jumped down out of the truck and started to walk towards the spot that he'd told me to hitch from. As I neared the spot, I turned and waved goodbye one last time, he waved back as he drove on by and headed up a side road. "What a lovely man" I wish all people were as warm, and kind as him" I thought to myself.

I glanced down at the record he'd given me, and saw printed on the cover "Whitey Carson Sings" and what looked like a picture of Whitey taken a few years earlier. "Oh, my goodness, it's him! He must be Whitey Carson! I thought feeling pleasantly surprised. I got my bearings and got ready to start hitching, with a warm feeling of love in my heart for all the good people in the world.

Within a few minutes, a large truck drove out of the truck stop and turned to head my way. I stuck out my thumb, and it stopped for me. I ran to the front of it and climbed up the steps and opened the door to see who the driver was, and ask if he was heading west.

As usual, I stood on the steps for a few seconds to check the vibes of the driver and to see if it felt safe to get inside. The driver was a friendly-looking Native American man, and his vibes felt very safe. "Hi, where are you heading?" he asked with a warm smile. "Hi! West!" I answered, not really sure exactly where I was heading. "OK, I'm heading west too!" he said grinning, as if he understood that I didn't actually know where I was heading, just that it was west! "Great, thanks!" I answered as if we had some kind of unspoken understanding of what West meant.

I climbed inside and sat in the passenger seat and slammed the door shut behind me. I now only had a small tote bag with the few clothes and toiletries that Billy's mum had given me which I placed on the floor between my feet. Although I missed my old rucksack, I enjoyed feeling a little freer somehow.

"My name's Al, what's yours?" He said as we were picking up speed. "Hi Al, I'm Della!" I answered with a smile. "Good to meet you Della, you're from England, right?" asked Al casually. "Yes, I was born in England, but I've been travelling for about six months now and I'm starting to feel at home everywhere!" I answered, with a laugh. He looked impressed and laughed along with me.

He told me that he had been all over the States on this latest trip, but was now on his way back home. "Shame I didn't meet you earlier, I could have gone with you!" I joked. "You sure could have!" He joked back.

I asked him about his life and his travels, and he told me that he had been delivering produce across the country for the past 20 years or so, since leaving high school. He told me that he was a Hopi Native American, and I felt honoured to meet him. He was very friendly and had a nice easy-going disposition, so I felt very comfortable and at ease with him.

He asked me about my travels I explained that I simply wanted to see the world! He didn't laugh like some of the others I'd told had done, he seemed to consider what I'd said very seriously and told me that I must be a very brave girl to be taking on such a task at such a young age.

"How old are you?" he asked curiously. "Seventeen" I answered. "Wow! You are a true pioneer, but one of the good ones! My people would call you a scout" He answered, looking impressed. "Oh, nice! I like that description!" I answered with a smile, and we both laughed. Al switched on the radio, to a country blues channel, and soon we were enjoying the music and the scenery we were passing through.

Al told me that his home was in a place called Redlands, California and that the journey would take about five hours or so, adding that I was welcome to come along and meet his family, and even stay for a while if I wanted to. "My family would love to meet you!" he said warmly. "Thank you, I'd love to meet them too!" I answered, once again, my heart touched by the kindness of the American people, and being that Al was a Native American this felt all the more special.

As we drove along, he opened up a pack of cigarettes and offered me one. Aside from a few light puffs on a cigarette with Janie in Toronto, when I was hungover, I had quit smoking over a year ago. I'd noticed that a lot of the truck drivers smoked cigarettes, and I suddenly thought 'Why not, it's something to do, if you can't beat 'em, join 'em!!'

"OK, thanks Al" I replied, as I accepted his offer. He flicked his lighter to light my cigarette first, and then he lit his. Within seconds I felt dizzy and started to cough. "New to smoking?" asked Al, looking a little concerned. "New again!" I answered with a laugh. "Ah!" he answered, seeming to understand what I meant and nodded knowingly. Despite feeling dizzy and coughing, I enjoyed the cigarette, although I hoped that it would just be an occasional thing, as I didn't want to get addicted again!

As we drove along the highways, I realised that not long after Whitey and I had reached the El Paso area of Texas, I'd been mainly travelling through desert land, and I loved it! I admired the magnificent other-worldly landscapes and rock formations set against the blue sky. 'What a beautiful country!' I thought to myself as we glided along. I felt so happy to be travelling again, while always putting the sadness I felt at the memories of the family and friends I'd left behind at the back of my mind as best as I could, I figured that they were always in my heart whether near or far.

Al pulled up at the next Truck-Stop diner for lunch, and once again we received a warm welcome from the staff and diners inside. I was loving the friendliness of the American people. They reminded me of the way my dad Geoff and I were together, always upbeat and fun, with lots of laughs! This felt like my kind of place! - It was similar to the feeling I had in Canada, but the weather was warmer!

I saw a calendar on the wall, and out of curiosity, I went over to check the date. I was surprised to see that it seemed to be the January 26th - My 18th Birthday! "Excuse me, is this the date?" I asked a waitress as she passed by, while I pointed at the date I thought it was. "Sure is, January 26th" she answered. "Thanks!" I answered before hurrying back to Al.

"Hey, Al, guess what?" I said excitedly! "What?" he asked with a big grin. "It's my birthday, I'm eighteen! I just checked the Calendar!" I answered with an equally big grin. "Wow, happy birthday Della!" Al exclaimed as we headed to a booth for some food. "This calls for a celebration!" said Al, as we both picked up a menu. "What do you want? Have whatever you want birthday girl!" he added with a big smile. The waitress must have overheard and came hurrying over to our table. "Happy Birthday Hun!" she exclaimed, as she poured our coffees, and got ready to take our orders. "Thanks!" I answered, suddenly realising that I had just become an official adult! The next hour or so we pigged out on a massive fry-up meal, with coffee cake, and coffee for dessert. I felt so happy to be spending my eighteenth birthday in the USA.

"Hey Al, you know when a baby is born in a certain country, and that place becomes their birth country?" "Yeah?" answered Al, looking curious to hear what I was going to say next. "Well, I've just become an adult in the USA, does that mean it's my adult country?" I asked laughing, half joking, half serious. "Yeah, I reckon it does!" Answered Al, joking back, but looking as if he got where I was coming from. "I like that!" I answered with a big smile.

After our delicious birthday meal, it was time to continue on with our journey, so we headed back to Al's truck and were soon cruising along, listening to some good ole country and blues music. I kept thinking about how I was eighteen now, officially an adult! "I'm so happy to be here!" I exclaimed dramatically, feeling a sense of pure joy as if my being was in perfect balance with the world. "And I'm happy you're here too!" exclaimed Al dramatically, and we both laughed and continued on down the highway.

"So, if I'm now an adult, what's twenty-one all about?" I asked Al, remembering that there was something about getting "The key to the door" at twenty-one. "I don't know?" answered Al, sounding as puzzled as I was. We went on to have a conversation about how different countries might have different coming of ages, and how young people can go to war at sixteen, but they can't vote or have a beer until they're eighteen, or twenty-one in some cases!

"It's crazy! Who makes these rules?" I exclaimed with a bemused look on my face while imagining some doddery old professor in his study making up random rules just to pass the time away while he waits for his wife to cook his dinner. I laughed and smiled to myself at this image, and decided that the cool blues music playing on the radio, and the beautiful scenery outside was much more worthy of my attention!

CHAPTER 21:

NATIVE AMERICAN FAMILY

After a couple of hours, we came to the town of Redlands and Al drove to the neighbourhood where his home was and parked up. "Come and meet the family!" Exclaimed Al with a big smile. "Are you sure your family will be okay with me visiting?" I asked, suddenly feeling unsure. "Yes, they will love to meet you! It is Hopi tradition to be a good host!" he answered back warmly. "OK, if you're sure?" I answered, with a smile, as I followed him towards his house.

As we neared the front door, it slowly opened, and a Native American woman around the same age as Al, with a big warm smile, greeted us, and ushered us both inside. He briefly explained who I was to his wife, and she nodded and smiled at me, as they hugged and kissed in reunion. "Come on, I'll make you both some coffee, are you hungry?" She asked as she led the way to the kitchen. "I'm not hungry, but coffee sounds good thanks" I answered as I followed her along. "Oh, I love your accent!" she exclaimed, as Al and I sat down at the kitchen table while his wife made some coffee. "This is my beautiful wife Cali, short for Caroline" said Al with pride. "Oh wow, so Al and Cal!, how cool!" I answered realising that their names went together really well. "Yeah, I guess you could say that!" answered Al, looking lovingly at his wife. She looked back at him with the same look of affection, which I found so heart-warming.

As we sat drinking our coffees around the kitchen table two skinny teenagers, a boy and a girl, joined us, and Al introduced them as Cindy - thirteen, and Lee – fifteen. They both looked like a perfect blend of their parents; Al and Cali, with their jet-black hair, dark brown eyes, and exotic good looks. They both smiled and said hi, as they grabbed some snacks from the cupboards. They hovered for a few moments to catch up with their dad before disappearing off to their rooms again, smiling and waving at me as they went. "Nice kids! I said, feeling all grown up, now that I was eighteen. Al and Cali nodded and smiled proudly. "Yeah, they're great kids, but they're at that age when they want their own space.

When they're not in School they spend most of their time in their rooms listening to music, watching TV, or chatting to friends on the phone, but at least they are safe!" said Al with a laugh.

I felt instantly at home with them all, as we sat around the kitchen table drinking our coffees. "You know you are welcome to stay as long as I like, Cali would be glad of the company, especially when I'm away, right Cali," said Al warmly. "Oh yes, I would be glad of the company" answered Cali, sincerely. "Thanks, it would be lovely to stay for a little while, while I figure out what I'm doing!" I joked, and the three of us laughed. "…I'd be happy to help out with chores and whatnot too!" I added, wanting them to know that I was willing to pitch in as thanks for their hospitality. "Thank you" answered Cali with a warm smile. I got the feeling that both Al and Cali, had a natural wisdom and that too many words weren't necessary.

The following two weeks I slept on the sofa at night, and in the daytime, I would help Cali out with chores, or shopping for an hour or two, before going out for a walkabout to explore the surrounding area. Apparently, the Redlands area of California was only a semi-desert, so there was still plenty of greenery around, although I noticed that quite a bit of it had turned brown! I absolutely loved the climate there. It was dry and sunny with blue skies, and it seemed to energise me somehow. I felt as though I could walk for hours on end during my daily rambles around. There wasn't a whole lot to do there, as they didn't have a town centre like in the UK, or Canada, instead, it had a few small shopping precincts, with car parks scattered about, as most people seemed to drive everywhere. I missed having a local pub or café to go to, but we would all enjoy family movies together most evenings which was lovely. There was a library nearby which I found myself moseying around in most days. I would usually head there to do a little journalling and pick out a book that took my interest, and find a seat in a cosy corner of the library to sit and read. As usual, I was drawn to books on philosophy, psychology, mysteries, and science. I found these kinds of books the most mentally stimulating, and I loved pondering on the content, often adding my own take on things, and wishing that the author was there to discuss ideas with.

All-in-all I felt very content and at home in Redlands, and Al's family were ever so lovely, but after a couple of weeks, I became restless once again. On my travels, I'd discovered that I could only spend a few weeks, at most, based somewhere before I started to physically miss the motion of moving along the road in a vehicle and seeing the world glide by. I wondered if this was a similar craving that sailors often developed for the sea. I felt as though, after I had seen all there was to see in an area, it was simply time to move on. It seemed to be a part of my travelling momentum, and nothing personal to the people or place I was visiting. I hoped they would understand.

I remembered that Al had mentioned Los Angeles on our journey, as it was the nearest big city to Redlands, and I had told him that I was curious to go and have a look around. I figured I could bring it up again at some point during one of our kitchen coffee chats so that my leaving wouldn't come as such a shock to them, but when I mentioned this to Al and Cali they looked at each other with worried faces, and in a concerned tone they told me that it was a very dangerous place. They added that they were planning to move over to Arizona in a few weeks because Cali's mother had arthritis and believed that she would be healthier there because the weather was a lot dryer. They told me that I was most welcome to go with them and become a part of their family.

I was so touched that they had accepted me as one of their own, but I knew that I wanted to get moving again, danger or no danger, it was all part of the adventure! I thanked them and told them I appreciated their offer, but I wanted to travel some more, I added that I would miss them all a lot, as they were such a lovely family, and I didn't want them to be offended that I'd declined their offer. They continued to look concerned, but slowly nodded their heads in agreement. "Well, OK, but keep in touch!" said Al, as if coming to terms with the fact that I was leaving. "Yeah, keep in touch" echoed Cali, looking sad. "I will do and hopefully, we can still visit each other in time too! I'm not sure where though?" I answered, with a laugh.

The day before I was due to leave, I took a shower, and coloured my hair my usual red/brown shade, with a hair dye I'd found at a drug store near the library. It wasn't my usual henna dye, but it was better than nothing, and it felt good to get a little tidied up. That night Al treated us all to some burgers, and fries to save Cali from cooking. It felt like we were having a little Bon Voyage party of sorts, as even the kids joined us!

The next morning, I packed up my little tote bag and said goodbye to everyone. Cali gave me a bag full of snacks, and a can of soda, and Al gave me $10 as he was telling me that there was a highway near the library that I could walk to. "Come right back if I don't get a lift" Exclaimed Al, still looking concerned for me. "…and call us if you need anything!" added Cali in her lovely gentle manner, as we headed outside. "Thank you both!" I answered feeling touched by how kind they were. Cindy and Lee came out of their rooms followed us outside, and stood quietly near their parents. I thanked Al and Cali once again, and hugged all four of them goodbye, before heading down the drive toward the street. I turned and waved at them all one last time, before continuing on. I felt sad to be leaving them, but I also felt happy to be on the move again. Once again, I pondered on what a strange dynamic my travels were creating. It seemed to be made up of a never-ending series of bonding with people, having a relationship, or friendship start to bloom, and then saying goodbye shortly afterwards which created a repeated pattern of joy and sadness. I wasn't sure what to make of it all, it seemed very bitter/sweet, and again I wondered if one day I would find a place that I would feel completely content to stay put in. 'Keep travelling, and find out!' I told myself, grinning at the irony of this notion, and with a newfound skip in my step I arrived at the highway and stuck out my thumb.

CHAPTER 22:

WESTWARD BOUND

Within a few minutes, a truck stopped and I jumped up the steps and opened the door to check out the driver. "Hi, thanks!" I said with a smile. He was a friendly average-looking guy, with brown curly hair and a bit of a beard. I guessed he was about thirty-something. His vibes felt safe, so I got inside the cab, put my tote bag on the floor, and sat down. "Where are you heading?" He asked in a breezy manner. "Los Angeles" I answered, feeling excited at the prospect of checking out a new place. "I'm heading right past downtown LA to Long Beach if that'll do you?" He asked, as he put the truck in gear and started to drive. "Perfect!" I answered with a big smile.

"My name's Neil what's yours?" He asked, smiling back. "Hi Neil, nice to meet you too, I'm Della!" I answered as I got comfy in my seat. "Hey, you're from England! Cool! Let's hit the road!" He exclaimed as he stepped on the gas pedal. "Great, let's go!" I exclaimed with a laugh as we took off down the highway, leaving my short-lived life in Redlands to fade away into the distance.

"So, you're from England, how come you're hitching to LA?" asked Neil with a curious laugh as the truck picked up speed along the highway. "Good question!" I answered, laughing too, and thinking I wasn't exactly sure what the answer was. "So do you have family and friends here in the US?" he asked, sounding genuinely curious. "Well, yes and no, I mean, I've made friends since I've been here, and I'm meant to be meeting up with my Aunt Freda at some point, so I thought I'd have a look around first" I answered, hoping that I was making some sort of sense to him.

"Ah, I see, so you're on some kind of adventure holiday?" He replied as if trying to wrap his head around what I'd just said. "Yeah, kind of!" I answered, with a laugh, while thinking it best not to mention my world travel ambitions and to keep it as simple as possible to save from having to try and explain things, that I'd yet to figure out for myself! Neil had good pop music playing on his radio, which we soon found ourselves singing along to in between lots of good, fun and interesting chats as he drove along. I noticed that we were still driving through Semi-desert, and I found it hard to imagine a big city like Los Angeles in the middle of this desert terrain!

After a little while driving, Neil stopped for a food break at a rest stop, in a more built-up area, and I assumed it was the LA suburbs, even though there was still quite a lot of desert land around us. He treated me to lunch, and once again I was touched by the generosity of the American people. I had protested several times, telling him that I could treat us, but he had insisted, telling me that he was glad of my company and that I was such a cool chic to be travelling all the way from England like I was!

As we ate our burgers and fries, he asked me about my travels and looked impressed at the places I'd been so far. We both laughed at my story of trying to ask people for the way out of New York City. "Hell, I wouldn't even want to go there in the first place!" He said with a laugh. "So where are you from ?" I asked curiously. "Nevada, but with my job, I drive all over the United States!" He answered proudly. "Wow, truck driving sounds like such a cool job, maybe that's what I should do? Get paid to travel! That would really suit me, but trucks are huge, maybe I could drive something smaller?" I answered, seriously considering the idea. "I'm sure you could!" answered Neil optimistically. "Yeah, I just need to learn how to drive first!" I joked back. We both laughed and headed back to his truck to continue on with our journey.

After a half hour or so, more buildings started to appear, and the roads got busier with traffic. "This is "The Valley" it's the northern part of LA!" announced Niel, as we drove along. "Gosh, I only thought of Valleys as having rivers, greenery and trees, set in between two mountains, I've never thought of a city Valley before!" I answered, looking around in amazement. "Not this Valley!" laughed Neil, as if he got where I was coming from. "Downtown LA isn't far now!" he added with a smile. I suddenly felt a surge of excitement at the idea of visiting a city that I'd only ever heard about in films, and I couldn't quite believe that I was actually there!

As we drove, the surrounding area got more and more built up and busy with traffic. "So, as I said, I'm gonna be continuing on past LA and down to Long Beach, so where do you wanna get dropped off?" asked Neil as we zoomed along, what looked like an intercity motorway. "Downtown would be good if that's ok?" I answered, feeling the excitement of arriving in LA growing more and more by the second. "Downtown? Nobody goes downtown!" he answered, looking shocked. "But isn't that the centre where everybody goes and where all the fun things are?" I asked, feeling confused by his reaction

"No, LA's very spread out, downtown has a business district in one part, which is ok, but kinda boring, and the other parts can be dangerous with winos, homeless people, and gang members on the streets" answered Neil as if trying to put me off going there. "Surely there are some normal people there too!?" I answered, my mind flashing to how cosmopolitan London, Toronto, and New York were. "Not too many! They're all afraid to go down there unless they're in cars!" He answered matter-of-factly.

"Hmmm?" I answered, finding it hard to believe. "Well, I guess I'd like to go and see for myself!" I added equally matter-of-factly, with a shoulder shrug, which he found amusing, "Sure thing!" he answered as if understanding my need to see for myself. "I can drop you off bang in the centre of downtown Los Angeles if you like?" He said as if in support of what may have seemed to him like a dare that I was about to partake in. "Great, thanks!" I answered. Suddenly looking even more forward to my upcoming exploration!

We were soon driving down busy city streets with lots of traffic, and a mixture of modern and classic-style old buildings of theatres, shops, and businesses. The sidewalks were mainly full of Hispanic people looking like they were going about their daily routines. I saw a few black people and one or two white people in the crowd, but the majority of the people looked Hispanic. They all looked busy with one thing or another, but none of them looked dangerous.

Neil pulled up at a convenient spot, scribbled his phone number on a piece of paper, and said, "Well, here we are! Call me if you need anything!" I took the piece of paper and thanked him, then I picked up my tote bag and opened the door to climb down the steps. "Good luck to ya!" shouted Neil looking at me with admiration. "Thanks, Neil, you too!" I called out, as I waved, slammed the truck door shut, and jumped down the steps to the sidewalk. We waved goodbye to each other one more time as he drove away with the rest of the downtown traffic.

CHAPTER 23:

LOST ANGELS

As I walked along the streets of downtown Los Angeles, all around me seemed to be just regular working people, who happened to be mainly Hispanic, none of them seemed bad at all, so I wondered what Neil had meant with his warning about downtown Los Angeles being dangerous. I wondered if maybe some white people assumed it to be dangerous because it was predominantly Hispanic, rather than white. but I couldn't make sense of this logic. 'People are people, and criminals are criminals whatever race they belong to!' I thought to myself, as I walked along feeling happy to be in a new place.

I soon found a small park in the centre of downtown and sat down on a bench to collect my thoughts and absorb the general atmosphere. So far, it just felt very busy, with lots of traffic and Hispanic people milling about, there were rows of shops and businesses on the surrounding city streets, but I had yet to notice any fun-looking stuff - No cafes, bars, or clubs, no record shops, vintage shops, or art galleries, I figured things like that must be somewhere in LA, if not downtown?

I wondered where young people like me hung out. Where were all the fun, creative, arty, hippy, punky, alternative types? My mind flashed to my friends back in my home town, they were such a fun and creative crowd, then my mind flashed to my friends in Toronto, again such a fun and creative crowd. I hoped I would find some kindred spirits here too. 'Oh well, this isn't so bad for a park to take a breather in!' I thought to myself, as I sat enjoying my rest on the park bench surrounded by lush greenery. A sign nearby read "Pershing Square"

Just as I was wondering what Pershing means, and pondering on if there was a connection to Persia, and if maybe they sold Persian Rugs in the neighbourhood, a friendly-looking, chubby Hispanic guy, maybe a year or two older than I was, walked over towards me. "Hi, how are you doing?" he asked with a friendly smile. "I'm ok thanks, just taking a breather, how are you doing?" I answered, smiling back.

"Hey, you're from England! What's your name, I'm Manny!" He exclaimed, as he instantly noticed my accent and an even bigger smile appeared on his face. "Hi Manny, nice to meet you, I'm Della!" I answered as we both shook hands. He sat down next to me on the bench, and asked me loads of questions about England; the food, the music, the people, the fashions... which I did my best to answer. We had a good chat for about twenty minutes.

"So, do you have anywhere to stay?" he asked, glancing at my tote bag, and looking a little concerned for me. "Not yet!" I answered, and we both laughed. "It's dangerous to be alone in downtown LA man, you're welcome to come over to my hood to stay if you want?" He said, sounding like he was genuinely concerned for my safety. "Sure, lead the way!" I answered, feeling interested to know more about this "hood" that he spoke of. I could tell by his tough guy style, that he was probably part of a gang, but he seemed to be a truly good person at heart, and the "anthropologist" in me was curious to see what his background was like. He laughed and seemed to like my attitude. "Ok, let's go English girl!" He answered as he led the way...

He flagged down as bus, and we both jumped on board. He mumbled something about just coming out of jail to the driver, and the driver nodded, and let us ride for free. I said nothing, as I felt it was best to just stay quiet, and follow his lead. After about a half hour or so we got off the bus, and he led the way to a poor-looking neighbourhood, down a side street, and to a ground-floor apartment. Manny knocked loudly on the door, as we walked inside and he called out some Spanish-sounding names.

Two guys and a girl looking in their late teens and early twenties appeared, and Manny quickly introduced us all to each other. "This is my older brother Julio, my younger brother Rico, and my sister Dolores! This is Della, from England!"

They all looked a little confused as to why I was there, but we all smiled, said hi to each other and shook hands. "Our parents are at work, they work at a factory across town," Said Manny, as if noticing that I was looking to see who else might be home. He explained that his mother and father were out at work at a factory across town. "Ah right!" I answered with a smile.

Manny quickly explained to them who I was and why I was there, and they seemed to warm up to me a little, but they continued to look confused, and going by the tone of their voices, while chatting to Manny in Spanish, I gathered that they were a little concerned, for me being in that neighbourhood. I had the feeling that they were instinctively taking me under their wing, as every so often they were shooting concerned-looking glances my way. I stood there, feeling quite awkward, with half of me wanting to just leave, and get out of what was quite an uncomfortable situation, and the other half of me feeling curious to stay and see what would happen if I stayed.

Manny suddenly asked if I wanted a beer, which seemed like a good idea to me. I said yes please, and he went to the fridge and took out a couple of beers. He asked the others if they wanted one too, but they were on their way out, and said they would join us later. Manny and I opened our beers and went to sit at the kitchen table to drink them. I felt comfortable with Manny, and as the beer buzz kicked in, we were soon chatting and laughing about all sorts of fun random stuff.

Over the next few hours, a few of his friends came around and joined us. "No messing, she's good people!" Manny had told each of them as they'd arrived, and I'd stood there nodding, smiling and shaking their hands as we met. They all seemed to be in the same gang, as they had the same clothing style, tattoos, and either near skin-heads, or hairnets covering their greased back hair, they all had tough attitudes, but they were not hostile towards me, they were very friendly, and fun spirited and seemed genuinely happy to meet me, and I felt honoured to see a side of them that the average white people might never get to see.

That night I met Manny's parents briefly, but they seemed very quiet and reserved, and after Manny had introduced us, and we'd politely shaken hands, they disappeared off to another room in the apartment. Manny followed them, and a few moments later I heard Manny rowing with them, and I got the feeling that he was in trouble for bringing me home with him.

After a few more minutes of heated discussion, it went quiet, and Manny appeared back in the living room looking a little disheartened. He let out a sigh, and then apologetically told me that I could stay on the sofa that night, but in the morning, he would take me up to Hollywood. "Hollywood?" I responded, not understanding what he meant. I had a vague notion that movies were made in a place called Hollywood, but I thought it was a studio, not a place. "It's where your people are" Manny answered with a reassuring smile. This confused me even more "What people?" I asked, laughing, and feeling genuinely puzzled. "You know, punks, artists, musicians, it's where all the fun clubs and stuff are!" he added, and the penny dropped, only the day before while I was sitting on the bench in the downtown park at Pershing Square, I'd been wondering where all the fun people and things were!

"Ah right!" I answered, totally understanding what he meant, but suddenly feeling sad that the city of Los Angeles seemed to be so segregated. I was used to places that were more cosmopolitan, where all sorts of people mixed. "Thanks, Manny, it's a shame LA is so segregated! The cities in England and Canada have all sorts of people in the centres, young, old, artists, punks, trendies, office workers, students, black, white, etc…" I exclaimed proudly. "That sounds fun!" answered Manny looking impressed. "Yeah, it is!" I answered, and we both laughed.

That night Manny gave me a towel to take a shower, and I got changed into some black sweatpants, and a long grey and black top that Sally-Anne had given me. I shoved the clothes I'd been wearing into my tote bag and headed back to the living room feeling refreshed. "Me and Julio are going out now, we probably won't be back until late. My parents and Rico and Delores will stay in their rooms, they won't bother you, so you can get some sleep" Said, Manny caringly, as I joined him and his brother Julio on the long sofa. "OK thanks, sorry to be a bother to everyone!" I answered while pulling a cringy face. "No, bother! See you in the morning!" answered Manny giving my arm a gentle rub. "OK, thanks Manny, have a good night, see you both tomorrow!" I called out, as they both headed out of the front door. "Bye/Adios!" they both called out, as the door closed behind them.

I felt odd being left alone in a stranger's house, especially as the rest of Manny's family were home, but holed up in their rooms hiding out from me! Or at least that's how it felt, although I was grateful for the fact that left me in peace to get a good night's sleep on the sofa in the living room, and I couldn't help but appreciate how respectful they were of giving me my privacy, as they never once bothered me the whole night. I had the impression that they were all good people at heart, but they had lived hard lives, and they'd had to toughen up in order to survive.

The next morning I woke up, and Manny appeared from another room looking like he hadn't had much sleep. "Good Morning Della, would you like a coffee? " he asked politely. "Yes, please, is it ok to use the loo?" I asked, sitting up, and blinking my eyes trying to get my bearings. "The loo, you mean the bathroom, sure!" He answered with a laugh, as he headed towards the kitchen. "Yeah, the bathroom!" I answered with a laugh, as I headed towards the loo.

I washed up and headed back to the living room to join Manny in drinking a strong cup of coffee. He shared some Mexican flatbread and melted cheese with me, which went well with the coffee, and helped to wake me up some more.

232

BOOK 1: TO SEE THE WORLD

"Where is everybody?" I asked as the place was still very quiet. "Oh, they're all out at work or school, and Julio is still sleeping!" He answered as he took a sip of his coffee.

"Oh, I see, will you thank your parents for letting me stay the night, and tell them I was sorry to be a bother!" I answered, feeling bad about putting them out. "I told you, you are not a bother! I'm sorry for them being a little unfriendly with you, it's nothing personal. They just didn't trust strangers in general!" he answered as if trying to smooth everything out. "Well. I guess I am a bit strange!" I joked, and we both laughed and finished our coffees.

"Hollywood is about eight miles away, so we will need to catch a couple of buses to get there!" said Manny, as I was getting my bag ready to leave. "Don't worry, you don't have to go the whole way with me!" I answered, feeling bad that Manny felt he had to escort me to Hollywood. "No, I will take you there, I want to make sure that you are safe!" he insisted. "Aw, thanks, Manny!" I answered, feeling touched by his kindness.

We left his house and headed down the street towards the bus stop. As we walked along, a few neighbourhood gang types weighed me up suspiciously, as Manny shouted out greetings and flashed hand signs to them. I felt as though he was my bodyguard as I followed him along giving sheepish little smiles, waves, and nods to the on-lookers.

At the bus stop, we jumped on the bus heading downtown, and once again Manny mumbled a few words to the driver and gestured for me to go and sit down. I did as he said, wondering if he ever actually paid for a bus ride. I had to laugh at his cheek!

We got off the bus downtown, and Manny said that we would have to walk a few blocks to get to the Hollywood bus. I was amazed that there was such a thing as a Hollywood bus, as in my mind Hollywood was still a movie studio! I followed Manny along. just enjoying the energy of the new day. The streets were bustling with mainly Hispanic people milling about doing their daily things. It reminded me a little of New York 'Although at least I found Pershing Square to rest up here, I didn't find anywhere to rest up in New York!' I thought to myself with a grin.

As we were passing what looked like a blue movie cinema, Manny slowed down and turned to approach a sleazy-looking white guy, aged about forty, who was about to pay for a ticket at the booth. Much to my shock and dismay, Manny suddenly grabbed his wallet out of his hand and took out a $10 dollar bill, then he threw the wallet back to the dumbfounded-looking white guy.

I stood there frozen in disbelief, but Manny did this act of robbery in such a smooth way that I couldn't help but be a little impressed! 'At least he didn't assault the guy, or take his whole wallet, or even more cash, and besides the guy was paying to go into a blue movie, so maybe he wasn't such a good guy himself?' I thought to myself, as I realised that the guy was one of the few white people I'd seen downtown. 'Figures!' I joked to myself.

Manny continued to walk cooly on leading the way. He had a confident, protective swagger about him as if to tell others not to bother me, and I felt as though he was acting as a kind of guardian angel to me, which was very touching.

We jumped on a bus that was Hollywood bound, and once again Manny told the driver that he had just come out of jail, so would need to ride for free, and again as he did this, he guided me past him and ushered me towards the seats, as if to say to the bus driver "She's with me!" and again the driver just nodded, and Manny came and sat down next to me.

We chatted a little bit about volunteer gigs I may be able to do in Hollywood, like nannying, or au-pairing. I told him that I'd been a nanny in Canada, and had enjoyed it.

As we chatted, I looked out of the window at the low-level buildings, zooming by, and the busy lanes of traffic around us. So far Los Angeles was looking like a very busy place in the sense that everyone seemed to be either coming or going, but I couldn't help but wonder exactly where they were all coming from and going to.

About an hour later Manny led the way to get off the bus. I followed him, waved and thanked the driver, and jumped off the bus. I looked up at the nearby street signs. Apparently, we were at the junction of Santa Monica Boulevard and La Cienega Boulevard.

I looked around me hoping to see some of the fun stuff that Manny and I had been chatting about, but I couldn't see anything really fun-looking in particular. There were just lots of cars and buildings, and maybe a restaurant or two, but no cosmopolitan centre buzzing with life.

"We'll have to walk up last La Cienega to Sunset, that's where you'll find your kind of people!" Exclaimed Manny, as if noticing my look of disappointment.

"Sounds good!" I answered as he led the way up a steep street. Curiously I followed him. "So, what exactly is Sunset?" I asked Manny, thinking that it sounded nice, whatever it was! "It's a Boulevard, it runs from downtown LA out to the coast, but the place we're heading to is called The Sunset Strip, it's got lots of clubs, and cafes, record stores, and like I said, your kind of people!" answered Manny earnestly.

"Sounds fun, and I'm curious to see what my kind of people look like?!" I answered laughing! "You know; cool like you! Punks, musicians, artists, actors… they look more like you, that I do, let's put it that way!" said Manny matter-of-factly, and we both laughed, but deep down I still felt kind of sad that the people in LA didn't seem to mix.

As we trundled along up the hill I pondered on the possible reasons for the LA divide, and I assumed it must be a case of "like attracts like" which I supposed was natural to a point, and not necessarily a bad thing unless it starts to create hate and division.

We arrived at Sunset Boulevard about ten minutes later. Both of us were a little out of breath after the walk up the steep hill. As we stood at the corner of La Cienega and Sunset I looked around me and to the right I saw lots of bars and restaurants and loads of young fashionable people milling around.

I understood what Manny had meant about them being "My kind of people" although the people here looked a little more on the glamourous edge of the fun spectrum to me! I was more on the free-spirited, alternative side, but still, it was great to see such a fun, upbeat, lively-looking area!

"Let's take a walk!" Said Manny, as he started to cross the street. "Sounds good!" I answered as I followed him quickly. We headed towards where a lot of the activity was, and it felt good to be seeing American young people who were into pop culture for the first time in real life. "This IS more my scene!" I said to Manny with a big smile. "What did I tell you?" He said smiling back.

We walked for a few more minutes, just taking in the sights of fun-looking bars, restaurants, and clubs. A lot of the people looked like they were into mainstream rock music, whereas I was more into punk and new wave music, but it was still a fun atmosphere.

I followed Manny along with a smile on my face and a skip in my step. We must have looked quite the odd couple; A young colourful dressed punky new-wave teenage girl, with shoulder-length wild and wavy, red-brown coloured hair, and a hard-core looking, tattooed, skinhead Hispanic gang member from east LA, both just walking along, side by side as if without a care in the world - chatting, laughing and joking. "This is what my travels are about, meeting people from ALL walks of life!" I thought to myself, feeling so happy to be on my continually unfolding adventure.

As we were walking past a gas station Manny approached a rich-looking guy who was pumping gas into his car "You need a housekeeper?" he asked, as he got nearer. "Maybe?" said the guy looking over at me, and seeming interested. Manny told the guy that I was from England and that I was travelling the world volunteering as a nanny or housekeeper, and that I'd be able to help him out in exchange for room, board and a little pocket money. "How long is she here for?" Asked the guy looking back my way. Manny looked over at me for an answer. "Um, a few weeks I guess" I answered, not really sure, as I hadn't actually thought about it. I was just enjoying being in each moment.

The guy nodded and strolled over towards me. "Mike, Movie Producer!" He said as he reached out his hand. "Della, explorer!" I answered with a laugh, as we shook hands. "So, you're in LA for a few weeks huh? You're welcome to try out as a housekeeper at my place, and see how it goes!" He said looking pleased to have found some help.

"Sounds good, thanks!" I answered, nodding at him and glancing over at Manny. "My place is up in the Hollywood Hills, I'll be heading up there after I get some gas, you're welcome to come along and see what you think" added Mike with a smile. "Yep ok!" I answered, feeling pleased with the possibility of a volunteer gig in the centre of Hollywood, and figuring that now was the best time to go and check out his house, rather than making arrangements for later.

"Thanks for all of your help, Manny!" I exclaimed, feeling truly grateful for Manny's hospitality, and LA guidance. "You're welcome English girl!" answered Manny, as he stepped forward to give me a big hug. After we finished hugging, he took the ten-dollar bill, that he'd taken from the guy at the blue-movie cinema, out of his pocket, and shoved it in my hand. "I got this for you!" he said generously.

"Oh gosh, thanks, Manny! Are you sure?" I exclaimed, while loosely holding the ten-dollar bill, as if ready to give it back to him. "Of course I'm sure, take it!" He exclaimed while closing my hand on the ten-dollar bill with both of his hands. "Aw, thanks, Manny!" I answered as I popped the ten-dollar bill into to small zip pouch on the front of my tote bag, while feeling as though Manny had now transformed from being my guardian angel to my own personal Robin Hood!

Deep down I had mixed emotions about his gesture, as he had done a bad thing to do a good thing, but what shone through above all else was his genuine kind spirit. "You got a pen and paper?" Manny called out to Mike suddenly, as he strolled over towards where he was pumping gas. "Sure" answered Mike, as he reached into his jacket and pulled out a notepad and pen, tore a page out of his notepad, and passed the pen and paper to Manny. "Thanks, man!" answered Manny, as he quickly scribbled down his number as he walked back over towards me. "Call me if you need anything!" said Manny, as he pressed the piece of paper into my hand, before casually strolling away. "Thanks, Manny!" I shouted after him, feeling so touched by his kind help. He waved without looking back as if to say, "My work here is done!"

I turned and strolled over towards Mike, just as he finished pumping his gas. "Jump in!" He exclaimed as he headed for the driver's seat of the open-top sports car. "OK, thanks!" I answered, feeling thrilled at the potential of having a live-in volunteer gig in this fun-looking part of LA for a while. 'I hope he doesn't turn out to be a sleaze bag though!' I thought to myself as he started the car up. So far it was hard to tell what he was really like. On the surface, he seemed friendly and intelligent, but the fact that he had such a fancy sports car gave me shallow vibes. I figured I would find out what he was really like soon enough!

Mike drove out of the gas station. "Now we're heading up into The Hollywood Hills!" exclaimed Mike as we zoomed along. "Nice name" I answered enjoying the overall atmosphere of the area. 'This must be where a lot of the "Beautiful People" live - The Rich, Successful and Carefree, I can tick one of those boxes at least!' I thought to myself with a grin.

"You ever thought about being in movies?" asked Mike as we sped higher and higher up the bendy roads into the Hollywood Hills, passing large fancy-looking houses as we went. "No, why?" I answered, thinking that it was an odd question. "You're a pretty girl, I could probably get you some movie work if you want it?" He answered confidently. "Huh? I'm not sure I would want to be in movies!" I answered, pulling a confused face.

"Why not?" He asked, looking surprised by my reaction. "Well, my main goal is to travel and see the world, and being in movies isn't something I ever thought about" I answered, with a shoulder shrug. "Right! But you're in Hollywood now!" He answered laughing nervously as if not knowing what to say. "Well yeah, but I didn't actually plan to come to Hollywood, it's just this is where my adventures have brought me so far!" I added in an attempt to explain why I was there in the first place.

"Oh, I see... So how exactly did you get here?" He asked looking as confused as I'd been looking at his movie question a few moments earlier. "Well, I took off from my home town in England with a fiver in my pocket about eight months ago, and one thing led to another, and here I am!" I answered with another shoulder shrug. Mike looked amazed and burst out laughing. "Wow, you got balls girl! Forget acting! We need to do a movie about YOU!" he exclaimed, shaking his head in disbelief. I laughed along too, although, to me, it didn't seem such a bizarre thing for a person to have a look around the planet they were living on!

"So, what exactly would you want me to help you out with?" I asked, feeling curious about my next potential volunteer gig. "Well, I could do with a little help around the house, just general housework, you know, keep everything clean and tidy!" He answered casually. "No problem!" I answered with a nod, while still feeling pleased at the idea of having a volunteer gig and a place to stay all rolled into one, although deep down I couldn't help but feel a bit suspicious of his motives. He just didn't have genuine vibes like Manny, or Al and his Hopi Indian family, and so many of the other good people I'd met so far on this journey, but I wanted to give him the benefit of the doubt, and see...

We arrived at a private gate and Mike typed in a code on a panel in the gate post. The Gate opened, and revealed a big beautiful house! Mike parked up and led the way inside. "Well, if you like it here, this is your home too now!" exclaimed Mike proudly, as he opened the front door into a beautiful hallway. "Nice!" I answered, with a smile. "...I'll show you to your room!" He exclaimed as he led the way through more beautiful pristine rooms, full of stylish furniture. "OK," I answered with a smile, but deep down I still felt wary of him. He led the way to a beautiful guest room, and for a moment I pictured myself staying there and thought how wonderful it might be. "Come on, I'll show you the rest of the house!" Mike exclaimed proudly, as he continued to lead the way on a tour of his home.

He seemed very pleased to have a chance to show his house off. It was a beautiful house, but it looked immaculate, so I assumed that he already had a cleaner, which heightened my suspicions towards him, as it was plain to see that he didn't actually need a housekeeper!

BOOK 1: TO SEE THE WORLD

"So, what exactly would my job would entail?" I asked, while looking around me with a puzzled expression, as if to say - You don't need a housekeeper that's for sure! "Well, you know - you take care of me, and I'll take care of you!" he answered with a wink. My heart instantly sank. "No thank you, I was looking for a proper volunteer gig, and nothing else!" I answered, feeling upset and disappointed. I could tell that he was thrown off by my response, but all I felt was annoyed.

"You should be ashamed of yourself! You may have a nice home, but you don't have a nice heart!" I shouted at him as I swiftly walked towards the front door, opened it, headed back outside, and slammed the door shut behind me. Thankfully I was able to open the gate from the inside, so I carried on walking and I did not look back!

CHAPTER 24:

ANGEL LEN OF SUNSET BOULEVARD

It took me about a half hour to get back down to The Sunset Strip, on Sunset Boulevard. I looked around at the Cafes bars, clubs, gas stations, shops, and liquor stores all teaming with life. Only an hour or so before I had felt as though I was so smoothly becoming one of the Hollywood "In crowd" but now I felt as if I was back out on the outside looking in.

I found a bus bench to sit on and pondered on how fickle some of the people in this world were. I told myself that I shouldn't let others have the power to make me feel good or bad, after all, we were all just people, and circumstances can fluctuate, what matters is that we treat each other as we would like to be treated. I sat for about twenty minutes lost in thought and feeling down - but not out. One way or another I would jump back into the game!

I took a deep breath and tried to think what the best thing to do next would be. My first instinct was to just hitchhike away! Carry on as I was, out on the road, living in the moment, with new adventures unfolding as I went, but despite my disappointing experience with Mike, I really did like the general atmosphere in LA, especially where I was now, up on the Sunset Strip, so I had the counter-urge to stick around and see what adventures might unfold there!

 I suddenly remembered my race car driver pal; Skid Martin who I'd met in Southampton. He had mentioned that his address was on Sunset Boulevard! 'Oh my goodness! This IS Sunset Boulevard!' I thought to myself feeling shocked at the realisation. '...He would be so astonished to see me here!' I thought with a grin.

I started to laugh to myself at the thought of his face if I turned up at his doorstep, although, I wasn't sure if the address he'd given me was an apartment or just a mailing address. Besides, I no longer had my address book, and all I remembered was that he'd written a lot of numbers, followed by: Sunset Boulevard as his contact details. I looked up at the numbers on the buildings, and they were all very long, which gave me hope that I was at the right part of the boulevard. I decided I would ask just around and hope that someone I asked would know of him, and where he lived. He was a race car driver, so hopefully somebody would know of him.

I saw what looked like an office-type building, so I walked inside and asked the receptionist if she knew of a race car driver who lived in the area called Skid Martin. She looked puzzled, shook her head and said the name didn't ring a bell sorry. I thanked her and carried on up the road and popped my head in several more businesses asking if they knew of Skid Martin the race car driver, but much to my disappointment none of them had heard of him.

As I strolled along, I spotted a long blond-haired, hippy-looking guy in his twenties heading my way, and figured there was no harm in asking him too. "Excuse me, have you heard of Skid Martin the race car driver by any chance?" I asked as we got near each other. "Who?" he answered, looking puzzled. "Um, Skid Martin, he's a race car driver, I met him in England, and he gave me an address on Sunset Boulevard, but I lost my address book!" I answered, hoping that I was making some kind of sense.

"Oh, I see! No sorry, never heard of him. So, you're from England huh? Cool, how come you're here?" He asked in a friendly way. "Well, I've been travelling for the past eight months, and my travels brought me here!" I answered, not knowing how else to put it. "Cool, I guess that's as good a reason as any! Nice to meet you, I'm Len!" He answered as he put out his hand. "Nice to meet you Len, I'm Della" I answered, as we shook hands.

"So where are you staying?" he asked as if hoping I was staying nearby. "Well, I would have been staying up in the Hollywood Hills, as a housekeeper for a movie producer, but he turned out to be a sleaze bag so I legged it back down the hill!" I answered with a laugh.

"That sucks! So, what will you do now?" He asked, looking concerned for me. "I'm not sure yet, I was hoping to find Skid Martin, and thinking that maybe he would let me stay for a while, while I regroup, and find out when my aunt Freda is coming over because I'm meant to be meeting up with her at some point!" I answered, once again hoping that I was making sense, as I was finding it hard to explain my bigger adventure picture, with simple answers.

"Well, you're welcome to crash out in my van if you're stuck!" answered Len looking at me earnestly. "Thanks, Len, that would be great!" I answered. Feeling that he came across as very sincere, as I didn't get any weird vibes from him at all. "Cool, let me show you where my van's parked!" he answered cheerily, as he turned and started to lead the way back up Sunset Boulevard and past all the fun bars, restaurants, and clubs.

Once again felt as though I was being let back into the Hollywood in-crowd. I wondered if any of the people dining and drinking at some of the outdoor restaurants had seen my comings and goings so far that day; from my first arriving on the sunset strip with a hardcore Hispanic gang member, and next zooming off up into the Hollywood hills with a movie producer in a fancy convertible sports car with the top down, and now strolling along with a cool looking blonde hippy guy. I laughed to myself, at what they would make of it all if they had noticed.

We walked until we came to a cross street where Len turned right. I followed him a short way until we reached a large van parked up on a residential side street. Len slid open the side door to reveal a large living area inside the van.

"Wow, you've got it really nice! It's like a little house! I exclaimed, feeling impressed! "Thanks, yeah and these side sofas can stay as they are as single beds, or they can be rolled out together to make a double. We can keep 'em as singles - one each!" He answered proudly. "Thanks, Len! This is great! I wish I had a van like this!" I answered excitedly. Loving the look and feel of the space inside, and imagining how wonderful it would be to have a home on wheels.

"Yeah, I'm happy with it! Do you want something to drink?" He asked, as he leaned over and opened up a small fridge. "Wow, you have everything!" I exclaimed, feeling more impressed by the second at his cool camper van. "Coke?" He asked as he was about to grab a couple of cans. "Yes please" I answered as he opened up the two cans of Coke and passed one to me. "Thanks, Len!" I answered, as I took a swig.

We sat at the little table in the centre of the van, while Len drew up a map of LA for me. Once the map was finished, he started pointing out various places: The Valley was over the Hollywood Hills in the north, and was a safe, mainly residential area, Watts was in the south and was a dangerous area. The coast was to the west and was mainly safe, he explained that Santa Monica had a large British population, and would be worth a visit as it was a lovely beach town. He went on to explain that Downtown Los Angeles was to the east, and was dangerous and not worth a visit. I nodded, and mumbled in agreement, while my mind flashed to my first arrival in downtown LA, although my experience there had been ok, I could see why the average white person would be wary.

"…And this is West Hollywood, where we are. It's mainly a safe area, and I would advise sticking around this area, at least until you get more familiar with LA" he exclaimed earnestly, which seemed paradoxical to me, but I didn't want to come across as contrary, so I just kept on nodding and mumbling sounds of agreement. "…And, if you do venture down to Hollywood, do not go east of Vine Street!" He warned with a serious look on his face. "Why not?" I asked curiously. "It's too dangerous down there! There are a lot of drug addicts, winos, and gangbangers! Innocent people get hurt over that side of town!" He answered as if to scare me from going down there. "Right, thanks so much for drawing up the map, and explaining all that!" I answered while feeling a little shocked by his warning. I picked up the map, folded it, and popped it into my tote bag. "You're welcome, just stay safe!" he answered, with a kind smile. "I will!" I answered, hoping to reassure him.

"Hey, do you need any clothes? A girlfriend of mine from back home left a bag of clothes for me to take to Goodwill!" He asked as he put a full-looking binbag on the table. "Oh thanks, I'd love to have a rummage!" I answered, feeling that the clothes that Sally-Anne had given me were nice in a practical way, but hopefully Len's girlfriend would have some fun clothes. "Sure, knock yourself out, leave whatever you don't want in the bag! I've gotta get going, I'm meeting a music biz friend soon, and I'm hoping to get some DJ work out of it!" he said, as he went about getting his things together. "OK, thanks Len, I'll probably catch up with some journaling, and have a rummage through the clothes before I venture out for a look about" I answered, looking forward to having a little alone time, and seeing what clothes were in the bag.

"So you're journaling about your travels huh? great! You're recording history too you know?!" answered Len, looking impressed. "I guess so, it's more like the ramblings of a mad woman! - Good therapy though" I joked, and we both laughed. "Here's a spare key for the van, make yourself at home, you're welcome to come and go as you, please. Oh, and here's my mobile phone number if you want to call me for anything!" he said in a caring tone and once again, my heart was warmed by how kind and hospitable a lot of North Americans were.

"Thanks, Len, what's a mobile phone?" I asked, curiously, as I glanced at the number on the piece of paper he'd given me. "Oh, they came out recently. and because I'm living in a van it was a must-have!" He answered. "Oh yeah, I bet!" I answered, with a nod, impressed that such a gadget existed.

"OK, see you later!" he said, as he started to open the van door. "See ya later, good luck with the DJ gig!" I called out after him. "Thanks, Della!" he called back, as the door slid shut behind him. I sat for a few moments just relaxing and thinking how lucky I was to have met two really nice guys in a row since my arrival in LA: Manny, and Len. I felt that they were both true Angels at heart. - I decided to put the sleazy movie producer Mike out of my mind, as he wasn't worth my thoughts! I took out my journal and wrote down the latest stories from my travels.

After catching up with my journaling, I packed my journal away, feeling pleased to be all caught up. 'OK, let's see what clothes are in the bag!' I thought to myself, as I picked up the bin bag, and tipped the contents out on the table. I straight away spotted a few clothes that were totally my style: A pair of black "Drainpipe-Jeans" a black and white striped T-shirt, some red pedal pusher-cotton trousers, a black T-Shirt, a purple and grey triangle patterned T-shirt, a red top, a short black cardigan, a pair of black leggings, some white leggings, a lilac t-shirt dress, a long red button shirt-dress, a short black blazer, and a short white denim jacket.

'Wow, I'll have fun mixing and matching these!' I thought to myself, as I quickly went about getting changed into the red pedal pushers, and the black t-shirt. I folded up the black cardi and put it to the side to put in my bag to take out with me. The rest of the clothes in the bin bag looked a bit too much on the glam side for me; some short dresses and skirts, and tiny skimpy tops, so I put them back in the bin bag and went about putting my new clothes in with the clothes that Sally-Anne had given me in my tote bag.

I suddenly realised that I would want my tote bag with me as a day bag when I went out, so I quickly shoved all of my clothes into an empty grocery bag that was lying on the side on the seat, then stuffed it into a small gap between the sofa and the front seats. I put my purse and new black cardi in my tote-bag, and was ready to go! I picked up the map that Len had drawn for me and quickly popped it into a side compartment of the tote bag, opened the side door, and jumped out of the van.

I made sure the van was securely locked before strolling off down the road. I started walking back down towards the area Len and I had come from when we met, but this time I was feeling happy to have a place to rest my head - albeit a van!

I headed, what I now knew as, east on Sunset Boulevard and just kept walking. The strip was a lively as ever, the sun was shining, and the atmosphere was great! "What a fab place!" I thought to myself, as I strolled along feeling so excited to be there! I decided to explore Hollywood, and to just go with the flow... 'If I can't live in the moment at eighteen, when can I?!' I thought to myself as I glided along feeling on cloud nine.

I walked until I reached a cross street called Fairfax, where I spotted what looked like some kind of large cosmetic and toiletries store, so I headed inside to browse around. I was so pleased to find some on sale, discount hair and make-up products, and even a lightweight army-style khaki shoulder bag, which would be more practical as a day bag than my tote bag. I paid for the items at the cash register, feeling excited to feel as though I was getting back to a little bit of normal living again. I packed everything up in my tote bag and headed outside.

The street signs read Sunset Boulevard and Fairfax Avenue. I stood for a moment trying to decide which way to walk, as I had no idea where to go from there, after a moment or so, I decided to head North on Fairfax, and just kept walking. I'd left the area where all the people, restaurants, bars and clubs were, but it was such a lovely day, I didn't care. I was feeling eager to just keep going, and see what there was to see... and after a few minutes, I came to the sign that read: Hollywood Boulevard 'Wow! I didn't know there was an actual street, named Hollywood Boulevard!' I thought to myself feeling excited. I wondered if this was what Len meant when he'd mentioned if I go down to Hollywood. I wondered it was where all the movie studios were. I turned right and carried on walking, to go and find out!

Soon I was in the heart of Hollywood, on Hollywood Boulevard! It had a different atmosphere from the Sunset Strip, and there was no sign of any studios. It was quite touristy, and a little tacky, but lively, which I liked. As I walked along, the street got busier with more and more people milling about, I noticed that there were gold stars on the pavements, lots of souvenir shops and crowds of tourists clustered around various spots taking pictures, there were also lots of street people - Homeless people, punk rockers, musicians, older people, younger people, students, bikers, hippies, break-dancers, black people, white people, Hispanic people, Chinese people... it reminded me more of the city centres in England and Canada.

'This is more like it!' I thought to myself! Feeling happy to see a good cross-section of people at last! I enjoyed the cosmopolitan atmosphere, despite it being a tad on the tacky side. I was just so pleased to discover that LA did have a cosmopolitan centre, of sorts, after all!

I kept walking until I came to a main junction and looked up to see the street signs they read: Hollywood Boulevard, and Vine Street. I suddenly remembered Len warning me not to go beyond Vine Street. I looked across the road to see if there were any dodgy-looking muggers, drug dealers, or just plain crazy people lurking about, but it looked exactly the same as the side of the road that I was on, so naturally I crossed the street to explore some more...

I walked along without a care in the world for a few blocks, until I came to an area where three Hispanic boys around my age were hanging out on a wall outside of a liquor store. They were having fun, laughing and joking, so I couldn't help but smile as I neared them.

"Holla!" one of them exclaimed. "Hello!" I answered back with a smile. "Are you from England?" one of them asked looking at me curiously. "Yes, but I'm having a look around the world!' I joked as I waved my arms around dramatically. "Cool!" answered the guy, and they all laughed. "You're welcome to join us for a beer if you want?" said one of them with a smile. "OK, thanks!" I answered, as I jumped up and sat on the wall with them.

They introduced themselves as Carlos, Miguel, and Juan, and I told them my name was Della as I shook hands with each of them, and soon we were all chatting, laughing and joking like old friends. I felt so at home and comfortable in LA, it didn't seem to matter to me what type of people I was with, or which part of town I was in, I just seemed to resonate with the vibe there, and I loved the feel of it!

We carried on chatting, laughing, and joking about all sorts of things, and at one point we were all being silly trying to do each other's accents and were cracking up with laughter at each other's efforts. Len's warning not to go east of Vine Street was still at the back of my mind, but I was having such a fun time, and these guys did not feel dangerous, so I trusted my instincts and was glad to have some fun company.

During our varied conversations, I told them that I thought it was strange that not many people seemed to be walking in LA, and they agreed. They said in their neighbourhood in east Hollywood people walked about more, and also back in

Mexico where their families were from, the cities were more like European cities, and each had a busy central area, which sounded great to me.

"Who knows, I may be heading there next!" I answered with a smile. "You will love Mexico!" exclaimed Miguel. "I bet!" I answered, feeling excited by the idea of maybe exploring Mexico next, and feeling that it was so nice to have people who I could relate with about the LA walking thing.

"Shall we get some Tacos?" asked Juan, looking across the street at a small Mexican food stand. "Sure, you wanna join us?" asked Juan enthusiastically. "Yeah, OK!" I answered, suddenly feeling a bit hungry. Soon we were all sitting on benches outside the food stand, and tucking into Mexican food. It was the first time I'd ever tried it, aside from the tortilla and cheese wraps that Manny had made for us. I had refried beans and cheese, with giant tortilla chips, and it was delicious and very cheap at $.39 cents!

"Well, I guess I'll head back into Hollywood. It was lovely to meet you guys. I hope I see you all again!" I said, as we all finished our food, and stood up to throw our paper plates in the trash can nearby. "Sure, look out for us, we're usually around this end of town!" answered Miguel, as he leaned over to give me a little hug. "Yeah, drop by again! /Yeah!" added Juan, and Carlos, as they each took a turn to give me a little hug. "I will! Thanks for your hospitality!" I answered as I started to stroll away.

We all waved goodbye to one another one last time, and I took off heading west, towards the main drag on Hollywood Boulevard where all the action was, as the east side beyond the taco stand didn't look like there was much going on, just large car lots, garages, and plain looking buildings. I was soon back in the hub of it all, and I enjoyed just strolling and browsing some of the shops on Hollywood Boulevard once more.

Eventually, I found my way back up to The Sunset Strip and headed towards Len's van. As I got near the van, I could see that the doors were open, so I called out Len's name. He popped his head out and greeted me with a big smile. "Hey Della, come and meet my friend Dave!" He exclaimed excitedly, as he gestured towards someone sitting inside his van. "Hi, Dave!" I said, as I climbed in the van and shook the skinny, long dark-haired guy's hand. "Hi Della, good to meet you!" answered Dave with a smile.

"I like this music, what is it?" I asked, curiously "It's an LA garage band, I've got a whole storage unit full of obscure records, I want to be a DJ, and produce music, so people give me all sorts of stuff to listen to!" answered Len earnestly.

"Cool!" I answered, feeling like I'd just got home from a day out as they made room for me to sit on the sofa with them. "Wanna can of coke?" asked Len. "Yes please!" I answered, with a thirsty grin.

"So, where did you go today?" asked Len curiously, as we sat around sipping on our cokes, and listening to the music. "I went for a walkabout, and wound up just past Hollywood and Vine hanging out with some really nice Hispanic boys around my age" I answered with a smile, as I recalled the fun we'd had chatting on the wall.

"You shouldn't have gone past Vine, they were gang-bangers you were hanging out with!" exclaimed Len, his face looking full of fear and somewhat annoyed with me. I wasn't sure how to take this, as on the one hand I was touched that he was so concerned for me, but at the same time, he wasn't the boss of me! I'd already been travelling around the world solo for the past eight months, what made him think I suddenly needed him to tell me what to do?

Len was such a nice guy though, and I know he meant well, and I didn't want to fall out with him, so I just calmly told him that the guys were absolutely fine, and explained to him that they were just nice normal people! "So, what did they look like?" asked Len curiously, as if trying to decide if they were good guys or not. "Well, I don't know, they just looked like regular Hispanic guys, dark hair combed back, jeans, T-shirts" I answered, with a shoulder shrug. "They sound like gang-bangers to me!" exclaimed Len, going back to his reproachful mode.

"Well even if they were, they were okay to me, and by the law of averages, not every single one of them would be a psychopath! They were just normal people!" I answered passionately defending my newfound Hispanic friends. His friend Dave laughed at my reasoning, and it broke the tension, and even Len laughed a little. "Well just be more careful next time!" Len said sounding like a big brother who didn't want to lose face. "I will!" I answered calmly, even though I wasn't sure what I was agreeing to, but it felt good to keep the peace.

At the back of my mind, I was thinking that maybe a big part of how people treat us is affected by how we treat them. Maybe if I'd been rude and standoffish towards the Hispanic boys, they might have been nasty in return, but because I was just warm, friendly, and non-judgemental with them, it had helped to bring out the best in them, rather than the worst? I decided to keep these thoughts to myself though, as I knew there was no way that Len would be open to such a theory!

Len put some more music on and we all sat listening to it. Once again, I was aware of how comfortable I felt in LA so far. I felt completely in my element, something I'd never experienced quite so fully before, although Toronto came a very close second. The music was very good, and we all listened while tapping our hands and feet, and bobbing our heads along to it. It was kind of like progressive rock, but a little more edgy sounding. Len told me that it was more garage rock, which was one of his favourite genres. He seemed to be a music connoisseur, as did his friend Dave, and I felt honoured to be hearing such cool, obscure tunes!

Around seven in the evening, Len said he would drop by the liquor store and pick us up some snacks for us. The liquor store was only a short walk away, so Dave and I stayed listening to music in the van. Dave was fun to chat with and not quite as serious as Len could be at times. He was much more easy-going, and like me seemed to see the funny side of most things.

"So how's England? I'd love to visit one day!" said Dave as the record we'd been listening to ended. "It's ok, I think you'd enjoy a visit for sure, hey if I'm back by then you and Len would both be welcome to stay at my place!" I answered, with a smile, while imagining how fun it would be to meet up on the other side of the pond! "Cool, thanks! So, what are your plans for LA?" Asked Dave, as he looked for another record to put on. "I don't know yet, I'm just waiting to see what happens!" I answered, with a laugh. "Cool!" he answered, seeming to like my style. "How about you Dave?" I asked, feeling curious about his life. "I love music, and I want to make a living in music, maybe producing, or sound engineering, something like that!" he answered optimistically. "Oh, sounds fun! Hey, anything is possible if you set your heart and mind to it! Good luck!" I exclaimed, loving that he was following his dreams. "Thanks, Della, good luck to you too!" he answered with a big smile, as he put another record on.

I suddenly remembered the make-up and shoulder bag I'd bought earlier, so I went about regrouping my clothes back into my tote bag from the plastic bag I'd stashed them in earlier, and putting my make-up, purse, and cardi into my new army-style shoulder bag. I liked the khaki colour, and it had loads of space for my bits and bobs which was great! I put on a little make-up, and tidied up my hair a bit, while Dave was busy lining up some more tunes to put on.

Len arrived back at the van with bags of food from a nearby deli and some beers and snacks from the liquor store. He poured his goods onto the little table, passed Dave and me a cheese and salad baguette with mayo each, and put the rest of the snacks to the side of the table. "Wow, thanks, Len! What a fantastic feast!" I exclaimed, before taking a big bite of my baguette. "Yeah, this is great! Thanks, Len!" exclaimed Dave, as he too started to tuck into his baguette. "You're welcome, guys!" answered Len looking pleased to see us both so happy.

"So, do you need me to run any errands for you or anything tomorrow?" I asked Len, so I could make myself useful as thanks for his generosity, and kindness. "Sure, I have some mail you can post for me if that's ok?" he answered, before taking a bite of his baguette. "Ok!" I answered with a smile, feeling good to be able to do something to help out. "Thanks, Della!" He answered, and I got the feeling that he was just obliging to try to make me feel useful which I found so heartwarming.

We hung out for a couple more hours in the van, enjoying our food, drinks, music and chats, and then Len suggested we go to a nearby club called The Rainbow Bar and Grill. "That sounds fun! Does it cost anything to go in?" I asked, feeling excited at the prospect of going out to a club in LA. "Not before 10 pm!" answered Len with a grin. "Great!" I answered. 'What a cool city LA is!' I thought to myself.

"You'll like it, it's a great club, with good tunes, and a fun crowd, and you never know who's going to be there, it's a favourite with actors and a lot of big-time rockstars!" added Dave, cooly. "Sound good to me!" I answered curiously.

CHAPTER 25:

MEETING A HOLLYWOOD STAR

We headed down to the Rainbow and as we walked Len told me that if we lost each other, I was welcome to just go back to the van any time. He added that he may not be there tonight, and for me not to worry about him. I got the impression that he had a date, so I thanked him and said ok. Dave said he wouldn't stay out too long but he was happy to join us for an hour or so. We all walked along like three old friends, and I felt so happy to be there in such good company.

As we rounded the corner into the Rainbow car park, we were suddenly met with a bounty of glamorous-looking rocker types all standing around, chatting, laughing, joking, and most of all posing! "Wow! There's a lot of people here!" I exclaimed, not really sure what else to say. "Yeah, it's a popular LA club!" answered Len proudly, while Dave nodded, and smiled, also looking proud, and pleased with the scene ahead of us.

They weren't like the heavy rockers and bikers that I was familiar with in the UK, they had a kind of over-the-top, dolled-up look about them as if it was all just a glamorous fashion show, rather than a lifestyle. It all seemed a bit fake and shallow to me, and I wasn't sure that it was really my cup of tea, as I preferred a more real-looking alternative crowd, but at the same time, I figured, as long as they were nice people, then "To each their own!" as all in all, whatever the style, it's about having fun - which was my cup of tea!

"Mario, this is my friend Della, she's from England!" Exclaimed Len to the friendly-looking man standing near the entrance. "Welcome to the Rainbow Bar and Grill!" exclaimed Mario as he reached out his hand. "Thank you!" I answered as we shook hands. "See you later!" said Len, as he led the way inside, and we all smiled and waved to Mario as we followed Len inside. "He was nice!" I exclaimed to Len and Dave, over the loud rock music that was playing. "Yeah, he's the owner, he's a cool dude!" answered Len proudly.

I noticed that there was a fun-looking bar area to the right and a stylish Italian-looking restaurant to the left. My mind flashed to Karina up in Toronto, and memories of us both helping out at the Italian Restaurant there. I hoped she, and my other friends up there were doing well.

Len led the way through the party people who were standing around drinking and upstairs to a club area where there was another bar with a small dancefloor to the right, and down a few steps. "Let's have a dance!" I exclaimed as I headed down the steps to the dance floor, as the music they were playing was good to dance to.

The guy's smiled, and gestured for me to go ahead, as they headed towards the bar to order some drinks. As I danced a friendly-looking guy joined me on the dance floor, his dance moves were just as fun and silly as mine were, and we were soon making up mad dances with each other and having a great laugh.

"Joe, what's your name?" He said, as one tune ended. "Della! Nice to meet you, Joe!" I answered as we shook hands. He suddenly made up a fun poem about Delightful Della Dancing at the Disco with Dancing Joe, and somehow, by the end of it, he'd nicknamed me Deli!

We both laughed, and I loved that we enjoyed the same silly creative type of humour. Some more good music played so we automatically danced some more while having random little chats here and there. He told me that he worked at a newsstand down at Hollywood and Cahuenga, and he would often come up to the rainbow after work for a dance. He was a really nice guy, just a pure fun-spirited type, and I really liked him as a person and felt very comfortable with him, as felt like a true kindred spirit.

After a while, Len came over and looked happy to see us both dancing together. Len seemed to know Joe's face and grinned knowingly. "I'm heading off to meet someone soon, but I may see you later, if not, I'll see you tomorrow!" said Len, as he passed me a glass of beer. "Oh, thanks, Len! Ok, see you sooner or later then!" I answered, feeling touched that Len had brought me a beer. "OK, see ya later, have fun!" exclaimed Len, before he turned and took off up the steps from the dancefloor.

Dave was waiting for him by the bar and they both waved at me as they took off. I smiled and waved goodbye to them. I felt happy to be dancing with Joe. I had no interest whatsoever in having a look around to see if any of the film or music bigwigs that Dave had mentioned were around, as to me Joe was a true Hollywood star! He was the real thing, not someone acting as him!

We continued with our fun dancing, which we took turns leading, and seemed to include every dance step under the sun, from the twist to the bunny hop, and a million made-up moves in between, which we cracked each other up laughing.

Every so often we would take a break, and lean at the side of the dance floor, with our drinks on a small shelf that surrounded the walls and chat away about all sorts of fun and interesting things. As we chatted, I noticed that some people would make song requests to the DJ through the small hatch on the dance floor which I would keep in mind for another time. At the end of the night, I said goodbye to Joe and headed back to Len's van. Len wasn't around, so I flaked out on the sofa bed and fell asleep straight away.

The next morning, I woke up feeling energised for the day. Len had left a pack of baby wipes on the table top which I used to freshen up with. I did my hair and make-up, grabbed my new shoulder bag, made sure my main tote bag was still safely hidden in the corner of the van, and took off to explore Los Angeles some more...

The brightness of the blue sky and the feel of the warm LA sun on my skin seemed to create an instant feel-good factor in me that I'd never quite experienced before. Florida had been sunny too, and had lifted my spirits a lot compared to the cold and grey weather in England, but it was more of a humid heat. The LA weather was bright, warm and dry, which I quickly discovered I preferred, as it made everything feel more alive and magical to me somehow. I felt as if I was experiencing life instantly as it happened - and I loved it!

As I walked along Sunset Boulevard a bus was coming along with Westwood written on the front. It stopped at a bus stop a few feet away from me, so I decided to jump on board and see what this place called: Westwood was like. LA was such a big place. It seemed to be a thousand cities in one!

The bus journey took about 30 to 45 minutes. The scenery was a mixture of residential, and built-up city areas. There were very few high-rise buildings, most were one story; and very modern or stylish Spanish-looking buildings, with palm trees accentuating most streets, which created a relaxing atmosphere. I got the impression, that the sunny weather helped things to run smoothly, as almost everyone I spotted seemed to be in a good mood, which was infectious. 'I really do like it here!' I thought to myself with a smile, as the bus glided along down Wilshire Boulevard.

"Westwood!" called out the bus driver, suddenly breaking me out of my relaxed state of mind. I quickly stood up and jumped out of the open back door. "Which way is Westwood please?" I asked the driver, as I arrived at the front of the bus just as the last person was boarding. "Straight up!" he answered with a smile. "Great, thanks!" I answered and turned and walked in the direction that he had pointed. On my right, I noticed an unusual, almost UFO shaped restaurant with a big neon sign reading "Ships" which straight away told me that this was a fun area!

Within a couple of minutes, I came to an area that reminded me of a mini-London! Especially the West End and Piccadilly Circus. Maybe this is why it was called Westwood? I thought, thinking that the words West End, and Westwood weren't too far apart!

The streets were laid out differently from the grided parts of LA that I'd seen so far. They were curved and seemed to twist and turn, and loop back around, similar to European streets. There were also lots of people walking around! This was very unusual, as aside from the centre of Hollywood, on most LA streets I had mainly seen people in cars, as very few people walked.

There were lots of cafes, restaurants, bars, arts and crafts shops, novelty shops, T-shirt shops, record shops, and a cinema! 'Wow, this really does feel like a UK or Canadian town centre, but with a strong American flavour!' I thought to myself, feeling pleased to have found such a lively place.

I really liked the vibrant atmosphere, although as I walked around, I started to notice that most of the people looked on the young, white, and rich side! I didn't see the usual cross-section of people that I would expect to see in UK and Canadian towns, which seemed a little odd, and unreal, as if the whole town had been built solely for privileged rich kids between the ages of fifteen to twenty-five.

'Gosh, what the heck am I doing here?' I laughed to myself, as I walked up the street feeling like some kind of raggle-taggle vagabond who was gate-crashing a posh party. Nevertheless, it was still nice to be in a city centre type of environment, even though it all seemed a tad artificial. I strolled along, soaking up the atmosphere, and enjoying a little window shopping as I went.

BOOK 1: TO SEE THE WORLD

As I turned a corner a regular-looking person, holding a clipboard and pen, approached me and asked if I would like to see a free movie? "Maybe, what's it about?" I asked him curiously. "Well, I can't tell you that, but it's a free movie, all you have to do is give your opinion at the end!" he answered persuasively. "OK, thanks! What have I got to lose?!" I answered with a laugh. "Great, there you go, oh and you can bring a guest too!" he added with a smile, as he passed me an invite.

"Thanks!" I answered, wondering where I might find a guest. "You're welcome! Enjoy the movie!" he exclaimed, as he started to continue on his way. I liked the way that he was working for a living, and not living off his rich parents, as most of the young people in Westwood seemed to be doing, going by the trendy clothes, and fancy cars they were driving.

I continued browsing around Westwood until I came across a novelty store and strolled inside. I spotted a young guy around my age who looked a lot like Simon LeBon from the new wave band Duran-Duran. I suddenly wondered if he would fancy being my movie guest, so I approached him as he was looking at a hologram toy.

"That's neat!" I exclaimed. "Yes, it is, have a look!" he answered in a foreign-sounding accent as he passed it over for me to look at. "Cool!" I answered, as I took it off him, and held it up to look at. He smiled and nodded, and we were soon chatting away about all the fun-looking things in the shop.

The conversation soon flowed into other things, as he was very easy to talk with. It turned out that he was a student at LACC originally from Greece, and his name was Petros Regos. "Ah Petros, that means Peter, in English right?" I asked curiously. "Yes, that's right!" He answered, looking impressed.

"Peter is one of my favourite boys' names, do you mind if I call you Peter? I asked, curious to know if the two names were interchangeable to him, now that he was living in LA. "Sure, that's ok, I don't mind!" He answered pulling a couldn't-care-less face and shrugging his shoulders. "Ah, nice!" I answered with a smile. He smiled back, and it felt as though we automatically clicked.

We continued to browse around together, and afterwards, we strolled out of the shop together and over to a nearby doughnut shop. We found a booth and sat down and got comfortable. "Hey, do you fancy coming to a free movie with me? All we have to do is fill out a form at the end, saying what we thought about the movie!" I asked enthusiastically, as tucked into our doughnuts, and coffees.

I only liked him as a friend, as I didn't feel a spark between us, so it wasn't meant to be a romantic date, and I think he could tell that, as he probably felt similar to me, but we each seemed glad of each other's company, especially as we were both from out of town. "Yes, I would like that!" he answered, looking pleased with the idea. "Great!" I answered, feeling pleased to have found someone to go to the movie with. "It's in Hollywood, but it's not for another three hours so there's no rush!" I said as we sat sipping away at our coffees, and eating our donuts. "That's good, I don't like to rush!" he answered nonchalantly, and we both laughed.

"So, do you miss Greece?" I asked curiously. "Well, yes, but I had to leave because I didn't want to join the army!" he answered, looking a little upset at the thought. "So would you have had to join the army if you'd stayed in Greece?" I asked, feeling shocked at the idea. "Yes, I would have no choice, so I decided to become a student in Los Angeles instead!" he answered, with a sad shoulder shrug. "Good idea, much preferable than going off to war!" I answered, feeling sorry for him being forced into such a big life-changing decision. "Yes, and I like it here!" he answered with a smile. "Me too, cheers!" I answered holding up my cup. We both clinked cups and laughed.

"And what about you, why are you here?" He asked looking genuinely interested. "Oh gosh, where do I begin!" I answered, with a laugh. "So, are you a student too?" he asked, looking puzzled. "Nooo, I'm just a traveller! I just wanted to have a look around the planet!" I answered, deciding to try and keep things simple.

"Oh, so do you have family or friends here?" He asked, still sounding confused. "Yes, I do have friends here now, and I have an aunt that's coming over from England at some point, and I'm meant to be meeting up with her to go and look at some property, she has a ranch in England, but I think she'd prefer to have a ranch in America!" I answered, hoping to make my loose plans sound a little tidier than they were. "Oh, I see" he answered, while still looking a little confused.

"I hope the movie's good!" I exclaimed, thinking it was best to change the subject. "Yes, although I don't really care, I have nothing else to do!" answered Peter casually. "Me too!" I answered, and we both laughed. "I guess we should start heading up to Hollywood soon," I said, as we finished off our doughnuts and coffee. "Yes, ok" answered Peter, as we both stood up and took our rubbish to the trash can.

BOOK 1: TO SEE THE WORLD

We strolled out of Westwood and down to Wilshire Boulevard to wait for the bus to Hollywood. A bus soon turned up, and Peter and I joined the queue and boarded the bus. We both paid our fairs, then found a seat together. As we rode on the bus along Wilshire Boulevard, I noticed that there were a lot of Hispanic people on the bus. I got the impression that they had all just clocked off from work and we're heading back to the downtown area to their homes.

I assumed that the rent must be a lot cheaper downtown. I remembered that the majority of people I'd seen downtown upon my arrival to Los Angeles were Hispanic, and once again I felt saddened that Los Angeles seemed so segregated. From what Len had told me, I had the impression that the majority of white people lived in the North part of LA known as "The Valley" and the majority of Hispanic people lived in the east, while the majority of the black people lived in the south, with a little bit of a mix in the middle around Hollywood, and out to the west coast.

I was staring out of the window pondering on the segregation of people by race, and riches, when Petros suddenly started telling me that he was studying film at LACC. "That sounds fun, and you're in the right city for it!" I answered encouragingly. "Yes, but I really want to be a DJ because I love music" he answered, sounding fed up with having to study film. "Can't you do both?" I asked curiously. "Yes, that's what I'm doing, but I'd rather just focus on music, but my college grant covers my hotel room, so I have to do so much film" He answered with a sigh. "Gosh, you get a hotel too?" I asked, feeling surprised that his grant covered a hotel for him, rather than just a room in someone's house to lodge in, which was what most students' live-in situations seemed to be in England.

"Yes, but it's not a nice hotel. It's near downtown LA, and I have to share a room, but at least it is near to the college I go to" He answered. "Wow, I love to study film! I have tons of ideas for stories, but I don't know what to do with them, and even if I write them out, where do I go with them? Finding the right publisher, or producer seems like trying to find a needle in a haystack!" I said, remembering my brief stint on a media course back in my home town. "Oh, you should do something with your ideas! Not everyone has a lot of ideas like that. Most people in my class, and myself just stare at a blank page for hours!" he answered "Yeah, but sometimes I feel that having too many ideas can be just as bad!" I answered, and we both laughed.

"Well, hopefully, I will be a DJ someday, and you will be a writer!" he exclaimed. "Yeah, that would be nice! I just don't understand how people get their books and movies out there. I guess they go through the usual route of college, and university, and get placements from there, but a lot of creative types don't like being confined to the school system, so they must either get a lucky break, or they just aren't bothered about commercialising their work? I don't know, it's all a bit of a mystery to me!" I answered, feeling baffled by it all. "Yes, and a lot of artists' work is not discovered until a long time after they are dead!" answered Peter in a serious tone. "Oh, that's motivating!" I joked, and we both cracked up laughing.

"I think we have to get off the bus here and walk down to the movie theatre!" I exclaimed, suddenly noticing that getting near to the area of Sunset shown on the movie invite map. "OK, let's go!" answered Peter, as he rang the bell, and we both stood up to get off the back of the bus. "Thanks!" I called out, as I waved to the driver, and followed Peter off the bus.

"So how come you have platinum blond hair, fair skin and blue eyes? I thought Greek people were dark?" I asked Peter, as we walked along Sunset Boulevard. "because my mother's side is German, and they are all very fair, so I am like them." answered Peter matter-of-factly. "Oh, I see!" I answered with a nod.

"What about you, you look more Mediterranean than English, you look Italian, or Spanish, or maybe even Maltese!" Peter asked, looking at me as if trying to figure out my ancestral roots. "Yeah, I probably do have some Mediterranean in me, seeing as most Brits came from mainland Europe originally, and a lot of them probably came up from Southern Europe, although on my dad's father's side, they're very fair and very Anglo' looking, so they're probably from northern Europe, although on my dad's mother's side there is also some Romany Gypsy, and they're quite dark looking. I guess I'm a mix of all sorts!" I answered, with a laugh. "Yes, probably me too, but I just look fair!" answered Peter with a nod.

We eventually got nearer to where the people were gathering for the movie, and as we walked along I noticed that Peter turned a lot of girl's heads. I guessed it was because he was very good-looking, and also maybe because he looked so much like Simon LeBon! He seemed mildly amused by this, but also a little annoyed, as if he didn't want to be bothered by strangers staring at him.

He was a sweet guy, but he came across as somewhat of a slightly pampered "mummy's boy" type, as he was squeaky-clean looking, and his clothes and shoes looked immaculate. His demeanour was a tad on the pompous side, and he seemed a little out of place and naïve to be in such a big city as LA, but at the same time, he did have a genuine quality about him that I couldn't help but like, and overall I found his character to be quite endearing.

We arrived at the movie theatre and joined the long queue waiting to go inside. "I hate long lines!" moaned Peter after about three seconds of standing in the queue. "So do I!" exclaimed a punky new-wave-styled girl with shoulder-length dark-brown hair standing in front of us as she turned around to face us. She had big brown eyes and a cheeky, but friendly face. We all laughed and introduced ourselves to each other.

"Gabby Guardino!" she announced as she reached out her hand. "Hi Gabby, that's Peter, and I'm Della!" I answered as we all shook hands. "So, are you two guys going out together?" she asked with a cheeky grin. "No, we're just friends, we only met today!" I answered, with a laugh, as Peter nodded along. "Cool! Mind if I hang with you both?" she answered, giving us another cheeky smile. "Sure, the more the merrier!" I answered as Peter continued to nod as if he wasn't bothered either way, he just wanted to get out of the queue and sit down!

Gabby looked pleased and turned a little more our way to face us so that she could talk with us as we all shuffled along in the queue. "You look like Simon Lebon!" Gabby suddenly exclaimed after looking at Peter for a few seconds, as if she knew him from somewhere. "I know, that's what I thought too!" I answered with a laugh, as Peter just shrugged his shoulders, and seemed unfazed by his similarity. I got the feeling that he probably felt that he was superior to Simon LeBon, so he didn't quite see what all the fuss was about! I chuckled to myself at this thought, and kind of liked his unique style of down-to-earth arrogance. It was a strange combination of traits. He was a one-off, that was for sure!

Finally, we made it into the building and got to see the movie, not that we paid that much attention to it, as the three of us were being silly, chatting, laughing and joking most of the time. We filled out a survey before leaving the theatre and dropped it in a box. We had all thought the comedy movie was quite bad, and had mainly been laughing because it wasn't funny!

Afterwards, we went to get a snack at a taco place and carried on getting to know one another. "You guys wanna go to a free club tonight?" Gabby asked suddenly. "Yeah/Why not?" Peter and I answered in unison. "...and if it's free, we can afford that!" I added, and we all laughed. "Yeah it's a cool punk and new wave club, it's called The Seven Seas, it's on Hollywood Boulevard, but the entrance is around the back!" said Gabby enthusiastically. "Sound's good to me, I could do with a dance after sitting in that movie theatre!" I answered, suddenly looking forward to checking out a new club. "Sure, let's go, I think it's open by now!" answered Gabby, leading the way back up towards Hollywood Boulevard.

As the three of us walked along, I once again became aware of how comfortable I felt in LA regardless of where I was, or who I was hanging out with. We all seemed to go with the flow, which suited me to a tee! We arrived at the club and made our way inside. "I know some people in here, I'll go score us some beers!" announced Gabby, as she took off towards the bar area, while Peter and I gravitated towards the large dance floor that already had quite a few funky-looking punk, new wavers, and funky disco types dancing around on it. "Nice club, I like this music!" exclaimed Peter, looking happy to be there. "Yeah, me too, let's dance!" I answered as we both started to dance around on the floor.

Peter wasn't a mad dancer like me and "Rainbow Joe" he was more of a normal side-to-side, cool new wave style dancer, but it was still fun to be having a dance with him. Gabby suddenly arrived back on the dance floor with a couple of glasses of beer. "Do you guys mind sharing?" she said, as she passed one of the beers to me, and took a swig of the other. "No, I don't do you?" I asked Peter before I took a sip of beer. "No, I do not mind!" answered Peter, as I passed him the beer, and he took a sip.

As the night went on Peter got so much attention from the girls at the club, that Gabby and I found it hilarious, especially as Peter was so shy and awkward and not a typical ladies man at all! - He just happened to look really cool! but rather than enjoy the attention, he seemed irritated by it. "Oh, it must be so awful to have all those girls after you!" I teased Peter as we danced "Yeah, that must really suck man!" added Gabby with a grin. He didn't look amused at all, and pulled a face, that made it obvious that he just wanted to dance and enjoy the music - without girls bothering him.

At the end of the night, we all headed out towards the parking lot at the back of the club. "You can both stay at my hotel room tonight if you want to, my Chinese roommate is away," said Peter, as the cool air outside hit us, and the crowds headed off in different directions. "Sounds good/ Cool!" answered Gabby and I, as if we wanted to keep hanging out together. "OK, let's go" answered Peter, as he led the way.

We travelled on various busses, until we reached an old hotel building with several floors, on Wilshire Boulevard just a few blocks away from the downtown area, which I thought was interesting, as it taught me that some cosmopolitan types do live in the downtown after all! There were two single beds in the room, so I slept with Peter in his bed, and Gabby slept in Peter's roommate's bed. There were no weird vibes between us, it just felt as though we were all old friends camping out together.

The next morning, I woke up around 11 am and went down to the lobby to phone Len to let him know that I was okay. On the way down the hallway I bumped into a Chinese guy, and I said hello and asked him if he was Peter's roommate. He looked confused and seemed to give me a slight nod.

I called Len, and he was happy to hear that I was okay. I told him about my two new pals: Gabby and Peter, and he was pleased to hear that I'd made some new "non-gang-member friends" As he jokingly put it, before saying he would see me whenever I got back up to Sunset!

"Don't forget you're welcome to treat the van as your home too, you can come and go as you please!" he reminded me, just before we were about to hang up. "Thanks, Len! See you sooner or later then!" I answered, feeling touched by his kind hospitality. "Have a good one!" he answered before we both hung up.

I headed back up to Peter's room feeling pleased with my life, my travels, and the lovely people I'd met along the way so far. I thought how wonderful it was that I felt so at home in so many places, especially: Toronto and LA, and I was so happy that I had ventured out of the known world of my small town in England into the unknown of the wider world, and that somehow, I had still managed to find kindred spirits, along the way. I strolled along the hotel corridors with a spring in my step, wondering what adventures my new friends and I would get up to today.

As I neared Peter's room, I could hear raised voices coming from inside. I gave a little knock as I opened the door and gingerly stepped inside. The Chinese guy was shouting at Peter, apparently, he was very angry that Gabby and I had stayed there overnight. I glanced a look at Gabby, who was sitting in a chair in the corner of the room looking bemused by the situation. As soon as we caught each other's eye we both instantly burst out laughing, which didn't help matters, as the Chinese guy suddenly turned his attention towards us, and started shouting for us to leave his room! This, of course, made us laugh even more, as the two of us quickly grabbed our belongings, and hurried out of the door doubled up in fits of laughter.

Peter quickly, followed us and shouted something back at the Chinese guy, before the three of us ran, and stumbled our way to the lift, laughing our hats off, like three drunks, who'd just been booted out of a pub "What's his problem?"

asked Gabby as we rode down in the lift. "Forget him! He doesn't like anybody in "his place" Pay him no attention!" Peter answered, somewhat arrogantly. Gabby and I found the situation somewhat bizarre, so we pulled puzzled-looking faces at each other, as we shook our heads, and continued to laugh it off.

"My goodness, we've done no harm, we only slept there, big deal!" I exclaimed shaking my head, while feeling a little indignant, but amused at the same time. I had the feeling that Gabby and myself, were both friendly and hospitable to others, so we found such uncalled-for inhospitality bewildering. "...but it takes all sorts. I guess!" I added, as I shrugged my shoulders, and shook my head. "I guess!" Answered Gabby, rolling her eyes, and we both cracked up laughing again. while Peter stoically led the way out of the building. We found a place to eat nearby and continued with our getting to know one another chats. It was fun to have a couple of friends to hang out with, and the feeling seemed mutual.

After eating we decided we would go to Santa Monica beach. There were regular busses running down Wilshire Boulevard that went all the way there, which according to Peter was about an hour's bus ride depending on traffic. We hopped on a beach-bound bus and found seats at the back to continue our chit-chat. The city flew past us as we laughed and joked our way to the coast. I found it interesting that the whole of LA seemed to come to an abrupt stop at the beach, as Wilshire Boulevard ran directly to it with just one boulevard running across it parallel to the ocean. 'Wow, so this is the Pacific Ocean!' I thought to myself in silent awe, as I admired its beauty.

We meandered around the busy streets near the ocean, chatting away, and enjoying the atmosphere. Much to my surprise Santa Monica was another little cosmopolitan pocket, with people walking around, shopping, enjoying cafés and bars, while some people were sitting on the grass lawns that overlooked the beach and ocean. This area felt more cosmopolitan than Westwood, as the people here did seem to be from all walks of life, which I liked.

We soon found ourselves strolling down towards the pier and down the ramp that led to it. We were surrounded by people having a fun day out, and it felt as if we'd suddenly gone on holiday from our street life, and were now part of the jolly beach crowd! The sand below the pier looked enticing, and we soon found some steps to take us down to it. "This is nice!" I exclaimed, feeling like a kid again. "Yes/ Sure is!" Gabby and Peter agreed, and all three of us couldn't stop from smiling as we strolled along, without a care in the world!

We had a fun afternoon hanging out at the beach, and at some point, it dawned on me that all three of us were just eighteen years old. We were each shiny brand-new adults! No wonder we still felt like kids at heart though, as we had been kids only weeks, or months earlier! I also loved that all three of us were from different countries in the world, but we had somehow managed to find each other and become friends. It felt like a little LA magic was at play!

After a while, we found ourselves automatically strolling back towards Wilshire Boulevard. "Wanna go get some free food?" asked Gabby suddenly. "Yes!" answered Peter and I in unison, and the three of us laughed. "Sure, there's a club near here called: The Green Onion, and during happy hour they put out a free buffet" said Gabby cooly. "Lead the way!" I exclaimed as I ushered her in front of us with a grin. We all laughed, as Gabby strode on ahead, and sure enough, led the way to a very plush-looking café-bar.

"The Green Onion" read the sign above the door. Peter and I followed Gabby inside. As we entered, I glanced around to get a feel for the place, it looked to be a major "Yuppie" type of hangout, as all of the local office workers seemed to be there. I assumed they went there after they finished work. There was a small dancefloor with music playing and some of the office workers were dancing. "What a great idea! A fun place for people to come to right after work and have some drinks and food and let their hair down!" I exclaimed, with a big smile. "Yeah, but this isn't really my scene" said Gabby looking "Too cool for school" as she stood back. "I prefer punk, but free food is free food!" she added. We all agreed and laughed, as we shuffled our way towards the buffet.

"My taste in music is more eclectic than just punk and new-wave, I like all sorts, as long as it sounds good!" I exclaimed as we nibbled away at the snacks. "Fair enough!" Gabby answered, looking like she understood where I was coming from, but I got the feeling that she still preferred Punk. "Yes, I like all sorts of music too!" agreed Peter, nodding his head. "Come and dance with me!" I exclaimed to Gabby and Peter, as some upbeat new-wave music came on. Gabby laughed and declined my offer as she wanted to go and get some more food, but Peter was game, so we headed over to the dance floor and started dancing.

We were trying to blend in, although I was sure we stood out. What with Peter looking exactly like Simon Le Bon with his blond hair, and fashionable new-wave clothes, and me with my punky, new-wave colourful clothes, and my long wavy burgundy hair, and Gabby with her hard-core punk look. The locals must have wondered where we'd sprung from!

After a few dances I went to use the bathroom, and much to my delight when I came back out Gabby and Peter were dancing together on the dancefloor which made me smile. "That's the spirit!" I said to them as I joined them, and we all had a fun, silly dance. The place started to fill up, and soon we were chatting with all sorts of friendly people and were being offered drinks, left, right and centre!

The tipsier we got, the wilder we danced on the dancefloor, but no one seemed to care that we weren't office workers like them. In fact, most of them seemed to like us for being a little different, and I just loved this American attitude! They seemed to cheer on each other on, in a "Viva la difference!" kind of way, which made them seem super-cool to me.

After a couple of hours, I asked Gabby and Peter if they wanted to come with me up to Hollywood to meet Len, and maybe go to the rainbow afterwards. They both said sure and we all jumped on the next bus back up to Hollywood!

CHAPTER 26:

LA CLUBBING

Len was inside his van listening to some music and seemed very happy to see me with my two new friends: Gabby and Peter. I introduced everyone, Len welcomed us, told us to find a seat, and passed around some beers. Len and Peter seemed to click instantly and were soon chatting away, while Gabby and I touched up our make-up, chatted, and laughed at the idea of us getting dolled up to go to the rainbow, especially as we were not typical "rainbow gals."

"I'm just gonna get changed" I whispered to Gabby, as I reached down into my tote bag and pulled out the black drainpipe jeans, and black and white T-shirt. Gabby pulled a face that said, how are you going to manage that, as I discretely switched my red pedal pushers, for the black jeans, then ducked down under the table and swapped tops. "Like that!" I announced, as I slowly slid back in my seat, as if nothing had happened. "Slick!" exclaimed Gabby, and we both cracked up laughing.

"So what would you do if one of those rich plastic rockers wanted to date you?" asked Gabby mischievously, as I topped up my black eyeliner. "Hmm, not really my cup of tea, but I guess if he was a nice person, I may give him a chance!" I answered, feeling not sure what I would do. "How about you?" I asked Gabby, curiously. "Sure, I'd go out with him as long as he wanted to spend a ton on me!" She answered with a big belly laugh, and I joined in laughing. I loved Gabby's mischievous sense of humour.

I glanced over to see what Len and Peter were chatting about. It turned out they had discovered that they were both Greek AND they both wanted to be DJs! I was pleased to see they had hit it off so well, and I was happy for Peter to have some male company - at last!

We all seemed to be ready to leave at the same time, and one by one we jumped out of the van and headed down to the Rainbow Bar and Grill. Gabby was cringing and pulling "Throw-up faces" at me from behind the backs of some of the "plastic-rocker" guys, as she called them, and I was trying not to laugh as I felt bad about it, but I could see the funny side too.

'Don't make fun of them! We are all just human beings trying to enjoy our lives! Live and let live!' I told myself, as we were all pushed and shoved about, as we made our way through the crowd toward the Rainbow entrance, and inside the club.

We followed Len upstairs to the small bar that wasn't as crowded as the downstairs bar. Len swiftly bought us all some drinks, and we all stood around as if in some kind of nightclub limbo. We weren't ready for dancing yet but didn't want to sit down either, so instead we hovered somewhat awkwardly while glancing around the club curiously at the other people, as if in hope of them entertaining us somehow!

Len seemed more relaxed than the three of us, and he was soon casually chatting away to someone at the bar. I could tell by Gabby's face that this was not her scene at all, and as usual, Peter looked a little out of place in his suave and sophisticated preppy-looking attire.

"Wanna go to The Cathy DeGrand?" Asked Gabby suddenly, looking bored with The Rainbow already. "What's that?" I asked, wondering if it was a café or a club. "It's a Punk Rock Club, it's way more real than the Rainbow, and the punks there are super cool!" She answered persuasively.

"Sure, OK!" I answered, feeling curious about what other nightlife LA had to offer. "Cool!" answered Gabby looking pleased. "What about you Peter, do you want to come to a Punk club with us, or would you rather stay here?" I asked, thinking that Peter may prefer to stay at the Rainbow and hang out with his newfound friend: Len. "OK, I go with you!" He answered, much to my surprise. I guessed because he saw that Len was preoccupied talking with someone else, and maybe Peter would have felt awkward just hanging about like a lemon.

I gingerly interrupted Len and his company to tell him that we were taking off to the Cathay de Grand with Gabby. "OK, have a good time!" He answered with a smile. He gave me an earnest little look as if to say: "Remember everything I told you about staying safe!" "Thanks!" I answered with a smile. "Don't forget, you're welcome to crash at the van anytime!" he added, just as we were taking off. "OK, thanks again, Len!" I called back as I smiled and waved, before turning round to follow Peter and Gabby back down the stairs, and out of the club, pushing our way against the tide of people squeezing to get in, as we went.

BOOK 1: TO SEE THE WORLD

We eventually made it outside, and into the parking lot, which was full of dolled-up rockers, fancy cars and motorbikes. It was quite an exciting atmosphere, although I couldn't quite pinpoint why. I assumed that everybody was just happy to be out to see and be seen. They reminded me of a bunch of peacocks parading around, all vying for the attention of one another, which I found both fascinating and amusing.

"We have to catch a bus heading east on sunset" said Gabby as she led the way through the crowd and onto the main street. "Right/OK" answered Peter and I, as we followed along, both of us looking eager to explore this city of LA that seemed to be full of surprises.

We jumped on the next eastbound bus that came along, and about twenty minutes later we jumped out and made our way up a side road until we arrived at a large building just a little way east of Vine, and south of Hollywood Boulevard. Loud Punk Rock Music was playing inside the building, and lots of hard-core-looking punk-rockers were hanging about outside.

They certainly looked more "real" as Gabby had put it, than the dolled-up "Plastic Rockers," as Gabby had called them, at the rainbow! "Follow me!" Said Gabby as she led the way to the club entrance. "Three bucks," said the guy at the door as we approached. "Nah, we don't pay, I'm a friend of El Duce!" answered Gabby confidently, while Peter and I stood there trying to look as if we knew who she was referring to.

"...His band The Mentors is playing tonight, I'm on the guest list, and these guys are with me!" added Gabby authoritatively, as she glanced our way, and gave us a wink. Peter and I tried to keep poker-faced as if we were both hoping that we would get to join Gabby in the club if she was let in for free.

The guy quickly checked the guest list. "OK!" He said, as he nodded and stood to the side to let us all in. 'Yay!' I thought to myself, as Peter and I flashed each other a triumphant grin. "Let's head down to the mosh pit, maybe we can do some moshing!" Shouted Gabby above the music. "Yeah maybe!" I shouted back, while Peter and I gave each other a puzzled look.

We followed Gabby inside and to the right, and headed down some dimly lit stairs. The walls were painted black and the atmosphere was very grungy. The Punk music was playing loud in a large basement type of room, and there were lots of punk rockers crammed in there all looking way "too cool for school!" or for anywhere for that matter!

The music was fast and rough, and I wasn't sure if this was my scene, or not. I liked that it was "real" but it was all a bit too aggressive for my liking. I preferred the fun creative new-wave stuff like Kate Bush, Human League, Talking Heads, Fun Boy Three, Bananarama, Kraftwerk etc... Plus the people at the clubs I liked were usually fun, and friendly. The people at this club all looked pretty hostile and angry! I figured I would only stay for a little while, but more as an "anthropologist" than an audience member, as I was curious to see how these hard-core punks had fun.

The room was very hot and sweaty, and I found it uncomfortable, so I could only imagine how painful Peter must be finding it! At the front of the stage were a bunch of guys throwing themselves around and smashing into each other, full-on slam-dancing as it was called in England, or "Moshing" as Gabby called it. There was a band on stage playing very fast metal punk, and the "Moshers" seemed to love it!

"Wanna dance?" said Gabby mischievously looking over at Peter and me. Peter looked horrified and shook his head as he backed away, but I found the invite quite funny, so I took her up on the offer. "Ok, hold on!" I answered grinning back mischievously at Gabby, as I asked Peter to hold my army shoulder bag.

Peter took my bag off me, and I jumped into the mosh-pit with Gabby, but just as quick as we jumped in, we were pushed back out, we both found this hilarious, so we dove back in, only to be rapidly expelled again, we dove in repeatedly, but were bounced back out time and time again by the crazed moshing slam-dancers.

We were both laughing hysterically at the absurdity of it all, but Peter stayed far away and had by now backed himself up against a wall in a less active part of the room, as if for his own safety. He stood there looking like a little boy lost, and I felt a little bit sorry for him, but ultimately, I figured that we were all having the same life experience, but we were just dealing with it differently!

Gabby and I were having such a laugh trying to get into the centre of the mosh-pit, that it started to feel like a challenge we just couldn't let go of. Eventually, we succeeded and spent a good few minutes slamming around like people in straight jackets. We both found it absolutely hilarious, although I could see that some of the guys were taking it all very seriously and were quite rough as they slammed and pushed hard into one another, but miraculously nobody was seriously injured, and all in all, it was quite fun!

When the music finished, Gabby and I went to find Peter and catch our breath. He was standing in the far corner of the room on his own looking miserable.

BOOK 1: TO SEE THE WORLD

"Thanks for looking after my bag!" I exclaimed as I took my bag off him. "No problem, I don't like it here, I am going now!" He answered glumly. "OK Peter, hopefully we'll see you soon, and maybe we can go somewhere that you want to go next time!" I answered, hoping to make him feel better. "Yes ok, bye!" He answered, with a nod, as he took off. "See ya/Bye Peter!" Gabby and I called out after him as he headed for the door. He gave a wave, then disappeared out of the door.

I felt a little concerned for him, and I hoped that he would make it through the crowds of hard-core punk rockers safely. I wondered if I should go with him, but Gabby and I were having a fun time, despite it not really being my scene either. 'He'll be fine, he's a big boy!' I told myself, with a sigh.

Gabby blagged a beer off some guy, and generously shared it with me, which was perfect timing as I was so thirsty after the slam dancing. Suddenly the main band appeared on stage. "This is El Duce's Band - The Mentors!" exclaimed Gabby excitedly, as she gulped down the last of the drink. "Who?" I asked, glancing up at the stage to see a bunch of guys with guitars wearing what looked like black executioner hoods! "The Mentors! Wanna go mosh?" shouted Gabby over the music with a grin. "OK!" I answered with a laugh, as I quickly hid my army bag in a dark corner of the room, and followed her back towards the front of the stage.

I was looking forward to another mad slam-dance, but this time it was impossible to get anywhere near the centre as the mosh-pit wash jam-packed, so we pogo-jumped around on the edges instead. The music was fast and furious, and a bit too hard-core punk for me, but I enjoyed a fun dance with Gabby non-the-less, as the two of us mock slammed-danced into each other as we pogoed about, cracking up with laughter, once again, at the madness of it all! 'If Peter could see us now, he'd probably be horrified!' I thought to myself with a laugh.

We had a fun time at the club for another hour or so, Pogo-dancing, drinking, and chatting to random people, and afterwards, we were invited to join the band and some others in the back room for drinks. Gabby seemed to know a lot of people there, and I just went along with her as a kind of "wing gal"

Although it wasn't really my scene, I was still curious enough to hang in there. I imagined that Peter was home safe, and tucked up in bed by now, I hoped his Chinese roommate wasn't giving him any more hassle. I laughed to myself at the memory of the morning in the hotel room, with Peter's roommate shouting at us all, and us all running off down the hallway. I hoped I would see Peter again at some point.

"El Duche this is Della, she's from England, Della this is El Duche!" exclaimed Gabby as a slightly older, stocky, bald-headed tough-looking guy with a beard came over towards us. "Hey, Della!" said El Duche with a smile, as he reached out his hand. "Hi, El Duche!" I answered as I shook his hand. "So what's up Gabs, wanna beer?" asked El Duche as we all sat down at a small table nearby. "Sure, can you get one for Della too?" answered Gabby, flashing me her mischievous grin. "No problem!" answered El Duche, as he gestured to a blond-haired punk guy at a nearby table to bring us some beers. The punk guy pulled a few cans from a box and brought them over to our table. "Drink!" exclaimed El Duche. "Thank you/ Thanks" Gabby and I answered, as we grabbed a can each.

Another black-haired, skinny punk guy joined us at our table and started chatting to me about all sorts of random things which made me think he was on some kind of drugs, but he was funny with it, so I humoured him and chatted along, while noticing that Gabby looked so happy to be having some time with El Duche that I didn't want to bother them. El Duche looked happy to be spending time with Gabby too, and I smiled to myself, as I realised that they actually looked good together, as if they were a couple of book ends.

The party continued down the road at a nearby recording studio and went on into the wee hours. Eventually, I fell asleep on a sofa in the main room, and Gabby disappeared off into another room with El Duce.

I woke up a few hours later with a massive hangover. I got up and staggered away to find the bathroom where I washed my face to try and wake up some more. Next, I went in search of coffee. I found some in a small kitchen area and spotted a jar of instant coffee, so I made myself a cup and went back to sit on the sofa to continue to wake up.

After a while punk rockers started to emerge from different rooms. I vaguely recognise some of them from the night before. As they neared me on their way to the kitchen, or bathroom, I asked if any of them had seen Gabby. They shook their heads, as if not sure who I meant, and just as I started to ask another punk who had appeared from the other side of the studio, Gabby suddenly appeared grinning at me from across the room.

"Gabby!" I exclaimed, and we gave each other a big smile, as she headed my way. "Hey Della, where did you get the coffee?" she asked, looking like she could do with a gallon of coffee to help sober her up. "Over there!" I answered in a croaky voice, as I pointed towards the kitchen and held my head as if to say I have a bad hangover and this coffee is essential and highly recommended! "Thanks!" answered Gabby, as she nodded, and disappeared into the kitchen area.

About five minutes later, with a cup of coffee in hand Gabby appeared again, and came and sat next to me on the sofa. She looked very pleased with herself and was grinning from ear to ear. "So, where'd you go last night?" I asked curiously. "I was hanging with El Duce!" she answered, as she gave me a cheeky wink. "Oh right!" I answered, with a grin.

After an hour or so of coffee refills, and chats with a few other punks, Gabby told me that El Duce will probably crash out for a few more hours yet, so we may as well get going. "OK, let's go!" I answered, as I grabbed my shoulder bag, and followed Gabby out of the building, and into the street.

We turned the corner onto Hollywood Boulevard, and I noticed that it was full of life as usual. "Would you rather live in a big city with new faces every day, or a small town with the same faces every day?" I asked Gabby, as we walked along. She thought about it for a few seconds then answered: "Big city! How about you?" she answered emphatically. "I'm not really sure... there are pros and cons to both!" I answered, with a shoulder shrug. "I guess so!" she answered, and we both laughed.

"Want an ace lunch?" Said Gabby suddenly. "Sounds good to me!" I answered curiously. Gabby seemed full of knowledge of places to go and things to do in LA. "I'll call my dad; he'll treat us out!" She said proudly. I was surprised that she was in touch with her dad as she seemed like a full-time street kid in her looks and ways.

"When we meet my dad you should put on your poshest English accent, it will totally freak him out!" she exclaimed with a big grin, as we walked along looking for a pay phone. "Hhh-wot, lake thees?" I answered jokingly, sounding like a cross between Queen Elizabeth and Inspector Clouseau. "Yeah, like that!" answered Gabby laughing. We spotted a payphone and she went to make a call to her dad. I stood away to the side, soaking in the beautiful LA sun, as she chatted away for a few minutes.

CHAPTER 27:

"WELCOME TO THE USA!" – John Candy

"He's going to meet us at swabs!" she said looking pleased with herself as she hung up the phone, and strolled over towards me. "Great!" I answered, looking forward to meeting Gabby's dad. "Yeah, we'll need to catch the bus on Sunset to get there, it won't take long!" answered Gabby looking pleased. "Sounds good!" I answered, as we headed south down a side street to Sunset Boulevard, and jumped on the first bus that came along heading west.

"Your dad sounds nice, it's good that you get along with him!" I said as we rode along on the bus up Sunset. "Yeah, he's a nice guy, he left my mom because she's an alky, but he keeps in touch, his brother is Harry Guardino, have you heard of him?" answered Gabby matter-of-factly. "Um, the name rings a bell, but I'm not sure?" I answered, trying to remember where I may have heard the name. "He was in the movie: Dirty Harry, and a bunch of other films" answered Gabby, as if trying to jog my memory. "Yeah, rings a bit of a bell, was the movie about him?" I asked, clocking the title was the same as his name. "Nah, Clint Eastwood plays Dirty Harry, it's a cop film, my uncle Harry plays a police lieutenant" answered Gabby. "Oh right, I'm not sure if I've seen it, but my dad and my brothers probably have!" I answered, feeling curious to see the movie, mainly to see if Harry Guardino looked like Gabby!

"He's still an actor but he was better known in the seventies, he used to go out with Lauren Bacall!" added Gabby, as if that would finally jog my memory. "My parents have probably heard of him, I haven't really watched that many films, but people used to say my mum looked a lot like Lauren Bacall when she was younger!" I answered, remembering how loads of family and family friends had told me that. "Cool!" answered Gabby, as if giving up on trying to jog my memory on Harry Guardino. We both laughed and soon it was time to jump off the bus.

We arrived at Swabs, found a table and sat down at it facing each other, and within seconds Gabby's dad joined us. "Hey girls, great to see you!" He exclaimed as he arrived at our table. Gabby stood up to give him a big hug. "This is my friend Della from England!" said Gabby, looking pleased to introduce us. "Hey Della, great to meet you!" exclaimed Gabby's dad, as he reached over to shake hands. "Nice to meet you too! I answered, completely forgetting to put on an extra posh English accent, besides, even if I'd remembered, I probably would have just laughed instead, and ruined it!

Gabby's dad sat down next to Gabby, picked up the menus and passed two of them to us. "Order whatever you want girls!" He exclaimed generously. "Thank you/Thanks Dad!" answered Gabby and I, as we set about studying the menus. 'What a treat!' I thought to myself feeling pleased as I read the fab-looking menu.

"Ok, girls so what are you having?" asked Gabby's dad, as he put his menu down. "Grilled cheese and a hot fudge sundae, you should get a sundae too, they're ace!" answered Gabby excitedly, as she glanced my way. "Oh yeah, it does sound delicious! I may have an egg salad sandwich with mine if that's ok?" I answered, feeling a little cheeky to be making such a request. "Sure, thing Girls!" answered Gabby's dad as if it was nothing, as he turned to look around for a waiter.

"Hey Johnny!" shouted Gabby's dad suddenly as he waved over a large guy who was chatting to a server at the counter. The man turned, waved and smiled knowingly at Gabby's Dad as he made his way over to our table. "Hey Johnny, good to see you! This is our friend Della from England, Della, this is my friend John Candy, he's an actor!" announced Gabby's dad, as John and I smiled at each other.

"Welcome to the USA!" exclaimed John, as he reached out his hand to shake mine. "Thank you!" I answered with a big smile, as we shook hands. I suddenly realised that this was my first welcome to the USA, and it couldn't have been more perfect. My heart felt so happy to be in such good company with Gabby and her dad, and even though I wasn't familiar with who John Candy was, he seemed like a lovely guy, and that was what counted!

We all had a fun little chat about what we'd each been up to lately, and then the server at the counter waved at John with what looked like his take-out order. "I'd better get going guys!" Said John, looking like he was torn between hanging out with us, and getting on with his daily to-do list. "Ok, Johnny, see you around!"

answered Gabby's dad warmly. "See ya Joe, See ya girls, good to meet you Della, have a great day everyone!" he exclaimed, as he turned to head back to the counter. "Thanks! You too bye/See ya!" called out Gabby and me as we waved our goodbyes. He picked up his order at the counter, then turned and waved one last goodbye to us all, before taking off out of the front door.

"What a lovely guy, hey and that was my first welcome to the USA!" I exclaimed to Gabby and her dad. "Cool!/Yeah, he's a great guy!" answered Gabby and her dad looking pleased to have seen him. I really enjoyed the friendliness of the people in LA. They were very easygoing and seemed full of an optimistic "You can do it!" attitude, which reminded me of my dad and me whenever we got together to chat about our ideas. It was totally my kind of wavelength and I was starting to feel like I had truly found my kind of people in the world!

The general mood of the people in LA was very upbeat and cheerful, not downbeat and dreary as some people in the UK seemed to be. I supposed the sunshine helped! Toronto had been a kind of hybrid of the two, it had the UK type of down-to-earthiness, but it also had a similar friendliness to LA, which I was starting to see was just the North American way.

We ordered our food, which swiftly arrived at our table not long afterwards. We continued chatting, laughing and joking as we ate. "So what movies has your friend John Candy been in?" I asked curiously, as I bit into a delicious egg salad and mayo sandwich. "Oh too many to remember!" answered Gabby's dad before going on to rattle off a bunch of movie names that I'd never heard of. "Gosh, I'm terrible, here I am in the heart of Hollywood, and I don't recognise the names of any actors or movies!" I answered with a laugh. "Hey, you're too busy living life that's why!" answered Gabby's dad with a grin. "Yeah, and travelling the world! There should be a movie about YOU!" joked Gabby, reminding me of what the sleazy movie producer Mike had said. "Well, as long as you're both in it too, it sounds like fun!" I answered with a laugh.

"The Blues Brothers! Surely, you've heard of THAT movie?" exclaimed Gabby's dad, as if suddenly remembering another John Candy movie. "Oh yes, I have heard of that one! I'm pretty sure I even saw it at the cinema, although I was with friends and I think we were running late, and missed some of it. It's about two guys dressed in black and white suits, and they sing and dance a lot right? What was John one of those two guys?" I asked, feeling impressed, as I recalled some fun dance moves in the movie. "Nah, but he's one of the characters in the movie!" answered Gabby's dad with a laugh. "Oh, I'll have to watch it again and look out for him!" I answered, looking forward to seeing The Blues Brothers, and John Candy again!

We finished our sandwiches, and not long afterwards two delicious-looking hot fudge sundaes arrived on our table. "Wow, they look amazing! Aren't you having one?" I exclaimed to Gabby's dad, feeling sorry for him to be missing out. "No, I'm fine, you girls go ahead, enjoy!" answered Gabby's dad looking happy for us. "OK, thank you!" I answered before tucking into my ice cream delight!

"So I was up at Jack Nicholson's house recently, and there were loads of torn-up dollar bills in a bowl on the coffee table! What do you girls make of that?" asked Gabby's dad, looking dumbfounded. "Oh, I have heard of him!" I exclaimed.

"So were they real dollar bills?" asked Gabby looking bemused. "Yeah, I'm pretty sure they were!" answered Gabby's dad, still looking dumbfounded by what he'd seen. "Well, Gabby and I can fix them back together, and spend them if they're a bother to him!" I joked, and we all laughed. "Weird!" exclaimed Gabby as she finished her sundae. "Yep, I guess that's what rich people do?!" answered Gabby's dad, and we all laughed and shook our heads in bewilderment.

Gabby's dad seemed to be well-in with a lot of Hollywood actors, and I wondered if he was an actor too, although Gabby hadn't mentioned him being an actor, only his brother Harry, so maybe he knew people through Harry? He didn't seem starstruck at all though, which I liked. If anything, he seemed to find the show biz folk amusing.

"I told Della about Harry going out with Lauren Bacall, and she said her mom used to look a lot like her when she was younger!" said Gabby, before taking a sip of her root beer. "Really, wow! She should have come to Hollywood and got an agent!" answered Gabby's dad with a grin. "Yeah, but then I probably wouldn't be here now!" I answered, and we all laughed.

"You girls need a ride anywhere?" asked Gabby's dad, as we all shuffled in our seats as if ready to get going. "Nah, we're good thanks!" answered Gabby. Glancing at me as if to say "Right?" "Yeah, we're fine thanks!" I answered, thinking how it would be fun to just ramble about freestyle as we were accustomed to doing - That way we were open to just going with the LA flow, seeking new adventures on route! "OK, let's go!" answered Gabby's dad, as he put a few dollars down on the table next to the bill.

We all stood up and walked outside together. "Well, see you later gals!" exclaimed Gabby's dad as he gave us each a big hug. "Sure, thanks for lunch

Dad!" answered Gabby, giving him another little hug. "Yeah, thanks it was delicious!" I exclaimed as I reached out to shake his hand goodbye. "You're welcome, girls!" He answered, as we started to turn to go in different directions, just before he turned, he discretely handed Gabby some money and she thanked him and gave him a little kiss on his cheek. He gave her one more big hug and then headed towards his car which was parked nearby alongside the curb. "Bye/See-Ya/Bye!" We all called out, before giving one another one last wave. Gabby's dad jumped in her car and sped off down Sunset.

Gabby and I continued to walk South on Sunset Boulevard, just enjoying the day. "Your dad is really nice, and you both get along great, so how come you're virtually living on the streets?" I asked, feeling genuinely intrigued. "Oh, he does his own thing, and I stay at my mom's sometimes, but because of her alcohol issues and mood swings, I prefer to be out on the streets most of the time!" answered Gabby in her usual matter-of-fact way. "Oh, right" I answered, as I felt a wave of sorrow for Gabby sweep over me, but at the same time I could see that for the most part she was having a great time freewheeling out and about town, and at least her dad was around when she needed him.

CHAPTER 28:

RICHARD "RISHARD" KANDA

"Let's go visit Rishard!" Gabby suggested excitedly. "Who's Rishard?" I asked curiously. "Oh, he's this lovely guy from Africa – Zaire, the French Congo part! His name is Richard, but he prefers to pronounce it the French way, so it sounds like Rishard. He's like a big brother to me, you will like him, he's very sophisticated! He only drinks fancy wines and Heineken beer, and listens to jazz music! He's a photographer in his spare time, but he works as a manager of a wine store and deli. He will love you!" Exclaimed Gabby, as she led the way to the next bus stop. "He sounds great!" I answered, feeling curious to meet this person who Gabby spoke so highly of.

We rode the bus for about 20 minutes until Gabby led the way to get off the bus at Hollywood Boulevard and Sycamore Avenue. "This way!" She said, heading up Sycamore Avenue Northwards. A few seconds later she stopped outside an apartment block and turned left from the street. This led inside a peaceful courtyard area, surrounded by two levels of apartments in a square U-shape. The top-level apartments had a railing around the veranda which was very ornate and had a Spanish style to it.

Gabby led the way to the far-left corner of the courtyard and knocked on the door. There were dark screens on the windows and doors, and it looked very private and secluded "Who's there?" Said a French male voice. "Hi, Rishard it's Gabby!" She called back, sounding pleased that Rishard was home. "Oh Gabby!" answered Rishard, as he opened the door with a big smile on his face, and looked very happy to see her and me!

"Come in, come in!" He exclaimed, in a welcoming manner. As he headed back inside, and we followed him. "Rishard this is my friend Della, from England, Della this is my friend Rishard from Zaire!" Gabby announced as we got inside. "Ah Della, lovely to meet you!" said Rishard as he reached out his hand. "You too Rishard, do you prefer to be called Richard, or Rishard?" I asked as we shook hands. "Oh, RISHARD, of course! - I am French!" he exclaimed dramatically with a laugh. "Ok, RISHARD it is!" I answered back dramatically, and we all laughed.

"What would you girls like to drink?" Asked Rishard, in his French accent, in a warm and hospitable tone. "Beer please!" answered Gabby with her usual cheeky grin. "Same please!" I answered grinning back. "Certainly! Have a seat girls!" answered Rishard as he headed towards his kitchen fridge, in the small kitchen to the side of the living room.

He soon appeared back in the living room with two open bottles of Heinekens which he passed to us with a big smile. "Thank You/Thanks!" we both said, as we took them off him and each took a swig. "So, Gabby, where did you meet Della? – You are from England correct?" Asked Rishard, smiling over at me. "Yeah!" I answered, as I nodded and smiled back. "Tell me all about it!" He said smiling warmly at us both, as if we were both his long-lost family.

"Well, all I know is, I was born in England and by the time I grew up, I wanted to get away from there and go travelling!" I answered with a laugh, not sure what he wanted to know. "Oh interesting, so where have you been so far?" He asked, looking genuinely interested. "Um, well when I first took off from my home town I travelled around a little bit in Southern England; New Forest, Bournemouth, Southampton, London, and then I went on to Canada; Montreal, Toronto, Niagara Falls, and after that the United States; All over the place! …and now here I am in Los Angeles with you two - It's great!" I answered with a laugh, and Rishard and Gabby cracked up laughing too. "Yeah, we were worth the journey right!" exclaimed Gabby, still laughing. "Absolutely!" I answered.

Rishard grinned over at me looking impressed, and I got the impression that he loved the fact that I was on such a grand adventure. "That is amazing!" he said in his elegant French accent while looking somewhat bewildered at the same time. "So, how are you surviving?" He asked, with a curious look on his face. "Let me think… Um, I've been getting by on a combination of hotel work and cocktail waitressing in England to save up money, and then hitchhiking and taking on various volunteer gigs to keep afloat as I go along!" I answered, feeling that I was explaining it to myself, as well as to him!

"You have a very adventurous spirit! I'm honoured to meet you!" he answered, still looking impressed. "Likewise! Cheers!" I answered as I raised my glass in the air. "Cheers!" exclaimed Rishard and Gabby, and we all clinked our glasses together. "I knew you guys would get along!" Exclaimed Gabby, looking pleased with herself "Yeah/Of course!" Rishard and I answered as we all sat around smiling at each other looking happy to be in one another's company. In my heart, I felt as if we were old friends finally reunited.

"So, how did you wind up in Los Angeles from Zaire Rishard?" I asked curiously, before taking a sip of beer. "Oh, I was a photography and film Student in Washington, and afterwards I decided to stay on with my brother, who is a doctor in Washington, and after a time I became a permanent resident" He answered in his nonchalant French accent. "Wow, that's great!" I answered, feeling happy for him.

"Yes, I am happy here, although I do have family all over the world, and I do miss my family at home too. My father is also a Doctor in Zaire, he is a lovely man. I call him my Dada, and I miss him so much, but hopefully, he will come and visit one day." he answered affectionately while looking a little sad.

I assumed that his mother had passed away, so I didn't want to ask him questions about her that might upset him. I could tell that he came from a decent family, as he was very well-mannered and a good conversationalist. He also had a creative air about him, and as he sat looking relaxed in his director's chair, sipping on his Heineken, I felt that he could easily have been a film director if he'd pursued a career in film.

I looked over at Rishard's bookshelf and noticed lots of books on photography, philosophy, art, and religion. All topics that I was also interested in. I knew that he was a kindred spirit, as his personality and his books reflected this.

"What's that all about - Waiting for Godot?" I asked pointing at a poster on his wall. "Oh, it is my favourite play – Waiting for Godoh" He answered, pronouncing Godot a French-sounding way, without sounding the T. "Oh, what's it about?" I asked curiously. "It is about two hobos sitting under a tree discussing life and waiting for someone named Godot who never turns up. You will have to see it some time I'm sure you will like it!" he answered with a smile.

"So is Godot a metaphor for God?" I asked, wanting to know more. "Maybe, there are many interpretations" answered Rishard, with a mischievous grin. "Hmm, so there are two hobos sitting under a tree discussing life, do any other people turn up?" I asked, trying to at least get a sense of what was going on in the play. "Oh yes, there is a man named Pozzo, and he has a slave named Lucky, and a boy also turns up, you have to see it, it's hard to explain!" answered Rishard with a chuckle.

"Yeah, I am curious to see it. So, what are the Hobos names?" I asked, trying to figure out if the names of the characters were significant. "Vladimir, and Estragon, but they call each other Didi and Gogo" answered Rishard smiling, and looking pleased with the memory of the play. "Hmm, so they took the di in the middle of Vladimir, and the go from near the end of Estragon, and repeated them to make Didi and Gogo, I wonder if the names mean anything? I mean, Godot gives me the impression of God, and Lucky is connected to fate and chance, and boy could represent anyone, not sure about Didi and Gogo though?" I laughed. "...and you say Godot never turns up?" I asked, still trying to understand the concept at least. "That's right he never shows up!" answered Rishard, chuckling some more. "Maybe it's purgatory, maybe the character Godot himself is in purgatory, or in some kind of dream, and all of the other characters are reflections of himself, from the life he's led, or in his dream?" I answered enthusiastically, feeling as though I was on to something.

"Ah, that is very good! You are a thinker! You must see the Play one day!" answered Rishard, looking impressed with my theories on the play. "Yeah, it sounds interesting, have you seen it Gabby?" I asked, bringing Gabby into the conversation. "Nah, I've seen a few musicals though - Tomorrow! Tomorrow! I love ya, Tomorrow!" she answered, bursting into song, and we all laughed. "I'll get us another beer!" exclaimed Rishard, as he jumped up, and headed to the kitchen "Thanks Rishard!" we both called out to him.

The three of us continued to drink beer and chat away through the evening. I loved how our conversation just flowed as we chatted with ease about various topics, thoughts and theories. The three of us seemed to share a sort of worldly wisdom, along with a childlike wonder, and I felt as though we could chat forever, and never get tired.

"Wanna go to a party in East LA?" asked Gabby suddenly as she finished her beer. "Oh, not East LA!" Exclaimed Rishard pulling a face, and we all laughed. "Sounds good to me!" I answered, feeling game for another night out with Gabby. Rishard continued to shake his head and sigh as if to say he didn't know what to make of us both, but in a fun big brotherly manner, which I found endearing.

"Is it ok if we use the bathroom to take a quick shower?" asked Gabby eagerly, as she looked over at me as if to say, ok? "Yeah, that would be good!" I exclaimed. "Of course, let me get you both some towels!" answered Rishard, as he got up and headed behind a bamboo screen, that separated his sleeping area from the living area.

He soon appeared back and passed us a large fluffy towel each. "Thanks, Rishard, shall I go first?" asked Gabby, as she started to make her way towards a small hallway that turned off to the left of where his bed was. "OK!" I answered, feeling happy to just stay chatting with Rishard, and finish off my beer.

Rishard and I continued to chat about all sorts of interesting things from science to spirituality, and it seemed like no time at all had passed before Gabby was back in the living room, and it was my turn to go and take a shower.

About twenty minutes later I was back in the living room, with the same clothes on, but feeling a lot fresher, especially after a hair wash, and a make-up top-up. "You both look lovely!" exclaimed Rishard elegantly. "Thank you/Thanks Rishard!" we both answered with big smiles. "OK Rishard, we'll see ya soon!" exclaimed Gabby as we started to head towards the front door. "Yes, and thanks for your hospitality!" I added as I followed Gabby towards the door.

"It was a pleasure to meet you, Della. You are both welcome, come back anytime! ...even late at night if you both need somewhere to crash out, my home, is your home!" He answered gracefully, as we hurried off out of the door. "Thank You Rishard, it was lovely to meet you too/Thanks!" We both shouted back, as we took off into the night and on to our next adventure.

"He's really nice! I said to Gabby as we strolled down Sycamore Avenue. "Yeah, he's cool! Hey wanna stop by the Cafe de Grand first, coz it's too early to go to the party yet!" answered Gabby as we headed towards the nearest bus stop on Hollywood Boulevard. "Yeah, OK!" I answered, figuring, why not? "Cool!" answered Gabby, as we jumped on the next eastbound bus that came along.

About fifteen minutes later we were jumping off the bus at Argyle and strolling down towards the club, which was only a few minutes South. As we got near to the club, Gabby seemed to recognise a guy sitting on the wall. "Hey, Ed!" She called out, as she headed over towards him, and jumped up on the wall next to him. I jumped up on the wall too, and sat on the other side of Gabby while looking around at all the punks that were milling about outside the club.

"This is my friend Della from England, Della this is Ed!" said Gabby loudly, so I turned to say hello, Ed and I shook hands and said hi to each other. Despite his hardcore punk style he turned out to be a really nice, easy-going guy. He shared his beers with us, and we all wound up having such a fun time sitting on the wall that we didn't even think to go inside the club!

281

"Don't go to East LA guys! Stay and hand with me!" exclaimed Ed, as he cracked open three more beers. "What do you wanna do?" asked Gabby looking at me, as if she was fine either way. "I don't mind, this is fun though!" I answered, with a shoulder shrug. "Cool, ok we're staying with you Ed!" exclaimed Gabby with a laugh. "Cheers Ed!" I exclaimed, holding up my beer can. "Cheers!" answered Ed and Gabby as we all clinked cans and took big swigs from them.

We spent the next few hours chatting, laughing, joking, and drinking cheap beer on the wall, with other acquaintances of Gabby and Ed's dropping by to hang out with us at random intervals.

Later on, we got wind that there was another party on over at the same studio that we'd been at the night before, so, of course, we went to it and we had another great night there partying with El Duche and other hardcore punk musicians while listening to the latest punk music to come out of the LA underground scene.

Although it wasn't totally my scene, I did love the realness of it all, and the enthusiasm that the punk musicians had as they talked about music. I loved how fresh it all was. We partied all night, as slowly but surely the punks took off to various other rooms in the studio, and once again I crashed out on the same sofa I'd slept on the night before.

The next morning I woke up, used the bathroom then tottered over to the kitchen to hopefully find some coffee. Ed was already in there getting himself a coffee together. "Morning, or afternoon Ed!" I said with a sleepy smile. "Hey Della, good to see you, you were out like a light when I passed by you on the way to the kitchen!" He said, looking happy to see me. "Yeah, I was zonked!" I answered with a grin.

"Oh, Gabby went somewhere else with El Duche and some others. She told me to tell you that she'd see you back at Rishard's!" exclaimed Ed, as if suddenly remembering. "Ah ok, thanks!" I answered, as I made myself a cup of instant coffee from the hot water that Ed had left in the kettle. "No problem!" answered Ed, as we both headed back into the main room and sat down next to each other on the sofa.

We sat sipping on our coffees, and chatting about this and that as we woke up. "Well, I guess I'd better get going!" I said as I stood up to take my cup back to the kitchen to give it a rinse. "Sure, hopefully, I'll catch you again!" answered Ed, as he stood up and followed me to the kitchen with his cup.

"Yeah, I'll probably see you at the Café de Grande with Gabby!" I answered with a smile. "Cool!" he answered, as he leaned forward and he gave me a quick hug. "OK, see ya!" I called out, as I started to head out of the studio. "Catch ya later!" He called back with a wave.

I headed down the studio steps, out of the building, and made my way back up to Hollywood Boulevard. After a short walk along the boulevard, I found a cheap food place for my late breakfast. They were offering: Eggs "Sunny side up" Hash browns, Toast and Coffee all for just $1.99.

I took my tray of food and cup of coffee to a window seat, and dug in, adding salt, pepper, and tomato ketchup as I ate. I sat feeling content while watching the world go by. There seem to be very extreme types in Hollywood, ranging from the super-rich to the dirt poor, and every type in between!

One of the main divides seemed to be between the car-folk and the street-folk. The people in the cars were often very glamorous looking and gave off an air of superiority which gave the impression that they were simply cruising about to be seen. Whereas most of the people walking around were more down-to-earth looking and I got the impression that they were struggling artists and students, or aspiring actors and musicians, quite a few of the people walking about seemed to be homeless or have addiction problems, and others seemed to be street hustlers, out and about looking out for opportunities that may come their way.

There were only a few people who looked kind of in between all the types, like Gabby and me! It wasn't quite like Toronto or London where there was always a big cross-section of people from all walks of life, but it was similar, although I got the impression that people in the cars would not walk around much, if at all, and the street people were probably rarely in cars! I wasn't sure what to make of it all, and couldn't decide which type of person I preferred if I had to choose between the LA "Street People" and the LA "Car People"

Suddenly Ed appeared walking past, and waved at me as soon as he spotted me. I smiled and waved back and he headed inside the café. "Hey, Della. I'll just grab a coffee!" he exclaimed, as he headed over to the counter. "OK, I answered, as I finished off the rest of my food.

He ordered a coffee and came and sat down next to me. "Long time no see!" I joked, feeling happy to see him again. These kinds of chance meetings with friends and acquaintances felt good, as it was what I was used to in England and Canada, as it brought a sense of normality to me, which helped me to decide there and then that I preferred the LA "Street People" to the LA "Car People" as so far, they seemed more real, and down to earth, which was familiar to me!

"So what are you up to today?" asked Ed, before taking a sip of coffee. "Nothing in particular" I answered, looking down at my empty plate. "Hey, I'm getting hungry too, I think I'll grab breakfast, do you want anything?" He asked as he stood up to head back to the counter. "No, I'm fine thanks" I answered, going back to my people watching, and pondering while he made his order at the counter.

He was soon back at the table with a similar plate of food to the one I'd just finished, and we sat chatting about various things as he ate. He was interested in the UK music scene, and I told him that it was very mixed from punk to pop, and that was fine with me, because I enjoyed all sorts of music, depending on my mood. "That's cool! I mainly only like punk, and some metal, but I don't like that old dinosaur rock!" He answered giving a look of disdain.

"What's dinosaur rock?" I asked curiously. "Oh you know The Eagles, Aerosmith, Led Zeppelin…t that kind of stuff!" he answered, sounding as if he hated all of it. "Oh, I like some of that too!" I answered with a laugh. "Really, but you look like a Punk Rocker?" He answered, sounding confused as he glanced at my black drainpipe jeans and black and white striped t-shirt. "I guess I dress this way because I like it, and because I do like a bit of punk and new-wave too, but that doesn't mean I don't like other stuff, why be limited to one type of music?" I answered defiantly. "Good point!" he answered as if taking what I'd said on board.

"Wanna go play pool down at Western?" he asked as he finished off his food. I guessed Western was a boulevard or street, as just the street name was how most people seemed to refer to streets in LA. "Sounds good!" I answered, liking the way things just seemed to just keep on flowing in this city. "Cool, let's go!" exclaimed Ed as we finished the rest of our coffees, and stood up to put our rubbish in the trash can.

"We can walk, it's not far!" said Ed, reminding me of my preference for the LA "Street People" that I'd decided on earlier. "Sounds good!" I answered with a grin. We crossed the street and walked for about ten minutes until we arrived at a large cross street, that read "Western Avenue" on the sign.

"It's in here!" said Ed, as he led the way inside the pool club, downstairs and into a big room full of pool tables. "I'll get us a beer, you hang there," said Ed, as he swaggered over to the bar. I sat on a high stool next to the wall and checked out the room, it was pretty large with about ten pool tables in it, with a mix of young street-kid punks, hippies, students, regular Joe's, and musicians all just hanging out and enjoying shooting some pool, and sipping on some beers. 'Maybe some worlds do collide here after all?' I thought to myself, loving the diversity of the people in the pool hall.

It didn't take long until Ed and I were playing pool and drinking beers too. I liked the atmosphere. It was very laid back and friendly, and it reminded me of Toronto. I suddenly missed Jeff and my friends back at the tropical paradise, but I told myself to be strong and focus on my new friends in LA!

Ed taught me what he called the "American way" to play pool, and I really enjoyed it, and because neither of us took the game too seriously, we had fun playing, both of us just laughing and joking at our bad shots, and showing off at our good ones! All in all, we were having a good time.

"I'm gonna have to go home and check on some things, I may see you and Gabby at the Cathay later if you're around?" said Ed, as we finished off a game of pool. "Yeah, ok Ed, thanks for a fun afternoon. I enjoyed learning to play pool the American way, not that I ever knew how to play it any other way!" I answered with a laugh. "Sure, it was a blast!" answered Ed, as we started to head out of the pool room, and back upstairs to the street.

"See ya later!" exclaimed, Ed as he leaned over and gave me a hug. "See ya later!" I answered as I hugged him back. He took off towards the east, and I headed west along Hollywood Boulevard and back towards the main drag.

The Hollywood Street life was as vibrant as ever and I enjoyed soaking in the atmosphere. Eventually, I arrived at Rishard's Street – Sycamore Avenue and headed for his apartment. His door was slightly open so I called out "Rishard!" as I got nearer. "Hey, Della!" called back Gabby's voice, much to my surprise, as she opened the door to me with a big smile on her face. "Come on inside, Rishard's at work!"

"How's it going?" asked Gabby with a big smile. "Good thanks I've been hanging out playing pool with that guy Ed from last night, how about you?" I answered as I flopped down on one of the soft futon chairs in the living room. "He's a nice guy! I went with El Duche and a few others back to some apartment in East Hollywood and got wasted. I got to Rishards and crashed for a few hours. Are you hungry? We can help ourselves to food, Rishard always says it's ok" said Gabby, as she strolled towards the kitchen.

"I'm ok for food thanks, but I'll have a beer if there are a few in the fridge if Rishard wouldn't mind?" I answered. "Sure, Rishard always has a few beers to spare!" answered Gabby with a laugh. "There ya go!" she said, as she passed me an open beer, then went about making herself a cheese sandwich. "Thanks, Gabby!" I answered, then took a swig. It felt good to be back at Rishards again after our night out.

"Wanna watch TV?" asked Gabby, as she landed on the other futon and put her beer and cheese sandwich plate down. "Yeah ok, I'll switch it on!" I answered, feeling it was easier for me to jump up, and let Gabby eat. "Sure" answered Gabby as she took a bite of her sandwich.

We spent the next couple of hours watching old black and white re-runs of The Honeymooners, vegging out, and having random chats, until Rishard arrived back around seven that evening, looking happy to see us once again. We drank and hung out for a couple more hours with Rishard, chatting, listening to his jazz tapes, and drinking Heineken beer. I loved how I felt so at home at Rishard's, and in LA in general.

CHAPTER 29:

LA HARD-CORE PUNK-ROCK SCENE

I spent the next few weeks partying at a variety of hard-core underground punk-rock clubs, parties and venues with Gabby and rode it out like some kind of wild alternative rollercoaster ride. We had all sorts of experiences from fab to bad, from ludicrous to downright dangerous!

One night at an East LA garage party with Gabby, we were drinking some strong alcohol; Whiskey with a little bit of Coca-Cola, and someone gave me what I thought was a cigarette - because it looked just like a normal cigarette. I thanked them and took a drag and suddenly it seemed to have a bad effect on me, as I passed the cigarette back, I instantly felt unwell and found myself curling up into a ball in the corner of the large garage.

I was overwhelmed with the feeling of missing my family and friends back in England, and suddenly I felt very scared, lost and lonely. It was as if I had suppressed my feelings while travelling and suddenly my emotions had been released like a great dam, and it had hit me how far away from my hometown and my family and friends I was – Thousands and thousands of miles!

I'd been travelling for about ten months now. It was the longest I'd ever been away from home before. I'd only ever had sleepovers with friends for a night or two in my hometown, so to be gone for this long by myself, must have been taking some kind of toll on my psyche, especially after the last few weeks of living on the edge with Gabby. I was feeling highly distressed, and I didn't like the feeling at all. All I could do was stay curled up in a ball in the corner of the garage, and hope it went away soon.

None of the punks around me seemed to notice that I was having a bad time, and Gabby had disappeared into the main house a little earlier, so my feeling of being all alone in the world was intensified and the realisation that none of the punks cared, made me also realise that this hard-core punk-rock scene was not for me! My first impression at The Cathay De Grande had been right, most of the hardcore punks there seemed very angry and aggressive, which created a negative, downbeat atmosphere, which was not my scene at all. I preferred the "Love and Peace" Hippy scene, and the creative and fun "New-Wave Scene, not this hell!

I stayed curled up in the corner of the garage, while the punks partied on around me. I reminded myself that not all the punks were bad, some of them were nice people, and to be fair they probably thought I'd just crashed out in the corner, that was if they even thought about me at all. But the truth was, I was just waiting for this horrible state of mind to pass.

Eventually, I felt a little better, so I uncurled, got up and headed inside the main house, and into the kitchen where I found a jar of instant coffee, and got chatting with a thin leather-clad, skinhead guy who was guzzling water straight from the tap.

"How's it going?" asked the skinhead guy after he'd finished drinking from the tap. "Not too good, I took a drag of a cigarette and it knocked me for six! I answered, feeling good to have someone to chat to, as I put the kettle to boil. "It was probably dipped in angel dust!" he answered with a laugh. "What the heck's that?" I answered feeling confused. "Strong stuff!" he exclaimed, as he staggered off out of the kitchen. "Oh right!" I called after him, as I found a cup, and made myself a strong cup of black coffee.

'Whatever that cigarette may or may not have been dipped in, I didn't like it!' That's for sure! I thought to myself, as I took my cup of coffee and sat down on a rickety old chair next to a dirty old kitchen table.

Around 5 am I left the party and headed up the street in search of a bus to get me away from there. As I walked away from the party house, I felt my old familiar sense of freedom start to rise inside of me, as I decided to continue on with my travels, and seek out healthier environments, reminding myself that although it's interesting to explore the lifestyles of all sorts of people, it didn't mean that I had to join them, and get stuck in their world!

I reminded myself that I saw myself as a kind of independent anthropologist explorer and reminded myself that I was keeping my travel journals so that one day I would maybe write about my adventures and share my stories of human nature and the places I've seen with the world, so I always had to keep a somewhat objective point of view on my surroundings, and never get too involved. This helped to remind me of the bigger picture of my travels and instantly made me feel better. 'I'm a world explorer and writer! Not some wasted suicidal punk! Be strong, and keep on going!' I told myself as I marched onwards, feeling my previous fears and sense of loneliness start to fade away, as it was gradually replaced by a sense of inner strength and calm.

As I walked down the street, I remembered what the skinhead had told me about the cigarette probably being dipped in what he called "Angel Dust" 'Nah, that stuff was more like devil dust than angel dust!' I thought to myself with a chuckle, feeling my old sense of humour coming back to lift my spirits. A bus suddenly appeared with "Venice Beach" written on the front, so I jumped on it, paid my fare and found a seat. I was curious to see what Venice Beach was like.

CHAPTER 30:

VENICE BEACH AND ANGEL XAVIER

I missed the main stop for Venice Beach, so I jumped off the bus a bit further down the street. I instinctively headed down towards the boardwalk so that I could walk along the beach, rather than the road with its noisy traffic, and car fumes.

As I arrived at the boardwalk, I looked around to get my bearings; to my right, I noticed that I was quite near to the Santa Monica pier, and my mind popped to my fun day out in Santa Monica with Gabby and Peter a while back.

I was tempted to revisit the pier, but I decided that seeing as I had already been there, I would stick with my original plan and head for Venice Beach, which I guessed must be south of the pier judging from the direction the bus had been going when it dropped me off.

I asked a friendly-looking man for directions and he told me to keep walking for another twenty minutes or so. I thanked him and continued on with my walk. It was such a lovely morning. The sky was blue, and the air felt fresh, and just cool enough to wake me up some more and to clear away my hangover.

The ocean and beach were to my right, and I strolled along feeling on cloud nine once again. Pleased to be back on my journey. I felt happy to have left the hard-core punk-rock scene behind me, as it was definitely not for me, but I was grateful for having my chance to explore it, and for the good people I'd met.

I kept walking until the Boardwalk slowly but surely started to get more and more crowded. All sorts of people started coming into view, I noticed lots of very colourful hippie types, funky music was playing from various areas, artists were sitting painting, bongo players were beating on drums, the smell of incense was in the air, restaurants, cafes and bars full of happy looking people lined the side. 'Wow, this is a fun neighbourhood, and all right next to the beach! This is more like it!" I thought to myself, while mentally comparing the upbeat colourful scenes before me, to the downbeat, dark hard-core punk rock scene behind me.

I kept walking, and enjoying the atmosphere until I found some grass to sit on. I sat down, let out a happy sigh, and watched the Venice Beach world go by. This was the perfect spot to take a breather and collect my thoughts. I was so happy that the terrible feeling created by that dodgy cigarette had worn off, and although I still felt tired and hungover, it was a good feeling to feel the fresh air on my skin and to have the freedom to enjoy a new day.

I started thinking that my next plan of action should be to find maybe some kind of volunteer au-pair gig for a while to give myself time to regroup, and afterwards, I would continue on with my travels. My mind flashed to my Aunt Freda, and I wondered when exactly she would make it over to meet up with me. I wondered what she would make of my adventures so far, and had to laugh at the thought of her being shocked that I was already in the US, and having a great time exploring! I imagined that she would be concerned for my well-being, but would be a little impressed too, as she also had an adventurous spirit and a love for America. I wondered where I might head next. San Francisco wasn't too far away, and it looked like a beautiful city, plus I was sure that my Aunt Freda had some ranches she wanted to look at in Oregan and Northern California, so maybe we would meet up somewhere in those parts, but until then, I had to do something, the question was what?

One thing I knew for sure, was that I did not want to go back to Gabby's hard-core punk scene, because I was feeling kind of traumatised by it all at this point, and as much as I liked Gabby and enjoyed her company, I also loved diversity in life. I was once again simply enjoying the feeling of being free, and not belonging to any clique, class, or group of people when a Hispanic guy came and sat near me. We smiled at each other, said hello, and soon got chatting. He sounded quite effeminate and had an artistic flare about him. "My name is Xavier, what is your name?" He asked in his Hispanic-sounding accent. "Nice to meet you, Xavier, I'm Della" I answered, as we shook hands. We both soon found out that we shared a fun sense of humour, and found ourselves laughing at all sorts of silly things throughout the conversation. We got along great and felt very comfortable together. He told me that he was a hairdresser from south LA, and I told him about some of my travels so far, including the party I was at the night before, and the bad cigarette.

"So, what are your plans for the rest of the day?" He asked curiously. "I'll probably start looking for a volunteer au-pair gig that I can do in exchange for room and board while I regroup a little before continuing with my travels" I answered, feeling good to have a plan of sorts to be able to talk about. "Tomorrow I am styling a lady's hair at a halfway house, maybe you can help out there?" he answered optimistically. "Oh, that sounds good, where is it?" I asked. "It's at Pico and Crenshaw. If you want you can come along with me tomorrow, and I will introduce you to Mary the house mother, and maybe she will call Larry the owner and you can talk to him on the phone" answered Xavier, as if having it all worked out in his mind. "Yeah ok, thanks!" I answered, with a big smile.

"So, do you have somewhere to stay tonight? If not, you are welcome to stay at my place if you want to?" he asked earnestly. I could tell he was very genuine. "Yes, that sounds good, thanks!" I answered, enthusiastically. We stayed sitting on the grass chatting for a little longer, and after a while Xavier suggested that we head over to his place, and he led the way. It was quite a long bus ride, followed by a long walk to his apartment block, which was some kind of project housing that reminded me of army barracks. Xavier's apartment was humble but clean and tidy. He told me that he had a couple more roommates and that they were travellers like me and had travelled from Latin America.

"I admire you all, it is such a brave thing to do! To leave one's home country and go somewhere else halfway across the world - Especially alone, and with no family or friends to meet with at the other end! I could never do that!" He exclaimed, looking at me with admiration. His words reminded me of the distressful experience I'd had after taking a drag on that bad cigarette, and I was so glad that the effects had completely worn off and that I was back to feeling my usual upbeat self. I wondered if the loneliness, and fear I felt while under the influence of the cigarette, was what most people feel when faced with the idea of travelling solo around the world, especially on a budget, "with no family or friends to meet at the other end" as Xavier put it?

"I guess, I just feel that the world is my home, so I feel at home wherever I go. Maybe your friends feel similar? - That's not to say that I don't miss my family and friends though! I just enjoy making more!" I said with a laugh. "Well now, you've added me to your collection!" exclaimed Xavier, and we both laughed. We spent the evening watching sitcoms on television, both of us laughing like two kids through most of them. Xavier was such a gentleman that he let me have his bed and told me that he would sleep on the sofa. I protested, but he wouldn't take no for an answer, so I was soon tucked up in his comfy bed drifting off to sleep.

The following morning, I met Xavier's roommates. They were two nice young Hispanic guys. They were all very friendly and generously made me a delicious breakfast of scrambled eggs, flatbread and coffee. I think they felt as if I was in the same boat as them and they wanted me to feel welcome. I was made to feel like a very special guest and my heart was warmed by their humble hospitality I felt so grateful and knew that I would remember them with fondness always. After breakfast, we got ready to leave. This time we found a shorter way to catch the bus and Xavier led the way to the halfway house at Pico and Crenshaw.

CHAPTER 31:

PICO & CRENSHAW

"Here it is!" said Xavier pointing at what looked like the back of a big house and warehouse type of building. We walked up the steps to the side of the house, where a metal cage surrounded the front door area. Xavier rang the bell, and a few seconds later the inner door opened and a friendly-looking chubby man, maybe in his late twenties, or early thirties, with light brown, chin-length wavy hair and a big smile stepped out.

"Hi Michael, I've come to style Eileen's hair, and this is my friend Della, from England" said Xavier excitedly. "Hi guys, I'll open the gate!" Said Michael warmly. "Thank you Michael/Thank you!" answered Xavier and I, as Michael went about unlocking the gate while glancing and smiling at me the whole time.

"Come in!" Exclaimed Michael, as he opened the gate, and gestured for us to enter the open living room door, while he stayed to lock the gate back up. "Thank you/Thanks" we both answered, as we stepped into a cosy-looking living room.

"You wanna coffee?" asked Michael as he hurried back inside the living room to join us. "Oh yes please/Sure thanks Michael" Xavier and I answered at the same time. Sure, you both want milk and sugar?" asked Michael, as he headed towards the back of the living room. "Yes please!" we both answered, again at the same time, and burst out laughing. "Sure, take a seat!" answered Michael, sounding pleased to have visitors. "Thanks! Thank you" Xavier and I called after him, as we both sat on the long sofa next to the door.

"Hi, Sonny!" exclaimed Xavier, as a tall skinny man, with a bald head, appeared from what looked like a stairway that led down from the side of the kitchen. "Hi Xavier!" mumbled Sonny, looking a little shy of me. There you go guys!" said Michael coming back from the kitchen with two mugs of coffee in hand. "Thank you/ Thanks!" we both answered while smiling at Michael and Sonny, who were now both hovering over us and looking at me with mild bewilderment.

"This is Della, she's from England, and this is Michael and Sonny from here!" Said Xavier with a laugh. "Hi, Michael! Hi Sonny!" I exclaimed, giving them both a big smile. "Hi Della, you can call me Mike!" answered Michael excitedly. "OK, thanks, Mike!" I answered. "Hi, Della!" mumbled Sonny shyly.

They stood over us somewhat awkwardly for a few seconds, as if none of us were sure what to say or do next, when suddenly a couple of young women - one taller, and larger built, with straight platinum-blonde hair and a dark suntan, the other shorted, and slimmer with short dark-blond curly hair, appeared in the living room, from the same stairway that Sonny had come up.

They looked at me in the same curious way that Michael and Sonny had looked at me, which was a look of surprise, combined with friendly smiles. I could tell these people had some kind of mental disability, but they all seemed friendly and not aggressive, so I felt safe.

"Della this is Suzi and Darleen!" announced Xavier. "Hi Suzi and Darleen!" I said standing up to shake their hands. "Hi Della!" they both replied, looking pleased to see me. "Hi Xavier!" exclaimed a woman's voice from the kitchen area, and I looked over to see a large-built lady, who looked in her early thirties, with a round smiley face, and long straight light brown hair appearing at the top of the stairs.

"Hi Mary, you're looking lovely! This is my friend, Della, she's from England! This is Mary she is the house-mother" exclaimed Xavier, looking pleased to introduce us. "Hi, Mary!" I said as I smiled and gave her a little wave. "Hi Della, nice to meet you!" answered Mary, with a sweet little smile. "Do you need some help? could you ask Larry if Della could help out in exchange for room and board? She's travelling and needs to be based somewhere for a while to regroup" asked Xavier earnestly. I stood there nodding and smiling, and hoping that the answer would be yes.

"Well, I would like some time off, so maybe she could cover for me some days!" answered Mary, looking over at me, as if to see if I liked the idea. "That would be great!" I answered, enthusiastically. "OK, let me call Larry, and see what he thinks?" answered Mary, as she walked past me to a phone on the wall in the corner of the room and started dialling.

The rest of us stood and sat around in the room until Mike asked if anyone wanted a coffee or a top-up. Everyone said yes please, and seemed to instantly relax and find seats to sit on. The two women sat at the large dining table that was at the left side of the room, and Sonny sat on a comfy-looking armchair by the TV, while Xavier and I stayed sitting on the sofa nervously waiting to hear the results of Mary's phone call. Meanwhile, Mike clanked around in the kitchen making more coffee, and getting cups together.

"Hi Larry, Xavier has an English girl named Della with him, and she says she can help out here for a while, as she needs to regroup from her travels. I thought maybe she could cover for me some days when I want some time off?" said Mary enthusiastically.

"He wants to speak to you" said Mary holding out the phone towards me. "OK!" I answered, as I jumped up, and took the phone from her hand. "Hi, Della!" said a friendly male voice casually, as if he knew me well.

"Hi, Larry!" I answered in a similar tone, with a little chuckle. Larry went on to ask me some questions about my life and travels so far. He seemed amused that I had travelled all the way there from England. "Well, how else was I going to see the world?" I joked back, and we both laughed.

"So, you're free to cover for Mary when she wants time off?" he asked suddenly. "Yes, I am!" I answered enthusiastically, as I turned and smiled over at Mary and Xavier. "Good! Mary will show you your room and show you what to do. You can cook can't you?" he asked, sounding as if he wasn't sure of what my reply was going to be. "Yes, I can" I answered, figuring that I could do basic cooking and would learn the rest as I go!

"Good, do you smoke?" He asked curiously. "Yes!" I answered, as by now, I was accepting more cigarettes from people when they offered me one, than I was turning down, even though I wasn't yet fully addicted. "OK, so as thanks in exchange for you covering for Mary, how does: room and board, a carton of cigarettes and $15 a day pocket-money, for the days you help out sound?" he asked warmly. "Sounds great! Thanks, Larry!" I answered feeling really pleased with the arrangement.

"Sure, no problem. I'll see you next time I visit!" answered Larry in a laid-back LA way. "Great thanks, I look forward to meeting you!" I answered excitedly. "Likewise!" he answered, "Bye for now / See Ya!" we both exclaimed before hanging up.

"Larry said YES!" I exclaimed, and everyone looked pleased for me, Xavier even gave a little clap of excitement. "Hooray!" I cheered, and we all laughed. "Let me show you your room." said Mary, as she started to head past me, and into a hallway at the back of the wall where the phone was.

"OK!" I answered, as I quickly followed her along. She led me down a short hallway and through a large bedroom on the left, and into another smaller bedroom on the right, which I worked out was at the very front of the building. I noticed that it had its own little sink which I liked as it gave it a mini bedsit feel. There was a single bed to the left of the room, which was next to a window. It was very small and cosy, but it was perfect for me!

"This is great, thanks" I exclaimed to Mary, feeling pleased to have my own little digs again, after so long. "You're welcome, I'll show you the ropes tomorrow, but you won't have to do anything for a few days" answered Mary with a smile. "Ok, thanks, Mary!" I answered, smiling back. "Sure, make yourself at home, you're welcome to make the room however you want it, and I'll get you some keys sorted out tomorrow as well" answered Mary with a smile. "Great, thanks!" I answered, excitedly. "OK then!" said Mary, as we headed back towards the living room.

The others all looked happy to see us back in the living room, and I noticed that Xavier was now starting to trim a lady's hair as she sat on a chair in the centre of the room. "Della, this is Eilene, Eilene this is Della!" said Xavier proudly. Eilene and I said hi to each other, and Mary suggested I follow her, and she would show me around the rest of the place.

"Downstairs is where I live" Mary said, as she led the way towards the stairway in the kitchen that most of the people had appeared up from. "I see" I answered, as I followed her past the others, who were now sitting around looking relaxed and sipping on their coffees.

Mary was a lovely easy-going lady, and I felt instantly comfortable with her. "So where are you from Mary?" I asked, noticing that her accent was a little different from the LA people I'd met. "I'm from Idaho, I moved here with my two sons Timmy and Danny a couple of years ago, and now we all live downstairs." She answered with a little laugh. "Great, isn't there a famous potato from Idaho?" I asked with a chuckle. "Oh yes, the very best!" she answered chuckling back.

"Here's the pool table, you're welcome to play in your spare time, Mike and Sonny like to play" Said, Mary as she led the way past a large pool table in the centre of the room. "Thanks! Sounds fun!" I answered, feeling pleased that we had a rec' room of sorts. "...And here's the freezer. Larry buys in bulk, so we freeze it all up, bread, cheese, meats, if you need anything, you'll find it here!" exclaimed Mary, as we walked past a large oblong freezer. "Ok, great" I answered. 'I certainly won't go hungry here!' I thought to myself.

"And this is where me and my sons live, come on in" exclaimed Mary, as she opened up a door, and led the way into another room. I followed her into a massive long room, which seemed to run from the front of the house to the back, with some areas sectioned off to create separate rooms at the front. There were no windows and I figured that the outside wall must be the warehouse-looking part of the building that I'd seen from the outside.

"Wow, this is huge!" I exclaimed as I looked around in awe. "Yeah, there's plenty of room for us here! Take a seat!" Said Mary as she sat down on her bed. "Thanks!" I answered, as I sat down on a nearby seat and looked around the room.

It was a little cluttered but lived-in and comfortable looking. "My sons Timmy, and Danny sleep in the back rooms, they're at school now, but you'll meet them later" she said gesturing towards the partitioned area of the building that backed onto the sidewalk, so although it seemed like the front, technically it was the back. "It's great!" I answered, feeling impressed with the whole set-up.

she reached over and took out a can of coke from a small fridge next to her bed "Want one?" She asked, generously. "Yes please" I answered, suddenly feeling thirsty. We spent the next hour or so, chatting about our lives, and how we had both wound up at Larry's halfway house. She told me that she was so glad to have me there to give her some days off. We finished off our cokes and headed back upstairs.

Xavier was just finishing styling Eileen's hair, and she was looking very pleased with the results. "Your hair looks lovely / Great!" exclaimed Mary as we sat back down in the living room. "Thank you!" answered Eileen with a smile.

"Well, I suppose I should get going!" exclaimed Xavier as he started to pack up his hairdressing kit. "Thanks so much for bringing me here, and to you and your housemates for your hospitality!" I exclaimed, to Xavier with a big smile. "You are welcome sweet Della!" he answered as he turned to give me a big hug.

"I will see you next time!" He exclaimed as he went on to hug the others goodbye. "Yes, I'll look forward to it!" I answered, still smiling. It felt funny to be staying, while Xavier was leaving, but my mind popped to the lovely little room that was to be my new base, and I felt so happy to be left there.

"Here is my phone number, if you need anything call me!" exclaimed Xavier, as he scribbled his number on a piece of paper. "Will do, thanks again, Xavier!" I answered, giving him another little hug goodbye. "You're welcome!" he said once again, as he headed for the door.

Mike and Sonny got up to see him out, while the others and I all waved and shouted out goodbye as he went. 'Another LA angel!' I thought to myself while feeling so happy about my decision to head to walk away from the hardcore punk scene and hop on a bus to Venice Beach. 'Every day is an adventure!' I thought to myself with a smile.

The next day after Mary loosely showed me the ropes, and because I wouldn't have to start helping out for a week or so, I popped up to Lens van to pick up my tote bag. My pen wasn't working so I couldn't leave him a note, but I knew he would figure out that I must have needed my things, and I planned on dropping by another time soon.

I spent the next few days getting settled into my new home. Mike and Sonny, especially Mike, became my two main buddies. They were both so easy-going, and I felt comfortable and safe with them. We would go for little walks down to the local Thrifty's store for ice creams; My favourite was the chocolate mint chip, Mike liked strawberry, and Sonny liked Vanilla. We would each walk out of Thrifty's with an Ice cream in hand, and leisurely stroll back up the hill to the halfway house.

The neighbourhood was made up of mainly Black and Hispanic working-class people who were just going about their daily duties, as we were. One day as we were passing a food stand with benches outside with mainly guys sitting at them someone shouted out "England!" while the others stood around laughing and grinning. "USA!" I shouted back, and they all cracked up laughing.

Mike, Sonny and I strolled over to the food stand to say hi to the guys, and as it turned out the one who had shouted out "England" was a really friendly black guy, with an upbeat jolly demeanour which I liked. He told us that his name was James, and from then on whenever we walked past, if James was at the food stand he would call out "England, how are you doing!" and I would wave, and shout back "Great thanks USA!" and we would all laugh and carry on walking.

Some days James would call out "Hey, New-Wave England!" because of my New-Wave look. So, I would call back "Hey, Funky USA!" because James' style was on the stylish and funky-disco side. He would crack up laughing at some of my responses, and our spontaneous banter and shoutouts to each other were always quite amusing for others within earshot. Mike would usually laugh, and sometimes join in our chatter, while Sonny would stand back, and look mildly amused, but would never engage in our silly shenanigans.

One day as we were passing the food stand, James called us all over to chat and have a drink with him. We all got a coke, and made ourselves comfortable at one of the picnic tables outside of the food stand, amongst the other diners; mainly black and Hispanic local workers, and street people.

"So New-Wave, tell me about England, have you seen the Beatles?" asked James excitedly, while Mike sat smiling at everyone around us and rocking back and forth, which was something he did when he was nervous. Sonny sat with his usual bemused stare, glancing around anxiously from time to time.

"Well, I'm no expert on England, but from what I experienced there, it rains a lot, but most of the people are friendly, and it has an eclectic music scene, so it's not all bad! I've never seen The Beatles, but apparently, an aunt of mine used to live next door to John Lennon's aunt according to family history!" I answered with a mock proud head nod.

"That is so cool! but you never saw, or met any of The Beatles though?" answered James enthusiastically. "Not that I'm aware of!" I answered, and we all laughed, even Sonny. We all relaxed into general conversation, and it felt good to be spending time with some of the neighbourhood locals, even Michael and Sonny seemed to be having a fun time and would add a little to the conversation here and there, which was lovely to see, as after years living in institutions and halfway houses, they had largely missed out on socialising with people outside. After we finished our drinks, we bid our farewells to James and headed back to the halfway house, each of us with an extra spring in our step.

The people at the halfway house were mainly suffering from schizophrenia. They were a lovely, interesting mixture of people from all walks of life. There were sixteen of us in total living between the main halfway house at the front and the two little houses at the back we were:

Mike and Sonny: Mike: A little chubby, late twenties, early thirties, with wavey brown hair, and sparkling blue eyes, and a friendly disposition. Sonny: Tall and thin, late thirties, with balding brown hair, Shy, with a seemingly permanent look of bewilderment on his face.

Mary and her two sons: Danny and Timmy: Danny was about 10, and was chubby and blond and quite street-wise, Timmy was about 12, he was dark-haired and slimmer, and more reserved. They were at a neighbourhood school most days, and with Mary in the evenings, so, I mainly only saw them at weekends, both were great kids.

Eileen: A middle-aged Mediterranean-looking lady, who had a room to herself downstairs, and who stayed in her room watching TV for most of the time.

Chico and Sheila: A loving couple who both looked to be in their late twenties. He was Hispanic and she was Asian. They kept to themselves, but they were always very pleasant whenever I saw them.

Linda: A dark-haired Irish American woman in her early thirties. I wasn't sure if she was also schizophrenic, because her main problem seemed to be alcohol, but she was friendly, albeit in a slightly prickly way which I found amusing.

Cathy: A young woman with jet-black hair, who was in her early twenties, and went by the nickname "Cathy Crude" She was into punk rock and often spoke of getting a punk band together, but I was never sure if she was serious, or if it was just one of her delusions?

Betty: An older lady in her late 60's or early 70's who was very sweet, and seemed like everybody's Grandmother. She seemed well in mental health, just older, and I presumed she'd been in need of a home, so Larry had arranged for her to live in one of the little houses at the back of the halfway house.

Darlene and Suzi: Two women who used to pal around together. Darlene was about 30, she had platinum blonde hair and a very dark tan and would love to sunbathe for most of the day. She was very laid-back in nature, and I had the impression that her meds helped to make her even more laid-back! Suzi was in her mid-twenties, she was highly strung, but also very sweet-natured and bubbly.

Ron: An older man in his 70's who was blind. He was very passive and gentle-natured and stayed in his room most of the time.

Mike 2, or "Angry Mike" as I sometimes thought of him, as he was the opposite to my friend Mike, as he could get very aggressive at times. He shared a room with Ron, and they both kept to themselves for most of the time.

And there was me; An eighteen-year-old, Punky-New-Wave, slim build, with brown eyes, and wavy reddish-brown hair, female explorer from England.

When it came time for me to start covering for Mary I found it a pleasure to spend time with all of the halfway house residents even when I wasn't cooking or cleaning. I enjoyed chatting, playing games, and going walks with them. Mary was the full-time "House Mother" and I felt that I was the part-time "House Sister." And my heart was in the small part I played in keeping things running as smoothly as possible.

At dinner times some of them would ask me questions about England. They seemed curious to find out as much as possible, and I was happy to oblige. I was also interested in their backstories, and how they came to be living in a group halfway house at Pico and Crenshaw in Los Angeles.

We would have many conversations, asking about one another lives. They each had their own unique ways, and it taught me that despite having schizophrenia, they were still all very different people with different personalities to match and that their illnesses did not define them.

Mike would sometimes knock on my door and invite me to join him for a peanut butter and jelly sandwich and to watch television with him, and I was always happy to take him up on his offer, as he was very good company. I loved his upbeat, enthusiastic disposition, and his childlike sense of fun, which was similar to my own.

Physically Mike was like a chubby teddy bear, with chestnut brown hair that grew in bouncy curls down to his shoulders. He always had a big smile, and a sparkle in his blue eyes whenever he would see me, and in some ways, he reminded me of an adult-sized cherub, which was so endearing. The two of us clicked like long-lost friends, and if he wasn't looking for me to hang out with, I would be looking for him!

We would often go on long walks together and would enjoy our chats about this-and-that, and having a laugh at all sorts of silly things. One day he showed me a street a couple of blocks south of Pico, called Washington Boulevard where I was able to buy bargain toiletries and clothing. I was pleased with this, and during our first shop, I decided to buy a box of blue-black hair dye with my pocket money. That evening, I coloured my hair with my newly bought hair dye, and couldn't wait to go and show it off to Mike.

"Hey Mike, what do you think of my blue-black hair?!" I exclaimed as he opened up his room door to me. "I love it! It really suits you black! Maybe I can colour my hair some time too?" He exclaimed excitedly. "Yeah, that would be fun, what colour?" I asked, just as excitedly. "I don't know, maybe blond?" he answered with a big grin. "Yeah, blond would suit you, Mike, because you've got lovely blue eyes, I'll help you with it if you want?" I answered grinning back.

"Cool thanks! Shall we go get some coffee and play some games?" asked Mike, looking a little restless. "Yeah, let's go do that!" I answered as we both headed upstairs towards the living room, while giggling at the idea of us both having new hair colours.

We got ourselves some coffee, and brought the card and board games out of the cabinet that the tv stood on. I spotted a map book of the USA and got it out to have a look at some of the places I'd been. "Hey Mike, I've just realised I turned eighteen the same day that I entered California from Arizona! That must make me a Californian adult!" I exclaimed, pointing out Redlands California, the town I'd stayed in with Al's Native American family. "You sure are!" exclaimed Mike, with a big smile. "I like it!" I exclaimed. "Me too!" answered Mike with a big smile. He was such a lovely, fun person.

One night when I went to bed I lay there and started thinking about Gabby and the hard-core punk crowd she was hanging out with, and the dodgy substances that some of them were into. One drag on a bad cigarette had been enough to put me off that scene for life, but she seemed happy enough to be a part of it. I said a little prayer for her and hoped that she would be safe.

I called Len after a couple of weeks of staying at the halfway house just to let him know that I was okay, and confirm that I'd picked up my tote bag. By then, he was used to me disappearing for days on end either doing my own thing or with various newfound friends, so he wasn't too worried about me.

I told him all about the halfway house and my role of helping out whenever Mary needed time off, and he was very happy for me. I asked how his DJ gigs were doing, and he sounded very busy, so I too, was very happy for him. He was such a genuine good guy; he deserved a good life. I told him that I would pop up and see him over the next couple of days to have a catch-up. He said ok, and told me the best times to drop by, and we both hung up, looking forward to seeing each other.

CHAPTER 32:

RICHARD FROM THE BAND: JAPAN, AND ANGIE BOWIE

The next day I was free, so I decided I would head up to Hollywood, and pop by and see Len. I would only have to catch one bus to get there, and depending on traffic, it would take about twenty minutes or so.

The bus was half full of working-class Black and Hispanic people who were mostly quietly sitting lost in their own daydreams, with some of the younger ones sitting at the back, chatting away animatedly with their music players blasting out all sorts of funky tunes, which nobody, including the driver, seemed to care about.

As I rode along on the bus to Hollywood from Pico and Crenshaw, I once again realised how at ease and at home I felt in Los Angeles. I marvelled at how it didn't seem to matter what part of LA I was in, if I was alone, with friends, or with strangers. I was in my element there and felt completely at one with the city, which I was growing to love more and more each day.

I thought about my plans to travel and see more of the world and started to feel very torn once again. I reminded myself that my plan was to travel, see the world, and have many adventures, so for now, seeing as I was happy with my LA adventure, I should just go with the flow, and enjoy it!

I got off the bus at Sunset and Vine and decided to walk up to the Sunset Strip, rather than take another bus. I would enjoy the walk as it was a beautiful sunny day, with blue skies and a gentle breeze. My favourite kind of weather!

As I walked along up Sunset Boulevard I spotted a large record store with a bright yellow banner, and the words: Tower Records across it, so I decided to stroll inside and have a look around. I entered the building and was hit by the sound of loud pop music playing, so automatically started dancing my way over to look at the endless rows of records they had on offer. In each Aisle all sorts of fun and interesting-looking people were browsing; Punks, Rockers, Hippies, Black Funk and Soulsters…

I was soon engrossed in flicking through some interesting-looking records and loving the groovy atmosphere of the record store. "Do you like New-Wave music?" asked a male English voice. I turned to see a good-looking guy about twenty-something, dressed all in black with black spiky hair. "Yeah, I do, but I also like all sorts of other music too, as long as it sounds good!" I answered with a grin. "Right, what's your name? He answered with a curious smile.

"Della, what's yours?" I answered as we shook hands. "Richard, I'm here with my band: Japan, have you heard of them?" He asked, looking pleased about his situation. "Oh yeah, I think so, they do that song "Quiet Life" don't they?" I answered, feeling pretty sure that I had that record, among the hundreds of singles I'd bought over the years, back at my mum's flat in England.

Yeah, that's us!" he answered, looking pleased that I'd heard of his band. "Great, I think I've got that record! What do you do in the band then?" I asked curiously. "Keyboard player!" he answered with a smile. "Great! The keyboard is kind of the core of Electronic-New-Wave music, so you're kind of like the lead singer then!" I answered while looking impressed. "Kind of" he answered, and we both laughed.

"How about you, how come you're over here?" he asked, looking genuinely interested. "No special reason, I'm just travelling, and going with the flow, and the flow brought me here!" I answered, and we both laughed. "Must be fun, to be able to do that!" He answered with a smile. "Yeah, it has its ups and downs, but all in all it's fun!" I answered smiling back.

"Hey, it's great to meet an English girl in LA! Here's the hotel I'm staying at, drop by tomorrow about twelve if you fancy hanging out" he said, giving me his hotel's business card. "Yeah ok, sounds good!" I answered as I took the card off him. "Great!" he answered, as he looked around him, as if ready to take off. "OK, see you tomorrow!" I answered while thinking it would be fun to hang out with someone fresh from England after being away from England for so long. "Great, I'd better get going. See you tomorrow at twelve!" he exclaimed, as he took off. "See ya!" I called after him, as he disappeared around the corner of the aisle. I browsed the record store for a little longer, then headed up to Len's Van.

Sadly, Len wasn't around, I was about a half hour later than the time that he'd told me was best for him, so he must have taken off out and about as usual. I wrote him a note telling him I was sorry that I'd missed him, but would hopefully catch him next time. I told him how things were going well for me. I thanked him once again for his kind hospitality, and wished him well, then signed off with a smiley face.

I suddenly remembered I should leave the spare van key he'd given me, although he'd previously mentioned having a couple of spares so I knew it wasn't crucial for him to have the one he'd given me back, but I still thought it best to leave it for him, so I placed it on top of the note. I took one last look around the van and asked the creator to please take care of Len always, then I jumped out of the van. Slammed the door shut, made sure it was all locked up and secure, and strolled away, and back down the hill towards Sunset Boulevard feeling pleased with my current circumstances. I decided to head back to the halfway house at Pico to have a night in.

I spent the evening catching up with some journalling, and watching TV comedies with Mike and Sonny, which was very relaxing until Sheila suddenly came running up the stairs screaming that the place was on fire! We all instantly jumped up and ran downstairs only to be met with Chico and Mary, who told us not to worry, there was no fire, and that Sheila was hallucinating. Feeling relieved we all laughed it off, as Chico and Mary helped calm Sheila down, and disappeared off to their rooms. Seeing as Mike and I were now standing next to the pool table we instinctively picked up cues, and started playing pool, while Sonny bid us goodnight, and tottered off to his room.

"So, when did your medical condition start Mike, was it slow, or sudden?" I asked curiously, as we played pool. "I started hearing voices while driving a truck" He answered. "Oh, when was that?" I asked, curiously. "Well, I started driving trucks right after I left school, and it started a couple of years after that" he answered, seeming ok with chatting about his health. "How exactly did it start then?" I asked, feeling genuinely interested. "Well to start off with the general sounds of the truck slowly started sounding like words, and it freaked me out!" he answered, looking a little alarmed at the memory.

"So, you mean things like the sound of the wheels going around, and the sound of the air passing by, and the engine running etc..." I asked feeling intrigued. "Yeah, I started hearing words in the noises the truck was making!" Answered Mike, as if he could tell that I was genuinely interested, and he was happy to indulge my interest.

"But, doesn't everybody hear those sounds? I mean isn't there a rhyme or something about a train going along and it sounds like it's saying – Over the points, over the points!?" I asked, trying to understand, and hoping to make Mike feel a little better. "Sure, but I started hearing full sentences, and after a while, it just wouldn't stop" he said, as if trying to get across how intense it was.

"Gosh, that would be kind of annoying!" I answered, and we both laughed. "It sure was!" He said, in his usual upbeat way. "So, what did you do?" I asked, curious to hear more. "Well, I got home, and it still didn't stop, so I went to the docs the next day, and he sent me to see a shrink, and after a couple of weeks of going here and there they diagnosed me with schizophrenia" He answered matter-of-factly.

"Wow, but the whole time you were aware of the voices being separate from yourself? I mean you were fully conscious of what was going on, you didn't lose your mind so to speak?" I asked, trying to get my head around it all. "Yeah, I knew what was going on. I was hearing voices, and they wouldn't shut up!" answered Mike, and we both cracked up laughing.

"Gosh, that would do anyone's head in!" I said as our laughter eased. "Did you ever think it could be spirits or something like that?" I asked, starting to think of other possibilities. "Sure, but whatever it was, it wouldn't shut up!" answered Mike, and we cracked up laughing again.

"So does the medication stop the voices?" I asked. "Sure, it helps a lot, but it makes me sleepy, that's why I drink a lot of coffee!" he answered with a laugh. "I guess, I've got no excuse, other than I like coffee!" I joked back.

"So, what about the others here, what are their stories?" I asked sympathetically. "Sonny was in a motorcycle wreck, Chico was in a gang and got shot in the head. His girlfriend Sheila is a recovering alcoholic, not sure about the others?" He answered, sounding happy to fill me in on some of the residents' backgrounds. "Oh, I see" I answered while nodding my head.

I wasn't sure if these things were health issues separate from the schizophrenia, or if they'd triggered it. Either way, it gave me a greater understanding as to both the fragility and strength of human beings.

"I'm going to head to bed to get an early night. Thanks for hanging out with me and telling me about your medical challenges!" I said, with a yawn, as we finished off our game of pool. "No, thank you for hanging out with me, it was fun as usual, and great to have someone who genuinely cares to chat with about things!" answered Mike sincerely.

"Hey you're fun too Mike, and interesting to chat with. I'm so glad you got help for your health, and now you live here and we are one big happy family!" I answered with a big smile. "Yeah, except for Mike McCulloch!" he answered with a mischievous grin. "Oh yeah, well we are nearly all one big happy family!" I answered, and we both cracked up laughing.

"Nighy night Della, sweet dreams! Said Mike sweetly, as he took off towards his room. "Thanks, have a good night Mike, and sleep well! I'll probably see you tomorrow sometime!" I exclaimed as I took off upstairs, and headed to my room while looking forward to meeting up with Richard from the pop band Japan the next day.

The next day I got up and got ready to go and meet Richard. Once I was showered and dressed, with my hair and make-up done I headed to the living room to have a coffee and cigarette, I wasn't yet hungry, and figured that I would eat a little later in the day.

"Hi Mike, hi Sonny!" I exclaimed as I entered the living room, to see Mike and Sonny hanging out together as usual. "Hi Della, you look nice, are you going out?" asked Mike, looking pleased for me. "Thanks, yeah, I'm going to meet a new friend named Richard, up in Hollywood!" I answered with a smile, as I headed to the kitchen to pour myself a cup of coffee. I quickly added a lot of cold water to it, so that I could drink it fast, and get going.

"Great, have fun!" answered Mike with a big smile, while Sonny gave just a little smile, but mainly looked concerned and a little bemused, as usual. "Thanks, Mike!" I answered, before drinking the coffee down in one. "Well, I'm gonna get going, say hi to the others for me!" I called out as I headed towards the front door. "Will do!" answered Mike, as he and Sonny gave me a little wave. I waved goodbye to them, ran down the steps, and made my way over to the nearby bus stop at Pico and Crenshaw.

The Hollywood bus appeared within a few minutes, so I jumped on it, paid and found a seat. By now I was fully aware that the passengers on this bus route were pretty much always Hispanic and African American, with the occasional Asian or White person onboard. I wondered what they made of me, if anything? - Here I was; a white teenage punky/new-wave English girl. I certainly looked out of place on the bus and if they'd heard my accent as well, they would have been really confused!

BOOK 1: TO SEE THE WORLD

I suddenly felt kind of amazed that somehow, I had managed to travel away from my hometown of Oswestry, starting off with only a fiver in my pocket, and wind up all away across the other side of the world, and now here I was in Mid-City LA, casually riding along on a bus surrounded by local working-class Black and Hispanic people, feeling as if I was one of the locals myself. I loved the feeling of being a part of the greater human family, and not limiting myself to my birth family back in England.

I jumped off the bus on Hollywood Boulevard and headed up the cross street that was on the Hotel card that Richard had given me and headed towards Richard's hotel. I soon spotted Richard standing on the steps outside of the hotel as if looking out for me. "Hi, Della/Hey Richard" we both called out, as we waved at each other. We were both dressed up somewhat, and it felt a little bit as though we were on a date, although I wasn't really sure if I liked him in that way, as so far, he just seemed a nice guy as a potential new friend, and maybe he only thought of me as a potential friend also. I wasn't sure if either of us expected anything more than a friend to hang out with. I guessed we would find out as we went along.

Richard sat down on the wide hotel steps, so I sat down on the same step a few feet away from him, to take a breather. "Good to see you, I'm glad you found the hotel ok!" said Richard with a smile. "Yeah, it was easy enough. Good to see you too!" I answered, smiling back. "My band's had some good news! I got a call from the manager earlier, he's confirmed the US tour! It'll cover Los Angeles and San Francisco, and maybe a couple of other places too! He exclaimed, sounding really pleased.

"Wow, that's great news! Congratulations!" I exclaimed, feeling really happy for him. "You should come along too!" he exclaimed, with a big smile. "Hey, maybe I will!" I answered, jokingly and we both laughed. "Fancy a walkabout?" Said Richard, still smiling. "Sounds good!" I answered, liking the fact that walking about in a city was as normal to him, as it was to me!

We spent the day hanging out in Hollywood, just strolling about, and checking out various music and clothing stores. He was a good-looking guy, so he got quite a few looks from the girls, but sadly, I just didn't feel a spark between us and guessed he probably felt similar, but I decided it was still nice to have a new friend, especially a fellow Brit, which felt special somehow, after being away for so long.

"Wanna go to The Rainbow?" asked Richard, as our walk about Hollywood started to slow down. "OK! Sounds good!" I answered, thinking it would be fun to have a bit of nightlife again, as I hadn't been out at night in a while.

"Have you been there before?" asked Richard, as we strolled up Sunset from Fairfax. "Yeah, have you?" I answered, curiously. "Yeah, when we first arrived a couple of days ago" he answered with a grin. "So, what did you make of it?" I asked, curious to hear if he picked up on the somewhat fake vibes that some of the people that went there had, along with the fun cool vibes of the actual club.

"It was ok, not really my scene though, it's all a bit too glam-rock for me!" he answered with a laugh. "Yeah, I know what you mean, it's a fun club though, they always play a good mix' of music, and the owner Mario is lovely. He's so cool, and always lets me and my friends in - even after ten! Actually, I think it's "Ladies Night" tonight, so it'll be free anyway for me, yay!" I answered, with a smile. "What about me?" Richard answered in a mock sad tone. "Wear a dress, and see?" I answered, and we both laughed.

Eventually, we arrived at the Rainbow and strolled into the parking lot. As usual, the crowd of dolled-up rockers were milling about, looking like proud peacocks at a fashion show. Richard and I must have looked like quite hard-core punk in comparison, as we were both dressed all in black; T-shirts, and skin-tight jeans, held up with metal studded belts. We both had punky-looking earrings, and spikey black hair, although his hair was short, and mine was longer - with a hint of blue!

"There's Stuart!" exclaimed Richard suddenly, and I looked to see who he was pointing at. "Stuart Copeland, from the band The Police!" he added, seeing my confused face. "Oh right!" I answered curiously. "He's a nice guy, we recorded together last year, let's go and say hi!" he exclaimed, as he led the way across the parking lot, and walked towards Stuart.

"Hi, Stuart!" exclaimed Richard, as we got nearer. Stuart looked at Richard and didn't seem to recognise him, which was kind of embarrassing for Richard, and I cringed at the awkwardness of the situation. Richard quickly reminded him of where they knew each other from, and Stuart suddenly remembered him, much to my relief!

They shook hands while looking pleased to see each other again. Richard introduced me and Stuart to each other, so we shook hands and smiled and nodded at each other, then Richard went back to chatting to him about music, and his band's upcoming tour.

I started to feel a little awkward just standing there like a lemon and wondered if I should head inside the club alone. Richard seemed to sense this and suddenly told Stuart that he would catch him later, so we both waved goodbye to Stuart and headed inside the club.

Mario was standing outside the club's entrance and gave us both his usual lovely smile as he ushered us inside. It was still before ten, so I guessed that neither one of us had to pay. "Hey. I'm sure that was Lemmy from Motorhead!" I exclaimed as we passed by a rocker on his way outside. "Probably!" Shouted back Richard over the music. "Yeah, probably!" I shouted back, and we both laughed.

We headed upstairs, and Richard got us a couple of beers, and we headed straight to the little dance floor down the steps, and started dancing to the heavy funky disco music that was pumping out from the surrounding speakers. It was fun to have someone to dance with, especially a fellow music lover, and the two of us soon got lost in the music.

Suddenly Len appeared dancing next to me, and we were both so happy to see each other. I introduced Richard and Len to each other, and they smiled and shook hands, and we all kept on dancing. As we danced Len and I had a good catch-up chat over the music, and he thanked me for leaving the key and such a nice note for him. I thanked him again for letting me stay. I wanted him to know that I really appreciated him, and all he had done for me, as he was such a genuine good guy.

Len told me that he was happy to help and that I was also such a genuine gal and great company to be around, so it had been his pleasure! His kindness was heartwarming, and I was so grateful that people like him existed in this world. Suddenly Joe turned and joined us all on the dance floor, and he and I automatically started doing our usual fun, silly dances together ranging from our version of the bunny hop to the whirling dervish, and all sorts of freestyle moves in between!

Richard and Len must've thought we were both quite mad, but we were having such a great time laughing at each other's outlandish moves, and trying to out-do each other in the most comical of ways, that neither one of us seemed to care, and I loved it! After a while, we all went to sit down, catch our breaths, and have a drink with Len and Richard who were both in good spirits and were getting along well with each other. Joe and I were having a fun catch-up chat too, so all in all, we were all having a great night.

"There's a party down the road if you all fancy going?" said Richard, after one of his trips to the bar to pick up drinks for everyone. "Sounds fun, why not? Do you two wanna come along?" I answered, looking over at Len and Joe. "Nah thanks, I'm meeting someone here soon, have fun though" answered Len, as he glanced around the room, as if looking out for whoever he was meeting. "Can't, gotta get going soon, up early tomorrow, have a dance for me though!" answered Joe, with a big smile. "OK well, I hopefully catch you guys next time then!" I answered, before taking a sip of my beer. Richard and I soon finished our beers and stood up to leave, wishing Len and Joe all the best as we went.

We headed out of the Rainbow, waved goodbye to Mario who was at the door welcoming people, and strolled east down Sunset. Richard seemed to know the way and led us around the corner of a cross street called Larrabee towards an apartment block that overlooked Sunset.

We soon found ourselves in a modern-looking apartment, where a vivacious blonde-haired woman was holding court, and loudly telling anecdotes while everybody was sitting and standing around attentively listening to her. When she would laugh, they would all laugh, and when she was speaking, they would go quiet.

"That's Angie Bowie, David Bowies Ex" Richard whispered to me, to fill me in. "Oh, I wonder if that song "Angie" by David Bowie is about her - It would make sense!" I whispered back, with a little giggle. "I think so" answered Richard, with a nod.

Feeling tipsy, I started to have a little dance to the cool music that was playing, and Richard joined me in dancing too. I liked how the two of us didn't follow the crowd, and although we both seemed to appreciate the whole Hollywood rock music scene, we weren't swept away with it, we enjoyed doing our own thing - which was dancing!

It was a fun night and we met lots of fun and interesting people. We danced, chatted, laughed, joked, and got tipsier by the minute until we both felt exhausted and found a place to crash out in one of the rooms.

The next morning, I woke up, used the bathroom to freshen up, and then groggily made my way to the kitchen to find some coffee. A couple of minutes later Richard appeared looking worse for wear, and I figured I probably looked in a similar state. We sleepily mumbled hi to each other as I sipped on my coffee. Richard started to pour a coffee for himself, so I finished my coffee and went back to the bathroom to sort out my hair and make-up.

A few minutes later I came back to the kitchen, to make another coffee, and to see how Richard was doing. By now he was looking a little more alert, so we hung out drinking our coffees and chatting about various things as we both woke up some more. "Well, I guess I'd better head back soon, as the "Pico-Gang" are probably wondering where I am!" I exclaimed, as I finished my coffee, and headed towards the sink to wash my cup.

The who?" asked Richard looking confused. "Oh, it's the people where I live!" I answered, not sure if that clarified things or made them more confusing, but I was too tired to explain. "Well, see ya then, I may see you at The Rainbow one of the nights!" I said, as I grabbed my army shoulder bag, and started heading towards the door.

"Yeah, ok!" answered Richard as he started to pour himself another coffee, which made me feel not too bad about leaving him there on his own, as he obviously wanted to stay and have another coffee. "Bye/See Ya!" we called out to each other, as I found my way out of the apartment, without bumping into anyone else. I assumed that Angie and the other guests were still sleeping, or they had left already.

The cool LA air hit me as I exited the building in the shade and made my way towards the street, and into the warm sunshine. I decided to walk back to Pico as it was such a lovely day, I figured that I could always jump on a bus if I got too tired to walk any more.

I headed east on sunset until I reached La Brea, and then I headed south. I walked for about ten minutes until I reached Melrose Avenue. Instinctively, I suddenly decided to turn right onto Melrose Avenue to have a look around, as I'd heard that it was a fun street, and now seemed the perfect time to check it out!

I walked for a few seconds, and was surprised to see Richard heading towards me! It felt kind of awkward to see him again so soon, as we had said our goodbyes to each other less than an hour ago.

"Hi, long time no see!" I joked. "Hi, yeah!" he answered, and we both laughed. "I just decided to have a quick look around Melrose on my way home, I've heard it's a fun street, but keep forgetting to check it out!" I said, to make conversation.

"Yeah, it's got a lot of cool punk and new-wave shops, you'll like it!" he answered, with a smile. "Great, I guess I'll go and have a look then!" I answered, feeling a bit unsure as to whether I should invite him to join me, or just let him carry on his way.

"Yeah, hey don't forget I've got a few gigs coming up, you're welcome to come to any of them, just give my name at the door, and you'll get free entry" said Richard enthusiastically. "Great thanks, I may just do that! Well, see ya then!" I answered as I started to walk away. "OK, bye then!" he answered, as he started to walk away in the direction he'd been heading.

As I walked away, I felt a little confused about bumping into each other so soon after I'd left him at Angie Bowie's apartment. He'd only just poured himself another coffee, but somehow, he had managed to cover nearly the same distance as I had, and I was quite a fast walker. I couldn't help but wonder if he'd followed me after I'd left, and had maybe taken a shortcut with the aim of catching up with me so that he could remind me of his gigs - although it was possibly just a coincidence too. I would never know for sure. Either way, he was a nice guy, and I wished him well.

I strolled along Melrose enjoying the new day, and after a few minutes, lots of fun shops, cafés and colourful-looking young people started to appear. I loved how cool and funky everyone looked, although it was a little similar to Westward, in that most of the people strolling about seemed more like rich-kid "fashion punks" than real working-class-kid "street-punks" but it was a fun street nevertheless, and I liked it. I decided I would definitely come back another time!

Fatigue suddenly hit me like a ton of bricks, and I decided that I'd walked enough, especially after a night of partying and only a couple of hours of sleep, so I jumped on an eastbound bus over to Vine Street, then caught the Pico bus south, and back to basecamp on Pico and Crenshaw.

Back at the halfway house, I walked in the front door to hear Mike and Sonny bickering over something. They both paused to greet me, and Mike looked especially happy to see me as usual, and then they went straight back to bickering. From what I could gather, it seemed they had been ripped off on a bag of weed. It was only half full, and they were blaming each other, but in a very gentle way, and seeing as they were both such nice guys, they soon forgave each other and made friends again and turned their attention towards me, asking how my night out had been.

The three of us were soon sitting around the living room, catching up with one another's latest stories. They generously shared their munchies with me, which I appreciated, although I declined the weed, as my mind flashed back to how rough I'd felt from the weed in Toronto. I suddenly wondered how Jeff, Karina, Brian and the others at The Tropical Paradise Café-Bar in Toronto were doing, and I felt a wave of missing them all sweep through me. I hoped they were all well, and quickly put my feeling of missing them to the back of my heart and mind.

"I think I need a coffee, do you two want any!" I exclaimed as I headed towards the kitchen. "Yeah, I'll help you, want one Sonny?" answered Mike, as he started heading to the kitchen with me. "Sure" mumbled Sonny, and a few minutes later the three of us, were sitting around the living room chatting, laughing and joking about all sorts of things as usual.

Because they were high on weed, they were chatting about ridiculous ideas and theories which I was enjoying and adding to. The conversation got more and more far-fetched and outlandish as we went, and the three of us seemed to be riding a wave of the surreal, bizarre and ludicrous.

"Who knows, maybe the whole universe exists in the bacteria of some giant's throat!" I exclaimed with a big grin. Mike found this concept hilarious and we both cracked up laughing, but poor Sonny looked terrified. "Only Joking Sonny!" I said, hoping to ease his fears. "Sure" answered Sonny, looking a little relieved.

 "Well, I need to catch up with some sleep, so I'll say "goodnight" guys!" I called out as I trotted off to bed still laughing as I went. I could hear Mike still laughing too, and I loved how we always got along so well. I was happy to be back home with my "Pico-Gang."

CHAPTER 33:

LARRY ZUKERMAN

One day Mary asked me to cover for her for a few days, and I was happy to oblige, as by now I was in the full swing of things, and quite enjoyed making myself useful. The meals were very easy and ranged from big giant pots of pasta with either pasta sauce or tuna and mayonnaise, or grilled cheese sandwiches with tinned tomato soup, The coffee pot was always on the go, thanks to Mike, and if the residents got peckish, they could help themselves to snacks.

I'd only cooked a little for myself, and my mum before, I'd never cooked for a large group of people, but I enjoyed it, and thankfully, they all seemed to enjoy it too! - Much to my relief, and surprise!

Sometimes as I prepared the meals my mind would wander, and I would think about my family and friends back in England, and my friends over in Florida, Niagara Falls, and up in Toronto, and the lovely friends I'd made on the road. My heart would feel a little sad, as I would naturally miss them all, but I would remind myself that I was doing what I had set out to do, I was travelling the world, and had already seen quite a big chunk of it, and I had only recently turned eighteen, so it was not bad going!

I pondered on the idea of getting a local home-town job, or going to college like most kids my age would be doing, but in my heart of hearts I knew I had made the right choice, because, after travelling, my second passion was writing, and I was in essence gathering experiences to write about, so all in all, I was happy with my lot!

One day, after I'd finished giving the living room a clean-up, I decided to take a breather in a comfy armchair and watch a little TV with Mike, when "Angry Mike" suddenly charged at my armchair and pushed it over with me in it, while yelling at me that he was the devil!

BOOK 1: TO SEE THE WORLD

"Get lost! She's a nice girl, don't give her any shit!" shouted my friend Mike, as he jumped up from the sofa to my defence and stood between "Angry Mike" and me, as I climbed back up to my feet, feeling a little shaken up. "Angry Mike" stepped back, and staggered off looking defeated, and I was so proud of my friend Mike, he was such a good guy, and it was so heart-warming that he had stepped up to protect me as he did.

"Thanks, Mike, the next Thrifty's Ice creams are on me!" I exclaimed with a big smile. "No problem! Thanks, Della!" he answered, as his face lit up with a big smile, and the two of us continued to chill out and watch TV, in peace.

After being at the Pico halfway house for a few weeks, one morning I suddenly heard Suzi calling out Larry, the halfway-house owner's name, as I'd yet to meet him I quickly jumped out of bed, got dressed, and headed to the living room while feeling excited to finally be on the verge of meeting him.

"Delilah!" he exclaimed when he saw me, as he instantly reached out a hand to shake mine. "Hi, Larry!" I answered as we shook hands, and stood grinning at each other. He reminded me a little bit of an English actor called Ronnie Corbett, as he was short and stout, with glasses and a big smile. "So good to meet you at last!" exclaimed Larry, as he finished handing out cigarettes and money to the residents. "You too, we kept missing each other!" I exclaimed, liking his easy-going manner.

"So, you're on your travels huh? Whereabouts are you from in England, I'm an Anglophile, by the way. I visit England regularly!" he exclaimed, looking pleased to finally be meeting me. "Oswestry in Shropshire, not too far from Liverpool, do you know it" I answered with a smile. "Oh sure, I'm into antiques too, and I love old towns, You're not too far from Chester, and Shrewsbury right?" he answered knowingly. "Yeah, that's right! My dad's into antiques as well. He has a stall in Shrewsbury market hall, you may have bought something from him!" I answered, with a laugh. "Oh, quite likely!" he answered casually, and we both laughed.

"I love antiques, flying too!" he answered enthusiastically. "Oh wow, my dad is also into planes, he doesn't fly, but he was in the Air Force, and loves going to air shows, he's into all things aviation! You two would get along great, maybe you're my long-lost uncle!" I joked, and we both laughed. Michael and Sonny, who were still in the living room, laughed too.

"Here, this is for covering for Mary on her days off!" exclaimed Larry as he suddenly handed me some pocket money and a carton of cigarettes. "Great, thanks, Larry!" I answered feeling so grateful with the arrangement, especially as I could tell that he didn't have any ulterior motives, which was refreshing after some of the sleaze bags I'd met so far on my journey!

He truly did seem like a fun friendly older brother or uncle type, and the fact that he loved England made me feel an affinity and familiar connection with him, which was comforting and gave me a sense of security.

He spent a little more time checking on things around the halfway house and chatting with everyone, then he bid his farewells to everyone and headed off towards the front door.

"Bye Della, great to meet you, bye everyone!" He called out as he disappeared out of the front door, through the open metal door, and down the steps. "You too Larry/Bye Larry!" We all called back. Everyone's mood seemed lifted by his visit, and I felt pleased to have such a good base to stay - It certainly wasn't the Ritz, but I was happy!

CHAPTER 34:

GETTING TO KNOW THE ANGELS

Over the next few days, I went for walks alone and explored the local area in the opposite direction that I was used to going with Michael and Sonny, and I was surprised to find Buddhist temples on a street not too far away. Judging by the various signposts, it was the Korean part of town, which was on the northeast side of Crenshaw, and only a couple of blocks down from the halfway house.

As I walked along admiring these Buddhist temples, I was reminded of how Los Angeles seemed to be full of surprises, yet once again sadly it seemed to be segregated by race and nationality, rather than the melting pot that I would have expected it to be. Each race and class seemed to have their section of the city, aside from small diverse pockets here and there like: Hollywood, Santa Monica, and Venice Beach.

I pondered on my perception of the differences between segregation, and integration. For me, integration represented cooperation, harmony, and peace, but it would mean that individual cultures might stand to lose their identities, and customs, which wasn't necessarily a bad thing, as collectively they would most likely create new customs and traditions, whereas segregation seemed to represent national and cultural-centricity, and often some level of hostility with cultures that were different from their own. If left as they are they would stand to keep their cultural identities and customs but would lose out on the greater benefits of integration. I concluded that in time people would ultimately evolve towards what was best suited to their chances of survival. Either way, I hoped that peace would prevail.

I continued to walk along admiring the architecture. The Buddhist temples were beautiful, but sadly they seemed a little cold and uninviting as the gates were all locked up and there was no sign of life around them. I wondered when people went to them and assumed they must have set opening times for gatherings, rather than an open-door policy for people to just walk inside and pray at any time, which was the norm, for most Western churches. I didn't belong to any organised religion, but I did believe in a creator because creation could not be denied.

I thought about asking if Mike and Sonny would want to come with me for a walk this way for a change of scenery next time, as I felt that they would enjoy seeing the Buddhist temples too. I felt blessed to have them for company at the halfway house and for walks around the neighbourhood. It reminded me of my childhood explorations around my home town and surrounding countryside. Mike and Sonny seemed to enjoy exploring too, so together, we were the perfect trio!

A few days later I took Mike and Sonny on a walk to see the Buddhist Temples, and while Mike seemed impressed, Sonny was nonplussed as usual. I got the impression he just didn't see the point of them, which I found amusing, and could see where he was coming from a little bit, especially as the temples never seemed to be open! On our way back to the halfway house we decide to head down to Wilshire Boulevard to loop around on Wilshire, and come back up Crenshaw, rather than stroll back past the same Buddhist Temple buildings again.

As we neared Crenshaw Boulevard, I spotted a sign that read "Wilshire Acting School" and I was instantly curious about it, and thought it might be fun to join for a laugh. "Hey, guys maybe I'll take some acting classes!" I said, half-joking, and nodding towards the sign. "Go for it!" answered Mike in his usual upbeat way, while Sonny nodded in agreement. I got my pen and notepad out of my shoulder bag to write the number down but much to my annoyance, my pen wasn't working.

"Damn, my pen isn't working!" I exclaimed, frustratedly. Mike and Sonny looked disappointed for me. "Hey, what if we each remember a part of the phone number until we get back to the house, then I can jot it down?" I suggested, enthusiastically. "OK/Sure!" answered Mike and Sonny obligingly. "OK, so I'll remember 879, Mike can you remember 38, and Sonny can you remember 62?" I asked, with a grin, finding this phone number-remembering technique to be quite fun. "Sure 38, 38, 38" answered Mike grinning back. "62" mumbled Sonny, as if it was no big deal. "Great, can we practice a few times before we head back, so mine is 879, Mike:" I exclaimed, "38" he answered, still grinning, as if finding it as funny as I was. "Sonny?" I exclaimed, "62" he answered again, as if it was nothing. We all repeated our numbers a couple more times then started walking back up Crenshaw to the halfway house, repeating the number, and laughing as we went.

Despite Mike and I laughing more than repeating our numbers, miraculously the technique worked, and once we got back at Pico I quickly grabbed a pen and wrote down the number."That's great, I'll have to treat you both to a thrifty Ice cream as thanks for helping me to remember the number!" I exclaimed, feeling happy that we accomplished our mission. "Thanks, Della/ Sure" They both answered, looking pleased. Thrifty's Ice Cream seemed to be my way of thanking them for various deeds, and it was always fun to have a little outing, and walk down to Thrifty's, and back. The next day I phoned The Wilshire Acting School and arranged to start classes. It seemed like it would be a fun hobby, and handy for me to get to, as it was only a twenty-minute walk away straight down Crenshaw.

Over the next couple of weeks, I would cover for Mary on her days, off, and spend the evenings either at the acting class, out in Hollywood, or home at the halfway house; journaling, or watching TV and playing card games with Mike and Sonny. Sometimes Darlene, Cathy Crude and Suzie would join us, whereas "Angry Mike" and the others would mainly keep to themselves watching TV in their rooms.

On the days I covered for Mary I was up at 7:30 to make breakfast for 8 am. It was just coffee and cereal, so it was very easy to get it together, it was mainly just a matter of putting the cereal, milk, bowls and spoons on the dining table, and making sure enough cups were clean for coffee, and plastic glasses for cool-aid - which was a drink made from mixing an orange-coloured powder and water together. It was very sweet, and I wasn't too keen on it, but the residents seemed to love it. Mike often turned up to help me. He was such a good friend, and I always appreciated his physical, and moral support.

After breakfast, I would be free until around 11.30 am when it was time to make lunch ready for 12 noon. After lunch, I would be free again until 5 pm when I would make dinner, and my evenings were free. Some nights if I was up very late, I would put the breakfast cereal, bowls and spoons on the table ready for breakfast in the morning and totter off to bed and have a lie-in until it was time to make lunch around 11.30 in the morning. I figured, as long as they had things ready for them in the morning, what difference did it make if I was there or not?

I had explained to Michael and Sonny about this, and they seemed to understand and be ok with it, as after all, the residents would only go back to bed after

321

breakfast, so it wasn't like I had to entertain them or anything. The only difference was they didn't get to see me until late morning when I would wash up the breakfast dishes, and make them lunch. Everyone seemed pretty laid-back about things, and no one complained, including Mary, who seemed to take everything in her stride, and cooly coast along. Sometimes I did feel a little bad about my late nights, and lie-ins, but not too bad, as I reminded myself that I was still only eighteen, and making meals for 12 adults was quite a responsibility, whereas most kids my age were still living at home, and having their meals made for them! – I didn't envy them though, as I much preferred my circumstances.

One night I went to bed early as I was tired after a busy day. I didn't sleep straight away, instead, I just lay there thinking about my journey so far. I thought again about how I wasn't feeling the same urge to continue on with my travels that I was used to feeling after a while in a place, now that I was in Los Angeles, or "The Angels" as one of the halfway house residents: Chico, had told me the name meant in English.

I wasn't sure why I wasn't feeling the usual pull to keep on travelling, I wondered if it was because of the combination of having a nice little basecamp, a good gig with a lovely 'boss' and residents, good friends, a fun and interesting city which was full of never-ending things to do, and beautiful feel-good weather! 'Yeah, why travel, when I'm so happy here!' I thought to myself. I suddenly remembered that my aunt Freda would be heading over to the US soon, according to a recent letter I'd received from my mum, she had given my aunt Freda my phone number and address in LA, so I was expecting to hear from her any day.

I pondered if, after my aunt Freda's visit, I should fly back to England with her, stay in LA for a little while longer, or continue on with my travels. Which, reminded me that I would need to get a new passport soon! My mind flashed to the day Ray had left me stranded in Virginia, taking off with all my stuff, and leaving me with only the clothes I was wearing. I thought about how Billy and his lovely family had come to my rescue, and how I'd wound up staying with them at their cosy farmhouse, just over the border from Virginia in North Carolina, and I realised that despite the ups and downs on my US travels so far, I was still developing a strong love for America and her people, and the thought of leaving a place where I felt so happy and at home deeply saddened me, and pained my heart. I wasn't sure what to make of these feelings, as I still had a strong desire to travel and see the world. When I'd first set off on my travels I'd had no idea that I would become so bonded to various people and places along the way. 'All part of the adventure!' I told myself, trying to keep an objective point of view.

As I lay there in bed pondering on my life and my travels so far, I realised that I was particularly falling in love with Los Angeles. I took stock of my time there so far and thought about all of the fellow free-spirited dreamers I had met since being there. Each of them doing what they could to put their dreams into action and make them come true. A lot of the people I'd met in Los Angeles had felt like true kindred spirits, although many of them had ambitions of being actors, singers, musicians and the like, although I wasn't really sure of what my ambitions were - Only that I wanted to travel and write.

I pondered on the idea of becoming an actor, and my mind went back to my first evening at the Wilshire Acting School. I had taken the bus there and walked inside feeling a mixture of nerves and curiosity. The teacher had greeted me and said his name was Dan. There were about 15 other male and female students of all ages, and they all looked friendly and fun-spirited. The lesson had started straight away as Dan told us to "Shake your bodies!... keep shaking!" As we all stood around laughing and shaking our bodies. Next, he told us to pull silly faces, keep shaking and walk around!

We all started to laugh even more, as it was quite hilarious. Next, he told us to stretch our bodies as big as we could make them, and then to run around the room! We all followed his instructions, most of us laughing hysterically as we went, I couldn't help thinking it was crazier than the halfway house, and the thought of the residents seeing me running around pulling silly faces with a bunch of other people doing the same cracked me up even more! Suddenly Dan shouted "Stop!" and we all stood still laughing, and catching our breaths. "That's enough warm-up! ...Tom pretend you're taking a shower!" Dan instructed looking over at a slim guy standing to my right. Tom quickly made the movement of taking a shower and when he was done everybody clapped. "Della you're next!" Dan said quickly looking my way. I felt a bit silly but made an effort to act as if I was taking a shower. After I was finished everybody clapped for me too. This felt good, and helped my confidence to grow a tad, although I wasn't sure if I was actually gaining acting experience, or just wasting time, but either way, it was fun!

That night I'd arrived home, after the acting class, to be welcomed by Mike and Sonny they celebrated my new hobby with goodies that Mike had brought from the liquor store, and we played card games and watched TV until the early hours, and I'd gone to bed feeling happy and content, these memories seemed to help me drift off to sleep – finally!

CHAPTER 35:

ENGLISH GAL IN HOLLYWOOD

One evening I was feeling restless, so I decided I would head up to Hollywood and mosey around with no plans, and see what happens. So, I got myself showered and dressed up a little, and headed out to catch the Hollywood bus. As the bus was passing Sunset and Vine, I spotted a sign that read "Gino's New-Wave Nightclub" It sounded like my cup of tea, so I decided to jump off at the next bus stop and go and check it out.

As I strolled along, I figured that the booze in the club was probably expensive, so I crossed over the street to a liquor store and bought a pack of "Olde English 800 Malt Liquor." It was cheap and the cans were taller than regular beer cans, so I felt it was a great bargain. Feeling pleased with my find, I crossed back over the street and looked for a spot to have a beer before heading to the club. I wandered around the back of a fast-food place called "The Beef Bowl" and found a large area of bushes growing. I figured that there might be a nice spot it the bushes, to sit and have a beer.

I glanced around to make sure no one spotted me, then ducked inside the bushes, while feeling like I was on some kind of stealth army mission! I soon found a small clearing in the centre of the bushes, with enough light from the nearby lamppost shining down to light it up. 'Ah perfect!' I thought to myself, as I spotted a concrete slab to sit on.

I sat down and opened up a can of beer and took a sip. It was very strong, but it tasted ok. I continued to sip away on my beer and felt myself relaxing more and more, with every sip I took. I looked around at my surroundings, it was like I was in my own little secret den, and I liked it! It reminded me of some of the dens me and my friends created as kids during our rambles around my home town and surrounding countryside.

I drank the rest of the can of beer and stashed the rest of the cans in the bushes, then headed over the street to "Gino's" The beer had gone to my head fast, and as I walked, I could feel myself getting tipsier. I turned the corner into the parking lot of Gino's to see loads of punk rockers and new-wavers milling about. 'Wow! This is great!' I thought to myself, and I couldn't stop myself from smiling as I strolled through the crowd, feeling happy to be there, and become a part of such a cutting-edge scene!

It was amazing to see all the different creative styles of punk and new-wave clothes and colours, from blacks and greys, to vibrant. The kids were mostly around my age, and I noticed that they had a tad more of a wholesome look than the Cafe de Grand hard-core street punks. I guessed that these kids still lived at home, and probably shopped at Melrose, but it was still an alternative music crowd and it felt a lot more my scene than the hard-core punk-rock scene for sure.

A cute guy in the crowd suddenly caught my eye and I wondered who he was. He was dressed in typical punk-rock clothes: mainly all black with a studded belt, and studded wristband, and a red tartan shirt tied around his waist. He had jet-black spiky hair and gorgeous big brown eyes, and I felt my heart skip a beat as he glanced my way. I quickly looked the other way and continued on towards the entrance of the club.

I climbed up the steep stairs into the club and could hear the Thompson Twins music playing loudly inside the club. "Yeah, this is more like it!" I thought to myself, as I started to dance to the music as I moved along up the stairs.

I entered the main club room at the top of the stairs and looked around. It was getting full as more of the kids from the outside were heading inside. It was an oblong-shaped club. About 40 feet over to my right was the dancefloor, and about 40 feet to my left were the bathrooms, and directly across the room from me was the bar.

I suddenly needed to pee, so I quickly headed over towards the bathroom. "Excuse me!" I said, as I entered the bathroom, and tried to get past the girls standing about chatting the entranceway in there. Suddenly, everyone stopped chatting and looked at me. "Oh my God, are you from England?!" squealed one of the gals. "Uh, yeah, Oswestry, towards Liverpool way" I answered, feeling self-conscious, as all eyes seemed locked on me.

I'd learned earlier on my travels with the truckers, that Liverpool seemed to be the nearest city to my hometown of Oswestry, that most Americans had heard of, so I figured it was quicker to say than I was from a place that was not too far from Liverpool, than try to explain the tiny town that I was from, that not even a lot of people in England had heard of, never mind people abroad! I had a quick chat with the gals in the bathroom about England, all while bursting to go for a pee, and then finally excused myself, and popped into a cubicle to use the loo.

"Oh my God an English girl in Hollywood!" "Aww, and she said see-ya, with such a cute accent!" I heard a couple of the girls say. I had never given much thought to my accent before and wondered how it must sound to them. When I came out of the loo two ethnic-looking girls were standing as if waiting to chat with me.

"Hi, I'm Sylvia and this is Julie. We heard your accent, and wanted to stay and say hi!" said one of the girls, as I washed my hands, and checked my hair and make-up in the mirror. "Hi!" added the other girl with a big smile. "Oh hi, I'm Della, nice to meet you both!" I said as I shook their hands. I noticed that Sylvia looked a little Spanish, whereas Julie looked Chinese, but they both had strong American accents, so I guessed they were born in the States.

"We're planning a trip to England soon, so we wanna know all about it!" exclaimed Sylvia excitedly, and the three of us laughed. "Well, I'm not sure if I knew all about it myself, but I'm happy to help if I can!" I answered, and they laughed. "So, who are you here with?" asked Julie curiously. "Myself!" I answered with a grin. "Good for you!/Yeah!" they answered while looking impressed. "You're welcome to join us if you want?" said Sylvia with a big smile, as Julie nodded, and smiled over at me enthusiastically. "Yeah ok, thanks!" I answered as I followed them out of the bathroom.

The three of us instinctively headed over towards the dancefloor and started dancing. We were getting along great, chatting, laughing, and dancing in a fun-spirited way. As we danced Julie took out a bottle of booze from her handbag and took a swig before passing it over to me.

"Thanks!" I exclaimed as I took a swig too. It tasted like Bacardi and Coke, and it instantly boosted my tipsy state. "Woo-hoo!" I called out, before passing the bottle over to Sylvia, as I twirled around to dance some more. The gals laughed, and as I twirled, I spotted the cute guy with black spiky hair and big brown eyes again. He reminded me of "Sid Vicious" It was a look that a lot of punk guys seemed to go for, but this guy really stood out to me, and I wondered who he was. Sylvia, Julie and I carried on dancing and drinking and having fun, and at some point, I tipsily confided in them that I had my eye on the Sid Vicious guy and asked if they knew his name.

They didn't know his name, but we all giggled as I gestured for them to keep hush about my secret crush. We carried on dancing, and at one point I twirled around and bumped right into him! We all laughed as I pulled a cringey "Help me!" face. "We'll get his name for you!" announced Sylvia mischievously, as Julie stood by grinning and nodding. "OK!" I answered, grinning back mischievously. "Let's go over there!" suggested Julie, pointing to the other side of the club. "OK" answered Sylvia, looking ready for a change of scenery. "Yeah, let's mingle!" I tipsily joked back.

As we walked across the club, Julie and Sylvia spotted the Sid Vicious guy and boldly headed over towards him. I stood back cringing with embarrassment, and decided to keep on walking to the other side of the club. I wondered what they were saying to him, and although I felt embarrassed by the thought that they might be telling him I liked him, I found it kind of funny as well, especially being as tipsy as I was.

Suddenly Sylvia and Julie came rushing over towards me, and I braced myself curious to hear what they had to say. "His name is Johnny, he says he'll come over and say hi later!" exclaimed Sylvia excitedly, while Julie stood to the side grinning, and looking pleased with the interaction.

A sense of pressure kicked in, and I suddenly felt an intense urge to leave the club, but at the same time, I knew it was all just good fun. "Great, ok thanks!" I answered as we all started dancing to the song: "Hungry Like the Wolf" by Duran Duran. I wondered how my Greek friend Peter - The Simon Lebon lookalike was doing? and made a mental note to tell him about Gino's as I was sure he would like it.

The three of us carried on drinking and dancing, chatting and laughing for the next hour or so, and I forgot all about Johnny. Eventually, it was time to leave, "I'll give you a lift home if you want?" said Syliva as we started heading towards the exit. "Great thanks, I stay down by Pico and Crenshaw if that's ok?" I answered thinking it would be nice to ride home in a car, rather than on the bus for a change. "Sure, no problem at all. We live in Santa Monica, so we can just head west from there!" answered Sylvia, as Julie smiled in agreement. "Great thanks!" I answered, feeling happy to have made two lovely new friends.

As we neared the crowds by the exit, Johnny suddenly appeared from nowhere. "Hi, they said you wanted to meet?" he said cooly. "Nah, I wanted two veg!" I answered flippantly, by now feeling very drunk, cocky, and devil-may-care! He looked really puzzled, and the girls cracked up laughing as we left him behind, and carried on walking down the stairs, and out into the parking lot at the front.

"Two veg!!!" quoted Sylvia, and we all cracked up laughing again, as we headed through a walkway that led to another parking lot at the back. Sylvia and Julie led the way, chatting to each other, and I followed along. On the surface, I was having a great time, but deep down I started to feel bad for giving Johnny the cold shoulder.

'Why did I do that?' I wondered to myself, as a sense of regret swept through me. 'Maybe it's because I know that if I get stuck with a guy, then I won't be free to travel, and he's the type of guy I would definitely get stuck with!' I thought, trying to make sense of my aloof behaviour, as I tipsily followed Sylvia and Julie along towards their car.

Once again, I felt torn between relationships, and travel, and felt as though I was on the verge of drunkenly falling down to the ground and crying out in despair when Sylvia shouted out that her car was the one on the end. I suddenly came out of my spiralling thoughts, took a deep breath, and followed them to the car.

We all jumped inside the car, and Sylvia put the radio on. The new-wave music instantly lifted my mood, and as we drove away, I caught a glimpse of Johnny and his friends standing around in the parking lot and felt a pang of sadness for messing up our introduction. My mind suddenly flashed to Jeff up in Toronto. The alcohol seemed to have stirred up all of my suppressed emotions to the surface, and I missed him. I hoped that he was doing ok.

As we drove along the music kept on playing, and soon we were all chatting, laughing and joking, and once again I felt happy to have made some fun new friends. They seemed much more my type than the hardcore punk kids. They were more fun-spirited, and light-hearted which I liked.

They dropped me off outside of the halfway house, and we quickly swapped numbers. "Thanks so much for the lift! See you next time!" I exclaimed as I jumped out of the car. "See you later!/See ya!" called out Sylvia and Julie, as I slammed the door shut. We waved goodbye to each other, and I tottered up the steps towards the caged porch.

Just as I was fumbling to open the gate a bleary-eyed Mike appeared from the other side of the living room door to help let me in. "Michael! I'm sure you're my guardian angel!" I exclaimed tipsily, as I trundled on inside. "I just wanted to make sure you got home safely, want some coffee?" He answered as he headed towards the kitchen. "Yes please, thanks, Mike!" I answered as I flopped down on the sofa. 'What a good soul he is' I thought to myself as Mike clanked around in the kitchen getting our coffees together.

"There you go, did you have a good night?" asked Mike as he arrived in the living room carrying two cups of coffee. "Yeah, it was fun, I made a couple of friends named Sylvia and Julie!" I answered, as Mike sat down on the sofa next to me, and handed me a cup of coffee. "That's so cool, it's because you're such a nice girl!" answered Mike looking pleased for me. "Aw, thanks Mike, they're nice girls too, and you're a nice guy! Thanks for the coffee!" I answered as I took a sip of strong-tasting coffee. Figuring that Mike could see I needed sobering up!

"We stayed sitting next to each other on the sofa chatting for hours. Mike was always curious to hear about my outings and adventures, and I was always interested to learn more about his life, especially before he got ill. Soon it was 7 am, so Mike helped me put the breakfast things out, then we wished each other goodnight, and we headed off to our rooms to crash out.

"Della wake up! wake up! you've gotta make lunch!" I suddenly heard Darlene shouting as she banged on my bedroom door. "OK, I'll be there soon!" I called back, as I jumped out of bed from a deep sleep and threw on some clothes. I glanced at the clock and saw that it was just after twelve noon. I felt bad for oversleeping, but I was glad that Darlene had woken me up when she did, as it wouldn't take me long to throw some food together for the residents.

I opened my bedroom door, and ran down to the living room, greeting the hungry-looking residents as I whizzed by them on my way to the kitchen. I quickly put a tuna casserole together, as this was a fast, easy dish to make, and everyone seemed to love it, so my slightly late lunch was soon forgotten, and forgiven.

Mary suddenly appeared up the stairs into the kitchen and handed me some pocket money. "From Larry, as thanks for helping!" she said in her usual laid-back manner. "Thanks, Mary!" I answered as I poured myself a coffee to help clear my hangover and wake up some more.

None of the residents, or Mary and Larry seemed bothered that I sometimes had late nights and lie-ins, and liked to go out and about. It was as if they expected that kind of behaviour, as after all I was still a teenager, and as long as I did my best to help out at the halfway house, they seemed satisfied. Which made me feel that I was appreciated, despite my sometimes slightly loose schedule.

After lunch, I cleared up the table, washed the dishes, and made myself another cup of coffee to take to my room. I sat propped up on my bed with my coffee and suddenly wondered what the latest was with my aunt Freda.

I decided to write her a letter to see when she would be in the States? and to update her on some of my recent travels and my current situation. I mentioned that my mum had told me that she had passed on my contact details to her, and added that she would probably be welcome to stay at the halfway house for a few days if she wanted to, as there were at least two bedrooms free, and I felt sure that Larry and Mary wouldn't mind. I made a mental note to ask Larry about it at some point.

Later that day Mike and Sonny accompanied me on a walk to the post office at Crenshaw and Washington Boulevard to post the letter. I was happy to have finally got around to writing to Aunt Freda and was sure that she would appreciate the update.

"So do you miss England?" asked Mike as we strolled back to the halfway house. "I do miss my family and friends, but I feel so at home in LA, that I don't feel homesick or anything like that" I answered, with a shoulder shrug. "Yeah, that's cool! This is your home now, you're a California adult remember!" answered Mike, with a big smile, looking pleased to hear that I wasn't homesick for England. "Yeah, that's right, I am!" I exclaimed, and we both laughed.

"My aunt Freda will be coming to the States to look at some properties soon, do you think Larry would mind if she stays at the halfway house? I've noticed the bedroom next to mine, and the one at the end of the hallway are both empty right?" I asked Mike, hoping to get a positive reply.

"Yeah, I'm sure Larry wouldn't mind!" Answered Mike in his usual optimistic manner, while Sonny nodded in agreement. "Ah great, I'll ask him at some point then!" I answered, feeling pleased. "Sure, it'd be cool to meet your auntie!" Mike answered with a smile, as we headed around the corner at Pico and Crenshaw, and back to base.

CHAPTER 36:

LA FAMILY

I covered for Mary for the next few days, so I stayed home, catching up with my journalling, playing games with the residents, and going on local walks with Michael and Sonny in my spare time. All in all, I was feeling happy and content. The days flew by, and soon I was to be free for the following week, so I decided to head up to Hollywood and visit Rishard, as I hadn't seen him in a few weeks, so it would be fun to have a catch-up, and maybe ask how Gabby was doing.

I took the bus up to Hollywood, and soon arrived at Rishard's apartment and knocked on the door. "Della, come in, come in!" Exclaimed Rishard with a big smile as he opened the door, and gestured for me to follow him inside. "DELLA!!!" Yelled Gabby as she jumped up to give me a big hug. "Hi, Gabby!" I exclaimed, hugging her back and glancing around the room at Rishard's other guests, who all looked a tad inebriated.

"These are my friends, Felix and Anna, this is my friend Della." Said Rishard as he gestured towards the handsome black guy, who looked around the same age as Rishard, and the good-looking dark-haired white woman who looked to be in her late twenties. We all smiled and said hi to each other, as Rishard headed towards the kitchen looking pleased to have his friends around.

"Where have you been!" Exclaimed Gabby, looking at me as if she couldn't believe it was really me. "I've got a little au pair volunteer gig at a halfway house down on Pico and Crenshaw, what have you been up to?" I asked, feeling pleased to see her again. "Would you like a beer, Della?" called out Rishard from the kitchen. "Yes, please Rishard!" I called back, feeling happy with the warm welcome.

"There you are Della, so how are you, I have not seen you lately," said Rishard, as he passed me an open bottle of Heineken. "Thanks, Rishard, I've just been busy helping out at the halfway house, and not venturing too far. How are you doing?" I answered, before taking a sip of beer.

"Oh, very well thank you, my good friend, Felix is also from Zaire, and he's had some free time to come and visit me, which has been nice" answered Rishard, smiling over at Felix. "It is also a pleasure to spend time with my brother Rishard" answered Felix, in a similar French accent as Rishard's, while smiling back at Rishard and me with a slightly arrogant expression on his face, which added to his character. "Yes, Rishard is great company!" I answered in agreement.

"So, tell me all about what you've been up to lately?" interrupted Gabby excitedly. "Not a lot really, like I said, mainly staying around the halfway house at Pico, and hanging out with the residents!" I answered with a laugh. "What are they crazy people?" asked Gabby. "Of course!" I answered, and we both cracked up laughing.

"So, are they safe, they are not dangerous, are they?" asked Rishard, looking concerned for me. "Yeah, they're very safe, that's why they're in a halfway house and not locked up. They just need a little support is all. They're actually all very different, and good people. My main friend is a guy named Mike. He is so sweet, and fun, we have a great laugh!" I answered, smiling at the memory of some of my and Mike's times together. "Oh, that is good, as long as they are not dangerous!" answered Rishard, looking a little more relaxed.

Rishard had some of his favourite jazz music playing in the background, and I had the sense of being with family. Gabby kept asking me what I'd been up to for the last few weeks, and Rishard and his friends seemed curious to know too, so they listened in as I did my best to answer Gabby's questions. "So what about you Gabby, what have you been up to?" I asked once I'd filled her in on the last few weeks. "Oh, same ole, same ole!" she answered nonchalantly, and we all laughed.

Rishard once again introduced me to his friends, this time with more details. "So, this is Felix he is a graphic artist, we met in college, and this is Anna, she is a photographer like myself, and guys, this is Della, the intrepid explorer, she is also my little sister, like Gabby," said Rishard proudly. We all smiled at each other and started chatting about all sorts of random, and interesting things. It didn't seem to matter what we were chatting about because the vibes felt good.

At some point Rishard and his friends got into an in-depth conversation about photography and film, so Gabby and I headed to the kitchen to grab ourselves another beer each and sat down at the Kitchen table and continued on with our catch-up chat.

"I've been worried about you! You disappeared man! I thought you took off back to England! It's so great to see you!" Exclaimed Gabby, still looking like she couldn't believe it was me. "Yeah, well I didn't want to say in front of Rishard, but remember that Garage-Party we went to in East LA, at some point we lost each other and I wound up in the garage with a bunch of punks, and someone gave me a cigarette to take a drag off, and it knocked me for six, especially on top of the booze! A skinhead in the kitchen told me that it was probably dipped in "Angel Dust" I felt so rough that I just wanted to get out of there, I didn't like that scene at all, so I did a runner at 5 am, and jumped on the Venice bus! Down at the beach, I met a hairdresser named Xavier who got me the volunteer gig helping out at the halfway house!" I answered, hoping that Gabby would get why I left the party when I did.

"Yeah, that was probably Angel Dust, man, it's nasty stuff, I'm just so glad you're ok! It's great to see you man!" answered Gabby, looking elated. "It's great to see you too Gabby!" I answered feeling happy to see her again.

"Wanna go to Seven Seas?" asked Gabby as we finished our beers. "Yeah, OK!" I answered, thinking it would be fun to have a dance. We bid out farewells to Rishard and his friends and took off into the night. I loved how Los Angeles always had a fun feel to it, daytime or nighttime, it didn't seem to matter! We headed down the street chatting, laughing and joking as we went.

As we neared Hollywood Boulevard the music from the cruising cars boomed out and the usual motley crew of tourists, street people and partygoers came into view. A bunch of black teenagers were breakdancing on the sidewalk, and a crowd had gathered around to watch.

We both smiled and grinned at the fun scene, but kept on walking across Hollywood Boulevard towards the club. "Moses!" Shouted Gabby, as we got over on the other side of the street. I looked over to see a Rastafarian guy looking to be in his thirties turning to look our way.

"Hey Mon, how you been living, irie?" he said as he strolled over towards us with a big smile. "Yeah, good Moses, this is my friend Della from England" answered Gabby as we shook hands. "Hey girls, what gives? I've been doing the love thing!" exclaimed Moses, looking as if he was on cloud nine. "Moses is all about the love!" Gabby exclaimed, with a grin. "That's nice!" I said, smiling at them both, while not sure what else to say to that.

334

BOOK 1: TO SEE THE WORLD

"You're welcome to visit me anytime. Keep it love!" Moses exclaimed, as he went into some kind of ramble, which gave the impression that he was maybe high on something. He seemed a nice guy, but I found it hard to make sense of what he was saying, so I stood there smiling and looking bemused. Gabby seemed amused by this and told him we would catch him later. We both waved goodbye and ran off giggling down Sycamore.

We headed around to the back of the club, as that was the main entrance, and where most of the clubgoers hung out in the large parking lot at the back. As soon as we reached the parking lot, I spotted Johnny amongst the crowds of punks and new-wavers hanging out around the parked cars, listening to music and sipping on drinks.

It felt too soon to be seeing him again after our last disaster of an introduction, so I tried to hide at the side of Gabby so he wouldn't see me. I noticed a blonde girl hanging around him and felt a pang of disappointment that he may be seeing someone, yet at the same time, I felt a sense of relief. 'More freedom, less stress!' I thought to myself with a laugh, as I followed Gabby inside the club.

The atmosphere inside was flat, as it was still relatively early and things hadn't kicked off yet. "Wanna go to Cathay de Grand instead?" suggested Gabby, looking bored. "Sounds good!" I answered, as we turned around, and took off out of the club.

Gabby and I arrived outside the Cathay de Grande, and as I looked around at some of the kids hanging out there, I suddenly realised that I had a new appreciation for the hard-core punk scene, as compared to the rich kids, and fashion punks that were obviously still living at home with mummy and daddy, this scene felt way more gritty and real.

Most of these kids were out in the world all alone. They were living in squats, or sharing cheap apartments in bad neighbourhoods, and working low-pay jobs to get by, and although it still wasn't really my cup of tea, I felt that I could relate to them on some level. I wasn't really sure what my cup of tea was, as I felt I didn't really fit into any of the categories, and refused to join any groups or cliques. I was simply an explorer, and I liked it that way!

"All I want is a room somewhere!" sang Gabby suddenly, in a strong cockney accent, and I cracked up laughing. "Wow, you have a great voice, Gabby! You should be on the stage!" I exclaimed, feeling impressed. "I know it's my calling!" she answered laughing. "You are really good!" I answered, feeling amazed by how strong and in tune her voice was. "Yeah, hey I would love some drugs!" She answered, with a mischievous look on her face.

"Oh right?" I answered, not sure what she was planning to do next. I wasn't into drugs, but I couldn't help but love her freewheeling, fun-spirited ways. "Let's head back to the boulevard, and see if I can score some!" she exclaimed enthusiastically. "OK!" I answered, as we turned around and headed back up to Hollywood Boulevard.

We were soon back up on "The Boulevard" as locals called it, and as we walked along Gabby asked random people if they had some goods. "Yeah" answered a black guy who looked like he lived on the streets, and Gabby's eyes lit up. "What have you got?" asked Gabby, as they moved to the side and started to chat. I moved away a little bit to give them some privacy and slowly started to stroll up the Boulevard.

"Hey, Della!" called out Gabby a few seconds later, as she gestured for me to follow them down a nearby side street. I followed them down the side street but hung back a little, ready to run and get help if things took a bad turn.

They made a left into an alleyway, and Gabby called out "Della will you keep a look out for us, while I get this deal sorted?" "OK!" I shouted back, not feeling good about the situation, and suddenly remembering why I'd parted ways with Gabby in the first place! She was a great gal, but her lifestyle was way too dangerous for me, as she seemed to enjoy taking unnecessary risks, just for fun. I guessed it boiled down to her being a somewhat neglected, and bored teenager, so I felt compassion for her, but I wasn't sure that I wanted to be taking the same kinds of risks along with her.

We all walked a little ways into the alleyway, and after going about thirty feet or so, I hung back, while they continued on towards a dark doorway at the back of a building. I turned around and stood there, not knowing what I was "looking out" for. I guessed it was just to warn them if anyone came along, but I was not enjoying just standing there in the dark, that much I did know! I could hear Gabby and the guy chatting away, and they sounded like they were negotiating a deal.

After a few moments passed, I suddenly realised that they had gone quiet, so I glanced back to see if everything was ok. I saw their silhouettes in the doorway of the building, and could just about make out that they were getting it on.

'Oh my God!" I thought to myself feeling shocked and sickened. I couldn't believe what Gabby was doing just for some drugs! I felt extremely disheartened and sorry for her to think that she would be so desperate! But I told myself that it was her choice, and this was her scene, but it certainly wasn't my scene! I suddenly lost all interest in hanging out with her and just wanted to go home to the halfway house on Pico. I slowly walked back to the entrance of the alleyway feeling disappointed and fed-up.

"Wait up! I got a good score!" Shouted Gabby triumphantly as she ran to catch up with me. "God, how could you do that with that guy?" I said feeling disgusted. "Oh, easy! No problem! He wasn't a good lay though; it was over in three seconds!" said Gabby, so matter-of-factly that I had to laugh.

"Wanna come to the studio and shoot it?" she asked as if it was the next fun thing to do for the night. "No thanks, you go ahead. I'm gonna go home and catch up with some sleep. I may see you next week" I said trying not to sound as bothered as I really was.

"Sure" she answered flatly as if she could sense my mood. We headed back down to The Boulevard and split. "See ya Gabby!" I called out, as I ran across the street, and waved goodbye. "See ya!" She called after me, as I jumped on a bus bound for Pico. As the bus took off, I caught a glimpse of Gabby heading back towards the Café de Grand and hoped that she'd be ok.

I couldn't wait to get back to the halfway house and be greeted by Mike and Sonny. It was dawning on me more and more that, so-called normal people and crazy people weren't always what they seemed to be.

I arrived back at the halfway house, and sure enough, Mike and Sonny were there to greet me at the door. I suddenly felt happy and safe, and glad to be away from the crazy Hollywood rollercoaster ride - especially when shared with Gabby! We had a little chat about their day and mine, and then I bid them goodnight and went to crash out in my bed. I spent the next few days at home, preferring the so-called crazy people inside the halfway house, to the so-called normal people outside of it!

CHAPTER 37:

THE MAGICAL PATTY MARTINEZ

The following Tuesday, I was finally feeling rejuvenated and ready for another dose of Hollywood nightlife, so I headed back to Gino's Nightclub. It was "Ladies' Night" so it was free to get in. I bought some Bacardi and Coke at the liquor store down the street from the club, headed across the street to my little den in the bushes at the back of the Beef Bowl, and kicked back to enjoy my little party for one!

Just as I was starting to feel a little tipsy and relaxed, a slim blonde girl suddenly appeared as if by magic through the bushes tiptoeing her way into the small clearing where I was, carrying a bottle of booze in a brown bag. "Oh hi, how are you?" she said as if it was absolutely normal to find a young gal in the bushes sipping on Bacardi and Coke. "Oh hi, I'm okay thanks, how are you?" I answered nonchalantly, but laughing a little because it was kind of bizarre that we had both headed to the same spot in the bushes to drink our booze.

"Have a seat!" I exclaimed with a laugh, as I made some space for her to sit down on the concrete slab next to me. "Thanks" she answered, as she came and sat down. "Looks like we're both here for the same reason!" I joked "Yeah, what's your name?" she said laughing.

"Della, what's yours?" I asked, reaching out my hand. "Patty" she answered, as we shook hands. "I'm going to Gino's I heard it's a good club, and I figured it would be cheaper to catch a buzz from the liquor store, than inside the club!" exclaimed Patty cooly, as she opened up her can of beer. "Yeah, me too, Cheers!" I exclaimed as I held up my bottle of Bacardi and Coke. "Cheers!" exclaimed Patty, as we knocked our drinks together.

338

We got tipsy in the bushes and were soon chatting away like old pals. She was twenty-one, so she was three years older than me, but we got along great, as she was very fun and easy-going and even though she commented on my English accent, she didn't make too much of a fuss about it, which was cool. I liked her style.

When my Bacardi and Coke ran out, I suddenly remembered the Olde English Malt Liquor beers that I'd stashed in the bushes the last time I was there. "I've got some more booze in here somewhere!" I announced, as I tipsily crawled into the bushes to find it. Patty found this hilarious, and we both cracked up laughing.

I retrieved the beers passed Patty a can, and opened one for myself. "Cheers!" we exclaimed again, as we clinked our cans together, before swiftly drinking them down. "Shall we go to Gino's!" I asked as we finished off our beers. "Yeah, let's go! To Peter O'Toole!" exclaimed Patty tipsily. "To Peter O'Toole!" I exclaimed back, and the two of us stumbled our way out of the bushes.

As we turned the corner from the street into the club's front parking lot. Patty looked impressed to see all the dressed-up punk rockers, and new-wavers milling about. "Cool!" she exclaimed, as we walked through the crowd and up the steps into the club.

As soon as we entered the club room we automatically headed over to the bathroom, chatting about this and that as we went. On hearing my accent, I experienced the same kind of reaction as the last time I'd been there from some of the girls in the bathroom, much to my embarrassment!

"You look too tanned to be English! You look more Italian or Spanish!" Exclaimed one of the girls, in a confused tone. "Not all English people are lily-white you know!" I answered with a laugh. "Yeah, some people in England are brown too!" added Patty, and we both laughed. "I guess the LA Sun has gotten to me!" I exclaimed before disappearing into a toilet cubical, and everyone laughed. Once again I felt happy to be in LA, it was a place where strangers chatted to each other like friends - it was my kind of place!

After using the loos Patty and I left the bathroom laughing at the girl questioning my tan, as we headed over to the dancefloor for a boogie. We had a fun dance, and I noticed that there was a good crowd there, but there was no sign of Johnny. I wasn't sure if I was disappointed, or relieved.

After a while, Patty and I got restless and started chatting about the LA nightclub scene and where else there was to go. "What about the Rainbow, have you been there?" asked Patty enthusiastically. "Yeah, I've been there a few times, it's a fun club!" I answered. "Yeah, it is, shall we go there?" said Patty, looking ready to take off. "Yeah, sounds good!" I answered, so off we went!

"We can hitchhike, it's only a couple of miles up Sunset!" exclaimed Patty, as we turned the corner from Vine onto Sunset Boulevard. "Yeah ok!" I answered as we both stuck out our thumbs while we walked along and continued chatting as we went.

I loved the way things just seemed to flow in LA. I wasn't sure if it was because of the LA people and the city itself, or if it was because of the kind of LA people that I was drawn to, or maybe it was because of the way that I was when out and about, which was very friendly and outgoing. I felt that it was probably a combination!

We hitchhiked for what seemed like less than a minute before we were picked up by two rocker types playing loud rock music in their car. "Thanks Guys/Thanks!" we both exclaimed, as we jumped in the back of the car. Patty and I soon got into the party mood, as we started rocking our heads to the music, the guys seemed to like this and turned the music up more.

As we cruised up Sunset and neared the rainbow, it was fun to see the Sunset Strip from a car for the very first time. Glam-Rockers swanned around outside of the clubs and in the parking lots dressed to the nines. "Cool!" exclaimed Patty as she beamed a big smile at the partygoers around her. 'What a fun place this is!' I thought to myself, as I laughed, and smiled back at a very happy-looking Patty.

The guys parked the car down a side street, and Patty and I jumped out telling the guys we may see them at the club later. The guys nodded and shouted "Later!" As Patty and I took off across the street. Patty and I spotted an alcove with an ATM on one side and a little wall with bushes and flowers on the other side, and we instinctively headed there and sat up on the wall to drink the rest of our booze.

We had a great time sipping on our beers and chatting away. It felt like we were having part two of our "bush party" I loved how our main focus was on having fun and chatting about interesting things like our theories on whether there is life on other planets, and if reincarnation is real, rather than chatting about the latest fashions, materialistic things, and guys.

We were laughing, joking and getting tipsy when suddenly a bright spotlight shone on us. It startled us so we looked to see what it was and saw a police car parked on the road nearby. "Come out with your hands up!" Shouted a loud intimidating voice through some kind of loudspeaker. "Is that for us?" I asked Patty, feeling bewildered by their sudden appearance.

Patty nervously nodded and threw her beer into the bushes. I followed suit, although I still didn't know what the problem was. "They must be bored!" I said to Patty laughing and shaking my head in disbelief. Patty and I jumped down off the wall and walked out of the alcove and onto Sunset Boulevard with our hands held up in the air.

Suddenly we were both grabbed, handcuffed and thrown against the police car. "What on earth!" I shouted as I saw one of the Policemen grabbed my shoulder bag and emptied out its contents all over the police car's bonnet. "What the heck are you doing!?" I shouted in disbelief. I looked over at Patty to see her being treated in a similar way at the other end of the Police car.

"Shut up!" shouted the policeman, as he rummaged through the contents of my shoulder bag. "Why are you doing this?" I asked feeling absolutely dumbfounded by the situation. "What are you doing here?!" the policeman asked angrily, completely ignoring my questions. "We're having a night out, aren't people allowed to have a night out in this country?!" I exclaimed, feeling totally shocked at his bizarre conduct. "Only hookers do that here!" He replied, sounding a little calmer.

"Well, maybe you should see a little more of the world then because in other countries it's normal to have a night out!" I exclaimed indignantly. I could see Patty cringing over towards me and from the look in her eyes, I got the impression that she was trying to tell me to shut up, but I felt completely within my rights, as we'd done nothing wrong, we'd been keeping to ourselves and causing no harm to anyone! So, it was absolutely absurd that they were treating us so roughly, for no reason whatsoever!

The clubgoers from the Sunset Strip started to gather around us to see what was going on. They could see my indignation at the situation, and I was glad to have some witnesses. "Okay, you can go!" said the policeman suddenly changing his tune as he removed my handcuffs. The other policeman removed Patty's handcuffs at the same time. "Keep moving in future!" exclaimed the Policeman as he gave me back my shoulder bag. Then both policemen jumped back in their Police car and took off.

"Oh my God, there are people being murdered and raped, and armed robberies are going on, and all they can think to do is hassle two harmless girls for having a fun night out! Is this some kind of police state?!!!" I shouted out at the crowd around us while feeling shaken up after their assault.

"What the hell was that all about?" I asked Patty feeling utterly dumbfounded, as the LA shine started to instantly fade for me, and I had an intense desire to leave. "I don't know?" answered Patty looking embarrassed, as she shook her head in disbelief "Shall we go to the rainbow, and dance to forget it!" exclaimed Patty suddenly, with a big grin "Good idea, let's go!" I answered, grinning back, as we walked on through the crowd of onlookers on the sidewalk.

"You go, girl! / You told him! / It is a police state man!" Exclaimed some of the people in the crowd as we walked past. I didn't know how to respond, and felt a little embarrassed by all the attention, especially as I was still in a state of shock and confusion from the incident. I'd only ever seen football hooligans, and the like, being handcuffed by the police on the streets of England, I'd never seen normal civilians, especially young girls, being harassed by the police. 'They must have zero sense of discretion here!?' I thought to myself as we headed around the corner and into the rainbow.

We were soon dancing away our ordeal on the rainbow dancefloor, and I spotted Len up at the bar. "Come and meet Len!" I said to Patty as I led the way up to the bar. "Hi Len, this is my new friend Patty, Patty, this is Len!" I said, feeling happy to introduce them. "Hi Patty, you two look like you're having fun!" said Len, as he and Patty smiled and shook hands.

"Well, we are now! But not so much earlier! The police handcuffed us, and searched our bags on the street!" I exclaimed shaking my head in disbelief. "Oh yeah, they do that here" replied Len, as if it were the norm' "Really??" I answered while pulling a puzzled face, and still shaking my head in disbelief. Just then some of Len's friends joined us, and we all headed to the dance floor, and quickly forgot all about the police encounter, as we were having so much fun, and the drinks kept flowing.

"Tommy Lee's at the bar!" exclaimed Patty excitedly, as she came back from one of her bathroom trips. "Who's Tommy Lee?" I asked, not having a clue who he was. "He's in the band: Motley Crue, he's really cute. See that guy with black hair at the far end of the bar on the right?" said Patty glancing over at the bar. I looked over to where she was looking to see a good-looking, black-haired rocker guy surrounded by dolly-bird, band-groupie types. It wasn't my scene at all, but I was happy to see Patty so happy!

After a while, Patty and I decided to go for a walkabout and pop to the loo on our way. Inside the bathroom, looking at herself in the mirror was a dolled-up blonde woman wearing all pink. Patty and I looked at her, and then at each other with raised eyebrows, and surprised grins. We quickly used the loos, then headed outside to hang out in the car park and see who was about.

The parking lot was full of glammed-up rockers milling around as usual. Patty and I soon got chatting to a friendly older rocker type. "Do you know who that blonde woman all dressed in pink is?" asked Patty curiously. "Yeah, her name's Angeline. She's on billboards all over town. She's famous for being famous!" answered the rocker raising his eyebrows, and shrugging his shoulders as if to say "Beat's me?"

"Cool!" Exclaimed Patty. "Oh right?!" I answered, as I smiled in amazement, and tried to grasp the concept of being "Famous for being famous!" I chuckled to myself, and couldn't help but love the fun, creative, and somewhat whacky off-beat side of LA. – Despite the insane police search!

"Wanna drink girls?" asked the older Rocker guy, as he looked like he was about to head inside the club. "Sure/Thanks!" we answered, and we were once again back inside the rainbow, drinking, getting tipsy, dancing on the tiny dance floor and having fun!

'This is such a fun club, but it's a shame that a lot of the people here seem so fake! It's like they dress like rebels, but they act like Royals, what's with that?!' I thought to myself with a laugh. '...So if this scene is a little too fake for me, and the Café de Grande Scene is too hardcore for me, what scene actually suits me?' I tipsily pondered to myself as I danced around on the dancefloor. 'Remember I'm still only eighteen, and that the whole point of exploring the world is to see what it has to offer, some things will suit me, and some things won't, but it's all part of the journey, just enjoy it!' I told myself, as I went into a twirl to the music.

As I danced, I continued to look around the club at some of the "plastic-rocker" types, as Gabby called them, and I suddenly felt honoured to be there on my journey. I felt like a true modern-day explorer. I smiled to myself and continued to dance. 'Remember it takes all sorts! They probably think I'm not dolled up enough! - differences go both ways ya know!" I told myself, with a laugh, while trying to be fair and non-judgmental.

Suddenly my dancing pal Joe appeared, and I felt so happy to see him, especially because he WAS one of the real people, and not fake at all! The two of us were soon doing our usual silly dances, which always seemed to include a whirling dervish-style dance, and a bunny hop or two!

Patty was leaning against the wall on the side of the dance floor crying with laughter watching us, so I beckoned for her to join us, but she gestured that she was about to request some songs from the DJ hatch at the back of the dance floor, so Joe and I carried on dancing. Patty soon joined us, she was a fun dancer too, although her dance moves were a little smoother and conventional compared to mine and Joe's ridiculously mad, over-the-top dances!

"Hey gals, the night is still young, David Lee Roth is having a party, and the whole of the Rainbow Club is invited!" Exclaimed Len suddenly appearing on the dance floor as the lights came on. "Cool!" exclaimed Patti gleefully, "Sounds like fun!" I answered, feeling in the mood for a house party. We all headed outside, jumped in Len's friend's car, and followed the caravan of cars up to an area of Beverly Hills called Bel-Air. We had good rock music playing and were all in great spirits as we cruised along Sunset.

After a long time of following the stream of cars up and down streets lined with fancy big houses, but having to loop back around each time because no party was found, the cars started to thin out and go in different directions as if giving up on the party quest.

Eventually, the car we'd been following slowed down and parked to the side of the road as if the driver was lost and had given up too. "We're not gonna find this party guys! - Denny's Diner?" exclaimed Len, sounding a little disappointed. " Yep, I'm up for getting some food!" I answered. "Sure dude/Yeah, let's go to Denny's!" answered Len's friend and Patty, as Len made a swift U-Turn, and started heading back towards Sunset.

I suddenly realised how hungry I was, and started to look more forward to going to Denny's Diner, than going to David Lee Roth's Party! Patty seemed to take it all in her stride as usual and seemed non-fazed by the change of plan.

As we entered Denny's, I recognised a lot of the other Rainbow Club people who must have had a problem finding the party too. "Gosh, I hope at least some people found the party! Poor David Lee Roth will be all alone otherwise!" I joked, and we all laughed.

We spent the next couple of hours or so eating, drinking, chatting and winding down. Until around 5.30 am, when Len's friend gave Patty and me a lift back to the halfway house. There were still two unused beds in the room next to mine, and I was sure that no one would mind if Patty crashed out on one of them. It was about 6. am when I put my head on the pillow and instantly fell asleep.

I woke at 11 am with the start, jumped up, and quickly got dressed. I headed out of my room, through the bedroom next door, and noticed that Patty was gone from there. I headed to the living room hoping that she was ok. As I entered the living room, I found Patty and Mike chatting away. I was relieved that everything was fine, and I was happy to see that they were getting along so well.

Sonny was there too, just sitting looking content and nodding along with Patty and Mike's chat. "Hi Della!" they all said as I entered the room. "Hi everyone!" I answered, noticing that Mike, forever the good host had given Patty some breakfast and coffee, and I was so thankful that they were okay with her being there. It reminded me of what good people my halfway-house family were.

"Mike's been showing me some card tricks, he wants to know if we will bleach his hair blond later?" Said Patty with a big smile. My mind flashed back to the day when I'd bought some blue-black hair dye and Mike had said that he may like to dye his hair some time. "Yeah, OK!" I answered, smiling back. "Cool!" answered Mike and Patty in unison, both looking pleased.

Mary appeared and gave Mike his meds. He thanked her and washed them down with a swig of coffee. "Hi Mary, this is my friend, Patty, I hope it's ok that she stayed in the room next to mine last night?" I asked, pulling a timid face. "Sure, no bother to me, as long as you make the bed up afterwards, nice to meet you Patty!" answered Mary, as she started to make her way back downstairs. "You too, thanks!" called out Patty, looking pleased. "Thanks, Mary!" I called out after her, as I made my way to get myself a coffee, as the others already had one.

"So, what meds do you take Mike?" asked Patty curiously as I entered back into the living room with my coffee in hand. "Just Lithium" answered Mike cooly. "Oh, yeah, I take that too. I'm on a low dose, how about you?" She asked Michael casually. "I'm not sure, I think it's just a regular dose?" He answered, looking puzzled. "So, why do you take Lithium Patty?" I asked feeling a little surprised, and curious by this revelation. "I have mild schizophrenia with delusions, but the doctors could be wrong though, they just don't see what I see!" she said matter-of-factly.

"Yeah, that's a good point. Even Scientists say that most humans are only capable of seeing and understanding a tiny fraction of what actually exists in creation. So what kind of things do you see Patty?" I asked, feeling intrigued. "You know like the pictures in magazines and on billboards of people who all look the same, to me they seem like they could have been cloned test-tube babies, and the bright lights in the stores, that are just too bright! Why are they so bright? I'm sure it's to make us buy more, or something like that?!" She exclaimed, looking slightly perplexed. "Yeah, I see what you mean" I answered, taking on board what she was saying while wondering if she was just highly sensitive to things.

"Yeah, who's to say what's normal?" exclaimed Mike in agreement. "Yeah, too right!" answered Patty, and they went into a long conversation about so-called crazy versus normality. I found their conversation to be very interesting and I had to agree with some of what they were saying, although some parts of it were a little too out there, even for me!

After a while we all headed downstairs to dye Mike's hair blond, apparently, he'd bought a blond peroxide kit the day before and had been waiting for me to help him with it. Mike sat on a chair in his room, and Patty and I took turns combing and putting the peroxide in his hair. The fumes made us cough, but we all had a good laugh as we did it, making jokes about how he was going to be so good-looking once we were finished.

After timing the process, he went to take a shower and wash out the peroxide. He was dressed again, and towel-drying his hair when he came back into his bedroom. "Let's see!/What's it like?" Exclaimed Patty and I, in eager anticipation to see his new hair-do.

"OK!" answered Mike, as he dramatically removed his towel in one swift swoop. "Oh my god, you look like Jesus!" I exclaimed. "That's what I thought too!" Exclaimed Patty and the three of us cracked up crying with laughter. "Cool, I like it!" Exclaimed Michael, looking pleased with his new look in the mirror.

"We'll have to call you "Blond Jesus" from now on!" I exclaimed, and the three of us roared with laughter again. The other house-mates must have wondered what was going on down in Michael's room, but we didn't care, as we were too busy laughing, although they all found out soon enough, when we headed back upstairs to the living room to show off Michael's new look!

Patty spent the rest of the day hanging out with us, and Mary was kind enough to invite her to join us for dinner. We all sat around the dining table tucking into our food. Some of the residents looked a little bit bemused by Patty being there with us, but no one made a fuss, and after dinner, they just headed back to their rooms, while Patty and I helped Mary to clear up the table and wash the dishes. I was happy to have Patty as a new friend. She was so fun and light-hearted and our time just flowed so easily together.

In the evening Patty and I decided to head back up to Hollywood. I felt bad leaving Mike and asked him if he wanted to join us, but he wasn't up to it. "Maybe another time then?" I said as Patty and I headed to my room to get ready to go out. "Sure!" he answered as we disappeared down the hallway.

Patty borrowed some of my clothes, and we took showers and got a little dolled up for our night out. "Bye Mike, bye Sonny!" Patty and I called out, as we were heading out the front door. "Bye!" mumbled Sonny. "Have fun girls!" shouted Mike. "Thanks, blond Jesus!!" we both called out in unison, and we all laughed.

CHAPTER 38:

BIKERS, AIR SUPPLY & PARTY PEOPLE!

Patty and I had no set plans for the evening, we were just going to go with the LA flow as usual! We hopped on a bus bound for Hollywood and found a seat among the usual Black and Hispanic passengers. I always got the impression that most of them were either heading to or from work, as the majority of them usually seemed in a vegged-out state, although occasionally a few young African American or Hispanic teenagers would get on board in a party mood, playing funky music at the back of the bus on their ghetto-blasters, which created an uplifting fun vibe.

Patty and I decided to jump off the bus at Sunset and Vine and found ourselves automatically walking west on Sunset in the direction of the Rainbow Club. A little ways up Sunset we spotted a bunch of bikers hanging out in a parking lot outside a convenience store. They looked really fun and friendly, so we strolled inside the parking lot to say hi to them. They were very welcoming and invited us to join them for a drink. We accepted their offer and had a great time shooting the breeze with them.

They generously shared their beers with us and told us to keep them on the down low from the police. I didn't understand why, as in England it was ok to drink alcohol outside in public places. Patty and I told them about the Police bothering us a while back, and they told us that they had a trick they would use to stop the cops from bothering them, and went on to explain how they would just freeze on the spot whenever a police car drove by. Patty and I found this hilarious and wanted to try it out for ourselves, so when the next police car went cruising by, we joined in with the bikers, and froze on the spot, while trying our hardest not to laugh. It seemed so ridiculous, but miraculously worked. I couldn't help but wonder what the police made of it.

BOOK 1: TO SEE THE WORLD

As we were chatting with the bikers, I told them that it was okay to drink outside in public in England, and they couldn't believe it. They joked about moving to England, but then one of them remembered that it was cold and rainy in England, and loudly exclaimed "Well, the cops may be assholes in LA, but at least we have the Sun!" and we all laughed. I couldn't help but agree!

More bikers, male and female joined us to party and soon they got ready to go for a ride around Hollywood. They invited us to go along with them "Cool/Sounds good!" we exclaimed, as we each jumped on the back of a motorbike.

Patty and I had made friends with an Asian biker named Lee, who had long brown curly hair and a smiley face, and his friend John, a stocky White guy, in his late twenties, early thirties, with short dark brown hair, and a long dark brown beard.

We felt very safe and at ease with these guys and girls, as the atmosphere was clearly about having fun, we sensed no ulterior motives or bad vibes at all, and it was definitely my and Patty's cups of tea!

The Chinese biker Lee was my pilot, and Patty jumped on the back of his friend John's bike. We all took off out of the parking lot at high speed to cruise the streets of Hollywood. "Cool!" shouted Patty as we went. "Woo Hoo!" I called back, loving our free-spirited ways.

Speeding along on the back of a motorbike was great fun! None of us wore helmets, so I could feel the wind in my hair. We were only on the surface streets, not on the freeway, so it didn't feel dangerous at all, just fun!

As we rode down Hollywood Boulevard, I wondered if Gabby, and some of my other Punk, and New-Wave friends and acquaintances would see me, and if so, what they would make of me hanging out with the bikers. I found the thought of this scenario very funny and figured I would just wave if I saw anyone I knew!

After a fantastic cruise around Hollywood, we headed back to the parking lot to drink some more beers. Feeling exhilarated, and in high spirits, we were having a great time! After a while, Patty suggested that we head up to the Rainbow, and Lee said that he and John would give us a lift up there on their motorbikes, but they wouldn't come in the club, as they preferred to party out in the streets. "You should definitely move to England!" I joked, and everyone laughed.

Lee and John swiftly drove us up to the rainbow, and like two knights in shining armour, they dropped this off by the Whisky and gallantly rode off into the night waving goodbye and shouting to join them again any time as they went.

As Patty and I were walking along the strip, I spotted a police car heading our way, "Hey Patty, are you ready?" I joked. "...One, two, three, FREEZE!" We both cracked up laughing and froze for a second as the police car whizzed by. Feeling in high spirits Patty and I headed to the liquor store up past the Rainbow, to buy some beers, then headed over to sit on the wall in "our little alcove" by the ATM machine, to drink them. We hoped that we wouldn't be rudely interrupted by the police this time!

Patty and I sat, sipping on our beers, chatting, laughing and joking, on the wall feeling happy with the night so far. I loved the feel-good atmosphere that surrounded us. As we were engrossed in our fun little party on the wall, two guys passed by and glanced our way, and then came back a split-second later.

"Hi girls!" said the dark curly-haired guy in a strong Australian accent "Got a good little hideaway here!" said the blond guy, in a milder somewhat English-sounding Australian accent. I was sure I recognised the dark curly-haired guy from somewhere

"Yes, as long as the police don't come along!" I joked back. "I know the police are real sticklers out here, aren't they?" said the blond guy. We all laughed. "Would you like a beer?" I asked, glancing at Patty for the ok. "Yeah, have a beer and join us!" added Patty warmly. "Sure/Yeah, thanks girls!" answered the guys as they came nearer, and we passed them both a can. They stood opposite us, and we continued on with our little party.

They both seemed like nice genuine guys and Patti and I had instantly warmed to them. "I know your face from somewhere?" I said to the dark curly-haired guy, "But you don't know mine!?" said the blond-haired guy in a sad jokey way.

"Sorry, so where do I know your face from?" I said grinning. "Air Supply, Graham and Russell" he answered with a grin, and then it clicked these were the two singers in the band Air Supply! Their faces were currently on billboards all around town! - That's where I knew them, well at least the dark curly-haired guy, from!

"Cool!" said Patty grinning at them as she took a sip of a beer, I guessed she had no clue who they were, but was still impressed that they had a famous band. But overall, I got the impression that she saw them as our new friends for the evening's amusement, famous or not.

"So, what's that famous song you do?" I asked excitedly, as the song "Piano Man" popped to mind. "Oh, I remember!" I said, before they had a chance to answer, as I burst into song, and tipsily sang "Sing us a song you're the piano man!" They both laughed and were too polite to tell me that it wasn't their song.

"That's really good!" said Russel adding "Make sure you sing it from the diaphragm!" He took a deep breath and started singing a couple of lines with me to demonstrate. "Oh, like this?" I said copying him and trying to sing from the bottom of my stomach instead of my throat "Great, great!" he said encouragingly. "You try too Patty!" I said hoping that Patty would join in the singalong, but Patty only managed to sing one word before bursting into laughter. We all followed suit and cracked up laughing hysterically.

Passers-by were staring into the alcove to see what was going on, suddenly a police car cruised by and shined a bright light at us, so like a group of startled rabbits we quickly jumped down off the wall and scurried around the corner and up the hill.

We found a car park a few yards on, which we all ducked into just in time to see the police car cruising back down sunset towards our alcove. "Ha ha, we tricked 'em!" exclaimed Graham, and we all burst out laughing. "I know, it must be a crime to have fun here!" I joked, still not understanding why the police were so intent on picking on people who were just having a night out, and obviously doing no harm! It just didn't make sense, especially in such a fun city!

We shared the rest of our beers with the guys and carried on with our little party; chatting, laughing, joking and singing all sorts of random songs, from Air Supply songs to Beatles. We were having such a great time that when Patty suggested we head down to the rainbow, it felt a bit of a downer to leave.

The guys said they'd already made plans to meet up with their manager, and explained it was where they were heading when they'd first spotted us, but they may come back and join us at the Rainbow later. We said our farewells and Patty and I headed down the hill, around the corner, and to the Rainbow.

We had another great night at the Rainbow and wound up at a nearby house party afterwards. We had been invited by some guys we'd met on the dance floor, they gave us a lift to the party, and seeing as it was just a short way up into the

Hollywood Hills at the back of the rainbow it only took a few minutes to drive up there.

The party was already in full swing when we arrived, and we instantly started dancing to the funky music that was playing. A smooth-looking dark-haired, slightly older guy joined us and started dancing, and Patty and I welcomed him. "Brian, what are your names girls?" said the guy as the music stopped playing. "Della!/Patty!" we called back, as we all shook hands. "Great to meet you both, would you both like a drink?" he asked, looking pleased to have met us. "Sure/Yes please!" we answered, as we followed him to the kitchen area.

There were partygoers everywhere, and the kitchen worktops were covered with alcohol of all sorts. Patty and I spotted a big bowl of punch with delicious-looking fruit floating on the top and decided that's what we would have. "That looks nice/Yeah!" exclaimed Patty and I, as the guy picked up a couple of glasses, placed them next to the bowl of punch, took a scoop, poured us both a large glass of punch each and passed them over to us.

"Thanks!" we exclaimed, as we took the drinks off him, and both took a sip. "Wow! Strong!" exclaimed Patty. "Woah! Really strong, nice though!" I exclaimed, as the fruity aftertaste kicked in. "Yeah!" exclaimed Patty, looking pleased. "Follow me," said the guy, as he led the way on through the kitchen, Patty and I gave each other a look that said "Don't laugh, just follow" as we followed him out of the kitchen down a hallway, and up some stairs.

As we walked, I spotted a guy I quite liked the look of standing on the stairway casually chatting to a girl. He looked a little edgier than the usual "plastic" rock crowd. He was kind of a cross between a rocker, and a punk, but not a punk rocker! His long jet-black hair was spiked out gloriously, and he wore jet-black eyeliner, that accentuated his striking dark brown eyes. He was wearing a red dress shirt, with drainpipe black leather jeans and a short leather jacket. 'Oh my god, he's like Sid Vicious on steroids!' I thought to myself with a laugh and felt my heart flutter as he glanced my way. 'Uh-Oh!' I thought to myself, as I gave him one more glance before following Brian and Patty onto the landing hallway.

"Come in girls," said Brian, as he opened a back bedroom door, where about seven people were sitting around a large glass table with white lines on top of it. "Ever done Coke before?" asked Brian with a big smile. "Nope/No!" answered Patty and I as we gave each other a puzzled look.

"You're gonna love it!" exclaimed Brian joyfully, and Patty and I burst out laughing. Brian laughed along with us, then introduced us to the people sitting around the table as they started to make space for us to join them. I got the impression that this was Brian's house from his general manner, and from the way the others responded respectfully towards him.

Patty and I stood there awkwardly as if we weren't sure that we wanted to join them at the table, but we didn't want to be rude and decline their invite either. "I gotta go Pee!" exclaimed Patty suddenly. "Me too!" I said, thinking what a perfect excuse! "Ok, guys, the bathroom is down the hall on the right, we're right here if you want to come back and join us!" said Brian casually. "OK Thanks/Thanks!" we called out, as did a runner from the bedroom back down the hallway.

We ducked inside the bathroom, and burst out laughing "Gosh, the punch is strong enough! I don't need anything else!" I said as I took a sip of my drink. "I know, and you never know what's in that stuff' said Patty sounding genuinely concerned. "Yeah right, shall we head back downstairs for a dance?" I asked, feeling that dancing was more our thing. "Sure" answered Patty with a grin. We both took a few more swigs of our punch and snuck out of the bathroom, hoping that no one from the back bedroom would spot us as we went.

David Bowie's "Let's Dance!" was playing in the dance room and it seemed a perfect synchronicity as we hit the dance floor. Patty and I started dancing and having fun, and as I twirled around I spotted the Sid Vicious on steroids guy again, but much to my disappointment, he was still with the same girl from the stairway.

'Oh well, at least I'm free!' I thought to myself, as my mind suddenly flashed to Johnny and the girl he'd been chatting to at the Seven Seas. I decided to "Dance to forget it" as Patty would have said, and was soon lost in the music, and having a great time.

"Hey girls, wait for me!" called out a male voice, and we turned to see Brian joining us on the dancefloor. "You didn't want to party upstairs then?" he asked with a grin. "Nah, this punch is enough for us!" I answered, and the three of us laughed. "Yeah, it's really strong, what's in it?" asked Patty, with a slightly wary, but mischievous grin. "Oh, now that would be telling!" exclaimed Brian, and the three of us laughed, and carried on dancing.

The punch was kicking in, and I was feeling very tipsy, and on cloud nine from dancing. I was so happy that my travels had led me to such a warm, wonderful, fun, and friendly place in the world. I felt as though everyone in the room, including myself and Patty were sparkling with the joy of life, as we danced the night away high up in the Hollywood hills.

"I love this song!" exclaimed Brian suddenly grabbing my hand, and twirling me around and under his arm. I laughed, and danced with him, while Patty went wandering off somewhere. I enjoyed the dance with Brian, but the song was a bit on the cheesy side for me, and it got me pondering on the fact that music in general these days seemed to be so simple and shallow compared to the traditional and classical music of times gone by. 'Oh well, it's still fun to dance!' I told myself as a funky James Brown song came on, and Patty came running back to the dance floor to join us.

After a while Patty and I realised that we were both really tired, so we told Brian we'd see him later, and took off from the dance floor, to find somewhere to crash out in the quieter part of the house. We went back upstairs and walked along the long landing in the opposite way from the party-room, and eventually found a bedroom with coats piled up on top of the bed, surrounded by a comfy looking wall-to-wall carpet.

"That area looks good!" I said to Patty, noticing a large space between the bed and the far wall where the window was. It looked like an ideal spot for us to crash-out, and not be bothered by anyone. "Yeah, cool!" answered Patty in agreement. We both tiptoed over and found a little space each. We used our jackets as pillows, and like two little kittens we each curled up in our spots and fell fast asleep.

We both woke up around the same time and sat up looking around the room as if dazed and confused. I was aching all over from sleeping on the floor and felt very hung-over. Patty looked to be in similar discomfort. "Good Morning, Patty!" I croaked. "Good Morning, Della!" Patty croaked back.

The clock on the wall read 12.05, I wasn't sure what time we'd crashed out, but guessed it was around 6 am. 'At least I have the day off today!' I thought to myself, suddenly feeling happy to have a free day to recover from the Party the night before.

We both stretched out our arms, yawned and slowly stood up. Patty went to use the bathroom that was attached to the bedroom, and I grabbed my shoulder bag, and went to use the bathroom in the hallway - the same one that we'd escaped to from the party room the night before.

BOOK 1: TO SEE THE WORLD

It felt so good to splash my face with cold water. I put a little soap on a damp folded piece of toilet tissue to tidy up my smudged eyeliner, then used another piece of folded damp toilet paper to rinse the soap away. Afterwards, I wet my hands and rubbed some of the water through my hair in effort to tidy it up a tad. It was still jet black with blue hues, and I'd recently cut it sort of spikey on top and left it long underneath. It was naturally wavy though, so even though I teased it, and sprayed loads of hairspray on it, I could never get the proper spikey look that I was going for, but it was still fun to play with. I dug into my shoulder bag and pulled out some make-up to touch up my old make-up, and try and look more awake, or more alive as the case may be!

After tidying myself up, I strolled back to the bedroom and found Patty tidying herself up in the mirror too. We smiled at each other as if to say that we were both happy with our situation. "Shall we go and look for some coffee and food in the kitchen?" I croaked to Patty, feeling that some sustenance would help to revive us some more. "Sure!" croaked Patty, and the two of us gingerly strolled down the long hallway, down the stairs and into the kitchen.

"Morning girls!" exclaimed Brian who was sitting drinking coffee at the breakfast bar and looking wide awake. I wondered if he'd slept at all. "These are my friends Diane and Rick...Patty and Della, right girls?" exclaimed Brian, gesturing towards his friends. We all gave each other a little wave and said hi.

"We're heading to the beach, wanna come?" Brian exclaimed enthusiastically. "Yeah!" answered Patty and I together, as we shot each other a "Why not?" glance "Coffee and waffles? - Help yourselves girls!" said Brian gesturing towards a pot of coffee sitting on a coffee maker, and a pile of hot waffles freshly made. "Mmmm, thanks! Thank you!" we both exclaimed excitedly and helped ourselves. "Enjoy, it's just a little snack for now, we'll have lunch at the beach!" said Brian cheerily. "Cool/sounds Good!" Patty and I answered as we tucked into the waffles.

Brian was a really nice, easygoing, friendly guy, and I wasn't sure if he liked one of us, or if he was just being friendly. It didn't seem to matter in LA, as the main goal seemed to be to just have fun and enjoy life! Which suited Patty and me just fine!

After breakfast the five of us headed outside and jumped into Brian's jeep, and sped off down the hill to Sunset Boulevard, then headed west on Sunset for the beach. Brian put some fun music on, and the breeze woke me up fast!

It was such a beautiful day that I felt on a natural high as we sped along. Blue skies above, sun shining, uplifting music playing, and surrounded by fun people. 'This is living!' I thought to myself as Patty and I grinned across at each other, looking pleased, as we threw our heads back to catch the wind in our hair.

It suddenly dawned on me that there seemed to be a lot of mysteriously rich people in Hollywood, with both time and money on their hands, which was a rare combination. I wondered how that had happened for them, and assumed that maybe some had got rich from the film industry, and their families had benefited from it too. Whatever it was, I was happy to be experiencing a taste of it! My mind flashed to my dad and his side of the family. They were natural entertainers, often playing music, singing songs, dancing, acting out skits, telling jokes etc...just for fun in their spare time. 'They would have been in their element here!' I thought to myself with a smile.

We arrived at Venice Beach, Brian parked up his jeep, and we all jumped out. The air felt fresh, and the atmosphere was vibrant. "Let's go get some lunch!" exclaimed Brian as he led the way down one of the little side streets that led towards the boardwalk. "Cool!/Sounds good/Sure man/OK!" we all answered as we walked along. Rick and Dianne seemed preoccupied with each other, so Patty and I walked side by side, chatting about what a fun night we'd had, and how the guys from Air Supply had been great company. We both hoped to bump into them again one day!

Brian continued to lead the way until we reached the sidewalk café. We found an available table on the patio with a view of the beach and ocean, and all sat down in jolly spirits. "Order whatever you like!" exclaimed Brian. "Thanks, Brian!" we all answered in unison, as we each picked up a menu.

Patty and I decided on a Caesar salad, with a large glass of orange juice each, and we were soon all tucking into our lunch and merrily chatting away. Rick and Dianne were fun and friendly, but they were not really my type of people, they were more on the trendy than the alternative side, but they were nice which was the main thing!

I suddenly noticed that Diane had shaved her legs, but not her arms - which had a thick layer of dark brown hair growing on them. It wasn't something I would normally notice, or think about, but it was hard not to notice because the hair was so thick and dark, and her legs looked bare in comparison. It didn't bother me at all, I just found it curious that someone would shave their legs, but not their arms if they too were very hairy. I went into a daydream about our apparent monkey ancestry and started pondering if we would have been happier if we'd stayed in the trees.

"Volleyball anyone!" asked Brian enthusiastically as he finished his orange juice. Patty and I looked at each other as if to say "No thanks!" it all seemed a bit too normal and preppy for us wild "street-urchins" "Thanks, but I think we're gonna go for a walk, we may see you later though, thanks for lunch, and for letting us crash last night, it was a fun party!" I answered, glancing at Patty, as we gave each other the "Let's go!" look, and started to stand up and get our jackets and shoulder bags together. "Yeah, it was cool, thanks!" added Patty with a smile.

"OK, no problem girls!" answered Brian, looking a little disappointed, as he scribbled his number down on a napkin. "There you go, give me a call sometime!" he added, as he passed me the napkin. "Thanks! Ok, see ya then!" I answered, as I started strolling away to catch up with Patty who was by now a few yards ahead of me and was looking very antsy to get going. "See ya girls!/Bye!/Bye!" they all called out as we left. "Bye guys!/Thanks!/Seeya!" we shouted back, as we strolled off out of the restaurant, and disappeared into the crowds milling about on the Venice beach boardwalk.

CHAPTER 39:

VENICE BEACH BIKERS

"They were nice, but not our scene huh?" said Patty as if she was feeling as relieved as I was to have broken away to do our own thing again. "Yeah, they were really nice, but yeah, not our scene - Especially when it got to the volleyball bit!" I replied, and the two of us burst out laughing.

Patty and I walked for a while just taking in the wonderful sights and sounds of Venice Beach. The usual mix of hippies, artists, families, and tourists meandered up and down the boardwalk amidst the vendors and street performers. It was strange how it felt so good to be free from Brian and company. I couldn't pinpoint exactly why though, as they were really nice people, I figured they were just a little too boring for us, then wondered if that was why they needed to do drugs.

'Patty and I have a good time, with or without booze, we just seem to have our own special take on things, which makes life fun!' I thought to myself with a smile as the two of us dance-walked along the boardwalk. We carried on until we came across some bikers who were sitting on their bikes partying on a main side street. We automatically strolled over towards them. "Hi, Leo!" exclaimed Patty, looking pleased to see someone she knew.

"Hey Patty, how's life?" answered Leo, looking pleased to see Patty. "Good thanks, this is my friend Della" answered Patty in her usual sweet and friendly way. "Hey Della, great to meet you!" answered Leo, as he reached out his hand. "You too!" I answered as we shook hands. Leo and the rest of his biker friends welcomed us, just as the Hollywood bikers had done, they were very open and friendly and seemed to have a "More the merrier!" attitude, which Patty and I loved.

There were about ten bikers in this group, made up of both men and women. They seemed to have a similar ethos to Patty and I, which was to just enjoy life and have a good time! They were drinking beers hidden in brown bags and generously shared them with us. They had hard-rock music playing, and Patty and I were soon partying away with them as part of their crowd.

We had a great time with the Venice Beach Bikers, and I appreciated how genuine and friendly they were. They felt like my kind of people. I pondered if it was because my family on both sides of my parents were always very open and welcoming too. I thought about the stories I'd heard as a child, about how my mum's family had opened up their home to US soldiers during World War 2, and how they had always kept an open door for all.

Even years after the war, my grandpop who was a dentist, rarely took money for dental treatment, if people were too poor to pay for their treatment, they would bring him fresh produce from their gardens instead – Potatoes, green beans, eggs etc… He had grown up in a privileged family in Liverpool, and he'd said that the extrema poverty he's seen there had made him want to share his wealth.

On my dad's side, my grandfather was a coal miner by day, and a local entertainer by night. He would often lead pub and club singalongs playing the piano, or his accordion and singing. My dad was similar, and music was one of his favourite pastimes.

My grandmother on my dad's side came from a Romany-Gypsy family, and they too were all very musical and fun-spirited, and this combination led to my grandparents on my dad's side having a "Life is a party!" type of attitude in their spare time as my grandad played the accordion and led singalongs in the local pub and clubs. I guessed that was why I gravitated towards unconventional free-spirited, creative types - either that or because they were just great fun!

"Wanna go for a cruise?" asked Leo, gesturing towards his Trike-Motorbike, with a bench at the back and enough room for two people. "Cool!/Yes please, looks fun!" Patty and I exclaimed excitedly. "Cool! Jump on!" exclaimed Leo, as he jumped on his Trike and started revving up the engine, and we both jumped on the back bench. We all waved goodbye to the others, and Leo zoomed off up the side street, turned left, and headed towards Pacific Coast Highway, or PCH, as the locals called it.

Patty and I were hooting and hollering with glee, and we couldn't stop ourselves from smiling and laughing the whole time as we sped along. I loved how Patty and I would just go with the flow, and wind up having such fun adventures. They didn't have a dark side to them, unlike my adventures with Gabby, they were just pure, innocent, wholesome fun, and I loved it!

Soon we were speeding along PCH with stunningly beautiful scenery around us. The Pacific Ocean was to our left, and the Santa Monica Mountains were to our right. We passed through the affluent town of Malibu where stylish-looking beach bars and cafes appeared and surfers milled about looking like they were living a life of pleasure.

Eventually, we stopped next to a beach cliff-top lookout spot to admire the view. We all stood in silence and gazed around us. I was feeling full to the brim with happiness, and on a pure and natural high.

We'd spent the next ten minutes or so, just being in the moment enjoying the scenery around us, and commenting on various things that caught our eyes. "Wanna head back? There's a cool club in Santa Monica we can stop by if you guys are up for it?" asked Leo looking ready to move on. "Yeah Cool!/great!" Patty and I answered as we all got on board his Trike, ready for our next adventure!

We were soon cruising the streets of Santa Monica, getting lots of looks from passers-by. Most of them seemed to be giving Leo's Trike and all of us looks of admiration. So, feeling like some kind of Biker-Royalty, Patty and I nodded our heads, waved and smiled back at our admirers as we glided on by.

We pulled up outside what looked like a biker bar. Parked up next to the other Motorbikes and headed inside with Leo leading the way. The club was crowded, rock music played loudly from the jukebox, and male and female bikers of all ages were playing pool, drinking and dancing.

"Cool!" exclaimed Patty looking happy to be there. "Looks fun!" I answered. I liked the feel of the club, it reminded me of some of the bars from my earlier travels. My mind flashed to Jeff, and some of the other friends I'd made along the way, and I felt a pang of sadness as I missed them all, but then I looked over at Patty and Leo laughing and joking, and my spirits picked up. 'Enjoy the now!' I told myself, feeling happy to have kept on travelling.

We had a fun night at the biker club dancing, laughing, joking, and drinking beers. I pondered on what it would be like to actually join the bikers, as they really seemed like my kind of people, but then my mind kept going back to my other friends in England, Toronto, Florida and LA, and it made me realise that as much as I enjoyed the company of the bikers, I still wanted to mix and mingle with all sorts of people! 'After all, "Variety is the spice of life!" as they say!' I thought to myself, but either way, I knew that the bikers would always have a special place in my heart, as they were the true rough diamonds of the world.

We stayed at the club until around 2 am when Leo offered to drop us off at home. We thanked him, and he gallantly drove us back to Pico and Crenshaw and dropped us off outside the halfway house like the typical biker gentleman that he was.

"Catch you girls again!" He called out, as he waved goodbye and sped off into the night, like a knight in black leather. "Thanks, Leo!" we both shouted after him, as we waved goodbye, then headed up the steps, and into the halfway house. We headed straight to our beds and crashed out.

CHAPTER 40:

DECISIONS, DECISIONS!

At 7.30 am Michael woke me up gently knocking on my door. It was my turn to cover for Mary, so I had to jump up, get dressed, use the loo, and rush to make breakfast, as I'd forgotten to get it ready when Patty and I had come home. Patty got up not long after me and joined us all at the breakfast table.

We had a lazy day just hanging out at the halfway house until Patty went home around late afternoon. I spent the next few days at the halfway house covering for Mary and relaxing in my bedroom journaling, and listening to music. I realised that I loved my alone time, just as much as I loved my social time, if not more in some ways, as it was lovely to just relax in my own space, and rejuvenate.

I would have made it to acting class to meet the actress Lindsay Wagner, but sadly I came down with a bad cold. One day as I was filling in some details, from notes I'd made, in my journal, I realised that I was enjoying my time in LA so much, that my travel plans had all but faded from the forefront of my mind! I wasn't sure what to make of this and hoped that at some point I would figure out what I truly wanted to do - Keep on travelling, or see if I could get based in LA, maybe I could become a student like Peter or something like that? I decided that I would continue to go with the LA flow and see what happens.

One Morning I arrived in the living room to see a letter from my aunt Freda on the dining table. I excitedly opened it and read it. Her news was that she would be arriving in America in a few weeks to look at some properties in Northern California, and Oregan, and to let her know if I wanted to meet up with her, and she would send me the details of where she would be staying, or if I would rather she just come and visit me in LA after she finishes looking at the properties, and she would have a few days holiday with me, and afterwards maybe I would travel back to England with her.

BOOK 1: TO SEE THE WORLD

The notion of going back to England with her suddenly hit me like a ton of bricks! I felt nowhere near ready to go back to England! For the most part, I just wanted to continue doing what I was doing - just going with the LA flow! But the more I thought about it, the more I realised, that I would have to head back to England in early June, as our passports had been stamped from early December to early June. Once again, I remembered that I would need to get a new passport, as mine had been forever lost on the border of Virginia and North Carolina.

I got myself a coffee and sat outside on the roof walkway to think about everything. Although in some ways it felt way too soon to be heading back to England, in another way I was starting to warm up to the idea, as I realised that it would be lovely to spend time with family and friends again and to rest up and regroup, and ultimately get some money together for more travels! Maybe I could see my visit back to England as a part of my overall adventure!

I wondered what I would do to get some more travel money together, and remembered that my dad had an antique stall at a market hall in Shrewsbury. Maybe I could watch the stall for him while he was out at antique auctions? Also, I knew from past experience that hotel and other seasonal work was also a handy way to get some travel cash together. I'd read somewhere that a lot of backpackers made quite good money for their travels by picking fruit! I was sure I could do that! Also, meeting fellow travellers would be fun too. My mind flashed to Heidi back at the hotel in Swanage, and I hoped she was doing ok wherever she was. I was sorry that we hadn't swapped contact details.

I lay on my bed, feeling full of a cold and not moving my body an inch, but in my mind, I was here, there, and everywhere! There seemed to be lots of possibilities, but I still really wasn't sure what I wanted to do, in my heart, I felt I would rather just stay where I was happy - which was LA, but there were many other practicalities to consider, so I just hoped that things would just fall into place as I went along.

I finally recovered from the cold, and just as I was starting to feel restless Sylvia and Julie phoned me up to ask if I wanted to go out clubbing with them, so of course I eagerly accepted their invite. They said they would pick me up at 7.30, so I thanked them, hung up the phone, and rushed to get ready as it was already nearly 6. I felt as though I was bursting for a night out, after what felt like an eternity of staying in with a cold.

Sylvia and Julie turned up at 7:30 and waited for me in their car while I said my goodbyes to the Pico gang, then ran out and down the steps. I always felt a little sad waving goodbye to Michael as he was such a lovely person with such a sweet and helpful nature. It seemed unfair that I could be part of his world but he couldn't be part of mine.

We went to Gino's, and the usual punks and new-wavers were there hanging out in the parking lot and dancing inside. Johnny was there too, although by now I wasn't too bothered about him, as he hadn't made an effort for us to get to know each other, although now he seemed more friendly than ever, and as soon as he saw us he headed our way to say hi. We all said hi to him, but I remained aloof towards him for most of the night, and just had fun getting tipsy with Sylvia and Julie, chatting, laughing, joking and dancing… as usual!

When it came time to leave the club, Sylvia and Julie had somehow arranged for Johnny to join us in the parking lot. "Would be ok for us all to party back at the halfway house for a bit?" asked Sylvia with a mischievous grin. "Sure" I answered, and we all piled in Sylvia's car and sped off down Vine Street.

Johnny and I were sitting close together in the back seat, and I felt self-conscious and a little uncomfortable as he was so quiet, and was making no effort to chat. It felt as though Julia and Sylvia were trying to help get us together, which was nice of them, but it also felt really awkward, and the quieter Johnny was, the more aloof I became – If he wasn't going to make an effort, why should I?

Back at the Pico halfway house, or "Pico" as I'd started calling it for short, we were greeted by Mike and Sonny. They seemed excited to have guests, although they didn't hang around too long, as after a while, they left us all to it.

We had a fun couple of hours in the living room, playing music and drinking some of the cheap beers that Larry always stocked the fridge with. Eventually, I felt really tired and told the others that they were welcome to crash out in the living room, but I was going to bed to crash out. By now they were all flaked out on the armchair and the sofa and mumbled their tipsy goodnights to me.

When I got up in the morning Sylvia and Julie had gone, but Johnny was fast asleep, stretched out on the sofa. I tiptoed past him to get some coffee. Breakfast time had already been and gone, and the residents, including Mike and Sonny, were nowhere to be seen.

I guessed they'd all been decent enough to leave Johnny sleep in peace. I wondered what they had made of seeing a Sid Vicious look-alike, clad in all black, with a studded leather jacket, and black spikey hair asleep on the sofa.

Although they were all so laid-back, they'd probably barely raised one eyebrow between them!

As I was pouring myself a coffee I heard Johnny cough, so I went to see if he was awake. He was slowly sitting up and looking like he'd just crawled through a hedge backwards. "Good morning, would you like a coffee?" I asked politely. "Please" He answered, his voice sounding raspy. "OK, milk and sugar?" I asked as I headed back to the kitchen. "Sure" he mumbled, as if he was having a hard time waking up. "Can I use your bathroom?" he asked, sounding like he was now standing up.

"Yeah, it's just here" I answered, as I nipped back to the living room to show him the bathroom that was nearby in the hallway. "Thanks" he answered, as he staggered inside the bathroom and closed the door behind him. I headed back to the kitchen and continued making some coffee. Just as the coffee was ready, I heard Johnny, come out of the bathroom and land back on the sofa. I couldn't believe that the guy I'd had a crush on for what seemed like ages was now sitting in the living room! I felt kind of nervous, yet at the same time curious to see what he was actually like as a person, as going on the car ride back to Pico with him, his personality seemed a little on the flat side to put it politely.

I poured us both a coffee and went to sit on the sofa next to him. "There you go!" I said as I passed him a large mug of coffee. "Thanks" he answered and took a big sip. "Are you hungry, would you like some cereal or toast?" I asked, thinking that coffee might not be enough to wake him up. "No thanks." he answered, again making no effort at conversation. "OK, if you're sure" I answered, as I adjusted to his silence, and sipped on my coffee.

He still looked as cute as ever to me, but I felt that if he wasn't the type of guy to make any effort whatsoever, then there was no way I was going to initiate anything! I wondered if he was so passive because he was a very good-looking guy and maybe he was used to the girls initiating things. I also considered the possibility that he just wasn't attracted to me, but if so, what the heck was he doing on my sofa? Either way, it wasn't my problem!

Things felt shy and awkward between us, as we both sat in our hangover silence sipping on our coffees. In some ways, it felt as if maybe we were both just too cool to flirt, or maybe deep down we were both too shy and acted cool as a cover. I had no idea what the problem was, all I knew was, that we were both sitting in some kind of painfully self-conscious silence, and I wasn't enjoying it one bit!

"Are you sure you don't want anything to eat?" I asked, finally breaking the silence. "No thanks." he mumbled, which brought the conversation to a swift stop once again. We both spotted a pack of cigarettes at the same time. "Is it ok to have one?" he asked as he picked it up. "Yeah, they're probably Mike or Sonny's, they won't mind, I'll have one too!" I answered as we both took a cigarette out of the pack, Johnny used his lighter to light my cigarette, then his, and we continued sitting in awkward silence on the sofa next to each other for a little longer as we smoked our cigarettes.

After I finished my cigarette, I got up to go and wash our coffee cups. It felt great to escape to the kitchen! So, I took my time washing the coffee cups, and staring out of the window wishing Johnny would leave soon, because the awkward tension between us was too much for me to bear. I couldn't understand how for some reason we were like a couple of deer frozen in headlights in each other's company, all I knew was, it wasn't fun!

"I'm gonna take off!" said Johnny suddenly appearing in the kitchen. "OK!" I answered, as I dried my hands on a tea towel and walked him to the front door. "Bye then, I'll probably see you around" said Johnny as he headed out of the door, looking a little down. "Yeah, ok! See Ya!" I called after him, as I closed the door behind him.

I felt so relieved that he had finally left. I sat on the sofa and let out a sigh of relief, before taking another cigarette out of the pack, finding a lighter at the end of the sofa, and lighting it up. I sat and pondered on why Johnny and I just didn't click. We did seem to like each other, but it felt as though we both expected the other to make the first move or something like that. 'Strange life!' I thought to myself, then jumped up and carried on with my day.

CHAPTER 41:

LA KNIGHTS

A few days later I picked up the phone to call Patty and bizarrely, she was already on the line. "Hello!" we both said, then burst out laughing "That was weird!" we both said in unison. "It didn't ring/I was just going to call you!" We both blurted out laughing, before arranging to meet up at the Beef Bowl at 7:30 that night.

We both arrived at the Beef Bowl around the same time and headed over the street to the liquor store to buy some beers to drink in our little den in the bushes behind the Beef Bowl. As we chatted, we decided that we had both had enough of the punk and new-wave scene for a while, the punks and new wavers were fun, but some of them seemed a little immature for our tastes, so we decided we would rather party with the bikers and the rockers as they seemed more grown-up in comparison.

My mind flashed to how awkward my time spent with Johnny had been, and I couldn't imagine any our biker or rocker friends acting like that. 'If one of them had been in Johnny's position, they would have taken the lead in the conversation if I'd have been a little shy, and they would have helped to create a fun-spirited friendship, and who knows, maybe if the circumstances were right, romance might follow, but if both people are just going to sit together in awkward silence, then obviously nothing is going to happen!' I thought to myself, as Patty rummaged in her bag for her face powder.

"Shall we go?" asked Patty once she'd powdered her face, and topped up her lipstick. "Yeah, let's go!" I answered, and we both put our empty beer cans in the brown bag they'd come in, picked them up, grabbed our shoulder bags, and made our way out of the bushes, and over towards the parking lot towards Sunset.

I threw the rubbish in the nearest trash can, and we started hitchhiking up towards the Sunset Strip. Some guy who seemed a little on the cheesy side stopped to give us a lift. We jumped into his car, both of us giving each other a look that said we were both fully aware that he was not the type of guy we would normally hitch a lift with, but taking a little risk all the same, and sure enough as soon as he propositioned us as if we were hookers, we both told him to get lost and jumped out of his car before it had a chance to take off.

"We're not hookers!" I shouted as he started to drive away. "No, we're party girls!" Shouted Patty. "Sleaze bag!" I added as he sped off, and Patty and I cracked up laughing. "God, you think he'd know the difference!" I said to Patty. "I mean, look at us! You're dressed in jeans, a regular tee shirt, and a blue fluffy cardi, with dark-blonde hair and make-up - like a cool rock chic, and I'm wearing funky looking colourful new-wave clothes, with long blue-black spikey-hair, and punky make-up! Hookers are dressed like hookers, not like us!!" I exclaimed, sounding exasperated. Patty and I instantly saw the funny side and started falling about the sidewalk crying with laughter.

Next, a pick-truck of rocker types slowed down near us "Need a ride?" One of them called out. We could tell they were okay, and that they were just out to party like us. "Sure/Yeah thanks!" we answered, as we jumped in their pickup truck with them. 'This is more like it!' I thought to myself, as Patty and I bobbed our heads to the rock music they had playing. The guys parked up near the Sunset Strip, and we headed over to the rainbow. "Thanks, guys! We may see you later/Thanks!" Patty and I called out as we went. "Sure/No problem, catch you later!" the guys called out as we went.

The Rainbow was as busy as always, and Patty and I soon got busy dancing away on the small dance floor. At one point Patty popped to use the bathroom while I stayed dancing. "Hey what's your name?" asked a quite good-looking guy, with cheesy vibes. "Della, what's yours" I answered politely, while feeling like I'd rather be dancing than chatting to him. "Dave, do you like coke?" He asked, and before I had a chance to answer, he lifted my left arm and put a line of Coke on the back of my hand as if trying to impress me.

"No thanks!" I answered, feeling insulted as I blew the coke off my hand. "What the hell! Do you know how much that cost?" Shouted the guy looking angry. "Not enough to buy me! See-Ya!" I exclaimed, before marching off to find Patty and tell her all about what had just happened.

"It's so cool that you blew the coke off your hand!" said Patty, grinning, and looking impressed. I loved how Patty and I got each other so well, and although we were part of the Hollywood party scene, we were also detached from it somehow, as if we could see it for what it was - just a fun night out, and wouldn't be swept away by the glamour that surrounded us. It all seemed so shallow to us, and we didn't need any of it to have a good time! We headed back over to the dancefloor to dance some more, until we felt hot, and needed to get some fresh air, so we headed outside.

In the club's parking lot, there was extra excitement in the air as Billy Idol and his entourage arrived, although Patty and I were more pleased to see that our Hollywood Biker pals were parked up nearby, so we went over to say hi, and after a fun catch up chat they offered us a lift, so off we went into the night, with our LA Knights.

We cruised east down Sunset until we reached a fast food place on the right, where the biker crowd hung out. I admired how they were just as fun and friendly as ever, but they also had a cool edge and weren't easily fazed by anything which I really liked - plus they weren't sleazy or cheesy! They never tried anything on with us, and always treated us with respect, if anything they looked out for us as true gentleman should. I once again realised how things were not always what they seemed to be in this world. – The ones who look "bad" on the surface, are often good, and vice versa.

Patty and I always enjoyed their company and the feelings seemed mutual as they always seemed happy to see us too, although we usually chatted to the couple of male bikers that we were acquaintances with, even the biker gals were friendly and welcoming towards us. They seemed as though they were already hooked up with certain bikers in the pack, and at least our biker guy pals were single.

After a couple of hours of hanging out and having fun at the fast-food place, our two biker pals: Lee and his friend John offered us a lift home which we gratefully accepted. "See you in Hollywood girls!/Later!" They shouted after dropping us off. "Thanks, guys!!" we called after them, as they sped off into the night.

Mike was at the door waiting to greet us as usual. He was watching the honeymooners on TV and invited us to join him, so we watched TV with him for a while, before heading to our beds and crashing out.

CHAPTER 42:

YOB IN THE OINTMENT!

The next day Patty took off home, and I spent the day at Pico. I went for a nice walk with Mike and Sonny to get us all a thrifty ice cream, and after we came out of Thrifty with our ice creams, we decided to sit on a nearby wall to eat them.

A couple of young, slim, friendly Mexican guys from a food store near by approached us and started speaking to me in Spanish. "She doesn't speak Spanish, she's from England!" said Michael in a friendly way, as if trying to help avoid confusion between me and the guys.

"How come you look Spanish!" asked one of the guys looking confused. I'd never realised I looked Spanish before these last few LA encounters where people had mentioned it. "I guess it's because I have brown hair, and brown eyes, and I tan easily?" I answered with a grin, and everyone laughed.

"What are your names, I'm Jose and he's Pedro" asked one of the guys. "I'm Della, and this is Mike and Sonny!" I answered, and we all shook hands. "Cool, do you guys smoke?" asked Jose. "Yeah, we do!" answered Mike eagerly. "Yes" mumbles Sonny. "What about you?" asked Jose, looking at me curiously. Only Cigarettes, but I don't care if others do!" I answered, with a grin. "Why not man?" asked Pedro, with a laugh. "I just don't like it, it knocks me out!" I answered with a laugh.

"OK, but you don't mind if we do huh?" asked Jose, as he took out a pack of weed and some papers, and started rolling a joint. "No, I'm not against it, it's no different to booze as far as I'm concerned, I just don't like it for me, but if others enjoy it, that's fine with me, I'm happy for them!" I answered, and we all laughed.

"Cool, there you go guys!" said Jose, as he lit up the joint and then passed it over to Mike. "Thanks, man!" answered Mike, before taking a long drag, and then passing it to Sonny. we spent the next hour so shooting the breeze with our new pals, and once again I loved how in LA everything just seemed to flow...work, play, fun, friendships, traffic...

"So, guys, shall we head back and get some food?" I asked Mike and Sonny when it felt like time to move on. "Yeah, I'm hungry" answered Mike with a laugh. "Yeah" mumbled Sonny. "Well, it was great to meet you both!" I said to Jose and Pedro, as we stood up ready to leave. "Yeah, thanks for the smoke guys!" added Mike, as he reached out and shook their hands. "Yeah, thanks guys" mumbled Sonny, following Mike's lead and shaking their hands too. "Sure/No problem, guys!" answered Jose and Pedro, standing up to say goodbye. "Bye then!" I said, as I too shook their hands, and turned to walk away. "Bye/Take care!" answered the guys, as the three of us headed off back towards the halfway house.

"Hope we see you again English girl!" shouted one of the guys across the parking lot. "Probably!" I called back, giving them one last wave, before turning around and heading home with Mike and Sonny.

As soon as we entered the living room, I spotted a letter with my mum's handwriting on it, so while Mike went about making us some coffee, and looking in the fridge and cupboards for snacks, I excitedly opened the letter. It was always a special treat to receive a letter from my family and friends back home.

My mum said that she was missing me and that she hoped that I was doing ok, and eating well. She went on to tell me that she was moving house, from the village on the outside of town; Morda, back to a flat in Oswestry town centre. She seemed happy about this and added that I would still have my room, as the new flat had two bedrooms. It was so nice of her to think of keeping a bedroom for me, but I felt that over time it would simply become a guest room for whoever might be visiting, including me! She mentioned that a couple of my school friends had been asking about me, and that she had given them my address to write to, and that my brothers were all doing well. My oldest brother Steve was still happily married, and working as a groundsman for the local council. My second oldest brother was doing well working as a Life Guard at the local Leisure Centre and had apparently been winning lots of Squash tournaments, and my youngest brother, Carl, who was four and a half years older than me, was doing great working as a classroom assistant and was thinking about applying to art school to develop his passion for photography. She mentioned that she'd also bumped into my dad Geoff in town and that he would be writing me again soon, and she ended the letter by reminding me that her cousin, my Aunt Freda, would be in the States soon and that she was looking forward to meeting up with me. I felt happy to know that my family and friends were doing ok, and excited at the thought of seeing my Aunt Freda again soon.

"Hey Della, wanna try a peanut butter and mayonnaise sandwich?" asked Mike excitedly. "A what?" I asked, feeling like I must have misheard him. "A peanut butter and mayonnaise sandwich, they're really good!" exclaimed Mike as he headed my way, offering me half of the sandwich on his plate. "Um ok, thanks" I answered, as I picked the sandwich half.

"Are you sure it tastes ok?" I asked, wondering if he was playing a little prank on me. "Honestly, they're one of my favourites!" exclaimed Mike, taking a big bite of his sandwich half. "OK, here goes!" I exclaimed dramatically, before taking a small bite of the sandwich. "Oh my god, it is nice!" I exclaimed, as the unusual blend of peanut butter, mayonnaise and bread flavours came together and created a delicious flavour I'd not tasted before. "I told ya, want another one!" Exclaimed Mike excitedly.

"I'm ok for now thanks Mike, I'll just get a coffee though" I answered, as I nipped to the kitchen to get a cup of coffee to go with my tasty sandwich half. Sonny was in the kitchen, making himself a peanut butter and jelly sandwich, and soon the three of us were sitting at the dining room table, eating our sandwiches, sipping on our coffees, and chatting about what nice guys Jose and Pedro were. Just as I was about to go and wash up the phone rang, so I went to answer it.

"Hi Della, wanna come on a picnic with me and Julie tomorrow?" asked Sylvia's friendly voice. "Yeah, that sounds good, thanks!" I answered, knowing that I was free the next day. "Great, we'll pick you up at about twelve noon, we're going to Griffith Park, have you been there before?" asked Sylvia curiously. "No, I haven't even heard of it, where is it?" I asked while trying to imagine what part of LA it might be. "Oh, you'll like it. It's where the observatory is. It's just east of Hollywood, its got hiking trails, and large park areas where a lot of LA locals go on weekends to have picnics and barbeques" answered Sylvia enthusiastically.

"Wow, it sounds great! Can't wait!" I answered, suddenly looking forward to checking out a new part of LA. "OK, see you tomorrow at noon!" answered Sylvia. "Great, see you then! Say hi to Julie for me!" I answered as we both hung up.

"Hey, have you guys ever been to a place called Griffith Park?" I asked Mike and Sonny, as I picked up our empty cups and plates and headed to the kitchen with them. "Yeah, it's massive! They got an observatory up there, it's really famous, it was in a James Dean movie!" answered Mike, sounding excited for me, while Sonny nodded along in agreement. "Wow, I can't wait to check it out!" I answered as I went about washing up the dishes. We spent the rest of the day playing board games on the dining room table before dinner, and watching TV after dinner, then headed off to our rooms to catch some Z's.

The next day, just before noon I quickly made a couple of peanut butter and jelly sandwiches (I didn't think peanut butter and mayo would be a good idea for a picnic in the sun, as the mayo' might go off fast!) I grabbed an empty pop bottle and filled it with water, shoved it all in my army shoulder bag, said goodbye to the Pico gang, and headed downstairs to wait for Sylvia and Julie.

Their car pulled up just as I reached the bottom of the steps, and we all gave each other a big wave, as I ran and jumped in the back of the car. "Hi girls, thanks for inviting me to the picnic! How are you both?" I asked as I got comfy in my seat. "Good thanks/Great!" answered Sylvia and Julie, looking pleased to see me.

"Mike tells me Griffith Park is really nice, and that there's a famous observatory from a James Dean movie up there or something?" I exclaimed excitedly. "Oh yeah, Rebel Without a Cause!" answered Julie knowingly. "Oh gosh, is it about Johnny?! I joked, and we all laughed. "How did things go with him when he stayed over?" asked Sylvia curiously. "Oh god, awful!! When I got up the next day he was still crashed out on the sofa, thankfully the residents had left him sleep, and when he woke up I made us both a coffee, and we both sat next to each other in silence on the sofa for what felt like forever! Every time I tried to start a conversation he would just give a one-word answer, it was torturous! So, I thought if he's not gonna bother, neither am I! So, we both just sat there in silence!" I exclaimed, and we all cracked up laughing.

"That does sound painful!" exclaimed Julie. "Yeah, it was, it was awful!" I answered, still laughing. "I think he does like you, but he's shy!" exclaimed Sylvia, between her bouts of laughter. "Maybe, I don't know, but nothing is ever gonna happen between us if the two of us just sit together in silence the whole time. What's the point of that!" I exclaimed as we all continued crying with laughter.

"Griffith Park!" exclaimed Sylvia as we arrived at what looked like a large park, surrounded by people picnicking on the grass and at picnic tables, working out, or hiking and jogging on various pathways. Some people had music playing, others were just chatting, and everyone seemed in great spirits. "Wow, this is lovely!" I exclaimed, feeling surprised to see so much greenery in the city of LA.

"Yeah, we love to come up here some weekends and just chill!" answered Sylvia as she parked up.

We soon found a nice spot on the grass, and Sylvia spread out a large picnic blanket for us to sit on, with our picnic. We each put out our various snacks in the centre and told each other to help themselves. I'd cut my sandwiches into fours and explained that it was all I had to hand. The girls didn't seem to mind, as they had an abundance of food to share.

"So are you both from LA originally?" I asked as we sat enjoying the fresh air, and scenery. "Yes, I'm an LA local, but Sylvia is from Oxnard right?" answered Julie, smiling over at Sylvia, as Sylvia nodded back, not yet able to answer after taking a big bite of a sandwich. "Oxnard, that's a weird name, where's that?" I asked with a laugh. "It's just northwest of LA, not too far!" answered Sylvia, laughing too. "West? How can it be West? Is it an Island?" I asked, picturing a small Island off the coast of LA. "No, the coastline goes West from LA, it doesn't go straight up. Oxnard isn't an Island!" answered Sylvia, and the three of us laughed at the idea of Oxnard being an Island.

"Jim and Frankie will be here soon, Jim's from England too. We'll introduce you!" exclaimed Julie excitedly. "Oh really! So are these your boyfriends?" I asked. "Yeah, I've been seeing Jim for a couple of months now, and Sylvia has been seeing Frankie a bit longer, it's nothing too serious, but it's fun!" answered Julie with a smile, as Sylvia nodded in agreement.

"Here they come!" exclaimed Sylvia suddenly, as she looked over towards the car park. I looked to see two guys who looked in their early twenties heading our way. Julie jumped up to run and give the guy who I presumed to be Jim, a big hug, while Sylvia slowly stood up and let her guy; Frankie come to her.

"Hey Jim, this is Della, the English girl I told you about!" exclaimed Julie excitedly. "Hi, Jim!" I said as I stood up to shake his hand. "'Ello, nice to meet a fellow limey!" he answered, in a London-sounding accent. "Yeah, you too!" I answered as we all sat down in a circle on the picnic blanket.

We had a great time at the picnic, and later on, we all headed back to Sylvia and Julie's apartment in Santa Monica to wrap up the day. "Wow, what a lovely apartment!" I exclaimed as we entered a small, but very stylish apartment, only a couple of blocks from the beach. "Yeah, and because it's rent-controlled the rent is only four hundred bucks a month too!" answered Julie, with a grin. "That's great!" I answered, feeling impressed.

"Does everyone want a beer?" asked Sylvia, as she headed towards the kitchen. "Sure/Yeah/Yes please!" we all called back. Sylvia soon arrived back in the living room with a cold six-pack of beers, and a big bag of potato chips that she placed on the coffee table in the centre of the room. We all thanked her, as she moved on to putting on a fun new wave tape on her music system.

We were having a fun time listening to music, drinking beers, and eating snacks when at some point Julie and Jim left the living room together. Julie mumbled something about they were going to her room to discuss something. A couple of minutes later, Julie and Jim started shouting at each other, and Sylvia, Frankie and I went quiet to listen if everything was ok, while pulling "What's going on?" faces at each other.

Suddenly we heard the bedroom door fly open, followed by a loud crash, so the three of us automatically jumped up and ran out of the room to see what was going on. We were met with the site of Julie lying curled up in a ball on the floor crying in pain, as Jim stood over her looking enraged.

We were all frozen in shock and suddenly Jim started kicking her in the stomach! We all yelled at him to stop and together we managed to drag him off of her "Asshole!" shouted Sylvia, as Jim took off running out of the front door. I was flabbergasted that Jim had turned out to be a low-life yob! Especially as Sylvia and Julie loved England and the English people so much. 'Maybe not for long, after this!' I thought to myself, feeling mortified by the whole incident.

We guided Julie to the living room to comfort her, and Sylvia and I sat with our arms around her on the sofa, while asking her what had happened. "He was jealous, he thinks I'm seeing someone else" sobbed Julie. "Well, you will be now!" I joked and we all laughed, even Julie. "I'll make some drinks, Coffee or booze?" asked Sylvia suddenly jumping up off the sofa. "Booze!" we all shouted in unison and burst out laughing.

"Voda and Cranberry!" announced Sylvia as she arrived back in the living room a few minutes later carrying a large jug of purple-looking juice in one hand and a stack of four glasses in the other hand. We spent the rest of the evening getting drunk, and listening to music while doing our best to comfort Julie. I explained to her that most English guys are fine, but the "yobs" are not so fine, and Jim was obviously a "Yob!" She seemed to understand what I meant and nodded as if trying to decide if she wanted to carry on seeing him.

"Hey guys, thanks for a lovely day, aside from the bit where Julie got beaten up! I'm gonna head home, I'm tired" I announced, as I stood up, feeling ready to leave. "You don't have to go, you can crash on the sofa if you want!" exclaimed Sylvia, looking surprised that I was leaving. "No, really I'm fine, I need to get back to do some stuff in the morning" I answered, feeling I wanted to give Julie some time to recover, and Sylvia and Frankie some time to themselves. "OK, if you're sure!" answered Sylvia, standing up to see me to the door. "Thanks for your help Della!" called out Julie with a sweet smile. "You're welcome, see you both, and maybe you as well again soon!" I answered, glancing at Frankie, as I waved goodbye. "Yeah, nice to meet you, Della!" called out Frankie, as I headed out of the front door. "See you soon!" said Sylvia from the doorway. "See ya!" I called back and took off.

It felt good to be on the bus back to Pico, I'd enjoyed the day out, but it had been a long day, so I was very tired, and Jim beating up Julie had left me feeling shaken up and stressed on top! I couldn't wait to get to bed and crash out!

The next morning I woke up surprisingly hangover-free and looking forward to the day ahead. I had some laundry to do, and some journalling to catch up with, and a letter to write to my mum. I figured I could write the letter, and catch up with my journaling at the same time as doing my laundry at the laundromat across the street.

I took a quick shower, got dressed, did my hair and make-up, and headed to the living room to grab a bowl of cereal and a cup of coffee. No one else was around, so after I finished, I washed up, then got my things together and headed to the laundromat.

The Laundromat was empty, so I had the place to myself to do my laundry, journalling, and letter writing. A Spanish radio station played romantic-sounding Spanish music in the background of the laundromat, and occasionally a shy-looking, middle-aged Hispanic lady would appear from a back room as if to check on things, picking up any litter she spotted, and giving various areas a little mop, before disappearing back into the back room.

She never came near enough for us to smile or say hello to each other, but I presumed that the Spanish radio station was her choice. I enjoyed the music, which reminded me of how near Mexico was to California, and my possible future plans to travel there, although I wasn't sure when that was going to happen next.

I wrote my letter to my mum and finished catching up with my journalling, just as the laundry drier stopped. "Perfect timing!' I thought to myself, as I grabbed my black bin bag, and threw my laundry inside in one big heap. I put my journal, and letter in my army shoulder bag, and headed back over across the street to the halfway house.

"Hi, guys!" I exclaimed as I entered the living room to see Mike and Sonny sitting at the dining table eating sandwiches. "Hi Della, been doing laundry? You should have said, I would have gone over there with you!" answered Mike, while Sonny. Checked out my bin bag of laundry with his usual bewildered look. "Aw, thanks, Mike! Maybe next time then!" I answered with a smile, as I headed back to my room.

I put my journal away, quickly folded my clothes up, put them in the chest of draws in the corner of the room, and put the bin bag under the tiny sink, I touched up my hair and makeup and decided to head up to Hollywood for a walkabout. I grabbed my army shoulder bag and headed back towards the living room.

"I'm off to Hollywood for a walkabout, see you guys later!" I exclaimed as I breezed past the dining table towards the open front door. "OK Della, have fun!" called out Mike, "Bye!" mumbled Sonny. "See ya later!" I called back, as I hopped down the steps to the sidewalk, and headed towards to bus stop at Pico and Crenshaw.

I loved days like this, where I had no plans at all, except to just roam about and see what happens! the gorgeous LA weather made it so easy to do so. The bus arrived swiftly, and I jumped on board, paid my fair and found a seat at the back, amongst my fellow passengers.

I jumped off the bus at Hollywood and Vine and just meandered west enjoying the vibrant Hollywood Boulevard atmosphere. As I walked along I suddenly came across some street punks who were hanging out on a wall opposite the Manns Chinese theatre. They seemed friendly, so I strolled over and got chatting with them.

A couple of them made a space for me on the wall in between them and introduced themselves as Ed and Jennie. Ed was white, and kind of tough looking, with brown spikey hair, and Jennie looked slightly Hispanic and had lovely dark brown shoulder-length hair and a warm smile. They both seemed around my age and generously shared their beer with me.

"So, you're from England right?" asked Ed. "What's the punk scene like there?" asked Jennie enthusiastically, the two of them talking over each other. "Yeah England, the punk scene is good as far as I know, I was always into all sorts of music though, not just the punk scene" I answered, not wanting them to think that I was some kind of English punk-scene specialist! "That's cool!" answered Ed with a smile. "Yeah, whatever floats your boat!" added Jennie.

We sat on the wall just shooting the breeze, and watching the world go by for the next half hour or so when suddenly a fabulously-dressed, black punk-rock girl came walking along the boulevard and stopped to chat with a couple of the punks who were on the sidewalk.

"Who's that?" I asked as she seemed like she may be some kind of artist. "Oh, that's Tequila Mockingbird, she's cool!" Answered Jennie. "Is she an Artist?" I asked. "I think so, she's got a band too" answered Jennie, while smiling over at Tequilla.

"Cool!" I answered hearing myself sound like my friend Patty. Tequilla glanced our way, and we all smiled and waved. I got the impression that she probably had a lot of creative stuff going on, and was one of the more productive punks, as opposed to the panhandling punks sitting nearby. 'Takes all sorts!' I thought to myself, feeling happy to be more of an independent type and free-spirited enough to be a part of all scenes, yet belonging to none!

"Gonna get some smokes!" announced Ed, as he jumped down off the wall, and headed towards the liquor store. Just then a cute-looking skinhead guy appeared, and jumped up on the wall next to me where Ed had been sitting, so I shuffled over a little towards Jennie to make room for him.

"Hi, I'm Jay, what's your name?" He said with a bold, yet somewhat shy expression. "Della" I answered, as we shook hands. He had lovely eyes, and I felt a little spark between us, as we started chatting with ease to each other about how we had both come to be in Hollywood.

He told me that he was a homeless, seventeen-year-old runaway, as were most of the other street punks hanging out around us and although they were all around my age, I didn't identify myself as a "homeless runaway" I truly saw myself as an explorer, who was out on an exciting adventure to see the world! I pondered on these labels and wondered if mental dispositions were simply a state of mind, as we were all in a similar boat, we were just seeing it differently.

"We're gonna go a walk down the Boulevard, wanna come along?" asked Jay, with his cute smile, as all the punks started to stand around as if ready to move. "Yeah ok!" I answered, as I glanced to see where Jennie was, and saw that she was now standing nearby chatting with Ed.

378

BOOK 1: TO SEE THE WORLD

We slowly but surely started to walk east down Hollywood Boulevard, about fifteen of us in total. I felt as if I was suddenly in some kind of spontaneous Punk Parade, and wondered what Rishard would make of it if he happened to drive by. I chuckled at the thought but tried to keep a serious face on, as these punks looked like they meant business, as they walked along, some of them holding out white Styrofoam cups begging for money as they went.

Begging for cash, was not my scene, but I was curious to see how the punks were being treated by the people passing us by. Most people just ignored them, but some people were kind and would drop a few coins into their Styrofoam cups, and wish them well.

At some point, as we all strolled along, I was propositioned by some cheesy-looking guy. "No thanks!" I exclaimed as I pulled an offended face. "Punks aren't hookers!" shouted Jay, quick to defend my honour, which I found very endearing. I didn't really consider myself to be a punk, but I guessed, compared to some of the other styles out there, I was definitely more on the punky side.

After a while of hanging out on the boulevard with the street punks, I got bored and decided to head back to Pico to do my own thing. "Well, I guess I'm gonna head home on the bus!" I said to Jay, as I got ready to get going. "I'll walk you to your bus stop if you want?" said Jay chivalrously, which I found heart-warming. "OK, thanks!" I answered with a smile. "See ya another time!" I called out to Jennie and Ed. "Yeah See ya/Come and hang with us any time!" they called back, as they waved goodbye. Some of the other punks gave little waves too, so I gave them all one last wave and started strolling with Jay towards the bus stop.

"Would you like to hang out sometime?" asked Jay as we sat at the bus stop, waiting for my bus. "Yeah, that would be nice, you can always visit me down at Pico, it's the halfway house I help out at, they don't mind if I have visitors" I answered, as I dug into my bag to jot down the Pico address and phone number.

"Great, I can drop by tomorrow night if that's ok?" he answered, looking pleased. "I have an acting class, but you're welcome to drop by after that, around 9 pm ish" I answered, as I handed him the piece of paper with the Pico details written on it. "Great ok, see you just after nine tomorrow then!" answered Jay, as the bus neared, and we both stood up. "Yep, see you then!" I answered, with a smile. "See ya then" he answered, giving me a little hug, just before I jumped on the bus. I paid my fair, found a seat, and Jay and I gave each other a little wave as the bus took off.

'Wow, he's really nice!' I thought to myself, thinking about how he treated me the way I like to be treated, with a little chivalry. I wasn't sure if I was attracted to him though. He was good-looking, had a strong-looking body, and was a little taller than me, but he was a skin-head, and I wasn't attracted to skin-heads, I liked a good head of hair of a guy, which I'd recently realised going by my last couple of Sid Vicious, and Sid Vicious on Steroids crushes! 'Oh well, see what happens I guess' I thought, looking forward to his visit the next night.

The acting class was fun, but the whole time I couldn't wait to leave and get back to Pico to see Jay. I went through the various motions as directed by the coach, but was most looking forward to the motion of taking off through the exit at the end of class!

I arrived back at Pico and quickly ran to the bathroom to touch up my hair and make-up. "Della, there's a guy here to see you!" called out Mike suddenly. 'Wow, he's on time too!' I thought to myself feeling that he was ticking all the right boxes so far.

"Hi, Jay!" I exclaimed, as I entered the living room to see Jay standing near the doorway chatting to Mike, while Sonny stayed a safe distance away observing the going's on from the armchair. "Hey Della, you look lovely!" exclaimed Jay, as he headed my way to give me a big hug. "So do you!" I answered, feeling my a flutter of butterflies in my stomach as we hugged. "I got you this," said Jay, as he handed me a little yellow flower. "Aww, thank you!" I exclaimed taking it off him and holding it to my chest lovingly. "I'll put this in a glass of water!" I exclaimed as I headed to the kitchen to find a small glass to put the flower in.

As I filled the glass with water, I had a strong feeling that I could really fall for Jay if things continued to go well between us, which felt both exciting and scary at the same time. "You guys wanna a beer?" asked Mike, as he headed to the fridge. "Sure/Yes please!" we all answered.

I headed back to the living room and put my flower on the table, then Jay and I automatically sat down on the sofa next to each other and got comfy. Jay put his arm around me, and we snuggled up closer together. 'He could teach Johnny a lesson or two!' I thought to myself, as the butterflies fluttered around my stomach some more.

The two of us hung out in the living room with Michael and Sonny for a couple of hours, chatting, drinking cheap beers and listening to music. I liked how Jay was easygoing and the way that he was ok with just hanging out, creating no sense of pressure towards me to entertain him. We were simply comfortable together, and I liked it.

"Well, I guess I'd better get going!" announced Jay around 11 pm. "OK, well thanks for calling round, where are you heading to?" I asked, curious to know where he stayed. "Thanks, it was lovely to spend some time with you Della. I usually crash out with the other punks up at "Hotel Hell" on the boulevard" he answered matter-of-factly.

My mind flashed to a massive abandoned hotel that was just set back on Hollywood, boulevard, and I felt bad for not inviting him to stay over, but I'd only just met him, plus it didn't seem fair to the residents to have a complete stranger crashing on the sofa. Johnny crashing over had put me off that whole idea!

"I'll see you up on the boulevard, or call you soon!" said Jay giving me a little hug and a kiss on the cheek, as if not wanting me to feel pressured to invite him to stay over. "OK, take care!" I answered as he headed out of the front door, and we waved goodbye to each other.

"He was a nice dude!" exclaimed Mike, while Sonny nodded, and mumbled in agreement. "Yeah, he's really nice!" I answered as I started tidying up the room. I spent a couple more hours watching TV with Mike and Sonny, then I bid them both goodnight, picked up the glass with my flower in, and headed off to bed.

I lay in bed awake for a while, thinking about what a lovely guy Jay was, but at the same time not sure how things would, or could develop between us, what with him being a homeless seventeen-year-old street punk, and me being an eighteen-year-old world explorer, who might be heading back to England to regroup soon. These thoughts kept me awake for another hour or so, and eventually, I got sleepy, giving the yellow flower that Jay had given me one last little glance before I dozed off.

CHAPTER 43:

AUNT FREDA IS ON HER WAY! SHOULD I GO, OR SHOULD I STAY???

The next day I received another letter from Aunt Freda. She told me that she had bought a ticket for the QE2 from Southampton to New York and that she would take the trains, and busses to travel across the USA to check out some potential ranch properties to buy, and then she would come and visit me in Los Angeles in a few weeks' time.

I had told her in my last letter that Larry had said that she would be welcome to stay at the halfway house, which would be better than me travelling up to meet her somewhere, and she seemed pleased with that. She ended the letter by telling me that if I wanted to fly back to England with her she would make the arrangements for us to fly back together from Los Angeles.

The thought of flying back to England with my Aunt Freda created a mental whirlwind in my mind, and once again I felt so confused as to what to do. On the one hand, it felt more natural to stay in LA, especially now that I'd met Jay, and to just continue going with the LA flow... but at the same time, I knew I would have to leave by early June anyway, because of my passport stamp.

I toyed with the idea of just exploring Mexico for a while and then coming back to LA, but I was missing my family and friends, also I knew I would need to top up my travel funds and hopefully do some more world travels at some point. Once again, I felt completely torn between these various possibilities, and spent the next few days, ruminating.

Suddenly I had the realisation that I didn't have to choose just one of the possibilities, I could do ALL of them! - I could fly back to England with Aunt

Freda, spend some time with family and friends, do some seasonal work to boost the travel funds, do some more world travels, AND make regular visits to LA to spend more time with Jay, and my other LA friends!

Over the next few days, I stayed at Pico, covered for Mary on her days off, and spent my spare time going on local walks and hanging out playing board and card games with Michael, and Sonny. Sometimes Suzy, Cathy Crude, and Dalene would join us, which added to the fun. I was enjoying being a bit of a homebody for a change, after spending so much time out and about around the city.

I also enjoyed spending some time to myself in my room, just listening to music, writing down various passing thoughts, prose and poems, and catching up with my journals. One night, I thought about how I'd often thought I would maybe one day turn my journals into a travel memoir about my adventures, and maybe share them with the world – 'That's if I wasn't too busy still travelling the world!' I chuckled to myself.

One night I was watching TV in the living room with Mike and Sonny, and the phone rang. "Hi, how you doing Della, I haven't seen you up on the boulevard lately?" said Jay's sweet voice. "I'm ok thanks' Jay, I've been busy covering for Mary so I haven't been out and about much, how are you doing?" I asked, feeling the butterflies again. "I'm glad you're doing ok, I'm good too thanks! Would it be ok to come and visit you again sometime?" he asked sweetly. "Yes, of course!" I answered while glancing a happy smile over at Mike, as he grinned back over, looking pleased for me.

"How about tomorrow around nine again, you have an acting class earlier right?" He asked, sounding upbeat. "Yeah ok, that would be great!" I answered, already looking forward to seeing him again.

"Great, see you at nine tomorrow!" he exclaimed. "Great, see you then!" I answered as we both hung up the phone. "Jay's coming over to visit me again tomorrow night about nine!" I exclaimed to Mike excitedly. "That's great news, he's a nice guy. I think he really likes you!" answered Mike, beaming me a big smile, while Sonny nodded in agreement. "Yeah, I think I like him too!" I answered with a laugh.

The acting class was okay, but I was starting to go off it a bit, mainly because I was realising that pretty much everyone there wanted to be a star, or a friend of a star at least, going by the way they name dropped! Whereas I was just there to have fun, so I was starting to feel a little like the odd one out as I wasn't taking it seriously at all, besides, I had Jay to look forward to seeing!

I headed back to Pico and quickly rushed to the bathroom to tidy my hair, and top up my makeup. Just as I arrived back in the living room, the house bell rang, and I excitedly ran to open up the front door, and metal gate, knowing that it was most likely Jay who had rang the bell. I couldn't believe how happy I was at the thought of seeing him again, I hadn't felt like this about a guy since Jeff up in Toronto.

My happiness instantly turned to shock, when I saw that he was covered in blood! "Oh my god, what happened?" I exclaimed, feeling instantly stressed and uneasy at the sight of him in such a scary state. "Got jumped!" he answered, sounding down, as I opened up the metal gate, and let him in. "That's awful!" I answered, as I gestured for him to sit on the sofa. "Thanks" he mumbled, as he sat down on the sofa looking in a bad way. "I'll get you some paper towels to stop the bleeding!" I exclaimed as I ran to the kitchen, and grabbed a whole roll of paper towels.

"There you go! So what happened?" I asked him, as I gave him the roll of paper towels, and sat next to him. "Thanks," he said as he took a few paper towels, and dabbed the blood on his head with them. "I just got jumped by some black guys when I got off the bus at Pico and Crenshaw, it's because I'm a skinhead!" he said matter-of-factly. This confused me, as most of the skinheads that I knew in England weren't racist, they were just into the Ska music scene, which was made up of black, white, and brown people, and most of the bands had a lot of black members.

"I don't get that, in the UK skinheads and black people are all part of the Ska music, and reggae scene, which is predominantly black, and being a skinhead isn't a racist thing, it's a fashion thing unless someone is some kind of national front football hooligan!" I exclaimed.

"Huh?" he answered, as if in disbelief. "Yeah, I mean Ska and Reggae bands like The Specials, Madness, UB40 and The Beat are made up of black AND white band members, and fans. I've been to clubs where everyone was just having fun dancing together because it was about the music, not race!" I explained enthusiastically. "Hmm?" he mumbled as if still not convinced.

Although, like I said there is also another type of skinhead, that is racist, they're usually not very bright football hooligan types, who support the national front, but just being a skinhead alone, doesn't mean a person is racist. I mean, are you racist?" I asked, suddenly wondering why he was a skinhead if he thought it had racist connotations.

"I'm not racist, but I was in juvy for six months when I was 15, and the kids in there automatically stuck together by race, so I guess I just got in the habit of it" he answered sounding very sincere. I reasoned that he was still only 17, and probably didn't know any better. He was basically just trying to fit in to survive.

"So why were you in that place?" I asked curiously. "I messed up!" He answered matter-of-factly. My heart went out to him, as I could tell he was a sweet soul by nature, and I got the feeling that things must have been bad for him at home. "Hey, everybody messes up!" I answered, hoping to make him feel better. He reached out and held my hand, and I felt butterflies in my stomach again, we just sat together sharing a moment of love between us, amidst the sorrow.

Mike and Sonny suddenly arrived upstairs into the kitchen and looked across at me and Jay sitting on the sofa together. They both seemed delighted to find a visitor in the living room, even a bloody one! "Man, what happened to you?" asked Mike looking wide-eyed and curious, as he rushed into the living room.

"Hi guys, I got jumped" he answered, looking pleased to see them too. "Aw, that sucks man, wanna coffee?" asked Mike, looking as if he wanted to help make things better, while Sonny stood on the spot looking worried, and rocking back and forth, as if he wasn't sure what to do. "Got a beer Man?" asked Jay, looking like he needed one. "Sure!" said Mike as he rushed towards the fridge.

"Anyone else wanna a beer?" Asked Mike as he opened the fridge door. "Sure/Yes Please!" said Sonny and I, as the atmosphere instantly relaxed. Soon the four of us were sat around the living room sipping on our cans of beer and listening to Jay's story. Sonny and Michael seemed to be enjoying hearing a guy's take on the outside world, and they sat listening intently, and asking questions here and there, in between head nods, and mumbling such things as "I hear ya man!" and "That sucks!"

It was touching to see them interacting this way, and it reminded me that before they got ill, they too were regular guys themselves. I noticed how good Jay was so good with them, and how he spoke to them in just the same way he would speak to any other guys, which was another thing I liked about him. Wanna play cards?" asked Mike, after Jay's story was fully exhausted, and he seemed to be feeling better. "Sure man" answered Jay. "Sounds fun!" I answered while Sonny nodded.

The four of us got up from the sofa, and armchair, and sat around the dining table. Michael grabbed us all another beer, put a music station on the radio and grabbed a deck of cards. We went on to have a good evening of drinking beer, playing cards, and shooting the breeze. Occasionally one of the other residents would appear to get a snack or a drink from the kitchen. They would say hi to us, but they didn't stick around, and would swiftly disappear back downstairs, and to their various rooms.

Around 2 am Mike and Sonny, bid us goodnight, and headed off down the stairs to bed. It suddenly dawned on me that Jay was still with me. I felt I couldn't send him back to "Hotel Hell" in the state that he was in, and it would seem kind of rude to suggest he crash on the sofa, especially as we'd had such a good night, despite the shocking start, so I guessed he could crash in my bed, because by now we'd had more time to bond, and felt very comfortable together. Plus, we were both tipsy on cheap beer!

"Do you wanna crash in my bed? I think there's enough room!" I said with a laugh. "Thanks, Della, if you're sure?" answered Jay. "Oh course!" I answered, thinking, I'd only said "crash" I wasn't sure" about anything else… "OK, thanks" answered Jay, as we both stood up. I quickly tidied up the table, and Jay helped me, before the two of us tottered off down the hallway towards my room, with our arms around each other. I quickly changed into my nighty, and Jay undressed to his T-shirt, and boxers, and the two of us crawled into bed and snuggled up together. It felt so perfect to cuddle, that anything more would have seemed wrong somehow. I felt a sense of pure love between us as we fell asleep.

The next morning Jay and I woke up around the same time and just lay snuggled up together until around 11 am. I stretched out, jumped out of bed, grabbed some clothes and popped to the bathroom to take a shower and get dressed for the day. Afterwards, Jay took a shower, got dressed, and we headed to the living room together to get some coffee and food. Jay helped me get our breakfast of cereal and coffee together, and soon the two of us were sitting at the dining table having breakfast and trying to wake up. No one else was in the living room, so it felt special to have a little time to ourselves.

"I'm thinking of heading up to Frisco for work soon, you're welcome to visit me. Who knows, maybe if you like it you will move up there with me?" said Jay with a sweet smile. "You mean San Francsico, right? I'd love to visit, I've yet to go there!" I answered, feeling not sure about the "moving there with him" bit, due to the fact that I would probably be leaving California soon, although it pained my heart to even think about leaving at this point. "Well, I guess I'd better get going," said Jay, after we finished our breakfast, and he helped me to clear the table. "Don't worry I'll wash up!" I told him, not wanting to hold him up if he had things to do. "If you're sure!" he answered earnestly. "Yeah, it's fine!" I answered as the two of us started heading towards the front door.

"I'll see you soon!" he said, giving me a hug and a sweet kiss on my cheek. "Yeah, I'll probably see you on the wall!" I answered with a grin. "I hope so!" he answered before he turned and ran off down the steps and up the street, turning back just before he disappeared, so that both of us could give each other one more wave goodbye. I really liked him, and he seemed to really like me too.

I didn't make it up to Hollywood for a few days, and what with one thing and another it slipped my mind to go and hang out with Jay on the wall, which made me question if I only liked him as a friend after all. He didn't phone me, or come down to visit me at Pico either, so I assumed he was too busy, and maybe he had realised that he also only liked me as a friend as well? Either way, I wasn't too bothered, as I was enjoying spending some quality time with the Pico crew, going on little walks around the neighbourhood, playing cards and board games, and spending time to myself in my bedroom listening to music, drawing, and journal writing. I certainly enjoyed my own company just as much as going out, so I was happy either way!

CHAPTER 44:

PATTY AND I DID IT AGAIN!

One night I got restless and decided to go up to Hollywood and hang out, and maybe visit Rishard and ask how Gabby was doing lately. I'd been keeping my distance from Gabby because the last time I hung out with her was not fun for me and the scene she was into was not really my thing, but she was a good person, and in some ways, she felt like my wayward sister, and I couldn't help but like her.

I got ready to go out and told Michael and Sonny that I'd see them sooner or later, and headed off down the street to catch the Hollywood bus. I decided that I wouldn't go straight to Rishard's, instead, I would spend a little "Go with the LA flow" time, which was one of my favourite things to do in my spare time.

As the bus turned left onto Hollywood Boulevard from Vine Street and cruised along, I jumped off at a random stop and headed over to the nearest liquor store. I bought some cans of Olde English Malt Liquor Beer, and figured that I would find a private spot to drink them, catch a buzz, and then go for a walkabout! I spotted an alleyway that looked safe enough as there were lots of stores at the front of it and lots of people around.

I headed down the alley, and around the back of the stores, and found a nice place to sit on a large concrete block that looked almost like a bench. There were palm trees nearby, and just enough light to feel comfortable. Feeling excited to be out on a mini adventure, I opened a can of beer and took a swig.

I could feel the booze kicking in as I relaxed a little, sat back looked up at the LA sky, and let out a sigh. 'Gosh, I even feel at home in an alleyway here!' I thought to myself with a laugh. Just then I heard footsteps and felt an instant sense of "fight or flight" as I wasn't sure what or who was about to come around the corner so I sat tensed up ready for action.

"Hey Della!" called out Patty's voice, and in the shadows, I could just about see Patty heading my way. "Oh my God, we've done it again! We found the same booze hideaway!" I joked, feeling in a state of surprise and disbelief that Patty had somehow appeared in this one tiny spot where I was in the whole of LA?!

"Cool!" she answered, with a laugh. "Yeah, great minds, eh?!" I added still not really believing that Patty had somehow magically joined me. I wondered if she had been driving, or walking along Hollywood Boulevard, and had spotted me heading down the alleyway with my booze, although, at the same time nothing struck me as bizarre when it came to the way Patty and I hung out. Together we seemed to create some kind of childlike magic where anything could happen!

"How did you find me here?" I asked, thinking that she must have at least had some kind of clue as to where I was. "I phoned the halfway house, and Mike told me you'd gone up to Hollywood, so I knew you were out and hoped I'd find you, but I didn't expect to find you here!" she laughed, looking as surprised as I was, as she cracked open one of her beer cans.

We each drank a couple of beers and continued our catch-up chat, and when we were feeling ready, we decided to head over to The Rainbow. I figured I would visit Rishard and co another time.

We headed back down Vine and jumped on the Sunset bus, and in no time, we arrived at The Rainbow. It was as vibrant as ever, with its usual mix of "Plastic-Rockers" and a few alternative types, and more real-looking rockers, like Patty and me. We headed upstairs to get some drinks. Just as we were heading down to the dance floor, I spotted Len, so I went over to say hi, while Patty continued on towards the dance floor.

It was great to see Len again, as it felt like it had been a while. I asked him how he was doing, and if he'd seen Peter. He said he hadn't seen him lately but had heard that he was seeing a girl in Westwood. "That's great news! To Peter!" I exclaimed as I raised my glass, reminding myself of Patty's "Peter O'Toole" cheers! "To Peter!" answered Len, as he raised his glass to clink mine. "Catch you later!" I told Len, as I headed back to the dance floor to join Patty.

CHAPTER 45:

JOHN GOODSALL, GOODSOUL

"Wanna come and visit Rishard with me?" I asked as the two of us seemed to start feeling a bit bored and restless after an hour or two of hanging out. "Sure!" answered Patty with a smile. So we headed out of the club onto Sunset Boulevard and hitchhiked east.

A rich-looking hippie guy, with dark brown curly hair, a moustache and a beard, stopped in a Bentley and picked us up. He had a friendly face and good vibes, so we both felt he was ok. He also had good music playing which Patty and I both liked. "Can you give us a lift anywhere near to Hollywood and Sycamore please?" I asked with a smile. "No problem girls!" he answered in an easy-going manner. "Thanks/Cool" we answered as we jumped inside his car. "Hi girls, I'm John!" said the guy, as he drove off. "Hi John, that's Patty, and I'm Della" I answered, giving Patty a grin.

"I like this music, what is it?" I asked curiously. "Yeah, it's cool!" added Patty. "Thanks, Girls, It's Jazz fusion, I'm playing the guitar!" answered John proudly. "Cool!" exclaimed Patty, "Yeah, I like it!" I added while getting comfy, and sitting back to enjoy our lift to Rishard's.

We arrived at the corner of Hollywood and Sycamore, and John stopped the car. "Here's my card, give me a call if you're ever out and about. I'm usually around!" said John as he passed us his card. "Ok, thanks, John!" I answered, taking the card of him, as Patty was getting out of the car. "Thanks, John, see ya!/Bye!" Patty and I called after him, as he drove off, giving us a wave as he went.

We strolled up to Rishard's and knocked on his door. Rishard opened the door and gave us both a big smile. "Girls, so lovely to see you!" exclaimed Rishard, as he gave us both a little hug, and kiss on the cheek. "You too Rishard, this is Patty!" I exclaimed, feeling happy to see him again, and not remembering if I'd taken Patty to visit Rishard before. "Wonderful" answered Rishard with a smile.

BOOK 1: TO SEE THE WORLD

"Rishard's name is actually Richard, but he prefers it to be pronounced the French way: Rishard!" I told Patty, in case she was wondering why I was pronouncing Richard differently. "Cool, I like it pronounced that way!" Patty exclaimed with a smile.

Rishard had soft lighting and jazz music playing, as usual, which was the perfect atmosphere to wind down to, after a night out dancing. "Hey Rishard, you like Jazz, have you ever heard of this guy?" I asked, handing him the card that John had just given us.

"Yes, that's John Goodsall, he's an excellent jazz guitarist" answered Rishard nodding and looking impressed by the card. "Ah, he's got a good soul too! He just gave us a lift" I joked back. "Yeah, he was cool!" exclaimed Patty. "Amazing!" said Rishard, as he gave us both an impressed smile as if to say "You never cease to surprise me!"

"Gabby has been asking about you, would you both like a beer?" He said politely as he made his way to the kitchen still smiling. "Sure/Yes Please!" we both answered, as we each found ourselves a futon to sit on in his cosy living room. We could tell that Rishard had been sitting on his director's chair, so neither of us sat there.

We spent the next couple of hours chatting, drinking beer, and listening to Jazz. It was nice to have such a lovely welcome. Rishard truly felt like a big brother to me, which was comforting. I felt that if I was ever in need, he would always be there to give me "Shelter from the storm"

"So, what's Gabby been up to lately?" I asked, curiously. "Oh, she has been living with some punk rockers near downtown LA, but she told me to tell you that she is still at the Café de Grand a lot if ever you wanted to catch up with her." Answered Rishard, in his usual laid-back French accent. "I'm glad she's ok, but that scene isn't really for me. Some of the people, like Gabby, are really nice, but overall, I just find it all too aggressive and negative, and it's just not my cup of tea. I prefer fun clubs, not angry clubs!" I answered, with a laugh. "Yes" answered Rishard nodded knowingly, as if he understood exactly what I meant. I found it interesting how Rishard had so many different types of friends, from all walks of life, yet he always stood firm and true to himself, with his own style and tastes, which I found to be an admirable quality about him.

"Well girls, I will go to sleep now. You are both welcome to stay over on the futons" said Rishard, as he stood up and yawned. "OK, thanks Rishard!" I answered, as Patty and I each folded out the futon chair beds we'd been sitting on, as Rishard popped to use the bathroom. "Domir bien!" called out Rishard, as he jumped into his bed behind the bamboo screen that separated his sleeping area from the living room. "Domir bien!" I called back. "Good night, Rishard!" called out Patty. Patty and I both got comfy on our futon beds and fell fast asleep.

Early the next morning I caught a glimpse of Rishard as he was opening the front door to leave. "There's food in the kitchen, and $10 on the side if you need to buy more" he whispered, upon noticing me waking up. "Thanks, Rishard" I answered, before falling back to sleep.

The next time I woke, it was nearing 12 noon. I could hear Patty washing up in the bathroom, so I headed to the kitchen, to make us some coffee. "Hey, Della," said Patty, as she entered the kitchen looking all scrubbed up. "Hey Patty, I've made us some coffee and found some pop-tarts that we can have for breakfast. I'll just pop to the loo to wash up!" I answered before I took off to use the bathroom. "OK, thanks, Della!" Patty called out after me.

I soon joined Patty back in the kitchen for breakfast, and as we sat drinking our coffees and eating our pop-tarts we chatted about how nice a guy Rishard was, and how he must come from a very nice family in the Belgian Congo. "He's so sophisticated!" said Patty in admiration. "Yeah, but down to earth at the same time. He has the perfect balance!" I answered as we both nodded in agreement. "Oh, and Rishard left this money for us to get some food if we want to?" I said to Patty as I held up the ten-dollar bill. "Cool!" said Patty looking pleased. "So, shall we go food shopping then?" I asked standing up and starting to feel like getting going. "Sure!" answered Patty as she finished her last bite of pop-tart, and drank the last drop of coffee. I quickly washed up our cups and plates, and we headed out of the door, I grabbed the spare key from the hook as I went.

We decided not to go straight to the grocery store, we would hang out for a bit first. As we both walked down Hollywood Boulevard, I was feeling high on life. The general atmosphere in LA always seemed to lift my spirits, and Hollywood in particular felt like a land where dreams and reality merged and became one! Patty seemed to be in a similar mood, as we both meandered along without a care in the world.

We suddenly bumped into the punks that were friends of Jay and I looked around to see if Jay was with them. "Hey Della, are you looking for Jay!" said a female voice, and I turned to see Jennie, the punk girl I'd hung out with on the wall when I first met Jay. "Not really, how's he doing?" I asked curiously. "He's good! He'll be back soon, he's on a beer run!" answered Jennie as if suggesting that we hang around a little longer. "OK, it'll be nice to see him!" I answered, as Patty and I jumped up and sat on the wall with the rest of the street-punks.

Jay soon arrived carrying a load of beers, and our eyes lit up to see each other. "Hey Della, great to see you, I was gonna call you later. I've made some cash working at a pen sales place, and wanted to ask you out to dinner" he said somewhat shyly. "Aw, thank you, that would be nice!" I answered, feeling the butterflies in my stomach, as my heart started to melt at his sweet gesture, although I also felt a little embarrassed by the idea of a proper dinner date, as I had become quite the wild child over these last few months, and partying on the streets with the bikers, rockers, and punks seemed to be more my scene.

I suddenly realised I'd never been on a proper date before, in the past I'd just hung out with guys, and sometimes the friendship turned into a romance, and sometimes it didn't, so to go on an actual date would be new territory for me, and I wasn't sure if I was comfortable with it, but at the same time it did seem so sweet of Jay to invite me, and it made me realise that maybe he did like me after all.

"So is seven o'clock at the Indian Restaurant at Sunset and Vine, ok?" asked Jay with a smile. "Yeah, that sounds great, see ya there!" I answered as Patty and I started to walk away. "Great, see ya there!" called back Jay. "See ya, Jennie!" I shouted as we headed off down the boulevard. "See ya Della!" called back Jennie, looking pleased for me and Jay.

Patty and I continued on with our walkabout along Hollywood Boulevard, just taking in all of the vibrant sights and sounds. "What did you think of Jay?" I asked Patty as we strolled along. "He was cute!" answered Patty cooly. "Yeah, he is" I answered with a grin. I liked how Patty didn't quiz me about him, she was very laid back about everything, including guys. "I guess I'll see him later!" I added, with a grin. "Cool!" answered Patty, grinning back. After a while, we went grocery shopping, then headed back to Rishard's apartment to stock his fridge and cupboards, relax and hang out.

Patty and I spent the afternoon hanging out at Rishard's just watching TV, chatting and eating snacks, until around six o'clock when Patty headed home to Long Beach and I got ready and headed off for my date with Jay. Rishard still hadn't come home yet, so I left a note for him, thanking him for his hospitality, and saying I'd see him soon.

393

CHAPTER 46:

FIRST EVER DATE - WITH JAY CONNER

I arrived at the Indian restaurant and headed inside. I spotted Jay sitting at a window seat and strolled over towards him. "Hey Della, good to see you, you look great!" exclaimed Jay as he jumped up, and gave me a big hug and a kiss on the cheek. "You too Jay!" I answered as I hugged him back. "Come and sit down" he said, as he led me to his table, and pulled out the seat for me to sit opposite him.

"Thanks, Jay!" I said, feeling happy to be on a proper date with him, although I did feel a little self-conscious as we were essentially two raggle-taggle street punk kids in a fancy restaurant surrounded by properly dressed-up grown-ups.

"I think you may like the vegetable biriani, it's not too strong," said Jay, as he opened up a menu and passed it to me. "Sounds good to me, thanks, Jay!" I answered as I went about reading the menu. The waiter came over to our table, and Jay ordered some Chardonnay for us both. I was impressed at Jay's sophisticated side, especially as he was a year younger than me and only seventeen.

"So how is the pen sales job?" I asked as we both sipped on our glasses of wine. "It's ok, you just call people up and sell 'em pens. Some people make hundreds a week doing it, but I only do it part-time, and make enough to get by" he answered matter-of-factly. "Do you think I could do it?" I asked, half joking, half curious. "Sure, they're always looking for people!" he answered with a grin. I wasn't sure I would fancy sales, especially after my short-lived jewellery selling career, although I assumed I would maybe enjoy sales if I truly believed in the product, I doubted I would enjoy selling just for selling's sake!

BOOK 1: TO SEE THE WORLD

We were having a lovely time and the restaurant, but I was finding it a little challenging to eat and talk at the same time. I wondered why couples chose such an awkward combination of actions, especially for a first date!

"How's the halfway house gig and your acting classes going?" he asked, as if genuinely interested. "The halfway house is fine, but I'm going off the acting classes! The people are nice, but they all seem a bit pretentious to me, it's as if their main goal is to be famous, or at least to know someone who's famous, they're always name-dropping famous actors as if it's some big deal, but I don't get it, we're all just people doing different jobs! I only went there for a bit of fun, but this superficial stuff isn't my cup of tea!" I answered, pulling a disgruntled face. "Have a glass of wine instead then!" Said Jay with a cheeky grin. "Don't mind if I do!" I answered pretending to be posh. We both laughed and sipped on our drinks, and I felt the butterflies flutter once again.

"So, how are you doing? Are you still staying at Hotel Hell, is San Francisco still on the cards?" I asked, curious to know what he'd been up to for the past week since I'd seen him last. "Things are going ok thanks. Yeah, still crashing at "Hotel Hell" but making enough money at the pen place to head up to Frisco soon. Would you consider joining me up there?" he answered, with a sweet smile.

I wasn't sure what to say, as on the one hand, we were still only friends, but sometimes it felt like he maybe wanted more than just friendship, but he'd yet to initiate anything, and neither had I, so we technically we were still just friends who were maybe testing the dating-waters with each other, but we were not yet an item, so why would we move to San Francisco together? It was way too soon for plans like that, plus I may be heading back to England soon! "I'd love to come up and visit!" I answered neutrally. "Great!" He answered with a big smile that melted my heart just a little more.

We finished our meals, drank the rest of the wine, and got ready to leave. Jay left a generous tip, and once again I was touched by what a nice guy he was. He had a tough-looking exterior, but he was a true gent' on the inside, and so mature for his age. We bid our farewells to the restaurant staff, and they told us to come back again soon. As far as a first proper date goes, or any date for that matter, it was a ten out of ten!

We took the bus back to Pico, and as usual, we were greeted by Mike and Sonny at the door. "Hi guys, want a beer?" asked Mike, looking pleased to see us, as Sonny shuffled about behind him, looking relatively pleased too. "Sure/Yes please!" Jay and I answered in unison. "You guys up for some card games, it was fun last time!" asked Mike, as he bought us our beers. "Thanks, Mike, yeah I am!" I answered, glancing at Jay, to see if he was up for it too. "Sure man!" answered Jay, looking pleased with our welcome.

We spent the next few hours drinking beers, playing card games, chatting, laughing and joking with Mike and Sonny. Around 2 am Mike and Sonny bid us both goodnight and headed off to bed. Jay and I tidied up the living room, took turns to use the bathroom to get ready for bed, and then headed down the hallway to my room. Once again it felt so lovely to just cuddle up together, as we fast fell asleep.

I woke in the morning and Jay was gone. He had left a note on the bedside table, reading that he would see me later. He also added the name and address of the pen place, telling me that Jennie would probably be glad if I could cover for her as she was off sick. He told me I'd need to speak to a guy named Brian Redland about it, and hopefully, I would be able to make a little pocket money. He'd signed off with a load of X's and O's which I remembered stood for kisses AND hugs in the States. In the UK they just put X's for kisses, so the hugs were a bonus!

I sat up in bed staring at the note and pondering on my feelings for Jay. I really wasn't sure how I felt. We did seem to like each other a lot, and my feelings for him were definitely developing, which felt like a good sign, but so far neither one of us had initiated anything, which created a strange sense of limbo between friendship and romance. I knew that deep down I was wary to get involved because of my travel plans, and he was such a sweet guy, that he would not want to rush anything. 'Oh well, coffee time!' I thought to myself before jumping out of bed, throwing some clothes on, and heading to the bathroom for a wash. After breakfast, I decided to head over to the pen place and see if they would let me cover for Jennie for a bit of pocket money. I took the busses, and it took about an hour to get there, which gave me plenty of time to daydream about sweet Jay.

I found the pen sales place and walked inside. "Hello, is Brian Redland here please?" "That's me!" Said a friendly-looking, slightly older, white Guy, with a big smile. "Oh, that was quick!" I joked, and we both laughed. "Um, Jay Conner said I may be able to cover for Jennie for a few days because she's off sick," I said smiling back.

"Ah, maybe!" he answered, seeming to like this idea. "Have a seat!" he said, gesturing towards some nearby seats. "Thanks" I answered, as I sat down, and he sat down near me. "So, do you have any phone sales experience?" he asked, as he got comfy in his chair. "Um, no not phone sales, but I did sell jewellery on the beaches in England" I answered, positively. "Oh, good, good!" he answered, sounding impressed. "Would you mind reading this?" he asked, picking up a piece of paper that looked like some kind of script. "OK!" I answered as I took it off him, took a deep breath and read the script while feeling kind of silly, yet enjoying it at the same time. "Ok, great! Wanna call some phone numbers and give it a go?" He asked enthusiastically. "OK!" I answered, feeling curious to try out. "Great, follow me!" he exclaimed. "OK!" I answered as I followed him.

He led me to a room where there was a big long table with people sitting around talking on telephones. They sounded as if they were speaking to potential customers. He placed a list of phone numbers on the table and pulled out a seat for me next to a young, good-looking, brown-haired guy who looked a couple of years older than me. I thanked him and sat down.

The good-looking guy and I smiled at each other, and I felt butterflies in my stomach. I wasn't sure what to make of that, especially as I was kind of going out with Jay. I picked up a phone handset and called a number from the list. A man answered and I started to read the script, as I was starting on the second part of the script, the man hung up on me. I blushed with embarrassment while feeling not sure that I wanted to carry on.

"Don't worry about it, just keep going!" exclaimed Brian in a hushed tone. "OK," I answered, as I dialled the next number. This time a woman who apparently couldn't hear me answered the phone and just kept saying hello. I burst out laughing, and the good-looking guy sitting next to me started to look over at me and grin, but he managed to keep his composure and carry on with his call. "Sorry wrong number!" I exclaimed as I hung up the phone. "She couldn't hear me, she kept saying hello!" I explained to Brian in a whisper, not wanting to disturb the others.

"It's ok, we get all sorts of people on the other end, it's best to just keep going. Want a coffee?" he asked in a relaxed way, which made me feel better. "Yes please" I answered. "Sure!" he answered, as he took off out of the room. I continued to dial numbers. Each time I hung up with a sigh, feeling that maybe I was just no good at it. "Don't sweat it!" said the good-looking guy sitting next to me, as he hung up his phone at the same time as me. "Thanks" I answered, feeling myself blush a little. I picked up the phone again and dialled the next number.

"How's it going?" asked Brian as he arrived back with my coffee. "Not too well!" I answered, feeling really bad as if I was there just wasting everyone's time.

"Don't worry, you'll soon get in the swing of it!" he answered optimistically. "Thanks!" I answered, feeling that the combination of embarrassment from making cold-phone calls, while sitting next to a good-looking guy made me feel like I just wanted to get out of there, never mind get in the swing of it!

The good-looking guy sitting next to me hung up his phone, and stretched out, as if ready for a breather. "Great work Johnny!" Exclaimed Brian to the good-looking guy. 'Oh no, not another one!' I thought to myself, as my mind flashed to "Sid Vicious Johnny" although this guy seemed a lot warmer and laid-back by miles. "So, Della, I've got some paperwork for you to fill out" Said Brian, gesturing for me to follow him just as it felt like "New Johnny" and I were on the verge of having a little chat. "OK," I answered, as I stood up to follow him. "See ya" I mumbled to "New Johnny" as I turned to follow Brian to his office.

"So, how long do you think you can stick around?" Brian asked enthusiastically. "Um, well I'd only be covering for Jennie, I'm an au pair at a halfway house, and I'm probably heading back to England soon" I answered, not sure what he meant by stick around. "Ah, too bad, well if you ever want a job here, come and see me!" he said looking disappointed. "...I know you haven't made a sale yet, but you have a lovely voice, and a great phone manner, so you will definitely make sales if you stick with it!" he added as if trying to convince me to stay. "Oh, thanks, maybe if I come back after England!" I answered with a smile, feeling pleased that somehow I'd got the job, even if I wasn't available for it! "No problem!" he answered with a big smile.

"Is there anywhere I can get some food near here?" I asked, suddenly feeling hungry. "Sure, if you wanna go get some lunch down the street, feel free! Just head east, there are a few places, you'll see!" He answered casually. "OK, great thanks!" I answered as I picked up my army shoulder bag. "No problem, see you later!" he answered, as he headed back towards the phone room. "See ya!" I called out after him, as I took off out of the front door. 'Pen sales are not for me!' I thought to myself, as I picked up speed. I suddenly realised that I didn't have to go back if I didn't want to! I was feeling so happy to be free again, that my decision was pretty much made for me – I wasn't going back!

I suddenly felt a pang of sadness that I wouldn't see "New Johnny" if I didn't go back, which was followed by a feeling of instant guilt at my liking another guy when Jay was being so nice to me. 'Yeah, but we're not a proper couple yet' I told myself, trying to ease the guilt.

CHAPTER 47:

JAZZ

A bus soon came along heading east, so I decided to jump on it. I figured that I would explain to Jay that it just wasn't for me, and ask him to give my apologies to Jennie and Brian. I headed back to Hollywood and found the punks at the wall. I was surprised to see Jennie there, so I went over to say hi and ask her how she was doing, and tell her about my time at the pen sales gig.

"Hi Della!" exclaimed Jennie looking pleased to see me as she gave me a big hug. "Hi Jennie, I thought you were sick! I kind of covered for you today" I said laughing, "I was sick, I felt better this morning though, but I still wanted a day off!" She answered, and we both laughed. "I know what you mean, I wanted the day off too, and it was my first day - so I quit!" I answered, and we both cracked up laughing.

"Panhandling is easier!" she joked back. "Yeah, I bet!" I answered while thinking that Panhandling was a curious name for begging. I assumed it originated from maybe passing a pan around for people to put money in, similar to the way some musicians pass around a hat after busking.

I looked around to see if Jay was about, but there was no sign of him "Jay's at the church!" Said Jennie, as if reading my mind. "The church?" I answered, feeling confused as to what he would be doing at a church. "Yeah, there's a TV crew over at the church interviewing street punks, do you want to go see?" she asked enthusiastically. "Yeah ok!" I answered, curious to see what it was all about.

It took us about ten minutes to walk over to the church. I followed Jennie inside. The room was full of street punks and street kids. I recognise some of them from the wall. The atmosphere felt quite heavy and serious, and the room was very still and quiet.

There was a TV camera crew interviewing one of the kids. I suddenly felt like some kind of imposter hanging out with these real runaways, but then it dawned on me that I was only just 18 myself, and around six thousand miles away from home, so I was sort of in a similar situation to these kids, but by now I was convinced that it was all just a state of mind, besides my family and friends knew where I was… Kind of!

I listened to the kids being interviewed and heard some really sad stories of abuse and neglect at home, and how many of the kids felt safer on the streets than at home. From what they were saying, even staying at "Hotel Hell" was a better option, than the hell they had lived through at home. I wondered what Jay had maybe gone through at home, and my heart hurt for him, and all of the other kids who had suffered abuse at the very place where they were meant to be loved, nurtured and kept safe.

One punk guy told the TV crew a sad story about a girl named Jazz. She had hitchhiked with some guy and he had murdered her. The punks were all very upset and angry about this as she had been a good friend of theirs. I was sickened that someone would do something so horrific to someone who was already in a vulnerable position, and simply in need of help.

When they broke from filming Jennie and I got chatting to some punks, and she asked if they'd seen Jay. They told her that he hadn't stuck around long, because he had to get to work. I suddenly felt embarrassed at what Brian might be saying to Jay about me doing a runner! "Oh no, I wonder what Brian will say to Jay about me taking off?" I exclaimed to Jennie pulling a cringing face. "Don't worry about it, most people take off after five minutes, sounds like you stayed longer!" She answered as if trying to make me feel better. "Oh yeah, I stayed a whole twenty minutes!" I joked, and we both laughed. "Wanna go get some beers?" asked Jennie suddenly. "Sounds good!" I answered as we joined the line of punks funnelling back out of the church.

We went to a nearby liquor store bought some beers, and then headed back outside the church to hang out with some of the punks there. Everyone was chatting about the TV interviews, and some were saying they hoped their folks didn't see them on TV.

As Jennie chatted with some of her friends I sat on the paving stones next to her and sipped my beer while wondering how on earth I had got there. It all felt like a strange dream. My mind went back to that morning I left my hometown with a fiver in my pocket, and how I had just hitchhiked off from my cousin's place down to my Aunt Freda's the new forest. Suddenly I remembered that my Aunt Freda would be arriving in a few weeks and that I would probably be heading back to England with her. I felt so sad at the thought of leaving LA, as by now it truly felt like my second home, and my friends there felt like family, also something special seemed to be developing between Jay and me. Once again, that old familiar feeling of being torn between people, places, and things came back with a vengeance. I reminded myself that I would be making regular trips back to LA to visit, which made me feel just a little better.

I got out my pen and notepad from my army shoulder bag and jotted down a note to remind me to get a new passport. I hoped it wouldn't be too expensive. "Wanna head back to the wall?" asked Jennie, as most of the punks started leaving the church car park, and heading back down towards the boulevard. "OK," I answered, jumping up and finishing my beer. We threw our empty beer cans in the nearest trash can and started heading back down the street. I'd noticed that it seemed to be ok to drink in public as long as the booze was concealed in a brown paper bag. It seemed a curious little game to me, but it was normal to my LA friends, so naturally, I went along with it.

Jennie and I headed back down to the wall on Hollywood Boulevard, jumped up and sat on it. By now the boulevard was in full swing for the evening with the usual carnival of cars cruising past playing loud music, partygoers, street kids, and tourists all milling about, with the occasional mentally ill person shouting out random things, just for good measure!

"There you go!" Said Jennie passing me another beer in a brown paper bag. "Thanks!" I answered, as I opened it, and took a sip. We sat shooting the breeze, sipping on our beers, and watching the Hollywood world go by with the rest of the street-punks. I liked how I felt comfortable with all sorts of people, from all walks of life, as long as they were nice. I wondered if Rishard was similar, and that was why he was also friends with all types of people. We seemed to value the essence of people, rather than their status in life.

We were all having a laugh about something or other when Jay arrived looking out of breath. He looked happy to see me and came straight over and jumped up on the wall next to me, and gave me a nice big hug and a kiss on my cheek. "Brian said you took off!" exclaimed Jay with a big grin. "Yeah! I couldn't stand it!" I answered, pulling a horrified face. "Don't worry, it's not for everyone!" said Jay in an understanding tone, as he put his arm around me. I loved how caring and wise he was, and once again I felt my heart melt.

As we chatted, I saw the name Jazz written on the wall in black marker and I realised that it must be the girl who was murdered. "I heard the sad story about Jazz at the church," I said, as we sat snuggled up to each other. "Yeah, the guy that did that can rot in hell!" said Jay suddenly looking very upset and angry. I could tell that Jay and his friends had all been very fond of Jazz. "What a terrible thing to have happened to a girl who was already having a rough time at home," I said feeling on the verge of tears. Jay squeezed his arm tighter around me, and we both leaned our heads against each other and sat in silence for a few moments.

"I hope you can come and visit me in Frisco!" said Jay, suddenly breaking the silence. "I hope so too" I answered, genuinely looking forward to visiting him there. "So do you know where you'll be staying up there?" I asked, curious if he had any family or friends to stay with. "Not sure yet, I'll probably rent a cheap hotel room in the Tenderloin, I'll send you my address, once I get one!" answered Jay, and we both laughed.

"I'll probably be working for a courier company called: Quick Silver" He added, looking as if he was looking forward to it. "Oh right, let me jot that down, just in case we lose each other somehow, I can always go there to ask about you!" I answered, as I dug out my pen and notepad from my bag, and wrote: Jay – Quick Silver. "I hope we don't lose each other!" said Jay, as he held my hand. "Me too!" I answered as a wave of sadness swept through me. "I'll write you as soon as I get situated up there, I hope you'll write me back?" he said with a cheeky grin. "Of course I will!" I answered, grinning back, as we sat cuddled up on the wall, watching Hollywood go by.

"I'd better head home," I said, suddenly feeling tired. "OK sweetie" said Jay as we gave each other a big hug, and a little kiss. I jumped down off the wall and, waved goodbye to the others. "See ya soon!" I called out, as I took off. "Bye/See ya!" they called back, as I headed down Hollywood Boulevard to catch the Pico bus.

CHAPTER 48:

FRISCO – PART 1

A few days later a letter arrived from San Francisco. It was from Jay telling me about his new job, his hotel room and the friends he'd made. He ended it by saying that he hoped I would visit soon. I was really happy to hear from him, but I was still feeling very confused about us and didn't really have a clue what we were to each other. For me, it felt like we were affectionate friends, with the potential for more, but he was writing to me as if I were his girlfriend, and he was my boyfriend and I wasn't sure how to respond, so I decided that I would just go with the flow, as usual!

We wrote to each other for a couple more weeks, and then one day I decided I would surprise-visit him in San Francisco, or "Frisco" as he and the other punks called it. I picked up the phone and called Larry, hoping that he would be ok with me taking off for a couple of weeks. "Hi Larry, how are you?" I asked when he answered his phone. "I'm well thank you, Della, how are things going for the English girl on Pico?" answered Larry, in his usual jokey way.

"I'm ok thanks Larry, I was wondering if it would be ok for me to take a couple of weeks off, as I'd like to see some more of California and I've been invited to visit a friend up in San Francisco. My aunt Freda isn't free to visit for a few more weeks, and hopefully, Mary won't mind" I asked enthusiastically. "Sure, you can go for a month if you like! Linda can cover for Mary! She's already asked me about helping out sometime. I'll ask Mary to give you some extra pocket money, because you've been a great help at the halfway house, and the residents love you. You deserve a break, dear Delilah!" exclaimed Larry.

"Aww, thanks Larry, and I love them too!" I answered, feeling touched to hear that the residents thought so well of me, and pleased that he thought I'd been a great help too. "OK Della, have a good "Holiday" my dear!" he exclaimed, putting on an English accent for the word: Holiday. "Fank you guvna!" I answered, putting on a cockney accent, and we both laughed. "Bye dear!" said Larry. "See ya!" I replied, and we both hung up.

I suddenly felt really excited at the thought of my little getaway to visit Jay, even though I wasn't sure about us as a couple, I still really liked him as a person as he was so sweet and lovely. I also looked forward to visiting "Frisco" for the first time!

The next day, I got ready and packed up my tote bag to use as a holiday bag. As I was packing, Mary knocked on my door and gave me £30 dollars extra pocket money from Larry, and wished me a fun visit to San Francisco. I thanked her and put the money safely in my army shoulder bag.

Once I was ready to go, I headed to the living room to say goodbye to the Pico crew. "Have a great time!" exclaimed Mike, looking happy for me, as usual, while the others stood around smiling, and looking a little confused as if they thought I was leaving. "Thanks, Mike, I'll see you all in a couple of weeks or so" I answered, as I headed for the door. "Bye Della/Have a good time/See ya!" they all called out as I left. "See ya!" I called back, as I walked out of the open front doors, and trotted down the steps.

Mike came out to stand at the top of the steps to wave, so I waved goodbye one last time, then headed off down the street and jumped on the Hollywood bus. I decided that I would go and see if Jennie was about in Hollywood, and ask her if she wanted to hitch with me up to Frisco.

I soon found Jennie sitting on the wall on Hollywood Boulevard. "Hey Jennie, do you fancy hitchhiking up to San Francisco with me to surprise Jay?" I asked enthusiastically. "Sure! He'll be stoked to see us!" she answered, with a big smile, as if loving the idea.

"Wanna beer first?" asked Jennie, as she pulled a beer can from her bag. "Yeah ok, thanks!" I answered, as I jumped up on the wall and sat next to her. "There ya go!" she said, handing me a can of generic beer. "Thanks!" I answered, as I took the can, and opened it up. "Here, put it in this!" she said, passing me a brown paper bag. "Thanks!" I answered, as I popped my beer into the bag, and took a sip.

Jennie and I sat on the wall drinking beers for a bit longer with the other punks, while chatting about our plan to surprise visit Jay. The tipsier we got, the more I looked forward to seeing him. 'Maybe I do really like him after all?' I thought to myself tipsily. It was strange to have the sense that I really liked someone but was holding my feelings back, but deep down I knew it was because of my travel plans. 'Oh no, not again!' I thought to myself, suddenly feeling really mixed up and confused, as my mind flashed to Jeff in Toronto, and the similar struggle I'd had between my feelings for him, and my longing to travel.

"When shall we go?" I asked Jennie as I finished my beer "Now?" she answered, in a questioning tone, while laughing. "Yeah, why not now? ...how do we get there?" I asked, laughing back. "The freeway! it's not far, we can walk over there" answered Jennie with a grin. "let's go!" I said feeling excited at the thought of a San Francisco adventure! We both jumped down off the wall, said goodbye to the other punks, and feeling high on cheap booze and life, we headed over towards the freeway.

We walked for about ten minutes until we reached a freeway on-ramp, then we stuck out our thumbs and started hitchhiking. I loved that the two of us were so free-spirited. We were two new-wave/punk-rock girls, both of us eighteen years old, hitchhiking from Los Angeles to San Francisco around midnight, and the sense of pure freedom it brought, made me feel on top of the world!

Soon a truck stopped with a friendly-looking guy driving it. He reached over to open up the passenger door for us, and we spent a few seconds chatting with him, and getting a feel for if he was ok. He didn't have any bad vibes, so we both climbed up the steps and jumped in.

He took off driving down the freeway and we all continued our chat. His name was Bill, he was about twenty-something, with dark hair and a dark beard. He seemed more like a fun-spirited rocker than a trucker, as he had upbeat rock music playing songs like Bye-Bye Silver-lining, Money Honey, and We Got to Get Out of This Place, as we zoomed along, and before we knew it we were all singing along to the songs at the tops of our lungs, and having a blast!

After a while, Bill pulled in at a rest station for us to go use the bathroom, and have a coffee break. While we drank our coffees in the restaurant area Bill offered us some caffeine pills to help us stay awake. This seemed a good idea, so we both said ok and washed them down with our coffees. We enjoyed the rest of the ride and stayed wide awake for the duration.

"So why are you going to San Francisco?" Bill asked curiously, during a lull in the music. "To surprise our friend Jay!" I answered excitedly, while Jennie nodded in agreement. "That's great! I'm sure your friend Jay will be happy to see you both! Said Bill. "I hope so!" I answered, and we all laughed.

As we rode up Pacific Coast Highway, the three of us singing along to the radio, I spotted a sign that read: Oakland, and I suddenly remembered that that was the name of the place I'd pinned on my dad's world map, and I couldn't believe that I was actually there, it felt like a dream, especially as I was already feeling a little delirious from lack of sleep, and on a fun high from our singalong. 'I can't wait to tell Geoff!' I thought to myself excitedly, knowing that he would be chuffed to hear that I'd passed by Oakland on route to San Francisco!

We were all in great spirits as we rolled into the San Francisco Bay area at dawn. We suddenly came to a large bridge that looked like it led directly into the city. "Oh wow, is this the Golden Gate Bridge?!" I asked Bill excitedly, as I was sure I'd seen it in movies and on posters before.

"Nah, it's the Oakland Bay Bridge. The Golden Gate Bridge is further down the bay" he answered, as he merged with the other traffic, and started to drive across the bridge. "Oh well, this bridge will do! It's still just as fab looking!" I exclaimed, feeling elated to be arriving at such an iconic city as San Francisco! "Yep/Sure is!" answered Bill and Jennie in agreement.

As the San Francisco skyline came into view, including a slim pyramid-shaped building, I still felt as though I was in a dream, and it was the best feeling ever. "I enjoyed your company girls" said Bill as he parked up. "Thanks, Bill likewise/You too man!" answered Jennie and I as we got our bags ready to leave. "Here, call me if you need anything!" said Bill, as he handed us a piece of paper with his contact details on it. "Thanks, Bill/Thanks man!" answered Jennie and I, as Jennie took the piece of paper off him.

We both jumped down out of his truck, and onto the streets of San Fransico. Bill pulled his truck out, and we all waved goodbye. He honked his horn and took off. "What a lovely guy!" I exclaimed. "Yeah, he was cool!" answered Jennie, as we headed off down the street, not sure exactly where we were going.

The air was fresh and breezy, and cooler than the LA air, and although we were tired it was invigorating to my senses. Jennie seemed to know the area a little, and after asking a female passerby for directions she led the way down the awakening city streets until we arrived at the block where Jay was staying.

We soon found his hotel and rang the bell. A doorman opened the front doors, left them wide open, and went back to his desk. "Hi, we're here to see Jay!" announced Jennie, as we stepped inside the reception area. "We have his address, is it ok to use the lift?" I asked, showing the doorman the piece of paper I had with Jay's name and address on it, and feeling as though we maybe needed permission to go any further. "Sure, go ahead" answered the doorman, gesturing towards the lift. "Thank you/Thanks!" we both answered, as we headed for the lift.

"I can't wait to crash!" exclaimed Jennie leaning back against the wall of the lift, and looking tired. "Yeah, me too!" I answered, also leaning back on another wall of the lift. "Oh my god, what if he's with someone else!?" I exclaimed to Jennie, suddenly realising that could be a possibility. "We'll see!" said Jennie with a laugh, and I suddenly felt like taking off back to LA!

We found room 11, and Jennie knocked on the door. We both stood there waiting for a few moments, but there was no answer, so I knocked a little louder. "Who's there?" called out Jay's sleepy voice. "Surprise!" shouted Jennie, while I stood there cringing, half of me feeling I wanted to be there, and the other half of me wanting to run away - hoping that he wasn't with anyone!

"Oh wow!" exclaimed Jay with a big smile, as he opened the door. When he looked at me his face lit up. "Wow, it's great to see you both, come in!"! he exclaimed giving us both a massive hug. "Great to see you too Jay, but we need to crash!" exclaimed Jenni. "Yeah, it's great to see you, but we're so tired!" I added as I nodded in agreement. "You can both crash on my bed, I have to go to work soon!" he answered obligingly.

"Thanks, Jay/Thanks man!" answered Jennie and me. "No problem guys, it's so good to see you both!" Jay answered, as he came over and gave us both another hug, this time with a little kiss on the cheek for each of us. He was such a sweet, loving guy, albeit in a tough-looking shell.

Jennie and I took turns to use his bathroom, and while Jennie was in the bathroom Jay came and sat next to me on the bed. "Thanks for coming up," he said, as he gave me another hug and a sweet kiss on my forehead. I hugged him back, and we sat for a moment cuddled up together in silence, and I wondered what our futures held.

Jennie came back out of the bathroom, and Jay jumped up to use the bathroom and get ready for work. "Night Jay/ Goodnight!" Jennie and I called out, as we both flaked out on his bed. "Sleep well girls, I'll see you both later!" he called back, just before I heard the shower start up.

A few hours later we were woken by someone in the hallway outside shouting "No Deal! No Deal!" at someone. "What's going on?" I said to Jennie as we both slowly sat up rubbing our faces, and heads and pulling faces at the shouting noises coming from the hallway. "I don't know, but I wish they'd shut up!" answered Jennie, and we both laughed.

We took turns using the bathroom and made ourselves some coffee in the tiny kitchen area, then we sat on a couple of chairs sipping our coffees like two zombies waiting for the caffeine to kick in. The only view we had from Jay's room was of an alleyway, so after a while, we decided to go out and about. We left Jay a note and took off.

The streets of San Francisco reminded me of London and Toronto. There were all types of people mixing and milling about, and it was very vibrant and upbeat, with a gritty edge to it. "This is the Tenderloin, it's a rough area, but it's fun!" said Jennie as we walked along. "I like it!" I answered, and we both laughed and set off to explore.

I loved the diversity that surrounded us! There were; arty types, tough guys and gals, students, punks, old people, young people, and quite a few Jewish guys in Cafes looking like they were having serious discussions.

Just as I was soaking in the atmosphere, an animal rights march came around the corner and I was handed a flyer showing a dog wired up to a machine "This is sickening!" I exclaimed, showing the flyer to Jennie. "Sure is!" she answered, as she pulled a face, and nodded in agreement.

We walked on for a while until we found a community arts centre, with all types of people hanging about in and around it "Dinner at 5 pm - free" read a sign in the window. Just then a group of cool-looking artist types trundled inside carrying books, and what looked like their art gear in large bags. "Wow, I like the vibes here!" I exclaimed to Jennie. "Yeah, it's cool man!" she answered looking as impressed as I was. We spent the rest of the afternoon, strolling the street of San Francisco taking in the eclectic sights and sounds, and eventually, we headed back to Jay's hotel.

Just as we got to the doorway of the hotel Jay arrived back too. "Great timing!" he joked, flashing us his cute smile, and we all laughed. We all went inside together and greeted the doorman. He nodded hello back to us as we passed by on our way to catch the lift upstairs to Jay's room.

Jay opened the door to his room, and we all piled inside and sat around. "I'm treating you both to a Chinese dinner tonight! Chinatown is nearby, and it's excellent!" exclaimed Jay, looking pleased to be able to treat us. "Wow/Cool, thanks Jay!" we answered with big grins on our faces. We each took turns to take a shower and get freshened up, and then we headed back out and onto the streets of San Francisco.

As we walked along, I noticed that Jay suddenly seemed very hyper. He started walking erratically, while nervously swinging a long black umbrella up and down like a walking cane, randomly swinging it around and striking out at the air, as if ready to attack any thugs that may come our way. At one point he nearly lashed out at a passing car with the tip of the umbrella, which seemed totally uncalled for as the car was simply just driving by. He suddenly started talking very fast, about nonsensical stuff, and I gave Jennie a confused look.

"Speed, he was hooked on it before he did time, now he's back on it!" whispered Jennie quietly. My heart sank, as I felt myself going off him. It seemed such a shame, especially as I was truly starting to develop feelings for him. Drugs were not my thing at all. I enjoyed getting a little tipsy, but that was about it, as I liked to keep my faculties about me. Besides, I always had such a great time sober, so I didn't really need anything to get me high! I wasn't against others partying on occasion, it was their business, and as long as they weren't hurting anyone, I was very "Live and let live" in attitude, but to get involved with someone who was apparently hooked on stuff was not for me at all! It would be way too much hard work, and I was sure that ultimately it would bring more grief than joy.

The three of us walked along in silence, and I started to regret making the trip up there. 'Oh well, may as well make the most of it now that we're here though!' I thought to myself, as I took a deep breath, and carried on walking.

We soon arrived at Chinatown, and it was an amazing sight to see! The streets were lined with beautiful Chinese-style architecture, and the buildings were fabulously decorated with Chinse lanterns, colourful lights and street signs. Normally I would have expressed my joy at such a sight out loud, but Jay's behaviour had led to me clamming up somewhat.

Jay led the way into a Chinese restaurant "Hello, Mr Jay" said a friendly Chinese man as he came to welcome us. "Hi, Mr Yow, this is my friend Jennie, and my girlfriend Della" answered Jay putting his arms around both of us. I felt embarrassed as this was the first time he had referred to me as his girlfriend, and it happened to be just as I was going off the idea of being with him! Jennie and I stood smiling politely and shook hands with Mr Yow. "Come, sit down, sit down" Said, Mr Yow as he pulled out chairs for us around a table.

We went on to have a lovely meal, and a good night chatting, laughing, and joking, although with Jay being high on speed, it made me feel somewhat uneasy and uncomfortable throughout. Jennie was very cool though, and just went along with things. One thing I noticed, and liked, about these street-punk kids, was that they were often wise beyond their years. I guessed they'd had to be, bringing themselves up in homes that were lacking love, protection, and guidance. Later we all headed back to Jay's, and Jay let us crash on his bed, while he crashed on the floor. He was such a true gentleman, despite his apparent addiction issues.

The next morning Jennie and I woke up. I noticed the bathroom door was wide open. There was no sign of Jay, so I guessed that he'd gone to work already. I spotted a note he'd left on the side table reading that he would see us later, he'd signed off with an x for a kiss, which made my heart flutter a little, even though, for the most part, I felt that it would not be a good idea to carry on with our seedling relationship.

Jennie and I got ready, drank coffee, and went out to explore San Francisco some more. It was such a fun city to walk around. I enjoyed the atmosphere, and in some ways, it seemed more real than LA, maybe it was because there was such a diverse mix of people everywhere, as it wasn't as segregated as LA was, and I didn't see any of the plastic-looking, beautiful people swanning around looking to see and be seen.

We just meandered around, found cheap food places for snacks and drinks, sat around in various parks and squares watching the world go by, and had random chats with local street punks, some of them were acquaintances of Jennie's, who had moved up from LA. Around 4 pm, we headed back to Jay's.

We had another good night out at a local Pizza place, eating pizzas, drinking beers and playing pool. This time Jennie and I insisted on treating Jay, which he eventually went along with. Afterwards, we headed back to Jay's place, all of us exhausted after another action-packed day. This time Jennie insisted on crashing out on some cushions on the floor so that Jay and I could share the bed. We soon fell asleep, with our arms wrapped gently around each other. I still felt a love between us, but wasn't sure if it would have a chance to grow.

The next day I woke up and both Jay and Jennie were gone. I used the bathroom, got dressed, got myself a coffee, and sat staring out of the window at the alleyway wall thinking about our visit so far, while slowly waking up.

"Hey Della, I've got to get back to LA, they need me at work!" exclaimed Jennie, as she suddenly appeared through the front door. "Oh really?" I answered, feeling a little surprised that we may be leaving so soon. "Yeah, but you can stay here with Jay, he's so happy to see you!" answered Jennie, as if trying to convince me to stay on.

For a moment I felt confused as to what to do, but I decided I didn't want to stay on with Jay and let Jennie hitchhike alone back to LA, especially as she had hitched up with me in the first place. "Nah, it's ok, I'll hitch back with you, it's only fair, I mean, you hitched up with me!" I answered with a little laugh. "Honestly man, I'll be fine, stay with Jay, you two need some alone time!" answered Jennie convincingly.

"No really, I'd rather go back with you, I'm not even sure I want to see Jay any more if he's hooked on speed!" I answered, with a sigh. "Aw man, I don't know if he's hooked - he just does it a lot!" answered Jennie, and we both cracked up laughing.

"Well, either way, I'd rather go back to LA with you!" I answered as Jennie grabbed her things together, and I started packing up my little tote bag. My instinct was to leave. I felt that there would be no point in my staying on, as things would only be awkward between us, plus there was no way I would let Jennie hitchhike back alone. "OK man, Jay's not gonna like it though, he is SO stoked that you're here!" answered Jennie, as if in one last-ditch attempt to persuade me to stay.

Jay arrived home early afternoon, and we broke the news that we would be leaving soon. "Aw man, I thought you would both stick around a while, what about you Della, can you stay for a while?" asked Jay, looking disappointed. "Nah, it wouldn't be fair to let Jennie hitchhike back alone, she only came up here with me because I asked her to, so I should go back with her" I answered, feeling like it was a smooth exit for me that would hopefully not involve hurting Jay's feelings. "I'm fine man, honestly!" exclaimed Jennie, before popping to the bathroom, as if to give us some privacy.

"I'll buy Jennie a bus ticket back if you like?" answered Jay, with a glimmer of optimism shining from his eyes. "Thanks, but I should probably get back anyway because my Aunt Freda will be visiting in a few weeks' time, and I'll probably be flying back to England with her, and I need to get a new passport sorted, as mine was taken with all my stuff in Virginia" I answered, feeling that now was as good a time as ever to let him know my travel plans.

Jay looked devastated at my news. I guess I hadn't mentioned going back to England before now, so the news must have come as a shock to him. I felt terrible for letting him down, and for a moment I felt like I wanted to stay with him, and just make everything alright between us, but instead, I kept a cool front, as I started getting my things together. "OK Della, well stay in touch" answered Jay, flatly, as if resigning himself to the fact that I was leaving. "I will" I answered.

"OK guys, what's the deal?" asked Jennie, as she appeared out of the bathroom. "We're hitching back to LA, it's for the best because I've just remembered I need to get my passport sorted before my aunt arrives in a few weeks" I answered, feeling it best to put the focus on my things to do, as the main reason for leaving, rather than Jay's erratic speed episode from the night before. "OK cool, let's go!" answered Jennie, as she grabbed her bag. "OK," I answered, as I grabbed my bag, and Jay led the way out.

Jay walked with us up to a street that we could hitch from, and we all said our goodbyes. Jay gave me a big hug, and I found myself pulling a face at Jennie as if to say I didn't want to hug him, I instantly felt bad about it, because deep down I did want him to hug me, and I wanted to hug him back, I was just put off by his speed taking. I hoped that Jennie would realise that.

Jennie and I walked away and waved goodbye. As we started heading towards the freeway a group of Punks, who I recognised from the Hollywood wall jumped out of a van across the street and waved over at us in recognition. We smiled, waved back, and carried on walking for the freeway on-ramp. As we neared the entrance to the freeway, we started sticking out our thumbs, and within seconds a big rig truck stopped for us, so we ran to catch up with it.

"Bills Big Rig" was written on the side of it, which cracked us both up. Jennie climbed up to check him out and asked if he was going anywhere near LA. "Sure am!" he answered, and she climbed on in. I followed suit, figuring that he must be ok if Jennie was ok with him. "Bill!" he exclaimed, reaching out his hand. "Jennie and Della!" Jennie answered, as they shook hands and I waved and nodded hello. Bill was very fun and friendly, similar to most of the truckers that I'd met before. He was also very hospitable and seemed glad of our company.

As we neared the outskirts of LA, I suddenly felt a sense of homecoming, which was a pleasant surprise to me. I looked forward to getting back and spending time with the Pico gang and my LA friends, as by now, they all felt like family to me.

The Pico gang looked very happy and somewhat surprised to see me, as they welcomed me back. Mike, Sonny and I spent the evening catching up with our latest stories while drinking coffee, eating food and watching TV. Then we bid our goodnights to each other and headed off to our rooms. I slept like a log!

The next morning, I phoned Larry and told him that I was back from San Francisco. "That was quick! You can save the rest of your "holiday" for another time if you want to?" he said, seeming surprised that I was back so soon. "OK, thanks, Larry!" I answered, figuring that I would spend some of those free days with Aunt Freda when she arrived. I hadn't mentioned that I'd probably be going back to England with her yet, as I felt it best to wait until nearer the time. "Sure, no problem, tally ho!" answered Larry with a chuckle. "Jolly good! Pip Pip!" I joked back, and we both hung up the phone laughing. I loved how Larry was so fun and easy to get along with.

Over the next few days, I phoned my grandad's house and managed to speak to my dad Geoff on the phone. It was great to hear his voice again after so long. "Hey Geoff, guess where I kind of was the other day?" I asked with a giggle. "Um, Disneyland?" guessed my dad. "Nooo, better than that; OAKLAND! Remember the place on the map I pinned as my "goal destination" near San Francisco?" I answered excitedly. "Oh yes, that's great news! Well done Angel!" he exclaimed, sounding really happy for me.

"Thanks! I didn't visit, because we were on our way to San Francisco, but it was great to be so near! Oh, by the way, would you be able to send my birth certificate over please, my old passport got lost, so I need to get a new one" I asked, not wanting to worry him with the backstory as to how my passport got "lost." "Sure Del, I'll get you one sorted as soon as possible, I'll post it out by registered mail!" he answered obligingly. "Thanks, Geoff! Give my love to everyone!" I answered, feeling excited at the prospect of having a passport again. "OK Angel, stay safe, happy travels!" he exclaimed. "Thanks, See ya!" I answered before we both hung up.

CHAPTER 49:

FRISCO - PART TWO!

Over the next few days, I soon got back into my LA routine which was a combination of my Pico halfway-house duties, alone time for journaling and the like, and hanging out in Hollywood with friends.

One day I received a letter from Jay, saying that he was sorry if he'd messed up by taking speed during our visit, and hoping that I would still visit again soon. I'd gone off the idea of seeing him, so I felt it best not to reply, as I wasn't sure what to tell him. I also missed a couple of his phone calls, and all in all, I felt it was probably for the best to just move on. I felt that maybe one day I would contact him again as a friend, but for now, I needed a little time to get over our sweet little romance that had been developing slowly, but surely.

My birth certificate arrived safely, and the local British Consulate was swift to send my passport replacement. It felt good to have a passport again, and it quickly reminded me of the bigger picture of my travels, yet I couldn't deny the fact that I loved California, and felt happy to be where I was in LA. I figured that my aunt Freda's arrival would help me to get into travel-gear, and get ready for another pond-hop!

One day my aunt phoned to say that she may be delayed by a week or so, as she had some more properties to look at in Oregon. Rather than be disappointed, I felt pleased that I would have some more time to spend in LA, hanging out with my friends before her arrival.

One night I popped up to Hollywood for one of my usual moseys around, and bumped into Johnny at the Seven Seas. We both acted too cool for school and barely said hello to each other. My mind and heart suddenly thought of Jay and how sweet, kind, warm, and loving he was, and I realised that I missed him.

BOOK 1: TO SEE THE WORLD

I thought about how much we liked each other, and how disappointed he'd been to hear that I was leaving for England. I suddenly realised that despite his speed issues, I did still have feelings for him. 'I should at least give him a chance!' I thought to myself, as I took off from the Seven Seas, without even looking to see where Johnny was, and jumped on a bus back to Pico.

The next morning, I decided that I would hitchhike alone up to "Frisco" to see Jay. I packed up my tote bag again, and wrote a note to Larry explaining that I was taking a few more days out of my "owed holiday days" and hoped that he would be ok with it.

I headed to the living room all ready to go. "Hi Mike, will you give this note to Larry please, I'm heading back to San Francisco for a few days" I asked with a smile. "Sure! You're going again? you get around!" answered Mike, looking surprised and smiling, as if impressed by my 'truck-setting' lifestyle!

"Yep, the open road doth calleth!" I exclaimed as I dramatically waved my arm high in the air, and we both laughed. "Good for you Della, I hope you have a fun time!" answered Mike with a big smile. I liked the way he was always so positive and supportive, and not at all possessive of his friendship with me. As long as I was happy, he was happy for me. He was a true friend indeed.

"Thanks, Mike, see ya soon!" I said as I headed outside. "See ya soon!" he called back, coming out to the top of the steps to wave at me, as I went. I gave him one last wave, then took off south on Pico, towards a Northbound freeway not too far away.

I arrived at the freeway on-ramp and stuck my thumb out. A big rig stopped straight away, and a chubby guy reached over and opened the passenger door. "Going near Frisco?" I asked with a smile, as I reached the top of the truck's steps. "All the way to Seattle, jump on board!" He answered smiling back. "Great, thanks!" I answered, sensing no bad vibes, as I climbed into the rig with my tote bag slung over my shoulder, and reached over to shake his hand.

"Gary, good to meet cha!" he exclaimed with a big smile. "Della, good to meet you too!" I answered as we shook hands. I got comfy in my seat, as Gary hit the gas and we took off up the freeway. Gary turned the radio up, and we had some fun pop tunes as background music as we chatted away.

It turned out that Gary had a great sense of humour, and was full of funny stories, with a variety of silly voices to help tell them! "You should get a job doing voiceovers!" I exclaimed, feeling impressed at how talented he was. "Sure, but

415

then who's gonna drive the truck!" he joked back, and we both laughed. He was great company and I enjoyed every moment of the journey back up PCH.

"San Francisco my lady!" announced Gary as he parked up on a side street in the Tenderloin district. "Thank you, kind sir!" I exclaimed as I got my bag ready to go. "Any time, here's my number, call me if you need anything!" he answered with his usual big smile.

"Thanks, Gary!" I answered, as I took the paper off him, put it in my tote bag, opened the cabin door, and jumped down from his truck. We waved goodbye to each other one last time as he drove off into the distance. I felt the usual mixture of happy and sad feelings over making a lovely new friend - who I would probably never see again.

I made my way to Jay's feeling that it was finally time to reveal my true feelings to him. I took a deep breath and rang the doorbell of his hotel. The doorman came out said hello, and smiled as if he recognised me. "Hi, do you know if Jay's in?" I asked, excitedly. "No sorry, Jay moved out about a week ago" he answered, looking a little sorry for me. "Oh, do you have his new address by any chance? I asked, feeling my heart sink, "Sure" he answered as he limped back over to the back of the desk. "Here," he said, after jotting it down for me. "Thanks, can you tell me whereabouts it is please?" I asked, glancing at the address, and not having a clue which way to go. "Sure, you'll have to catch a couple of trams to get there." He answered, as he led the way back outside, and gave me directions. I thanked him, and jumped on the nearest tram heading in the direction he'd said to go.

I eventually arrived at Jay's new address on Oak Avenue and nervously rang the doorbell. After a few moments, Jay opened the door. His face instantly lit up when he saw me, but then dropped a split second later. "Hi Della, I'm with someone now" he whispered awkwardly, as he nodded his head, and rolled his eyes towards the inside of the building.

"Who's that Jay?" shouted a female voice from upstairs. "Just a friend!" shouted Jay, giving me a "please play along!" look "Come in, come and meet my girl!" Jay exclaimed as if trying to sound like nothing was awry. "This is Della, Jennie's friend" announced Jay, as he led the way upstairs and inside the apartment. I played along and smiled politely, while my heart felt as though it was crumbling inside. "Della this is my girl Chrissy," said Jay pleasantly. "Hi, Chrissy!" I said as I reached out my hand, "Hi Della" said Chrissy, as we shook hands. "Have a seat, I'll make some coffee?" said Chrissy in a friendly way. "I'll help you!"

exclaimed Jay, as he stood up to go and help her, and I sat down feeling like I just wanted to get out of there!

They soon both came back with the coffees and sat down with me. "I thought you'd be back in England by now?" Said Jay, as if secretly trying to let me know why he'd moved on. "No, not yet! my aunt isn't even in the States yet!" I laughed, and even when she does get here, she's going to be a while touring around and looking for a ranch to buy before coming down to LA. She says she wants to take me to the San Diego Zoo, maybe she's planning to leave me there!" I answered, and we all laughed.

Although I felt upset that Jay had moved on, in a way, I felt happy that he'd found someone nice, especially as I wasn't able to commit. "So, how's Jennie, and the other punks doing down in Hollywood?" asked Jay, as if feeling it best to get back to a general catch-up chat. "They all seemed ok the last time I saw them, how's Frisco, are you liking it?" I asked curiously. "Yeah, things are good now, especially since Chrissy and I met at work a couple of weeks back, we just hit it off, didn't we Chrissy!" Jay answered as he gave her a little side hug as if wanting to reassure her that all was well. "We sure did" answered Chrissy, looking at Jay lovingly. "That's great!" I answered with a smile, even though I felt sad inside.

"Well, I guess I'd better get going, I only popped by to say hello, I want to go and see some of the sites that I didn't get to see last time!" I exclaimed, as I finished my coffee, and stood up. "It was nice to meet you, Della!" said Chrissy, as she stood up, and started heading towards the kitchen with the empty coffee cups. "You too, thanks for the coffee!" I answered as Jay started leading the way to the door.

Jay walked me down the stairs, and out onto the sidewalk. Once we were outside, he pulled the front door closed behind us. "I'm so sorry Della, I didn't hear back from you for a while, so I guessed it was over between us. I thought you'd gone back to England!" He said in a hushed tone while looking as if he was about to cry. "No worries, take care then!" I answered, trying not to show how hurt and sad I was feeling deep down, as I started to stroll away backwards. "Bye Della!" Jay called after me. "See ya!" I called back. We waved to each other and I turned and walked away.

As I walked, I wondered if he'd phoned Jennie, and she'd told him about the face I pulled when he'd hugged me goodbye the last time and he'd taken it to mean I wasn't interested, or maybe he really did think that I'd gone back to England, especially as I hadn't replied to his letter, or returned his calls. I took a deep breath, and jumped on a tram without knowing where it was going, I figured I would jump off when it arrived somewhere that I liked the look of. As the tram rode along through various neighbourhoods, I sat gazing out of the window feeling sad about Jay and me, while at the same time admiring the views of the picturesque bay windowed architecture and the vibrant mix of people who helped to create such a diverse and collective atmosphere. It was strange to be feeling sad over Jay, yet happy about being in San Francisco, all at the same time!

As I breathed in the fresh salty air, I felt as though I certainly would enjoy spending some more time there, with or without Jay! I suddenly saw a sign that read Height-Ashbury and automatically jumped off the tram. I remembered hearing somewhere that Height-Ashbury was the place where the hippies, artists, and bohemian types hung out. Even though I was still feeling very sad about Jay, I was happy to be back out exploring the world once again. 'I'm travelling to see the world, not to see a guy!' I reminded myself, as I walked along. I felt my spirits lift a little, although I couldn't help but think about how this was probably going to continue to be an ongoing problem, as my mind flashed back to Jeff in Toronto. Once again I wondered if I would be forever torn between my love of travel and various potential relationships. 'Don't worry, if I meet "The One" for me, and I'm "The One" for him, then we'll naturally work all that other stuff out - I hope!' I thought to myself with a sigh.

I strolled around the Haight-Ashbury area soaking in the wonderful sights, sounds and colours. Everywhere I looked were cool-looking record stores, clothes stores, tattoo workshops, vintage stores, bars, coffee houses, band posters, art exhibitions, and a variety of punks, hippies, bikers, artists, workers, students, and regular-looking people milling about.

The song lyrics "What we need is a great big melting pot, big enough to take the world and all it's got!" by Blue Mink, started playing in my mind as I walked along, and I couldn't help but smile. I remembered how my mum had always had a soft spot for the hippy era, and how she used to play that song, and "If you're going to San Francisco, be sure to wear some flowers in your hair" by Scott McKenzie, a lot as she did her chores, when I was a kid. 'Wow, I'm actually here! I'm in San Francisco!" I thought to myself, with a smile, my joy of life feeling stronger than my sadness about Jay.

CHAPTER 50:

GOODBYE JAY! HELLO HAIGHT ASHBURY AND THE FABULOUS HIPPIES OF SAN FRANCISCO!

I slipped into a relaxed dreamlike state and felt as if I was in a waking dream as I meandered along feeling on cloud nine. "Hi how are you doing?" said a big-hair, big-bearded, older hippy guy wearing dark glasses and standing on the corner. "Hi, I'm ok, how are you?" I answered as I strolled over towards him "There looks like a lot to do here!" I exclaimed enthusiastically. "Best place in the world!" he replied with a big smile "Is this your first time up at Height-Ashbury" He asked. "Yeah, I came to visit a friend on Oak Avenue, but he's not available, so I came up here to look around instead" I answered.

"It's a little bit of heaven on Earth!" said the Hippy guy with a big smile. "Do you smoke? Would you like a tote?" He asked starting to roll a joint "No thanks, I'm going to have a look around, I may see you later though!" I answered as I started to stroll away. "Sure thing, my name is Al" he shouted after me. "My name's Della!" I shouted back as I headed off to explore.

The area reminded me of a mix between the Sunset Strip in LA, Kensington Market in Toronto, and Camden Town in London. It was a fun, happening scene and I loved it! I found a cafe bar, where a guy was sitting up on a little stage playing guitar, so I strolled inside and bought myself a coffee. There was an interesting mix of bohemian-looking people in there, sipping away at their coffees, quietly chatting, reading, writing, playing board games, or simply listening to the musician.

"Okay guys, I need your help with this one!" said the punky-arty-looking singer up on the little corner stage. "When I say who, you say You! You! You!" We all laughed and nodded. 'This is fun!' I thought to myself as I sipped on my coffee and got ready to sing along. The guy went on to sing some sort of political punk-folk song about who is to blame for the state of the world today. "…So, who's to blame?" He sang loudly. "You, you, you!" we all sang back, with some of us laughing, including me. 'I REALLY liked this town!' I thought to myself feeling totally in my element and very comfortable as I looked around at the eclectic creative-looking crowd around me. 'These are my people!!' I thought to myself. "Thank you so much!" said the guy as he finished his set. We all clapped and cheered, as the goatee-bearded barrister ran up from the serving counter, and grabbed the mic.

"Next up is Arizona!" he announced, before scurrying off, back behind the serving counter. We all clapped, as a tall skinny girl with long straight fair hair and round glasses got up on the platform and adjusted the mic. "Hi I'm Arizona, I'm going to do you some poetry, it's about when I first moved here," she said, giving the room a sweet smile.

I thought about how I would love to do what she was doing. I did write a bit of poetry from time to time. 'I'm not sure that I'm ready to share it with others though, and I'm not sure others are ready to hear it!' I thought to myself with a chuckle, before taking a big sip of coffee.

"San Francisco! The mother of all towns! The birthplace of revolution and the centre of LOVE!!!" exclaimed Arizona loudly. "Cool!" I thought to myself, as I sat back, sipped on my coffee and enjoyed the rest of the poem. When Arizona finished we all clapped and cheered, and the goatee coffee-barrister guy ran back up on the stage and announced that that was the end of the open mic session until later that eve.

'I love it here!' I thought to myself while trying to work out if I preferred San Francisco to Los Angeles. I concluded that I loved both equally and that they were like two different flavours that I loved, not one better, just different! '…and it's all California, maybe I just love California!' I thought to myself, feeling pleased with that concept.

I sat just sipping on my coffee, thinking about Jay, pondering on various things, and enjoying the atmosphere. 'Where am I going to stay tonight?' I suddenly thought to myself as I finished my coffee. 'Maybe my new hippy friend Al might know of a place I can crash?' I thought to myself, as I stood up, grabbed my tote bag, and left the café.

I strolled back down Haight Street and made my way back to Ashbury Street. "Hey Della you came back to me!" Exclaimed Al, looking happy to see me. "Of course!" I answered smiling, as I sat down next to him. "So where did you go, what did you see?" asked Al, in a fun exaggerated manner. "I just strolled around and wound up at a coffee house that had an open mic session going on. It was great fun. I love it here!" I answered, excitedly.

"Yeah, no need for me to move, the world comes to me here!" said Al looking as cool and laid-back as ever. "You came to me didn't you Della, all the way from England! See, I didn't have to move an inch" he continued. "True!" I exclaimed, and we both laughed and nodded our heads in agreement.

"Do you know anywhere I could stay tonight?" I asked, hoping that he might know of somewhere cheap, as my funds were low because I'd been expecting to crash at Jay's. "Stay?" he answered as if he didn't know what I meant. "You know, somewhere to crash, sleep, catch forty winks!" I answered with a laugh. "Oh well, STAY wherever you happen to be at the time!" he answered dramatically, and we both laughed at the simple logic of his answer.

"I guess that's pretty much what I have been doing on my travels, staying wherever I happen to be at the time!" I answered, and we burst out laughing like two crazy fools. - I didn't need to smoke weed to see the funny side of life, that was for sure!

"Most of us hippies "stay" in Golden Gate Park!" exclaimed Al, after we finally stopped laughing. "Oh really?" I answered curiously. "Sure, it's just a few blocks away, wanna go see?" asked Al, with a smile. "Yeah, great!" I answered, feeling curious to see the park where the San Francisco Hippies crash out at night, and feeling pleased to have made a new friend!

As we walked along almost everybody said hi to Al as if he was an old friend of theirs. He was such a warm, friendly, open person, that I couldn't help but feel fond of him. I guessed that others felt the same way. As he virtually danced his way along the sidewalk waving and greeting those we passed by, he reminded me of some kind of jolly hobgoblin. He wasn't very tall, and he was slightly chubby in stature. His hair was frizzy and stuck straight out from his head as if he'd just had an electric shock. and his face had whiskers that stuck out from all over his chin in a similar fashion. I loved his unique look and free-spirited somewhat magical personality!

At the end of the street, I saw an archway that read: Golden Gate Park. Al led the way inside the park. "Wow, this is beautiful!" I exclaimed, admiring how green and spacious it was. "Yep, and you can sleep like a baby in here! and no one will bother you, because everybody is cool!" exclaimed Al proudly, as we gazed around the park. "Wow, I love it!" I answered in admiration of such a beautiful place.

Al's words reminded me of how so many of the people I'd met on my travels had been very cool too! Most people I'd met were friendly, helpful, and kind. It was such a shame that a tiny handful of "bad apples" seemed to exist everywhere and tried to ruin things for the good people. '...but we still have to enjoy life, and make the most of it, we can't let them win!' I thought to myself, as I gazed around the park, trying to imagine what it would be like to sleep there for the night!

Although I was curious about experiencing a night crashed out in the park with the hippies, I wasn't really keen on being completely at the mercy of the elements, and whatever "bad apples" just might happen to be about, so although I was sure that Al meant well, I wasn't too sure of what I was going to do later just yet.

As we strolled around the park, Al told me all about the good spots to visit in San Francisco. He mentioned a place called The Fisherman's Warf which sounded quaint. He'd added that I'd be able to see the world-famous Alcatraz prison from there too, which I found amazing, as I'd seen the movie "Escape from Alcatraz" as a kid, and was fascinated that it was still around!

I noticed how the other hippies greeted Al respectfully wherever we strolled in the park, and knew that I was in safe hands with him. "Who is the lovely lady?" exclaimed a red-haired hippy guy as he neared us. "This is Della! ...All the way from England to hang out with the coolest people, in the coolest city!" answered Al, dramatically.

"Tis a pleasure to meet you! Jack here!" exclaimed the red-haired hippy guy, as he reached out his hand. "Hi, Jack, a pleasure to meet you too!" I answered as we shook hands. "Why don't you join us for a walk around!" exclaimed Al, with a big smile. "Don't mind if I do!" answered Jack, as the three of us meandered along.

Eventually, we came to an interesting mixture of characters sitting around on the grass in a chilled-out area of the park. "Della, these are my very good friends, my very good friends, this is Della, all the way from England!" announced Al joyfully. They all looked up at me in amazement, as if they couldn't believe that

BOOK 1: TO SEE THE WORLD

I was there, and I gazed back at them as if I couldn't believe that I was there either! I smiled and gave them all a little wave, and they all smiled back, while some gave peace signs and others threw salutes our way.

Most of them looked to be around fifteen to twenty years older than me, and it suddenly dawned on me that these were the original San Francisco hippies that had started the worldwide hippy movement, and I suddenly felt honoured to be in their company.

"Come join us!" exclaimed a guy with long dark brown hair and round sunglasses. "Sure, wanna sit for a while?" asked Al with a smile. "Yeah!" I answered as the three of us found a spot on the grass near among the hippies.

The guy who'd invited us to join them started to play guitar, and a few others started to play little bongo drums, and maracas, while one of the women started to sing a beautiful song. "They're good!" I whispered to Al, as the three of us started to sway and hum along to the music.

Gradually other hippies, a few bohemian types, and punks started joining us – young, old, male, and female. They all shared their drinks and smokes, and the vibes were very happy. A few of them had musical instruments: guitars, harmonicas and drums, and joined in with the jam. There was a strong sense of the collective spirit of love, which was beyond beautiful.

'This is life!' I thought to myself feeling completely alive and in the moment. Joints were being passed around, and although I passed them up, the air was still thick with smoke. Someone shared some beers around, and as I felt myself getting tipsy from the beer, I was also feeling high from the atmosphere. - in more ways than one!

As the day turned into night time the party continued. I felt very happy and safe with these truly beautiful people. I couldn't believe that I was in The Golden State Park, in Height-Ashbury, hanging out with the world-famous hippies of San Francisco! 'This is what my travels are all about! Not about getting hung up on some guy!' I thought to myself with a big smile, as I lay down on the grass surrounded by good vibes and good people, put my head on my army shoulder bag as a pillow, and fell asleep.

I woke up as the Sun was rising, and lifted my head a little to see what was going on around me. I could see the outlines of a few hippies & punks sleeping peacefully nearby. The air was cool but refreshing. I sat up properly to get my bearings and see exactly who was sleeping around me. I could see that there were two hippy females, three hippy males, and a few punk guys and gals a little further down.

Three hippy guys nearby were all lying in a row snoring like there was no tomorrow, I noticed that one of them was Al, the other was his red-haired friend Jack, and the third was an Al lookalike, and had similar bushy hair and beard. They all looked so cute together like they were out of some kind of Disney scene. "The Seven Dwarfs" suddenly popped to my mind, and I chuckled to myself at the thought.

'What a great night we all had!' I thought to myself, feeling so pleased that I had really got to experience what the San Francisco hippies stood for – Love, Peace and Harmony! 'That's who Al and his two friends are! Not the seven dwarfs!' I thought to myself, smiling at them fondly. Again, I thought about how these guys were the originals! They had started the Hippie movement, that went worldwide. Some of them were probably even a little older, and may well have been part of the previous beatnik scene of the 1950s, and here was little ole me: Della, an eighteen-year-old girl from a small town in England, spending time with them at the epi-centre of the hippy world! Or "The centre of Love!" as Arizona had called San Francisco. 'If only the whole planet was like this, the world would be perfect!' I thought to myself, as I stood up and stretched.

I wondered what to do for the day. Maybe I would head over to check out the Fisherman's Warf, and see Alcatraz, and afterwards head to the Tenderloin district to have a look around, and see if any of the LA punks were about? I'd heard Jay and Jennie chat about how a lot of them would hitchhike back and forth between LA and San Francisco regularly, and Jennie had bumped into a few of them the last time we came up. I felt that it would be fun to see some familiar LA faces!

As much as I'd enjoyed my night in Golden Gate Park singing songs, getting tipsy with the hippies and punks, and later crashing out there, I knew that I wouldn't want to make a habit of it. I craved change and diversity to keep me mentally stimulated, but I would treasure the memory of my night there always, that was for sure!

I wrote out a note to Al, thanking him for being such a perfect host, adding that hopefully, I would see him again - sooner or later, and stuck it under a rock near to where he lay sleeping peacefully, with a golden ray of sunlight shining softly above his head. 'Aw, he's not a hobgoblin after all, he's one of my Angels" I thought to myself with a smile. I gazed at him fondly for a moment. "Thanks, Al" I whispered, and then I took off out of the park.

Once I got back out onto the street, a "Wino," as they called homeless alcoholics in the US, was sitting on a bench with a bottle of something in a brown paper bag, staring into space, so seeing as he was the only awake person around, I politely asked him for directions to The Fisherman's Warf, and he politely answered me, and then he politely asked me for a quarter. I thanked him, and gave him 50 cents instead, before taking off in the direction he'd sent me.

It didn't take long to get to Fisherman's Warf by tram, and I was soon strolling around enjoying the salty sea air, and admiring the local architecture. There were lots of seafood restaurants, cafes, bars, and a few tourist shops, and it was all very stylish, and not tacky, like some seaside places can be.

I walked to the edge of the docks and looked out at the bay. I knew the massive building on a small island in the middle of the bay just had to be Alcatraz! 'Wow, there it is!' I thought to myself, gazing at it in awe. I wondered what it must have been like for the prisoners who were held there, and how fascinating it was that the guys they'd made the movie about had actually escaped from there! I wondered if they'd survived. I couldn't remember what happened in the movie. I couldn't wait to write to my dad and tell him that I'd actually seen Alcatraz!

After a while, I decided to head back to the Tenderloin for a walk about, so I jumped on the BART train going that way. It was very clean, I noticed that there were no crisp bags, or empty lager cans like I'd seen on some of the trains in the UK.

I asked a sleepy-looking passenger if he knew how many stops away the tenderloin was, and he pointed to a map which showed the stops. I thanked him, checked the map, and went to sit down. I found a window seat and sat looking out at Market Street speeding by. No ticket collector turned up, so I didn't have a chance to buy a ticket and was pleased to be able to keep the cash. I spotted the stop for the tenderloin and jumped off the train. I noticed that people were putting tickets in a machine that opened a turn-style. I didn't have a ticket, so I cheekily popped through a turn-style close behind someone else to get out! 'What else could I do?" I joked to myself.

I felt like a mole coming up from underground as I popped out into the daylight on Market Street. It was not yet buzzing with life, but I still liked the atmosphere. Things were just starting up, so I strolled along, still feeling in my element, and enjoying exploring brand-new places, sights and sounds once again. I saw a sign that read "Plasma donors wanted - Paid" and as I was getting low on cash, I decided to follow the sign.

The building was pale blue and looked like an old army barrack building. Outside the doorway was a small gathering of homeless people, street kids, punks, students, artists and hippies. All obviously also low on funds and in need of a top-up!

I joined the queue, curious to see what would happen next. The doors suddenly opened and we were all called inside. Once again, I felt as though I was in my "Independent Social experimenter" mode as I trundled along at the back of the queue, not sure what to expect next.

We were all instructed to take a seat in the reception area, and not long afterwards a nurse appeared who explained the procedure to us. We would each have a bed to lie down on in the ward, and blood would be taken from our arms. Next, they would extract the plasma, and afterwards, they would put the blood back into our arms.

This alarmed me somewhat, as I'd assumed they would keep the plasma AND the blood, so I wasn't sure if I fancied the blood being put back into my arm. 'What if they put the wrong blood in my arm!' I thought feeling sick at the thought, yet at the same time curious enough to go along with it.

I was given a bed to lie down on in the corner of the room nearest to the exit. Other people were lying down on the beds that lined the dorm. Soon a nurse appeared and swiftly stuck a needle in my arm, took out my blood, then whisked it away to another room at the far end of the dorm. 'At least it didn't hurt that much!' I thought, feeling pleased to get the first part over with.

After a while, the nurse came back with a bag of blood that she hooked up to a stand next to my bed. I debated on telling her that it was ok, they could keep my blood too as I watched her pop the needle in my arm, that would allow for, hopefully, my blood, to flow back into me. I didn't fancy this at all, so I closed my eyes and imagined I was lying on a lovely beach somewhere.

The nurse left, and suddenly I could feel a terrible pain in my arm where the needle was. I looked at my arm to see what was going on and saw that it was swelling up like a mini volcano - with scary-looking colours of pink, purple and yellow building up around it.

"Nurse!" I cried out, but she didn't hear me. Somebody in a bed near to her told her that I was calling for her so she immediately rushed over to me. She looked a little alarmed to see the state of my arm, and quickly pulled the needle out. "I'm sorry this happens sometimes, it'll go down," she said apologetically. "That's ok!" I answered, as I grimaced, while nodding and trying to smile, in an understanding way. while inside I was regretting the whole thing!

I told her that I didn't need the blood that was left in the bag, and sat up feeling ready to leave. "OK, please take your form to the office for payment, thank you for your donation!" she answered, as I grabbed my tote bag off the nearby chair. "You're welcome, thank you!" I answered as I headed for the office.

I was paid $15 as a thank-you for my donation, which soon cheered me up a little. Although my arm was very sore, I was happy to have some extra pocket money on me. I thanked them, said goodbye, and got out of there - fast!

I strolled around just enjoying the general San Francisco atmosphere, which took my mind off my sore arm. 'I really do love it here!' I thought to myself, as I imagined being based there for a while. I turned a corner and spotted some of the LA punks who had arrived from the freeway as Jennie and I were hitchhiking out the last time I was there. 'They must have stayed on for a few weeks or they've been back and forth a lot – like me!' I thought to myself, as I strolled over towards them to say hi.

"You're back!" said a skinny guy with a purple mohawk looking pleased to see me. "Yeah, I came back to see Jay, but he's with someone else, so I crashed out with the hippies in the park and donated blood plasma instead" I answered, with a laugh. "…Something went wrong though, and I wound up with a swollen arm!" I added, giving my arm a rub. "That sounds painful! I'm glad you're ok! It's too bad that Jay's hooked up with someone else, don't worry you can hang with us. My name's X, what's yours?" He answered warmly. "Thanks, I'm Della!" I answered as we shook hands. I appreciated his and the other punks' hospitality albeit - Street hospitality!

As we chatted a few more punks came and joined us. Gals and guys, all with wonderful colourful spiky hair and punk rock clothing. We all sat around and they told me the best places to get free food and gave me the addresses of squats they were staying at. "Yeah, hang with us!" said one of the others sitting on the outside of the group. "Thanks" I answered with a smile, and although I truly did appreciate their welcome, I also really liked doing my own thing a lot of the time and wasn't really a pack joiner.

"Well, I guess I'm gonna go for a walk!" I exclaimed after hanging out with them for an hour or so. "Where are you going man?" said one of the guy punks sounding alarmed. "Just for a walkabout, I fancy doing my own thing for a bit, I'll probably see you all later though!" I answered with a smile, hoping that I wasn't offending them. "Right!" he answered while nodding, but looking as if he didn't understand why I would take off from them on my own. "See ya!" I called out as I strolled away. "Later man!" he called after me, his voice sounding flat. The others waved and shouted "See ya/later" too, as I took off down the street to look around some more.

I felt a strong sense of freedom as I walked away. I realised as much as I liked hanging out with them, I was used to being free to explore, have interesting experiences, and meet a variety of people. I would be bored to tears sitting around with the same group of people all day!

As I headed down a tree-lined pathway just enjoying the fresh air, and enjoying feeling completely in the moment, I spotted a bag lady sitting on a park bench, swigging something from a brown paper bag and I wondered what her life story was.

"Hi, nice day?! I said smiling, as I neared her "Yes it's wonderful! are you from England?" she answered with a big smile. "Yes, I am," I said as I sat down next to her on the bench. "I'm Della, nice to meet you!" I said as I reached out my hand. "Hi Della, I'm Liz Holloway, nice to meet you too!" she exclaimed, as we shook hands.

She asked me the usual questions about the UK; mainly about the weather, the music, and The Queen. We continued to chat and joke about life in general. She seemed to be a down-and-out bag lady, who was just living day to day and staying at various mission houses around San Francisco at night.

"Want some vodka?" she asked passing me her bottle. "Thanks!" I answered and took a swig, feeling happy to have made another new friend. "So, what if I like a drink!?" she exclaimed to the world rebelliously as she took another swig of her vodka. I smiled and nodded in agreement.

Her face looked quite tired and weather-worn, and she had ratted blonde hair and was wearing ragged old clothes. I guessed she was in her late forties, and would probably be an attractive-looking lady when scrubbed up.

We spent the next couple of hours just shooting the breeze, laughing, joking and drinking vodka. Me taking little sips, her taking big swigs. I told her all about my night with the hippies in Golden Gate Park, and how I'd popped over to the Fisherman's Warf and had seen Alcatraz earlier. She seemed to love my sense of adventure and listened with a look of admiration.

"Wanna go to dinner?" she asked, suddenly standing up. "Sounds like a plan lead the way!" I answered with a big smile while standing up and feeling a little tipsy! "Sure will!" she said as she grabbed her bundle of bags and led the way down the tree-lined avenue towards the Tenderloin.

As we turned into the main street, we bumped into some of X's punk friends "Hey Della, what's up?" asked one of the punks smiling over at me, but giving Liz a judgemental look. "Liz and I are off to get something to eat!" I answered with a smile. "You don't want to hang with her man, she's wrecked!" whispered one of the punks in my ear. 'Pots and Kettles!' I thought to myself, not liking my new friend being spoken badly of. "I do what I want!" I answered defiantly, feeling annoyed at how rude, shallow, and judgemental they were being. "Come on Della!" said Liz grinning and leading the way across the street. "See Ya!" I shouted to the punks as I followed Liz across the street.

We arrived at a big food hall. There was a diverse crowd inside. I felt a strong sense of solidarity between everyone which I found admirable. I also loved how it seemed that we were all simply being. We were all simply there together in the now! It reminded me of the sense of freedom I had found out on the road, and I started to wonder if I was maybe getting a little too comfortable at Pico, and in LA in general. But then I remembered that I'd probably be heading back to England with my Aunt in a few weeks, so it didn't really matter!

I looked forward to seeing my family and friends back in England, but at the same time, I was already looking forward to my future travels! 'Maybe it's my Romany genes from my grandmother's side kicking in?' I thought to myself, as I followed Liz across the room, both of us nodding, and smiling at the fellow diners as we went.

We sat at a table and got chatting with an older guy. There was a young guy at the table too, but he was engrossed in reading a newspaper and didn't even say hi back to us. Liz and I laughed at him ignoring us, and after putting Liz's bags on our chairs to save our seats we headed over to the food counter and got a plate full of food and a drink of punch put on our trays. We headed back to the table to eat and drink, mainly in silence. - I noticed that Liz really liked to focus on her food while she was eating, as she paid very little interest to anyone, or anything else.

"Right back to the park?" asked Liz after we'd finished eating. "Sure!" I answered, standing up and following suit as she took her tray and put it in a pile on the side. We said goodbye to anyone who was looking our way, got our things together and headed out of the building, across the street, and back to the park.

We soon found a bench and sat down. We chatted about all sorts of things from what life was like in my town in England, to what her life was like on the streets of San Francisco. I liked how our conversation just flowed, and I could tell she was an educated woman, as she was very knowledgeable about all sorts of topics.

"Hey Liz, I'm gonna go for a walkabout, so I'll probably see you later!" I said, after a couple of hours of hanging out with Liz, and suddenly feeling restless. "Sure, here's the address of the mission I'll be staying at tonight" She answered, giving me a piece of paper with an address scribbled on it. I guessed; she didn't need it anymore. "OK, thanks, Liz!" I answered, as I took it off her, and turned to leave. "See you there, if not before!" she shouted after me, as I strolled off. "Ok!" I shouted back, feeling good to have some time to myself again! I liked how she wasn't fazed by my decision to take off for a walk-about, she just seemed to understand, no explanations needed!

I enjoyed my little walkabouts alone to collect my thoughts, and would often stop and jot down notes for my journal as I went. I guess, not everyone would understand that, as they weren't on my journey, and they had their own journeys to focus on. I thought about how I enjoyed Liz's company, and for the most part, I felt a lot more of an affinity with her free spiritedness, than I did with some of the punks. I know they meant well, but a lot of them seemed to almost enjoy carrying chips on their shoulders. Whereas people like Liz, and I just enjoyed being free and having fun! I guessed we chose to focus on the positives, instead of the negatives, so maybe to a certain degree, it was about internal disposition, rather than external circumstances.

My mind flashed to the feeling I'd had about Jay probably having a not-so-good home life, and I suddenly realised why some of the punks might be carrying chips on their shoulders, as most of them were still in their teens. I suddenly felt a wave of sorrow and a strong compassion in my heart for them. I prayed a little prayer that their lives would get better.

As I walked along, I thought about Jay, and although I felt sad that things hadn't worked out. Deep down I knew that it just wasn't the right time for us, and hopefully, he and Chrissy would be a good match. He was a lovely guy, and he deserved some happiness in his life, and Chrissy probably did too! I wished them both the best of luck, then carried on with my walk.

I spotted a library and automatically strolled inside, I had my library card from LA in my purse and wondered if I'd be able to use it in San Francisco, as it was also in the State of California. "Excuse me, hello, I was wondering if my LA library card is valid here?" I asked the library assistant behind the desk, holding my library card out for her to see. "Ummm, yes it is!" she answered, after taking it from my hand and giving it a thorough look. "Great, thanks!" I answered, feeling pleasantly surprised. "You're welcome!" she answered, as I turned to walk away.

I browsed around looking for something interesting to read. I found the philosophy and psychology section and flicked through a few pages of a handful of books. One book held my interest over the others, so I took it to the counter and checked it out.

As I left the building, I got some strange looks from the normal-looking people going inside the building and I got the feeling that they were wondering why a new-wave/punky-looking street kid had checked out a book.

I found some steps to the side of the entrance and sat down to read my book. The first chapter was about the power of the mind and how psychology plays a big part in how we deal with the ups and downs of life. It stated how our mindset is a co-creator in each of our individual realities. For example: If we think we will lose a race, then we probably will! but if we think we will win the race, then we just might! I loved this theory, as it was in line with my way of thinking. I had also become very aware on my travels, of how my friendly disposition seemed to help to make MY world a friendlier place.

The book went on to expand on the different personality types, and why they're drawn to various jobs, lifestyles, and even politics. I found this most interesting and soon got lost in the book's pages. I seemed to be bang in the middle of these personality types with most of my ways, as I liked a sense of balance in things and always tried to see things from all angles.

I was enjoying reading a section on how being a pessimist or an optimist may affect various human tribal instincts - The pessimists might see newcomers as a threat, bringing disorder to the tribe, whereas an optimist may see the newcomer as an asset to the tribe "More hands on deck" so to speak! - I was definitely an optimist!

I was just in the middle of imagining welcoming various newcomers to my tribe in a remote jungle somewhere when someone suddenly shouted: "Wow a punk rocker reading a book!" in a rude tone. I glanced up to see some preppy-looking guy and his friends heading up the library steps "Yeah you should try it sometime!" I shouted back. His friends laughed and teased him and he looked a bit sheepish as they strode on inside. 'What small-minded people!' I thought to myself feeling annoyed that my reading had been disturbed. 'He would definitely get booted out of my tribe!' I thought to myself with a laugh.

"What are you reading?" said a white-whiskered homeless person sitting on a bench nearby. "Oh, just a book on psychology, about the power of the mind and how our mindset helps to create our reality" I answered, with a smile. "Good stuff! The mind is a powerful thing!... it can also drive you crazy though! He answered laughing. "True!" I answered, laughing along with him

"My name is Harry what's yours?" He said as he got up, stumbled towards me and sat down next to me on the step. "Della, nice to meet you, Harry!" I answered reaching out my hand. "Nice to meet you too Della!" he answered, as we shook hands.

We were soon chatting away about "life, the universe, and everything" as they say. He had been a successful businessman at one time in his life, but his wife had left him, and alcohol had taken her place. "Do you have any family or friends to help you get back on your feet?" I asked curiously. "Not sure I like being on my feet, I kind of like lying down!" He answered, and we both cracked up laughing.

"But I mean, wouldn't you like a home, friends, a partner ...and a good life again?" I persisted. "Had all that, and it didn't work out! I like it this way, it's easier!" he answered matter-of-factly. "I see, I guess the less stuff you have, the less stuff you have to worry about!" I answered, starting to see things from his point of view. "Yeah!" he answered as he suddenly started to cough violently which I found quite distressing. I felt helpless, so I just sat next to him trying to act normal and taking my mind off his coughing by thinking about the book I'd been reading.

It suddenly dawned on me that my life and Harry's were not a whole lot different, and again, it was just our outlooks that were different. I saw myself as an intrepid explorer, off having adventures around my little home planet, and he saw himself as homeless, but free from responsibilities alcoholic. The only actual difference was that I, thankfully, wasn't an alcoholic, and I wasn't an older guy, I was a teenage girl from England, but aside from those things, there wasn't a whole lot of difference between us. We were both not conforming to societal norms – Life was way too short for that!

I pondered on how people became alcoholics, I wondered if it was genetic, circumstantial, or both. Just then Harry took a swig of his booze from his brown paper bag and sat staring into space. He suddenly seemed ok with not chatting, so I slowly picked up my book and started to read again.

"Hey Harry, how's it going?" said a gruff male voice. I looked up to see one female and three male homeless people standing in front of us. 'Gosh, I sure know how to hobnob! Or Hobo rather!' I joked to myself. "Good, this is my new friend Della! My friends Brian, Dave, Billy and Sandy!" exclaimed Harry proudly. We all said hello to each other, then they went about sharing out their tobacco and booze with Harry, which I found heart-warming. They seemed like good people. I also found it a relief that they didn't make a fuss about me being from England, and I got the impression that it would take a lot to faze them!

"You're gonna have to move along now please!" exclaimed a serious-looking security guard, who suddenly appeared from around the corner, as if back from walking his beat. "Isn't it ok to sit here?" I asked, wondering what the problem was, as we were on the far side of the steps, and not blocking the way at all. "Can't sit there! Move along please!" exclaimed the security guard, as if in robot mode. "That's very unkind of you!" I answered, as I stood up, and put my book in my tote bag. The security guard didn't say anything, but instead started to awkwardly turn around and look the other way, as if not sure what to say or do next.

"Well Della, we're going to get some eats, wanna come?" said Harry "Sounds good!" I answered, as I jumped up, and started to follow them away from the library. "Bye, have a lovely day!" I called out to the security guard, giving him a big smile as we passed him by. He looked a little embarrassed and turned away again as if to avoid any interaction with us. I suddenly felt sorry for him, and the small-minded little world that he must live in.

As the five of us walked along together, we got funny looks from passers-by, which I found amusing. 'People are people, we are all human beings having different life journeys, big deal! What is your problem?' I thought to myself as we passed them by.

On our way to eat, we bumped into the punks again, and they looked at my company in utter disbelief 'What must they be thinking? First, I'm hanging out with a homeless "bag-lady" and now I'm strolling around with a gang of homeless hobos' I thought, laughing to myself.

They obviously didn't see the irony that we were ALL homeless, we were just doing it in different ways! 'At least the conversations are more interesting with the "bag-lady" and the hobos, that's one thing for sure! - Just moaning and complaining about how everyone and everything sucks gets boring after a while!' I thought to myself as we all walked along together.

I recognised that we were heading back to the food hall that Liz had taken me to and I wondered if she would be there. As we entered the building, Liz was the first person I spotted. She was fully engrossed in eating her food, "as usual" and not looking up from her plate once.

The other diners seemed to be doing the same, and I realised that food must be very serious business when you're living on the streets. I joined the queue behind Harry and his friends and got some food. "Hey Harry, I've spotted my friend, Liz, so I'm gonna go and say hi, I'll probably see you later!" I said as I passed by Harry's table. "OK, see ya later!" answered Harry casually, while his friends focused on their food.

"Boo!" I exclaimed to Liz as I arrived at her table, "Oh boo yourself!" she answered, looking a little startled, but happy to see me. I sat next to her and told her about my day so far, and asked her about hers. By now she'd finished eating and was ready to chat again.

As we chatted away, I told her about my visit to the library and the interesting book I'd taken out. The other diners sitting around our table seemed to take notice of our conversation, and they also seemed curious as to where I'd sprung from! They looked happy to see me, and I had the impression that they were somehow being woken up by my youthful energy at the table!

"It's the best library in the state, you can get a book on any subject there!" said a large-built older man. "Yes, agreed!" said another "What do you like to read?" I asked. "Mysteries, politics and history…" he answered passionately. This was followed by a chat about the history of the American; North and South divide, and a debate on whether or not the United States should have stayed divided. "I don't care, as long as I can get some good vodka, and that comes from Russia!" exclaimed Liz, and we all laughed.

BOOK 1: TO SEE THE WORLD

"Okay kiddo, wanna head out for a smoke?" Asked Liz, looking restless. "Yeah, sounds good" I answered, as the two of us stood up, took our empty food trays over to a trolly on the side, strolled outside, and continued on with our chit-chat.

"Wanna head over to the mission, we can probably both sleep there tonight?" asked Liz, after we finished our cigarettes. "Yeah ok!" I answered, thinking 'Why not? I've already experienced sleeping in the Golden Gate Park! Why not see what it's like to sleep overnight at a homeless shelter?'

We strolled down a few streets until we arrived at the mission and Liz rang the buzzer "Two beds please" She stated. "Come in" answered a soft-spoken man, as the door made a buzzing sound and we entered the building.

Inside we were greeted by the same soft-spoken man, who seemed quite a shy and retiring type to have such a job. He was of a slight build, with dark brown hair to one side, and I guessed he was in his forties. "Follow me please, we only have two beds available tonight," he said, as he led the way. "That's great, cos there's only two of us!" exclaimed Liz, and the two of us laughed.

"Yes, this way" he answered, not cracking a smile, as he opened the door to a dorm room. "Your beds are in the centre, keep your possessions with you at all times, and if you want to smoke, please use the reception area," He said, as he turned to leave. "Ok, thanks/thank you!" Liz and I answered, as we gingerly stepped inside the dimly lit dorm room.

The room was large with about forty camp' beds on the floor. We made our way to our camp beds in the middle of the room. The air smelled of various body odours, and the people were snoring loudly, coughing, mumbling and making other strange noises in their sleep. I wondered if we would actually manage to get any sleep there. I guessed I would soon find out!

"Let's put our bags on our beds, and go for a smoke!" suggested Liz. "Yeah ok!" I answered, as the two of us put our most valuable things in our smaller shoulder bags and put our larger bags onto our camp-beds, and covered them with the blanket that was there. Then we headed over to the small reception area.

I was glad to have a little area to hang out and wind down for a while, as going straight to bed after a day of rambling around on the streets was way too abrupt for me! A few others joined us, and we had sporadic efforts at conversation, but we were all too tired and worn out to chat. All we had energy for was to smoke our cigarettes while sitting and staring into space.

"I'm off to catch some z's!" said Liz suddenly. "Me too!" I answered, following her, and giving a little wave to the other people in the reception room as we left. We both put our main bags underneath our camp' beds, and put our smaller hand and shoulder bags on the camp' beds and lay down next to them. "Good night Liz" I whispered, as I stretched out on my camp' bed, and tried to get comfy. "Goodnight, Kiddo!" Liz whispered back, before rolling over and instantly falling asleep.

I lay there staring at the ceiling, and taking in the reality that I was actually spending the night in a San Francisco homeless shelter! I could still hear the snoring and other noises going on around me, and I was amazed at how easily Liz had fallen asleep. I stretched out again and tried to get comfortable, but the mattress was lumpy, the sheet was scratchy, and the blanket was rough. I tossed and turned, and tried to relax, figuring that if I could just rest, it would be better than nothing. Eventually, I fell asleep.

I suddenly woke up in the morning and glanced around me. Most of the other people were up and leaving already. I looked over and saw that Liz was still fast asleep. 'Evidentially we're not morning people!' I thought to myself with a chuckle.

"Ten minutes!" Shouted a stocky-looking guy, who appeared from the reception area. I realised that he meant we had ten minutes to get up and out, so I sat up and gave Liz a gentle tap on her shoulder. I couldn't wake her, so I went to use the bathroom. When I came back Liz was sitting on her bed looking totally wrecked and confused.

"Hiya Liz! I said as I got near her. "I need a cigarette!" she growled back at me. "Yeah, me too! shall we head to reception?" I answered. "Where are my effing shoes?" she growled some more. I helped her look for her shoes and spotted them under the far end of her bed. "Here they are Liz!" I said as I grabbed them and passed them to her. "I'm going to reception for a cigarette," I told her as I headed off to give her a space to wake up. "Yeah, whatever!" she growled.

Inside the reception area was a mixed group of people sitting around looking half asleep, sipping coffee, and smoking cigarettes. I grabbed myself a coffee from the pot on the counter, sat down, nodded hello to whoever glanced my way and lit up a cigarette.

After a few minutes, Liz appeared and joined us. "Hi, Liz!" I said smiling. "Hi yourself!" she answered gruffly. I found her grumpy mood amusing and tried to suppress a chuckle. "I need a drink fast!" exclaimed Liz looking amused at my grinning face.

She sat next to me and lit up a cigarette. We sat in silence slowly waking up for a few minutes, and I pondered on what I might do that day. I wondered if I should head back to LA, or explore San Francisco some more. I was in no rush to get back to LA, as my aunt wouldn't be over for a few more weeks yet, and Larry had ok'd me to have a "Holiday" as he put it, so I was free to do whatever I fancied, which felt great!

I wondered where my aunt might buy a ranch. She had spent her childhood with relatives in Montana and seemed to love it there, although she was curious about other States too. I wondered if she would want me to help her look after the ranch. I was just envisioning myself gearing up to help out as a ranch hand when Liz suddenly said "Ok kiddo let's hit the street!" "OK!" I said, as we both grabbed our bags and said goodbye to the others.

The streets of San Francisco were as vibrant as ever. I absolutely loved the fresh cool salty air that flowed gently around us, and as ever, the fabulous cosmopolitan mix of people going about their daily lives. Liz popped into a liquor store while I stood outside admiring the city and her people. Liz soon appeared holding a large brown paper bag, and I grinned at her, knowing exactly what was inside of it.

We headed back over to "Liz's park bench" and we both sat for a while. Liz sipping vodka from her brown paper bag, and me just enjoying being. After a while I got restless. "Fancy a walk?" I asked Liz "No you go ahead, you know where to find me, here, the mission, the eating place, OR the liquor store!" she answered with a loud laugh. "OK, see ya later!" I answered, laughing with her, as I turned and strolled away.

I enjoyed exploring the city some more. I just walked and walked, not knowing if I was in good or bad neighbourhoods, but trusting my instincts to guide me. I came across an amazing zigzag Street and stood there for a while admiring it, and marvelling at human ingenuity. I suddenly spotted a gift store nearby, so I went inside, and I bought some postcards to send to my parents and friends back in England.

I found a café to sit and have a coffee while I wrote the postcards, and afterwards, I sat some more, enjoying watching the world go by. As the people rushed by, on foot, in cars, and on trams, it fascinated me that we were all strangers, living completely different lives, with various things to do, yet we were all sharing the same space. I pondered on my ancestors, the start of creation, and how many billions of years had passed before I'd popped into the world eighteen years ago. I was aware of how relatively short human life was, and felt as though I wanted to make the most of my time and try and see and do as much as possible while I was here! I felt so grateful just to be.

After a while I wondered how Liz was doing, so I headed back to "her park bench." She wasn't there, so. I headed over to the community centre and there she was sitting in a big comfy chair sipping on a coffee and smoking a cigarette.

I sat down in the chair next to her and she looked surprised to see me. "Hi, Liz!" I exclaimed. "Hi Kiddo!" she answered, with a smile. "I'm gonna get a coffee!" I said, as I jumped up, and headed over to the coffee maker that seemed to be topped up, most of the time.

I went back to sit with Liz. Although she could be prickly, I liked her company. I found her comfortable to be around. I liked that she was very down to earth, with no false airs or graces. She was real, warts and all!

"Hey Della, fancy coming home to Sacramento with me?" asked Liz as I sipped on my coffee. "How do you mean home?" I asked puzzled. "You know, home!" she answered, sounding frustrated. "I can get Brian to drive my car back, it's parked on Maple Avenue outside of town. We'll be there in a couple of hours, and you can meet my dog Bo, and my friends Lyn and Paul! They're looking after the house for me while I'm away" said Liz casually. I felt confused, and blown away to find out that my friend Liz the "Bag Lady" had a home, a car, friends, and even a dog named Bo!

Liz waved over a guy from the other side of the room and introduced us. "This is my friend, Brian, he drove me down here, he's been in Oakland taking care of business. This is my new friend Della" Said Liz, smiling, looking pleased to be introducing us.

"Hi, Della!" said Brian as he reached out his hand. "Hi Brian!" I answered as we shook hands. He was a slim, dark-haired guy, and looked to be in his mid-twenties, and I wondered where Liz had met him. "I'm off to use the John!" exclaimed Liz, suddenly jumping up, and heading towards the bathroom.

"Wow, I didn't know that Liz had a home, or a car, or you!" I exclaimed to Brian while feeling surprised by such revelations. "Oh sure, she has a big house in Sacramento! She just likes to get away from it all! So, every once in a while, she comes down here and lives on the streets." Answered Brian matter-of-factly.

438

"Gosh, I never knew that, she never told me!" I answered, feeling a whole new light shining on Liz. 'I guess she's a fellow adventurer of sorts too!' I thought to myself.

"So, are you coming with us?" asked Liz as she returned from the bathroom. "Yes, sounds great!" I answered, looking forward to seeing some more of California, and seeing where Liz lived.

CHAPTER 51:

SACRAMENTO LADIES OF LEISURE!

"OK, so we need to take the Fifth Street bus over to Maple, that's where the car is" Liz exclaimed, suddenly sounding very sober, sensible and well-organised, which I felt was possibly giving a glimpse to Liz's personality before alcohol moved in. Brian and I followed her out of the door of the community centre, waved goodbye to the others, and off we went.

After a while, Brian took over the lead as Liz dropped back to walk by my side. Brian had a serious disposition - the opposite of me! I seemed to find the funny side of most things, which worked as a great life raft and helped to keep me afloat.

The three of us piled onto the number five bus, found some seats, and sat in silence as it trundled along, "So what's Sacramento like Liz?" I asked curiously. "Beautiful! So green! With a river running through it! It's my home and I love it! but sometimes I get so bored, I just gotta take off!" she exclaimed passionately. "Yes, like escape TO Alcatraz!" I joked. "That's right!" exclaimed Liz, and we both cracked up laughing.

"So where do you know Brian from?" I asked, in a hushed tone. "Oh, he's a neighbour of mine, he has a business in Oakland, and often uses my car to give me a ride to Frisco whenever I feel the urge to take off!" She answered in a similar hushed tone. "That's handy!" I answered, wondering if Brian took a bus or a train the rest of the way to Oakland, or if he borrowed the car for the rest of his journey, and just drove back, and parked up in the spot we were going to. "Sure is!" she answered, and we both chuckled.

Once again my mind flashed to Oakland on my dad's map, and I felt a little sense of pride in myself, that not only had I passed right by a place I had once only dreamed of visiting, but I was now in the company of someone who actually had a business there! I smiled to myself and looked forward to writing to my parents, especially my dad, about my latest adventures.

"He seems a bit quiet?" I whispered to Liz nodding back towards Brian, who was sitting far enough away not to hear me. "Yeah, that's just Brian. He is sound though! Sound as a bell!" she answered, with a motherly type of pride. "That's good!" I answered with a smile. The bus rolled on and we sunk back into our thoughts and daydreams.

"This is it!" exclaimed Liz, as she suddenly jumped up. Brian and I stood up also, and we all quickly got off the bus. "My car is parked up here!" said Liz as we walked up a side street. Brian walked ahead of us and was soon opening the doors, to a big classic-style American car, for us.

Liz jumped in the front, and I jumped in the back, and we set off. Liz put the radio on and we all went back into our thoughts and daydreams and glided along the city streets. My heart was still missing Jay, but I continued to wish him all the best, and I decided to think about other things instead, as what was the point of being sad?

I decided to focus my thoughts on my travels instead. I was pleased at how well they were going so far. Somehow in less than a year, and on the tiniest of budgets, I had managed to see quite a bit of England, Canada, and the USA! I thought about how each place seemed to have its own special atmosphere and people to match it, and I loved that I was getting to experience such a diverse variety of people and places. It taught me that neither way of living was right or wrong, it was just different.

I thought about how I seemed to be falling in love with California, as it seemed to suit me in every way! but I reminded myself that there was still a big wide world out there to continue exploring, including more of the Americas! I wondered what my final decision would be once my Aunt Freda arrived, would I go back to England with her, or would I go on to explore Mexico, and then maybe on to Central and South America, and after that maybe over to the Caribbean, or across to Asia, who knows? but for now, I would enjoy exploring California - especially Sacramento!

The car hit the highway and was now travelling at high speed, with lively pop music playing on the radio that Liz was humming along to, in between swigging on her vodka. Brian looked deep in thought and was focused on the road ahead. He drove fast but in control.

As we sped along, I felt as though I was in a kind of limbo between worlds, and life experiences, literally transferring from one reality to another as we went. It was a wonderful feeling to be free enough to do such a thing. It fascinated me how one's life was so wrapped up in the people and things around us, yet it all seemed so temporary, like a thin veneer of props on the world's many stages. It was a little scary to think how fragile it all is, but I decided to relax into the experience and enjoy it. I sat back and watched the scenery whizz by while looking forward to my next destination. I hoped Jay was doing ok.

After a time we stopped at a rest station "Let's stretch our legs!" exclaimed Liz, and we all jumped out of the car. Liz and I automatically headed over to use the bathroom. "See you in the store!" Liz shouted to Brian as we went. Brian nodded, then headed over towards the male bathrooms.

After using the bathrooms, we all headed over to the store for some refreshments. Other drivers had the same idea, and once we'd bought our snack and drinks we all headed back outside and stood, or sat around next to our cars making light conversation. It felt like some kind of low-key roadside party, as we all transitioned between destinations.

"Ready to roll?" exclaimed Brian, just as we all finished eating. "Let's roll!" Liz exclaimed back, and the three of us said our goodbyes to our fellow carpark diners and jumped back in the car and took off along the highway once again.

After another hour or so we turned off the highway onto regular streets and drove into an upscale residential area. We continued on down various side streets until we reached a street with trees lined on either side of it and parked up outside of a big house.

The house was beautiful, with well-kept lawns, flower gardens, and a gorgeous cherry tree to the side. I glanced around to see if I could see the name of the street and noticed the sign nearby read Cherry Avenue which filled me with a sense of wholesomeness. "Home Sweet Home!" exclaimed Liz, sounding pleased to be home.

'The punks would never believe this! Liz the homeless, drunk "Bag Lady" lives in a mansion! It just shows that being judgemental like they were, means that people often miss out on getting to know the real person!" I thought to myself, as the three of us grabbed our bags and got out of the car. I was looking forward to meeting Liz's friends - and Bo the dog!

BOOK 1: TO SEE THE WORLD

"Hi there!" said a blonde female as she appeared at the front door. "Susie baby! How are you? And how are my babies Bob and Bo?" exclaimed Liz excitedly. "All good!" answered Susie with a big smile. "Susie and her boyfriend Bob live with me, the house is too big for me, I'd be lonely! ...and besides they take care of my pooch Bo!" Exclaimed Liz dramatically. "Yeah, she's out back! I'm not sure where Bob is, I think he's upstairs" answered Susie, looking happy to see Liz home safe and sound.

"This is Della, my new friend from England!" exclaimed Liz excitedly. "Hi! Susie!" I said as I got nearer. "Hi Della, nice to meet you!" Susie answered as we shook hands "Come on in!" Exclaimed Liz, as she led the way into the house.

The house was just as grand looking on the inside, as it was on the outside: The décor was stylish, with beautiful furniture and ornaments elegantly arranged. We didn't stay inside for long though, as we all shuffled on through the house, and outside to the garden on the other side of the house, because Liz was longing to see her dog: Bo.

Bo was very excited to see Liz again and exhibited his joy with lots of jumping, yelping and tail wagging. It was lovely to see Liz so happy to be with Bo again, as she hugged, petted, and kissed him. I looked around at the beautiful large garden with a well-kept lawn, more flower beds, a tree swing in the centre, and a bar in one corner, just to the side of the house. 'What a lovely home!' I thought to myself as I stood there smiling, feeling happy to have gone along for the ride!

"How about a welcome back drink!" exclaimed Liz as she headed towards the bar in the corner of the garden. We all followed her and jumped up on barstools on either side of her. Bo sat nearby, slowly calming down, but still wagging his tail, and looking very happy to see Liz again.

"You have a beautiful home, Liz!" I exclaimed as Brian went behind the bar to pour the drinks. "I sure do kiddo, and my home is your home for as long as you want to stay!" answered Liz exuberantly. "Aw, thanks Liz, cheers!" I answered as Brian slid us a couple of drinks over. "Cheers Kiddo!" Liz exclaimed as we clinked glasses.

"Put some music on Brian!" exclaimed Liz, and Brian switched a pop radio station on the radio. Soon we were all sat at the bar laughing, joking, and telling stories about our San Francisco adventures. It was a great atmosphere, and even Brian cracked a smile or two. 'I think I'm going to like it here!' I thought to myself with a big grin, as I felt the vodka orange cocktail kicking in.

"Bobby baby!" exclaimed Liz, as a slim, short, brown-haired, guy suddenly appeared from the house. Liz jumped up and hugged him. "Hi Liz, did you have a good time?" asked Bobby, as he gave her a hug and a kiss, then climbed up on a seat at the end of the bar, the other side of Susie. "Sure did, and I made a new friend - Della!" exclaimed Liz, giving me a little side hug. "Hi, Della!" said Bobby, stretching his arm behind Susie and Liz. "Hi, Bobby!" I answered as I also stretched my arm and we shook hands. Then Bobby turned and gave Susie a big hug and a kiss, as if not wanting her to feel left out. "Young love!" exclaimed Liz loudly, and we all laughed.

Later on, Brian went on a Pizza run, and we ate, drank and were merry until the wee hours of the following morning. "Time to go to bed!" exclaimed Liz suddenly. "Yeah/Sure is!" we all agreed. "Susie, take Della to the guest room, goodnight!" said Liz, before disappearing off into the house. "Goodnight Liz/Sleep well!" We all called after her. "I'll show you the guest room!" said Susie, as we all stood up and started heading back inside the house. "Thanks!" I answered as I followed her along.

Susie led me to a study with a comfy-looking sofa bed in the middle, which Susie helped me to set up. We wished each other good night, and I lay down, got comfortable, and instantly fell asleep!

After a few hours of sleep, I woke up feeling hung-over, but happy. The Sun shone gently through the window as if to welcome me to the new day. I slowly sat up and looked around me to see bookshelves lined with books, and a stylish oak desk, with a chair next to it. I wondered if Liz or her husband had been a lawyer or something similar, as I stood up and headed to the bathroom to wash up.

The bathroom was as immaculate and beautifully decorated as the rest of the house, and I was curious as to what Liz's background was to own such a palace! After using the bathroom, I headed for the Kitchen as quietly as possible, as I assumed that everyone, including Bo the dog, was still crashed out asleep.

I arrived in the kitchen to scc booze bottles and cans all over the countertops. I grinned at the sight of the mess, it felt so nice to be a guest at such a beautiful, and fun party house! I made a cup of instant coffee and rummaged for snacks in the kitchen cupboards.

"Hey Della, top of the morning to you!" Exclaimed Liz in her husky morning voice. I turned to see her looking as rough as I felt "Morning Liz!" I answered, feeling pleased to see her. "Where's my drink? I need a vodka!" she exclaimed suddenly. "I think I saw some on the countertop!" I answered, feeling obliged to help her search. "Where!? Where!?" She demanded, sounding very distressed as if finding the vodka was an upmost urgent matter. "Over there!" I answered. pointing to the countertop behind her.

Just then Bobby, Susie, and Bo joined us, Liz found her vodka instantly calmed down, and looked happy again. "Cereal everyone?" asked Bobbie, as he went to a cupboard that I'd yet to check. "Sure/Yes please" we all answered, as we sat down around the kitchen table.

"I'll help you!" said Susie, as she jumped up and helped Bobby get the breakfast things together. I felt a bit awkward not helping out, but I didn't have a clue where anything was and would have probably been more of a hindrance than a help. I figured that I would do the dishes afterwards, as it was only fair that I pitch in.

We were soon all tucking into bowls of cereal, followed by pop tarts and fresh coffee, as we all sat around the breakfast table slowly waking up, and chatting about what a fun night we'd had the night before, sharing our San Francisco tales for tales of how everything had been ok back at Liz's while she'd been away. I loved how none of them made a fuss about me being from England, it made me feel as though I was one of them.

"We gotta get ready for work!" exclaimed Susie, as she glanced at the clock on the wall, stood up and started heading out of the kitchen. "Gotta go!" exclaimed Bobby, as he jumped up and followed her. "OK/See you later/bye" we all called out to each other, as they headed off upstairs to get ready.

It was nearing 12 pm so I assumed they had afternoon jobs. Liz and I stayed chatting in the kitchen, and it was lovely to spend some quality time with her in her own home. "So why do you go and live rough on the streets Liz?" I asked, feeling a little puzzled, as to why she would leave such a beautiful home, with loving friends, and a cute dog. "I just get SO bored! I've always lived such a privileged life, I want to see what the real world is like, and what people are REALLY like! That's why I like you kiddo! You don't judge, you take people for what they are! You're a gal after my own heart!" exclaimed Liz, holding up her glass towards me.

"Aw, thanks Liz, yeah, I get it! I guess that's pretty much what I've been doing on my travels too - seeing the world, and its people for what they truly are. When you look like a street kid or homeless person, people treat you differently, you get to see their true colours, it's like a sneak peek behind the scenes of the world's various stages" I answered.

"You're a deep thinker kiddo! I hope you're going to write about all this one day!" exclaimed Liz, as if knowing me, inside and out. "Well yeah, I have been keeping a travel journal, so ya never know!" I answered, jokingly. "Good for you Kiddo! So, what are your plans for today? Do you wanna take Bo for a walk?" she asked, while looking around, I presumed, for Bo.

"Sounds good! I'll just do the dishes!" I answered, as I jumped up, and started clearing the table. "Thanks, Kiddo!" answered Liz, as she poured herself another Vodka, and petted Bo. "Would it be ok to take a shower?" I asked after I finished the dishes. "Of course! There are tons of towels in the guest bathroom drawer, just help yourself!" exclaimed Liz, generously. "Thanks, Liz! I'll go get ready then" I answered, as I headed off to the study, to get some fresh clothes. "Sure!" called out Liz after me as I went.

Once I was ready I went back to see Liz in the kitchen, who by now was quite tipsy and was singing along to pop music on the radio. "OK, I'm ready, where's Bo's lead please Liz?" I asked, feeling bad for interrupting her fun time. "Here it is Kiddo!" she answered, jumping up, and reaching for the dog's lead that was hanging at the back of the kitchen door. "Thanks! Come on Bo!" I exclaimed as Bo came running towards me. I put his lead on, and Liz walked us both to the front door.

Outside the front door, Liz gave me directions to a river that was nearby and added that it was a lovely walk, Bo loved it, and so would I. I thanked her for the directions, we said our goodbyes, and then Bo and I took off. I wasn't sure who was the most excited to be going on a walk! Bo, or me! I was really looking forward to having a walkabout to see the local area, and to spend some time with Bo!

Bo was a cute little sandy-coloured mongrel. He was a very happy dog with a friendly disposition. We walked along, both of us in a good mood, he led the way as I looked around and admired my new scenery.

Large stylish detached houses, with well-kept flower gardens, and lawns, were evenly spaced along the tree-lined residential streets. It was obviously a very affluent area, and once again, I couldn't help but wonder what Liz's background was. I got the impression that she may have come from "old money" and that possibly also her late/ex-husband had been/was well off. I didn't care about any of that, because I liked Liz for Liz, but I was intrigued.

BOOK 1: TO SEE THE WORLD

I loved that Liz had a whole lot more going on than what first meets the eye, but more importantly, I loved that Liz was a fellow free-spirit! I also liked the fact that we were of a different age group, but still on a similar wavelength in some ways so we got along just fine! I was happy to have a new friend, especially one with such character! 'So, what if she likes a drink!' I thought to myself, as I remembered one of the things, she'd said to me when we first met.

As I followed Bo along, I noticed that the way he was leading me matched Liz's directions, so he obviously knew the way well. We came to a busy main road, and I noticed Bo's tail stopped wagging, and he seemed nervous about the traffic. "Don't worry Bo, we'll be at the park soon" I said softly, as I stopped to give him a little hug and stroke his head. He seemed to understand and started to wag his tail a little again.

We didn't have to cross the main road; we only had to turn left and walk alongside of it. I could see that the path to the river wasn't far away, so we walked for a few moments until we were able to take off down a hilly pathway and into a big field that was next to the river.

We were soon both walking the river bank, and Bo's tail started wagging fast again. 'Paradise!' I thought to myself as we strolled along, surrounded by lush green grass, wildflowers, and trees. We headed towards the centre of the field, and once I found a space that seemed safe, with plenty of room for Bo to run free, I knelt down, petted him, and let him off the lead. He took off excitedly running around me in circles of joy! Seeing him so happy, made me feel happy.

I sat down on the grass, lay back and stared up at the blue sky, feeling a sense of pure happiness in the moment. The temperature was just right for me, not too hot, and not too cold. The trees near me had stunning branches, with just enough space to let the blue sky show through. I felt more relaxed than I'd felt in a long time, and a sense of pure gratitude took over me as I gave my thanks to the creator.

I had never joined an organised religion, but I did believe in a creator because creation existed, I could not deny that. I wasn't sure what god or the creator was exactly, but I felt it was simply the life force at the heart of all things, in creation.

I lay there staring up at the blue sky through the tree branches and thought about my journey so far. I thought of my family and friends back in England, and all the lovely friends I'd made along the way. I briefly thought about some of the bad people, or "bad apples" as I now called them, and prayed for them too. - They were obviously unwell, and I didn't want to dwell on negative things. I truly did appreciate all of the good things, and the good people in my life, and to have such a special time in Sacramento to reflect on everything was priceless to me.

I could hear Bo running around nearby happily panting, and I would lift my head to glance at him every so often to check that he was ok. After he'd exhausted himself running around, he came to lie down next to me, still panting happily. "Good boy Bo!" I said, as I reached over and stroked his head as we both lay side by side enjoying the moment.

I wondered how Jay was doing back in San Francisco, and hoped he didn't feel bad about what had happened. I felt it was understandable that he'd moved on, as I hadn't replied to his last few phone calls or his letter, plus he'd thought I'd gone back to England. I assumed that when he was working with Chrissy there must have been a spark between them, and maybe he was desperately trying to contact me before deciding whether or not to move on with Chrissy. This told me that he was a loyal type at least, so I couldn't fault him for anything really. I wished them both well and went back to daydreaming about my travels.

After a while, I sat up, and Bo followed suit and sat up too. "Do you want to walk a little more?" I asked him, with a smile. He looked at me excitedly and started wagging his tail, so I took that as a yes. I stood up, and we continued on with our walk.

After a while, we reached a nearby playground. There were no kids, or adults around, so for fun, I had a little ride on the roundabout and a little swing on the swings. Bo stood watching me as if trying to understand what I was doing, so not wanting to leave him out, I gently picked him up and took him on the slide with me which he seemed to love, as when I put him on the ground he ran fast back to the steps, so I took him on the slide with me a couple more times. He wagged his tail and I laughed, as we whizzed down the slide. I loved how the two of us were from different species, yet we were both happy with the same simple pleasures.

"OK Bo, let's walk some more!" I exclaimed, as I stood up from the slide, and gently placed Bo back on his feet. He wagged his tail excitedly, as we carried on with our walk through the field.

I'd always loved animals. I loved how pure they were. My thoughts turned to my childhood dog Kim, and I realised that I was playing with Bo the same way I'd played with Kim. I thought about how animals seemed to have the same emotional intelligence as children, and my mind flashed to the Animal rights march and the flyer I'd been handed in San Francisco the first time I visited with Jennie, and I couldn't understand why anyone would want to hurt them. They were so innocent, and harmless. If anything, surely it was our responsibility to help them?

I thought about farm animals, and how I'd always eaten meat without ever giving much thought to the suffering they might have gone through. I questioned myself on whether it was morally ethical to eat animals. My gut and heart said no, but my head said it's just the way it is! That didn't seem right, or fair, but I left it at that, for the time being.

Bo suddenly came running over towards me with a stick, so we played fetch until we were both worn out and had to sit down on the grass to catch our breath. "Wanna go home?" I asked Bo after it seemed we had rejuvenated. Bo jumped up looking excited, and started to wag his tail. So, once again, I took that as a yes, and we headed home.

"Hi. Liz!" I shouted as we entered the house, but there was no reply. I took Bo through the house, and out to the back garden, took his lead off, and put it away, then went in search of Liz. I was feeling a little concerned for her and hoped she was okay.

As I neared her bedroom, I heard snoring, so feeling relieved I headed back down to the kitchen, and made myself a grilled cheese sandwich and a glass of Kool-Aid, then went to the guest room/study to relax, do some journalling, and maybe read, as there were so many books around!

Once I was all caught up with my journalling, I browsed through the books and a book titled: "Flowers in the Attic"- By VC Andrews, caught my attention. I pulled it out and opened it to read a little. It had a good flow to it, so I decided I would read some more. I got comfortable on the sofa bed, which I'd left the bedding on, but had made the bed, and spent the next couple of hours, lying down, stretched out reading.

It was so lovely to have some time out just to relax and read. I felt as though I was having a holiday from my adventures, which although fun, could also be extremely stressful and exhausting at times. I felt blessed to have such a lovely home to take respite in, and I realised that none of it would have happened if I hadn't been friendly with a supposed "bag lady". It reminded me of a part of the Bible that read something like: "Be kind to strangers, because you may be in the company of angels" I felt that Liz and I totally got that, and I realised that she must have had a similar take on me - an eighteen-year-old, new-wave, punky looking free-spirit, all the way from England!

"Hi, anybody home?" called out Susie, as the front door opened, and slammed shut behind her. I put the book down, grabbed my empty glass, and got up to go and say hi. By the time I came out of the study, Susie was entering the kitchen. "Hi, Susie!" I called out, as I followed her, deciding to top up my drink of Kool-Aid.

"Hi Della, do you know where Liz is?" she asked, with a smile, as she put some groceries away. "The last time I checked she was fast asleep!" I answered. "Ah, that's good! I'm going to make some dinner if you'd like some?" she asked, as she started putting some food on the countertop to prepare. "OK, thanks, can I help with anything?" I asked, hoping to make myself useful. "Sure, can you chop up the salad while I make the pasta and sauce?" she answered, looking pleased to have some help. "Yep, ok" I answered, as I went about rinsing and chopping up various salad ingredients. Bobbie suddenly appeared, greeted us both, gave Susie a little kiss, and then went about getting the plates and cutlery together, and setting the table. I liked how we each had a little job to do.

"Ready for another round of living!" exclaimed Liz, followed by her hoarse laugh, as she came down the stairs, and we all cracked up laughing. "Dinner's nearly ready Liz!" called out Susie proudly. "Oh, wonderful! Wonderful! Thank you, my darlings!" answered Liz, as she arrived in the kitchen, looking refreshed after her nap.

Once dinner was ready, Bobbie suggested that we eat outside, so we all picked up our plates and utensils and headed out to the back garden picnic table. It was lovely to be in such a climate that eating outside seemed to be a normal everyday thing. After dinner, we all cleared up, and I helped do the dishes. Just as we were finishing putting everything away, a friend of Liz's named Frankie arrived at the house, and we all headed back outside to the garden bar for another night of partying.

I went to bed that night feeling happy with the day. I felt a strong sense of togetherness and belonging. I felt very much at home here, as I did pretty much everywhere I'd been so far, and it made me realise that the world truly is just one big house, with one big family - The human family. 'We just need to connect with one another more to realise it!' I thought to myself, as I dozed off.

Over the next couple of weeks, while Susie and Bob went about their daily routines, Liz and I mainly lived a life of 'ladies of leisure.' As Liz had told me I was welcome to stay for as long as I liked, in return I would usually help out with light housework, errands, and taking Bo for walks, but aside from that, I would mostly spend my spare time at Liz's nighttime garden-bar parties, playing with Bo in the garden, swinging on the garden tree swing, or lounging in the study: journalling and reading. I wanted for nothing!

There were lots more VC Andrews books, which by now I was steadily developing an addition to! After "Flowers in the Attic" I read "If There Be Thorns" and "Petals on the Wind." They were Gothic Mysteries, and I found them to be such the perfect read for my relaxation down-time. At some point, I realised that I'd read through them in the wrong order, but I enjoyed them nonetheless!

One day I rang the Pico halfway house to check if everything was ok, and Mary told me that everything was fine and that Linda was covering for her, so there was no need for me to rush back which was a great relief. My aunt Freda still wasn't due to arrive in LA for a few more weeks, so I was absolutely free to do as I pleased for a while, which was wonderful!

Staying at Liz's house in Sacramento helped me to gain a perspective on my time in LA. It showed me how quickly I had become wrapped up with various duties and responsibilities. I realised that it all seemed to go hand in hand with putting down roots in a place. I felt that I was a long way off wanting just one main home base, as I wanted to stay free for as long as possible, or at least until I felt ready to put down roots. I appreciated having my time at Liz's to take stock of such things.

Although I was having a lovely time staying at Liz's, one day I felt restless, and bored. I'd read all the VC Andrews books from the library, I was all caught up with my journalling, I'd had plenty of beautiful walks with Bo to last a lifetime, and I'd had enough partying with Liz and co' to keep me tipsy for the next three months! I felt that it was time to get going!

I soon realised that I was missing the excitement of city life! I missed the sense that anything could happen, I missed the noise of the traffic, the buzz of the crowds, and the random people I would meet. I decided I would head back to San Francisco the next day, and maybe spend a few more days there, before heading back down to LA. I wasn't sure how, or when I would tell Liz I was leaving, as I didn't want her to think that I wasn't grateful for her hospitality. I decided it was probably best to tell her at the bar in the evening, as that was when she always seemed at her most relaxed.

"I think I'm gonna head back to Frisco tomorrow Liz" I announced at the bar that evening, when the timing felt right. "You can't leave yet! You're the daughter I never had! Have Susie and Bobby been mean to you?" She exclaimed, sounding and looking distressed. "No, everything is fine! I'm just missing city life!" I answered honestly. "Don't I know it! but, so soon?" she answered, as if understanding where I was coming from, but still a little confused. "Well yeah, I've had a lovely time with you all, I just feel it's time to get going though. Nothing personal!" I answered, laughing nervously.

"I guess you are still very young, you're only eighteen, and two weeks must seem like two months to you! I remember how restless I used to be at that age, but you better write to me, and come and visit often okay?" she said caringly, looking like she was about to cry. "Yes, of course!" I answered, with a big smile. "You better kiddo! To Della! I'll miss you! We all will, won't we?" Liz exclaimed, raising her glass in the air. "To Della!" echoed the others. "To Liz and all of you!" I answered, as we all clinked our glasses together in cheers, and carried on drinking.

We had an extra big party that night and the next morning I woke up feeling hung-over, but ready to roll! Liz arranged for Brian to give me a lift over to the Greyhound Bus station and she insisted on giving me some money for the ticket. I'd tried to decline, but she'd forced it into my hand, and wouldn't take no for an answer. Liz, Frankie, Susie, Bob and Bo came out and stood about on the front porch to say goodbye to me, and they each gave me a big hug, before I turned, and followed Brian to his car.

I jumped inside, threw my tote bag down at the side of me, and looked out of the window. The sight of Liz, Frankie, Susie, Bobby, and Bo, all standing there was very moving, and I wondered when, or if I would ever see them again. We all waved goodbye to one another, and Brian started to drive away. I felt sad to be leaving Liz and company, but at the same time, I was happy to be on my way again. We all kept waving at one another until they were out of sight.

Brian drove me to the Greyhound station. "Thanks, Brian!" I exclaimed as we shook hands. "No problem, have a good trip!" he answered. "See ya!" I called out, "See ya, be good!" he called back, then jumped into his car and drove off. I looked around me to get my bearings, then strolled inside the Greyhound building to buy my ticket to San Francisco. I was feeling excited to be free to explore once again, and I couldn't wait to get back to the city!

CHAPTER 52:

FRISCO – PART 3!

I jumped off the Greyhound bus in San Francisco, feeling so happy to be back! The city seemed to give me a big warm welcome-back hug, as I breezed along its streets feeling on cloud nine. 'San Francisco, it's great to see you again!' I thought as I walked along with a smile, just soaking in the city atmosphere, with no plans whatsoever, and loving it! All around me were city streets, parks, flowers, trees, and beautiful people of mixed ages and races. 'Such diversity! What a great city!' I thought to myself, as I glided along. "Hey Della, is that you?" shouted a female voice. I turned to see a blonde punk girl around my age who I vaguely recognised from the LA and Frisco Punk crowd. I went over to say hi, and we sat down on a nearby bench and got chatting.

"What's your name again?" I asked, not wanting to seem rude, as she knew my name, but I didn't know hers. "Janie!" she answered, as we shook hands. "Ah yeah, I know your face, but I'm not great with names, sorry!" I answered. "No worries, so where have you been, I haven't seen you around lately, I thought you'd gone back to LA," she asked, looking pleased to see me. "Well, I made friends with who I thought was a homeless "bag-lady" named Liz, and she invited me up to her place in Sacramento, so I stayed there for a couple of weeks, how about you, what have you been up to?

"Same ole, same ole! Sacramento sounds like a blast, how cool that you thought she was a "bag lady" to start out with!" answered Janie with a laugh. "Yeah, well it's because she basically was a "bag-lady" when I met her! She was carrying loads of plastic bags, living homeless, getting drunk on vodka, and crashing at the mission house!" I answered, and we both cracked up laughing. "Oh, I think I saw you with her one day, yeah she totally looked like a homeless bag-lady!" answered Janie with a grin.

"So, what's been going on in Frisco? I missed it! Do you know Jennie and Jay?" I asked, hoping to hear some news about Jay. "Not a lot, a few of us are thinking

453

of heading back to Hollywood next week, yeah I know Jennie and Jay, I haven't seen them in a while though!" she answered, with a shoulder shrug. My heart sank at the news that she hadn't seen Jay, as that probably meant that he was spending his spare time with Chrissy, rather than out on the streets with the punks.

"So, what's your deal man, did you run away from your home in England?" she asked curiously. "No, I didn't run away, I turned seventeen and just felt ready to leave home. I was longing to see the world, so off I went!" I answered, with a laugh.

"But still, you were only seventeen! That's very young to be leaving home, especially to another country all on your own!" she added sounding really concerned for me. "Well, it just seemed natural to me!" I answered not sure what else to say. – In my mind, I was on a great adventure, and I didn't have a problem with it. If others couldn't understand it, that was their problem, not mine! - That was how I saw it. "Wow, good for you!" answered Janie, as if in admiration. "Thanks, I guess we all have our journeys, what about you, what's your story?" I asked curiously. "No big deal really, my folks live too far out in the valley for me to have any fun, so when I turned eighteen, I moved to Hollywood with a friend to go to beauty school, and one thing led to another, and I ended up here!" she answered, and we both laughed. "That's life, right!" I answered. "Right!" she answered.

Janie was easy-going, and fun to chat with, so we spent the rest of the day hanging out together and rambling around the streets of San Francisco. As we walked along, I thought about all the different street kids I'd made friends with around the world: Southampton, London, Toronto, Los Angeles, and now here in San Francisco, and I loved how in all these different cities, and countries the street-kids were so open and welcoming to each other. 'Maybe the world leaders could take some tips from them!' I thought to myself with a smile.

I spent the rest of the money that Liz had given me on food and drinks for the two of us, and at night time I blew the rest of my other money on getting us into an overrated punk club. We got drunk, danced, and had fun. Afterwards, Janie arranged for us to crash at one of the local crash pads.

We got a lift in an old van with some punks from one of the bands that had been playing and headed into a dingy old apartment full of musical instruments and band equipment. It turned out it was where the band lived. They put some old records on, and we partied on cheap beers, until the others took off to various bedrooms to crash, and I passed out on the sofa.

I woke up in the morning feeling wrecked. The room was spinning as I rushed to the loo to throw up. Afterwards, I drank cold water straight from the tap. I hadn't felt this bad in a while! I usually preferred to just catch a buzz and get tipsy, I didn't enjoy getting full-on drunk at all. I used the loo, washed my face, tidied my hair, topped up my makeup, and then headed back to the living room, trying to stop the room from spinning as I went.

One of the bedroom doors was half open and I could see Janie was passed out on a bed with a band member. I was glad to see that she was okay. I landed on a beanbag, found a cigarette in a pack lying about, lit it up, smoked it and just sat there completely vegged out and staring at the ceiling. I felt so rough and just wanted everything to stop moving.

Eventually, the room stopped spinning, and I felt the urge to get outside for some fresh air. I decided to go for a walkabout and find some coffee! I hadn't seen any in the kitchen of the apartment. Just empty beer cans, and ashtrays full of cigarette butts, so I tiptoed out, and closed the front door quietly behind me. I was feeling too rough to stop and write a note, but I figured I would see Janie about town later in the day.

It was good to be in the cool fresh air again. I was starting to feel hungry, and checked my purse, while hazily remembering blowing the last of my money when Janie and I were out and about the night before. I was surprised to see I had a dollar left, I thought I'd spent it all. I kind of liked the idea of having only a dollar to my name, and the strong feeling of living in the moment that it gave me. I was living on the edge, and loving every second of it! 'Things can only get better from here!' I thought to myself.

I suddenly spotted a hotdog stand with a big sign reading: "Hot Dogs and a Soda $1.00!!" "See, Perfect!" I thought to myself, as I swaggered over and bought myself a hotdog and a soda, then strolled along with my mobile feast, and not a care in the world.

I sat on a park bench and enjoyed the fresh air and the scenery around me. I was broke, but I was free! I suddenly missed Liz. It felt weird to be there without her. 'Liz the, supposedly, homeless person who had ironically made me feel at home in San Francisco and Sacramento! What a character she is!' I thought to myself, smiling at the memory of the two of us rambling around the streets of San Francisco together like a couple of hobos, and later on living a life of luxury at her place up in Sacramento. 'That's what life is all about, experiences and adventures! - To Liz!' I thought to myself with a smile.

I suddenly remembered that I could donate blood plasma for some pocket money, so I stood up, threw my hot dog tray and empty soda can in the trash, and started walking towards the area where the blood plasma donation building was.

As I walked along enjoying the sights and sounds of San Francisco, I suddenly felt a pang of homesickness, but not for England - for Los Angeles! I was suddenly missing my friends there, and my crazy halfway-house family on Pico! I missed them all - especially Mike. He was such a sweet soul, and I started to feel bad for leaving him for so long.

I thought about how LA was starting to feel like my second home. Toronto had felt like home too, but the LA sunshine and beaches gave it that little bit extra. I thought about how, in some ways, I did feel in my element in San Francisco too. I loved the slight edginess it had, and the strong socially-conscious vibes about town, which was reflected in the posters on the walls, the bands, the community centres and the people! I loved all of that, as it felt very familiar and similar to the UK, and Toronto in some ways, but for whatever reason, I felt more at home in LA.

I decided that San Francisco would be a fun city to visit from time to time, while I was visiting LA in the future, but until then I would be continuing on with my travels. I reminded myself, that I did not want to get tied down to any place, thing, or person, just yet!

As I continued to walk along my thoughts turned more and more towards LA and my friends there, and the feeling of missing them all built up so much that I suddenly decided to forget about the blood plasma donation, and instead, find a freeway and hitchhike 'home' to LA.

CHAPTER 53:

(SECOND) HOMEWARD BOUND!

As I walked along, I asked a few people for directions to the southbound freeway, made my way to it, and stuck out my thumb. Soon a big rig truck stopped, so I ran, climbed the steps, and opened the passenger door to check out the driver. I was greeted by a chubby guy with big friendly smile. "Hi, where are you heading?" He asked warmly. "LA!" I answered smiling back. "No, problem! I'm going to San Diego, my name is Fabe, what's yours?" he exclaimed enthusiastically. "Great thanks! I'm Della!" I answered, as I sat down in the passenger seat and slammed the door shut behind me.

Fabe had good vibes and I instantly felt comfortable in his company. "What does Fabe stand for?" I asked curiously. "Fabian!" he answered, still smiling. "I like it!" I said smiling back. "I was named after my great grandfather" Fabe continued. "Nice!" I answered, and we both smiled, nodded, and laughed as if there was nothing more to say about that!

We hit it off really well and chatted merrily as we zoomed off down the highways and byways. Around midway Fabe treated us to lunch at a roadside rest station. "That was a real treat, thank you!" I said as I cleared the last morsel of food off my plate. "You're welcome, darling!" Said Fabe, as he lit up a cigarette to have with his coffee. "I'm just gonna use the bathroom, I'll be back soon!" I said, as I jumped up, and headed towards the bathrooms. "Sure" he called after me, casually.

After I used the loo, I tidied up my hair and makeup in the mirror and was surprised to find some loose change in the bottom of my army shoulder bag, which I kept inside my tote bag with my most important stuff in. I suddenly had a memory flash of throwing the change in there during my night out with Janie.

After I finished doing my hair and makeup, I headed out of the bathroom and noticed that there was a gift shop over at the other side of the rest station so I strolled over there for a browse. The gift shop was a little on the tacky side, but fun, and cute. There were pens with the word the grapevine printed on them, so I decided to use the change to buy a pen each for Fabe and me as souvenirs.

Feeling pleased with my purchase, I headed back to the table to give Fabe his pen. "Little present for you!" I exclaimed with a smile. "Thank you so much!" answered Fabe, while looking genuinely surprised. "You're welcome, Fabe! Thank you for giving me a lift, your good company, and the great meal!" I answered cheerily, as I drank the rest of my coffee. "And thank you for your good company!" Fabe exclaimed with a big smile, and that moment reminded me of why I loved travel so much, it was because I got to meet such wonderful and special people who I would have otherwise never met, and the scenery was just a bonus.

Soon we were back on the road, and rolling back into the outskirts of LA. In no time at all we were back in LA itself. Fabe dropped me off at Venice and Crenshaw, right near my Pico home base. "Thank you, Fabe!" I said as he parked up his truck. "My pleasure! Let me know if you ever need a lift to or from Frisco!" he said, as he handed me a piece of paper with his phone number on it. "Will do, thanks again, Fabe!" I answered as I opened the truck door. "No problem, I go that way a lot! ...and thanks again for the pen!" He answered, with his lovely big smile. "OK, see ya!" I exclaimed, as I grabbed my tote bag, jumped out of the truck, and waved goodbye!

I felt a pang of sadness as Fabe drove away. I turned and started heading towards the halfway house. As I walked along, I slowly felt an extra spring coming back to my step, and I started to feel happy to be back in LA. I looked forward to seeing the Pico gang, especially Mike. I checked the time and saw that it was going on 11 pm, so it wasn't too late, Mike would probably still be up, and I couldn't wait to surprise him!

Just as I got to the front door of the halfway house, Mike coincidently, opened it. "Della! You're back!" he exclaimed sounding surprised. "Sonny, Della's back!" He called out, excitedly. "Yes, I was missing you all!" I exclaimed as I walked inside. "Wow, Della, it's so great to see you again! exclaimed Mike continually smiling, while Sonny stood behind him grinning and nodding. They both kept looking at me in disbelief as if they'd thought I was never coming back.

"You want some coffee?" asked Mike, slipping into his usual good host mode. "Yes please, thanks, Mike!" I answered, finding his sweet welcome so heartwarming. Mike quickly made us some coffee and we sat around the dining table for a catch-up chat. Sonny was too tired to stay up, so he bid us goodnight and headed downstairs.

"Xavier was here today, he was asking about you!" Said Mike, still looking pleased to see me. "Aw, I missed him again! How is he doing?" I answered, feeling sorry I'd missed Xavier's visit. "He's doing great, he's got his own shop now, not sure if he'll still be mobile. So, how was your trip?" answered Mike, eagerly. "I'll have to give him a call one of the days, he's a nice guy. The trip was great thanks! I saw some LA friends in San Francisco, and even wound up staying in Sacramento for a couple of weeks! How have things been here?" I answered, with a big smile, feeling happy to be back.

"Wow, Sacramento, it's beautiful there, I'm glad you had a good time! Everything has been good here, but I think Linda asked Larry if she can cover for Mary full time, so I don't know what's gonna happen now" Mike answered, as if embarrassed to tell me such awkward news. "Oh no, but Larry said it was ok for me to have a month for a holiday, and I've only used up about three weeks of it - I've saved the rest for when my Aunt Freda gets here!" I answered, suddenly feeling like I'd messed up somehow. "Don't worry about it, Larry's cool, you can still stay here!" answered Mike, as if trying to make me feel better. "Thanks, Mike, we'll see I guess" I answered. "Yeah, it'll be ok," said Mike reassuringly.

Well, I guess it's time for bed! Night, night, don't bite the bedbugs!" I exclaimed, with a little laugh. "Sure, sleep tight, sweet dreams, I'm happy that you're back!" answered Mike, as we both stood up and took off to our rooms.

I wasn't sure what to make of the news that Mike had just shared with me, so I went to bed feeling confused and a little dejected. It was good to be back, but it didn't feel quite the same if I wasn't going to be helping out in exchange for being there. I always liked to feel that I was pitching in, and doing my bit.

I felt as though I had done something wrong by going away, but I was only using up some of the weeks that Larry had already okayed. I wondered if he'd forgotten our previous conversation about it all, and when I had popped back briefly, he maybe thought that I was back indefinitely, and forgotten that I was still on my little holiday. 'Oh well, it's all part of the adventure!' I reminded myself as I rolled over, and fell asleep.

The next day I woke up around 11, got up, and went to grab a coffee from the kitchen. There was no one around, but I spotted a letter on the dining room table with my dad's handwriting on it. I quickly poured myself a coffee, then headed back to my room with the coffee and my dad's letter, feeling excited to read what he had to say.

I put my coffee on my bedside table, got comfy sitting up on my bed leaning on a pillow that was against the wall, and opened the letter. My dad had drawn a fun cartoon, and written a little joke under it, which was one of his hobbies - He had sold a few of his cartoons to national newspapers over the years – Just one of his many talents!

He asked how I was doing, and told me about various school friends of mine that he'd bumped into in town, and sent on their regards. His big news was that he'd managed to get the house he was renting recognised as a "listed building" for historical reasons. He'd included a newspaper article about it, which I put aside to read later when I was fully awake.

Feeling happy to have heard from my dad, I put his letter away and suddenly remembered, the emergency-cash fund that I kept hidden in my room. I went to check how much was there, as I'd lost track. I counted the cash and found that I was down to my last fifty dollars. 'It'll last me until Aunt Freda gets here at least!' I thought to myself with a laugh. I headed back to the living room to get a coffee top-up and wound up having a chat with Mary about the new situation. She said that I was still welcome to stay there as long as I liked. She sounded genuine which made me feel a little better.

"Della!" squealed Suzi, sounding happy to see me, as she appeared up the stairs. "Hi, Suzi!" I called back, happy to see her too. The others appeared one by one and greeted me, some loudly, others shyly, and I was touched, that they'd all, apparently, missed me! They all seemed very surprised that I'd come back, which I found amusing, and wasn't sure what to make of it. Mary made a big pot of tuna casserole and invited me to join them to eat at the table. I suddenly felt awkward about eating their food if I was no longer helping out there. "Thanks, Mary" I said, as I sat down and humbly took a small portion. "Have more! Have more!" she exclaimed. "Yeah, have more!" chimed in the others, as if they could tell I felt awkward about it. I felt this was very kind and insightful of them, and it told me that they had full sensibilities in ways that count as human beings, despite their disabilities.

We all had a friendly catch-up chat about my San Francisco visit and about Pico. Mary told me that she and her sons: Timmy and Danny were doing well, and about how Linda had really enjoyed helping out, and that she was glad of the extra pocket money, echoing Mike's words – She was currently out shopping, but I would probably see her later, Cathy told me she was going to be joining that punk band soon, Suzi said that she was looking forward to playing some more board games with me and Mike, and Darlene was a lot browner than before I left! They all seemed to be making an extra effort to welcome me back, and it felt good to be catching up with them all after my time away, even though deep down I still felt a little upset by the change in circumstances, I did my best to cover it up with lots of jokes and laugher, besides I would probably be leaving with Aunt Freda soon, so it was probably for the best.

After dinner, I told Mary I would clear up the dishes as a thanks for the meal. She graciously accepted my offer and headed back downstairs to her apartment. "Are you ok Della?" asked Mike, as I washed the dishes. "Yeah, I'm fine thanks Mike" I answered, turning to see him and Sonny hovering awkwardly in the kitchen behind me, as if they were both sensing, that deep down I was still feeling a little hurt and confused by the change at the halfway house. "Shall I make us some coffee!" asked Mike optimistically, and I got the feeling that they were doing their best to give me their moral support and take my mind off things. "OK, thanks, Mike!" I answered as I finished the last of the dishes.

'What sweet souls they are' I thought to myself as the three of us sat down in the living room together with our coffees. They both looked a little embarrassed by the situation as if they wanted to help me, but they didn't know how. I started to feel bad that they were feeling so bad for me, so as we chatted I told them that Linda taking over covering for Mary was probably from the best as I would most likely be heading back to England with my aunt Freda after her visit.

"Oh no, you can't leave! This is your home, you're a Californian adult, remember!" exclaimed Mike, as they both looked shocked and saddened by my news. "Yeah, this does feel like my home, and I'll always be a Californian adult, but it's for the best, as I only have a few dollars left, so I need to top up my travel funds, but don't worry, I plan to visit LA regularly, and I'll be sure to come and visit you all, whenever I'm back in town, and you're welcome to visit me in England too!" I answered, with a big smile. They both looked excited at the idea, and we all joked about having tea with the Queen! Afterwards, we tidied up, bid each other our goodnights, and then headed off to our beds.

Just as I was dozing off, I realised I hadn't seen Linda that eve, and I suddenly wondered if she had maybe asked Larry if she could take over covering for Mary some time back, basically take my gig! He'd casually mentioned that she'd offered to help out when I'd asked him for a couple of weeks off, so maybe that's why he'd been so quick to suggest I take a month off instead. This seemed quite likely, and suddenly I didn't feel so bad about my trip to San Francisco. Plus, I'd probably be leaving soon, so it truly was all for the best. I was glad that Linda would be in a sense taking over from me, and I felt happy that she would be able to make a little extra pocket money. Things felt as if they were falling into place just as they should! I lay there for a while thinking about my time up in San Francisco and Sacramento, and I felt that although I may have lost Jay, I'd gained a bounty of wonderful new friends, acquaintances, and memories.

"Della, your Aunt Freda's on the phone!" shouted Mike, as he banged on my door, waking me from a deep sleep. "What?" I called back, feeling all disorientated, as I sat up in bed, rubbing my eyes. "It's your aunt Freda!" He repeated anxiously. "OK, thanks!" I answered, as I jumped out of bed, threw some clothes on, opened my bedroom door, and ran past him down the hall, into the living room to pick up the phone.

"Hi, Freda!" I said, sounding all out of breath. "Hello Della, I've arrived in New York, off the QE2, I'll be motoring around America looking at potential ranch properties for a week or two, and then I'll arrive in Los Angeles. I want to take you to the San Diego Zoo!" she said, making it sound as if the Zoo visit was the most important part of her trip.

"Great OK, I'll look forward to it!" I answered, with a nervous laugh, as I remembered that she was quite eccentric and always full of drama. "Yes, it will be wonderful! Now will you be coming back to England with me? If so, I'll buy you a plane ticket so that you can fly back with me! She said earnestly.

"Um, yes ok, thank you. It'll be good to go back, and regroup before some more travels!" I answered, feeling that at this point the decision had made itself. "Ok, well I'll sort that from Los Angeles. See you soon!" She said loudly. "OK, see you soon, have a good journey, and good luck finding a property!" I said enthusiastically. "Thank you, god bless!" she exclaimed, before we both hung up our phones.

"Wow, she sounds like the Queen!" Said Mike, looking impressed, and rocking back and forth on his feet excitedly. Sonny sat in an armchair nearby anxiously looking over at us both as if trying to figure out what was going on. "Yeah, she does sound a bit posh, she looks more like a cowgirl though!" I joked back. "Cool! So, when will she be here?" asked Mike, excitedly. "In a week or two, I think, I guess she'll phone again nearer the time" I answered, as I headed towards the kitchen to grab a coffee.

"Hey Mary, my Aunt Freda just called to tell me she's arrived in the States, and she'll be here in a week or two if that's ok? I said as Mary appeared up the stairs. "Sure, the bedroom at the end of the hallway is still empty, and she's welcome to stay there" answered Mary in her usual laidback manner. "Thanks, Mary, would it be ok for us to phone Larry to confirm things with him?" I asked, just wanting to be sure that it was ok. "Sure!" she answered, as she headed over towards the phone on the wall, and picked up the receiver.

"Hi Larry, Della's back, I told her that Linda is covering for me now and that she's still welcome to stay here. She says her aunt will be here in a week or two, and she wants to know if it's ok for her to stay here. I told her that she can use the back bedroom down the hall" said Mary, as if wanting to fill him in that the news had been broken to me about Linda taking over covering for her. "He wants to speak to you!" said Mary Passing the phone to me. Feeling a little embarrassed at the latest change in circumstances. "Thanks, Mary" I answered, as I took the phone off her.

"Hi, Larry!" I said with a little laugh. "Delilah, you came back!" exclaimed Larry in his usual facetious way. "Well, yeah, why wouldn't I!" I answered, still feeling a little confused by his, and the other resident's reaction to my returning back to Pico, as it was slowly dawning on me that none of them actually expected me to come back!

"I did enjoy my little 'OLIDAY in San Francisco though!" I added, emphasising the word holiday in a cockney accent, and hoping that it would trigger his memory of our previous arrangement. "We didn't think you were coming back!" he exclaimed, not picking up on my hint, and we both laughed!

"I wouldn't just go like that! That's why I asked you for time off!" I answered, still hoping to jog his memory of our conversation before I'd left. "OK dear, welcome back, and of course, your Aunt Freda is welcome to stay! Hopefully, I'll get to meet her too!" answered Larry casually. "OK great, thanks, Larry!" I answered. "See you soon my dear!" exclaimed Larry. "See ya, Larry!" I answered as we both hung up our phones. "Yay, he says it's ok, thanks Mary!" I said as I headed to join Mary in the kitchen and top up my coffee. "Sure, no problem!" answered Mary, with a smile, as she left the kitchen, and headed back downstairs.

"I'll see you a bit later Mike, I'm gonna take this coffee to my room and wake up a bit" I said, as I passed Mike, who was by now sitting comfortably in the armchair, while Sonny hovered about on the steps outside. "Sure, see ya later!" answered Mike, looking happy for me.

I headed back to my room, and sat up on my bed, with the pillow propped up against the wall for back support. I let out a sigh of relief that it was ok for my Aunt Freda to stay at Pico, but I was still puzzled as to why they had all thought that I wasn't coming back. It wasn't like we'd had a row or anything. All was well! I had just fancied a little holiday to see Jay and some more of California. I'd even arranged it with Larry first, but going by the way they had all reacted to my return, I was starting to feel as if I was in the movie Gaslight! Still, at least everyone was still on good terms, and at least my Aunt Freda, and I, still had a place to stay!

CHAPTER 54:

WALKING UP TO HOLLYWOOD!

The next day I spent some time sorting out my things after my trip and headed across the street to do some laundry. It felt great to have a home base to come back to. I was starting to see trips and home bases as two sides of the same coin. They both had a place in my life and as long as I had a home base in a place I liked and was also able to go on regular trips, I was happy! I wondered where my next "home base" would be?

That evening, after dinner, Mike, Sonny, and I sat at the dining table drinking coffee and playing card and board games. Just as it was nearing midnight Sonny got sleepy, said goodnight, and tottered off to bed, but Mike and I were still feeling wide awake and full of energy due to drinking a lot more coffee than Sonny.

"Hey Mike, do you fancy seeing if we can walk up to Hollywood? We can always jump on a bus if we get tired!" I asked, thinking it would be a fun little challenge. "Sure, that sounds fun, okay, let's go!" answered Mike, enthusiastically, as if we were suddenly on an important mission. "Yeah, let's go! I've just gotta pop to the loo!" I exclaimed, just as enthusiastically. Mike stood up and shoved his cigarettes in his pocket, and I quickly went to use the bathroom, then ran to my bedroom, to grab my shoulder bag.

I arrived back in the living room, and a couple of seconds later Mike appeared back in the living room, from using the bathroom. "Ready?" I asked. "Ready!" answered Mike, and out into the night we both headed. "Shall we cut down the side streets to get there rather than go on the main streets?" I asked, thinking the side streets may be more relaxing, with less traffic. "Sure," answered Mike.

casually, as we headed south towards the nearest quiet side street, instead of east towards the usually busy Crenshaw.

As we walked down the side street it felt as if we were entering another world. There were no other people, or cars around, and it was very quiet. Cute bungalows with neat lawns at the front lined the sides of the street. Some houses had lights on and TV lights shining out which was comforting, as this was meant to be somewhat of a rough, dangerous area, but much to my surprise it was very neat, tidy, and peaceful.

I did notice that every window had bars across them, as if to keep the people inside safe though, and it saddened me to think that the crime rate must be so bad that people here had reached such a level of fear of the world around them.

As we walked along, the song: "Walking Back to Happiness!" by Helen Shapiro came to mind, but I changed the words to Walking up to Hollywood! and started singing it out loud, which Mike thought was very funny, and started to sing along. Soon we both cracked up laughing at our efforts and I loved how we always had such a fun time together. He was such a good-spirited, sweet friend, and as we walked, I felt as though we were Tom Sawyer and Huckleberry Finn off on another mini adventure together.

After walking for a while we came to a large square of grass, with a children's play park in the centre, this was a big surprise for me, as I hadn't expected to see such a playful thing in the middle of a supposedly dodgy area! Mike and I automatically headed for the swings, took one each, and like two big kids we sat swinging for a while, just looking up at the stars in the sky and calling out "Woo hoos! And Whees!" joyfully as we swung past each other.

"It's great to just do what you feel isn't it Mike?" I exclaimed as we Swung. "Sure, this is great fun!" answered Mike sounding really happy. We continued to just swing, hoot, holler, chit-chat, and sing songs for an hour or so, before we decided to carry on with our walk up to Hollywood. I guessed it was about five miles away, and we would get there eventually, as long as we kept heading North.

We strolled along without a care in the world, feeling as if we were the only people alive on the planet when suddenly a car appeared slowly heading towards us from the direction we were walking in. As it got nearer, I could hear that it had loud Rap Music playing, and I glanced to see that it was full of black gang members.

I suddenly felt a sense of panic, but instantly decided to cover it up by acting crazy and just staring around me wide-eyed in a detached way, as if I hadn't even noticed them. I was doing my best to emulate how Sheila, from the halfway house, had looked the time when she had come running upstairs, looking out of her mind with fear, after hallucinating that there was a fire in the house.

The car slowed down even more as it passed by as if to check out who we were, so I kept darting my eyes all over the place erratically and continued to act as if I hadn't even noticed them or the car. Mike just huffed and puffed, and marched on, staring straight ahead, and didn't glance at the car either. I caught a tiny glimpse of a couple of the gang members looking puzzled to see us, but thankfully they just kept on going. Maybe they knew that there was a halfway house in the neighbourhood, and assumed we were just a couple of the residents rambling around. - I suppose we were!

"Phew, thank goodness they're gone!" I said to Mike, as soon as the car was out of sight. "Yeah, heavy dudes!" answered Mike, which told me that he'd been totally aware of the situation, but like me had been playing it cool, by marching on and staring straight ahead.

Eventually, we reached Wilshire Boulevard. turned left, and headed west towards Vine Street. We reached Vine in about twenty minutes and then turned right heading north towards Hollywood. We continued marching onward, and chatting about random things as we went. I loved that there was still very little traffic around, and even fewer people!

Eventually, we reached the other side of Melrose Avenue. Well, we're here! Exclaimed Mike. "Yeah great!" I answered, feeling excited by the fact that we had actually walked to Hollywood! We continued to stroll Northwood some more for a little while until we found a bus bench to sit down on near Santa Monica Boulevard. I noticed a homeless person across the street stroll silently by as if he too was a resident of this other world that we'd entered.

"Well, we walked to Hollywood!" said Mike in disbelief. "Yep, I wonder how long it took?" I answered. We worked out that we'd set off just after midnight and we must have been gone at least three hours. "Not too long then, and we had a long rest stop at that park!" I joked. "Yep!" answered Mike, with a laugh. "Time to head back now then!" I exclaimed. "Sure!" answered Mike and the two of us started walking back towards Pico. This time, we took the main roads, as we didn't fancy bumping into the gang car again, or another one like it! Plus, we figured we could jump on a bus if we got tired. We got home around 5 am, bid each other goodnight, headed to our rooms, and crashed out.

The next day I woke up around noon feeling amazed by our midnight walk to Hollywood. It suddenly dawned on me that Mike was quite a large, chubby guy, whereas I was quite a slight, slim girl, so I hoped it hadn't been a harder walk for him than it was for me. He seemed strong though, and I hadn't seen any signs of him struggling, so I concluded that he must have been fine. I got up, got dressed, and went to see Mike to chat all about it! "Wow, we did it!" I exclaimed, as soon as I saw Mike in the living room!" "Yep, we walked to Hollywood!" answered Mike with a big smile. "I'm so glad we did that, especially as I'm going to be leaving soon, so it's nice to have such a special memory of the two of us!" I answered, smiling back, as I headed to the kitchen to get a coffee.

"It sure is! Shall we go and get some ice cream, my treat!" answered Mike, still smiling. This was so kind of him, as he was aware that I was down to my last few dollars. "Thanks, Mike!" I answered, with a smile. "Wanna come too?" Mike asked Sonny enthusiastically. "Sure" mumbled Sonny, and the three of us took off.

As we walked south on Pico, down towards Thrifty's, I tried to savour every second of my precious time with Mike and Sonny, as I didn't know if, or when, I'd be seeing them again, after I'd left. I loved the good vibes the three of us created as we walked along together, It was as if our collective energy created a calming sense of well-being, as we enjoyed some of the simple pleasures in life: good company, a walk, and ice cream. We had a wonderful time as usual, and I knew that I would always treasure my memories of the special times the three of us spent together.

"Wanna walk to Venice beach!" exclaimed Mike suddenly, as if inspired by our walk to Hollywood the night before. "Ummm, not really, let' not and say we did!" I joked. "Yeah, good idea!" Mike joked back, and the three of us laughed our way back to the halfway house, although I'm not sure that Sonny knew why he was laughing, but he seemed happy and that was the main thing! By the time evening rolled around, I was feeling restless for a night out and decided to take the bus up to Hollywood for a walkabout. It felt great to be back in Hollywood, and I felt instantly in my element as I strolled along the boulevard.

I suddenly spotted Jennie and the punks, so I went over to say hi. "Hey Jennie, how are you doing? I asked, giving her a big smile. "Hey Della, I'm good! How are you doing?" she asked, as the other punks nodded and smiled our way. "I'm ok thanks. I hitched up to Frisco to see Jay, and guess what? He was with someone!" I exclaimed, pulling a horrified cringing face, and the two of us burst out laughing. "Aw, that sucks man, he really dug you, he must have thought you weren't interested, and didn't you say you were going back to England?" Jennie asked as we headed over to the wall to sit down. "Well yeah, but...I don't know, he should have waited for me!" I exclaimed dramatically, and we both cracked up laughing again.

We sat on the wall, and Jennie leaned over the other side and dug out a couple of beer cans from a hidden stash. "Here, drown your troubles!" she exclaimed, handing me a can, and an old brown paper bag to put it in. "Thanks, Jennie, don't mind if I do!" I answered, and we both laughed some more. "So, what have you been up to?" I asked curiously. "Ah same ole, same ole, there's a party tonight over at Mystic Studios though if you wanna come along?" she answered enthusiastically. "Yeah, sounds good to me!" I answered, feeling up for anything! We drank a couple more beers on the wall while chatting with each other, and with random punks who would join us, while the rest of Hollywood scurried to-and-fro. Once again, I felt happy to just be. I was in no rush to be anywhere, see anyone, or do anything.

"Let's book it!" exclaimed Jennie, as we finished the last can of beer. "OK!" I answered as the two of us jumped down off the wall. Jennie told the other punks she'd see them later, and we took off heading east on the boulevard. "So where's Mystic Studio?" I asked curiously. "Oh, it's not far, it's just off Vine Street" answered Jennie, looking pleased to be heading over there. "OK," I answered, starting to look forward to a party!

We crossed the street at Vine and headed south. After we walked down a block, Jennie made a left turn, and it suddenly dawned on me that we were headed to the same studio that Gabby and I wound up at a few times after gigs at the Cathay de Grand. "Oh yeah, I've been here before!" I exclaimed, with a grin. "Yeah, it's cool. There's a record release party tonight!" answered Jennie excitedly. "Sounds fun!" I answered, as I followed Jennie inside the building, and up the steps.

The party was already in full swing, and I recognised a few punks from around town, especially from the Cathay de Grande, I wondered if Gabby was around. "Hey El Duche!" exclaimed Jennie, as she ran over and gave El Duche a big hug. "Meet my friend Della!" she exclaimed. I wasn't sure if he'd recognised me from hanging out with Gabby, but I didn't let on that I'd met him before, as I reached over and shook his hand. He mumbled some kind of greeting to me, and I mumbled a greeting back, but the music was too loud to hear much of what he said.

"Let's get some booze!" exclaimed Jennie, leading the way towards a table full of beers, spirits and mixers, with plastic tumbles stacked next to them. We both filled up a tumbler of Bacardi and Coke, with way more Bacardi than there was Coke! "Cheers!" I exclaimed to Jennie. "Cheers!" she exclaimed back, and we tapped our plastic tumblers together before each taking a swig. "Ugh, too strong!" I exclaimed, and we both laughed, as I went back to pour a bit more coke in mine.

We were soon getting tipsy and dancing around to the punk music that was playing. The atmosphere was relatively upbeat for the hard-core punk crowd, so I guessed that releasing an album had cheered them up! I glanced at some of the records and tapes by the sound system and saw a bunch of familiar LA band albums: Fear, Suicidal Tendencies, Black Flag, Dead Kennedys, Circle Jerks... and the punk style of the covers reminded me of Matt, the guy I'd been seeing in my home town before I set off travelling, as he'd been into similar bands, and had been talking about getting a punk band together. I wondered how he was doing. The last I'd heard, he was moving to London.

"Della meet Derf!" shouted Jennie, and I turned to see Jennie chatting to a cool-looking older punk wearing a trilby hat. "Hi Derf!" I shouted, thinking his name was unusual, or maybe I'd heard it wrong. "Hi Della!" he shouted back, and we shook hands. "Derf sez there's an after party at Bogart's house later, wanna go?" asked Jennie invitingly. "Yeah, why not!" I answered as we went to top up our drinks.

An hour or so later, Jennie and I joined a bunch of other punks and jumped into a posh looking large American car, and whizzed up to the Hollywood hills for the after-party. By the time we got there, I was feeling so drunk that all I could do was stagger over to the nearest comfy-looking chair and pass out. When I woke up a little while later, I caught a glimpse of Jennie and El Duche sitting across the room looking pretty snug together, while a bunch of other punks were scattered around the room, some still standing and drinking, others crashed out on various chairs and sofas. I turned over on the chair, got comfy, and fell back to sleep.

The next time I woke up, most of the people had left, aside from a few punks still crashed out around me on sofas, chairs and the floor. I slowly stood up, with my army shoulder bag still on my shoulder, and went in search of Jennie, but there was no sign of her. I suddenly felt sick, so ran to the hallway in search of a loo. Thankfully I found one, just in time to throw up! I drank a load of cold water from the tap, washed my face, tidied my hair, topped up my makeup, and decided to get out of there, as I needed some fresh air fast. I headed outside and saw that we'd been in a little cottage-type of house, that looked like it belonged in the English countryside. I headed out of the gate and made my way back down the hill until I eventually reached Hollywood Boulevard, where I found a café to grab a coffee and wake up. Finally feeling sobered up, I decided to jump on the next bus heading down to Pico and crash out some more. The bus ride was rough, and every little movement had me feeling queasy. I couldn't wait to get back to bed! After a half hour or so, I arrived back at the halfway house, and thankfully no one was around, so I tiptoed to my room, flaked out on the bed, and fell fast asleep.

I woke up around 2 pm, and went in search of more coffee, and some food, as my appetite was back. "Hi Mike" I moaned, still feeling rough, as I entered the living room. "Oh hi Della, did you just get up?" Mike asked, looking amused. "Yeah, I feel rough! I wound up at some guy named Bogarts party, and got way too drunk! I don't like getting drunk, tipsy is ok, but not drunk!" I moaned, as I got myself a coffee, and made some toast.

"That Sucks! Bogart, you mean like Humphry Bogart?" asked Mike curiously. "Oh yeah! It was a nice place, up in the Hollywood Hills!" I answered. "Oh wow, it was probably Humphry Bogart's old house!" exclaimed Mike looking impressed. "Really? It's funny, because when Jennie told me the party was at Bogart's house, I just assumed it was a punk rocker called Bogart, but your theory makes a lot more sense!" I answered, and we both cracked up laughing.

CHAPTER 55:

AUNT FREDA ARRIVES!

On the day that Aunt Freda was due to arrive, I quickly made sure that her room was nice and tidy for her. Mary told me that we should both feel free to help ourselves to food and drink, which I felt was very kind of her and Larry, and I was sure that my Aunt Freda would appreciate it too. Aunt Freda would be arriving at the halfway house by taxi, so Mike, Sonny and I stood outside on the sidewalk eagerly awaiting her arrival. Finally, her taxi turned up. "Della!" exclaimed Aunt Freda, as she jumped out of the taxi, ran towards me, and gave me a big hug, while Mike and Sonny stood to the side looking bashful.

"Hi Freda, great to see you! These are my friends Mike and Sonny!" I announced as Mike shuffled forward to shake her hand. "Lovely to meet you both!" exclaimed Aunt Freda, as she quickly shook their hands, before twirling back around, and heading back towards the taxi. The Taxi driver got her suitcase out of the trunk and plonked it down next to her. "Thank you ever so much!" she exclaimed, as she paid him. "Welcome to the Pico halfway house, this way please!" I exclaimed dramatically, as we all trundled up the steps together with Mike insisting on carrying her case.

"Oh, it's so wonderful to see you again Della!" exclaimed Aunt Freda. "You too Freda!" I answered as we all piled into the living room. "Have a seat, would you like a coffee and some food?" I asked, wanting to make her feel welcomed, and comfortable. "Just a coffee please!" answered Aunt Freda, looking pleased to have arrived. "I'll get it, milk and sugar?" asked Mike, as he headed towards the kitchen. "Oh yes, one sugar please!" answered Aunt Freda, as she got comfortable on the sofa. "Sure, would you like some coffee Della and Sonny?" asked Mike, as he hovered in the living room for a moment. "Yes please/Sure" answered Sonny and me, as we both sat down, Sonny on the armchair, and me on the sofa next to Aunt Freda.

Mike arrived back with our coffees and sat on the sofa on the other side of me. and soon we all sat around listening to my Aunt Freda's tales of her bus journeys across America looking at potential ranch properties. Mike couldn't keep the smile off his face, and I got the impression that he was really getting a kick out of her very English accent, while Sonny sat by looking dazed and confused as if he couldn't understand a word she was saying, which I found comical.

"And what about you Della? What have you been up to since I last saw you?" asked my Aunt Freda, after she'd finished telling us her journey tale. "Oh, this and that!" I answered, thinking I wouldn't even know where to begin to tell her of my travels since I'd last seen her! "Oh yes, it's good to keep busy!" she answered enthusiastically. "Yep!" I answered, as I just smiled and nodded back at her.

My aunt Freda's visit was a whirlwind of taking the local busses to show her some local LA sights, such as Venice Beach, and The Griffith Park Observatory, followed by her big treat of taking me to visit the San Diego Zoo, and in no time at all we were getting ready to head back to England, but I knew that I would be back, because I was missing California even before I'd left, and I felt it had many more adventures in store for me, and I couldn't wait to experience them...

MA LYDIA

PA GEOFF

BROSKIES: MARTIN, STEVE, CARL

PAULINE, DELLA, SUE LL, SUE L

DELLA & KIM

GABBY & DELLA

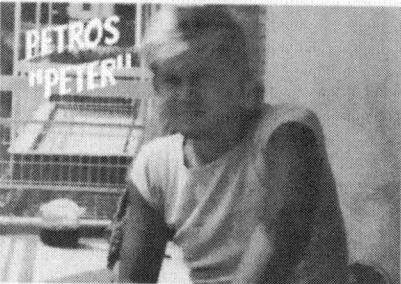

PETROS "PETER"

JONATHAN MORRIS, DELLA & BENEDICT TAYLOR

WHITEY CARSON SINGS

LARRY

DELLA & MIKE

SYLVIA, JULIE & DELLA

JOHNNY

DELLA & RICHARD

DELLA & AUNT FREDA: SD ZOO

Printed in Great Britain
by Amazon

47508401R00267